James Quiggle
Translation
New Testament

Copyright Page

James Quiggle Translation New Testament

Copyright 2023 James D. Quiggle. All rights reserved.

ISBN: 979-8-9871044-1-5

Revision 10f, 23 May 2024. Minor corrections including typos, missing verse number, and corrected translation of Acts 18:17.

Permissions: the scripture translations and translation notes in this book may only be reproduced as:

> part of a commentary on a Bible book or doctrine,
> part of Bible study materials,
> used for teaching-preaching in a local church setting,
> for the purpose of a review article, limited to twenty verses.

Identify individual scriptures or scripture passages used from this translation with the abbreviation JQTNT or JQT New Testament, which represents the *James Quiggle Translation New Testament*.

In a bibliography, on a copyright page, or in an acknowledgement of sources, please identify this book as: *James Quiggle Translation New Testament*, translated and published by James D. Quiggle, copyright 2023.

Some translations first appeared in James D. Quiggle, *Translations of Select Bible Books*, copyright 2018.

Dedication

Who is able to name or number all the influences in a man's life? Certainly this translation owes a debt to those who studied the language, or commented on the texts, or interpreted the words, whose works I read and profited from in the past forty-nine years.

Those with a more direct influence may be named. Pastor Hollies Lockaby, under whose ministry I was saved. Pastor Richard Wile, who began my journey as student of the Bible. Pastor David R. Hollingsworth, true friend and mentor, who encouraged me to write, and helped me learn to communicate clearly. These men are now with the Lord, enjoying their reward. Their influence lives on in my life and the lives of many others.

Kathleen Hollingsworth, wife of David, a good friend for forty-five years, and the copyeditor for this work. Your perceptive and useful corrections and comments made a significant contribution to the quality of the work.

Linda Marie Quiggle, best friend and wife. Without your love and friendship and counsel this book would not have come to fruition.

Thank You.

Contents

Dedication 5
Preface 9
The JQT New Testament 21
The Book of Matthew 23
The Book of Mark 70
The Book of Luke 100
The Book of John 151
The Book of Acts 190
The Book of Romans 239
The Book of First Corinthians 259
The Book of Second Corinthians 278
The Book of Galatians 291
The Book of Ephesians 298
The Book of Philippians 305
The Book of Colossians 310
The Book of First Thessalonians 315
The Book of Second Thessalonians 320
The Book of First Timothy 323
The Book of Second Timothy 329
The Book of Titus 333
The Book of Philemon 336
The Book of Hebrews 338
The Book of James 353
The Book of First Peter 359
The Book of Second Peter 365
The Book of First John 369
The Book of Second John 375
The Book of Third John 376
The Book of Jude 377
The Book of Revelation 379
    Matthew Translation Notes *404*
    Mark Translation Notes *412*

- Luke Translation Notes 419
- John Translation Notes 426
- Acts Translation Notes 435
- Romans Translation Notes 438
- First Corinthians Translation Notes 442
- Second Corinthians Translation Notes 448
- Galatians Translation Notes 455
- Ephesians Translation Notes 458
- Philippians Translation Notes 461
- Colossians Translation Notes 463
- First Thessalonians Translation Notes 468
- Second Thessalonians Translation Notes 471
- First Timothy Translation Notes 474
- Second Timothy Translation Notes 476
- Titus Translation Notes 477
- Philemon Translation Notes 478
- Hebrews Translation Notes 479
- James Translation Notes 487
- First Peter Translation Notes 490
- Second Peter Translation Notes 495
- First John Translation Notes 497
- Second John Translation Notes 501
- Third John Translation Notes 501
- Jude Translation Notes 502
- Revelation Translation Notes 504

Primary Translation Resources 509
Translation Notes Resources 510
BOOKS BY JAMES D. QUIGGLE 513

Preface

General Introduction

Augustine wrote, "In reading Scripture, men seek nothing more than to find out the thought and will of those by whom it was written, and through these to find out the will of God" [*City of God*, 12:16]. The *JQT New Testament* is for those seeking to read and understand what was written.

A translation is an attempt to reproduce the original language in a target language, in this case American English. To do so, most translations will change an expression in the original language to an equivalent expression in the target language. The intent is to express the words, thoughts, emotions, and literary style of the original text into the target language in a form suitable to the reader. Translation also extends to punctuation and capitalization.

The difference between a more literal translation and one less literal is illustrated by two versions of 1 Samuel 15:33. The NKJV translates, "Samuel hacked Agag in pieces before the Lord in Gilgal." The NIV translates, "Samuel put Agag to death before the Lord at Gilgal." The Hebrew text reads "and Samuel hewed in pieces Agag before the Lord in Gilgal." My preference, if I were translating that verse, would be to reproduce the Hebrew text as closely as possible.

A more literal translation is known as "formal equivalence," sometimes identified as "word-for-word." A less literal translation is known as "dynamic equivalence," sometimes identified as "thought for thought." A good translation achieves a balance between formal and dynamic equivalence.

My goal was to translate the New Testament scriptures as I believed the original readers would have encountered God's word in autographs of the gospels, Acts, letters, and the Revelation. The principle I have followed is to use formal and dynamic equivalence as may be required to clearly communicate the message of the Bible author.

I have not slavishly attempted to give a word-for-word translation of Greek-to-English, but to communicate the sense of the Greek words into English. For example, the word translated "walk" by other versions, when not used literally, has the figurative sense of conduct, behavior, the manner in which a person lives his or her life. In 2 Corinthians 4:2, the word others translate as "commend" or "commending" has the sense of "presenting ourselves as worthy."

Occasionally I have used modern words and concepts. For example, "impotent" (Romans 4:19; Hebrews 11:12), or "employees" (Mark 1:20) to clearly communicate the intent of the passage.

I have followed the example set by other Bible translators in comparing my translation work with that of others, using versions dating from 1535 to 2005. The primary versions used for comparison were the Tyndale, KJV, YLT, ASV, NKJV, ESV, HCSB, NIV, NLT, and occasionally the ERV, Wuest, and

Preface

translations by various commentators, lexicons, and grammarians. The intent was not to reproduce the work of others but to stay within the translation norms established by the history of New Testament translation, and still be true to my understanding of the Greek text.

The reader of my commentaries on the New Testament, and my work *Four Voices, One Testimony*, may notice an occasional difference between the translations here and the translations there. The maturing experience of continuing biblical exegesis and the possibilities inherent in the semantic range and synonyms of the New Testament vocabulary account for the variations.

The text of the *James Quiggle Translation New Testament* (JQTNT), is solely my work based on my translation choices to express the vocabulary, grammar, and syntax of the Greek text of the New Testament.

Translation Conventions

Style

I am following the guidance of the *Chicago Manual of Style*, 16th edition.

Word Order

The JQTNT will read a little differently than other versions. I have tried to preserve the vocabulary and syntax of the Greek text where it does not affect the sense to the English reader. For example, Hebrews 11:19, "having reckoned that God was able to raise even out from the dead, from where him also in a figure he received." That is the Greek text, and understandable as it was written by the Hebrews Author, but very different from the many variations in the several Bible versions.

I have followed the word order of the Greek text when that word order is sensible as an English translation. In English word order establishes meaning: Subject + Verb + Object. In Greek the order might be Verb + Object + Subject. Meaning in Greek is created by grammatical form. Words that go together in the Greek sentence have the same grammatical form, regardless of how they are placed in the sentence.

> Galatians 3:7 (Greek), Know then that those of faith these sons are of Abraham
>
> Galatians 3:7 (JQTNT), Know then that those of faith, these are sons of Abraham.

Here is how the Greek and the JQTNT compare with other translations.

> Galatians 3:7 (NKJV), *Therefore* know that *only* those *who are* of faith are sons of Abraham. (Italics not in Greek text.)
>
> Galatians 3:7 (ESV), Know then that *it is* those of faith *who* are *the* sons of Abraham. (Italics not in Greek text.)
>
> Galatians 3:7 (NIV), Understand, then, that those who believe are children of Abraham. (Wrongly translates "know" as "understand"

Preface

[two different Greek words], "sons" as "children" [two different Greek words], and the noun "faith" as a pronoun + verb.)

I tend to translate the Greek text as it is. If I add in a word, it is in italics and is required to understand the Greek text, e.g., when "recline" means "lying on a couch perpendicular to the table propped up on the left elbow eating with the right hand," I translate "recline *to eat*." I only change the grammar if necessary (rarely) to understand the Greek sentence as an English sentence. In the JQTNT, what you see is what the Greek text says.

Brackets, Italics, and Parentheses

Brackets [] are used to indicate Greek text disputed by textual critics as not part of the original text. See the appropriate Translation Note at the end of each Bible book for a particular text and explanation.

Italic font is used for words not present in the original text that I have inserted as an aid to understanding or good English. For example, "recline *to eat*." Another example is verses without verbs, where the reader or translator must supply a verb or verbs for the sentence to make sense.

Parentheses () are used to enclose a word, phrase, clause, or sentence in the original text which I thought an aside or comment made by the biblical writer, as parentheses might be used in an English sentence.

Transliterations

I have not transliterated certain Greek words, such as *ággelos*, *baptízō*, and *blásphēmos*, as is common in other Bible versions. I have translated these words: messenger, immerse, slander.

Most versions transliterate *ággelos* (plural *ángelos*) into "angel." The Greek *ággelos* translates to "messenger." Sometimes in the Scripture *ággelos* is a human messenger and sometimes *ággelos* is a spirit being (a being created suitable for habitation in the spirit domain, aka "angel"). In this translation, when the spirit beings are in view, I have translated *ággelos* as "messenger." Occasionally I have added the noun *God's* or the adjective *holy* to distinguish the messengers who remained faithful to God from the messengers who fell with Lucifer. Unless the context indicates otherwise, the word "messenger" points to the holy spirit beings *ággelos*.

Most versions transliterate *baptízō* and related words into "baptize, baptism, baptized," etc. The Greek *baptízō* and related words translate to "immerse, immersed," etc. That is how the original readers would have understood the words. In some passages the JQTNT and other versions translate *baptízō* et al, as "washings." In the JQTNT John the Baptist is named John the Immerser.

Most versions transliterate *blásphēmos* and related words into "blasphemy, blaspheme" etc. The Greek *blásphēmos* translates to "slander, revile, ruin a reputation."

Preface

Some transliterations have been maintained. For example, "apostle" from *apóstolos* [Zodhiates, s. v. 652], which translates to "one sent, ambassador."

Names are also a translation issue. Most names appearing in New Testament translations are transliterated, e.g., *Iēsoús* transliterates to "Jesus," *Ioudaíos* to Judas. I have followed this translation convention, with an exception, the name *Iakōbos* [Zodhiates, s. v. 2384]. *Iakōbos* transliterates to "Jacob," but almost all versions replace *Iakōbos* with "James." The name "James," is from the Old French *Gemmes*, which is a variation of the later Latin *Jacomus*, which is a variation of the early Latin *Jacobus*. I have transliterated *Iakōbos* to "Jacob," but have left "James" as the title for the New Testament letter by that name

Frequently Occurring Words

The translation "never no never" occurs fifty-four times. This is my translation of the double negative *ou mḗ* [Zodhiates, s. v. 3756, 3361, respectively]. In biblical Greek (and other languages) a double negative intensifies the negative sense. The *ou* is the absolute negative, the *mḗ* is a conditional negative. The combination *ou mḗ* may be understood as "Is it possible? No never!"

The plural translation, "heavens," occurring eighty-seven times, is not an error. The Greek word is used in the plural form more often than the singular form. Other versions change the plural form into the singular.

The plural translation, "Sabbaths," occurring nine times, is not an error. Other versions change the plural form into the singular.

The word "loaves," as in "loaves of bread," occurs twenty-two times in other versions. The translation "loaves" is anachronistic. The translation "loaves" by other versions is in the Greek text the plural form of *ártos* [Zodhiates, s. v. 740], "bread." The bread would have been comparable to small pancakes for size and shape; think pita bread. Bread is an uncountable noun, so the translation "bread" may be used as both singular and plural. I translate both the singular and plural forms of *ártos* as "bread."

The word "gospel" occurs about one hundred times in other versions. But when the New Testament's writers and original readers saw the word *euaggélion* [Zodhiates, s. v. 2098] they would have thought "good news." I have translated *euaggélion* as "good news.

The word *kúrios* [Zodhiates, s. v. 2962], "sir, master, lord" occurs 262 times in the four gospels. When the writer uses *kúrios* in a comment referring to Jesus Christ, I have translated it "Lord," because the writer, who is writing after the fact, understands Jesus the Christ as "Lord" in the sense of deity. In dialogue spoken by one of Jesus' disciples or apostles during the days of Jesus' earthly ministry, I have translated *kúrios* as "master," the word of a disciple toward his master. Other occurrences of *kúrios* as referring to Jesus have been translated "sir." In the parables, uses of *kúrios* by a servant referring to his

Preface

employer or owner are translated "lord" or "master." In the 489 occurrences in the Acts through Revelation, I have usually translated *kúrios* as "Lord," unless context indicates sir or master should be the translation.

The word *ekklēsía* [Zodhiates, s. v. 1577], a public assembly, occurs 116 times in the New Testament. The word has traditionally been translated "church," even where the New Testament church is not in view. I have translated *ekklēsía* as "church" when the whole New Testament church (which began at the AD 33 Pentecost), or a local New Testament church, is in view. I have translated *ekklēsía* as "public assembly" at 1 Corinthians 11:18, which better fits the context. Where the New Testament church is not in view I have translated *ekklēsía* as "public assembly." At Hebrews 12:23 I have translated the second use of *ekklēsía* as "called-out assembly."

Looking at 1 Corinthians 11:18 provides a good example of my translation process. At 1 Corinthians 1:2, I translate *ekklēsía as* "church." At 1:2 the text has a definite article: *tē ekklēsía,* giving the straightforward translation "the church." The context is Paul has addressed this letter to the congregation at Corinth: a local church. But at 1 Corinthians 11:18 I translate *ekklēsía* as "public assembly." At 11:18 the text is proposition+noun, *én ekklēsía*, no definite or indefinite article. Context is also important. In 11:18 the *ekklēsía* was not acting as a local NT church should act. For those reasons, I believed the meaning of *én ekklēsía* at 11:18 was best communicated by "in public assembly." Translation is not only grammar and vocabulary, but also context.

The word "law" occurs 212 times (in 166 verses) in the New Testament. Sometimes "law" means a law(s), a commandment(s), a precept(s), a regulation(s). Other times the word "law" means the Law as given to Israel by YHWH at the mountain of God, Exodus 20:1—23:19, as supplemented by the laws in Leviticus and Numbers, and as repeated and further supplemented by Moses in Deuteronomy. That "law" is commonly called the Law of Moses. When "law" refers to the Law of Moses, I have capitalized the word "law."

Figurative Language

The Scripture is full of figurative language. One example is the Greek word *peripatéō* [Zodhiates, s. v. 4043], which literally means "to walk." However, the New Testament writers frequently use this word figuratively as the manner in which a person lives out his/her life. Whereas other versions translate the figurative use of *peripatéō* with the literal "walk," I have translated "manner of life" or "behave" or something similar.

Pronouns

Occasionally I have used nouns in place of pronouns to clarify the sense. For example, when "he" occurs multiple times in a passage but refers to two different people.

I have not capitalized pronouns referring to deity. As noted earlier, capitalization is part of translation. The tradition begun by earlier versions is just that, a tradition. Most modern versions do not capitalize pronouns referring to deity.

The pronoun "you" in Greek has different grammatical forms for the singular and the plural. In English "you" is both the singular and plural form. When the Greek "you" is plural, but in context might be understood as singular or plural, I have usually translated in a way that recognizes the plural form, e.g., "you all."

I have translated some third person singular neuter pronouns as plurals. Most versions translate the third person neuter pronoun as a masculine pronoun. I have retained the neuter plural by translating "they, them, their." Modern English usage has agreed "they, them, their" may be used to reflect the singular or the plural.

The Definite Article

A definite article appearing in the Greek text is often untranslated in most versions. For example, when the word *theós* (God) appears in the Greek text, it is often preceded by the definite article. The same is true for the word "Christ." I have continued that tradition of not translating the definite article, in most places, because to translate it creates a sentence unusual to the English reader. For example, John 1:1, "In beginning was the word and the word was with the God and God was the word." However, when the specificity created by a definite article is useful to the meaning, I have translated that definite article.

In places where a definite article does not appear in the Greek text, other versions have often supplied a definite article. As a rule I have not supplied a definite article where none appears in the Greek text. For example, the Greek text of Luke 1:32 does not have the definite article: "son of Most High." Adding words to the text is one way other translations try to make the English translation more accommodating to the reader. I have not added a definite article where I believed the translation was understandable without adding the definite article. There are exceptions, e.g., John 1:1, "In *the* beginning was the word" etc. Occasionally the definite article is implied by the context, and in those places I have provided the definite article.

In other places, supplying a definite article where the writer did not use or imply a definite article, leads to a wrong translation. For example, the Greek word *pneúma* is used of both human spirit and Holy Spirit. When trying to decide which is which in a text, a definite article in the text preceding *pneúma* usually indicates the Holy Spirit is in view, whereas *pneúma* without a definite article usually means the human spirit in in view. Some versions supply a definite article and translate "Spirit," when "spirit" is meant. When the adjective "holy" is associated with *pneúma*, then with or without a definite article the Holy Spirit is in view. Identifying the distinction between "Spirit" and "spirit" by using, or not using, a definite article is particularly a characteristic of Paul's writing.

Verbs

The correct translation of Greek verbs sometimes makes the translation sound un-English. In many texts modern translations have turned the present tense into a past tense to make the sentence "read better." I have chosen to translate the biblical texts as written. For example, at John 11:21, "Martha said," is aorist tense. The aorist indicates something has occurred. At John 11:24, the present tense is used, "Martha says to him." At 11:25, "Jesus said," aorist tense. At 11:27, "Martha says," present tense. The dialogue sounds strange to the reader familiar with the passage because modern versions use the past tense, "said," to translate the present tense "says," in 11:24, 27. I have maintained the verbal tense in the text.

Some Greek verb tenses do not have an exact English grammar equivalent, e.g., the Greek perfect tense, which is properly translated "having been." The perfect tense speaks of a past completed action whose affects are felt in the present. I have usually translated the perfect as "having been" (204 occurrences) but occasionally gave the sense of the tense. For example, Hebrews 10:10, "By that will we were and are sanctified through the offering of the body of Jesus Christ once for all."

I have compared and followed the best advice of several Greek grammars.

Prepositions

Prepositions are incredibly important to translation. For example, there are doctrinal issues at stake if you were sealed with, by, or in the Holy Spirit, Ephesians 1:13. To properly translate Greek prepositions, I have followed Wallace, *Greek Grammar Beyond the Basics.* Where prepositions important to doctrine, I have applied doctrine to the translation. For example, Ephesians 1:13, the Holy Spirit himself is not the seal, because he is a person not a thing. Therefore, "having believed you were sealed by the Holy Spirit of promise."

Semantic Range and Synonyms

Translation is affected by two inescapable facts of vocabulary: semantic range and synonyms. Semantic range means a word has different meanings as used in a culture and its language. For example, the English "ran" has many meanings. Here are two: I ran a mile, I ran a business. Same word, different meanings. And every word has synonyms, which are a word or phrase that means exactly or nearly the same as another word or phrase in the same language. Here are synonyms of "ran." I sprinted a mile. I managed a business. A Scripture example, translations of Acts 8:37 from the same Greek text: What hinders me from being baptized [KJV]? What prevents me from being immersed [JQTNT]?

Paragraphing

Preface

The New Testament manuscripts were written without spaces between the words, without punctuation, and without paragraphs. Dividing the text into paragraphs is a function of translation. Some versions, e.g., the KJV, made each verse a paragraph. The general rule is begin a new paragraph when the subject or theme changes. The paragraphing in the JQTNT is my translation.

Capitalization

The Greek text was copied by scribes in all capitals or all lower case. Capitalization is part of translation, not the text. In this translation, pronouns referring to deity are not capitalized. Adjectives, such as "first" and "last" in Revelation 1:11, are not capitalized. Only proper nouns are capitalized (a proper noun does not usually have a definite article or other qualifier. For example, I am James, not the James. In Revelation 1:11 the Greek text is, "I am the alpha [noun] and the omega [noun], the first [adjective] and the last [adjective]).

With one exception (John 12:34) Jesus Christ is the only person who used the title, "Son of Man." In his mouth capitalization is appropriate. The title "Son of God" is rendered "son of God" when said by Jesus' enemies, unless, as in Matthew 26:63; Mark 14:61; John 19:7, it is an accusation of slander against God. Jesus' enemies certainly did not believe Jesus was the messiah and certainly did not believe Jesus was deity incarnate.

In the gospels, the title "Son of God" is rendered "son of God" when said by disciples, apostles, those healed, Jesus' enemies, or fallen messengers, because they did not know Jesus the Christ was deity incarnate. I understand how that statement goes against all you have been taught. I will make some extended comments. Hear me out.

The fallen messengers called him "son of God," because they had heard Gabriel say, "He will be called 'son of Most High,'" Luke 1:32. The fallen messengers knew he was the messiah, for they had heard Gabriel say, "the Lord God will give him the throne of David, his father," Luke 1:32, cf. 2 Samuel 7:13–16, and they knew "son of Most High" ("Most High" was a recognized title for YHWH, forty-seven uses in the Old Testament), was the messiah, Psalm 2:2, 7.

The fallen messengers did not have the New Testament revelation that told them "son of Most High" was God the Son incarnate. What the fallen messengers knew was what their master Satan knew. If Satan had thought Jesus of Nazareth, whom Satan believed to be the messiah, was in fact God incarnate, would Satan have offered God the kingdoms of the world in exchange that God worship Satan the creature? At Matthew 4:3. Luke 4:3, the request to turn stones into bread was not a test of deity, but a demand Jesus prove he was the Messiah. Intertestamental literature, e.g., *Ecclesisates* Rabbah 1.9, said the Messiah would cause manna to descend [Bock & Herrick, 216–217]. Satan did not know this particular son of God was God the Son incarnate. Satan thought he could corrupt Jesus of Nazareth just as he had corrupted other sons of God, such as Adam the son of God, Luke 3:38.

The Old Testament believers in God understood God as one person, not a Trinity of three deity persons, one deity essence. The revelation of God as a Trinity, although there were hints in the Old Testament (e.g., God's spirit; Genesis 1:26), waited for the completed New Testament revelation. This fact impacts how we understand gospel comments and dialogue concerning Jesus the Christ.

Those who believed Jesus was the messiah saw him as a "son of God," per Psalm 2:2, 7. Not deity incarnate, but a man anointed by God to be King and rule Israel and the nations. No one during Jesus' lifespan on earth understood Jesus of Nazareth to be God incarnate. Many believed he was the Christ. But in the Old Testament revelation—the only existing revelation in gospel times—the Christ was a man whom God had anointed to be king, Psalm 2:2, 7–12, per 2 Samuel 7:13–16. *You today* read that Psalm, and other Old Testament scriptures, in the light of the New Testament revelation that those in gospels times *did not have*.

Think on this: if any person had believed Jesus of Nazareth was God incarnate—his parents, his disciples, his apostles, his enemies, or anyone else—they could not have interacted with him in a normal manner as with any other human being; but they did, indicating they did not know.

Consider this also: "no one has seen God at any time," John 1:18. God is a unique spirit being. God did not create any creature with the ability to perceive his unique essence. No one can see God the Father, God the Son, or God the Holy Spirit as they truly are, a unique immaterial spirit essence. The immaterial essence of God the Son embodied in the human being Jesus of Nazareth is not visible to the holy or fallen messengers, just as it is not visible to any other created being. For God to have created a being with the ability to perceive the unique spirit essence that is God would violate the principle, "no one has seen God at any time." God the Son in his incarnation revealed himself (and continues to reveal himself) through his words and acts, but the deity essence that is God the Son cannot be perceived by human or messenger.

For a discussion of this issue see any of my commentaries on the four gospels, or appendices in my book *Four Voices, One Testimony*.

Other Conventions

Time

In the ancient world, telling the time of day was based on three factors. One, sunrise; two the position of the sun in the sky; three, sunset. The Romans began their new day at what they perceived to be midnight. The Jews began their new day at sunset and reckoned the daytime hours from sunrise. My translation assumes the gospel writers used Jewish reckoning.

As to the time of day, when the sun was directly overhead it was the sixth hour, or in modern reckoning, about noon. When the position of the sun was between sunrise on the horizon but halfway to directly overhead the time was the third hour, or in modern reckoning, about nine a.m.

In my translation I have converted the Jewish hours of the day into modern chronology. But one must always bear in mind this is an approximation by the gospel writers, in accordance with the customs of the times. Sunrise was about 6:00 a.m., the third hour was midmorning or about 9:00 a.m., the sixth hour was about noon, the ninth hour was midafternoon or about 3:00 p.m., sunset was about 6:00 p.m., and the third hour of the night was about 9 pm, all without regard to seasonal variations. The rooster crowing divided the hours after midnight. Apparently roosters crowed around midnight and again about 1:30 am to 2:30 am.

Distances

Distances in the New Testament are usually given in Roman *stadia*. One Roman *stadia* was about 606.9 modern feet. I have translated *stadia* into modern equivalents. A "Sabbath day's journey" is mentioned only in Acts 1:12. Because no one is certain of the distance in modern terms (believed to be .75 miles, aka 1.2 km) I have not given a modern equivalent. Again, as with reckoning time, modern precision in reckoning distances should not be expected. For example I know it was about one hundred miles from Jerusalem to Capernaum, but to the biblical writer it was about three days travel by foot.

Chronology

At the head of each book I have given a brief introduction, including assumed dates when each book was written. My dating is based on Hollingsworth and Quiggle, *New Testament Chronology* (Amazon KDP, 2014); David Alan Black, *Why Four Gospels* (2nd ed., Gonzalez, FL: Energion Publications, 2010); Frank J. Goodwin, *A Harmony of the Life of St. Paul* (Grand Rapids, MI: Baker Book House, 1951), and my own conclusions concerning these matters.

The order of the New Testament books in this work is the traditional order. However, reading the New Testament books chronologically has value in seeing the development of doctrine and testimony over the course of the fifty or so years of the apostolic age. See table, below. Dates are approximate.

Preface

The Date column reflects the best judgment of when the book was written.

Date	Book	Date	Book
AD 42	Gospel of Matthew	AD 62–63	Acts
AD 45	James	AD 62–64	1 Peter
AD 49–52	1 Thessalonians	AD 64–67	2 Peter
AD 50–51	Galatians	AD 66–67	Gospel of Mark
AD 53	2 Thessalonians	AD 67	1 Timothy
AD 57	1 Corinthians	AD 67	Titus
AD 57	2 Corinthians	AD 68	2 Timothy
AD 58	Romans	AD 67–70	Jude
AD 58–62	Gospel of Luke	AD 68–69	Hebrews
AD 62	Ephesians	AD 95	1, 2, 3 John
AD 62	Philippians	AD 95–96	Gospel of John
AD 62	Colossians	AD 95–96	Revelation
AD 62	Philemon		

There is a benefit to be gained, I believe, in reading the New Testament historical narratives, the gospels and Acts, as a unit, in the order written: Matthew, Luke, Mark, John, followed by Acts; then reading the development of church and doctrine as a unit, in the order written: James, 1 Thessalonians, Galatians, 2 Thessalonians, 1 & 2 Corinthians, Romans, Ephesians, Philippians, Colossians, Philemon, 1 & 2 Peter, 1 Timothy, Titus, 2 Timothy, Jude, Hebrews, 1, 2, 3 John; and then the Revelation, which stands by itself as a letter from Jesus Christ about the yet-future (John was not the author but was the scribe to Jesus and publisher of the book).

A note on dating Matthew, Luke, and Mark. I have followed Black's argument (*Why Four Gospels*) in dating the books. It seems likely to me Matthew was written to be the evangelistic document of the apostolic church, and so used by Paul. Having used Matthew, Paul commissioned Luke to write a gospel more suitable for evangelizing gentiles. The date is for Luke is its composition during the years Paul was under house arrest with Felix and Festus. Mark's gospel, which is really Peter's gospel (according to the church father Papias), was a series of lectures given by Peter, in response to reviewing Luke's gospel (so Black), stenographically recorded, and then published with Peter's approval. I also agree with Black that Mark was first published in Rome,

Preface

Italy, by Mark and Peter, without 16:9–20, then later published in Alexandria, Egypt by Mark with 16:9–20, to include post-resurrection events, as did Matthew and Luke (and with which Mark 16:9–20 agrees), and thus the section is as inspired by the Holy Spirit as the rest of Mark's gospel. See Black for a detailed discussion. See Black for a detailed discussion.

Translation Notes

Translation is, or should be, more than grammar and vocabulary. If the purpose of translation is to communicate the author's truth-intention through the words he selected, and it is, then the translator should consider the several contexts affecting the words, the passage, the paragraph, the book, the author, the original reader, and the historical-cultural circumstances in which the book was written. The Analogy of Scripture and the Analogy of Faith should also be kept in mind, so that any particular translation conforms to the teaching of the Scripture as a whole. If a translation or interpretation choice contradicts any other part of the Scripture, then the translator or interpreter should seek another solution. My goal was to communicate the author's truth-intention through the words he selected, by selecting appropriate English words and punctuation for the translation, that agreed with the teaching of Scripture as a whole.

Certain translation choices in the JQTNT are marked with superscript characters in the text, that correspond to translation notes located after the New Testament books. The translation notes are not text critical notes, for which see the works of the textual critics.

The translation notes are explanations why I chose to make certain translations that differ from others in popular use. In some scriptures there were textual reasons for my choices, but more often the choices were for lexical or syntactical reasons, or in some cases to properly communicate orthodox doctrine (e.g., at John 1:14) in a way agreeable to the Greek text. A few translation choices, e.g., Mark 13:24, where the preposition *metá* is translated "with" versus "after," were made to conform with the teaching of Scripture as a whole. Not every choice is explained by a translation note, only those that created a significant difference from other translations.

Most, but not all, of the translation notes are from my commentaries on the New Testament, which as of this writing does not include Romans, 1 Corinthians, and 2 Corinthians. Translation notes for those Bible books were generated during the act of translating.

The superscript characters used within the biblical text and the corresponding notes are lower case alphabet characters.

Translation Resources

Primary translation resources and translation notes resources are listed following the text of the *JQT New Testament*.

The JQT New Testament

The Book of Matthew

The good news according to Matthew was written ca. AD 42 as the primary evangelistic document for the New Testament church. Matthew's purpose was to prove to the Jews that Jesus of Nazareth was the Christ prophesied in the Old Testament Scripture. This is the document used by the Twelve, Paul, and others until Luke and Mark were written and published.

MATTHEW ONE

1 Book of the genealogy of Jesus Christ, son of David, son of Abraham.

2 Abraham fathered Isaac; and Isaac fathered Jacob; and Jacob fathered Judah and his brothers; 3 and Judah fathered Perez and Zerah of Tamar; and Perez fathered Hezron; and Hezron fathered Ram; 4 and Ram fathered Amminadab; and Amminadab fathered Nahshon; and Nahshon fathered Salmon; 5 and Salmon fathered Boaz of Rahab; and Boaz fathered Obed of Ruth; and Obed fathered Jesse; 6 and Jesse fathered David the king.

And David the king fathered Solomon of her of Uriah; 7 and Solomon fathered Rehoboam; and Rehoboam fathered Abijah; and Abijah fathered Asa; 8 and Asa fathered Jehoshaphat; and Jehoshaphat fathered Joram; and Joram fathered Uzziah; 9 and Uzziah fathered Jotham; and Jotham fathered Ahaz; and Ahaz fathered Hezekiah; 10 and Hezekiah fathered Manasseh; and Manasseh fathered Amon; and Amon fathered Josiah. 11 and Josiah fathered Jeconiah and his brothers at the time of the relocation to Babylon.

12 And after the relocation to Babylon Jeconiah fathered Shealtiel; and Shealtiel fathered Zerubbabel; 13 and Zerubbabel fathered Abiud; and Abiud fathered Eliakim, and Eliakim fathered Azor; 14 and Azor fathered Zadok; and Zadok fathered Achim; and Achim fathered Eliud; 15 and Eliud fathered Eleazar; and Eleazar fathered Matthan; and Matthan fathered Jacob; 16 and Jacob fathered Joseph the husband of Mariam, of whom was born Jesus, the one named Christ.

17 Therefore all the generations from Abraham to David were fourteen generations; and from David until the relocation to Babylon fourteen generations; and from the relocation to Babylon to the Christ fourteen generations.

18 Now of Jesus Christ the genealogy[a] was in this manner. Mariam his mother was betrothed to Joseph. Before they came together, she was pregnant from the Holy Spirit. 19 But Joseph her husband, being righteous, and not willing to expose her publicly, desired to secretly divorce her. 20 But these things he having thought (his spirit was agitated[b]), behold, a messenger[c] of the Lord in a dream appeared to him, saying, "Joseph, son of David, do not fear to receive

Mariam as your wife, for that conceived in her is from the Holy Spirit. 21 She will bear a son, and you will call his name Jesus; for he will save his people from their sins."

22 So all this was done that may be fulfilled that having been spoken by the Lord through the prophet, saying: 23 "Behold, the virgin shall be with child, and bear a son, and they shall call his name Immanuel," which is translated, "God with us."

24 Then Joseph, being aroused from sleep, did as the messenger of the Lord commanded him and took to him his wife, 25 and did not know her until she had brought forth her firstborn son. And he called his name Jesus.

MATTHEW TWO

1 Now Jesus, having been born in Bethlehem of Judea in the times of Herod the king, behold, wise men from the east arrived at Jerusalem, 2 saying, "Where is the one who was born King of the Jews? For we saw his star in the east and have come to do homage[d] to him."

3 But having heard, Herod the king was troubled, and all Jerusalem with him. 4 And having gathered together all the chief priests and scribes of the people, he asked them where the Christ was to be born.

5 And they said to him, "In Bethlehem of Judea, for thus it has been written through the prophet:

6 'And you, Bethlehem in the land of Judah, by no means are least in the rulers of Judah. For out of you will come forth a ruler who will shepherd my people Israel.'"

7 Then Herod, having secretly called the wise men, inquired exactly of them the time of the star's appearing. 8 And sending them to Bethlehem, he said, "Go. Search carefully for the child.[e] Then, whenever you have found him, make it known to me, that I might come and do homage to him."

9 Now, having heard the heard the king, they went. And they saw the star—the one they saw in the east—going before them until it came and stood over where the child was. 10 Now when they had seen the star they earnestly rejoiced with great joy.

11 And having come into the house, they looked at the child with Mariam his mother. And falling down they did homage to him. And opening their riches, they brought gifts to him: gold and frankincense and myrrh. 12 And having been warned by God in a dream not to return to Herod, they went into their country through another way.

13 Now after they left, behold, a messenger of the Lord appears in a dream to Joseph, saying, "Get up. Take the child and his mother and escape to Egypt, and remain there until I may tell you; for Herod is about to look for the child to destroy him."

14 Now getting up he took the

child and his mother by night and went into Egypt, 15 and was there until Herod's death, that might be fulfilled that spoken by the Lord through the prophet, saying, "Out of Egypt I have called my son."

16 Then Herod, when he understood that he had been deceived by the wise men, was very angry, and he sent to put to death all the male children that were in Bethlehem and in all its region, from two years old and under, according to the time which he had inquired from the wise men. 17 Then was fulfilled that spoken by Jeremiah the prophet, saying, 18 "A voice was heard in Ramah, great wailing and mourning, Rachel wailing for her children and would not be comforted, because they are no more."

19 Now Herod having died, behold, a messenger of the Lord appears in a dream to Joseph in Egypt, 20 saying, "Get up, take the child and his mother, and go into the land of Israel. For those seeking the life of the child have died."

21 Now Joseph got up, took the child and his mother, and came into the land of Israel. 22 But having heard that Archelaus rules Judea in place of his father Herod, he was afraid to go there. Having been warned by God in a dream, he turned in to the region of Galilee. 23 And having come he lived in a city called Nazareth, so that might be fulfilled what was spoken through the prophets, that "He will be called a Nazarene."

MATTHEW THREE

1 Now, in those times, John the Immerser comes preaching in the wilderness of Judea, 2 and saying, "Repent, for the kingdom of the heavens is near!" 3 For he is the one declared through Isaiah the prophet, saying: "the voice of one exclaiming in the wilderness: 'make ready the way of the Lord; make his paths straight.'"

4 Now John himself, his clothing was camel's hair, and a belt of leather around his waist; and his food was locusts and wild honey.

5 Then went out to him Jerusalem, and all Judea, and all the region around the Jordan, 6 and were immersed[f] in the Jordan by him, confessing their sins. 7 But having seen many of the Pharisees and Sadducees coming to his immersing, he said to them, "Generation of vipers! Who instructed you to flee from the coming wrath? 8 Therefore produce fruit worthy of repentance, 9 and think not to say in yourselves, 'A father we have, Abraham.' For I say to you that God is able from these stones to raise up children unto Abraham. 10 Even now the ax is being used against the root of the trees. Therefore a tree not producing good fruit is being cut down, and into the fire is thrown.

11 "I indeed immerse you in water unto repentance, but the one coming after me, he is

mightier than me, whose shoes I am not worthy to carry, he will immerse you inᵍ the Holy Spirit and with fire. 12 Of whom the winnowing shovel is in his hand, and he will thoroughly clean out his threshing floor and gather his wheat into the storehouse; but the chaff he will burn with unquenchable fire."

13 Then Jesus came from Galilee to the Jordan unto John to be immersed by him. 14 But John hindered him, saying, "I have need to be immersed by you, and you come to me?" 15 But Jesus said to him, "You let this pass for the present time; for thus it is proper to us to fully accomplish all righteousness." Then he allowed him.

16 Now having completed his immersion, Jesus immediately came up from the water. And behold, the heavens were opened to him, and he saw the Spirit of God as a dove descending and coming upon him. 17 And he perceived a voice out of the heavens, saying, "This is my son, the beloved, in whom I am well pleased."

MATTHEW FOUR

1 Then Jesus was led up into the wilderness by the Spirit to be tempted by the devil. 2 And having fasted forty days and forty nights, afterward he was hungry.

3 And having come, the tempter said to him, "If you are God's son, speak that these stones might become bread." 4 But answering he said, "It has been written, 'Not by bread alone shall the man live, but on every word that comes from the mouth of God.'"

5 Then the devil takes him to the holy city and sets him upon the highest point of the temple, 6 and says to him, "If you are God's son, throw yourself down. For it has been written: 'To his messengers he will give command concerning you,' and 'In their hands they will bear you so at no time may you strike your foot against a stone.'" 7 Jesus said to him, "Again it has been written, 'You will not put to the test the Lord your God.'"

8 Again, the devil takes him to a very high mountain, and shows to him all the kingdoms of the world and their glory, 9 and he says to him, "These things, to you I will give all, if falling down you will worship me." 10 Then Jesus says to him, "Go away, Satan! For it has been written, 'The Lord your God you will worship, and him alone you will serve.'"

11 Then the devil leaves him, and look, *God's* messengers came and ministered to him.

12 Now having heard that John had been arrested, he withdrew into Galilee. 13 And having left Nazareth, he came and dwelt in Capernaum, which is by the seaside, in the regions of Zebulun and Naphtali, 14 that might be fulfilled that spoken by Isaiah the prophet, saying, 15 "Land of Zebulun and land of Naphtali, way of *the* sea, beyond

the Jordan, Galilee of the gentiles, 16 the people sitting in darkness have seen a great light and those sitting in the country and shadow of death, a light has dawned on them."

17 From that time Jesus began to preach and to say, "Repent, for the kingdom of the heavens has drawn near."

18 Now walking by the Sea of Galilee he saw two brothers, Simon called Peter and Andrew his brother, casting a large net into the sea, for they were fishermen. 19 And he says to them, "Follow me and I will make you fishers of men." 20 Now immediately leaving the nets, they followed him. 21 And having gone on from there he saw others, two brothers, Jacob the son of Zebedee and John his brother, in the boat with Zebedee their father, mending their nets, and he called them. 22 Now having immediately left the boat and their father, they followed him.

23 And he went in all Galilee, teaching in their synagogues, and preaching the good news of the kingdom, and healing all disease and all sickness among the people.

24 And the news of him went out into all Syria. And they brought to him all the sick having varied diseases and pains, oppressed and being inhabited by demons,[h] and being epileptics[i] and paralytics; and he healed them. 25 And great crowds followed him from Galilee, and the Decapolis, and Jerusalem, and Judea, and beyond the Jordan.

MATTHEW FIVE

1 Now seeing the crowds, he went up on the mountain. And when he had sat down his disciples came to him. 2 And opening his mouth, he taught them, saying, 3 "Blessed the poor in the spirit, because theirs is the kingdom of the heavens.

4 "Blessed those mourning, because they will be comforted. 5 Blessed the meek, because they will inherit the earth. 6 Blessed those hungering and thirsting for righteousness, because they shall be filled. 7 Blessed the merciful, because they will receive mercy. 8 Blessed the pure in heart, because they will see God. 9 Blessed the peacemakers, because they will be called sons of God.

10 "Blessed those having been persecuted because of righteousness, because theirs is the kingdom of the heavens. 11 Blessed are you when they may revile you and may persecute you, and may say all kinds of evil against you, lying on account of me. 12 Rejoice and leap for joy, for great is your reward in the heavens, for so they persecuted the prophets before you.

13 "You are the salt of the earth; but if the salt is no longer salty, with what shall it be salted? It can be used for nothing any longer, except to be thrown out to be trampled by men.

14 "You are the light of the world. A city is not able to be hidden setting upon a hill. 15 Nor do they light a lamp and put it under a basket, but upon the

lampstand, and it shines for all those in the house. 16 Thus let shine your light before men, so that they might see your good works and they should glorify your Father in the heavens.

17 "Think not that I came to destroy the Law or the prophets. I have not come to destroy but to fulfill. 18 For truly I say to you, until the heaven and the earth may pass away, never no never will one iota or one point from the Law pass away until all may be accomplished.

19 "Whoever then may break one of these commandments, even the least, and may teach so to others, he will be called least in the kingdom of the heavens; but whoever may practice and may teach them, he shall be called great in the kingdom of the heavens.

20 "For I say to you, that unless your righteousness may abound above the scribes and Pharisees, never no never might you enter into the kingdom of the heavens.

21 "You have heard that it was said at the beginning, 'You shall not murder,' and 'whoever shall murder will be liable to the judgment.' 22 But I say to you, that any person becoming angry with his brother without cause will be liable to the judgment. Moreover, any person who may say to his brother, 'Raca'[j] will be liable to the Sanhedrin. Moreover, any person who may say 'Moros'[k] will be liable to the fire of Gehenna.[l]

23 "Therefore, if you should offer your gift at the altar, and there you should remember that your brother has something against you, 24 leave your gift there before the altar, and go away. First be reconciled to your brother, and having returned offer your gift.

25 "Become friends with your accuser quickly, while you are on the way with him, that the accuser never deliver you to the judge, and the judge to the officer, and into prison you will be cast. 26 Truly I say to you, you will never no never come out from there until you should pay the last coin.

27 "You have heard that it was said at the beginning, 'You shall not commit adultery.' 28 But I say to you that anyone looking upon a woman to lust for her has already committed adultery with her in his heart.

29 "But if your right eye leads you into sin, take it out and cast it from you; it is advantageous for you that one of your members should perish, and not all your body be cast into Gehenna. 30 And if your right hand leads you to sin, cut it off and cast it from you; it is advantageous for you that one of your members should perish, and not all your body be cast into Gehenna.

31 "Now it was said, 'Anyone who should divorce his wife, let him give her a written notice of divorce.' 32 But I say to you, that any man divorcing his wife except on account of sexual immorality causes her to commit adultery;

and whoever it may be should marry a woman having been divorced commits adultery.

33 "Again, you have heard that it was said at the beginning, 'You shall not swear falsely, but you shall keep your oaths to the Lord.' 34 But I say to you not to swear at all: not by heaven, because it is God's throne; 35 not by the earth, because it is the footstool for his feet; not by Jerusalem, it is the city of the great King; 36 not by your head will you swear, because you are not able to make one hair white or black. 37 But let your word be 'Yes, Yes'; 'No, No'; now more than these comes from evil.

38 "You have heard that it was said, 'Eye for eye and tooth for tooth.' 39 But I say to you, resist not the evil; but whoever might strike you on your right cheek, turn to him also the other; 40 and to the one willing to sue you and take your shirt, let him have your coat also; 41 and whoever may compel you to go one mile, go with him two. 42 To the one asking, give; and you should not turn away from the one desiring to borrow from you.

43 "You have heard that it was said, 'You will love your neighbor and you will hate your enemy.' 44 But I say to you, love your enemies, and pray for those persecuting you; bless those cursing you, do good to those misusing you and hating you, 45 so that you may be sons of your Father in the heavens. Because he makes his sun rise on evil and good, and sends rain on righteous and unrighteous. 46 For if you love those loving you, what reward have you? Do not also the tax collectors do the same? 47 And if you greet your brethren only, what more do you? Do not also the gentiles do the same? 48 Therefore you will be *as* mature^m as your heavenly Father is perfect."

MATTHEW SIX

1 "But beware your righteousness is not practiced before men in order to be seen by them; otherwise you will have no reward from your Father in the heavens. 2 Therefore when you practice compassion toward the poor, do not sound a trumpet before you, as the hypocrites do in the synagogues and in the streets, that they might have glory from men. Truly, I say to you, they have their reward. 3 But when you practice compassion toward the poor, do not let your left hand know what your right hand is doing, 4 so that your compassion toward the poor may be in secret; and your Father, the one seeing in secret, will reward you.

5 "And when you pray, do not be like the hypocrites, because they love to pray in the synagogues and in the corners of the streets, standing to pray, so that they may be seen by men. Truly, I say to you, they have their reward. 6 But you, when you pray, go into your room, and having shut your door, pray to your Father who is in secret; and your Father seeing

in secret will reward you. 7 Now when praying, do not repeat the same thing over and over again like the pagans; for they think that in their many words they will be heard. 8 Therefore do not be like them. For the Father knows of what things you have need before you ask him.

9 "You, therefore, pray in this manner: 'Our Father, who is in the heavens, your name be sanctified, 10 your kingdom come, your will be done, as in heaven also upon earth. 11 Our daily bread give us today, 12 and forgive us our offenses, even as we have forgiven those who offend us. 13 And bring us not into a state of trial,ⁿ but deliver us from the evildoers.' 14 For if you forgive men their wrongdoing, your heavenly Father will also forgive you. 15 But if you do not forgive men their wrongdoing, neither will your Father forgive your wrongdoing.

16 "Now, whenever you fast, do not be like the hypocrites with sad faces. For they disfigure their faces, so that they may appear to men to be fasting. Truly I say to you, they have their reward. 17 But you fasting anoint your head and wash your face, 18 so that you may not appear to men to be fasting, but to your Father, who is in secret; and your Father seeing in secret will reward you.

19 "Do not store up for yourselves treasures upon earth where moth and rust destroy, and where thieves break in and steal, 20 but store up for yourselves treasures in heaven, where neither moth nor rust destroy and where thieves do not break in nor steal. 21 For where your treasure is, there will be your heart also.

22 "The lamp of the body is the eye. Therefore if your eye is healthy, your whole body will be full of light. 23 But if your eye is evil, all your body will be full of darkness. If therefore the light that is within you is darkness, how great that darkness!

24 "No one is able to serve two masters; for either he will hate the one and the other he will love, or he will be devoted to the one and the other he will hold in contempt. You are not able to serve God and the god of materialism.º

25 "Therefore I say to you, do not be anxious about your life, what you should eat or what you should drink; nor your body, what you should put on. Is not one's life more than food and the body more than clothing? 26 Consider the birds of the air, that they sow not, nor do they reap, nor do they gather into barns; and your heavenly Father feeds them. Are you not much more valuable than they?

27 "Can any of you by being anxious add to his lifespanᵖ one hour? 28 And why are you anxious about clothing? Consider the lilies of the field, how they grow: they neither toil nor spin; 29 But I say to you that not even Solomon in all his glory was clothed like one of these. 30 Now if God thus clothes the grass of the field, being here today and tomorrow thrown into

the furnace, will he not you much more, you of little faith?

31 "Therefore do not be anxious, saying, 'What shall we eat?' or 'What shall we drink?' or 'What shall we wear?' 32 For all these things the gentiles seek to acquire. For your heavenly Father knows that you need them all. 33 But seek first the kingdom of God and his righteousness; and all these things will be added to you. 34 Therefore do not be anxious about tomorrow, for tomorrow will be anxious about itself. Sufficient to the day is its trouble."

MATTHEW SEVEN

1 "Do not judge, that you should not be judged. 2 For with whatever judgment you judge, you will be judged; and with whatever measure you measure, it will be measured to you. 3 But why do you look at the splinter that is in your brother's eye, but in your eye not notice the beam? 4 Or how will you say to your brother, 'Permit that I might take out the splinter from your eye,' and look, the beam is in your eye? 5 Hypocrite, first take out the beam from your eye, and then you will see clearly to take out the splinter from your brother's eye.

6 "Do not give what is holy to the dogs; nor cast your pearls before the pigs, so they may not treat them with contempt,q and then turn and tear you to pieces.

7 "Ask and it will be given to you; seek and you will find; knock and it will be opened to you. 8 Because everyone asking receives; and the one seeking finds; and to the one knocking it will be opened.

9 "Or which man of you, whom his son will ask for bread, he will not give him a stone, will he? 10 Or also he will ask for a fish, he will not give him a serpent, will he? 11 If therefore you, being evil, know to give good gifts to your children, how much more your Father who is in the heavens will give good things to those asking him.

12 "All things therefore, all that you might desire that men should do to you, so also you do to them, for this is the Law and the prophets.

13 "Enter through the narrow gate; because wide the gate and broad the way leading to destruction, and many are those entering through it; 14 because narrow the gate and difficult the way leading to life, and few are those finding it.

15 "Beware of false prophets, who come to you in sheep's clothing, but inwardly they are ravenous wolves. 16 By their fruits you will know them. They don't gather grapes from thornbushes, or figs from thistles, do they? 17 So every good tree produces good fruits; but a bad tree produces bad fruits. 18 A good tree is not able to produce bad fruits, nor can a bad tree produce good fruits. 19 Every tree not producing good fruit is cut down and into the fire is thrown. 20 Therefore then, by their fruits you will know them.

21 "Not everyone saying to

me, 'Lord, Lord,' will enter into the kingdom of the heavens, but the one doing the will of my Father who is in the heavens. 22 Many will say to me in that day, 'Lord, Lord, did we not in your name prophesy, and in your name cast out demons, and in your name perform many miracles?' 23 And then I will declare to them, those working lawlessness, 'Because I never knew you, you depart from me.'

24 "Everyone therefore, whoever hears these my words and does them, will be like a wise man who built his house upon the rock, 25 and the rain came down and the floods came and the winds blew, and fell against the house, and the house did not fall, for its foundation was upon the rock. 26 And everyone hearing my words and not doing them, he will be like a foolish man who built his house on the sand, 27 and the rain came down and the floods came and the winds blew, and fell against the house, and it fell, and its fall was great."

28 And so it was when Jesus had finished these words, the crowds were astonished at his teaching, 29 because he was teaching them as having authority, and not as their scribes.

MATTHEW EIGHT

1 Now he having come down from the mountain, great crowds followed him. 2 And look, a leper having come knelt before him,[r] saying, "Sir,[s] if you are willing, you are able to cleanse me." 3 And having stretched out the hand, he touched him, saying, "I am willing, be cleansed." And immediately his leprosy was cleansed. 4 And Jesus says to him, "See that you tell no one, but go, show yourself to the priest, and offer the gift that Moses commanded, for a testimony to them."

5 Now having entered into Capernaum, a centurion came to him, pleading with him, 6 and saying, "Sir, my servant is lying in the house, paralyzed, in terrible pain."[t] 7 And he says to him, "I will come and heal him." 8 But the centurion answering said, "Sir, I am not worthy that you should come under my roof. But only speak the word, and my servant will be healed. 9 For I also am a man under authority, having under me soldiers I set in order; and I say to this one, 'Go,' and he goes; and to another, 'Come,' and he comes; and to my servant, 'Do this,' and he does it."

10 Now having heard, Jesus marveled, and said to those following, "Truly I say to you, among Israel I have found no one with so great faith. 11 Now I say to you, that many from east and west will come and will recline at the table[u] with Abraham, Isaac, and Jacob in the kingdom of the heavens. 12 But the sons of the kingdom will be cast out into the outer darkness; there will be weeping and gnashing of teeth."

13 And Jesus said to the centurion, "Go. As you have believed, be it to you." And his servant was healed in that hour.

The Book of Matthew

14 And Jesus, having come to Peter's house, saw his mother-in-law lying sick and running a fever. 15 And he touched her hand, and the fever left her; and she arose and served them.

16 Now evening having come, they brought to him many inhabited by demons, and he cast out the spirits with a word, and he healed all those being sick, 17 so that might be fulfilled having been spoken through Isaiah the prophet, saying: "himself our sicknesses took, and our diseases bore."

18 Now Jesus, having seen a great crowd around him, he commanded to depart to the other side. 19 And one scribe coming to him, said to him, "Teacher, I will follow you wherever you may go." 20 And Jesus says to him, "Foxes have holes, and the birds of the air nests, but the Son of Man has no place where he might lay his head." 21 Now another of his disciples said to him, "Master, allow me first to go and to bury my father." 22 But Jesus said to him, "Follow me, and leave the dead to bury their own dead."

23 And having entered the boat, his disciples followed him. 24 And look, a violent windstorm arose on the sea, so that the boat was being swamped by the waves. But he was asleep. 25 And having come to him, they awoke him, saying, "Master, save us, we are perishing." 26 And he says to them, "Why are you fearful, you of little faith?" Then, having arisen, he restrained[v] the winds and the sea, and there was great calm. 27 But the men wondered, saying, "What kind of man is this, that even the winds and the sea obey him?"

28 And having come to the other side, to the country of the Gadarenes, two met him, inhabited by demons, coming out of the tombs. They were very violent, so that no one was able to pass by that way. 29 And look, they cried out, saying, "What are we to you, son of God? Are you come here before the time to torment us?"

30 Now there was far away from them a herd of many pigs, feeding. 31 Now the demons begged him, saying, "If you cast us out, send us away into the herd of pigs." 32 And he said to them, "Go." Now having gone out, they went away into the pigs, and look, all the herd rushed down the steep bank into the sea, and died in the waters.

33 Now those feeding them fled, and having gone away into the city, told everything, even about the men inhabited by demons. 34 And look, all the city went out to meet Jesus; and having seen him, they begged him that he would go away from their country.

MATTHEW NINE

1 And having entered into a boat, he crossed over and came to his own city. 2 And look, they brought to him a paralytic lying on a bed; and Jesus having seen their faith, he said to the paralytic,

"Have courage, my son, your sins are forgiven."

3 And look, some of the scribes said to themselves, "This man slanders God!"ʷ 4 And Jesus, having known their thoughts, he said, "Why are you thinking evil in your hearts? 5 For which is easier? To say, 'Your sins are forgiven,' or to say, 'Get up and walk.' 6 But in order that you might know that the Son of Man has authority on the earth to forgive sins" (then he says to the paralytic), "Get up, take up your bed, and go to your house." 7 And he got up and went away to his house. 8 Now having seen, the crowds were awed, and glorified God who had given such authority to men.

9 And from there, Jesus saw a man sitting at the tax office, named Matthew, and says to him, "Follow me." And getting up, he followed him.

10 And it happened, reclining at his table in the house, that behold, many tax-collectors and sinners, having come, were reclining at the table with Jesus and his disciples. 11 And having seen it, the Pharisees said to his disciples, "Why is it your teacher is eating with tax-collectors and sinners?" 12 Now having heard, he said, "The strong have no need of a physician, but rather those being ill. 13 But go, learn what is 'Mercy I desire, and not sacrifice.' For I did not come to call the righteous, but sinners." [ˣ]

14 Then came to him John's disciples, saying, "Why do we and the Pharisees fast often, but your disciples do not fast?" 15 And Jesus said to them, "The sons of the bride-chamberʸ cannot mourn as long as the bridegroom is with them, can they? But times will come when the bridegroom will have been taken away from them, and then they will fast. 16 But no one puts a piece of unshrunk cloth on old clothing; for the patch tears away from the cloth, and a worse tear is made. 17 Nor do they pour new wine into old wineskins; but if it is, the wineskins burst and the wine is spilled and the wineskins ruined. But rather they pour new wine into new wineskins, and both are preserved."

18 As he was saying these things to them, look, one of the leaders came and knelt before him, saying, "My daughter is at this moment dead, but come and lay your hand upon her and she will live." 19 And Jesus got up and followed him and his disciples.

20 And look, a woman having a flow of blood twelve years, having come behind him, touched the fringe of his garment.ᶻ 21 For she said in herself, "If only I might touch his garment, I will be delivered." 22 But Jesus, having turned and having seen her, said, "Have courage, daughter; your faith has delivered you." And the woman was delivered from that very hour.

23 And Jesus, having come into the ruler's house, and seeing the flute players and the crowd lamenting the dead, 24 says, "Go

away, for the girl is not dead, but sleeps." And they laughed at him. 25 But when the crowd had been put outside, having entered, he took her hand, and the girl sat up. 26 And this report went out into all that land.

27 And Jesus, passing on from there, two blind men followed him, crying out and saying, "Son of David, have mercy on us!" 28 Now having come into the house, the blind men came to him, and Jesus says to them, "Do you believe that I am able to do this?" They say to him, "Yes, sir!" 29 Then he touched their eyes, saying, "According to your faith be it to you." 30 And their eyes were opened. And Jesus sternly warned them, saying, "See that no one knows." 31 But, having departed, they made him known in all that land.

32 Now, as they were going out, look, they brought to him a mute man, inhabited by a demon. 33 And the demon having been cast out, the mute spoke. And the multitudes were astonished, saying, "Never was it seen like this in Israel!" 34 But the Pharisees said, "By the ruler of the demons he casts out demons."

35 And Jesus went to all the towns and the villages, teaching in their synagogues, and proclaiming the good news of the kingdom, and healing every disease and every infirmity. 36 But having seen the crowds he was moved with compassion for them, because they were wearied and scattered, as sheep not having a shepherd. 37 Then he says to his disciples, "Truly the harvest is plentiful, but the workers few. 38 Pray therefore the master of the harvest, that he might send workmen into his harvest."

MATTHEW TEN

1 And having called twelve of his disciples, he gave them authority over unclean spirits, so as to cast them out, and to heal all kinds of disease and all kinds of infirmity. 2 Now the names of the Twelve apostles are these: first, Simon, the one called Peter, and Andrew his brother; and Jacob the son of Zebedee, and John his brother; 3 Philip and Bartholomew; Thomas, and Matthew the tax-collector; Jacob the one of Alphaeus, and Thaddaeus; 4 Simon the Zealot; and Judas Iscariot, who also betrayed him.

5 These twelve Jesus sent out, having instructed them, saying, "Do not go into the way of the gentiles, and do not enter any city of the Samaritans. 6 But go rather to the lost sheep of the house of Israel.

7 "Now going proclaim, saying, 'The kingdom of the heavens has drawn near.' 8 Infirm be healing, dead be raising, lepers be cleansing, demons be casting out. You freely received; freely give. 9 Do not take gold, nor silver, nor copper in your belts, 10 nor food-bag for the journey, nor two tunics, nor sandals, nor a staff: for the worker is worthy of his hire.

11 "Now into whatever city or

town you may enter, ask who in it is worthy, and there remain until you may leave. 12 Now entering into the house, greet the family. 13 And if the house be worthy, let your peace come upon it; but if it not be worthy, let your peace return to you. 14 And whoever may not receive you, nor will hear your words, when going out of that house or the city, shake off the dust of your feet. 15 Truly I say to you, it will be more tolerable for the land of Sodom and of Gomorrah in the day of judgment than for that city.

16 "Look, I am sending you as sheep among wolves. Therefore you be wise as the serpents and innocent as the doves. 17 But beware of men. For they will deliver you to councils; and in their synagogues they will whip you; 18 and before governors and kings you will be brought on account of me for a testimony to them and to the gentiles. 19 But when they deliver you, do not be anxious how or what you might say. For it will be given you in that hour what you should say; 20 for you are not the ones speaking, but the Spirit of your Father is speaking through you.

21 "Now brother will deliver brother to death, and father child; and children will rise up against parents and will put them to death. 22 And you will be hated by all on account of my name. But the one having endured to the end, he will be delivered. 23 But whenever they persecute you in the one city, flee to the next. For truly, I say to you, by no means will you have completed the cities of Israel till the Son of Man may come.

24 "A disciple is not above the teacher, nor a servant above his master. 25 Sufficient for the disciple that he be as the teacher, and the servant as his master. If they called the master of the house Beelzebul, how much more the members of his household! 26 Therefore you should not fear them.

"For nothing is concealed which will not be revealed, and hidden which will not be known. 27 What I tell you in the dark, speak in the light; and what you hear in the ear, proclaim upon the housetops.

28 "And do not be afraid of those killing the body, but are not able to kill the soul; but fear rather the one being able to ruin both soul and body in Gehenna. 29 Two sparrows are sold for a brass coin,[aa] aren't they? And not one of them will fall to the ground apart from your Father. 30 But even the hairs of your head are all numbered. 31 Fear not, therefore; you are worth more than many sparrows.

32 "Anyone therefore who will confess in me before men, I also will confess in him in the presence of my Father who is in the heavens. 33 But whoever may deny me before men, I also him in the presence of my Father who is in the heavens.

34 "Think not that I came to bring peace to the earth. I came

not to bring peace, but a sword. 35 For I came to incite a man against his father; and a daughter against her mother; and a daughter-in-law against her mother-in-law; 36 and the man's enemies his household.

37 "The person loving father or mother more than me is not worthy of me; and the person loving son or daughter more than me is not worthy of me; 38 and he who does not take his cross and follow after me is not worthy of me. 39 He who having found his life will lose it; and he having lost his life on account of me will find it.

40 "The person receiving you receives me; and the person receiving me receives the one having sent me. 41 The person receiving a prophet in the name of a prophet will receive the reward of a prophet; and the person receiving a righteous man in the name of a righteous man will receive the reward of a righteous man; 42 and whoever might give one of the little ones of these a cup of cold water, only in the name of a disciple, truly I say to you he shall by no means lose his reward."

MATTHEW ELEVEN

1 And so it was when Jesus finished instructing his twelve disciples, he left there to teach and to preach in their cities. 2 Now John, having heard in the prison the works of the Christ, having sent two of his disciples, 3 he said to him, "Are you the Coming One, or are we to look for another?"

4 And answering Jesus said to them, "Go and tell to John what you hear and see: 5 blind see, and lame walk, lepers are cleansed, and deaf hear, and dead are raised, and to helpless poor good news proclaimed. 6 And blessed is he who may not be offended in me."

7 Now as they were going away, Jesus began to speak to the crowds about John. "What went you out into the wilderness to see? A reed waving in the wind? 8 But what did you go out to see? A man in soft clothing? Look, those wearing soft clothing are in the houses of kings. 9 But what did you go out to see? A prophet? Yes, I say to you, and more than a prophet. 10 For this is he of whom it has been written: 'Look, I send my messenger before your face, who will prepare your way before you.'

11 "Truly I say to you, there has not risen among those born of women any person greater than John the Immerser. But the least in the kingdom of the heavens is greater than he. 12 Now from the times of John the Immerser until now, the kingdom of the heavens is sought with haste, and the forceful seize it. 13 For all the prophets and the Law prophesied until John. 14 And if you are willing to receive it, he is Elijah who must come. 15 The person having ears, let him hear!

16 "But to what will I compare this generation? It is like little children sitting in the markets and calling out to others, 17 saying, we

piped for you and you did not dance; we wailed and you did not beat your breast.bb 18 For John came neither eating nor drinking, and they say, 'He has a demon.' 19 The Son of Man came eating and drinking, and they say, 'Look, a glutton and a wine-drinker, a friend of tax-collectors and of sinners!' But wisdom is justified by her works."

20 Then he began to reproach the cities in which his most mighty works had been done, because they did not repent: 21 "Woe to you, Chorazin! Woe to you, Bethsaida! Because if the mighty works having taken place in you had been done in Tyre and Sidon, then long ago they would have repented in sackcloth and ashes. 22 But I say to you, it will be more tolerable for Tyre and Sidon in the day of judgment than for you. 23 And you, Capernaum, who will be lifted up to heaven, will be brought down to hades. Because if the mighty works taking place in you had been done in Sodom, it would have remained until this day. 24 But I say to you, that it will be more tolerable for the land of Sodom in the day of judgment than for you."

25 In response to these things Jesus then said, "I glorify you Father, Lord of the heaven and the earth, that you did hide these things from the wise and discerning, and did reveal them to the unlearned. 26 Yes Father, because doing so was good in your sight. 27 All things have been delivered to me by my Father. And no one knows the Son except the Father. Nor does anyone know the Father except the Son, and to whom the Son may choose to reveal him.

28 "Come to me, all those laboring and being burdened, and I will give you rest. 29 Take my yoke upon you and learn from me, for I am gentle and humble in heart, and you will find rest for your souls. 30 For my yoke is easy and my burden is light."

MATTHEW TWELVE

1 At that time Jesus went through the grainfields on the Sabbath. And his disciples were hungry, and began to pull off heads of grain and to eat. 2 And the Pharisees having seen said to him, "Look, your disciples are doing what is not lawful to do on the Sabbath." 3 But he said to them, "Have you not read what David did when he was hungry, and those with him? 4 How he entered into the house of God, and he ate the bread of the Presence, which it was not lawful for him to eat, nor for those with him, but for the priests only? 5 Or have you not read in the Law, that on the Sabbath the priests in the temple profane the Sabbath, and are guiltless? 6 I say to you that a greater than the temple is here. 7 But if you had known what is, 'I desire mercy and not sacrifice,' you would not have condemned the guiltless. 8 For the Son of Man is Lord of the Sabbath."

9 And having left from there, he went into their synagogue. 10 And look, a man having a withered

hand. And they asked him, saying, "If it is lawful to heal on the Sabbath?" that they might accuse him. 11 But he says to them, "What man will there be among you, who will have one sheep, and if it falls on the Sabbath into a pit, will he not lay hold of it and lift it up? 12 How much, then, is a man more valuable than a sheep? Therefore it is lawful to do good on the Sabbath." 13 Then he says to the man, "Stretch out your hand." And he stretched it out, and it was restored whole as the other.

14 Now, having gone out, the Pharisees held a counsel against him, how they might put him to death.

15 But when Jesus knew, he withdrew from there. And great crowds followed him, and he healed them all, 16 (and warned them that they should not make him known), 17 so that it might be fulfilled that having been spoken by Isaiah the prophet, saying: 18 "Look, my servant whom I have chosen, my beloved in whom my soul is well pleased. I will put my Spirit upon him, and he will declare justice to the gentiles. 19 He will not quarrel nor will he cry out; nor will anyone hear his voice in the streets. 20 A bruised reed he shall not break, and a smoking wick he will not quench, until he has led justice to victory; 21 and in his name gentiles will hope."

22 Then was brought to him a person inhabited by a demon, blind and mute, and he healed him, so that the mute man spoke and saw.

23 And all the crowds were amazed, and said, "This is not the son of David, is he?"

24 Now the Pharisees having heard, said, "This person does not cast out the demons except by Beelzebul, the ruler of the demons." 25 But having known their thoughts, he said to them, "Every kingdom having divided against itself is brought to desolation, and every city or house having divided against itself will not stand. 26 And if Satan casts out Satan, he is divided against himself. How then will his kingdom stand? 27 And if I by Beelzebul cast out demons, by whom do your sons cast out? On account of this they will be your judges. 28 But if by the Spirit of God I cast out demons, then the kingdom of God has come upon you.

29 "Or how is anyone able to enter into the house of the strong and plunder his goods, if not first he bind the strong? And then he will plunder his house. 30 The person not being with me is against me, and the person not gathering with me scatters. 31 Because of this I say to you, every sin and slander will be forgiven men, but slander against the Spirit will not be forgiven. 32 And whoever speaks a word against the Son of Man, it will be forgiven him; but whoever may speak against the Holy Spirit, it will not be forgiven him, neither in this age nor in the one coming.

33 "Either make the tree good and its fruit good, or make the tree

bad and its fruit bad; for by its fruit the tree is known. 34 Generation of vipers! How are you, being evil, able to speak good things? For out of the abundance of the heart the mouth speaks. 35 The good man out of his good treasure puts forth good things, and the evil man out of his evil treasure puts forth evil things. 36 Now I say to you, that every insincere word that men will speak, they will give an account of it in a day of judgment. 37 For by your words you will be justified, and by your words you will be condemned."

38 Then some of the scribes and Pharisees responded, saying, "Teacher, we want to see a sign from you." 39 But answering he said to them, "A generation evil and adulterous seek for a sign, and a sign will not be given to it, except the sign of Jonah the prophet. 40 For just as Jonah was in the belly of the great fish three days and three nights, so will be the Son of Man in the heart of the earth three days and three nights.

41 "The men of Nineveh will stand up in the judgment with this generation and will condemn it, because they repented at the preaching of Jonah, and look, greater than Jonah is here. 42 The queen of the South will stand up in the judgment with this generation and condemn it, for she came from the ends of the earth to hear the wisdom of Solomon, and look, greater than Solomon is here.

43 "Now when the unclean spirit is gone out from the person, it goes through barren places,[cc] seeking rest, and finds none. 44 Then it says, 'I will return to my house from where I came out.' And having come, it finds it empty, and swept, and put in order. 45 Then it goes and takes with itself seven other spirits more evil than itself, and having entered in they dwell there; and the last of that person is worse than the first. So it will also be unto this evil generation."

46 While he was speaking to the crowds, look, his mother and brothers were standing outside seeking to speak with him. 47 Then someone said to him, "Look, your mother and your brothers are standing outside, seeking to speak with you." 48 But responding, he said to the person telling him, "Who is my mother? and who are my brothers?" 49 And having stretched out his hand to his disciples, he said, "Look, my mother and my brothers. 50 For whoever shall do the will of my Father who is in the heavens, he is my brother and sister and mother."

MATTHEW THIRTEEN

1 On that day, Jesus having left the house, he sat by the sea. 2 And great crowds were gathered together to him, so that he entered a boat to sit down; and all the crowd stood on the shore.

3 And he spoke many things to them in parables, saying, "Look, the one sowing went out to sow. 4 And in his sowing, some indeed fell along the road; and the birds having come devoured them. 5 Now others fell upon rocky places,

where they did not have much soil, and immediately they sprang up, on account of not having depth of soil. 6 But the sun having risen, they were scorched, and through not having root, were dried up. 7 Now others fell upon thorns, and the thorns came up and choked them. 8 But others fell upon good soil and yielded fruit, some indeed a hundredfold, but some sixty, but some thirty. 9 The person having ears, let him hear!"

10 And the disciples, having come to him, said to him, "Why do you speak to them in parables?" 11 Now answering he said to them, "Because it has been given to you to know the mysteries of the kingdom of the heavens, but to them it has not been given. 12 For whoever has, to him will be given, and he will have abundance; but whoever does not have, even what he has will be taken away from him. 13 On account of this I speak to them in parables, because seeing they see not, and hearing they hear not, nor do they understand. 14 And in them the prophecy of Isaiah is fulfilled, the one saying, 'In hearing you will hear and by no means understand, and seeing you will see and by no means perceive. 15 For the heart of this people has grown callous, and with the ears they heard dully, and their eyes they have closed, lest they should see with the eyes, and with the ears they should hear, and with the heart they should understand and return and I will heal them.' 16 But blessed are your eyes because they see, and your ears because they hear. 17 For truly I say to you, that many prophets and righteous desired to see what you see, and did not see, and to hear what you hear, and did not hear.

18 "You therefore, hear the parable of the one having sown. 19 Everyone hearing the word of the kingdom and not understanding, the evil one comes and snatches away that having been sown in his heart. This is that having been sown on the road. 20 But that having been sown upon the rocky places, this is the person hearing the word, and immediately receives it with joy. 21 But he has no root in himself, but is temporary; but tribulation or persecution having come on account of the word, immediately he falls. 22 Now that having been sown among the thorns, this is the person hearing the word, and the anxiety of this present age and the deceit of riches choke the word, and it becomes unfruitful. 23 But that having been sown on the good soil, this is the person hearing the word and understanding, who indeed brings forth fruit, and indeed produces a hundredfold, but some sixty, but some thirty."

24 Another parable he put before them, saying: "The kingdom of the heavens has become like a man having sown good seed in his field, 25 but while the men are sleeping, his enemy came and sowed darnel among the wheat, and went away. 26 But when the grass[dd] sprouted and produced fruit, then the darnel also

appeared.

27 "Now the servants of the master of the house, having come to him, said to him, 'Sir, you sowed good seed, didn't you? How then has it darnel?' 28 Now he said to them, 'A man, an enemy, did this.' So the servants said to him, 'Then do you want that we should go and gather them?' 29 But he said, 'No, lest gathering the darnel you might uproot the wheat with them. 30 Allow both to grow together until the harvest; and in the time of harvest I will say to the harvesters, "First gather the darnel and bind them into bundles in order to burn them; but the wheat gather together into my barn.""'

31 Another parable he put before them, saying: "The kingdom of the heavens is like a seed of mustard, which a man having taken sowed in his field, 32 which indeed is smallest of all the seeds. But when it is grown it is greater than the garden plants and becomes a tree, so that the birds of the air come and nest in its branches."

33 Another parable he spoke to them: "the kingdom of the heavens is like leaven, which a woman having taken hid in three measures of flour until all of it was leavened."

34 All these things Jesus spoke in parables to the crowds; and without a parable he did not speak to them, 35 so that might be fulfilled that having been spoken by the prophet, saying, "I will open my mouth in parables; I will utter things secret from the foundation of the world."

36 Then having dismissed the crowds, he went into the house. And his disciples came to him, saying, "Explain to us the parable of the darnel of the field." 37 Now answering he said, "The one sowing the good seed is the Son of Man, 38 and the field is the world. Now the good seed, these are the sons of the kingdom; but the darnel are the sons of the evil one. 39 Now the enemy having sown them is the devil, and the harvest is the consummation of the age, and the harvesters are God's messengers.

40 "As therefore the darnel is gathered and consumed in fire, so it will be at the consummation of the age. 41 The Son of Man will send his messengers, and they will gather out of his kingdom all that offends and those practicing lawlessness, 42 and they will cast them into the fire of the furnace. There will be the wailing and the gnashing of teeth. 43 Then the righteous will shine forth as the sun in the kingdom of their Father. The one having ears, let him hear.

44 "The kingdom of the heavens is like a treasure having been hidden in the field, which having found, a man hid, and for joy of it goes and sells all that he has and buys that field. 45 Again, the kingdom of the heavens is like a man, a merchant, seeking quality pearls, 46 and having found one valuable pearl went away and sold all, as much as he had, and bought

it.

47 "Again, the kingdom of the heavens is like a dragnet having been cast into the sea and having gathered of every kind, 48 which, when it was filled, having drawn it to shore, and having sat down, they gathered the good into vessels, but the bad they cast out. 49 So it will be in the consummation of the age. Messengers will go out and will separate the evil from among the righteous, 50 and will cast them into the furnace of the fire. There will be the wailing and gnashing of the teeth."

51 Jesus said to them, "Have you understood all these things?" They said to him, "Yes, sir." 52 And he said to them, "Because of this, every scribe having been discipled into the kingdom of the heavens is like a man, a master of a house, who brings out of his treasure things new and old."

53 And so it was when Jesus had finished these parables, he withdrew from there. 54 And having come into his native city, he taught them in their synagogue, so that they are astonished and are saying, "From what place to this man the wisdom and the ability? 55 Is not this the son of the builder?ee Is not his mother called Mariam? And his brothers Jacob and Joses and Simon and Judas? 56 And his sisters; are not all with us? From what place then to this man all these things?" 57 And they were offended at him. But Jesus said to them, "A prophet is not without honor except in his native city, and in his household." 58 And he did not many mighty works there because of their unbelief.

MATTHEW FOURTEEN

1 At that time Herod the tetrarch heard the report about Jesus 2 and said to his servants, "This is John the Immerser. He is risen from the dead, and on account of this mighty power works in him." 3 Because Herod having arrested John, he bound him, and put him in prison, on account of Herodias, the wife of Philip his brother. 4 For John had been saying to him, "It is not lawful for you to have her." 5 And wanting to kill him, he feared the crowd, because they regarded him as a prophet.

6 But when Herod's birthday had come, the daughter of Herodias danced in the midst and pleased Herod. 7 Whereupon with an oath he promised to give to her whatever she might ask. 8 Now having been urged by her mother, she says, "Give me here upon a platter the head of John the Immerser." 9 And the king, though grieved, on account of the oaths and those reclining with him, he commanded it to be given. 10 And having sent he beheaded John in the prison. 11 And his head was brought on a platter and was given to the girl and she brought it to her mother. 12 Then his disciples having come took the body and buried it; and having come they told it to Jesus.

13 Now Jesus, having heard, left from there by boat to a

deserted place to be alone. And the crowds having heard followed him on foot from the villages. 14 And having gone out, he saw a great crowd, and was moved with compassion toward them, and healed their sick. 15 Now evening having come, the disciples came to him, saying, "This place is desolate, and the time already passing. Dismiss the crowds, that having gone into the villages they might buy for themselves food." 16 But Jesus said to them, "They have no need to go away. You give to them to eat." 17 But they say to him, "We have here only five bread and two fish." 18 Then he said, "Bring them here to me."

19 And having commanded the crowds to recline upon the grass, taking the five bread and the two fish, looking up to heaven, he spoke a blessing; and having broken the bread he gave to the disciples, and the disciples to the crowds. 20 And all ate and were satisfied; and they took up the excess, twelve hand-baskets full of the fragments. 21 Now those eating were about five thousand men, besides women and children.

22 And immediately he made the disciples enter into the boat and to go before him to the other side, while he dismissed the crowds. 23 And having dismissed the crowds, he went up on the mountain by himself to pray. Now evening having come, he was there alone.

24 But the boat, in the midst of the sea, about three miles from land,[ff] was being tossed by the waves, for the wind was contrary. 25 Now in the fourth watch of the night, he went to them, walking on the sea. 26 And the disciples, having seen him walking on the sea, were fearful, saying, "It is a ghost!" And they cried out from fear. 27 But immediately Jesus spoke to them, saying, "Have courage, it is I, fear not." 28 Now Peter answering him said, "Master,[99] if it is you, command me to come to you on the waters." 29 And he said, "Come." And having descended from the boat, Peter walked upon the water and came to Jesus. 30 But seeing the wind boisterous, he was afraid. And having begun to sink, he cried out, saying, "Master, save me!" 31 Now immediately Jesus, having stretched out his hand, took hold of him, and says to him, "You of little faith, why did you doubt?"

32 And they having entered into the boat, the wind ceased. 33 Then those in the boat bowed to him, saying, "Truly you are God's son."

34 And having crossed over, they came to the land of Gennesaret. 35 And the men of that place having recognized him, sent to all that surrounding region and brought to him all those being sick, 36 and begged him that they might only touch the fringe of his garment. And as many as touched were healed.

MATTHEW FIFTEEN

1 Then Pharisees and scribes came from Jerusalem to Jesus,

saying, 2 "Why is it your disciples transgress the tradition of the elders? For they do not wash their hands when they eat bread." 3 Now answering he said to them, "And why is it you transgress the commandment of God on account of your tradition? 4 For God commanded, 'Honor the father and the mother' and 'the person speaking evil of father or mother, let him die the death.' 5 But you say, 'Whoever may say to the father or the mother, "Whatever it may be by me you might profit, it is a gift."'" 6 By no means will he honor his father or his mother, and you made God's word of no effect on account of your tradition.

7 "Hypocrites! Justly Isaiah prophesied about you, saying: 8 'This people draw near with their mouth and with the lips honor me, but their heart is far from me. 9 Moreover in vain they worship me, teaching as doctrines the precepts of men.'"

10 And having called the crowd, he said to them, "Hear and understand: 11 not that entering into the mouth defiles the man, but that coming out of the mouth, this defiles the man." 12 Then the disciples having come to him said to him, "Do you know that the Pharisees were offended when they heard this saying?" 13 But answering he said, "Every plant that my heavenly Father has not planted will be uprooted. 14 Leave them; they are blind leaders of the blind; but if blind lead blind both will fall into a pit."

15 Then Peter answered and said to him, "Explain to us this parable." 16 And he said, "Are you also still without understanding? 17 Do you not yet understand that everything entering into the mouth goes into the stomach and is cast out to the toilet? 18 But the things going out of the mouth come out of the heart, and these defile the man. 19 For out of the heart go forth evil thoughts, murders, adulteries, sexual immorality, thefts, false witness, verbal abuse. 20 These are the things defiling the man; but to eat with unwashed hands does not defile the man."

21 And having gone from there, Jesus withdrew to the area of Tyre and Sidon. 22 And look, a Canaanite woman from the same area, having come out, cried out, saying, "Have mercy on me, lord, son of David. My daughter is grievously inhabited by a demon." 23 But not a word did he answer her. And his disciples having come to him entreated him, saying, "Dismiss her, for she cries out after us." 24 But answering he said, "I was not sent except to the lost sheep of the house of Israel."

25 Now having come she bowed to him, saying, "Sir, help me!" 26 But answering he said, "It is not right to take the children's bread and throw it to the little dogs." 27 But she said, "Yes, sir, yet even the little dogs eat the crumbs that fall from their masters' table." 28 Then answering Jesus said to her, "O woman, great is your faith! Be to you as you desire." And her daughter was healed from that

very hour.

29 And having left there, Jesus went along the Sea of Galilee; and having gone up on the mountain, he was sitting there. 30 And great crowds came to him, having with them lame, crippled, blind, mute, and many others, and they placed them at Jesus' feet and he healed them, 31 so that the crowd marveled, seeing the mute speaking, the crippled made healthy, the lame walking, and the blind seeing; and they glorified the God of Israel.

32 Now Jesus, having called his disciples, said, "I have compassion toward the crowd, because already they continue with me three days, and have nothing that they might eat. And I am not willing to send them away hungry, lest they faint on the way."

33 And the disciples say to him, "From where to us in this wilderness so many bread as to satisfy so great a crowd?" 34 And he says to them, "How many bread have you?" And they said, "Seven, and a few small fish." 35 And having told the crowds to recline on the ground, 36 having taken the seven bread and the fish, and having given thanks, he broke and gave to the disciples, and the disciples to the crowd. 37 And all ate and were satisfied; and they took up seven baskets full of the fragments that were left. 38 Now those eating were four thousand men, besides women and children. 39 And having dismissed the crowds, he got into the boat, and came to the area of Magdala.

MATTHEW SIXTEEN

1 And having come, the Pharisees and Sadducees tempting asked him to show them a sign from heaven. 2 Now answering he said to them, "Evening having come you say, 'Fair weather, for the sky is red'; 3 and in the morning, 'Today a storm, for the sky is red being overcast.' Indeed you know how to discern the appearance of the sky, but signs of the times you are not able. 4 A generation evil and adulterous seeks a sign, and no sign will be given to it, except the sign of Jonah." And having left them he went away.

5 And the disciples having come to the other side, they had forgotten to take bread. 6 But Jesus said to them, "Take heed and beware of the leaven of the Pharisees and the Sadducees." 7 Now they reasoned among themselves, saying, "Because we took no bread."

8 But having known, Jesus, said, "Why reason you in yourselves, O you of little faith? Because you took no bread? 9 Do you not yet understand or remember the five bread for the five thousand and how many hand-baskets you took away? 10 Nor the seven bread for the four thousand, and how many baskets you took away? 11 How do you not understand that I did not speak to you about bread, but to beware of the leaven of the Pharisees and Sadducees?" 12 Then they

understood that he had not said beware of the leaven of bread, but of the teaching of the Pharisees and Sadducees.

13 Now Jesus having come into the area of Caesarea Philippi, he questioned his disciples, saying, "Who do men say the Son of Man to be?" 14 Now some said, "Indeed some John the Immerser"; and others, "Elijah," and others, "Jeremiah or one of the prophets."

15 He says to them, "But you, who do you say me to be?" 16 Now Simon Peter answering said, "You are the Christ, the son of the living God." 17 And Jesus in reply said to him, "Blessed are you, Simon son of Jonah. Because flesh and blood revealed this not to you, but my Father who is in the heavens. 18 Now I also say to you, that you are Peter, and on this the rock I will build my church, and the gates of hades will not prevail against it. 19 And I will give you the keys of the kingdom of the heavens; and whatever if you might bind on earth will be bound in the heavens, and whatever if you might loose on earth will be loosed in the heavens." 20 Then he commanded the disciples that to no one should they say that he is the Christ.

21 From that time Jesus began to show to his disciples that it is necessary for him to go away to Jerusalem, and to suffer many things from the elders and chief priests and scribes, and to be killed, and on the third day to be raised. 22 And having taken him aside, Peter began to rebuke him, saying, "Far be it from you, master;[hh] no, this will never be to you." 23 But having turned he said to Peter, "Get behind me, Satan! You are an offense to me, because your thoughts are not of the things of God, but the things of men."

24 Then Jesus said to his disciples, "If anyone desires to come after me, let him deny himself, and take up his cross, and follow me. 25 For whoever may desire to save his life will lose it, and whoever may lose his life on account of me will find it. 26 For what will it profit a man, if the whole world he gains, and his soul loses? Or what will a man give as an exchange for his soul? 27 For the Son of Man is about to come in the glory of his Father, with his messengers, and then he will give to each according to his conduct. 28 Truly I say to you, there are some of those standing here who shall not taste of death, until they might see the Son of Man coming in his kingdom."

MATTHEW SEVENTEEN

1 And after six days Jesus takes with him Peter, and Jacob, and John his brother, and brings them into a high mountain by themselves. 2 And his form was changed[ii] before them, and his face shone as the sun, and his clothes became white as the light.

3 And look, Moses and Elijah appeared to them, talking with him. 4 Now Peter responding said to Jesus, "Master, it is good for us to be here. If you so desire, we will make here three tabernacles: one

for you, and one for Moses, and one for Elijah." 5 While he was still speaking, look, a bright cloud overshadowed them; and look, a voice out of the cloud, saying, "This is my son, the beloved, in whom I am well pleased. You listen to him." 6 And having heard it, the disciples fell upon their faces, and were greatly afraid. 7 And Jesus having come to them and touching them, said, "Get up, and be not afraid." 8 Now having lifted up their eyes, they saw no one except Jesus himself alone.

9 And as they came down from the mountain, Jesus commanded them, saying, "Tell no one the vision until that the Son of Man is risen from among the dead." 10 And the disciples asked him, saying, "Why then *do* the scribes say that it is necessary that Elijah come first?" 11 And answering he said, "Elijah indeed comes and will restore all things. 12 But I say to you that Elijah is already come, and they knew him not, but did to him whatever they desired. Thus also, the Son of Man is about to suffer from them." 13 Then the disciples understood that he spoke to them about John the Immerser.

14 And they having come to the crowd, a man came to him, kneeling down to him, 15 and saying, "Sir, have mercy on my son, because he is an epileptic[jj] and miserably suffers. For often he falls into the fire, and often into the water, 16 and I brought him to your disciples, and they were not able to heal him."

17 Now Jesus responding said, "O generation without faith and perverse, how long will I be with you? How long will I bear with you? Bring him here to me." 18 And Jesus rebuked the demon and the demon went out from the boy and the boy was healed from that hour.

19 Then the disciples, having come to Jesus in private, they said, "What is the reason we were not able to cast it out?" 20 Now he said to them, "On account of your little faith. For truly I say to you, if you have faith as a mustard seed, you will say to this mountain, 'Move from here to there,' and it will move; and nothing will be impossible for you. [21[kk]]

22 Now as they were together in Galilee, Jesus said to them, "The Son of Man is about to be betrayed into the hands of men, 23 and they will kill him; and on the third day he will be raised up." And they were deeply distressed.

24 Now they having come to Capernaum, those receiving the double-drachma tax came to Peter and said, "Your teacher, does he not pay the double-drachma tax?" 25 He says, "Yes." And having entered into the house, Jesus anticipated him, saying, "What do you think, Simon? The kings of the earth, from whom do they receive customs or tax, from their sons or from strangers?" 26 Now he having said, "From the strangers," Jesus said to him, "Then the sons are free. 27 But in order that we might not offend them, having gone to the sea, cast a hook, and the first

fish having come up take, and having opened its mouth, you will find a four drachma coin. That having taken, give to them for me and yourself."

MATTHEW EIGHTEEN

1 In that hour the disciples came to Jesus, saying, "Who then is greatest in the kingdom of the heavens?" 2 And having called to a child, he set it[ll] in the midst of them, 3 and said, "Truly I say to you, if you are not converted and become as the little children, you will by no means enter the kingdom of the heavens. 4 Whoever therefore will humble himself as this little child, he is the greatest in the kingdom of the heavens. 5 And whoever may receive one such little child, in my name, receives me. 6 But whoever may cause offense to one of these little ones believing in me, it is better for him that a heavy millstone should be hung around his neck, and he be drowned in the depth of the sea.

7 "Woe to the world because of the offenses. For it is inevitable the offenses come; but woe to the person by whom the offense comes. 8 But if your hand or your foot causes you to sin, cut them off and cast them from you. It is better for you to enter into life crippled or lame, than having two hands or two feet, to be cast into the eternal fire. 9 And if your eye causes you to sin, take it out and cast it from you. It is better for you to enter into life one-eyed, than having two eyes to be cast into the fire of Gehenna. 10 See to it you not despise one of these little ones. For I say to you, that their messengers in the heavens who minister to the saved continually see the face of my Father who is in the heavens. [11^{mm}]

12 "What do you think? If some person has a hundred sheep, and one of them has wandered, will he not leave the ninety-nine on the hills, and having gone, seek the one wandering? 13 And if he should find it, truly I say to you, that he rejoices over it more than over the ninety-nine not wandering. 14 So it is not the will of your Father who is in the heavens that one of these little ones should be lost.

15 "Moreover if your brother sins against you, go and rebuke him, between you and him alone. If he will hear you, you have gained your brother. 16 But if he will not hear, take with you more, one or two, that on the mouth of two witnesses or of three, every word may stand. 17 But if he disregards them, tell it to the public assembly. But if he disregards also the public assembly, let him be to you as the pagan and the tax collector. 18 Truly I say to you, whatever you may bind on the earth will be bound in heaven, and whatever you may loose on earth will be loosed in heaven.

19 "Truly^{nn} I say again to you, that if two of you may agree on the earth, about any matter to be done, that if they might ask, it will be done for them by my Father who is in the heavens. 20 For where

two or three are gathered together to my name, there am I in the midst of them."

21 Then, having come, Peter said to him, "Master, how often will my brother sin against me, and I will forgive him? Up to seven times?" 22 Jesus says to him, "I do not say to you, up to seven times, but up to seventy times seven.

23 "On account of this, the kingdom of the heavens is like a man, a king, who desired to settle accounts with his servants. 24 Now, he having begun to settle, one was brought to him, a debtor of ten thousand talents. 25 But he not having means to pay, the master commanded him to be sold, and the wife and the children, and as much as he had, and payment to be made. 26 Therefore the servant, having fallen down to him, was on his knees, saying, 'Have patience with me, and I will pay all to you.' 27 Now having compassion, the master of that servant released him, and forgave him the debt.

28 "But having gone out, the servant found one of his fellow servants, who owed him a hundred denarii, and having taken hold of him, he choked him, saying, 'Pay what you owe!' 29 Having therefore fallen down, his fellow servant begged him, saying, 'Have patience with me, and I will pay you.' 30 But he was not willing, and having went away, he cast him into prison until when he should pay that which was owing.

31 "Therefore, having seen the things that occurred, his fellow servants were deeply grieved, and having gone, made known to their master all that had occurred. 32 Then having called to him, his master says to him, 'Evil servant. I forgave you all the debt because you begged me. 33 Should you not also have compassion on your fellow servant, as I had compassion on you?' 34 And being angry, his master delivered him to the torturers, until that he should pay all being owed to him. 35 Thus also my heavenly Father will do to you, if each of you does not forgive his brother from your heart."

MATTHEW NINETEEN

1 And so it was when Jesus had finished these sayings, he left Galilee and came to the area of Judea beyond the Jordan. 2 And great crowds followed him, and he healed them there.

3 And Pharisees came to him, putting him to the test, and saying, "Is it lawful for a man to divorce his wife on any grounds?" 4 Now answering he said, "Have you not read, that he who created them, from the beginning made them male and female, 5 and said, 'On account of this, a man will leave the father and the mother and will be joined with his wife, and the two will become one flesh'? 6 So that, no longer are they two, but one flesh. What therefore God united let not man separate."

7 They say to him, "Why then did Moses command to give a certificate of divorce, and to send her away?" 8 He says to them, "For the hardness of your heart, Moses

permitted you to divorce your wives, but from the beginning it was not this way. 9 Now I say to you, whoever shall divorce his wife, except for sexual immorality, and shall marry another, commits adultery; and he who marries her that is put away, commits adultery."

10 His disciples say to him, "If this is the case of the man with the wife, it is better not to marry." 11 But he said to them, "Not all receive this saying, but only to whom it has been given. 12 For there are eunuchs who were born thus from their mother's womb, and there are eunuchs who were made eunuchs by men, and there are eunuchs who made eunuchs of themselves on account of the kingdom of the heavens. The one being able to receive it, let him receive it."

13 Then little children were brought to him, that he might lay hands on them, and pray, but the disciples rebuked them. 14 But Jesus said, "Let the little children come to me and do not forbid them; for of such kind is the kingdom of the heavens." 15 And having laid hands on them, he departed from there.

16 And look, one having come to him, said, "Teacher,ᵒᵒ what good shall I do that I might have eternal life?" 17 But he said to him, "Why are you asking me about what is good? Only one is good. Now, if you desire to enter into life, keep the commandments." 18 He says to him, "Which?" And Jesus said, "You will not murder; you will not commit adultery; you will not steal; you will not bear false witness; 19 honor the father and the mother; and you will love your neighbor as yourself."

20 The young man says to him, "All these things I have kept. What yet lack I?" 21 Jesus said to him, "If you desire to be completely blameless, go, sell your possessions, and give to the poor, and you will have treasure in the heavens; and come follow me." 22 But the young man having heard this saying, he went away grieving, for he was a person having many possessions.

23 Then Jesus said to His disciples, "Truly, I say to you, that a rich man with difficulty will enter the kingdom of the heavens. 24 And again I say to you, it is easier for a camel to pass through the eye of a needle, than a rich man to enter into the kingdom of God." 25 Now having heard this, the disciples were greatly astonished, saying, "Who then is able to be saved?" 26 But having looked on them, Jesus said to them, "With men this is impossible, but with God all things are possible."

27 Then Peter responding said to him, "Look, we left all and followed you; what then will be to us?" 28 Now Jesus said to them, "Truly I say to you, that you having followed me, in the restoration, when the Son of Man will sit down upon his throne of glory, you also will sit on twelve thrones, judging the Twelve tribes of Israel. 29 And

everyone who has left houses, or brothers, or sisters, or father, or mother, or wife, or children, or lands for my name's sake, a hundredfold will receive, and will inherit eternal life. [v. 30 moved to chapter 20]

MATTHEW TWENTY

19:30 "But many first will be last, and last first. 20:1 For the kingdom of the heavens is like a man, the master of a house, who went out at dawn to hire workers for his vineyard.

2 "Now having agreed with the workers for a denarius a day, he sent them into his vineyard. 3 And having gone out about nine o'clock, he saw others standing unemployed in the marketplace, 4 and he said to them, 'You also go into the vineyard, and whatever is right I will give you.' 5 And they went. Now again having gone out about noon and three o'clock, he did likewise. 6 And about six o'clock, having gone out, he found others standing, and says to them, 'Why stand you here unemployed all the day?' 7 They say to him, 'Because no one hired us.' He says to them, 'You also go into the vineyard, and whatever is right you will receive.'

8 "Now evening having come, the owner of the vineyard said to his manager, 'Call the workmen, and give them the wages, beginning from the last unto the first.' 9 And those hired about six o'clock having come, they received a denarius each.

10 And the first having come, they thought they would receive more; and they received, they also, a denarius each. 11 But having received, they complained against the master of the house, 12 saying, 'These the last have worked one hour, and you have made them equal to us, those having borne the burden of the day and the scorching heat.'

13 But answering to one of them he said, 'Friend, I do not wrong you. Did you not agree with me for a denarius? 14 Take what is yours and go. For I have chosen to give to this last as also to you. 15 Is it not lawful for me to do what I will with that which is mine? Or is your eye evil because I am good?' 16 So the last will be first, and the first last.'"pp

17 As Jesus was going up to Jerusalem, he took the Twelve disciples aside, and on the way said to them, 18 "Look, we go up to Jerusalem, and the Son of Man will be betrayed to the chief priests and scribes; and they will condemn him to death, 19 and they will deliver him to the gentiles to mock and to scourge and to crucify; and the third day he will rise again."

20 Then came to him the mother of the sons of Zebedee, with her sons, kneeling, and asking something from him. 21 Now he said to her, "What do you desire?" She says to him, "Say that these two sons of mine might sit, one on your right hand, one on your left hand, in your kingdom."

22 But Jesus answering said, "You know not what you ask. Are

you able to drink the cup that I am about to drink?"qq They said to him, "We are able." 23 He says to them, "Indeed my cup you will drink. But to sit on my right hand and on the left, this is not mine to give, but to those for whom it has been prepared by my Father."

24 And having heard, the ten were indignant about the two brothers. 25 But Jesus, having called them, said, "You know that the rulers of the gentiles exercise dominion over them, and the great exercise authority over them. 26 It will not be so among you; but whoever among you may desire to become great, he will be your servant; 27 and whoever among you may desire to be first, he will be your servant; 28 even as the Son of Man came not to be served, but to serve, and to give his life a ransom for many."

29 And as they were going out from Jericho, a great crowd followed him. 30 And look, two blind men sitting beside the road, having heard that Jesus is passing by, cried out, saying, "Sir! Have mercy on us Son of David!" 31 Now the crowd rebuked them, that they should be silent; but all the more they cried, saying, "Sir! Have mercy on us Son of David!" 32 And having stopped, Jesus called them, and said, "What do you want I should do unto you?" 33 They said to him, "Sir, that our eyes may be opened." 34 Now having been moved with compassion, Jesus touched their eyes; and immediately they received sight, and they followed him.

MATTHEW TWENTY-ONE

1 And when they drew near to Jerusalem and came to Bethphage at the Mount of Olives, then Jesus sent two disciples, 2 saying to them, "Go into the village that is ahead of you, and immediately you will find a donkey having been tied, and a colt with her; having untied them, bring them to me. 3 And if anyone says anything to you, you will say, 'The Lord°° has need of them.' Now immediately he will send them."

4 Now this came to be that might be fulfilled that having been spoken by the prophet, saying, 5 "Tell the daughter of Zion, 'Behold, your King comes to you, meek, and mounted on a donkey, even upon a colt, the foal of a beast of burden.'"

6 Now the disciples having gone, and having done as Jesus commanded them, 7 they brought the donkey and the colt, lay their clothes upon them, and he sat on them.

8 Now the very large crowd spread their clothes on the road; but others were cutting branches from the trees, and were spreading them on the road. 9 Then the crowds going before him, and those following, were crying out, saying, "Hosanna to the Son of David! Blessed the one coming in the name of the Lord! Hosanna in the highest!" 10 And he having come into Jerusalem, all the city was agitated, saying, "Who is this?" 11 Now the crowds said, "This is the prophet, Jesus, the one

from Nazareth of Galilee."

12 And Jesus went into the temple court and cast out all those selling and buying in the temple, and overturned the tables of the money changers, and the seats of those selling the doves. 13 And he says to them, "It has been written, 'My house will be called a house of prayer,' but you have made it a den of robbers."

14 And blind and lame came to him in the temple, and he healed them. 15 But the chief priests and the scribes having seen the wonderful things that he did, and the children crying out in the temple court and saying, "Hosanna to the son of David!" they were indignant, 16 and said to him, "Hear you what these say?" But Jesus says to them, "Yes. Did you never read, 'Out of the mouth of babes and sucklings you have prepared praise'?" 17 And having left them, he went out of the city to Bethany, and lodged there.

18 Now in the morning, having come back into the city, he became hungry. 19 And having seen one fig tree beside the road, he came to it and found nothing on it except leaves only. And he says to it, "Let there be no more fruit from you for the age." And the tree immediately withered.

20 And having seen it the disciples marveled, saying, "How did the fig wither so quickly?" 21 Now Jesus answering said to them, "Truly I say to you, if you have faith and do not doubt, not only will you do what was done to the fig tree, but also, if to this mountain you might say, 'Be removed and be you cast into the sea,' it will be done. 22 And all things, as many as you might ask in prayer, believing, you will receive."

23 And he having come into the temple court, the chief priests and the elders of the people approached him as he was teaching, saying, "By what authority are you doing these things? And who gave to you this authority?" 24 But Jesus answering said to them, "I also will ask you one thing, which if you tell me, I also will say to you by what authority I do these things. 25 The immersion of John, from where was it? From heaven or from men?" Now they were reasoning with themselves, saying, "If we might say, 'from heaven,' he will say to us, 'Why then did you not believe him?' 26 But if we might say, 'from men,' we fear the crowd, for all hold John as a prophet." 27 And answering Jesus they said, "We know not." And he said to them, "Neither do I tell you by what authority I do these things.

28 "But what do you think? A man had two sons, and having come to the first, he said, 'Son, go today, work in the vineyard.' 29 Now he answering said, 'I will not'; but afterward having repented he went. 30 Now having come to the second he said in the same manner. Now he answering said, 'I go,'[pp] sir,' and he did not go. 31

Which of the two did the will of the father?" They say, "The first." Jesus says to them, "Truly I say to you, that the tax collectors and the prostitutes go before you into the kingdom of God. 32 For John came to you in the way of righteousness, and you did not believe him; but tax collectors and the prostitutes believed him; but you having seen, did not afterward repent to believe him.

33 "Hear another parable. There was a man, a master of a house, who planted a vineyard, and placed a fence around it, dug a winepress in it, and built a tower, and hired it out to vinedressers, and went away into a foreign country.

34 "Now when the season of the fruits drew near, he sent his servants to the vinedressers, to receive his fruits. 35 And the vinedressers having taken his servants, one indeed they beat, but one they killed, and one they stoned. 36 Again he sent other servants, more than the first, and they did the same to them.

37 "Now afterward he sent to them his son, saying, 'They will respect my son.' 38 But the vinedressers, having seen the son, said among themselves, 'This is the heir. Come, let us kill him, and possess his inheritance.' 39 And having taken him, they cast him out of the vineyard and they killed him. 40 When therefore, the owner of the vineyard shall come, what will he do to those vinedressers? 41 They say to him, "He will destroy miserably those wicked men, and the vineyard he will hire out to other vinedressers who will give to him the fruits in their seasons."

42 Jesus says to them, "Did you never read in the scriptures, 'The stone which those building rejected, this has become the chief corner; this was from the Lord, and it is marvelous in our eyes?' 43 On account of this I say to you, that the kingdom of God will be taken from you, and it will be given to a people producing its fruits. 44 And the one having fallen on this stone will be broken; but on whomever it may fall, it will grind him to powder."

45 And having heard his parables, the chief priests and Pharisees knew that about them he is speaking. 46 And seeking to lay hold of him, they feared the crowds, because they held him as a prophet.

MATTHEW TWENTY-TWO

1 And responding, Jesus again spoke to them in parables, saying, 2 "The kingdom of heaven may be likened to a man, a king, who made a wedding feast for his son, 3 and sent his servants to call those having been invited to the wedding feast; and they were not willing to come. 4 Again, he sent out other servants, saying, 'Tell those having been invited, "Look, I prepared my dinner; my oxen and the fatlings have been killed, and all things are ready. Come to the wedding feast."' 5 But not caring they went away, one indeed to his own field, but one to his business, 6 and the

rest having laid hold of his servants mistreated and killed them. 7 Now the king was furious, and having sent his armies he destroyed those murderers, and burnt their city.

8 "Then he says to his servants, 'The wedding feast is ready, but those having been invited were not worthy. 9 Go therefore into the highways, and as many as you may find, invite to the wedding feast.' 10 And those servants having gone out into the highways brought together all, as many as they found, both evil and good. And the wedding hall became full of those reclining *to eat*.

11 "But the king having come in to see those reclining *to eat*, he saw there a man not dressed in wedding clothes. 12 And he says to him, 'Friend, how did you come in here not having wedding clothes?' And he was speechless. 13 Then the king said to the servants, 'Having bound him, feet and hands, cast him into the outer darkness; there will be weeping and gnashing of teeth.' 14 For many are called, but few chosen."

15 Then having gone, the Pharisees took counsel how they might trap him in his words. 16 And they send to him their disciples with the Herodians, saying, "Teacher, we know that you are true, and teach the way of God in truth; and you do not care about anyone, for you do not look on the person of men. 17 Tell us, therefore, what do you think? Is it right to give tax to Caesar, or not?"

18 But Jesus having known their malice, said, "Why do you test me, hypocrites? 19 Show me the tax money." And they brought to him a denarius. 20 And he says to them, "Whose this image, and whose inscription?" 21 They say to him, "Caesar's." And he says to them, "Give therefore the things of Caesar to Caesar, and the things of God to God." 22 When having heard they marveled; and having left him went away.

23 In that day the Sadducees came to him, saying there is no resurrection. And they questioned him, 24 saying, "Teacher, Moses said that if anyone should die not having children, his brother will marry his wife, and raise up children for his brother. 25 Now there were with us seven brothers; and the first having married, died, and having no children, left his wife to his brother. 26 In the same manner the second also, and the third, even to the seventh. 27 Now the woman died last of all. 28 Therefore, in the resurrection, of which of the seven will she be wife, for all had her."

29 Now answering, Jesus said to them, "You are lead astray, not knowing the scriptures or the power of God. 30 For in the resurrection they do not marry, nor are given in marriage, but they are like messengers in heaven.

31 "Now concerning the resurrection of the dead, have you not read that having been spoken to you by God, saying, 32 'I am the God of Abraham and the God of

Isaac and the God of Jacob?' He is not God of the dead, but of the living." 33 And having heard, the crowds were astonished at his teaching.

34 Now the Pharisees, having heard that he had silenced the Sadducees, came together in the same place. 35 And one of them, a lawyer, questioned him, testing him. 36 "Teacher, which commandment is the greatest in the Law?" 37 Now he said to him, "'You will love the Lord your God with all your heart, and with all your soul, and with all your mind.' 38 This is the great and first commandment. 39 The second is like it: 'You will love your neighbor as yourself.' 40 On these two commandments all the Law stands, and the Prophets."

41 And the Pharisees having been gathered together, Jesus questioned them, 42 saying, "What do you think about the Christ? Whose son is he?" They say to him, "Of David." 43 He says to them, "How then does David in spirit call him 'Lord,' saying, 44 'Said the Lord to my Lord, "Sit at my right hand, until I may place your enemies as a footstool for your feet"?' 45 If therefore David then calls Him 'Lord,' how is he his son?" 46 And no one was able to answer him a word, nor dared anyone from that day question him anymore.

MATTHEW TWENTY-THREE

1 Then Jesus spoke to the crowds and to his disciples, 2 saying: "The scribes and the Pharisees, having sat down on Moses' seat, 3 all things, therefore, as much as they might tell you to do, that keep; but do not do according to their works, for they say and not do. 4 But they bind heavy burdens,ʳʳ and lay them on men's shoulders; but themselves with their finger they are not willing to move them. 5 But all their works they do to be seen by men. For they broaden their phylacteries, and enlarge their borders. 6 Now they love the chief place at the feasts, and the chief seats in the synagogues, 7 and the greetings in the marketplaces, and to be called by men, 'Rabbi.'

8 "But you, you may not be called 'Rabbi', for one is your teacher, and you are all brethren. 9 And you may not call anyone on the earth your 'father'; for one is your Father, who is in heaven. 10 Neither be called masters; for one is your master, the Christ. 11 But the greatest among you will be your servant. 12 Now he who will exalt himself will be humbled, and whoever will humble himself will be exalted.

13 "But woe to you, scribes and Pharisees, hypocrites! Because you shut up the kingdom of the heavens against men; for you neither enter, nor even those who are entering do you allow to go in. [14ˢˢ]

15 "Woe to you, scribes and Pharisees, hypocrites! Because you traverse the sea and the dry land to make one convert, and when he may become so, you make him a son of Gehenna twofold more than

yourselves.

16 "Woe to you, blind guides, those saying, 'Whoever might swear by the temple, it is nothing; but whoever might swear by the gold of the temple, he is obligated.' 17 Foolish and blind! For which is greater, the gold or the temple that sanctifies the gold? 18 And, 'Whoever might swear by the altar, it is nothing; but whoever might swear by the gift that is on it, he is obligated.' 19 You blind! For which is greater, the gift or the altar sanctifying the gift? 20 Therefore he who having sworn by the altar, swears by it and by all things that are on it. 21 And the one having sworn by the temple, swears by it and by the one dwelling in it. 22 And he who having sworn by heaven, swears by the throne of God and by the one sitting on it.

23 "Woe to you, scribes and Pharisees, hypocrites! Because you pay tithes of mint and dill and cumin, and have neglected the weightier matters of the Law: justice and mercy and faith. Now it is necessary to do these, and those not to neglect. 24 Blind guides! Those straining out the gnat but swallowing the camel!

25 "Woe to you, scribes and Pharisees, hypocrites! Because you cleanse the outside of the cup and of the dish, but inside they are full of robbery and self-indulgence. 26 Blind Pharisee! First cleanse the inside of the cup and of the dish that the outside of them might also become clean.

27 "Woe to you, scribes and Pharisees, hypocrites! Because you are like tombs having been whitewashed, which indeed outwardly appear beautiful, but inside are full of bones of the dead, and of all uncleanness. 28 Even so you indeed outwardly appear righteous to men, but inwardly you are full of hypocrisy and lawlessness.

29 "Woe to you, scribes and Pharisees, hypocrites! Because you build the tombs of the prophets and adorn the monuments of the righteous, 30 and you say, 'If we had been in the times of our fathers, we would not have been partakers with them in killing the prophets.' 31 Thus you bear witness to yourselves that you are sons of those having murdered the prophets, 32 and you fill up the measure of your fathers.

33 "Serpents, offspring of vipers, how may you escape from the condemnation of Gehenna? 34 Because of this, look, I send to you prophets and wise and scribes. Some of them you will kill and crucify, and some of them you will scourge in your synagogues, and will persecute from city to city, 35 so that upon you may come all the righteous blood being shed upon the earth, from the blood of Abel the righteous, to the blood of Zechariah son of Berekiah, whom you murdered between the temple and the altar. 36 Truly, I say to you, all these things will come upon this generation.

37 "Jerusalem, Jerusalem, killing the prophets and stoning

those having been sent to her! How often would I have gathered your children, as a hen gathers her chicks under the wings; and you were not willing! 38 Look! Your house is left to you desolate. 39 For I say to you, no, you shall not see me, from now until you say, 'Blessed the one coming in the name of the Lord!'"

MATTHEW TWENTY-FOUR

1 And Jesus having gone out was going away from the temple, and his disciples came near to point out to him the buildings of the temple. 2 Now he responding said to them, "Do you not see all these? Truly I say to you, there will be none left here, stone upon stone, which will not be thrown down."

3 Now as he was sitting upon the Mount of Olives, the disciples came near to him privately, saying, "Tell us when these things will be; and what is the sign of your coming; and the completion of the age?" 4 And answering Jesus said to them, "Beware lest anyone misleads you. 5 For many will come in my name, saying, 'I am the Christ,' and they will mislead many. 6 Now you will hear of wars and rumors of wars. See that you are not alarmed, for it is necessary to take place; but not yet is the end. 7 For nation will rise against nation, and kingdom against kingdom. And there will be famines and pestilences and earthquakes in various places. 8 But all these are the beginning of sorrows.

9 "Then they will deliver you to tribulation, and will kill you, and you will be hated by all the nations, on account of my name. 10 And then many will take offense, and they will betray one another, and will hate one another; 11 and many false prophets will arise, and will mislead many. 12 And because lawlessness is to be multiplied, the love of many will grow cold. 13 But the one having endured to the end, he will be delivered. 14 And this good news of the kingdom will be proclaimed in all the world for a testimony to all the nations; and then the end will come.

15 "Therefore when you shall see the 'abomination of desolation' spoken of by Daniel the prophet, standing in the holy place—the one reading let him understand—16 then those in Judea let them flee to the mountains. 17 The one on the housetop, let him not come down to take anything out of his house. 18 And the one in the field, let him not return back to take his garment. 19 But woe to those pregnant, and to those nursing infants, in those times! 20 Now, pray that your flight might not be in winter, or on a Sabbath. 21 For then there will be great tribulation, such as has not been from the beginning of the world until now, no, nor may be. 22 And if those times had not been shortened, there would not have been anybody saved *from death*, but because of the elect, those times will be shortened.

23 "Then if anyone says to you, 'Look, here is the Christ,' or 'Here,' do not believe. 24 For false

christs will rise and false prophets, and will give great signs and wonders, so as to mislead, if possible, even the elect. 25 Look, I have foretold it to you. 26 If therefore they say to you, 'Look, he is in the wilderness,' do not go; 'Look, he is in the inner rooms,' do not believe. 27 For just as the lightning comes from the east and shines as far as the west, so will be the coming of the Son of Man. 28 For wherever the carcass might be, there the vultures will be gathered.

29 "Now immediately during[tt] the tribulation of those times, the sun will be darkened, and the moon will not give its light, and the stars will fall from the sky, and the powers of the heavens will be shaken. 30 And then will appear the sign of the Son of Man in the heaven, and then all the tribes of the earth will mourn, and they will see the Son of Man coming on the clouds of heaven with power and great glory. 31 And he will send his messengers with a great trumpet call, and they will gather his elect from the four winds, from the ends of the heavens to the ends of them.

32 "Now learn the parable from the fig tree: when its branch is already become tender and it puts forth the leaves, you know that the summer is near. 33 And so you, when you see all these things, know that it is near, at the doors. 34 Truly I say to you, that this generation may by no means have passed away until all these things may have taken place. 35 The heaven and the earth will pass away, but my words by no means may pass away.

36 "But about that day and hour no one knows, not even the messengers of the heavens, nor the Son, except Father only. 37 For as were the times of Noah, so will be the coming of the Son of Man. 38 For as they were in those times, before the flood, eating and drinking, marrying and giving in marriage, until that day Noah entered into the ark, 39 and they knew not until the flood came and took all away; and so will the coming of the Son of Man.

40 "Then two will be in the field: one is taken and one is left; 41 two grinding at the mill: one is taken and one is left. 42 Therefore keep watch, because you do not know on what day your Lord is coming. 43 But know this, that if the householder had known in what watch of the night the thief comes, he would have watched, and not have allowed his house to be broken into. 44 And on account of this, you be ready, for the Son of Man comes in that hour you do not expect.

45 "Who then is the faithful servant, and wise, whom the master has set over his household, to give to them food in season? 46 Blessed that servant, whom the master having come, will find doing thus. 47 Truly I say to you, that he will set him over all his possessions. 48 But if that evil servant should say in his heart, 'My master delays,' 49 and should begin to beat his fellow servants, and to

eat and drink with the drunkards, 50 the master of that servant will come in a day in which he does not expect, and in an hour which he is not aware, 51 and will scourge him and will appoint him a place with the hypocrites; there shall be the weeping and the gnashing of teeth."

MATTHEW TWENTY-FIVE

1 "Then the kingdom of the heavens will be like ten virgins, who having taken their lamps, went out to meet the bridegroom. 2 Now five of them were foolish, and five wise. 3 For the foolish, having taken their lamps, did not take oil with them, 4 but the wise took oil in the vessels with their lamps.

5 "Now the bridegroom delaying, they all became sleepy and slept. 6 And at the middle of the night there was an outcry: 'Look, the bridegroom, go out to meet him.' 7 Then all those virgins arose, and trimmed their lamps. 8 But the foolish said to the wise, 'Give us from your oil, for our lamps are going out.' 9 Now the wise answered, saying, 'No, lest it might not even be enough for us and you; go rather to those selling, and buy for yourselves.'

10 "Now while going to buy, the bridegroom came, and those ready went in with him to the wedding feast; and the door was shut. 11 But afterward the other virgins also come, saying, 'Sir, sir, open to us.' 12 But answering he said, 'Truly, I say to you, I do not know you.' 13 Therefore watch, for you neither know the day nor the hour [ᵘᵘ].

14 "For it is exactly like a man going on a journey. He called his own servants and delivered to them his possessions. 15 And to one indeed he gave five talents, but to one two, and to one one, to each according to his own ability; and he left the region immediately. 16 Having gone, he who having received the five talents, traded with them, and made five more. 17 Likewise, he with the two gained two more. 18 But he having received one, having went away dug into the ground, and hid his master's money.

19 "Now after much time comes the master of those servants, and settled accounts with them. 20 And having come, he who having received the five talents, brought to him five other talents, saying, 'Sir, you delivered to me five talents; look, I have gained five more talents.' 21 His master said to him, 'Well done, good and faithful servant; you were faithful over a few things, I will set you over many things. Enter into the joy of your master.' 22 Now also having come, he with the two talents said, 'Master, you delivered to me two talents. Look, I have gained two more talents.' 23 His master said to him, 'Well done, good and faithful servant; you were faithful over a few things, I will set you over many things. Enter into the joy of your master.'

24 "Now also having come, the one having received the one talent

said, 'Master, I knew you, that you are a hard man, reaping where you did not sow, and gathering from where you did not scatter. 25 And I having been afraid, having gone away, I hid your talent in the ground. Look, you have what is yours.'

26 "But answering, his master said, to him, 'Wicked and lazy servant. You knew that I reap where I sowed not, and gather from where I scatter not. 27 Therefore you ought to *have* put my money with the bankers, and I having come, I should have received my own with interest. 28 Therefore take the talent from him, and give it to him having the ten talents. 29 For to everyone having will be given, and he will have abundance; but the one not having, even that which he has will be taken from him. 30 And the useless servant, cast out into the outer darkness.' There will be the weeping and the gnashing of teeth.

31 "But when the Son of Man comes in his glory, and all the messengers with him, then he will sit upon the throne of his glory. 32 And all the nations will be gathered before him, and he will separate them from one another, as the shepherd separates the sheep from the goats. 33 And indeed he will set the sheep on his right hand, but the goats on the left.

34 "Then the King will say to those on his right hand, 'Come, those blessed of my Father, inherit the kingdom prepared for you from the foundation of the world. 35 For I hungered, and you gave me to eat; I thirsted, and you gave me to drink; I was a stranger, and you took me in; 36 naked, and you clothed me; I was sick, and you visited me; I was in prison, and you came to me.'

37 "Then the righteous will answer him, saying, 'Lord, when saw we you hungering and fed you? Or thirsting and give you to drink? 38 Now when saw we you a stranger, and took you in? Or naked and clothed you? 39 Now when saw we you sick, or in prison, and come to you?' 40 And the King answering said to them, 'Truly I say to you, inasmuch as you did it to one of the least of these my brethren, you did it to me.'

41 "And then he will say to those on the left, 'Depart from me, you cursed, into the eternal fire prepared for the devil and his messengers. 42 For I hungered, and you gave me nothing to eat; I was thirsty, and you gave me nothing to drink; 43 I was a stranger, and you did not take me in; naked, and you did not clothe me; sick, and in prison, and you did not visit me.'

44 "And then they will answer, saying, 'Lord, when saw we you hungering, or thirsting, or a stranger, or naked, or sick, or in prison, and did not minister to you?' 45 Then he will answer them, saying, 'Truly I say to you, inasmuch as you did not do it to one of the least of these, neither did you to me.' 46 And these will go

away into eternal punishment, but the righteous into eternal life."

MATTHEW TWENTY-SIX

1 And so it was when Jesus had finished all these words, he said to his disciples, 2 "You know that after two days the Passover comes, and the Son of Man is handed over to be crucified."

3 Then the chief priests and the elders of the people were gathered in the courtyard of the high priest, who is called Caiaphas, 4 and consulted together in order that they might take hold of Jesus by trickery and kill him; 5 but they said, "Not during the feast, that there not be a riot among the people."

6 Now Jesus having been in Bethany, in the house of Simon the leper, 7 a woman came to him, having an alabaster vessel of very expensive fragrant oil, and poured it on his head as he was reclining. 8 But having seen, the disciples became indignant, saying, "For what purpose this waste? 9 For this could have been sold for much, and have been given to the poor."

10 But knowing this Jesus said to them, "Why do you cause trouble to the woman? For she did to me a beautiful work. 11 For the poor you always have with you; but me you have not always. 12 For this woman in pouring this fragrant oil on my body, she did it for my burial. 13 Truly I say to you, wherever this good news may be proclaimed in all the world, that which this woman did will be spoken of for a memorial of her."

14 Then one of the Twelve, who is called Judas Iscariot, having gone to the chief priests, 15 said, "What are you willing to give me, and I will deliver him to you?" Now they weighed out to him thirty pieces of silver. 16 And from that time he sought an opportunity that he might deliver him.

17 Now on the first *day* of Unleavened Bread, the disciples came to Jesus, saying, "Where would you like us to prepare for you to eat the Passover?" 18 Now he said, "Go into the city unto a certain man, and say to him, 'The Teacher says, "My time is near. With you I will keep the Passover with my disciples."'" 19 And the disciples did as Jesus directed them, and prepared the Passover.

20 Now evening having come, he reclined *to eat* with the Twelve disciples. 21 And as they were eating, he said, "Truly I say to you, that one of you will betray me." 22 And being exceedingly sorrowful, each one began to say to him, "Master, it isn't me, is it?" 23 And answering he said, "The person having dipped the hand in the dish with me, he will betray me. 24 Indeed, the Son of Man goes just as it has been written concerning him; but woe to that man by whom the Son of Man is betrayed. Better would it be for him if that man had not been born." 25 But Judas (who was betraying him) responding said, "It isn't me, is it, Rabbi?" He says to him, "You have said."

26 Now as they were eating,

Jesus having taken bread, and having blessed it, broke it, and having given it to the disciples, said, "Take, eat; this is my body." 27 And having taken a cup, and having given thanks, he gave it to them, saying, "Drink from it, all of you. 28 For this is my blood, of the covenant, being poured out for many, for forgiveness of sins. 29 But I say to you, I will not drink, from this moment, of this the fruit of the vine, until the day when I drink it anew with you, in my Father's kingdom." 30 And having sung a hymn, they went out to the Mount of Olives.

31 Then Jesus says to them, "You all will fall away because of me during this night, for it has been written: 'I will strike the shepherd, and the sheep of the flock will be scattered.' 32 But after I have been raised, I will go before you into Galilee." 33 Now Peter responding said to him, "If all will fall away because of you, I will never fall away." 34 Jesus said to him, "Truly I say to you that this night, before the rooster crowing, you will deny me three times." 35 Peter says to him, "Even if it is necessary for me to die with you, I will never no never deny you." In like manner also said all the disciples.

36 Then Jesus comes with them to a place called Gethsemane, and he says to the disciples, "Sit here while I go over there and pray." 37 And having taken with him Peter and the two sons of Zebedee, he began to be sorrowful and deeply distressed. 38 Then he says to them, "My soul is very sorrowful, even to death. Remain here and watch with me." 39 And having gone forward a little, he fell upon his face, and praying says, "My Father, if it is possible, let this cup pass from me. Nevertheless, not as I will, but as You."

40 And he comes to the disciples and finds them sleeping, and says to Peter, "So, were you not able to watch one hour with me? 41 Watch and pray, so that you do not enter into temptation. The spirit indeed is willing, but the flesh is weak."

42 Again for a second time having gone away, he prayed, saying, "My Father, if this is not possible to pass, unless I drink it, Your will be done." 43 And having come again, he finds them sleeping, for their eyes were indeed heavy. 44 And having left them again, having gone away, he prayed for the third time, having said again the same thing.

45 Then he comes to the disciples and says to them, "Sleep for the time remaining, and take your rest.

"Look, the hour has drawn near, and the Son of Man is betrayed into the hands of sinners. 46 Rise; let us go. Look, he who is betraying me has drawn near."

47 And as he is still speaking, look, Judas, one of the Twelve, came, and with him a great crowd with swords and clubs, from the chief priests and elders of the people.

48 Now the one betraying him gave them a sign, saying, "Whomever that I may kiss, he it is; seize him." 49 And immediately having come to Jesus, he said, "Greetings, Rabbi." and kissed him. 50 But Jesus said to him, "Friend, for this you come?" Then having come to him, they laid hands on Jesus and seized him.

51 And look, one of those with Jesus, having stretched out his hand, drew his sword, and having struck the servant of the high priest, cut off his ear. 52 Then says Jesus to him, "Return your sword to its place; for all having taken the sword, by the sword will perish. 53 Or think you that I am not able to call upon my Father, and he will provide to me right now more than twelve legions of messengers? 54 How then should the Scriptures be fulfilled, that it must be thus?"

55 In that hour Jesus said to the crowds, "Are you come out as against a robber with swords and clubs to seize me? Every day in the temple I was teaching, and you did not seize me. 56 But this is come to pass, that the scriptures of the prophets might be fulfilled." Then the disciples, all having forsaken him, fled.

57 Now those persons having seized Jesus led him away to Caiaphas the high priest, where the scribes and the elders were assembled. 58 But Peter followed him from afar, even to the courtyard of the high priest. And having entered within, he sat with the temple police to see the outcome. 59 Now the chief priests and the whole council sought false testimony against Jesus, so that they might put him to death, 60 but they found none, many having come forward as false witnesses. But at last two having come forward 61 said, "This man said, 'I am able to destroy the temple of God and in three days to rebuild it.'"

62 And having stood up, the high priest said to him, "Answer you nothing? What do these witness against you?" 63 But Jesus was silent. And the high priest said to him, "I adjure you by the living God, that you tell us if you are the Christ, the Son of God." 64 Jesus says to him, "You have said. Moreover, I say to you, from now you will see the Son of Man sitting at the right hand of the Power, and coming in the clouds of heaven."

65 Then the high priest tears his clothes, saying, "He has slandered God! Why have we any more need of witnesses? Look, now you have heard the slander against God! 66 What do you think?" Now answering they said, "He is deserving of death." 67 Then they spit in his face, and struck him. Others slapped him, 68 saying, "Prophesy to us, Christ, who is he having hit you?"

69 Now Peter was sitting outside in the courtyard, and a serving girl came to him, saying, "You also were with Jesus the Galilean." 70 But he denied before all, saying, "I know not what you say."

71 Now having gone out to the gateway, another female saw him, and says to those there, "This person was with Jesus of Nazareth." 72 And again he denied, with an oath, "I know not the man."

73 After a little while, those also standing close by, having come to him, said to Peter, "Surely you also are one of them, for even your speech gives you away." 74 Then he began to curse and to swear, "I know not the man!" And immediately a rooster crowed. 75 And Peter remembered the word of Jesus, having said, "Before the rooster crowing, you will deny me"; and having gone out, wept bitterly.

MATTHEW TWENTY-SEVEN

1 Now morning having come, all the chief priests and elders of the people took counsel against Jesus, so that they might put him to death. 2 And having bound him, they led him away and delivered him to Pilate the Procurator.ʷ

3 Then Judas (the one having delivered him), having seen that he was condemned, having regretted his actions, returned the thirty pieces of silver to the chief priests and elders, 4 saying, "I sinned, having delivered innocent blood." And they said, "What is that to us? You will see to it." 5 And having cast the pieces of silver into the temple, he left; and having gone away, hanged himself.

6 But the chief priests having taken the pieces of silver said, "It is not lawful to put them into the treasury, since it is the price of blood." 7 And having taken counsel, they bought with them the potter's field, for a burial place for strangers. 8 Therefore that field was called "Field of Blood" to this day.

9 Then was fulfilled that having been spoken by Jeremiah the prophet, saying, "And they took the thirty pieces of silver, the value of him having been priced, whom they set a price on, by the sons of Israel priced, 10 and they gave them for the potter's field, as the Lord directed me."

11 Now Jesus stood before the Procurator, and the Procurator questioned him, saying, "Are you the King of the Jews?" Now Jesus said, "You say." 12 And in his being accused by the chief priests and elders, he answered nothing. 13 Then Pilate says to him, "Hear you not how many things they witness against you?" 14 And he did not answer him, not even to one word, so as to greatly amaze the Procurator.

15 Now at the feast the Procurator was accustomed to release to the crowd one prisoner, whomever they wished. 16 Now they had then a notorious prisoner called Barabbas. 17 They therefore having been gathered together, Pilate said to them, "Whom will you that I release to you? Barabbas, or Jesus who is called Christ?" 18 For he knew that they delivered him through envy.

19 Now as he was sitting on

the Judgment Seat, his wife sent to him, saying, "Have nothing to do with that righteous man, for many things I suffered today in a dream on account of him."

20 But the chief priests and the elders persuaded the crowds that they should ask for Barabbas; but Jesus execute. 21 Now the Procurator answering said to them, "Which do you want of the two I might release to you?" Now they said, "Barabbas." 22 Pilate says to them, "What then should I do with Jesus who is called Christ?" They all say, "Let him be crucified." 23 But he said, "For what evil did he commit?" But all the more they cried out, saying, "Let him be crucified."

24 Now Pilate having seen that it availed nothing, but rather an uproar is rising, having taken water, he washed his hands before the crowd, saying, "I am innocent of the blood of this. You will take care for yourselves." 25 And responding all the people said, "His blood be on us, and on our children." 26 Then he released to them Barabbas; now having flogged Jesus, he delivered him that he might be crucified.

27 Then the soldiers of the Procurator, having taken Jesus with them to the Praetorium, gathered before him all the company. 28 And having stripped him, they put on him a scarlet robe. 29 And having twisted together a crown of thorns, they put it on his head, and a reed in his right hand; and having bowed the knees before him, they mocked him, saying, "Hail, King of the Jews." 30 And having spit upon him, they took the reed and struck him on his head. 31 And when they had mocked him, they took the robe off him, and they put on him his clothes, and led him away to crucify him. 32 Now going out, they found a man of Cyrene, named Simon. They compelled him that he might carry his cross.

33 And having come to a place called Golgotha, which is called, "Place of a Skull," 34 they gave him wine mingled with gall to drink; and having tasted, he was not willing to drink it.

35 Now having crucified him, they divided his clothing, casting lots; that might be fulfilled that which was spoken by the prophet: "They divided my clothing among themselves, and for my clothing they cast a lot." 36 Sitting down, they kept watch over him there. 37 And they put up over his head the accusation written of him: "This Is Jesus The King Of The Jews."

38 Then two robbers are crucified with him, one at the right hand, and another at the left. 39 Now those passing by reviled him, wagging their heads 40 and saying, "The one destroying the temple and building it in three days, save yourself. If you are son of God, also come down from the cross."

41 In the same manner also the chief priests, mocking with the scribes and elders, said, 42 "He saved others; he is not able to save himself. He is King of Israel; let him

come down now from the cross, and we will believe in him. 43 He trusted on God; let Him deliver now if He wants him. For he said, 'I am son of God.'" 44 Now also in the same manner the robbers, those having been crucified with him, reviled him.

45 Now from about noon darkness was over all the land, until about midafternoon. 46 Now about midafternoon Jesus cried out with a loud voice, saying, "Eli, Eli, lama sabachthani?" that is, "My God, my God, why have You forsaken me?" 47 Now some of those who were standing there, having heard, said, "This man calls Elijah." 48 And immediately one of them having run and having taken a sponge, having filled it with vinegar and having put it on a reed, gave him to drink. 49 But the rest said, "Let be; let us see whether Elijah comes to save him."

50 Now Jesus again having cried out with a loud voice, yielded up his spirit. 51 Then, look, the veil of the temple was torn from top to bottom, into two; and the earth was shaken, and the rocks were split, 52 and the tombs were opened, and many bodies of the saints having fallen asleep arose, 53 and having gone out of the tombs after his resurrection, they entered into the holy city and appeared to many. 54 Now the centurion and those with him keeping guard over Jesus, having seen the earthquake and the things taking place, greatly feared, saying, "Truly this was God's son."

55 Now there were many women from afar off, looking on, who followed Jesus from Galilee, ministering to him, 56 among whom was Mary the Magdalene, and Mary the mother of Jacob and Joses, and the mother of the sons of Zebedee.

57 Now evening having come, a rich man came from Arimathea, named Joseph, who also himself was discipled to Jesus. 58 He having gone to Pilate asked for the body of Jesus. Then Pilate commanded it be given. 59 And having taken the body, Joseph wrapped it in clean linen cloth, 60 and placed it in his new tomb, which he had cut in the rock; and having rolled a large stone to the door of the tomb, went away. 61 Now there was Mary the Magdalene and the other Mary, sitting opposite the tomb.

62 Now the next day, which is after the preparation, the chief priests and the Pharisees were gathered together before Pilate, 63 saying, "Sir, we have remembered how that deceiver said while living, 'After three days I arise.' 64 Command therefore the tomb to be secured until the third day, lest having come his disciples steal him away, and say to the people, 'He is risen from the dead'; and the last deception will be worse than the first." 65 Pilate said to them, "You have a guard; go make it as secure as you know how." 66 Now having gone they made the tomb secure with the guard, having sealed the stone.

MATTHEW TWENTY-EIGHT

1 Now after Sabbath, it being dawn toward the first day of the week, came Mary the Magdalene and the other Mary to see the tomb. 2 And look, there was a great earthquake; for a messenger of the Lord having descended out of heaven, and having come, rolled back the stone, and was sitting upon it. 3 Now his appearance was as lightning, and his clothing white as snow. 4 Now from the fear of him, those keeping guard trembled with fear, and became as dead.

5 Now responding, the messenger said to the women, "Fear not; for I know that Jesus, the one having been crucified, you seek. 6 He is not here, for he is risen, as he said. Come, see the place where he was lying. 7 And having gone quickly, say to his disciples, that he is risen from the dead; and look, he goes before you into Galilee; there you will see him. Look, I have told you."

8 And having gone out quickly from the tomb, with fear and great joy, they ran to tell his disciples. 9 Now as they were going to tell his disciples, also look, Jesus met them, saying, "Rejoice!" Now having come to him, they took hold of his feet and worshiped him. 10 Then Jesus says to them, "Fear not. Go tell my brethren that they should go into Galilee, and there they will see me."

11 Now they were going, look, some of the guard having gone into the city reported to the chief priests all things that happened. 12 And having been gathered together with the elders, and having taken counsel, they gave to the soldiers much money, 13 saying, "Say that, 'His disciples having come at night stole him, we being asleep.' 14 And if this may be heard by the Procurator, we will persuade him, and keep you out of trouble." 15 Now having taken the money, they did as they were instructed. And this saying is spread abroad among the Jews until this day.

16 Now the eleven disciples went into Galilee, to the mountain where Jesus directed them. 17 And having seen him they worshiped; but some doubted. 18 And having come to them, Jesus spoke to them, saying, "All authority in heaven and on earth has been given to me. 19 Having gone therefore, disciple[ww] all the peoples, immersing them in the name of the Father, and of the Son, and of the Holy Spirit, 20 teaching them to observe all things whatever I commanded you. And look, I am with you all the days, until the completion of the age" [xx].

The Book of Mark

The good news according to Mark, is really the good news according to the apostle Peter, with certain words by Mark, e.g., 1:1; 16:9–20, both men being inspired by the Holy Spirit (as for example Paul and Tertius, Romans 16:22, Peter and Silvanus, 1 Peter 5:12). The oldest testimony, Papias (AD 70–155) *Fragments* VI, states Mark "wrote down accurately" what Peter said of the sayings and deeds of Christ. Peter's purpose was not an orderly account, but "instructions accommodated to the necessities of his gentile hearers" [Papias]. The arrangement of those instructions in a narrative format is Mark's contribution to this gospel. Mark published the good news first in Rome, Italy, ca. AD 63, then in Alexandria, Egypt, ca. AD 66/67, giving rise to the version with 16:9–20, which is agreeable to the post-resurrection narratives of Matthew and Luke. The Book of Mark, though positioned after Matthew in our Bibles, was most likely published after Luke was published.

MARK ONE

1 Beginning of the good news of Jesus Christ God's Son.

2 As written in the prophets,[b] "See! I send my messenger before your presence, who will prepare your way. 3 'A loud exhortation in the wilderness: "Prepare the way of the Lord. Make his paths straight."'"

4 John came immersing in the wilderness and proclaiming an immersion of repentance for forgiveness of sins. 5 And all the region of Judea went out to him, and they of Jerusalem. And all were immersed by him in the Jordan River, confessing their sins. 6 And John was dressed in camel hair, and a belt of leather around his waist, and eating locusts and wild honey.

7 And he proclaimed, saying, "The one who comes after me, is mightier than me, of whom I am not worthy—having stooped down—to untie the string of his sandals. 8 I immersed you in water, but he will immerse you in Holy Spirit."[c]

9 And it came to pass in those times, Jesus (from Nazareth in Galilee) came and was immersed in the Jordan by John. 10 And immediately coming up out of the water, he saw the heavens split open, and the Spirit as a dove coming down upon him. 11 And a voice came out of the heavens: "You are my son, the beloved, in whom I am well pleased."

12 And immediately the Spirit urged[d] him out into the wilderness. 13 And he was in the wilderness forty days, being tempted by Satan, and was with the wild animals, and messengers cared for him.

14 And after John had been delivered up, Jesus came into Galilee, publicly proclaiming God's good news, 15 and saying, "The time has been fulfilled, and the kingdom of God has come near. Repent and believe in the good

news."

16 And passing by the Sea of Galilee, he saw Simon, and Andrew the brother of Simon, casting a net into the sea; for they were fishermen. 17 And Jesus said to them, "Come after me, and I will make you to become fishers of men." 18 And immediately having left the nets, they followed him. 19 And having gone forward a little, he saw Jacob, the one of Zebedee, and John his brother, and those[e] in the boat, mending the nets. 20 And immediately he called them. And having left Zebedee their father in the boat with the employees,[f] they went away after him.

21 And they entered into Capernaum. And immediately on the Sabbath, having entered into the synagogue, he taught. 22 And they were struck with astonishment at his teaching, for he was teaching them as having authority, and not as the scribes.

23 And shortly there came into their synagogue a man with an unclean spirit. And he cried out, 24 saying, "What do you have to do with us, Jesus of Nazareth? Are you come to destroy us? I know who you are, the holy one of God." 25 And Jesus rebuked him, saying, "Silence" and "Come out of him." 26 And the unclean spirit having convulsed the man, and having cried out with a loud voice, came out of him.

27 And all were astonished, so as to inquire among themselves, saying, "What is this new teaching? With authority he commands even the spirits, the unclean ones, and they obey him!" 28 And the report of him immediately went out into all the surrounding region of Galilee.

29 And immediately, having left the synagogue, they came into Simon and Andrew's house, with Jacob and John. 30 And Simon's mother-in-Law had lain down sick, fevering.[g] And immediately they speak to him about her. 31 And having come to her, having taken her hand, he healed her, and the fever left her, and she served them.

32 Now evening having come, when the sun went down, they brought to him all those who are ill and those demonized.[h] 33 And all the city was assembled together at the door. 34 And he healed many being ill with various diseases, and cast out many demons. And he did not allow the demons to speak, because they knew him.[i]

35 And very early in the morning, still dark, having risen up, he went out and went to a solitary place, and there was praying. 36 And Simon went after him, and those with him. 37 Now having found him they also said to him, "Everyone looks for you!" 38 And he said to them, "Let us go elsewhere into the next towns, that there also I might preach. This is why I have come." 39 And he was going, preaching in their synagogues in all of Galilee, and casting out demons.

40 And a leper came to him, imploring him, and kneeling down to him, and saying to him, "If you

are willing, you are able to cleanse me." 41 And having pity, and having stretched out his hand, he touched him, and said to him, "I am willing. Be cleansed." 42 And immediately the leprosy departed from him and he was cleansed. 43 And having sternly warned him, immediately he sent him away. 44 Now he said to him, "Take heed you speak nothing to none. But go show yourself to the priest and offer for your cleansing what Moses commanded for a testimony to them." 45 But having gone out, he began to proclaim much and to advertise the matter, so that no longer was Jesus able to openly enter into a city, but was out in solitary places; and they came to him from all sides.

MARK TWO

1 And after some days, entering again into Capernaum, it was heard, "He is in the house." 2 And many gathered together, so there was no more space—not even at the door; and he was speaking to them the word.

3 And they came, bringing to him a paralytic, being carried by four. 4 And not able to come near to him on account of the crowd, they removed the roof where he was. And having removed the roof tiles, they let down the bed on which the paralytic was lying. 5 And Jesus, having seen their faith, said to the paralytic, "Son, your sins are forgiven."

6 Now, there were some of the scribes sitting there and reasoning in their hearts, 7 "Why does this one in this manner speak slandering lies? Who is able to forgive sins if not one, God?" 8 And Jesus, in his spirit, immediately knowing that in this manner they are reasoning in themselves, said to them, "Why reason you these things in your hearts? 9 What is easier to say to the paralytic? 'Your sins are forgiven,' or to say, 'Get up, and take up your bed, and walk?' 10 Now that you might know that the Son of Man has authority on the earth to forgive sins (he says to the paralytic), 11 I say to you, 'Get up, take up your bed, and go to your house.'" 12 And he got up, and immediately having taken up the bed, went out before all, so as to amaze all and to glorify God, saying, "Never did we see it so!"

13 And he went out again, by the sea, and all the crowd came to him; and he taught them. 14 And passing by, he saw Levi of Alphaeus sitting at the collector's office. And he said to him, "Follow me." And getting up, he followed him.

15 And he was reclining[j] *to eat* in Levi's house, and many tax collectors and sinners were reclining with Jesus and his disciples; for they were many, and they followed him. 16 And the scribes of[k] the Pharisees, seeing him eat with the sinners and tax collectors, said to his disciples, "Why does he eat with the tax collectors and sinners?" 17 And Jesus, having heard, said to them, "Those who are robust have no need of a physician, but those who are ill. I came not to call righteous

ones, but sinners."

18 And the disciples of John and those of the Pharisees, they were fasting. And they came and they said to him, "Why is it the disciples of John and the disciples of the Pharisees fast, but your disciples do not fast?"

19 And Jesus said to them, "Are the groom's companions[l] able to fast when the bridegroom is with them? During the time they have the bridegroom with them, they are not able to fast. 20 But times will come when the bridegroom may be taken from them, and then they will fast—in those times.

21 "No one sews a new piece of cloth on old clothing. But if he does, the patch tears away from it, the new from the old, and a worse tear occurs. 22 And no one puts new wine into old wineskins. But if he does, the wine will burst the wineskins, and the wine will be ruined, and the wineskins; but new wine into new wineskins."

23 And it came to pass on the Sabbath, he is passing through the fields of growing grains. And his disciples began to make their way, pulling off the heads of grain. 24 And the Pharisees said to him, "Look! Why do they on the Sabbath that which is not lawful?"

25 And he said to them, "Did you never read what David did, when he had need and hungered, he and those with him? 26 How he entered into the house of God, during Abiathar the priest, and ate the shewbread, which it is not lawful to eat, except the priests. And he even gave to those who were with him?" 27 And he said to them, "The Sabbath was made for humankind,[m] and not humankind for the Sabbath. 28 So then the Son of Man[n] is master even of the Sabbath."

MARK THREE

1 And he entered again into the synagogue. And a man was there, having a withered hand. 2 And they watched him, whether on the Sabbath he would heal him, in order they might accuse him. 3 And he said to the man with the withered hand, "Stand up in the middle." 4 And he said to them, "Is it lawful, on the Sabbath, to do good or to do evil? To save life or to kill?" But they remained silent. 5 And having looked at all of them—with anger, grieving at the hardness of their heart—he said to the man, "Stretch out your hand." And he stretched out and his hand was restored to health. 6 And leaving, the Pharisees immediately took counsel with the Herodians against him, how they might destroy him.

7 And Jesus, with his disciples, withdrew to the sea; and a large number of people from Galilee followed; and from Judea, 8 and from Jerusalem, and from Idumea, and the other side of Jordan, and around Tyre and Sidon—a great multitude, having heard how much he was doing, came to him. 9 And he told his disciples to keep a small boat close by, on account of the crowd, lest they should press upon

him. 10 For he healed many, such that they pressed upon him, so that they might touch him, as many as had diseases. 11 And the unclean spirits, when they saw him, fell down before him, and exclaimed, saying, "You are the son of God." 12 And he censured them many times, in order that they should not make him known.

13 And he goes up on the mountain and calls those he wanted to himself; and they went to him. 14 And he appointed twelve, whom he named "apostles," that they should be with him, and that he might send them to preach, 15 and to have authority to cast out demons.

16 And he appointed the Twelve. And he gave the name "Peter" to Simon. 17 And Jacob of Zebedee and John the brother of Jacob he gave the name "Boanerges," which is "sons of thunder." 18 And Andrew, and Philip, and Bartholomew, and Matthew, and Thomas, and Jacob of Alphaeus, and Thaddaeus, and Simon the Zealot, 19 and Judas Iscariot, who also betrayed him.

20 And he comes into a house, and again a crowd comes together, so that they are not even able to eat bread. 21 And having heard, his kindred went out to take him. For they said, "He is out of his mind."

22 And the scribes, those having come down from Jerusalem, said, "Because he has Beelzebul," and "Because by the prince of the demons he casts out demons." 23 And having called them he said in parables to them, "How is Satan able to cast out Satan? 24 And if a kingdom is divided against itself, that kingdom is not able to stand. 25 And if a house is divided against itself, that house will not be able to stand. 26 And if Satan has risen up against himself and is divided, he is not able to stand, but is coming to an end. 27 But no one having entered into the strong man's house is able to seize his goods, unless first he binds the strong man, and then he will rob his house.

28 "It is so, I say to you, that all will be forgiven the sons of men, the sins and the slanders,° as much as if they might have slandered. 29 But whoever should speak evil against the Holy Spirit never has forgiveness forever, but is guilty of an endless act of sin"; 30 because they said, "He has an unclean spirit."

31 And his mother came, and his brothers. And standing outside sent to him, calling him. 32 And a crowd sat around him, and they said to him, "Look, your mother and your brothers and your sisters are outside, seeking you." 33 And he, responding to them, said, "Who are my mother and my brothers?" 34 And looking around him on those sitting in a circle around him, he said, "See my mother and my brothers. 35 For whoever should do the will of God, he is my brother, and sister, and mother."

MARK FOUR

1 And again he began to teach

beside the sea. And a great crowd came to him, so that he got into the boat to sit in the sea. And all the crowd was on the land facing the sea. 2 And he taught them many things in parables, and said to them in his teaching, 3 "All of you, listen, give heed! The sower went out to sow. 4 And it came to pass as he sowed, that some fell along the road. And the birds came and ate it. 5 And other fell upon the rocky ground, where it had not much soil. And immediately it sprouted, because the soil was not deep. 6 And after the sun rose it was burned. And because there was no root, it dried up. 7 And other fell into thorns, and the thorns grew and choked it. And it gave no fruit. 8 And other fell into the good soil. And sprouting and increasing gave fruit. And one bore thirty, and one sixty, and one a hundred." 9 And he said, "The one having ears to hear should listen!"

10 And when he was alone, those around him, with the Twelve, asked him about the parable. 11 And he said to them, "To you the mystery of the Kingdom of God has been given. But to those who are outside, all the things come in parables, 12 that seeing, they might see and not perceive, and hearing, they might hear and not understand—if ever they should turn and it should be forgiven them."

13 And he said to them, "Do you not understand this parable? And how will you understand all the parables? 14 The sower sows the word. 15 Now these are the ones beside the road where the word is sown. And when they hear, Satan immediately comes and takes away the word that was sown in them. 16 And in the same way, these are the ones who are sown upon the rocky ground. When they hear the word, they immediately receive it with joy, 17 and do not have root in themselves, but are temporary. Then tribulation or persecution, having come on account of the word, they immediately fall away. 18 And these are the ones sown among the thorns. They are those having heard the word, 19 and the anxieties of the times, and the deceit of riches, and other desires springing up, overpower the word, and it becomes unfruitful. 20 And these are the ones who are sown upon the good soil—the ones who hear the word, and receive it, and are fruitful: one thirty, and one sixty, and one a hundred."

21 Also he said to them, "A lamp is not brought so that it should be put under a basket or under the bed. Is it not put upon the lampstand? 22 For there is nothing hidden except that it should be made known. Nor a secret thing taken place but that it should come to light. 23 If anyone has ears to hear, let him listen."

24 And he said to them, "Consider what you hear. In what measure you measure it will be measured to you and added to you. 25 For whoever has, it will be given to him. And he who does not have, even that he has will be taken from him."

26 And he said, "In this manner is the kingdom of God: as a man should cast the seed upon the earth, 27 and should sleep and rise, night and day, and the seed should sprout and grow, he knows not how. 28 The earth of itself brings forth fruit. First a stalk, then a head, then abundant grain in the head.p 29 Then when the grain is ready, he immediately sends the sickle, for the harvest has come."

30 And he said, "By what means should we compare the Kingdom of God? Or with what parable should we describe it? 31 As to a mustard seed, which, when it may be sown upon the earth, is smallest of all the seeds which are upon the earth. 32 And whenever it may be sown, it grows and becomes larger than all the garden plants, and produces great branches, so that the birds of the air are able to nest beneath its shade."

33 And with many such parables he spoke to them the word, even as they were able to listen. 34 Now he did not speak to them without parables; but alone, to his own disciples, he explained all things.

35 And he said to them on that day, evening having come, "Let us go over to the other side." 36 And having dismissed the crowd, they took him as he was, in the boat; and other boats were with him. 37 And a violent wind storm came. And the waves beat into the boat, so that the boat is already being filled. 38 And he was in the stern, sleeping on the pillow. And they woke him and said to him, "Teacher, do you not care that we perish?" 39 And he, having been awakened, rebuked the wind and said to the sea, "Silence. Be still." And the wind ceased, and there was a great calm. 40 And he said to them, "Why are you fearful? Do you still have no faith?" 41 And they feared a great fear, and said to one another, "Who then is this, that even the wind and the sea obey him?"

MARK FIVE

1 And they came to the other side of the sea, to the country of the Gerasenes. 2 And he, having left the boat, immediately met him, out of the tombs, a man with an unclean spirit, 3 who had his dwelling in the tombs. And no one was able to bind him anymore, not even with chains; 4 because he had often, by means of shackles and chains, been bound. And he had torn the chains in two and had shattered the shackles. And no one had the strength to subdue him. 5 And throughout all night and day, in the tombs and in the mountains, he was crying out, and cutting himself with stones.

6 And seeing Jesus from a distance, he ran and kneltq before him. 7 And crying with a loud voice, he said, "What do you have to do with me, Jesus, son of God the Most High? I charge you to swear by God, torment me not." 8 For he was saying to him, "You, the unclean spirit, come out of the man." 9 And he asked him, "What

is your name." And speaking, he answered, "My name is Legion, because we are many." 10 And many times he exhorted Jesus, that he would not send them out of the country.

11 Now there was nearby the mountain a great herd of pigs grazing. 12 And they exhorted him, saying, "Send us into the pigs, that into them we may enter." 13 And he allowed them. And having left, the unclean spirits entered into the pigs. And the herd rushed down the steep place into the sea, about two thousand, and they were drowned in the sea.

14 And those grazing them ran away and told it in the city and in the countryside. And they came to find out what had been done. 15 And they came to Jesus, and saw the one demonized sitting, clothed, and in his right mind—the one having had the legion—and they were afraid. 16 And those who saw it told how it happened with him demonized, and about the pigs. 17 And they began to exhort him to leave their country.

18 And Jesus, having entered into the boat, the one who had been demonized was fervently asking him, that he might be with him. 19 And he did not permit him, but said to him, "Go to your home, to your own, and tell them how much the Lord did for you, and had mercy on you." 20 And he left and began to proclaim in the Decapolis how much Jesus had done for him; and all were struck with astonishment.

21 And Jesus, again having passed over to the other side in the boat, a great crowd gathered to him; and he was by the sea. 22 And one of the leaders of the synagogue, named Jairus, came. And seeing him, falls at his feet 23 and repeatedly appeals to him, saying, "My little daughter is holding on at the point of death—would you come and lay hands on her, that she might be healed and should live. 24 And he went with him, and a great crowd followed him, and pressed closely upon him.

25 And a woman, having a flow of blood twelve years, 26 and having suffered much under many physicians, and having spent her all, and in no way having benefitted, but having come more to the worse, 27 having heard about Jesus, coming up in the crowd from behind, touched his outer clothing.ʳ 28 For she said, "If I may only touch his outer clothing, I will be healed." 29 And immediately the flow of her blood was dried, and she knew that her body was restored to health from the disease.

30 And Jesus, immediately knowing in himself the power had gone forth out of him, turning around in the crowd, said, "Who touched my clothing?" 31 And his disciples said to him, "You see the crowd pressing upon you, and you say, 'Who touched me?'" 32 And he looked around to see the one who had done this. 33 Now she, being frightened, and trembling, knowing what had been done to her, came and knelt before him,

and told him all the truth. 34 Now he said to her, "Daughter, your faith has restored your health. Go in peace and be in health from your affliction."

35 While he was still speaking, they come from the leader of the synagogue's *house*, saying, "Your daughter is dead. Why yet trouble the teacher?" 36 And Jesus, having heard the word spoken, said to the leader of the synagogue, "Fear not, only believe." 37 And he did not allow any to follow him, except Peter, and Jacob, and John the brother of Jacob.

38 And he comes to the house of the leader of the synagogue, and observes loud mourning, and weeping, and loud wailing. 39 And entering, he says to them, "Why such noise and grief? The child is not dead, but sleeps." 40 And they ridiculed him. But he, having put all out, takes with him the child's father and mother, and those with him, and goes in where the child was. 41 And taking the child's hand, he says to her, "Talitha, koumi"; which translated is, "Little girl, I say to you, get up." 42 And immediately the girl got up and walked, for she was twelve years. And they were immediately overcome with great astonishment.

MARK SIX

1 And he went away from there and came to his hometown; and his disciples followed him. 2 And Sabbath having come, he began to teach in the synagogue. And many hearing were astonished, saying, "How to this one these things, and what is the wisdom given to him, also the miracles, such as by his hands are done? 3 Is this not the builder,[s] the son of Mariam, and brother of Jacob, Joseph, Judas, and Simon? And are not his sisters here with us?" And they were offended by him.

4 And Jesus said to them, "A prophet is not without honor, except in his hometown, and among his relatives, and in his household." 5 And there he was not able to do any mighty works, except a few sick, laying hands, he healed. 6 And he was amazed at their unbelief. Then he went round about the villages, teaching.

7 And he called the Twelve, and began to send them out two and two, and gave to them authority over the unclean spirits. 8 And he instructed them, that they should take nothing for the journey, except a staff only—not bread, nor bag, nor money in the belt, 9 but put on sandals, and do not put on two tunics. 10 And he said to them, "Whenever you might enter into a house, there remain until you should leave from there. 11 And any place that will not receive you, nor hear you, leave from there, shake off the dust which is under your feet, for a testimony against them." [t]

12 And having gone out, they proclaimed that they should repent. 13 And they cast out many demons and anointed many sick with oil and healed them. 14 And

king Herod heard, for his name became well known. And he said, "John, the one immersing, is risen out from the dead, and on account of this the powers are at work in him." 15 But others said, "He is Elijah." And others said, "A prophet, like one of the prophets."

16 Now Herod, having heard, said, "John, whom I beheaded—he is risen!" 17 For Herod himself, having sent, took John and put him in prison, because of Herodias, his brother Philip's wife, because he had married her. 18 For John said to Herod, "It is not lawful for you to have your brother's wife." 19 Now Herodias held it against him, and desired to kill him, but was not able, 20 because Herod feared John, knowing he was a righteous and holy man, and kept him safe. And hearing him he was greatly perplexed, yet would hear him gladly.

21 Now an opportunity came when Herod, on his birthday, gave a party. 22 And Herodias's daughter came in and, having danced, pleased Herod and those reclining *to eat* with him. The king said to the girl, "Ask me what you desire, and I will give it to you." 23 And he swore to her, "That you might ask of me, I will give you, up to half of my kingdom." 24 And she left and asked her mother, "What shall I ask?" Now she said, "The head of John, the one immersing." 25 And immediately, quickly returning to the King, she asked, saying, "I desire that you give to me as soon as possible the head of John the Immerser on a plate."

26 And the king was made very sorrowful—because of his oaths and those reclining *to eat* with him he did not want to refuse her. 27 And immediately the king sent a soldier, commanding his head be brought. And he, having gone, beheaded him in the prison, 28 and brought the head upon a plate, and gave it to the girl, and the girl gave it to her mother. 29 And his disciples having heard, they came and took up his body, and laid it in a tomb.

30 And the apostles gathered around Jesus and told him all things they had done and what they had taught. 31 And he said to them, "Come away with me by yourselves to a solitary place and rest a little." For there were many coming and going and they could not even find opportunity to eat. 32 And they left by boat into a solitary place by themselves.

33 And they saw them going, and many recognized them, and they ran together there on foot from all the cities and arrived before them. 34 And having arrived, he saw a great crowd, and had compassion toward them, because they were as sheep not having a shepherd. And he began to teach them many things.

35 And the hour being already late, having come to him, the disciples say to him, "The place is desolate, and the hour already late. 36 Send them away to go into the surrounding countryside and villages, so they may buy for themselves something to eat." 37

But responding, he said to them, "You give to them to eat." And they say to him, "Should we go and buy two hundred denarii of bread, and give them to eat?"

38 Now he said to them, "How many bread have you? Go see." And finding out, they say, "Five, and two fish." 39 And he told them to have all recline in groups on the green grass. 40 And they sat in groups, by hundreds and by fifties.

41 And taking the five bread and the two fish, looking up to the heaven, he blessed and broke the bread, and gave it to the disciples, that they might set it before them. And the two fish he divided to all. 42 And all ate and were satisfied. 43 And they picked up twelve handbaskets full of fragments and of the fish. 44 And those having eaten the bread were five thousand men.

45 And immediately he compelled his disciples to enter into the boat, and to go before to the other side, to Bethsaida-Galilee,[u] until he dismissed the crowd. 46 And leaving them, he went away to the mountain to pray. 47 And at evening the boat was in the middle of the sea, and he was alone upon the land. 48 And he saw them straining in the rowing, for the wind was set against them.

About the fourth watch of the night he comes to them, walking on the sea, and desired to pass by them. 49 But having seen him on the sea, walking, they thought, a spirit! and cried out. 50 For all saw him and were troubled. Now, immediately he spoke with them, and said to them, "Have courage; it is I; fear not." 51 And he went up to them into the boat, and the wind stopped. And they were astonished beyond measure. 52 For they did not understand about the bread, but their heart had been hardened.

53 And having crossed over, they came to the land of Gennesaret, and drew to shore. 54 And they, upon getting out of the boat, immediately he was recognized, 55 so that running through the whole country, they began to carry about on the beds those sick, upon hearing where he is. 56 And wherever he was going into villages, or into cities, or into fields, they laid in the marketplaces those sick, and begged him that if only they might touch the fringe of his clothing; and as many as did touch him were restored to health.

MARK SEVEN

1 And the Pharisees and some of the scribes, having come from Jerusalem, came together to him. 2 And they saw some of his disciples that are eating the bread with defiled hands, that is, not washed. 3 (For the Pharisees—and all the Jews—unless they carefully wash the hands, do not eat, keeping the tradition of the elders. 4 And coming from the market, unless they wash, do not eat. And many other things there are which they received to keep: washings of cups and pots and bronze vessels; and couches for reclining at meals.)

5 And the Pharisees

questioned him, and the scribes, asking, "Why do your disciples not conduct themselves according to the tradition of the elders, but with unwashed hands eat their bread?" 6 Now he said to them, "Rightly Isaiah prophesied about you—hypocrites! As it has been written, 'This people honor me with their lips, but their heart is distant, far from me. 7 Moreover, falsely they worship me, teaching as doctrines the precepts of men.' 8 Leaving the commandment of God, you keep the traditions of men.'"[W]

9 And he said to them, "Suitably do you void the commandment of God, that your tradition you may keep. 10 For Moses said, 'Honor your father and your mother,' and 'The one speaking evil of father or mother must die the death.' 11 But in addition you say, 'If a man says to the father or the mother, "Anything from me that might be useful is Corban"' (that is, a gift) 12 you no longer allow him to do anything for the father or the mother, 13 making void the Word of God for your tradition which you have handed down. And many similar things you do."

14 And again calling the crowd to him, he said to them, "All hear me, and understand. 15 There is nothing outside a man entering into him that is able to defile him. But that coming out of the man are the things defiling the man. 16 Anyone having ears to hear, let him hear."

17 And when he went into the house away from the crowd, his disciples asked him about the parable. 18 And he said to them, "Are you also without understanding? Do you not understand that anything from outside entering into the man is not able to defile him? 19 Because it does not enter into his heart, but into the belly, and goes out into the toilet, purifying all the foods." 20 He also said, "That coming out of the man, that defiles the man. 21 For within, from the heart of men, the evil thoughts go out: sexual immoralities, thefts, murders, adulteries, 22 greediness, wickedness, deceit, lewdness, an evil eye, slander, arrogance, foolishness. 23 All these evils go out from within and defile the man."

24 Now from there he left and went into the regions of Tyre [W]. And entering into a house, he wanted no one to know; and he was not able to be hidden. 25 But immediately a woman heard about him, whose little daughter had an unclean spirit, and coming, she fell at his feet. 26 Now, the woman was a gentile, a Syrophoenician by birth, and asked him that he might cast the demon out of her daughter. 27 And he said to her, "First let the children be satisfied. For it is not good to take the children's bread and cast it to the dogs." 28 But she answered and said to him, "Yes, sir. But the dogs under the table eat the children's crumbs." 29 And he said to her, "On account of this word, go. The demon has left your daughter." 30 And having gone to her home, she

discovered the child lying on the bed, and the demon gone.

31 And again, leaving the region of Tyre and Sidon, he went through Sidon to the Sea of Galilee, through the middle of the region of Decapolis.

32 And they brought to him a deaf man, who also spoke with difficulty. And they asked him earnestly that he might lay on him the hand. 33 And taking him privately aside from the crowd, he put his fingers into his ears, and then having spit, he touched his tongue. 34 And looking up to heaven he sighed deeply, and said to him, "Ephphatha!" (that is, "Be opened!"). 35 And his ears were opened, and immediately the ligament of his tongue was loosed, and he spoke plainly.

36 And he commanded them that they should tell no one. But as much as he commanded them, more and more they proclaimed it.

37 And they were astonished beyond measure, saying, "He has done all things well. Even the deaf he makes to hear, and the mute to speak."

MARK EIGHT

1 Again, in those days, the crowd being great, and not having anything they might eat, having called his disciples, he said to them, 2 "I have compassion on the crowd, because already they have continued three days with me, and they have nothing that they might eat. 3 And if I should send them away hungry to their homes, they will faint on the way; and some of them have come from afar."

4 And his disciples answered him. "From where will anyone here be able to satisfy these with bread in this desolate place?" 5 And he asked them, "How many bread have you?" And they said, "Seven." 6 And he commanded the crowd to recline on the ground. And taking the seven bread, giving thanks, he broke and gave to his disciples, that they might lay it before them. And they laid it before the crowd. 7 Also they had a few small fish. And having blessed them, he commanded these also to be laid before them. 8 And they ate and were satisfied. And they took up more than seven baskets of fragments. 9 Now there were about four thousand; and he sent them away.

10 And immediately getting into the boat with his disciples, he came into the region of Dalmanutha. 11 And the Pharisees went out and began to question him, seeking a sign from heaven from him, tempting him. 12 And, sighing deeply in his spirit, he said, "Why does this generation seek a sign? Truly, I say to you, no sign will be given to this generation."

13 And having left them, again leaving in the boat, he went away to the other side. 14 And they had forgotten to take bread, and except for one bread, they did not have any in the boat with them. 15 And he admonished them, saying, "Watch out, beware, of the leaven of the Pharisees, and of the leaven

of Herod." 16 And they were reasoning with one another because they have not bread.

17 And knowing, he said to them, "Why do you reason, 'Because we do not have bread?' Do you not perceive nor understand? Have you hardened your heart? 18 Having eyes, see you not? And having ears do you not hear? And do you not remember? 19 When I broke the five bread for the five thousand, how many hand-baskets full of fragments did you take up?" They said to him, "Twelve." 20 "When the seven to the four thousand, how many baskets full of fragments did you take up?" And they said, "Seven." 21 And he said to them, "Do you not yet understand?"

22 And he comes to Bethsaida-Julius. And they bring to him a blind man, and they implored him that he might touch him. 23 And taking hold of his hand, he led him out of the village. And having spit in his eyes, laying hands on him, he asked him if he could see anything. 24 And looking up he said, "I see the men, because as trees I see them walking." 25 Then again he laid the hands upon his eyes, and he opened his eyes, and was restored to health, and looked on all clearly. 26 And he sent him to his home, saying, "You may not go into the village, nor may you tell it to any in the village."

27 And Jesus and his disciples went out into the villages of Caesarea Philippi. And on the way he questioned his disciples, saying to them, "Who do people say I am?" 28 Now they told him, saying, "John the Immerser, and others, Elijah; but others, one of the prophets." 29 And he asked them, "But who do you say I am?" Answering, Peter said to him, "You are the Christ." 30 And he commanded them that they should tell no one about him.

31 And he began to teach them that it is necessary for the Son of Man to suffer many things, and to be rejected by the elders and the chief priests and the scribes, and to be killed, and after three days to rise; 32 and he spoke the word plainly. And Peter took him aside and began to rebuke him. 33 And turning about, and observing his disciples, he rebuked Peter, and said, "Get behind me, Satan. For your thoughts are not of the things of God, but the things of humankind."

34 And calling to himself the crowd and his disciples, he said to them, "If any person desires to come after me, let him deny himself, and let him take up his cross, and let him follow me. 35 For whoever might desire to save his life, will lose it, but whoever loses his life on account of me and of the good news, will save it. 36 For what will it profit a person to gain the whole world and to lose his soul? 37 For what might a person give as an exchange for his soul? 38 For if any might be ashamed of me and my words in this generation—adulterous and sinful—also the Son

of Man will be ashamed of him when he shall come in the glory of his Father, with the holy messengers."

MARK NINE

1 And he said to them, "Truly, I say to you, that there are some of those standing here, who absolutely shall not experience death, until they see the kingdom of God having come in power."

2 And after six days, Jesus took with him Peter, and Jacob, and John only, by themselves, and brought them up into a high mountain. 3 And his clothes became shining, extremely white, such as no launderer on the earth is able to whiten. 4 And Elijah with Moses appeared to them, and they were talking with Jesus.

5 And in response, Peter said to Jesus, "Rabbi, it is good for us to be here. And let us make three tabernacles, one for you, and one for Moses, and one for Elijah." 6 For he did not know what he should say; for they were greatly terrified.

7 And a cloud came, overshadowing them. And a voice came out of the cloud, "This is my son, the beloved: listen to him." 8 And suddenly, looking around, they saw no one, except Jesus only, with themselves.

9 Now when they were coming down from the mountain, he commanded them that they should not tell anyone what they had seen, until the Son of Man had risen out from the dead. 10 And they kept that saying among themselves, questioning, what is, "to rise out from the dead?"

11 And they asked him, saying, "Why do the scribes say that Elijah must come first?" 12 Then he said to them, "Truly Elijah coming first restores all things. And how it has been written of the Son of Man, that he should suffer many things and be rejected! 13 But I say to you, that also Elijah has come, and they did to him whatever they desired, as it has been written of him."

14 Now when they came to the disciples, they saw a great crowd gathered around them, and scribes arguing with them. 15 And immediately all the crowd, having seen him, were astonished, and running to him, greeted him. 16 And he asked them, "What do you argue with them?" 17 And one out of the crowd answered him. "Teacher, I brought my son to you. He has a mute spirit. 18 And whenever it may seize him, he is thrown down, and froths at the mouth, and grinds his teeth, and is withering away.[x] And I spoke to your disciples, that they might cast it out, and they were not able."

19 Then he, answering him, said, "O unbelieving generation! How long will I be with you? How long will I bear with you? Bring him to me."

20 And they brought him to Jesus. And seeing Jesus, the spirit immediately convulsed the man's son. And having fallen upon the ground, he rolled about, frothing at the mouth. 21 And Jesus asked his

father, "How long a time is it that this has been with him?" And he said, "Since childhood. 22 And often it throws him both into fire and into water, that it might kill him. But if you are able to help us, have compassion on us."

23 And Jesus said to him, "If you are able, all things are possible to the one believing." 24 Immediately the father of the child cried out, saying, "I believe! Help my unbelief." 25 Now Jesus, having seen that a crowd was running together, rebuked the unclean spirit, saying to it, "Mute and deaf spirit, I command you, come out of him, and you may enter into him no more." 26 And crying out much, and convulsing him, it came out. And he became as if dead, so that many said that he was dead. 27 Now Jesus, taking his hand, raised him up, and he stood up.

28 And having entered into a house, his disciples asked him in private, "Why were we not able to cast it out?" 29 And he said to them, "This kind is able by nothing to go out, except by prayer."ʸ

30 Leaving from there, they passed through Galilee. And he did not want any to know, 31 for he was teaching his disciples. And he said to them, "The Son of Man is delivered into the hands of men, and they will kill him; and having been killed, he will rise on the third day." 32 And they did not understand the saying, and were afraid to ask him.

33 And he came to Capernaum. And being in the house, he asked them, "What did you discuss on the way?" 34 But they were silent with one another, for on the road they had been discussing who was greatest. 35 And sitting, he called the Twelve and said to them, "If anyone desires to be first, he will be last of all and servant of all." 36 And taking a child, he stood it in the middle of them; and taking it in his arms he said to them, 37 "Whoever might receive one of such little children in my name, receives me; and whoever might receive me, receives not me, but the one having sent me."

38 John answered him, "Teacher, we saw someone casting out demons in your name, who does not follow us, and we restrained him, because he was not following us." 39 And Jesus said, "Do not forbid him. For there is no one who will do mighty work in my name and will lightly be able to speak evil of me. 40 For whoever is not against us is for us. 41 For whoever might give you a cup of water to drink in my name, because you are Christ's, truly I say to you that he should never no never lose his reward. 42 And whoever might cause to stumble one of these—the little ones believing on me—it is better for him, rather, if a heavy millstone is put around his neck and he is thrown into the sea.

43 "And if your hand might cause you to stumble, cut it off. It is better for you to enter into life maimed rather than, having two hands, to go away into Gehenna—

into the unquenchable fire 44 where their worm dies not, and the fire is not quenched. 45 And if your foot might cause you to stumble, cut it off. It is better for you to enter into life lame rather than, having two feet, to be cast into Gehenna—into the unquenchable fire 46 where their worm dies not, and the fire is not quenched. 47 And if your eye might cause you to stumble, cast it out. It is better for you with one eye to enter into the kingdom of God, than having two eyes to be cast into Gehenna, 48 where their worm dies not, and the fire is not quenched.

49 "For everyone will be salted with fire. 50 Salt is good, but if the salt becomes unsalty, with what will you season it? Have in yourselves salt and be at peace with one another."

MARK TEN

1 And he left there and came into the region of Judea, and beyond the Jordan. And, again, crowds came together to him. And as he was accustomed, again he taught them. 2 And the Pharisees came to him, asking him if it is lawful for a husband to divorce his wife, testing him.

3 Now answering he said to them, "What did Moses command you?" 4 And they said, "Moses permitted to write a bill of divorce and dismiss her." 5 And Jesus said to them, "For the hardness of your heart he wrote this commandment for you. 6 But from the beginning of creation God made them male and female. 7 Because of this, a man will leave his father and mother and will join with his wife. 8 And unto one flesh will be the two, so that no longer are they two, but one flesh. 9 Therefore what God has united together, let not man separate."

10 And in the house again, the disciples asked him concerning the same thing. 11 And he said to them, "Whoever may divorce his wife and should marry another commits adultery against her. 12 And if the woman has herself divorced the husband and should marry to another, she commits adultery."

13 And they brought to him little children, that he might touch them. Now the disciples rebuked them. 14 But seeing, Jesus was indignant, and said to them, "Permit the little children to come to me; do not restrain them. For of such is the kingdom of God. 15 Truly I say to you, whoever may not receive the kingdom of God as a little child, shall never no never enter into it." 16 And taking them in his arms, he blessed, laying hands on them.

17 And as he went out on the street, one running up and kneeling to him, asked him, "Good teacher, what might I do that I might inherit life eternal?"

18 Now Jesus said to him, "Why do you call me good? No one is good except one, God. 19 You know the commandments. Do not murder. Do not commit adultery. Do not steal. Do not bear false witness. Do not defraud. Honor your father and mother."

20 Now he said to him, "Teacher, all these I have kept, from my youth."

21 But Jesus, looking at him, loved him. And he said to him, "You lack one thing. Go, sell as much as you have, and give to the poor, and you will have riches in heaven; and come, follow me."z 22 And he was depressed at this word, and went away sorrowful; for he was one having many possessions.

23 And having looked around, Jesus said to his disciples, "How with difficulty those having riches will enter into the kingdom of God!"

24 Now the disciples were astonished at his words. But Jesus, responding, said to them, "Children, how difficult it is to enter into the kingdom of God, for those who trust in riches. 25 It is easier a camel to pass through the eye of the needle, than a rich man into the kingdom."

26 Now they were very much astonished, saying among themselves, "And who is able to be saved?" 27 Jesus, having considered them, said, "With men? Impossible. But not with God. For all things are possible with God."

28 Peter began to say to him, "Look, we have left all and followed you." 29 Jesus answered, "Truly I say to you, there is no one who has left house, or brothers, or sisters, or mother, or father, or children, or lands—for my sake and because of the good news—30 but that he shall receive a hundredfold now in this time: houses, and brothers, and sisters, and mothers, and children, and lands—with persecutions—and in the age which is coming, eternal life. 31 However, many first will be last, and the last first."

32 Now they were on the way, ascending to Jerusalem, and Jesus was leading them. And they were astonished; but those following were afraid. And again taking the Twelve to himself, he began to tell them the things about to happen to him.

33 "Look, we ascend to Jerusalem, and the Son of Man will be betrayed to the chief priests and to the scribes. And they will condemn him to death. And they will betray him to the gentiles. 34 And they will mock him, and they will spit on him, and they will flog him, and they will kill him. And on the third day he will rise up."

35 And Jacob and John, the sons of Zebedee, come to him, saying to him. "Teacher, we desire that whatever it might be that we may ask you, you would do for us."

36 So he said to them, "What do you desire me to do for you?"

37 Now they said to him, "Give to us, that one of us at your right hand and one at your left hand might sit in your glory."

38 But Jesus said to them, "You know not what you ask. Are you able to drink the cup which I drink and be immersed with the immersion which with I am immersed?" 39 And they said to him, "We are able." Then Jesus said to them, "The cup which I

drink you will drink, and the immersion with which I am immersed you will be immersed. 40 But to sit at my right hand or at my left hand is not mine to give, but it is to those for whom it has been prepared."

41 Now, having heard this, the ten began to be indignant about Jacob and John. 42 And having called them, Jesus said to them, "You know that those considered to rule the gentiles exercise lordship over them, and those of them who are important exercise authority over them. 43 However this shall not be with you. But whoever might desire to become great with you, will be your servant. 44 And whoever might desire with you to become first, will be servant of all. 45 For even the Son of Man came not to be served, but to serve, and to give his life as a ransom for many."

46 And they came to Jericho. And as he was leaving Jericho—and his disciples and a large crowd—a blind beggar, Bartimaeus the son of Timaeus, was sitting beside the road. 47 And hearing that it is Jesus of Nazareth, began to cry out and to say, "son of David, Jesus, have mercy on me."

48 And many rebuked him, that he might be silent. But much more he cried out, "son of David, have mercy on me!" 49 And having stopped, Jesus commanded he be called. And they call the blind man, saying to him, "Be of good cheer, rise up, he calls you."

50 And casting away his cloak, getting up he comes to Jesus. 51 And responding to him, Jesus said, "What do you desire I should do to you?" And the blind man said, "Rabbi, that I might receive sight." 52 And Jesus said to him, "Go. Your faith has healed you." And immediately he received sight and followed him in the way.

MARK ELEVEN

1 And as they approached Jerusalem, near Bethphage and Bethany at the Mount of Olives, he sent two of his disciples, 2 and he said to them, "Go into the village before you, and immediately entering into it, you will find a foal tied, on which no man has sat; untie it and bring it. 3 And if anyone says to you, 'Why are you doing this?' say, 'Because the Lord has need of it,' and immediately he will send it here."

4 And they left and found the foal, tied at the door, out in the street. And they untied it. 5 And some of those standing there said to them, "What are you doing untying that foal?" 6 But they said to them as Jesus had commanded them. And they let them go.

7 And they led the foal to Jesus. And they threw their mantles on it, and he sat on it. 8 And many laid their mantles on the road; but others cut branches from the fields. 9 And those going before and those going after were crying out, "Hosanna! Blessed is he coming in the name of the Lord! 10 Blessed is the coming kingdom of our father David. Hosanna in the highest!"

11 And he entered into Jerusalem, into the temple. And looking around on all things—the hour already being late—he went out of the city to Bethany with the Twelve.

12 And on the next day, as they left from Bethany, he was hungry. 13 And having seen a fig tree in the distance, having leaves, he went, if perhaps he would find anything on it. And coming to it, he found nothing but leaves. For it was not the time of figs. 14 And he responded, saying to it, "No more from you—to the age—no one may eat fruit." And his disciples heard.

15 And they came to Jerusalem. And entering into the temple court, he began to drive out those selling and those buying in the court. And he overturned the tables of the money-exchangers, and the seats of those selling the doves. 16 And he would not allow that anyone should carry a container through the temple court.

17 And he admonished them, and was saying to them, "Has it not been written, 'My house will be called a house of prayer for all the nations?' But you have made it a den of robbers."

18 And the chief priests heard, and the scribes. And they considered how they might destroy him. Because they feared him, because all the crowd was astonished at his teaching. 19 And when evening had come he left the city.

20 And passing by in the morning they saw the fig tree, which had dried up from the roots. 21 Now Peter, remembering, said to him, "Rabbi, look, the fig tree that you cursed is dried up."

22 And responding Jesus said to them, "Have faith in God. 23 And so it is I say to you, that whoever might say to this mountain, 'Be you taken away and be you cast into the sea,' and may not doubt in his heart, but may believe that what he says takes place, it will be done for him. 24 On account of this I say to you, all things whatever you pray and you ask, believe that you receive, and it will be to you.

25 "And when you stand praying, forgive if you have anything against anyone, in order that your Father who is in the heavens may forgive you of your wrongdoing." [26^{aa}]

27 And again they came to Jerusalem. And as he is walking in the temple courts, the chief priests and the scribes and the elders come to him. 28 And they say to him, "By what authority are you doing these things, or who gave you this authority that these things you may do?"

29 Now Jesus said to them, "I will ask you one thing, and you answer me, and I will tell you by what authority I do these things. 30 John's immersing, was it from heaven or from men? Answer me."

31 And they deliberated with each other, saying, "What should we say? If we say, 'From heaven,' he will say, 'Why then did you not believe him?' 32 But if we should

say, 'From men'"—they feared the people, for all held that John was indeed a prophet. 33 And answering Jesus they said, "We do not know." Jesus replied, "Neither will I tell you by what authority I do these things."

MARK TWELVE

1 And he began to speak to them in parables. "A man planted a vineyard, and placed a fence around it, and dug a pit for the winepress, and built a watchtower, and hired it out to vinedressers, and went to another country. 2 And he sent a servant to the vinedressers at the season, that he might receive of the vinedressers from the fruit of the vineyard. 3 But taking him, they beat him, and sent him away with empty hands.

4 "And again he sent another servant to them. And him they struck on the head and treated shamefully. 5 And he sent another and him they killed; many others also: some they beat, some they killed. 6 Having yet one beloved son, him he sent to them last, saying, 'Because they will respect my son.'

7 "But those vinedressers said to themselves, 'This is the heir. Come, we may kill him and the inheritance will be ours.' 8 And they took him and killed him and threw him outside the vineyard.

9 "What will the master of the vineyard do? He will come, and destroy the vinedressers, and will give the vineyard to others.

10 "Have you not read this scripture? 'The stone that those building rejected, this has become the chief corner. 11 This was of the Lord and it is marvelous in our eyes.'"

12 And they sought him, to lay hold of him; and they feared the crowd. For they knew that the parable he had spoken was against them. And leaving him, they went away.

13 And they sent to him certain of the Pharisees and Herodians, that they might ensnare him with words. 14 And having come, they said to him, "Teacher, we know that you are true, and care not for anyone—for you do not look to the appearance of men, but with truth teach the way of God. Is it lawful to give tribute to Caesar, or not; should we pay or should we not pay?"

15 But knowing their hypocrisy, he said to them, "Why do you test me? Bring me a denarius, that I might see it." 16 Now they brought it, and he said to them, "Whose is this likeness and the inscription?" And they said to him, "Caesar's." 17 Then Jesus said to them, "Give that of Caesar to Caesar, and that of God to God." And they were astonished at him.

18 And Sadducees come to him—who say there is not a resurrection. And they questioned him, saying, 19 "Teacher, Moses wrote for us, that if anyone's brother should die and leave behind a wife but not leave children, that his brother should take the wife and raise up offspring

for his brother. 20 There were seven brothers. And the first took a wife. And dying left no offspring. 21 And the second took her, and died, and left no offspring; and the third likewise. 22 And the seven left no offspring. And last of all the woman died. 23 In the resurrection, when they rise, of which of them will she be wife; for seven had her as wife?"

24 And Jesus said to them, "Do you not err because of this, you do not know the scriptures or the power of God? 25 For when they rise out from the dead ones, neither do they marry nor are given in marriage, but are like messengers in the heavens. 26 But concerning the dead, that they rise, have you not read in the book of Moses, in that of the bush, how God spoke to him, saying, 'I, I am the God of Abraham, and the God of Isaac, and the God of Jacob?' 27 He is not God of the dead but of the living. You err greatly."

28 And one of the scribes—having heard them reasoning together, perceiving that he answered them well—questioned him: "which is first of all the commandments?" 29 Jesus answered, "The first is, 'Hear, Israel, God our Lord is one Lord. 30 And you will love God your Lord with all your heart, and with all your soul, and with all your mind, and with all your strength.' 31 This second: 'You will love your neighbor as yourself.' Greater than these there is not another commandment."

32 And the scribe said to him, "Correct, teacher, you have spoken according to truth, that he is one, and there is not another besides him. 33 And to love him with all the heart and with all the understanding, and with all the strength, and to love one's neighbor as oneself, is more important that all the burnt offerings and sacrifices." 34 And Jesus, perceiving he answered wisely, said to him, "You are not far from the kingdom of God." And no one no longer dared to question him.

35 And taking the occasion, Jesus said, teaching in the temple court, "How say the scribes that the Christ is son of David? 36 David himself said by the Holy Spirit, 'Said the Lord to my Lord, "Sit at my right hand until I may put your enemies as a footstool at your feet."' 37 David himself calls him Lord, so how of him is he his son?" And the large crowd heard him gladly.

38 And in his teaching he said, "Beware of the scribes. They desire to walk about in robes, and greetings in the marketplaces, 39 and chief seats in the synagogues, and chief places at the feasts. 40 They are extorting widow's houses and as an outward show praying long. They will receive greater judgment."

41 And sitting down opposite the temple treasury, he saw the crowd put money into the temple treasury; and many rich were putting in much. 42 One poor

widow came and put in two leptons,[bb] which together are a *Roman* quadrans. 43 And having called his disciples, he said to them, "Surely I say to you, that this poor widow has put in more than all of those putting into the temple treasury. 44 For all put in out of their abundance. But she out of her poverty put in all she had, all her livelihood."

MARK THIRTEEN

1 And as he is going out of the temple court, one of his disciples said to him, "Teacher, see what stones and what buildings?" 2 And Jesus said to him, "See these great buildings? No not one shall be left here stone upon stone that shall not be thrown down."

3 Then, as he is sitting at the Mount of Olives, opposite the temple, Peter, and Jacob, and John, and Andrew asked him in private, 4 "Tell us when these things will be, and what is the sign when all these things are about to be accomplished?"

5 And Jesus began to say to them, "Be watchful, lest anyone mislead you. 6 Many will come in my name, saying, 'I am he,' and they will mislead many. 7 Now when you hear of wars and rumors of wars, be not troubled; it must come to pass, but it is not yet the end. 8 For nation will rise against nation, and kingdom against kingdom. There will be earthquakes in places; there will be famines. These are the beginning of sorrows.

9 "But you yourselves, be aware. They will deliver you to sanhedrins and you will be beaten in synagogues. And you will be brought before procurators and rulers because of me, for a testimony to them. 10 And it is first necessary the good news be announced to all peoples. 11 But when they may lead you, delivering you, do not be anxious what you should say. But what might be given to you in that hour, speak. For you are not speaking, but the Holy Spirit.

12 "And brother will deliver brother to death; and father, child; and children will rise against parents, and will put them to death. 13 And you will be hated by all on account of my name. Now the one having endured to the end, he will be delivered.[cc]

14 "Now when you see the abomination of the desolation—that spoken of by Daniel the prophet—standing where it should not (let the one reading understand), then those in Judea, let them escape to the mountains. 15 The one on the housetop, let him not come down, nor go in to take anything out of his house. 16 And the one in the field, let him not return to the things behind, to get his clothes.

17 "And woe to those having child in the womb and to those nursing infants in those times. 18 And pray that it might not be in winter. 19 For in those times will be tribulation such as has never been of this kind, from the beginning of

creation which God created until now; and never shall be. 20 And if the Lord had not shortened the times, no flesh would be preserved. But because of the elect whom he chose, he has shortened the times.

21 "And then if anyone says to you, 'See here the Christ, see, there,' you shall not believe. 22 For false christs will arise and false prophets, and will give signs and wonders so as to deceive, if possible, the elect. 23 Now you be aware. I have forewarned all things to you.

24 "But in those times, with[dd] that tribulation, the sun will be darkened, and the moon will not give its light, 25 and the stars will be falling out of the heaven, and the powers in the heaven will be shaken. 26 And then they will see the Son of Man coming in clouds with great power and glory. 27 And he will send the messengers and gather together his elect from the four winds, from the end of earth to the end of heaven.

28 "Now from the fig tree learn the parable. Even when the twig has become tender and it puts out the leaves, you know that the summer is near. 29 So also you, when you see these things coming to pass, know that it is near, at the doors. 30 Truly I say to you, that this generation shall not in any way pass away until that all these things shall have taken place. 31 The heaven and the earth will pass away, but my words will not in any way pass away.

32 "Now concerning that day or the hour, no one knows, not even the messengers in heaven, nor the Son, only the Father. 33 Be aware, watch. For you do not know when is the time, 34 like a man having left his house to go abroad, and having given his servants authority, to each his work, and commanded the doorkeeper that he should keep watch. 35 You watch therefore, for you know not when the master of the house comes, at evening, or at midnight, or when the cock crows, or morning, 36 lest having come unexpectedly he may find you sleeping. 37 Now what I say to you I say to all: watch."

MARK FOURTEEN

1 Now it was the Passover and the Unleavened Bread after two days. And the chief priests and the scribes were seeking, how having taken him by treachery, they might kill him. 2 For they said, "Not during the feast, lest at that time there will be an uproar of the people." 3 And he was in Bethany, in the house of Simon the leper, having reclined *to eat*. A woman came, who had an alabaster vessel of pure nard ointment of great price. She, having broken the alabaster vessel, poured it on his head.

4 Now some were indignant within themselves: "Why has this waste of the ointment been made? 5 For this ointment might have been sold above three hundred denarii, and that given to the poor?" And they murmured at her.

6 But Jesus said, "Leave her

alone. Why do you trouble her? She did a good work toward me. 7 For you always have the poor with you, and whenever you want you are able to do them good. But me you do not always have. 8 What she could she did. She anticipated to anoint my body for the burial. 9 Now truly I say to you, wherever the good news may be proclaimed unto the whole world, also what this woman did will be spoken for a memorial of her."

10 And Judas Iscariot, one of the Twelve, went away to the chief priests, that Jesus he might deliver into their power. 11 Now hearing, they rejoiced, and promised to give him money. And he looked for an opportunity, how he might deliver him into their power.

12 On the first day of the Feast of Unleavened Bread when they sacrificed the Passover lamb, His disciples say to him, "Where do you want us to go to prepare that you may eat the Passover?"

13 And he sends two of his disciples and says to them, "Go into the city, and you will meet a man carrying a pitcher of water. Follow him. 14 And wherever he may enter, say to the master of the house, 'The teacher says, "Where is my guest room where I may eat the Passover with my disciples?"' 15 And he will show you a large upper room, furnished and ready, and there prepare for us."

16 And his disciples left, and came into the city, and found as he said to them, and they prepared the Passover.

17 And evening come, he comes with the Twelve. 18 And as they reclined and were eating, Jesus said, "Truly I say to you, that one of you, who is eating with me, will deliver me into the power of another."

19 They began to be distressed, and to say to him, one by one, "Surely not I?" 20 Then he said to them, "One of the twelve who is dipping with me in the bowl. 21 Because, truly, the Son of Man goes as it has been written concerning him. But woe to the man that by whom the Son of Man is delivered up. Better for him if that man had never been born."

22 And as they were eating, he, taking bread, blessing, broke, and gave to them, and said, "Take. This is my body." 23 And having taken the cup, having given thanks, he gave to them, and they drank all of it. 24 And he said to them, "This is my blood of the covenant poured out for many. 25 Truly I say to you that no more, no never, will I drink of the fruit of the vine until the day when I drink it new in the kingdom of God." 26 And after singing hymns, they went out to the Mount of Olives.

27 And Jesus said to them, "All you will fall away, because it has been written, 'I will strike the shepherd and the sheep will be scattered.' 28 But after I have been raised I will go before you into Galilee."

29 Then Peter said to him, "Even if all fall away, yet not I." 30 And Jesus said to him, "Truly I say

to you, that you today, this night, that before the rooster crows twice, you will deny me three times."

31 Then Peter said passionately, "If it is necessary of me to die with you, I will never no never deny you." And in like manner they all spoke.

32 And they came to a place, of which the name is, "Gethsemane." And he said to his disciples, "Sit here while I pray." 33 And he took Peter and Jacob and John with him. And he began to be distressed and deeply burdened. 34 And he said to them, "My soul is overwhelmed with sorrow unto death. Remain here and watch."

35 And going a little further, he fell upon the ground and prayed, that if it is possible, the hour might pass from him. 36 And he said, "Abba, Father, all things are possible to you. Take away this cup from me—but not what I will, but what you."

37 And he comes and finds them sleeping. And he says to Peter, "Simon, are you asleep? Were you not able to watch one hour? 38 Watch, and pray, that you may not enter into temptation. Truly the spirit is willing but the flesh is weak."

39 And, again having gone away, he prayed, saying the same thing. 40 And again having returned, he found them sleeping. For their eyes were heavy. And they did not know what they might answer him.

41 And he came the third time, and said to them, "Still sleeping and resting? It is enough. The hour has come. Look, the Son of Man is delivered up into the hands of sinners. 42 Get up, let us go. See, he who is delivering me has come near."

43 And immediately, while of him he is yet speaking, Judas, one of the Twelve, comes, and with him a crowd—with swords and clubs—from the chief priests, and the scribes, and the elders.

44 Now he who was delivering him had given a sign to them, saying, "Whomever I may kiss is he; take him, and safely lead him away." 45 And arriving, immediately coming up to him, he said, "Rabbi," and kissed him. 46 And they laid hands on him and took him.

47 Now, a certain one of those standing by, having drawn the sword, struck the high priest's servant and cut off his ear.

48 And Jesus spoke, saying to them, "As against a robber you have come with swords and clubs to take me. 49 Every day I was with you in the temple teaching and you did not take me; but that the scriptures might be fulfilled."

50 And leaving him, all fled. 51 And a certain young man was following him, having put a linen cloth on his naked body; and they took hold of him. 52 Then he fled, naked, having left the linen cloth behind.

53 And they took Jesus to the high priest. And all the chief priests, and the elders, and the

scribes came together. 54 And Peter followed him at a distance, until within the courtyard of the high priest. And he was sitting with the temple police[ee] and warming himself at the fire.

55 Now, the chief priests and all the council sought testimony against Jesus—to put him to death—but none was found. 56 For many gave false testimony against him, but their testimonies were not sufficient. 57 And some rose up giving false testimony against him, saying, 58 "We heard him saying, 'I will destroy this temple, the one made with hands, and in three days I will build another not made with hands.'" 59 And none of their testimony was sufficient.

60 And standing up in the midst, the high priest questioned Jesus, saying, "Do you answer nothing to what these testify against you?" 61 But he was silent and did not answer, not a thing. Again, the high priest questioned him, and said to him, "Are you the Christ, the Son of the Blessed?" 62 And Jesus said, "I am. And you will see the Son of Man sitting at the right hand of the Power and coming with the clouds of heaven."

63 Now the high priest tore his clothes, and said, "What need have we of more witnesses? 64 You heard the slander against God. What do you think?" And all judged him to be deserving of death.

65 And some began to spit on him, and to cover up his face and strike him and say to him, "Prophesy!" And the temple police struck with him their palms.

66 And Peter, being below in the courtyard, one of the servants of the high priest, a young girl, comes. 67 And seeing Peter warming himself by the fire, stares at him, and says, "You also were with Jesus the Nazarene." 68 But he denied, saying, "I do not know nor even understand what you say," and he went out on the porch. And the rooster crowed.

69 And the servant girl, seeing him, again began saying to those standing by, "He is one of them." 70 But again he denied. And after a little *while*, again those standing by said to Peter, "Truly you are from them, for you also are a Galilean [ff]."

71 Then he began to curse and to swear, "I do not know this man of whom you speak." 72 And immediately, for the second time, a rooster crowed. And Peter remembered the word that Jesus had said to him: "Before the rooster crows twice, three times you will deny me." And falling down, he wept.

MARK FIFTEEN

1 Now early in the morning, the chief priests formed a council with the elders, and scribes, and all the Sanhedrin. They put Jesus in bonds, led him away, and delivered him to Pilate.

2 And Pilate questioned him. "You are the King of the Jews?" Now answering him, he said, "It is as you say." 3 And the chief priests continued to accuse him of many

things. 4 Then Pilate again questioned him, saying, "Do you not answer one thing? See how many things they witness against you." 5 But Jesus did not answer anything, and Pilate was amazed.

6 Now at the feast he would release one prisoner to them, whomever they asked. 7 Now there was one named Barabbas, bound with the rebels arrested, who had committed murder in the insurrection. 8 And the crowd began to call out, to beg him to do as he usually did for them.

9 Now Pilate responded to them, saying, "Do you desire I should release to you the King of the Jews?" 10 For he knew that because of envy the chief priests had delivered him. 11 But the chief priests stirred up the crowd, that instead he might release Barabbas to them. 12 And Pilate, responding again, said to them, "What, then, do you want I should do to him you name 'King of the Jews?'" 13 And they yelled out, "Crucify him!"

14 But Pilate said to them, "For what evil committed?" But they yelled all the more, "Crucify him!" 15 Now Pilate, inclined to do that which would satisfy the crowd, released Barabbas to them and delivered Jesus, having flogged him, that he might be crucified.

16 And soldiers led him away within the palace, that is, the Praetorium, and they called together all the troops. 17 And they put purple on him and placed on him a crown twisted from thorns. 18 And they began to salute him, "Hail King of the Jews!" 19 And they struck his head with a stalk, and spit on him. And kneeling, they bowed to him. 20 And after they had mocked him, they took off him the purple and put on him his own clothes, and they led him out, that they might crucify him.

21 And they compelled one passing by, Simon of Cyrene, coming in from the country (the father of Alexander and Rufus), that he might carry his cross. 22 And they took him to Golgotha, a place that translated is, "place of a skull." 23 And they gave him wine mixed with myrrh, but he did not take it.

24 And having crucified him, they also divided his clothes, casting lots for them, who should take what. 25 Now it was about midmorning,[99] and they crucified him. 26 And in the inscription of the accusation against him had been written, "The King of the Jews."

27 And with him they crucified two robbers, one on the right hand and one on the left of him. [28[hh]]

29 And those passing by insulted him, shaking their heads and saying, "Aha! You destroying the temple and building it in three days, 30 save yourself, come down from the cross!"

31 In the same manner also the chief priests mocking him to one another, with the scribes, said, "Others he saved. He is not able to save himself. 32 The 'Christ,' the 'King of Israel,' let him come down now from the cross, that we might see and believe." And those being

crucified with him insulted him.

33 About noon darkness came over all the land, until about midafternoon. 34 And about midafternoon Jesus cried out with a loud voice, "Eloi, Eloi, lama sabachthani?" which is interpreted, "My God, my God, why have you forsaken me?"

35 And some of those standing by, hearing, said, "Listen, he calls Elijah." 36 Now, one ran and filled a sponge with vinegar and, putting it on a stick, gave him it to drink, saying, "Let be. Let us see if Elijah comes to take him down." 37 But Jesus called out with a loud voice and then breathed his last. (38 And the veil of the temple was torn into two, from top to bottom.)

39 Now the Centurion standing in front of him, having seen in what manner that he died, said, "Truly this man was a son of god." 40 Also there were women observing from afar, among whom was Mary the Magdalene, and Mary mother of Jacob the younger and of Joseph, and Salome—41 who, when he was in Galilee, followed him and served him—and many others, those having come up with him to Jerusalem.

42 And about evening, since it was preparation day, that is, before Sabbath, 43 Joseph, who was from Arimathea, a prominent council member, who also himself was expecting the kingdom of God, boldly went to Pilate and asked for Jesus' body.

44 Now Pilate wondered if he were dead. And calling the centurion to him, he questioned him, if he had already died. 45 And knowing from the centurion, he freely gave the body to Joseph.

46 And having bought linen cloth, he took him down, wrapped him in the linen cloth, and laid him in a tomb which was cut out of rock. And he rolled a stone on the door of the tomb. 47 And Mary the Magdalene and Mary of the mother of Joseph saw where he was laid.

MARK SIXTEEN

1 And the Sabbath having ended, Mary the Magdalene, and Mary the mother of Jacob, and Salome brought spices, that coming they might anoint him.

2 And very early on the first day of the week, having risen with the sun, they come to the tomb. 3 And they said among themselves, "Who will roll away the stone for us from the door of the tomb?" 4 And looking up they see that the stone has been rolled away; for it was very large.

5 And entering into the tomb, they saw a young man sitting on the right, clothed with a white robe. And they were afraid.

6 Now he said to them, "Be not afraid. You seek Jesus the Nazarene, the crucified. He is risen! He is not here. See the place where they laid him. 7 But go, say to his disciples, and to Peter, that he goes before you into Galilee. There you will see him, as he said to you."

8 And running out they fled from the tomb. For trembling and

fear possessed them. And they spoke nothing to no one, for they were very afraid.

9[ii] Now having risen early on the first day of the week, he appeared first to Mary the Magdalene, from whom he had cast out seven demons. 10 She went and told it to those who had been with him and were now mourning and weeping. 11 And they, having heard that he is alive and had been seen by her, did not believe.

12 Now after these things he appeared to two of them, in another form, as they were walking, going into the country. 13 And they, having gone, told it to the rest; neither did they believe them.

14 Now later, as they were reclining *to eat*, he appeared to the Eleven. And he rebuked their unbelief and hardness of heart, because they did not believe those who had seen him risen from the dead.

15 And he said to them, "Go into all the world, proclaim the good news to all the creation. 16 He who having believed and having been immersed will be saved. But the one having disbelieved will be condemned.

17 "Now these signs will be done by those having believed: they will cast out demons in my name; they will speak new languages; 18 [ji] they will take up snakes; and if they drink anything deadly it shall not in any way hurt them; they will lay hands on the sick and they will be well."

19 Therefore, then, the Lord Jesus, after speaking to them, was taken up into the heaven and sat at the right hand of God. 20 Now they, going forth, preached everywhere, the Lord working with them, and confirming the word by the accompanying signs.

The Book of Luke

The good news according to Luke was written ca. AD 58–62, and published ca. AD 62, in Rome, Italy, during Paul's house arrest in that city. Luke's purpose was to provide an evangelistic document as suitable for evangelizing gentiles as Matthew's good news was for evangelizing Jews. Paul's experience using Matthew's good news on his several missionary journeys provided the impetus to write a good news for evangelizing gentiles. During the time he was under house arrest under Felix and Festus, Paul had Luke write that version of the good news. Luke's testimony is that he interviewed eyewitnesses and those who had known the eyewitnesses.

LUKE ONE

1 Inasmuch as now many attempted to compose in an orderly manner a history concerning the things accomplished among us, 2 as delivered to us by those who from the beginning were eyewitnesses and ministers of the Word, 3 so I believed myself also, having accurately investigated all these things from the first, to write an orderly account to you, most noble Theophilus,[a] 4 so that you may know the certainty of the words concerning which you were instructed.

5 There was in the times of Herod King of Judea a certain priest named Zacharias, of the course of Abijah, and his wife of the daughters of Aaron; and her name was Elizabeth. 6 Now they were both righteous before God, conducting their manner of life in all the commandments and laws of the Lord blameless. 7 And there was to them no child, because Elizabeth was barren, and both of them were advanced in years.

8 Now it happened in serving as a priest, in the order of his course before God, 9 according to the custom of the priesthood, it came to him by lot to burn incense, having entered into the temple of the Lord. 10 And all the multitude of the people were praying outside at the hour of the incense. 11 Then a messenger of the Lord appeared to him, standing at the right side of the altar of the incense. 12 And seeing him Zacharias was disturbed, and fear came over him.

13 Then the messenger said to him, "Fear not, Zacharias, because your prayer has been heard, and your wife, Elizabeth, will bear a son to you. And you will call his name 'John.' 14 And he will be great joy to you, and many will rejoice at his birth. 15 For he will be great before the Lord. Wine and strong drink never no never shall he drink. And of the Holy Spirit he will be filled, even from the womb of his mother.

16 "And many of the sons of Israel he will turn to the Lord their God. 17 And he will go before him in the spirit and power of Elijah, to turn the hearts of the fathers to the children, and the disobedient to the wisdom of the righteous, to make ready a people prepared for

the Lord."

18 And Zacharias said to the messenger, "By what will I know this? For I am an old man, and my wife is advanced in her years." 19 And responding, the messenger said to him, "I am Gabriel, the one standing before God, and I was sent to speak to you, and to announce these[b] good news to you. 20 Look now, you will be silent, and not able to speak until that day these things will happen, because you did not believe my words, which will be fulfilled in their season."

21 And the people were expecting Zacharias, and they were wondering at his continuing delay in the temple. 22 Then, coming out, he was unable to speak to them, and they understood that he had seen a vision in the temple. Also he was making signs to them, and continued speechless.

23 And it happened when the days of his priestly service were fulfilled, he went to his home. 24 Now after these days Elizabeth his wife conceived, and hid herself five months, saying, 25 "Thus to me the Lord has done, in the days in which he looked upon me to take away my disgrace among men."

26 Now, in the sixth month, Gabriel the messenger was sent by God to a city of Galilee, whose name was Nazareth, 27 to a virgin betrothed to a man, whose name was Joseph, of the house of David; and the virgin's name was Mariam. 28 And, having come to her, he said, "Rejoice, favored one. The Lord is with you."[c] 29 And at that word she was disturbed, and considered what manner this greeting might be.

30 And the messenger said to her, "Do not fear Mariam. For you have found favor with God. 31 Look now, you will conceive in your womb, and will bear a son, and you will call his name 'Jesus.' 32 He will be great, and will be called 'son of Most High.' And the Lord God will give him the throne of David, his father. 33 And he will reign over the house of Jacob to the ages, and of his kingdom there will not be an end."

34 Then said Mariam to the messenger, "How will this be, since I know not a man?" 35 And responding the messenger said to her, "The Holy Spirit will come upon you, and the power of Most High will rest upon you. Therefore also the holy begotten will be called, 'Son of God.' 36 Look now, Elizabeth, your relative, she has also conceived a son in her old age, and this month is the sixth to her who was called barren. 37 For not anything will be impossible with God." 38 Then Mariam said, "See the handmaid of the Lord. May it be to me according to your word." And the messenger departed from her.

39 Then Mariam arose in those days, going into the hill country with haste, to a town of Judah. 40 And she entered into the house of Zacharias and greeted Elizabeth. 41 And it happened as Elizabeth heard

Mariam's greeting, the baby in her womb suddenly moved. And Elizabeth was filled with the Holy Spirit, 42 and she cried out with a loud voice and said, "Blessed are you among women, and blessed is the fruit of your womb.

43 "And what is this, that the mother of my lord should come to me? 44 For, behold, as came the voice of your greeting into my ears, the baby in my womb suddenly moved in gladness. 45 And blessed is the one having believed that there will be fulfillment to the things spoken to her from the Lord."

46 And Mariam said, "My soul is praising the Lord, 47 and my spirit rejoices in God my savior, 48 for he had regard unto the humble state of his handmaiden. For, behold, from now all the generations will say I am blessed. 49 For the Mighty One has done great things to me, and holy is his name. 50 And his mercy is to generations and generations to those fearing him.

51 "He has shown strength with his arm, he has dispersed the arrogant in the thought of their heart. 52 He brought down rulers from thrones, and exalted the humble. 53 Those hungering he has filled with good, and those rich he has sent away empty. 54 He has helped Israel his servant, remembering mercy, 55 even as he spoke to our fathers, to Abraham and to his offspring, to the age."

56 Then Mariam remained with her about three months, and returned to her home.

57 Now, to Elizabeth the time was fulfilled for her to give birth. And she birthed a son. 58 And the neighbors and her relatives heard that the Lord was magnifying his mercy with her, and they were rejoicing with her.

59 And it happened on the eighth day they came to circumcise the child. And they named it after the name of his father, Zacharias. 60 And responding his mother said, "No, but he will be named 'John.'" 61 And they said to her, "No one is among your relatives who is called by this name." 62 Then they were looking to his father, what he might desire him to be called. 63 And, having asked for a writing tablet he wrote, saying, "John is his name." And they all marveled.

64 Now immediately his mouth was opened, and his tongue, and he was speaking, blessing God. 65 And fear came upon all. Those living near and in all the hill country of Judea, all talked of these things, these words. 66 And those having heard stored all in their heart, saying, "What then will this child be?" For the hand of the Lord was with him.

67 And Zacharias, his father, was filled with the Holy Spirit, and prophesied, saying, 68 "Worthy of praise the Lord God of Israel, because he has regarded and made deliverance for his people, 69 and has raised a horn of deliverance for us, in the house of David his servant, 70 even as he spoke by the mouth of his holy

prophets of old, 71 deliverance from our enemies, and from the hand of all those hating us.

72 "To cause mercy toward our fathers and to remember his holy covenant, 73 the oath that he swore to Abraham our father to give us, 74 so that without fear, having been rescued from the hand of our enemies, to serve him 75 in holiness and righteousness, before him all the times of our life.

76 "And you now, child, will be called "Prophet of Most High." For you will go before the Lord, to prepare his ways, 77 to give knowledge of deliverance to his people, in remission of their sins, 78 through the affectionate compassions of our God, in which will visit us sunrise from on high, 79 to shine upon those in darkness and sitting in the shadow of death, to direct our feet into the way of peace."

80 And the child continued to grow and became strong in spirit. And he was in the desolate places until the day of his appearance to Israel.

LUKE TWO

1 Now it happened in those times, a decree went out from Caesar Augustus to register all the world in a census. 2 And this earlier enrollment took place when Quirinius was Procurator[d] in Syria. 3 And all were going to be registered, each to their city.

4 Then also Joseph went up from Galilee, out of the town of Nazareth, to Judea, to the city of David, which is called Bethlehem, because he was of the house and family of David, 5 to register, with Mariam, the one being betrothed to him, she being with child. 6 Then it happened in their being there, the days of her giving birth were fulfilled. 7 And she birthed her son, the firstborn, and swaddled him, and laid him in a barn, because there was not a place for them in the lodging.[e]

8 And shepherds were in the same region, living in the fields and keeping watch by night over their flock. 9 And a messenger of the Lord stood by them, and the glory of the Lord shone around them, and they greatly feared. 10 And the messenger said to them, "Do not fear. For behold, I proclaim to you good news, great joy, which will be to all the people. 11 For has been born to you today a savior who is Christ Lord,[f] in David's city. 12 And this to you the sign: you will find a baby, swaddled, and lying in a barn." 13 And at once there came with the messenger a multitude of the heavenly host, praising God and saying, 14 "Glory in the highest to God, and on earth peace among men of good will."

15 And it happened, as the messengers went away from them into the heaven, the shepherds kept saying to one another, "Let us pass through the surrounding area, indeed as far as Bethlehem, and let us see this word that has come, which the Lord declared to us."

16 And they went quickly and

found both Mariam and Joseph, and the baby lying in the barn. 17 Then seeing, they proclaimed concerning the saying that was told them concerning this child. 18 And all those hearing marveled concerning the things spoken to them by the shepherds.

19 But Mariam was carefully keeping these matters, considering in her heart.

20 And the shepherds returned, giving glory and praising God for all which they had heard and seen, as had been said to them.

21 And when eight days were fulfilled to circumcise him, then he was called his name, Jesus, which had been called by the messenger before he was conceived in the womb.

22 And when the days of their purification were fulfilled according to the Law of Moses, they brought him to Jerusalem, to present him to the Lord, 23 as it is written in the Law of the Lord: every male opening a womb shall be called holy to the Lord, 24 and offer a sacrifice, according to that declared in the Law of the Lord, a pair of doves or two young pigeons.

25 And behold, there was a man in Jerusalem whose name was Simeon. And this man was righteous and devout, waiting for the Consolation of Israel, and the Holy Spirit was upon him. 26 And it was divinely revealed to him by the Holy Spirit not to see death before he might see the Lord's Christ. 27 And he came, by the Spirit, into the temple, and when the parents were bringing in the child Jesus, they to do for him according to that custom of the Law.

28 Then Simeon received him into his arms, and blessed God, and said, 29 "Now you are letting your servant depart, Lord, according to your word, in peace. 30 For my eyes have seen your deliverance, 31 which you prepared before the face of all the peoples, 32 a light for revelation to the gentiles and glory of your people Israel."

33 And his father and mother were marveling at the things having been spoken concerning him. 34 And Simeon blessed them, and said to Mariam his mother, "Consider this, he is appointed for the falling and rising of many in Israel, and for a sign spoken against, 35 and of you also a sword will go through your soul, so that the thoughts of many hearts may be revealed."

36 And there was Anna, a prophetess, daughter of Phanuel of the tribe of Asher. She was much advanced in years, having lived with a husband seven years from her marriage, 37 and she a widow, of about eighty-four years, who did not leave the temple, with fastings and prayers serving night and day. 38 And she at that hour, standing nearby, praising God, and was speaking concerning him to all those waiting for the deliverance of Israel.

39 And when they had

completed all according to the Law of the Lord, they returned to Galilee, to their town Nazareth. 40 Now the child continued to grow and become strong, filled with wisdom. And the grace of God was upon him.

41 And his parents went every year to Jerusalem at the feast of the Passover. 42 And when he was twelve years, they having gone according to the custom of the Feast, 43 and the days being completed, in their returning the boy Jesus remained in Jerusalem. And his parents did not know. 44 Now, having assumed him to be in their company of travelers, they went a day's journey, and began seeking him among their relatives and acquaintances.

45 And not finding him they returned to Jerusalem, seeking him. 46 And it happened after three days they found him in the temple, sitting among the teachers, both hearing them and questioning them. 47 Now all those hearing him were amazed at his understanding and answers. 48 And seeing him, they were astonished, and his mother said to him, "Child, why have you done thus to us? Look, your father and I were seeking you in distress."

49 And he said to them, "For what reason were you seeking me? Did you not know that it is needful for me to be in the things of my Father?" 50 And they did not understand the word that he spoke to them. 51 And he went with them, and came to Nazareth, and he obeyed them. And his mother carefully kept all these matters in her heart. 52 And Jesus progressed in wisdom and maturity,[9] and in favor with God and men.

LUKE THREE

1 Now in the fifteenth year of the reign of Tiberius Caesar, Pontius Pilate being Procurator of Judea, and Herod tetrarch of Galilee, and Philip his brother being tetrarch of Ituraea and the region Trachonitis, and Lysanias tetrarch of Abilene, 2 during the high priesthood of Annas and Caiaphas, the word of God came upon John, son of Zacharias, in the wilderness.

3 And he went into all the region surrounding the Jordan, announcing publicly an immersion of repentance for forgiveness of sins, 4 as written in the book of the words of Isaiah the prophet: the voice exclaiming in the wilderness, "Make ready the way of the Lord, make straight his ways. 5 Every valley will be filled, and every mountain and hill will be made low. And the crooked will become into straight, and the rough into smooth ways. 6 And all flesh will see the deliverance of God."

7 Therefore, he was saying to the crowds coming out to be immersed by him, "Offspring of vipers. Who taught you to flee from the impending wrath? 8 Produce therefore fruits worthy of repentance. And do not begin to say within yourselves, 'We have father Abraham.' For I say to you that God is able from these stones to raise up children to Abraham. 9

And now already the ax is ready to be applied to the root of the trees. Therefore, every tree not producing good fruit is cut down and thrown into fire."

10 And the crowds were asking him, saying, "What then shall we do?" 11 Now, answering he was saying to them, "The one having two tunics, share with the one having none; and the one having food, let him do the same." 12 Then came also tax collectors to be immersed, and they said to him, "Teacher, what shall we do?" 13 Now he said to them, "Collect no more than that appointed to you." 14 Then also those who were soldiers were asking, saying, "What shall we also do?" And he said to them, "Do not extort anyone, nor falsely accuse, and be satisfied with your wages."

15 Then all the people are expecting and wondering in their hearts concerning John, whether or not he might be the Christ. 16 John responded, saying to all, "I truly immerse you in water, but one mightier than I comes, of whom I am not worthy to untie the string of his sandals. He will immerse you in Holy Spirit, and in fire, 17 of whom the winnowing shovel is in his hand to cleanse his threshing floor and to gather the wheat into his granary. But the chaff he will burn in unquenchable fire." 18 Many other things truly exhorting, he proclaimed the good news to the people.

19 Now Herod the tetrarch, being reproved by him concerning Herodias, his brother Philip's wife, and concerning all the evils Herod had done, 20 and added to all this, he also confined John in prison.

21 Now it happened when having immersed all the people, and Jesus having been immersed, and having prayed, the heaven was opened, 22 and the Holy Spirit descended in bodily form as a dove upon him. And a voice came out of heaven: "You are my son, the beloved. With you I am well pleased."

23 And Jesus himself was beginning about thirty years, being son, as was supposed,[h] of Joseph of Heli, 24 of Matthat, of Levi, of Melchi, of Jannai, of Joseph, 25 of Mattathias, of Amos, of Nahum, of Hesli, of Naggai, 26 of Maath, of Mattathias, of Semein, of Josech, of Joda, 27 of Joanan, of Rhesa, of Zorobabel, of Salathiel, of Nen, 28 of Melchi, of Addi, of Kosam, of Elmadam, of Er, 29 of Joshua, of Eliezer, of Jorim, of Matthat, of Levi, 30 of Simeon, of Judah, of Joseph, of Jonam, of Eliakim, 31 of Melea, of Menna, of Mattatha, of Nathan, of David, 32 of Jesse, of Obed, of Boaz, of Sala, of Naasson, 33 of Aminadab, of Admin, of Arni, of Hezron, of Perez, of Judah, of Jacob, of Isaac, of Abraham, of Terah, of Nahor, 35 of Serouch, of Rhagau, of Peleg, of Eber, of Sala, 36 of Kainan, of Arphaxad, of Shem, of Noah, of Lamech, 37 of Methuselah, of Enoch, of Jared, of Mahalalel, of Kainam, 38 of Enos, of Seth, of Adam, of God.

LUKE FOUR

1 Then Jesus, Holy Spirit filled, returned from the Jordan and was led by the Spirit into the wilderness, 2 forty days being tempted by the devil. And he did not eat in those days. And they having ended he was hungry.

3 Then the devil said to him, "If you are 'son of God,' speak to this stone that it may become bread." 4 And Jesus answered him, "It has been written: 'Not on bread alone shall the man live.'"

5 And taking him up, the devil showed him all the kingdoms of the world in a moment in time. 6 And the devil said to him, "To you I will give all this authority and its glory, because it has been delivered to me, and to whomever I may desire I give it. 7 If, therefore, you will worship before me all will be yours." 8 And answering, Jesus said to him, "It has been written: 'You shall worship the Lord your God, and him only will you serve.'"

9 Then the devil brought him to Jerusalem, and set upon the apex of the temple, and said to him, "If 'son of God' you are, throw yourself down from here. 10 For it has been written, 'To his messengers he will command concerning you, to guard you, 11 and on their hands they will carry you, lest at any time you might strike your foot against a stone.'" 12 And answering, Jesus said to him, "It has been said, 'Never shall you put to the test the Lord your God.'"

13 And ending every temptation, the devil withdrew from him, until an opportune season. 14 Then Jesus returned in the power of the Spirit to Galilee. And a fame went out into all the region concerning him. 15 And he was teaching in their synagogues, being glorified by all.

16 And Jesus came to Nazareth, where he had grown up. And he entered according to his custom, on the day of the Sabbaths, into the synagogue, and stood up to read. 17 And the scroll of the prophet Isaiah was given to him, and having unrolled the scroll, he found the place where it was written: 18 "The Spirit of the Lord is upon me, because of which he has anointed me to proclaim good news to the poor. He has sent me to proclaim deliverance to captives, and to blind recovery of sight, to send the oppressed into deliverance, 19 to proclaim the year of the Lord's favor."

20 And rolling up the scroll, having delivered it to the attendant, he sat down, and all the eyes in the synagogue were fixed on him. 21 Then he began to say to them, "Today this scripture is fulfilled in your hearing." 22 And all were bearing witness to him and marveling at the words of grace that are coming out of his mouth. And they were saying, "Is this not son of Joseph?" 23 And he said to them, "Assuredly you will say to me this proverb, 'Physician heal yourself.' What we have heard was done in Capernaum, do also here in your hometown."

24 Then he said, "Truly I say to you, that no prophet is acceptable in his hometown. 25 Now in truth I say to you, many widows there were in the times of Elijah in Israel. The heaven was closed for three years and six months, when there was a great famine upon all the land. 26 And to none of them was Elijah sent, except to Zarephath of Sidon, to a widow woman. 27 And many lepers were in Israel in the time of Elisha the prophet, and none of them was cleansed, except Naaman the Syrian."

28 And all in the synagogue were filled with anger, hearing these things. 29 And getting up, they drove him out of the city, and led him to the edge of a precipice of the hill upon which their town had been built, in order to throw him over. 30 But he, going through the midst of them, walked away.

31 And he went down to Capernaum, a city of Galilee. And he was teaching them on the Sabbaths; 32 and they were astonished at his teaching, because his word was with authority.

33 And in the synagogue was a man who had a spirit of an unclean demon. And he cried out in a loud voice, 34 "Ah! What do we have to do with you, Jesus of Nazareth? Are you come to destroy us? I know who you are, the holy one of God." 35 And Jesus rebuked him, saying, "Be silent," and "Come out of him." And the demon having thrown him into the middle, it came out from him, not hurting him.

36 And all were astonished, and were speaking to one another, saying, "What word is this? Because in authority and power he commands the unclean spirits and they come out?" 37 And the fame spread concerning him into every place of the surrounding region.

38 Then leaving the synagogue, he entered into Simon's house. Now Simon's mother-in-law was afflicted with a great fever, and they appealed to him on her behalf. 39 And standing over her he rebuked the fever, and it left her. Then immediately she rose and served them.

40 Now, at the setting of the sun, all—as many as had any sick with various diseases—brought them to him, and on each one of them, having laid hands, he would heal them. 41 Now also demons were leaving many, crying out and saying, "You are the son of God." Now rebuking them, he did not allow them to speak, because they knew him to be the Christ.

42 Then day arriving, he having gone out, went into a lonely place; and the crowds were seeking him; and they came to him and kept detaining him, so he could not leave them. 43 But he said to them, "Also I must go to the other towns to proclaim the good news of the Kingdom of God; because for this I was sent." 44 And he was preaching in the synagogues of Judea.

LUKE FIVE

1 Now it happened, as the crowd pressed on him to hear the Word of God, and he was standing by the Lake of Gennesaret, 2 he saw two boats sitting by the lake. But their fishermen had left them to wash the nets.

3 Then entering into one of the boats, which was Simon's, he asked him to put out from the land a little. Then sitting down, from the boat he was teaching the crowds. 4 Then, when he stopped speaking, he said to Simon, "Put out into the deep and let down your nets for a catch of fish." 5 And responding, Simon said, "Master, we are worn with labor, having caught nothing through the whole night. But at your word I will let down the nets."

6 And having done this, they enclosed a great multitude of fishes; now their nets were breaking. 7 And they gestured to their partners in the other boat to come to help them. And they came and filled both the boats, so that they were sinking. 8 Then Simon seeing this, fell at the knees of Jesus, saying, "Go away from me, for I am a sinful man, master."

9 For astonishment had seized him, and all those with him, at the catch of the fish they had taken. 10 Now in the same way also Jacob and John, sons of Zebedee, who were partners with Simon. And Jesus said to Simon, "Do not fear. From now you will be catching men." 11 And bringing the boats to the land, leaving all, they followed him.

12 And it happened when he was in one of the cities, that look, a man fully covered with leprosy, when seeing Jesus, falling upon his face, begged him, saying, "Sir, if you might be willing you are able to cleanse me." 13 And stretching out the hand he touched him, saying, "I am willing. Be cleansed." And immediately the leprosy departed from him. 14 And he ordered him to tell no one but, "Go show yourself to the priest, and offer for your cleansing as Moses commanded for a testimony to them."

15 Then the word concerning him traveled, and great crowds kept on coming to hear and be healed from their sicknesses. 16 Now, he himself was withdrawing into the wilderness and praying.

17 And it happened on one of the times when he was teaching, and there were Pharisees and teachers of the Law sitting there, who had come out of every village of Galilee, and of Judea, and of Jerusalem. And the power of the Lord was with him to heal. 18 And look, men carrying upon a sick bed a man who was enfeebled, and they sought to bring him in and place him before Jesus. 19 And not finding a way to bring him in, on account of the crowd, they went up on the housetop. They let him down, on the sick bed, through the roof tiles, into the middle before Jesus.

20 And Jesus, seeing their faith, he said, "Man, your sins are forgiven you." 21 And the scribes and the Pharisees began to reason,

saying, "Who is this who speaks slandering lies? Who is able to forgive sins except God only?"

22 Now Jesus, knowing their reasonings, responding, said to them, "Why reason you in your hearts? 23 Which is easier? To say, 'Your sins are forgiven you,' or to say, 'Get up and walk?' 24 But in order that you may know that the Son of Man has authority on the earth to forgive sins," he said to the one who had been enfeebled, "To you I say, get up, take up your sick bed, go to your house." 25 And immediately he stood up before them, took up that on which he had been lying, leaving to his house, glorifying God. 26 And amazement seized all, and they were glorifying God, and were filed with fear, saying, "We have seen miraculous things today."

27 Now after these things, he went out and he saw a tax collector named Levi sitting at the toll booth. And he said to him, "Follow me." 28 And leaving all, rising, he began to follow him.

29 And Levi made a great banquet for him in his house, and there was a great crowd of tax collectors and others reclining *to eat* with them. 30 And the pharisees and the scribes, they were complaining to his disciples, saying, "For what reason do you eat and drink with the tax collectors and sinners?" 31 And answering Jesus said to them, "Those who are well have no need for a physician, but those being sick. 32 I have not come to call righteous but sinners to repentance."

33 And they said to him, "The disciples of John fast often, and make prayers; in the same manner those of the Pharisees. But those of you eat and drink." 34 Then Jesus said to them, "You cannot make the sons of the bridechamber fast in the time the bridegroom is with them, can you?" 35 But times will come, and when the bridegroom may be taken away from them, then they will fast in those times.

36 Now he was speaking a parable to them. "No one having torn a piece of new garment, puts it on an old garment, but if otherwise, also the new he will tear and the old will not match the piece from the new. 37 And no one puts new wine into old wineskins, but if otherwise, the new wine will burst the wineskins, and it will be spilled out, and the wineskins will be ruined. 38 But new wine must be put into fresh wineskins. 39 And no one having drunk old desires new, for he says, 'The old is better.'"

LUKE SIX

1 Then it happened on a Sabbath, the second after the first,[i] he is passing through grainfields, and his disciples were plucking and eating the heads of grain, rubbing them in their hands.

2 But some of the Pharisees said, "Why do you that not lawful on the Sabbaths?" 3 And answering to them Jesus said, "Have you not read this, that which David did,

when he himself was hungry, and those who were with him? 4 How he entered into the house of God, and taking the bread of the presentation, ate, and gave to those with him, which it is not lawful to eat, except only the priests?" 5 And he said to them, "The Son of Man is Lord of the Sabbath."

6 Then it happened on another Sabbath, he went into the synagogue and taught. And there was a man there, and his hand, the right, was withered. 7 Now, the scribes and the Pharisees were closely watching Jesus, whether on the Sabbath he will heal, that they might accuse him.

8 Now, he knew their thoughts. Then he said to the man with the withered hand, "Get up and stand in the middle." And getting up, he stood. 9 Then said Jesus to them, "I ask you, whether it is lawful on the Sabbath to do good or to do evil? To save life or to destroy?" 10 And looking around on all of them, he said to him, "Stretch out your hand." And he did and his hand was restored. 11 Then they were filled with rage, and discussed with one another what they might do to Jesus.

12 Then it happened in those times he went out to the mountain to pray; and he was spending the night in prayer to God. 13 Now when it became day, he called his disciples, and chose out from them twelve, whom he also named "apostles": 14 Simon, whom he also named Peter, and Andrew his brother; and Jacob and John; and Philip and Bartholomew; 15 and Matthew and Thomas; and Jacob of Alphaeus; and Simon the one called Zealot; 16 and Judas of Jacob; and Judas Iscariot who became the betrayer.

17 And descending with them, he stood on a level place, and a large crowd of his disciples, and a great multitude of other people from all Judea, and Jerusalem, and the sea coast of Tyre and Sidon, 18 who came to hear him and be healed of their diseases. And those troubled with unclean spirits were healed. 19 And all the multitude were seeking to touch him, because power was going out from him and healing all.

20 And he, lifting up his eyes upon his disciples, was saying, "Blessed the poor, for yours is the kingdom of God. 21 Blessed those hungering now, for you will be filled. Blessed those lamenting now, for you will laugh. 22 Blessed are you when men may hate you, and when they may exclude you, and may insult you, and may cast out your name as evil, on account of the Son of Man. 23 Rejoice in that day, and leap for joy, for behold, your reward is great in heaven. For according to these things their fathers did the same to the prophets.

24 "But yet, woe to you who are rich, because you are receiving your comfort. 25 Woe to you being filled now, for you will hunger. 26 Woe to those laughing now, for you will mourn and will lament.

Woe to you when all men speak well of you, for according to these things their fathers did the same to the prophets.

27 "But to you I say, to those listening: love your enemies, do good to those hating you, 28 bless those cursing you, pray for those insulting you. 29 To the one striking you on the cheek, offer the other also. And from the one taking away your outer garment, also do not withhold the tunic. 30 To all asking you, give, and from the one taking away what is yours, do not ask its return.

31 "And as you desire that men may do to you, do to them the same. 32 And if you love those loving you, what benefit is it to you? For even sinners love those loving them. 33 For if you do good to those doing good to you, what benefit is it to you? For even sinners do the same. 34 And if you lend from whom you expect to receive in return, what benefit is that to you? Even sinners lend to sinners, that they may receive the same amount.

35 "But rather, love your enemies, and do good, and lend, expecting nothing in return; and your reward will be great, and you will be sons of the Most High, because he is kind to the ungrateful and evil. 36 You be merciful, as also your Father is merciful. 37 And do not judge, that no, you should not be judged. And do not condemn, that no, you should not be condemned. Forgive and you will be forgiven. 38 Give, and it will be given to you. They will give into your lap good measure, pressed down, shaken together, running over; for with what measure you measure it will be measured in turn to you."

39 Then he also spoke a parable to them. "Is blind able to lead blind? Will not both fall into a pit? 40 A disciple is not above the teacher. But every one prepared will be like his teacher.

41 "Why now look you at the splinter that is in your brother's eye, and not notice the beam that is in your own eye? 42 How are you able to say to your brother, 'Brother allow I might take out the splinter that is in your eye,' yourself the beam in your eye not seeing? Hypocrite, cast out first the beam from your eye, and then you will see clearly to cast out the splinter in the eye of your brother.

43 "For there is no good tree producing bad fruit; nor again a bad tree producing good fruit. 44 For each tree is known by its own fruit. For not from thorns do they gather figs, nor from a thornbush do they gather grapes. 45 The good man out of the good treasure of his heart brings forth the good; and the evil out of the evil brings forth the evil. For out of the abundance of the heart speaks his mouth.

46 "Now why do you call me 'Lord, Lord,' and not do what I say? 47 Everyone who is coming to me, and hearing my words, and doing them, I will show you whom he is like. 48 He is like a man building a house, who dug and deepened and

laid a foundation on the rock. Then a flood having come the river burst upon that house, and was not able to shake it, because it had been well built. 49 But the one having heard, and not having done, is like to a man having built a house on the ground without a foundation, on which the river burst upon, and immediately it fell, and great was the ruin of the house."

LUKE SEVEN

1 Because he had finished all his words in the hearing of the people, he entered into Capernaum. 2 Now, a certain servant of a centurion, being ill, was about to die, who was highly valued by him. 3 Then hearing about Jesus, he sent elders of the Jews to him, entreating him that coming he might heal his servant. 4 And coming to Jesus, they were entreating him earnestly, saying that, "He is worthy to whom you will give this. 5 For he loves our nation, and he built the synagogue for us."

6 Then Jesus was going with them. Now already, he not being a great distance from the house, the centurion sent friends, saying to him, "Sir, do not trouble yourself, for I am not worthy that you might come under my roof. 7 Therefore I do not reckon myself worthy for you to come. Just say a word and my servant will be healed. 8 For I also am a man under appointed authority, having under me soldiers. And I say to this one, 'Go,' and he goes; and to another, 'Come,' and he comes; and to my servant, 'Do this,' and he does it." 9 Then hearing these things, Jesus was amazed at him. And turning to the crowd following, he said, "I say to you, not even in Israel did I find such great faith." 10 And upon returning to the house, those who were sent found the servant in good health.

11 And it happened on the next day, he went into a town called Nain; and the disciples went with him, and a great crowd. 12 Then, as he came near to the gate of the town, now look, one having died was being carried out, the only begotten son of his mother; and she was a widow. And a large crowd of the town was with her.

13 And seeing her, the Lord had compassion on her, and said to her, "Do not lament." 14 And coming, he touched the bier. Those bearing it stopped. And he said, "Young man, to you I say, 'Get up.'" 15 And the dead man sat up and began to speak; and he gave him to his mother.

16 Then fear seized all, and they began glorifying God, saying, "A great prophet has risen among us and God has visited his people." 17 And this word concerning him went out in all Judea, and in all the surrounding region.

18 And John's disciples told him about all these things. 19 And calling a certain two of his disciples, John sent to the Lord this saying, "Are you the Coming One, or are we to look for another?"

20 Then coming to him the men said, "John the Immerser has

sent us to you, saying, 'Are you the Coming One, or are we to look for another?'" 21 At that same hour he healed many of diseases, and afflictions, and evil spirits, and to many blind he bestowed sight.

22 And responding he said to them, "Go, tell John what you have seen and heard: blind receive sight, lame walk, lepers cleansed, and deaf hear, dead are raised, poor evangelized. 23 And blessed is he who, if he will not be offended in me."

24 Then the messengers of John having left, he began to speak to the crowds concerning John. "What did you come out into the wilderness to see?" A reed shaken by the wind? 25 But what did you come out to see? A man robed in fine clothing? Behold, those in splendid clothing and living in self-indulgence are in the palaces. 26 But what did you go out to see? A prophet? Yes, I say to you, and more excellent than a prophet.

27 "This is he concerning whom it was written, 'Look, I send my messenger before your presence, who will prepare your way before you.' 28 I say to you, no one is greater among those born of women than John. But the littlest one in the kingdom of God is greater than he." 29 And all the people hearing, even the tax collectors, proclaimed God righteous, having been immersed with John's immersion. 30 But the Pharisees, namely the experts in the Law,ʲ rejected the purpose of God for themselves, not having been immersed by him.

31 "To what, therefore, will I compare the men of this generation? And to what are they similar? 32 They are similar to little children sitting in the marketplace, and calling to each other, saying, 'We played the flute and you did not dance; we mourned and you did not lament.'

33 John the Immerser came neither eating bread not drinking wine, and you say, 'He has a demon.' 34 The Son of Man came eating and drinking, and you say, 'Look, a man, a glutton and a drunkard, a friend of tax collectors and of sinners.' 35 Yet wisdom is justified by all her children."

36 Now, one of the Pharisees asked that he should eat with him. And entering into the Pharisee's house, he reclined *to eat.* 37 And look, a woman who was a sinner in the city. And she, knowing that he had reclined *to eat* in the house of the Pharisee, took an alabaster flask of fragrant oil, 38 and standing behind him at his feet crying, with her tears she began to wet his feet, and with the hair of her head she wiped them, and was kissing his feet, and anointing them with the fragrant oil.

39 Now the Pharisee, the one having invited him, spoke within himself, saying, "If this man were a prophet, he would have known who and what the woman who touches him, for she is a sinner."

40 And Jesus responded to him. "Simon, I have something to

say to you." And he said, "Teacher, say it." 41 "There were two debtors to a certain creditor. The one owed five hundred denarii, and the other fifty. 42 They having nothing with which to pay, he forgave both. Therefore which of them will love him more?" 43 Answering, Simon said, "I suppose that one whom he forgave the most." And he said to him, "You have rightly judged."

44 And having turned to the woman, he said to Simon, "Do you see this woman? I entered into your house, you gave no water for my feet. But she with her tears wet my feet, and with her hair wiped them. 45 You did not give me a kiss. But she has not stopped kissing my feet from when I came in. 46 You did not anoint my head with oil. But she anointed my feet with fragrant oil. 47 Therefore I say to you, her many sins have been forgiven, because she loved much. But to whom little is forgiven, little he loves."

48 And he said to her, "Your sins have been forgiven." 49 And those reclining began to say within themselves, "Who is this who even forgives sins?" 50 Then he said to the woman, "Your faith has saved you. Go into peace."

LUKE EIGHT

1 Afterward this soon took place, that he was passing through city and village preaching and bringing good news of the kingdom of God. And the Twelve *were* with him, 2 and certain women who had been cured from evil spirits and sickness: Mary who is called Magdalene, from whom seven demons had gone out; 3 and Joanna wife of Chuza, a steward of Herod; and Susanna, and many others, who were ministering to them out of their own means.

4 Now a great crowd was coming together, and some from each town coming to him. He spoke through a parable: 5 "One sowing went out to sow his seed. And in his sowing, indeed some fell along the road, and it was trampled, and the birds of the air ate it. 6 And other fell upon the rock, and springing up it dried up on account of not having moisture. 7 And other fell in the middle of thorns, and springing up, the thorns choked it. 8 And other fell upon the good earth, and springing up produced fruit, a hundredfold."

9 Then his disciples asked him, "What does this parable mean?" 10 Then he said, "To you has been given to know the mysteries of the kingdom of God. But to the others in parables, so that seeing, they may not see, and hearing they may not understand.

11 "Now this is the parable. The seed is the word of God. 12 Now those along the road are those hearing, then comes the devil and takes away the word from their heart, lest having believed they should be saved. 13 Now those on the rock, who when they hear, receive the word with joy, and these do not have a root, who for a time believe, and in a time of testing fall away. 14 Then

that fallen into the thorns, these are those having heard, and as they go on their way under the cares, and riches, and pleasures of life, are choked and do not mature. 15 Now that in the good earth, these are those in a heart good and profitable, having heard the word, keep it, and bring forth fruit by perseverance.

16 "Now none lighting a lamp covers it with a vessel, or puts it under a bed, but puts it on a lampstand, so those entering may see the light. 17 For nothing is hidden which will not become plain, nor nothing secret which shall not be known and come to light. 18 Take heed, therefore, how you hear. For whoever may have will be given to him, and whoever may not have, even what he thinks to have will be taken away from him."

19 Then came to him his mother and brothers; and they were not able to come near to him, because of the crowd. 20 And he was told this: "your mother and your brothers are standing outside wanting to see you." 21 But then responding, he said to them, "My mother and my brothers are those who are hearing and doing the word of God."

22 Then it happened, on one of the days, he also got into a boat with his disciples. And he said to them, "Let us pass over to the other side of the lake." And they set sail.

23 Then as they sailed, he fell into a deep sleep. And a wind storm came down to the lake, and the boat was filling with water. 24 Then coming to him, they awoke him saying, "Master, master, we are perishing!" Then rising, he rebuked the wind and the raging of the water, and they stopped, and there was calm.

25 Then he said to them, "Where is your faith?" Then having been afraid, they were struck with astonishment, saying, "Who then is this, that even the winds he commands, and the water, and they obey him?"

26 And they sailed to the region of the Gerasenes, which is opposite Galilee. 27 Then, going out upon the land, he met a certain man out of the city, having demons, and a long time was not wearing clothing, and did not live in a house, but in the tombs.

28 Then seeing Jesus, and crying out, he fell down before him, and in a loud voice said, "What do you have to do with me, Jesus the son of God the Most High? I beg of you, you might not torment me." 29 For he was commanding the unclean spirit to come out from the man. For many times it had violently seized him, and he was bound, kept with chains and shackles. And breaking the chains, he was driven by the demon into the deserts.

30 Now, Jesus asked him, "What is your name?" And he said, "Legion," because many demons were entered into him. 31 And they were begging him, that he would not command them to go away

into the abyss. 32 Now, there was a herd of many pigs feeding on the hill, and they begged him that he would allow them to enter into them; and he allowed them. 33 Then the demons left from the man, they entered into the pigs, and the herd rushed down the steep bank into the lake and was drowned.

34 Then those feeding them, having seen what happened, they ran away and told *it* to the city and to the country. 35 Then they went out to see what had happened, and they came to Jesus and found the man sitting, from whom the demons had gone out, clothed and of sound mind, at the feet of Jesus. And they were afraid. 36 Then those having seen told them how the one inhabited by demons was healed. 37 And all the multitudes of the region of the Gerasenes asked him to leave them, because they were taken with great fear. Now he, entering into the boat, returned.

38 But the man from whom had gone the demons was begging to be taken with him. But he sent him away, saying, 39 "Return to your house, and tell all God has done for you." And he left, proclaiming through all the city all that Jesus had done for him.

40 Then when Jesus returned, the crowd received him, for all were looking for him. 41 And look, a man came whose name was Jairus, and he was a ruler of the synagogue. And falling at Jesus' feet, he began begging him to come to his house, 42 because he had an only daughter, about twelve years old, and she was dying. Then, as he went, the crowds were pressing around him.

43 And a woman with a flowing of blood for twelve years, who having spent all her living on physicians, neither was able to be healed by none, 44 coming behind touched the fringe[k] of his outer garment, and immediately the flowing of her blood stopped. 45 And Jesus said, "Who touched me?" But all were denying. Peter said, "Master, the crowd surrounds you and presses.'" 46 But Jesus said, "Someone touched me, for I know power has gone out from me." 47 Then the woman, knowing she was not hidden, she came trembling, and falling down before him, she declared before all the people why she had touched him, and how she was immediately healed. 48 Then he said to her, "Daughter, your faith has healed you. Go in peace."

49 As he was still speaking, one comes from the synagogue ruler's *house*, saying, "Your daughter has died. No longer trouble the teacher." 50 But hearing, Jesus responded, "Fear not, only believe and she will be made whole."

51 Then entering into the house, he did not allow anyone to go in with him, except Peter, and John, and Jacob, and the father of the child, and the mother. 52 Now all were lamenting and wailing for her. But he said, "Do not lament,

for she is not dead but sleeps." 53 And they were laughing at him, they knowing that she was dead. 54 Now he, taking hold of her hand, called out, saying, "Child, get up." 55 And her spirit returned, and she immediately stood. And he directed to her be given to eat. 56 And her parents were amazed; and he told them not to tell what had happened.

LUKE NINE

1 Then, calling together the Twelve, he gave them power and authority over all the demons, and to heal diseases. 2 And he sent them to proclaim the kingdom of God and to heal the sick. 3 And he said to them, "Take nothing for the journey, neither staff, nor bag, nor bread, nor money, nor to have two tunics each. 4 And into what house you may enter, there remain, and from there leave. 5 And as many as might not receive you, leaving from that city, shake off the dust from your feet as a testimony against them." 6 Then going out they passed through the villages, preaching the good news and healing everywhere.

7 Now Herod the Tetrarch heard of all the things being done, and was perplexed, because some were saying, "John has been raised out from among the dead." 8 Also by some that Elijah had appeared. Also by others that a prophet of old had appeared. 9 Then said Herod, "John I beheaded, but who is this about whom I hear such things?" And he was seeking to see him.

10 Upon returning, the apostles related to him all they had done. And taking them, he withdrew by himself into a town called Bethsaida-Julius.ᵐ 11 Now the crowds, knowing, followed him. And receiving them, he spoke to them concerning the kingdom of God; and those having need of healing he was healing. 12 Now the day began to decline, then the Twelve came to him: "Dismiss the crowd, that going into the surrounding villages and countryside they might find lodging and food. Because here we are in a desolate place."

13 Then he said to them, "You give them something to eat." But they said, "There are not to us more than five bread and two fish, except going we should buy food for all this people." 14 For there were about five thousand men.

Then he said to his disciples, "Make them recline *to eat*, in about groups of fifty." 15 And so they did, and made all recline *to eat*. 16 Then, receiving the bread and two fish, looking up to the heaven, he blessed and broke them, and he kept giving to the disciples to set before the crowd. 17 And they all ate and were satisfied. And they gathered to themselves fragments which remained, twelve handbaskets.

18 Now it happened as he was praying alone, the disciples were with him, and he asked them, saying, "Whom do the crowds say me to be?" 19 Now answering they said, "John the Immerser; also others Elijah; now others that a

prophet of old had appeared." 20 Then he said to them, "But you, whom do you say me to be?" Then Peter, answering, said, "The Christ of God."

21 Then having strongly admonished them, he commanded them to tell this to no one, 22 saying, "It is necessary the Son of Man to suffer many things, and to be rejected by the elders and chief priests and scribes, and to be killed, and on the third day to be raised."

23 Then he was saying to all, "If anyone desires to come after me, let them[n] deny themselves, and let them take up their cross every day, and let them follow me. 24 For whoever might desire to save their life, will lose it. But whoever might desire to lose their life because of me, they will save it. 25 For what is a person profited in having gained the whole world, but having ruined or lost themselves? 26 For whoever may be ashamed of me and my words, him the Son of Man will be ashamed of when he may come in the glory of himself, and of the Father, and of the holy messengers. 27 Now I say to you truthfully, there are some of those standing here who no, may not taste of death until they have seen the kingdom of God."

28 Now it happened after these sayings, about eight days, and taking Peter and John and Jacob, he went up on the mountain to pray. 29 And it happened in his praying, the appearance of his face changed, and his clothing white—sparkling. 30 And look, two men talking with him, who were Moses and Elijah. 31 They appearing in glory were speaking of his departure, which he was about to accomplish in Jerusalem.

32 But Peter and those with him were weighed down with sleep. Then, becoming fully awake, they saw his glory, and the two persons standing with him. 33 And then it happened their departing from him, Peter said to Jesus, "Master, it is good for us to be here. And let us make three booths: one for you, and one for Moses, and one for Elijah"; not understanding what he was saying. 34 Then, as he is saying these things, a cloud came and was overshadowing them; then they feared as they entered into the cloud. 35 And a voice came out of the cloud, saying, "This is my Son whom I have chosen; listen to him." 36 And as the voice came Jesus was found alone. And they were silent. And they told no one in those times anything of what they had seen.

37 Then it happened the next day, when they came down from the mountain, a great crowd met him. 38 And see, a man of the crowd cried out, saying, "Teacher, I implore you to look upon my son, for he is my only child. 39 And look, a spirit takes him, and suddenly he cries out, and it convulses him with foaming, and with difficulty it leaves from him, wounding him. 40 And I asked your disciples that they might cast it out, and they

were not able."

41 Now responding, Jesus said, "O unbelieving and perverted generation, how long will I be with you and bear with you? Bring your son here." 42 Then, as he was coming near him, the demon threw him down and into convulsions. Then Jesus rebuked the unclean spirit, and healed the boy, and gave him back to his father. 43 Then all were astonished at the majesty of God.

Then as all were wondering at all which he did, He said to his disciples, 44 "Let these words sink into your ears: for the Son of Man is about to be delivered into hands of men." 45 But they did not understand this saying, and it was hidden from them, that they should not understand it. And they were afraid to ask him concerning this saying.

46 Then an argument came up among them, this: who might be greatest of them. 47 But Jesus, knowing the reasoning of their heart, took up a child, set it by him, 48 and he said to them, "Whoever might receive this child in my name, receives me. And whoever shall receive me, receives the One having sent me. For the one being least among all of you, he shall be great."

49 But responding, John said, "Master, we saw someone in your name casting out demons, and we restrained him, because he does not follow with us." 50 Then Jesus said to him, "Do not restrain; for whoever is not against you is for you."

51 Then it happened in the days of his ascension to be fulfilled, that he firmly set his face to go to Jerusalem. 52 And he sent messengers before him. And having gone, they entered into a village of the Samaritans, so as to make ready for him. 53 And they did not receive him, because his face was going toward Jerusalem. 54 Now in seeing this, the disciples Jacob and John said, "Master, will you we should call fire down from heaven and consume them?"⁰ 55 But he turned and rebuked them. 56 And they went to another village.ᵖ

57 And they passing on the road, someone said to them, "I will follow you wherever if you may go." 58 And Jesus said to him, "The foxes have holes, and the birds of the air nests; but the Son of Man has not where he might lay his head."

59 Then he said to another, "Follow me." But he said, "Sir, allow me first to go and to bury my father." 60 Then he said to him, "Leave the dead to bury their own dead; but you, having gone, declare the kingdom of God."

61 Then another also said, "I will follow you, sir, but first let me bid farewell to those at my home." 62 Then Jesus said to him, "No one having laid the hand upon the plow, and looking on the things behind, is fit for the kingdom of God."

LUKE TEN

1 Now after these things, the Lord also appointed seventy-two[q] others and sent them in twos before his face into every city and place where he himself was about to go. 2 Then he said to them, "Truly the harvest is plentiful, but the workers few. Pray earnestly, therefore, to the Lord of the harvest, that he may send out workmen into his harvest.

3 "Go. See, I send you as lambs among wolves. 4 Do not carry money bag, or food sack, or sandals. And greet no one on the road.

5 "Now into whatever house you may enter, first say, 'Peace to this house.' 6 And if there is a son of peace, your peace will rest upon him. But if not so, to you it will return. 7 Now, remain in the same house eating and drinking the things they give. For worthy the workman of his wages. Do not go from house to house.

8 "And into whatever city you may enter, and they receive you, eat that set before you. 9 And heal in it the ill, and say to them, 'The kingdom of God has drawn near to you.' 10 Now into whatever city you may enter, and they do not receive you, having gone into its streets, say, 11 'Even the dust clinging to us out of your city, to our feet, we wipe off against you. Yet this know, the kingdom of God has drawn near.' 12 I say to you, that for Sodom in that day, it will be more tolerable than for that city.

13 "Woe to you, Chorazin! Woe to you, Bethsaida! For if the miracles having taking place in you had taken place in Tyre and Sidon, long ago they would have repented sitting in sackcloth and ashes. 14 But for Tyre and Sidon it will be more tolerable in the judgment than for you. 15 And you, Capernaum, you will not be lifted to heaven, you will go down to hades.

16 "The one hearing you hears me, and the one rejecting you rejects me. The one now rejecting me rejects the one having sent me."

17 Then the seventy-two returned with joy, saying, "Master, even the demons are subject to us through your name." 18 Then he said to them, "I was seeing Satan as lightening out of the heaven falling. 19 Behold, I give you the authority to trample upon serpents and scorpions, and upon all the power of the enemy, and nothing never no never will harm you. 20 Yet, do not rejoice in this, that the spirits are subjected to you; but rejoice that your names are written in the heavens."

21 In the same hour he rejoiced in the Holy Spirit and said, "I glorify you, Father, Lord of the heaven and of the earth, that you have hidden these things from wise and discerning persons, and have revealed them to the unlearned; yes, Father, because such was well-pleasing to you.

22 "All things have been delivered to me by my Father. And no one knows who is the Son, except the Father, and who is the

Father except the Son, and to whomever if the Son may intend to reveal."

23 And turning to the disciples in private, he said, "Blessed the eyes seeing what you see. 24 For I say to you that many prophets and kings desired to know what you see, and saw not; and to hear what you hear, and heard not."

25 And look, a certain one skilled in the Mosaic Law[r] stood up, putting him to the test, saying, "Teacher, what having done, will I inherit eternal life?" 26 Now Jesus said to him, "What has been written in the Law? How do you read it?" 27 Then answering he said, "You shall love the Lord your God with all your heart, and with all your soul, and with all your strength, and with all your mind, and your neighbor as yourself." 28 Then Jesus said to him, "You have correctly answered. This do and you will live." 29 But desiring to justify himself, he said to Jesus, "And who is my neighbor?"

30 Continuing, Jesus said, "A certain man was going down from Jerusalem to Jericho, and fell among robbers, who also having stripped him and inflicted wounds went away, leaving him half dead.

31 "Now, by chance, a certain priest was going on that road, and having seen the man, he turned out of the way and passed by. 32 Now likewise also a Levite, to the place having come and having seen, turned out of the way and passed by.

33 "But a Samaritan, one travelling, came to him, and having seen had compassion. 34 And approaching, he bound up his wounds, pouring on oil and wine. Then putting him on his own animal, he brought him to a khan[s] and took care of him. 35 And on the next day, he took out two denarii, gave them to the host and said, 'Take care of him, and whatever more you might spend, on my return I will repay you.'

36 "Which of these three seems to you to have been a neighbor of the one fallen among the robbers?" 37 And he said, "The one having shown compassion toward him." Then Jesus said to him, "You go and do likewise."

38 Now in their going, he entered into a certain village. Then a certain woman named Martha received him.[t] 39 And she had a sister called Mariam, who also, sitting down at the feet of the Lord, was listening to his word. 40 But Martha was distracted about much serving.

Now having come, she said, "Master, does it not concern you that my sister has left me alone to serve? Therefore speak to her that she may help me." 41 Then answering the Lord said to her, "Martha, Martha, you anxiously care and are troubled about many things. 42 But one thing is needful, even one; for Mariam has chosen the good position, which will not be taken away from her."

LUKE ELEVEN

1 Now it happened in his being

in a certain place praying, when he stopped, one of his disciples said to him, "Lord, teach us to pray, as also John taught his disciples." 2 Then he said to them, "When you pray say, 'Father, hallowed be your name. Your kingdom come. 3 Give us our daily bread each day. 4 And forgive us our sins, for also we ourselves forgive everyone indebted to us. And do not lead us into a trial.'"u

5 And he said to them, "Who among you will have a friend, and will go to him at midnight, and say to him, 'Friend, lend me three bread, 6 because my friend is come to me from a journey, and I have nothing what I will set before him.' 7 And he answering from within may say, 'Trouble me not; already the door has been shut, and my children are with me in the bed; I am not able to rise up to give to you.' 8 I say to you, even if he, having risen, will not give to him because he is his friend, yet because of his persistence he, having risen, will give him as much as he needs.

9 "And I say to you, continue to ask, and it will be given to you; continue to seek, and you will find; continue to knock, and it will be opened to you. 10 For everyone asking receives, and the one seeking finds, and to the one knocking it will be opened.

11 "Now which of you who is a father, the son will ask for a fish, and instead of a fish, a serpent he will give to him? 12 Or also, he will ask for an egg, will he give to him a scorpion? 13 If therefore you, being evil, know to give good gifts to your children, how much more the Father who is in heaven will give the Holy Spirit to those asking him?"

14 And he was casting out a demon, and it was mute. Then it happened, the demon having left, the mute man spoke. And the crowds marveled. 15 Then some of them said, "By Beelzebul the prince of the demons he casts out the demons." 16 Now others, testing, were seeking from him a sign from heaven.

17 Now he, knowing their thoughts, said to them, "Every kingdom being divided against itself will be made desolate; and house against house falls. 18 Now also if Satan is divi1ded against himself, how will has kingdom stand? For you say, 'By Beelzebul' I cast out the demons. 19 If now I by Beelzebul cast out the demons, by whom do your sons cast out? On account of this, they will be your judges. 20 But if by the finger of God I cast out the demons, then the kingdom of God has come upon you.

21 "When fully armed, the strong may guard his house, his possessions are in peace. 22 But when one stronger than he comes upon him, may overcome him, his whole armor he takes away, in which he had trusted, and his plunder he divides. 23 The one not being with me is against me, and the one not gathering with me scatters.

24 "When the unclean spirit is gone from the man, it passes through arid places[v] seeking inward tranquility. And not finding, then it says, 'I will return to my house from where I came.' 25 And having come finds it swept empty and put in order. 26 Then it goes and takes other spirits more evil that itself, seven, and entering they live there; and the last of that man becomes worse than the first."

27 Then, in saying these things, it happened one raised her voice, a woman from the crowd said to him, "Blessed the womb bearing you, and the breasts at which you nursed." 28 Then he said, "Yes, truly.[w] Blessed those hearing the word of God and keeping it."

29 Now, as the multitudes crowded together, he began to say, "This generation is an evil generation. It seeks for a sign, and a sign will not be given to it, except the sign of Jonah. 30 For as Jonah was a sign to the Ninevites, thus also will be the Son of Man to this generation. 31 The Queen of the South will rise up in the judgment with the people of this generation, and will condemn them. For she came from the ends of the earth to hear the wisdom of Solomon, and here behold greater than Solomon. 32 People of Nineveh will stand up in the judgment with this generation, and will condemn it. Because they repented at the preaching of Jonah, and here behold greater than Jonah.

33 "No one lighting a lamp sets it in a secret place, nor under the basket, but upon the lampstand, that those entering in may see the light. 34 The lamp of your body is your eye. When your eye is clear, also all your body is light. But when it be evil, also your body is dark. 35 Therefore give attention, lest the light that is in you be darkness. 36 If therefore your body is full of light, not having any dark part, it will be all light, as when the lamp may shine to give you light."

37 Then in the speaking, a Pharisee asked him that he might eat lunch[x] with him. Then entering, he reclined *to eat*. 38 Then the Pharisee, seeing it, was amazed that he had not first washed before the lunch. 39 Then the Lord said to him, "Now you Pharisees, you make clean the outside of the cup and of the dish, but the inside of you is full robbery and wickedness. 40 Fools, did not the One having made the outside also make the inside? 41 But of the things within *your heart*, give compassionately, and see, all things are clean to you.[y]

42 "But woe to you Pharisees, for you give tithes of mint and rue and every herb, and you neglect the justice and the love of God. These things *are* also proper to do, and those not to neglect. 43 Woe to you Pharisees, for you love the principle seat in the synagogues and the greetings in the marketplaces. 44 Woe to you, for you are like the unmarked graves, and men walking above do not know."

45 Now, responding, one of the experts in the Mosaic Law says to him, "Teacher, saying these things, you also insult us." 46 Then he said, "Also to you the experts in the Law, woe! For you overload the people with burdens hard to be borne, and yourselves do not touch the burdens with one of your fingers.

47 "Woe to you, for you build the tombs of the prophets, but your fathers killed them. 48 So you are witnesses and consent to the works of your fathers. Because they indeed killed them, now you build their tombs. 49 Because of this, the wisdom of God also said, 'I will send to them prophets and apostles, and out of them they will kill and persecute,' 50 so that the blood of all the prophets having been shed from the foundation of the world might be demanded against this generation, 51 from the blood of Abel to the blood of Zechariah, the one having perished between the altar and the house. Yes, I say to you, it will be required of this generation. 52 Woe to you, the experts in the Mosaic Law, because you have removed the key of the knowledge. You yourselves did not enter, and you hindered those who are entering."

53 As he left from there, the experts in the Mosaic Law and Pharisees began to vehemently press and provoke him to speak about many things, 54 watching him, to lay hold of something out of his mouth.

LUKE TWELVE

1 In these times crowds of thousands gathered together, so as to trample one another. He began to say to his disciples first, "Take heed to yourselves of the leaven of the Pharisees, which is hypocrisy. 2 Now, nothing is concealed which will not be revealed, nor hidden which will not be known. 3 Instead, that whatever you have said in the darkness, will be heard in the light. And what you have said in the ear in the inner rooms will be proclaimed upon the housetops.

4 "Now I say to you, my friends, you should not fear for those killing the body and after these things not able to do more. 5 But I will show you whom you should fear: fear the One who has authority after the killing to cast into Gehenna. Yes, I say to you, fear him. 6 Are not five sparrows sold for two assárion?[z] And not one of them is forgotten before God. 7 But even all the hairs of your head are numbered. Fear not, you have more value than many sparrows.

8 "Now I say to you, everyone who will confess in me before people, also the Son of Man will confess in that person before God's messengers. 9 Now the one having denied me before people, will be denied before God's messengers. 10 And everyone who will speak a word against the Son of Man, he will be forgiven. But the one having slandered against the Holy Spirit will not be forgiven.

11 "Now, when they bring you before the synagogues, and the

rulers, and the authorities, do not be anxious how or what you will speak in defense, or what you might say. 12 For the Holy Spirit will teach you in the same hour what is necessary to say."

13 Then one from the crowd said to him, "Teacher, say to my brother to divide with me the inheritance." 14 But he said to him, "Man, who made me a judge or divider over you?" 15 Then he said to them, "Beware, and keep yourselves from all greediness. Because no person's life is in the abundance of what he possesses."

16 Then he spoke a parable to them, saying, "The ground of a certain rich man abundantly yielded. 17 And he kept reasoning within himself, 'What shall I do, because I do not have where I will store my fruits?' 18 And he said, 'I will do this: I will demolish my barns and will build larger, and will store there all my grains and goods. 19 And I will say to my soul, "Soul, you have many good things laid up for many years; take your rest; eat, drink, be happy."' 20 Then God said to him, 'Foolish man! This night your soul is demanded of you; now what you did prepare, to whom will it be?' 21 So the one treasuring for himself and not being rich toward God."

22 Then he said to his disciples, "Because of this I say to you, do not be anxious for your life, what you should eat, nor for your body, what you should wear. 23 For the life is more than the food, and the body than the clothing. 24 Consider the ravens, that they do not sow or reap. To them there is not storehouse nor barn—and God feeds them. How much more you are valuable than the birds. 25 Now which of you by worry is able to add size to their height?[aa] 26 If then you are not able to do even the least, why are you anxious about the rest?

27 "Consider the wild flowers, how they grow—they do not labor, nor do they spin. But I say to you, not even Solomon in all his glory was clothed as one of these. 28 But if the plant in the field, here today and tomorrow thrown into the oven, God thus clothes, how much more you of little faith?

29 "And you, do not seek what you might eat and what you might drink, and do not be in suspense, 30 for all these things the peoples of the world seek after. But of you, the Father knows that you have need of these. 31 But you, seek his kingdom, and these things will be added to you. 32 Do not fear, little flock, for the Father delights in you to give you the kingdom.

33 "Sell your possessions and give money to the poor. Make to yourselves money bags not growing old, an unfailing treasure in the heavens, where thief does not draw near, nor moth destroy. 34 For where your treasure is, there also your heart will be.

35 "Let your clothes be pulled up and knotted about your waist,[bb] and the lamps burning, 36 and you as men awaiting their master, whenever he might return from the

wedding feasts; that he, having come, and having knocked, immediately they might open to him. 37 Blessed those servants whom the master, having come, will find watching. Truly I say to you that he will pull up and knot his clothes about his waist and will make them recline *to eat*; and having come, he will serve them. 38 And if in the second and if in the third watch he comes and finds them doing the same, blessed they are.

39 "But know this, that if the master of the house had known in what hour the thief is coming, he would have watched and not have allowed his house to be broken into. 40 You also be ready. For at an hour you do not expect, the Son of Man comes."

41 Then said Peter, "Master, speak you this parable to us, or also to all?" 42 And the Lord said, "Who, then, is the faithful and wise household manager, whom the master of the house will set over the care of his domestics, to give the measure of food at an appropriate time? 43 Blessed the servant that whom, his master having come, will find him doing likewise. 44 I say to you in truth, that he will set him over all his possessions.

45 "But if that servant should say in his heart, 'My master delays to come,' and should begin to beat the men-servants and the maid-servants, and also to eat and to get drunk, 46 the master of that servant will come at a day in which he does not expect, and at an hour he knows not, and he will scourge him, and will appoint his place with the unbelievers.

47 "Now that servant, the one having known the will of his master, and not having made ready, not having done according to his will, will be beaten much. 48 But the one not having known, but having done things worthy of blows, will be scourged little. Now to all to whom much has been given, much will be required from him; and to whom much more has been entrusted, much more they will ask him.

49 "I came to cast fire upon the earth, and how I desire it already be kindled. 50 But I have an immersion to be immersed, and how I am distressed until it should be accomplished. 51 Think you that I came to give peace on the earth? No, I say to you, but rather division. 52 For there will be now five in one house divided, three against two, and two against three. 53 They will be divided father against son and son against father, mother against daughter and daughter against mother, mother-in-law against the daughter-in-law and daughter-in-law against mother-in-law."

54 Now he was saying also to the crowds, "When you see a cloud rising up from the west, immediately you say, 'A heavy rain in coming,' and so it happens. 55 And when a southwest wind is blowing, you say, 'There will be heat,' and it happens. 56

Hypocrites, you know to discern the face of the earth and of the sky, but this the time, how do you not know to discern?

57 "And now why for yourselves do you not judge what is right? 58 For as you are going with your adversary before a magistrate, in the way make effort to be set free from him, lest ever he might drag you to the judge, and the judge will deliver you to the public officer, and the public officer will throw you into prison. 59 I say to you, you will never no never come out from there until even the last lepton you shall have paid."

LUKE THIRTEEN

1 Now some were present at the same time telling him about the Galileans whose blood Pilate had mingled with their sacrifices. 2 And responding, he said to them, "Think you that these Galileans were sinners beyond all the Galileans, because these things they suffered? 3 No, I say to you, but if you do not convert all you likewise will perish. 4 Or those eighteen on whom fell the tower in Siloam and killed them, think you that these were debtors beyond all persons living in Jerusalem? 5 No, I say to you, but if you do not convert, all you likewise will perish."

6 Now he was speaking this parable. "A certain man had planted a fig tree in his vineyard. And he came seeking fruit on it and did not find any. 7 Then he said to the vinedresser, 'Look, of these three years I came seeking fruit on this fig tree, and do not find. Cut it down. For what purpose does it use up the ground?' 8 But answering he says to him, 'Sir, let it alone also this year, until when I might dig around it, and put manure. 9 And if truly it should bear fruit, so be it. But if not, you will cut it down.'"

10 Now he was teaching in one of the synagogues on the Sabbaths. 11 And look, a woman having a spirit of infirmity eighteen years. And she was bent over and not able to fully raise herself. 12 Now, seeing her, Jesus called her near and said to her, "Woman, you are freed from your sickness." 13 And he laid his hands upon her, and immediately she was made to stand erect, and began to glorify God.

14 Now the ruler of the synagogue responded, indignant because Jesus had healed on the Sabbath. He said to the crowd, "Six days there are in which we need to work. In these therefore come to be healed, and not on the day of the Sabbath."

15 But the Lord answered him, and said, "Hypocrites. Each one of you on the Sabbath, does he not untie his ox, or the donkey from the stall, and leading it away give it to drink? 16 Now this being a daughter of Abraham, whom Satan has bound—look, for eighteen years—is it not right she to be loosed from this bond on the day of the Sabbath?" 17 And on him saying these things, all those

opposed to him were ashamed. And all the crowd was rejoicing at all the glorious things that were being done by him.

18 Then he was saying, "To what is like the kingdom of God? And to what shall I compare it? 19 It is like to a grain of mustard, which having taken, a person cast into his garden. And it grew and became a tree, and the birds of the air nested in its branches."

20 And again he said, "To what will I compare the Kingdom of God? 21 It is like leaven, which taking, a woman concealed in three measures of meal until all of it was leavened."

22 And he was going through towns and villages, teaching, and making his way toward Jerusalem.

23 Then one said to him, "Master, are those being saved few?" And he said to them, 24 "Make every effort to enter in through the narrow door. For many, I say to you, will seek to enter in and will not be able. 25 From what time the master of the house may have risen and may have shut the door, then you might begin to stand outside and to knock at the door, saying, 'Sir, open to us.' And he answering will say to you, 'I do not know you, from where you are.' 26 Then you will begin to say, 'We ate and drank in your presence, and you taught in our streets.' 27 And he will say, 'I tell you, I do not know you, from where you are; depart from me, all you workers of unrighteousness.'

28 "There will be weeping and gnashing of teeth when you see Abraham and Isaac and Jacob, and all the prophets, in the kingdom of God, but you are being cast out. 29 And they will come from the east and west, and from north and south, and will recline *to eat* in the kingdom of God. 30 And look, there are last who will be first, and there are first who will be last."

31 In the same hour certain Pharisees came near, saying to him, "Go out and leave from here, because Herod desires to kill you." 32 And he said to them, "Go, say to the fox that, 'Look, I cast out demons and perform healing today and tomorrow, and the third day I finish my work.' 33 But I must today and tomorrow and the following go my way, because it is not possible a prophet die outside of Jerusalem.

34 "Jerusalem, Jerusalem, killing the prophets and stoning those having been sent to it. How often I have wanted to gather your children, the way a hen her brood under her wings, and you were not willing. 35 Behold your house is left to you. I say now to you, never no never shall you see me until the time comes when you say, 'Blessed the One coming in the name of the Lord.'"

LUKE FOURTEEN

1 And it happened that he went into a house of one of the leaders of the Pharisees on a Sabbath to eat bread; and they were watching him closely. 2 And look, a certain man with the illness dropsy was there in front of him. 3

And responding, Jesus spoke to the experts in the Law of Moses, and to the Pharisees, saying, "Is it lawful to heal on the Sabbath, or not?" 4 But they were silent. And grasping the man's hand, he healed him, and let him go. 5 And he said to them, "Which of you, a son or ox will fall into a pit, will he not also immediately pull him up, on the Sabbath day?" 6 And they were not able to reply to these things.

7 Now he was speaking a parable to those having been invited, giving attention to how they were choosing the first places, saying to them, 8 "When you are invited by anyone to wedding feasts, do not recline *to eat* in the first place, lest at the time a more honorable than you might have been invited by him, 9 and you and him having come, the one who invited will say to you, 'Give your place to this one,' and then you will begin with shame to take the last place. 10 But when you are invited, having gone, recline *to eat* in the last place, so that when the one having invited you might come, he will say to you, 'Friend, come to a higher place.' Then to you will be glory in front of all those reclining *to eat* with you. 11 For everyone exalting himself will be humbled, and the one humbling himself will be exalted."

12 Then he was saying to the one having invited him, "When you make a breakfast or a supper, do not call your friends, nor your brethren, nor your relatives, nor your rich neighbors, and recompense be made to you. 13 But when you make a feast, call the poor, the crippled, the lame, the blind; 14 and you will be blessed because they have nothing to repay you. For it will be repaid to you in the resurrection of the righteous."

15 Then one of those reclining *to eat* having heard these things, he said to him, "Blessed is he who will eat bread in the kingdom of God." 16 Now he said to them, "A certain man was preparing a great supper, and invited many. 17 And he sent his servant at the hour of the supper to say to those having been invited, 'Come, because it is now ready.' 18 And as one all began to excuse themselves. The first said to him, 'I have bought a field, and I have need going out to see it. I beg of you, hold me excused.' 19 And another said, 'I bought a yoke of five oxen, and I am going to prove them. I beg of you, hold me excused.' 20 And another said, 'I have married a wife, and because of this I am not available to come.'

21 "And having returned, the servant reported these things to his master. Then becoming angry, the master of the house said to his servant, 'Go out, quickly, into the broad streets and narrow lanes of the city, and the poor, and crippled, and blind, and lame bring in here.' 22 And the servant said, 'Sir, it has been done as you commanded, and there is still room.' 23 And the master said to the servant, 'Go out into the highways and hedges and

persuade them to come in, so that my house may be filled. 24 For I say to you that not one of those men having been invited will taste of my supper.'"

25 Then great crowds were going with him. And turning he said to them, 26 "If anyone comes to me, and hates not his father and his mother and the wife and the children and the brothers and the sisters, yes and even his life, he is not able to be my disciple. 27 Whoever does not carry his cross and come after me, is not able to be my disciple.

28 "For which of you, desiring to build a tower, does not first sit down to count the cost, whether he has for its completion. 29 Lest having laid a foundation, and not being able to finish, all observing may begin to mock him, 30 saying, 'This man began to build and was not able to finish.'

31 "Or what king, going on to engage in war with another king, does not first sit down, taking counsel whether he is able with ten thousand to meet the one with twenty thousand coming against him. 32 But if not, while he is still far off, he sends an embassy to ask for peace. 33 So, therefore, each of you who does not give up all that he himself possesses, is not able to be my disciple.

34 "Now salt is good. But if also the salt becomes tasteless, with what will it be seasoned? 35 For neither for soil nor manure is it fit; they cast it out. The one having ears to hear, let him hear."

LUKE FIFTEEN

1 Now drawing near to him were all the tax collectors and the sinners, to hear him. 2 And both the Pharisees and scribes were complaining, saying, "This one receives sinners and eats with them." 3 But he spoke to them this parable, saying, 4 "What man of you, having a hundred sheep, and having lost one out of them, does not leave the ninety-nine in the open field, and goes after the one that was lost, until he finds it? 5 And having found it he lays it on his shoulders, rejoicing? 6 And coming to the house, he calls together the friends and the neighbors, saying to them, 'Rejoice with me, for I have found my sheep, the one having been lost.' 7 I say to you that in the same way there will be joy in heaven over one sinner repenting, rather than over the ninety-nine righteous ones who have no need of repentance.

8 "Or what woman having ten drachmas, if she should lose one drachma, does not light a lamp and sweeps the house, and seeks carefully until she finds it? 9 And having found, she calls together the friends and neighbors, saying, 'Rejoice with me, because I have found the drachma that I lost.' 10 Thus I say to you, there is joy in the presence of God's messengers over one sinner repenting."

11 Now he said, "A certain man had two sons. 12 And the younger of them said to the father, 'Father, give to me the part of the

substance falling to me.' Then he divided to them the living. 13 And after not many days, gathering all together, the younger son went away into a distant country, and there he squandered his substance, living extravagantly.

14 "Now having spent his all, there arose a severe famine throughout that country, and he began to be in want. 15 And having gone on, he joined himself to one of the citizens of that country; and he sent him into his fields to feed pigs. 16 And he lusted to fill his belly from the carob pods that the pigs were eating; and no one was giving to him.

17 "But having come to himself he was saying, 'How many hired servants of my father have bread, but here I am perishing with hunger? 18 I will get up and go to my father, and I will say to him, "Father, I have sinned, to the heaven and before you. 19 I am no longer worthy to be named your son. Make me like one of your servants."' 20 And getting up he went to his father.

"Now he still being far distant, his father saw him, and was moved with compassion, and having run, fell upon his neck and kissed him. 21 Then the son said to him, 'Father, I have sinned to heaven and before you. I am no longer worthy to be named your son. Make me as one of your hired servants.'

22 "But the Father said to his servants, 'Quickly, bring out the best robe and clothe him, and give a ring for his hand, and sandals for his feet, 23 and bring the fattened calf and kill it, and let us eat and be merry. 24 For this my son was dead and is again living, he was lost and is found.' And they began to be merry.

25 "But his son, the elder, was in the field. And as he was coming he drew near to the house, he heard music and dancing. 26 And calling one of the servants near, he began asking what these things might be. 27 Now he said to him, 'Your brother is come, and your father has killed the fattened calf, because he has received him in good health.' 28 But he became angry, and was not willing to go in. Now his father, going to him, was beseeching him.

29 "But answering he said to his father, 'Look, so many years I served you, and never a commandment of you I disobeyed, and never to me did you give a young goat that with my friends I might make merry. 30 But when this son of yours, the one having consumed your living with prostitutes, came, you have killed for him the fattened calf!'

31 "Then he said to him, 'Son, you are always with me, and all that is mine is yours. 32 But to make merry and to rejoice was right, because this your brother was dead, and is again alive, and he was lost, and is found.'"

LUKE SIXTEEN

1 Now also he was saying to the disciples, "A certain man was

rich, who had a manager, and he was accused to him as wasting his possessions. 2 And having called him, he said to him, 'What is this I hear concerning you? Give the account of your management; for you are no longer able to manage.' 3 Then the manager said within himself, 'What shall I do, because my master is taking away the management from me? I am not able to dig; I am ashamed to beg. 4 I know what I may do, so that when I might be removed from the management, they may receive me into their homes.'

5 "And having called each one of the debtors of his master, he said to the first, 'How much do you owe to my master?' 6 And he said, 'Nine hundred gallons of oil.' So he said to him, 'Take your bill, and sitting down, quickly write four hundred fifty gallons.'

7 "Then to another he said, 'Now how much do you owe?' And he said, 'one thousand and one hundred bushels of wheat.' He says to him, 'Take your bill and write eight hundred eighty bushels.'

8 "And the master praised the unrighteous manager, because he had acted shrewdly. Because the sons of this age are shrewder than the sons of the light, in their generation. 9 And I say to you, make for yourselves friends from the wealth of unrighteousness, in order that when it may fail they might receive you into the eternal dwellings.

10 "The one faithful in very little, is also faithful in much; and the one unrighteous in very little, is also unrighteousness in much. 11 If, therefore, you have not been faithful in the unrighteous wealth, who will entrust to you the true riches? 12 And if in that of another you have not been faithful, who will give to you that which is yours? 13 No servant is able to serve two masters. For either the one he will hate and the other he will love, or he will remain faithful to one and the other he will despise. You are not able to serve God and material possessions."[cc]

14 Now, the Pharisees were listening to all these things; and being lovers of money they were scoffing at him. 15 And he said to them, "You are those justifying themselves before people, but God knows your hearts. Because that which among people is exalted is abhorrent before God.

16 "The Law and the prophets were until John; from that time the kingdom of God is proclaimed, and everyone presses into it. 17 But it is easier the heaven and earth to pass away, than of the Law one point of a letter to fail.

18 "Everyone putting away his wife and marrying another commits adultery. And the one marrying her put away from a husband commits adultery.

19 "Now there was a certain rich man, and he was clothed in purple and fine linen, living merry every day in splendor. 20 Then a certain poor man named Lazarus was laid at his gates, having ulcers

on his skin, 21 and desiring to be fed from whatever was falling from the rich man's table; but even the dogs were coming and licking his sores. 22 Then it happened the poor man died, and he was taken away by the messengers into the bosom of Abraham.

"Then also the rich man died and was buried. 23 And in hades, having lifted up his eyes, being in torment, he sees Abraham from afar, and Lazarus in his bosom. 24 And he, crying out, said, 'Father Abraham, have mercy on me and send Lazarus, that he might dip the tip of his finger in water and cool my tongue; for I am suffering in this flame.'

25 "Now Abraham, said, 'Child, remember that you did fully receive the good in your lifetime, and Lazarus in the same manner the evil. But now here he is comforted; now you are suffering. 26 And in all these this, between us and you a great chasm has been fixed, so that those desiring to pass from here to you are not able, nor can they pass from there to us.'

27 "Then he said, 'I implore you then, father, that you would send him to my father's house—28 for I have five brothers—so that he might warn them, that they also might not come to this place of torment.' 29 But Abraham says, 'They have Moses and the prophets; let them hear them.' 30 Then he said, 'No father Abraham, but if one from the dead should go to them, they will repent.' 31 But he said to him, 'If they hear not Moses and the prophets, not even if one should rise out from the dead will they be persuaded.'"

LUKE SEVENTEEN

1 Then he said to his disciples, "It is impossible for stumbling blocks not to come, but woe through whom they may come! 2 Better for him if a millstone is hung around his neck and he is thrown into the sea, than he might cause to stumble one of these littles.

3 "Pay attention to yourselves. If your brother may sin, rebuke him. And if he may repent, forgive him. 4 And if seven times in the day he may sin against you, and seven times may return to you saying, 'I repent,' you will forgive him."

5 And the apostles said to the Lord, "Add to us faith!" 6 Then the Lord said, "If you have faith like a seed of mustard, you would have said to this sycamore tree, 'Be uprooted and be planted in the sea,' and it would have obeyed you.

7 "Now which of you having a servant, plowing or shepherding, who has come out of the field, will say to him, 'Now having come, recline *to eat*'? 8 But will he not say to him, 'Prepare what I may eat and prepare yourself to serve me while I eat and drink, and after these things you will eat and drink'? 9 Does he thank that servant because he did what he was supposed to do? 10 Thus you also, when you may have done all that you were supposed to do, say, 'Unworthy servants are we. That

which we were obligated to do we have done.'"

11 And it happened in the going up to Jerusalem, that he was passing through the midst of Samaria and Galilee. 12 And as he entered a certain village, ten leprous men met him, who stood afar off. 13 And they called out saying, "Jesus, master, have mercy on us." 14 And seeing them, he said to them, "In going, show yourselves to the priests." And it happened in their going, they were cleansed. 15 Then one of them, seeing that he was healed, turned back, with a loud voice glorifying God. 16 And he fell on his face at his feet, giving thanks to him; and he was a Samaritan. 17 Then responding, Jesus said, "Were not ten cleansed? But where are the nine? 18 Have none been found returning to give glory to God except this foreigner?" 19 And he said to him, "Get up, go; your faith has healed you."

20 Now, having been asked by the Pharisees, when the kingdom of God is coming, he answered them and said, "The kingdom of God does not come with attentive watching, 21 and they will not say, 'Behold here or there,' for look, the kingdom of God is in your midst."

22 Then he said to the disciples, "Times will come when you desire to see one of the days of the Son of Man, and you will not see. 23 And they will say to you, 'Look there, see here.' Do not go out nor follow. 24 For as the lightening flashing shines from one part of the sky to another part of the sky,[dd] so will be the Son of Man in his day. 25 But first, it is necessary him to suffer many things and be rejected by this generation.

26 "And as it happened in the times of Noah, thus will it also be in the times of the Son of Man. 27 They were eating, they were drinking, they were marrying, they were being given in marriage, until that day Noah entered into the ark, and the flood came and destroyed all.

28 "In the same manner, as it happened in the times of Lot, they were eating, they were drinking, they were buying, they were selling, they were planting, they were building. 29 Then in that day Lot left Sodom, it rained fire and brimstone from heaven and destroyed all.

30 "According to these will it be in the day the Son of Man is revealed. 31 In that day, one will be on the roof, and his goods in the house—let him not come down to take them away. And one in the field, in the same manner, let him not return to the things behind.

32 "Remember Lot's wife. 33 Whoever may seek to save his life, will lose it. But whoever will lose it will preserve it. 34 I say to you, in that night there will be two upon one bed: the one will be taken and the other will be left. 35 There will be two grinding at the same place: the one will be taken and the other will be left. 36 Two will be in the field: the one will be taken and the

other will be left."ee 37 And responding, they say to him, "Where Master?" And he said to them, "Where the body is, there also the vultures will gather together."

LUKE EIGHTEEN

1 Then he was speaking a parable to them about the necessity for them to always pray and not give up, 2 saying, "There was a certain judge in a certain city, not fearing God and not respecting man. 3 Now there was a widow in that city, and she was coming to him, saying, 'Support my right to justice against the accusation of my adversary.' 4 And for a time he would not. But after he said within himself, 'Even if I do not fear God nor respect man, 5 yet because this widow causes me trouble, I will support justice for her, to end her coming lest she exhaust me.'"

6 Then said the Lord, "Hear what the unrighteous judge says. 7 And should not God do justice for his elect, the ones crying out to him day and night, and be long-suffering for them? 8 I say to you that he will do justice for them quickly. But the Son of Man having come, truly will he find faith on the earth?"

9 Now he also spoke this parable to some trusting in themselves that they are righteous and despising the others: 10 "Two men went up into the temple to pray, the one a Pharisee, and the other a tax collector. 11 The Pharisee standing by himself was praying, 'God, I thank you that I am not like the rest of the men—extortioners, unjust, adulterers—or even like this tax collector. 12 I fast twice in the week; I tithe all things, as much as I gain.'

13 But the tax collector, standing afar off, was not willing even his eyes to lift up to heaven, but was striking his breast, saying of himself, 'God be merciful to me the sinner!' 14 I say to you, this one went down justified to his house, rather than that one. For everyone exalting himself will be humbled, but the one humbling himself will be exalted."

15 Then they were also bringing to him the infants, that he might touch them. But seeing this, the disciples were rebuking them. 16 But Jesus called to them and said, "Permit the little children to come to me, and do not forbid them; for of such is the kingdom of God. 17 Truly I say to you, whoever may not receive the kingdom of God as a child, may never no never enter into it."

18 And a certain ruler asked him, saying, "Good teacher, what having done, will I inherit eternal life?" 19 Then Jesus said to him, "Why do you call me good? No one is good, except God alone. 20 You know the commandments: you may not commit adultery; you may not murder; you may not steal, you may not bear false witness; you will honor your father and your mother." 21 And he said, "All these I have kept from my youth."

22 Now hearing this, Jesus

said to him, "Yet, you are missing one thing. All, as much as you have, sell, and distribute to the helpless beggars,[ff] and you will have treasure in the heavens; and come, follow me."

23 And hearing these things, he became very sorrowful, for he was extremely rich. 24 Then, seeing him, Jesus became sorrowful, saying, "With difficulty those having riches might enter into the kingdom of God. 25 For it is easier a camel to go through an eye of a needle than a wealthy person to enter into the kingdom of God." 26 Then those having heard said, "Then who is able to be saved?" 27 But he said, "The things impossible to man are possible with God."

28 Then Peter said, "Look, we having left our own, followed you." 29 And he said to them, "Truly I say to you that there is no one who has left house or wife or brothers or parents or children for the sake of the kingdom of God, 30 who may not receive much more in this time, and in the age that is coming, eternal life."

31 Then taking the Twelve aside, he said to them, "Look, we go up to Jerusalem, and all things will be accomplished written by the prophets concerning the Son of Man. 32 For he will be betrayed to the gentiles, and will be mocked, and will be treated shamefully, and will be spit upon. 33 And having flogged him, they will kill him; and on the third day he will rise up." 34 And they did not understand these things, and this word was hidden from them, and they did not understand the things being spoken.

35 Then it happened as he drew near to Jericho, a certain blind person was sitting beside the road, begging. 36 Then, hearing a crowd passing by, he asked what this might be. 37 Then they told him, "Jesus of Nazareth is passing by."

38 And he called out saying, "Jesus, son of David, have mercy on me." 39 And those along the way were rebuking him, that he might be silent. But he much more kept on crying out, "Son of David have mercy on me."

40 Then stopping, Jesus commanded him to be brought to him. Then drawing near, he asked him, 41 "What do you want I do to you?" And he said, "Sir, that I may receive sight." 42 And Jesus said to him, "Receive sight. Your faith has healed you." 43 And immediately he received sight, and began following him, glorifying God. And all the people, seeing it, gave praise to God.

LUKE NINETEEN

1 And having entered, he was passing through Jericho. 2 And see, a man called by name Zacchaeus, and he was a chief tax collector, and he was wealthy. 3 And he was trying to see Jesus, who he is, and was not able for the crowd, because he was small in height. 4 And running to the front, he went up into a sycamore tree, in order that he might see him, because he

would pass that way.

5 And as he came to the place, having looked up, Jesus said to him, "Zacchaeus, hurry and come down. For today I need to stay in your house." 6 And he came down in a hurry and received him, rejoicing.

7 And seeing this, all were grumbling, saying, "He has come to stay with a sinful man." 8 Then, standing, Zacchaeus said to the Lord, "Look, I give half of my possessions, sir, to the helpless poor. And if I have defrauded anything of anyone, I restore it fourfold." 9 Then Jesus said to him, "Today salvation has come to this house, because he also is a son of Abraham. 10 For the Son of Man came to seek and to save that having been lost."

11 Now as they were hearing these things, he added and spoke a parable, on account of his being near Jerusalem, and their thinking that immediately the kingdom of God is about to appear. 12 Therefore, he said, "A certain man of noble birth went to a distant country to receive for himself a kingdom and to return. 13 Now having called ten of his servants, he gave to them one hundred twenty ounces of silver and said to them, 'Do business until that I come back.' 14 But his citizens hated him and sent an ambassador after him, saying, 'We are not willing this man to reign over us.'

15 "And it happened on his returning, having received the kingdom, that he commanded his servants be called to him, those to whom he has given the money, in order that he might know what each had gained by business.

16 "Now the first came, saying, 'Master, your hundred twenty ounces of silver has produced one hundred twenty more ounces of silver.' 17 And he said to him, 'Well done good servant. Because you were faithful in very little, you are to have authority over ten cities.'

18 "And the second came, saying, 'The one hundred twenty ounces of your silver, Master, had made sixty ounces of silver.' 19 Then he said also to this one, 'And you are to be over five cities.'

20 "And another came, saying, 'Master, behold the one hundred twenty ounces of your silver, which I kept lying away in a piece of cloth. 21 For I was afraid of you, because you are an austere man. You take up what you did not lay down, and you reap what you did not sow.'

22 "'Out of your mouth I will judge you, evil servant. You knew that I am an austere man, taking up what I did not lay down, and reaping what I did not sow. 23 Then why did you not give my silver to the table of a money changer, and I having come might have collected it with interest?'

24 "And to those standing by he said, 'Take from him the one hundred twenty ounces of silver and give to the one having the one hundred twenty ounces of silver.' 25 'And they said to him, 'Master,

he has one hundred twenty ounces of silver.'

26 "'I say to you that to everyone having will be given; but from the one not having, even that he has will be taken away. 27 Furthermore, these enemies of mine, those not being willing for me to reign over them, bring them here and execute them before me.'"

28 And having said these things, he went on ahead, going up to Jerusalem. 29 And it happened as he came near to Bethphage and Bethany, nearing the mount called "Olivet," he sent two of his disciples, 30 saying, "Go into the village ahead, in which entering you will find a colt tied, on which no one yet of men has sat. And untying it, bring it. 31 And if anyone asks you, 'What is the reason you untie it?' This you will say: 'Because the Lord has need of it.'"

32 Then leaving, those being sent found as he had said to them. 33 Then on them untying the colt, the masters of it said to them, "Why do you untie the colt?" 34 And they said, "The Lord has need of it." 35 And they led it to Jesus, and throwing their cloaks on the colt, they put Jesus on it. 36 Then as he went, they were spreading their cloaks on the road.

37 Now as he began to draw near the descent of the Mount of Olives, all the multitude of the disciples began rejoicing to praise God in a loud voice for all the mighty works which they had seen, 38 saying, "Blessed the coming king in the name of the Lord. In heaven peace, and glory in the highest." 39 And some of the Pharisees from the crowd said to him, "Teacher, rebuke your disciples." 40 And responding, he said, "I say to you that if these were silent, the stones will cry out."

41 And as he drew near, seeing and considering the city, he wept over it, 42 saying, "If you had known in this the day, even you, the things for peace. But now they are hidden from your eyes. 43 Because times will come upon you that your enemies will build a fence around you, and they will surround you, and will hem you in on every side, 44 and raze you and your children within you, and will not leave a stone upon a stone within you, because you did not know the season of your visitation."

45 And entering the temple, he began to drive out those selling, 46 saying to them, "It has been written, 'And my house will be a house of prayer'; but you have made it a den of robbers." 47 And he was teaching every day in the temple. But the chief priests and the scribes and the leaders of the people were seeking to destroy him. 48 But they did not discover what they might do, for all the people were hanging on his words, listening.

LUKE TWENTY

1 And it happened on one of the days, as he was teaching the people in the temple and proclaiming the good news, the

chief priests and the scribes with the elders came up 2 and spoke, saying to him, "Tell us by what authority you do these things, or who is the one giving you this authority?" 3 Then answering, he said to them, "I also will ask you one thing, and you tell me. 4 John's immersing, was it from heaven or was it from men?"

5 Now they reasoned among themselves, saying, "If we might say, 'From heaven,' he will say, 'What was the reason you did not believe him?' 6 But if we might say, 'From men,' all the people will stone us. For they are persuaded John to be a prophet." 7 And they answered they knew not from where. 8 And Jesus said to them, "I will not tell you by what authority I am doing these things."

9 Then he began to speak to the people this parable. "A certain man planted a vineyard, and leased it to farmers, and traveled abroad a long time. 10 And in the proper season he sent to the farmers a servant, that they will give to him from the fruit of the vineyard. But the farmers sent him away, with empty hands, after beating him. 11 And again he sent another servant. But him they sent away with empty hands, having beaten and dishonored him. 12 And again he sent, a third. But him also, having wounded, they cast out.

13 "Then said the master of the vineyard, 'What shall I do? I will send my son, the beloved. Perhaps they will respect him.' 14 Now seeing him, the farmers reasoned among themselves, saying, 'This is the heir. Let us kill him so that the inheritance might become ours.' 15 And casting him outside the vineyard, they killed him. What, therefore, will the master of the vineyard do to them? 16 He will come and will destroy those farmers, and will give the vineyard to others." Then, having heard, they said, "May it never be!"

17 But looking at them he said, "What then is this that has been written? 'The stone which those building rejected, this has become head of the corner.' 18 Everyone falling on that stone will be broken, but on whoever it may fall it will make chaff of him."

19 And the scribes and the chief priests sought to lay hands on him in that hour; and they feared the people; for they understood that he was speaking this parable against them. 20 And they watched him, they sent spies, pretending to be righteous, that they might catch him in speech, in order to deliver him to the rule and to the authority of the Procurator.

21 And they questioned him, saying, "Teacher, we know that you speak and teach rightly, and not receive any person, but upon the basis of truth teach the way of God. 22 Is it lawful for us to give tribute to Caesar, or not?" 23 But understanding their shrewdness, he said to them, 24 "Show me a denarius. Whose is the image and inscription?" And they said, "Caesar's." 25 And he said to them,

"Therefore return the things of Caesar to Caesar, and the things of God to God." 26 And they were not able to censure his word before the people. And they being astonished at his answer, they became silent.

27 Then, some of the Sadducees having come near, the ones denying the possibility of a resurrection, they questioned him, 28 saying, "Teacher, Moses wrote to us if anyone's brother might die having a wife, and he is childless, that his brother should take the wife and raise up offspring to his brother. 29 Therefore there were seven brothers. And the first, having taken a wife, died childless; 30 and the second⁹⁹ 31 and the third took her; then in the same manner also the seven did not leave children, and died. 32 Finally also the woman died. 33 The woman, therefore, in the resurrection, of which of them does she become wife? For the seven had her as wife."

34 And Jesus said to them, "The sons of this age marry and are given in marriage. 35 But those counted worthy to obtain that age and the resurrection which is out from the dead, do not marry and are not given in marriage. 36 For they are not able to die anymore, for they are like the messengers; and they are sons of God, being sons of the resurrection. 37 But that the dead are raised, even Moses showed at the bush, when he calls the Lord, 'the God of Abraham, and the God of Isaac, and the God of Jacob.' 38 Now God is not of the dead but of the living, for all live to him." 39 Now responding, some of the scribes said, "Teacher, you have spoken well." 40 Then no longer did they dare to ask him anything.

41 Then he said to them, "How do they declare the Christ to be son of David?" 42 For David himself says in the book of Psalms, 'Said the Lord to my Lord, "Sit at my right hand 43 until I place your enemies a footstool for your feet."' 44 David therefore calls him 'Lord,' and how of him is he son?"

45 Now, all the people were listening, he said to his disciples, 46 "Beware of the scribes, desiring to walk in long robes and loving greetings in the marketplaces, and chief seats in the synagogues, and chief places in the evening banquets, 47 who devour widows' houses, and as a pretext pray at great length. These will receive greater judgment."

LUKE TWENTY-ONE

1 Now, looking up, he saw the rich ones casting their gifts into the treasury. 2 Then he saw a certain poor widow casting in two leptons.ʰʰ 3 And he said, "Truly I say to you that this poor widow has cast in more than all. 4 For all these out of their abundance cast in their gifts. But she out of her poverty did cast all the livelihood that she had."

5 And as some were speaking about the temple, that it was decorated with beautiful stones and consecrated gifts, he said, 6 "These things which you admire,

times will come in which will not be left stone upon stone which will not be thrown down."

7 Then they asked him, saying, "Teacher, when then will these things be, and what the sign when these things are about to occur?" 8 And he said, "Take heed, lest you be led astray. For many will come in my name, saying, 'I am he' and 'The time has drawn near.' Do not go after them. 9 Now when you should hear of wars and commotions, be not terrified. For these things must take place first; but the end is not immediately."

10 Then he was saying to them, "Nation will rise against nation, and kingdom against kingdom. 11 There will be both great earthquakes and famines and pestilences in different places; fearful sights also, and from heaven there will be great signs.

12 "But before all these things, they will seize you, and will persecute you, delivering you to synagogues and prisons, bringing you before kings and leaders on account of my name. 13 To you it will turn out for a testimony. 14 Therefore, settle in your minds not to premeditate a defense. 15 For I will give you a mouth and wisdom which all those opposing you will not be able to resist or contradict.

16 "Then you will be delivered even by parents and brethren and relatives and friends, and they will deliver to death from among you. 17 And you will be hated by all because of my name. 18 But never no never should a hair of your head perish. 19 By your endurance you will possess your souls.

20 "Then, when you see Jerusalem surrounded by army encampments, then know that her desolation has drawn near. 21 Then those in Judea, let them flee to the mountains; and those in the midst of her, let them leave; and those in the countryside, let them not enter into her. 22 For these are the times of judicial punishment, to fulfill all things that have been written.

23 "Woe to those who are pregnant, and to the ones nursing in those times. For there will be great affliction upon the land and wrath to this people. 24 And they will fall by the edge of the sword, and be led captive into the nations. And all Jerusalem will be trampled by gentiles until the times of the gentiles are fulfilled.

25 "And there will be signs in the sun and moon and stars. And on the earth anguish of nations in perplexity, roaring of the sea and rolling billows, 26 people faint of heart from fear and expectation of that which is coming on the earth. For the powers of the heavens will be shaken. 27 And then they will see the Son of Man coming in a cloud, with power and great glory. 28 Now these things beginning to happen, look up and lift up your heads, because your redemption draws near."

29 And he spoke a parable to them. "Behold the fig tree and all the trees. 30 When they put forth leaves, you see for yourselves, knowing that summer is already

near. 31 So also you, when you see these things taking place, know that the kingdom of God is near. 32 Truly I say to you, that never no never will this generation perish until all may have taken place. 33 The heaven and the earth will pass away, but my words will never no never pass away.

34 "Now take heed to yourselves, lest ever you burden your hearts with overindulgence in drink and partying and drunkenness and cares of life, and that day should come upon you unexpectedly as a snare. 35 For it will come upon all those sitting upon the face of all the earth. 36 Watch, then, in every season, praying that you may be strong to escape these things, all that are about to come to pass, and to stand before the Son of Man."

37 Now during the day he was in the temple teaching, and leaving in the evening he was lodging on the mount called Olivet. 38 And all the people would come to him in the morning in the temple to hear him.

LUKE TWENTY-TWO

1 Now the Feast of Unleavened was approaching, called Passover. 2 And the chief priests and the scribes were seeking how they might put him to death; for they were afraid of the people. 3 Then Satan entered into Judas, the one called Iscariot, being of the number of the Twelve. 4 And going his way, he spoke with the chief priests and chief officers, how he might betray him to them.

5 And they were happy and agreed to give him money. 6 And he agreed, and began seeking opportunity to betray him in the absence of a crowd.

7 Then came the day of Unleavened on which the Passover must be sacrificed. 8 And he sent Peter and John, saying, "Go and prepare for us the Passover, that we may eat it." 9 And they said to him, "Where will you we should prepare?" 10 And he said to them, "Look, when you enter into the city, you will meet a man carrying a pitcher of water. Follow him into the house into which he enters. 11 And you will say to the master of the house, 'The Teacher says to you, "Where is the guest room, where I may eat the Passover with my disciples?"' 12 And he will show you a large, furnished upper room; there prepare." 13 Then going, they found it as he had said to them. And they prepared the Passover.

14 And when the hour was come, he reclined *to eat*, and the apostles with him. 15 And Jesus said to them, "I have longed to eat this Passover with you before I suffer. 16 For I say to you, that never no never will I eat thereof until when fulfilled in the kingdom of God." 17 And receiving a cup he gave thanks, saying, "Take this and divide among yourselves. 18 For I say to you that never no never will I drink now of the fruit of the vine, until that the kingdom of God shall come."

19 And taking the bread, giving thanks, he broke it and gave

to them, saying, "This is my body, which is given for you. This do in the remembrance of me." 20 And the cup, after having eaten, in the same manner, saying, "This cup is the new covenant in my blood, which for you is being poured out.

21 "But behold, the hand of him betraying me is with me on the table. 22 For truly the Son of Man goes according to that appointed, but woe to that person by whom he is betrayed." 23 And they began to question among themselves, which of them it might be who is about to do this.

24 Also then there was a dispute among them, which of them is thought to be greatest. 25 Now Jesus said to them, "The kings of the gentiles rule over them, and those exercising authority over them are called benefactors. 26 But not you in that manner. Instead, the greatest among you, let him be as the younger. And the one who leads, as the one serving. 27 For who is greater? The one reclining *to eat* or the one serving? Is not the one reclining? But I am in the midst of you as the one serving.

28 "Now you are those who remained with me in my trials. 29 And I bequeath to you as the Father assigned to me, a kingdom, 30 so you may eat and may drink at my table in my kingdom, and may sit on thrones judging the Twelve tribes of Israel.

31 "Simon, Simon, look, Satan asked to sift all of you like wheat. 32 But I prayed for you all, that your faith might not fail. And you, when you have turned back, strengthen your brethren."

33 Then Peter said to him, "Master, I am ready with you to go both to prison and to death." 34 And he said, "I tell you Peter, the rooster will not crow today, until three times you will deny knowing me."

35 He said to them, "When I sent you without money bag and food sack and sandals, you did not lack anything, did you?" And they said, "Nothing." 36 Then he said to them, "But now, the one having a money bag, let him take it, and also a food sack. And the one not having, sell his cloak and buy a sword. 37 For I say to you, that this which has been written, it will be accomplished in me: 'And with the lawless he was counted.' For the things concerning me have an end." 38 And they said, "Master, look here, two swords." And he said, to them, "It is enough."

39 And leaving, he went according to custom to the Mount of Olives; then also the disciples followed him. 40 Then having come to the place, he said to them, "Pray not to enter into temptation."

41 And he withdrew from them about a stone's throw, and falling on his knees, he was praying, 42 saying, "Father, if you are willing, take away this cup from me. Yet not my will, but of you be done." 43 Then a messenger from heaven appeared to him, strengthening him. 44 And being in agony, he was praying more

intensely. And his sweat became like great drops of blood, falling down upon the ground.

45 And getting up from the prayer, coming to the disciples, he found them sleeping from sorrow, 46 and he said to them, "Why are you sleeping? Get up, pray that you might not enter into temptation."

47 While he was still speaking, look, a mob, and he who is called Judas, one of the Twelve, was leading them, and he came near to Jesus, to greet him with a kiss. 48 Then Jesus said to him, "Judas, do you deliver the Son of Man with a kiss of greeting?"

49 Then, having seen those around him, they said, "Master, should we strike with the sword?" 50 And a certain one of them struck the servant of the high priest, and cut off his right ear. 51 Now responding, Jesus said, "That is enough!" And touching the ear, he healed him.

52 Then Jesus said to those having come against him, chief priests and chief officers of the temple and elders, "Have you come as against a robber with swords and clubs? 53 Every day I was in the temple with you, and you did not lay hands on me. But this is your hour, and the power of darkness."

54 Then seizing him, they led him away, and led him into the house of the high priest; and Peter was following from afar.

55 Then they kindled a fire in the middle of the courtyard, and sat down together, and Peter was sitting among them. 56 Then a certain servant girl seeing him sitting by the light, and having looked intently at him, she said, "This one was also with him." 57 But he denied, saying, "Woman, I do not know him."

58 And after a little, another seeing him was saying, "You also are of them." But Peter was saying, "Man, I am not."

59 And about one hour having passed, a certain other strongly affirmed, saying, "Of a truth, this one was also with him, for he is also a Galilean." 60 But Peter said, "Man I know not what you say." And immediately while he was speaking, the rooster crowed. 61 And turning the Lord looked at Peter, and Peter remembered the word of the Lord, how he had said to him, "Before the rooster crows today, you will deny me three times." 62 And going outside, he wept bitterly.

63 And the men who are holding Jesus began mocking him, beating him. 64 And blindfolding him, they questioned him, saying, "Prophesy, who is the one striking you?" 65 And many other slanderous things, they kept on saying to him.

66 And when day came, the elder body of the people, they gathered together, both chief priests and scribes, and they led him into their council, saying, 67 "If you are the Christ, tell us." Now he said to them, "If I should tell you, you will never no never believe. 68

Now if I should ask you, by no means would you answer. 69 But from now the Son of Man will be sitting at the right hand of the power of God." 70 Then all said, "You then are the Son of God?" Then he said to them, "You rightly say that I am." 71 Then they said, "What need have we any more of witnesses? For we ourselves have heard it from his mouth."

LUKE TWENTY-THREE

1 And getting up, the entire multitude of them led him to Pilate. 2 Then they began to accuse him, saying, "We found this one misleading our nation and forbidding tribute to be given to Caesar, and saying himself to be Christ, a King."

3 Then Pilate questioned him, saying, "You are the king of the Jews?" Then answering him he was saying, "You rightly say." 4 Then Pilate said to the chief priests and the crowds, "I do not find guilt in this man." 5 Now they continued to insist, saying, "He stirs up the people, teaching throughout all of Judea, and he has begun from Galilee even to here." 6 Then Pilate, hearing this, asked if the man is a Galilean, 7 and having learned that he is from Herod's domain, he sent him to Herod, he himself also being in Jerusalem in those days.

8 Then Herod, seeing Jesus, was very glad, for he was a long time desiring to see him, because he had heard about him. And he was hoping to see some sign done by him. 9 Then Herod kept questioning him, with many words. But he answered him not a thing. 10 Now the chief priests and scribes had been standing nearby, vehemently accusing him. 11 Then Herod, with his soldiers, despised him. And having mocked him, putting on him splendid clothing, sent him back to Pilate. 12 Then both Herod and Pilate became friends with one another on that day, there having been enmity between them before that.

13 Then Pilate, calling together the chief priests and the leaders of the people, 14 said to them, "You brought me this man as misleading the people. And look, before you I have examined him. I found nothing in the man guilty of that accusation you brought against him. 15 No, not even Herod did, for he sent him back to us. And behold, nothing worthy of death is done by him. 16 Therefore, having chastised him, I will release him." [17ⁱⁱ]

18 But they all cried out together, saying, "Away with this man. Now release to us Barabbas," 19 who was on account of a certain insurrection made in the city, and murder, had been thrown into the prison. 20 Now again Pilate called to them, desiring to release Jesus. 21 But they were crying out, saying, "Crucify, crucify him." 22 Now a third time he said to them, "For what evil did this man commit? I found no cause of death in him. Therefore, having chastised him, I will release him."

23 But they were insistent,

with loud voices, asking for him to be crucified. And their voices were prevailing [ʲʲ]. 24 And Pilate adjudicated their demand to be done. 25 Then he released the one on account of insurrection and murder had been cast into prison, whom they asked for, and Jesus he delivered to their will.

26 And as they led him away, laying hold of Simon, a certain man of Cyrene, coming from the country, they put the cross upon Simon, to carry behind Jesus.

27 Now, a great crowd of the people were following Jesus, and of women who were beating their breasts and wailing for him. 28 Then turning to them, Jesus said, "Daughters of Jerusalem, lament not for me, but lament for yourselves, and for your children. 29 For behold, times are coming in which they will say, 'Blessed the barren, and the wombs that never did bear, and breasts that never nursed.' 30 Then they will begin to say to the mountains, 'Fall upon us,' and to the hills, 'Cover us.' 31 For if these things they do in the green tree, what might take place in the dry?"

32 Now also others, two criminals, were being led away with him to be put to death. 33 And when they came to the place called, "The Skull," there they crucified him and the criminals, one on the right, and one on the left. 34 Then Jesus was saying, "Father, forgive them, for they know not what they do." Then, dividing his clothing, they cast lots.

35 And the people stood, watching. Then also the leaders were mocking him, saying, "Others he saved, let him save himself, if this is the Christ of God, the Chosen." 36 Then also the soldiers mocked him, coming near, offering him sour wine, 37 and saying, "If you are the King of the Jews, save yourself." 38 Now there was also an inscription over him: "this is the King of the Jews."

39 Now one of the criminals being hanged was bad-mouthing him, saying, "Are you not the Christ? Save yourself and us!" 40 But the other, responding, rebuked him, saying, "Do you not even fear God, that you are under the same judgment, 41 and truly we justly? For we are receiving what we deserve for what we did. But this man did nothing wrong." 42 And he was saying, "Jesus, remember me when you come into your kingdom." 43 And Jesus said to him, "Truly[kk] I say to you, today you will be in Paradise with me."

44 Now it was about noon, and darkness came all over the land until about midafternoon. 45 The sunlight was failing; the veil of the temple was torn in the middle. 46 And calling out in a loud voice, Jesus said, "Father, into your hands I commit my spirit." Now having said this, he breathed his last.

47 Then the centurion having seen what happened, he began glorifying God, saying, "Certainly this man was righteous." 48 And all the crowds coming together to this

spectacle, having seen the things that took place, returned home beating their breasts. 49 Now all those who knew him stood far off, also women, those having followed him from Galilee, observing these things.

50 And look, a man named Joseph, a Council member, being also a good man and righteous—51 he did not consent to the counsel and their deed—from Arimathea, a city of the Jews, who was waiting for the kingdom of God. 52 He, going to Pilate, asked for the body of Jesus. 53 And taking it down, he wrapped it in a linen cloth and placed it in a tomb cut into a rock, in which no, no one, not yet had been laid. 54 And the day was of Preparation, and Sabbath was drawing near. 55 Then, having followed, the women who had come out of Galilee with him, saw the tomb and how his body was laid. 56 Then returning, they prepared spices and anointing oils. And indeed, on the Sabbath they rested according to the commandment.

LUKE TWENTY-FOUR

1 Now the first day of the week, earliest dawn, they came to the tomb, bringing spices that they had prepared. 2 Then they discovered the stone was rolled away from the tomb. 3 Then entering they did not find the body of the Lord Jesus. 4 And it happened while they were perplexed about this, that look, two men stood by them in shining clothing. 5 Now they became terrified of them and bowed their faces to the ground.

They said to them, "Why do you seek the living among the dead? 6 He is not here, but he is risen. Remember how he spoke to you, being yet in Galilee, 7 saying, 'The Son of Man must be delivered into the hands of sinful men, and to be crucified, and the third day to rise.'" 8 And they remembered his words.

9 And returning from the tomb, they declared all these things to the Eleven and to all the rest. 10 Now it was Mary the Magdalene, and Joanna, and Mary of Jacob, and the other women with them, telling these things to the apostles. 11 And their words seemed to them like an idle tale, and they did not believe them. 12 But Peter, getting up, ran to the tomb, and bending near, he sees only the linen strips of cloth. And he went away, wondering in himself what had happened.

13 And look, two of them on the same day were going to a distant village, seven miles from Jerusalem, whose name is Emmaus. 14 And they were talking with one another about all these things that had occurred. 15 And it happened in their talking and reasoning, that Jesus himself, drawing near, was walking with them. 16 But their eyes were held not to know him.

17 Then he said to them, "What words are these that you discuss with one another as you are walking? And they stopped,

looking sad. 18 Now responding, one named Cleopas said to him, "You alone visit Jerusalem and have not known the things that happened in it in these days?" 19 And he said to them, "What things?"

And they said to him, "The things concerning Jesus of Nazareth, who was a man, a prophet mighty in deed and word before God and all the people. 20 How then the chief priests and our leaders delivered him up to the judgment of death, and crucified him.

21 "But we were hoping it is he who is about to redeem Israel. But now also with all these things, this is the third day since these things happened. 22 But also certain women of ours astonished us, being early to the tomb. 23 And not finding his body, they came also declaring to have seen a vision of messengers, who say he is alive. 24 And some of those with us went to the tomb and found it so, as also the women said. Him, however, they did not see."

25 And he said to them, "Oh foolish and slow of heart to believe in all that the prophets have spoken. 26 Was it not necessary for the Christ to suffer and enter into his glory?" 27 And beginning from Moses and from all the prophets, he clearly and exactly explained to them in all the Scriptures the things concerning himself.

28 And they drew near to the village where they were going, and he seemed to be going further. 29 And they persuaded him, saying, "Abide with us, for it is toward evening, and now the day has declined." And he entered to abide with them. 30 And it happened in his reclining *to eat* with them, having taken the bread, he blessed it, and breaking it, he began giving it to them. 31 Then their eyes were opened, and they knew him. And he vanished from their sight.

32 And they said to one another, "Was not our heart burning within us as he was speaking with us on the road, as he opened the Scriptures?" 33 And getting up that same hour, they returned to Jerusalem, and they found the Eleven gathered together and those with them, 34 saying, "Truly the Lord has risen and he has appeared to Simon." 35 And they began telling the things on the road, and how he was known to them in the breaking of the bread.

36 Now, as they were telling them these things, Jesus himself stood among them, and said to them, "Peace to you." 37 But being frightened and filled with fear, they were thinking to see a spirit.

38 And he said to them, "Why are you troubled and why do doubts continue in your hearts? 39 See my hands and my feet, that I am he. Touch me and see, because a spirit has not flesh and bones, as you see me having. 40 And having said this, he showed to them the hands and the feet. 41 Now still, while they were unbelieving for the joy and

amazement, he said to them, "Have you anything here to eat?" 42 And they gave to him part of a broiled fish. 43 And taking it, he ate before them.

44 Now he said to them, "These are my words which I spoke to you still being with you, that all things must be fulfilled written in the Law of Moses and the prophets and the Psalms concerning me." 45 Then he opened their mind to understand the Scriptures.

46 And he said to them, "Thus it has been written: the Christ was to suffer, and rise out from the dead the third day, 47 and to be proclaimed in his name repentance and forgiveness of sins to all nations, beginning from Jerusalem. 48 You are witnesses of these things. 49 And look, I am sending the promise of my Father upon you. But you remain in the city until you should be clothed with power from on high."

50 Now he led them out as far as to Bethany, and lifting up his hands, he blessed them. 51 And it happened in his blessing them, he was separated from them and was carried up into heaven. 52 And they having worshiped him, returned to Jerusalem with great joy, 53 and they were continually all in the temple blessing God.

The Book of John

The good news according to John was written and published ca. AD 95–96. John states his purpose at 21:31. A comparison of John to Matthew, Mark, and Luke reveals John focused on details not found in those three accounts, specifically events and discourses that took place before the Galilean ministry, and in the later Judean ministry. John reports Jesus' AD 33 Passover discourses. John's good news does not have an eschatological discourse, but does declare the return of Christ for his NT church. In an epilogue, John 21, Jesus tells the NT church what it is to do until his return, "You follow me," 21:22. John's message may be summarized as "believe to be saved and then follow Christ."

JOHN ONE

1 In the beginning was the Word and the Word was with God and God was the Word. 2 He was in the beginning with God. 3 All things through him came into existence, and without him not even one came into existence that has come into existence. 4 In Him was life, and the life was the light of men. 5 And the light in the darkness shines, and the darkness could not comprehend it.

6 There came a man sent from God. His name was John. 7 He came for a witness that he should testify concerning the light, that through him all might believe. 8 He was not the light, but that he should testify concerning the light.

9 The true light is the one that coming into the world enlightens every person. 10 He was in the world: and the world came into existence through him; and the world knew him not. 11 He came to his own possessions, and his own people did not receive him. 12 But as many as did receive him—those believing on his name—he gave to them authority to be children of God: 13 who not of bloods, nor of will of flesh, nor of will of man, but of God were born.

14 And the Word became embodied[a1] and dwelt among us. And we saw his glory—glory as of a one and only begotten with the Father, full of grace and truth. 15 John did testify concerning him, and cried out, saying, "This was the one of whom I said, 'He who comes after me is before me because he was before me.'" 16 That out of his fullness we all received, even grace instead of grace,[a2] 17 because the Law was given through Moses; the grace and the truth came through Jesus Christ. 18 No one has ever seen God. The one and only begotten Son being in the bosom of the Father, he declared him.

19 And this is John the Immerser's testimony when the Jews sent to him priests and Levites from Jerusalem so that they might ask him, "Who are you?" 20 And he confessed and did not deny but confessed, "I am not the Christ." 21 And they asked him, "What then, are you Elijah?" And

he said to them, "I am not." "Are you the Prophet?" And he answered, "No." 22 Therefore they said to him, "Who are you?" that we might give an answer to the ones having sent us. What say you about yourself?" 23 He said: "I am, 'a voice crying in the wilderness: make straight the way of the Lord,' as the prophet Isaiah said."

24 And they had been sent from the Pharisees. 25 And they asked him and said to him, "Why then immerse if you are not the Christ, nor Elijah, nor the Prophet?"

26 John answered them, saying, "I immerse in water, but in your midst stands whom you do not know. 27 This is he who comes after me, who was before me, of whom I am not worthy that I should loose the string of his sandal." 28 These things took place in Bethabara across the Jordan, where John was immersing.

29 On the next day John sees Jesus coming toward him and says, "Behold God's lamb, he who takes away the sin of the world! 30 This is he about whom I said, 'After me comes a man who is before me, because he was before me.' 31 And I knew him not; but that he should be revealed to Israel, therefore I came immersing in water."

32 And John bore witness, saying, "I saw the Spirit descending as a dove out of heaven, and it remained upon him. 33 And I knew him not, but the one sending me to immerse in water that one said to me, 'On whom you see the Spirit descending, and abiding on him, this is the one immersing in Holy Spirit.' 34 And I have seen and have borne witness that this is God's son."[a3]

35 On the next day, John was again standing, and out of his disciples two; 36 and looking at Jesus as he walked, he said, "Behold the lamb of God!" 37 And the two disciples heard him speak, and followed Jesus.

38 Then Jesus turned, and seeing them following, said to them, "What do you seek?" And they said to him, "Rabbi" (which is to say, when translated, teacher), "where are you staying?" 39 He said to them, "Come and you will see." They came and saw where he was staying, and remained with him that day (now it was about four p.m.).

40 One of the two who heard John speak and followed Jesus was Andrew, Simon Peter's brother. 41 He first found his own brother Simon, and said to him, "We have found the Messiah" (which is translated, Christ). 42 And he brought him to Jesus. Having looked at him Jesus said, "You are Simon the son of Jonah. You shall be called Cephas" (which translated is Peter).

43 On the next day Jesus wanted to go into Galilee. And he found Philip, and said to him, "Follow Me." 44 Now Philip was from Bethsaida-Galilee, the city of Andrew and Peter. 45 Philip found Nathanael and said to him, "We

have found him of whom Moses in the Law, and also the prophets, wrote—Jesus the son of Joseph, who is from Nazareth." 46 And Nathanael said to him, "Can anything good come out of Nazareth?" Philip said to him, "Come and see."

47 Jesus saw Nathanael coming toward him, and said of him, "Behold, a true Israelite, in whom is no deceit!" 48 Nathanael said to him, "How do you know me?" Jesus answered and said to him, "Before Philip called you, when you were under the fig tree, I saw you." 49 Nathanael answered him, "Rabbi, you are the son of God! You are king of Israel!"

50 Jesus responded and said to him, "Because I said to you, 'I saw you under the fig tree,' do you believe? You will see greater things than these." 51 And he said to him, "I tell you the truth,^{a4} you shall see the heaven opened, and God's messengers ascending and descending upon the Son of Man."

JOHN TWO

1 And on the third day a wedding was in Cana of Galilee, and the mother of Jesus was there. 2 Now Jesus and his disciples were invited to the wedding. 3 And wanting wine, the mother of Jesus said to him, "They have not wine." 4 And Jesus said to her, "What *is that* to me and to you, woman? My hour has not yet come."

5 His mother said to the servants, "Whatever thing he may say to you, do." 6 Now there were in that place six waterpots of stone, according to the Jewish process of purification, each with space for about sixteen or twenty-five gallons. 7 Jesus said to them, "Fill the waterpots with water." And they filled them up to the brim. 8 And he said to them, "Draw out now and take to the master of the feast." And they took it.

9 Now when the master of the feast had tasted the water made wine, and did not know from where it came (but the servants knew, having drawn the water), the master of the feast called the bridegroom. 10 And he said to him, "Every man at the first sets out the good wine, and when the guests have drunk freely, the inferior. You have kept the good wine until now!" 11 This beginning of the signs, Jesus did in Cana of Galilee, and openly showed his glory; and his disciples believed on him.

12 After these things he went down to Capernaum, he and his mother, and his brethren, and his disciples; and they did not stay there many days.

13 Now the Passover of the Jews was near, and Jesus went up to Jerusalem. 14 And he found in the temple those selling oxen and sheep and doves, and the money changers sitting. 15 And having made a whip of cords, he drove all out of the temple, both sheep and the oxen; and poured out the coins of the money-changers, and overturned the tables. 16 And he said to those selling doves, "Take these things out of here. Do not

make my Father's house a market house." 17 His disciples remembered that it is written, "The zeal of your house will consume me."

18 Therefore the Jews responded and said to him, "What sign do you show to us, that you do these things?" 19 Jesus answered and said to them, "Destroy this temple and in three days I will raise it up." 20 Therefore the Jews said, "Forty and six years was this temple in building, and you in three days will raise it up?" 21 But he spoke about the temple of his body. 22 Therefore, when he was raised out from the dead, his disciples remembered that he had said this, and believed the Scripture and the word that Jesus had spoken.

23 Now when he was in Jerusalem at the Passover, during the feast, many believed in his name when they saw the signs which he did. 24 But Jesus, he did not entrust himself to them, because he knew all, 25 and that he had no need that any should testify about the human nature, for he knew what was in the human nature.

JOHN THREE

1 Now there was a man of the Pharisees, Nicodemus was his name, a leader of the Jews. 2 He came to him by night and said to him, "Rabbi, we know that you have come from God, a teacher; for no one is able to do these signs that you do if God should not be with him."

3 Jesus responded and said to him, "I tell you the truth, if anyone be not born from above, he is not able to see the kingdom of God." 4 Nicodemus said to him, "How is a man able to be born being old? He is not able to enter into the womb of his mother a second time and be born, is he?"

5 Answered Jesus, "I tell you the truth, if anyone be not born of water and of spirit, he is not able to enter into the kingdom of God. 6 That which is born of the flesh is flesh; and that which is born of the Spirit is spirit. 7 Do not wonder that I said to you it is necessary for you to be born from above. 8 The wind blows where it pleases, and you hear its sound, but do not know from where it comes and where it goes. So is everyone having been born of the Spirit."

9 Nicodemus responded and said to him, "How are these things able to be?"

10 Jesus answered and said to him, "You are the teacher of Israel and do not know these things? 11 I tell you the truth, that which we know, we speak, and that which we have seen, we bear witness; and our witness you do not receive. 12 If I have told to you the earthly, and you do not believe, how will you believe if I tell to you the heavenly? 13 And no one has ascended into heaven but only he having come down out of heaven, the Son of Man who is in heaven. 14 And even as Moses lifted up the serpent in the wilderness, so it is necessary the Son of Man be lifted

up, 15 that everyone believing in him may not perish but have eternal life.

16 "For God so loved the world that he gave the Son, the only begotten, that everyone believing in him should not perish but may have eternal life. 17 For God did not send his Son into the world to judge the world, but that the world through him might be saved.

18 "The person believing on him is not judged; the one not believing has been judged already, because he has not believed on the name of the only begotten Son of God. 19 Now this is the judgment, that the light has come into the world, and men loved the darkness rather than the light; for their works were evil. 20 For everyone habitually doing evil hates the light and comes not to the light, that his works might not be exposed. 21 But the person habitually doing the truth comes to the light, that his works may be known, that they have been done in God."

22 After these things, Jesus and his disciples came into the land of Judea; and he stayed there with them, and was immersing. 23 Now John also was immersing, in Aenon near Salim, because there was much water there; and they were coming and being immersed, 24 because John had not yet been cast into prison.

25 Then an argument occurred among John's disciples with some Jews about purification. 26 And they came to John and said to him, "Rabbi, he who was with you beyond the Jordan, to whom you bore witness—behold, he immerses, and all come to him!"

27 John responded and said, "A person is not able to receive anything, except it has been given to him from heaven. 28 You yourselves bear witness to me, that I said, 'I am not the Christ,' but that, 'I am sent before him.' 29 The one having the bride is the bridegroom. Now the friend of the bridegroom, the one standing and hearing him, rejoices with joy because of the voice of the bridegroom. Therefore in this my joy is fulfilled. 30 He must increase, but I decrease."

31 The one coming from above is above all. The one being from the earth is from the earth, and from the earth speaks. He coming from heaven is above all. 32 And what he has seen and heard, this he testifies; and no one receives his testimony. 33 The one having received his testimony has attested that God is true. 34 For whom God sent speaks the words of God; for not by measure he gives the Spirit. 35 The Father loves the Son, and has given all things into his hand. 36 The one believing on the Son has eternal life; but the one not believing the Son will not see life, but the wrath of God abides on him.

JOHN FOUR

1 When therefore the Lord knew that the Pharisees heard that Jesus made and immersed more disciples than John 2 (although Jesus himself was not immersing,

but his disciples), 3 he left Judea and went away again into Galilee. 4 But it was necessary he go through Samaria.

5 He came therefore to a city of Samaria named Sychar, near the plot of ground that Jacob had given to Joseph his son. 6 Now Jacob's well was there. Therefore Jesus, being worn out from his journey, sat down by the well. It was about noon. 7 A Samaritan woman came to draw water. Jesus said to her, "Give me a drink" 8 (because his disciples had gone into the city that they might buy food).

9 Therefore the Samaritan woman said to him, "How do you being a Jew, ask from a woman being a Samaritan, a drink?" For Jews do not ask anything from Samaritans.

10 Jesus answered and said to her, "If you had known[a5] the gift of God, and who it is saying to you, 'Give me a drink,' you would have asked him, and he would have given to you living water."

11 The woman said to him, "Sir, you have nothing to draw with and the well is deep. From where then have you the living water? 12 Are you greater than our father Jacob who gave us the well, and drank from it himself, and his sons and his livestock?"

13 Jesus answered and said to her, "Every person drinking of this water will thirst again, 14 but any person that might drink of the water that I will give him will never no never thirst, even to forever. But the water that I will give him will become in him a well of water springing up into life eternal."

15 The woman said to him, "Sir, give me this water, that I might not thirst, nor come here to draw." 16 Jesus said to her, "Go call your husband, and come here." 17 The woman responded and said, "I have not a husband." Jesus said to her, "You have spoken rightly, 'I have not a husband'; 18 for five husbands you have had, and now he whom you have is not your husband; this you have spoken in truth."

19 The woman said to him, "Sir, I perceive that you are a prophet. 20 Our fathers worshiped on this mountain, and Jews[b] say that in Jerusalem is the place where it is necessary to worship."

21 Jesus said to her, "Believe me woman, that an hour is coming when neither on this mountain nor in Jerusalem will you worship the Father. 22 Samaritans[c] worship what you know not; we *Jews* worship what we know, because salvation is from the Jews. 23 But an hour is coming and now is when the true worshipers will worship the Father in spirit and truth; yes, the Father seeks such as those to worship him. 24 God is Spirit, and those worshiping him must worship in spirit and truth."

25 The woman said to him, "I know that Messiah is coming, who is called Christ; when he comes he will tell us all things." 26 Jesus said to her, "I am he who is speaking to you."

27 And upon this came his disciples, and marveled that he was speaking with a woman; however, no one said, "What seek you?" or, "Why speak you with her?"

28 The woman then left her waterpot, and went away into the village, and said to the men, 29 "Come see a man who told me all things whatever I did. Is it possible this is the Christ?" 30 They went out of the city and came to him.

31 In the meantime his disciples were saying, "Rabbi, eat." 32 But he said to them, "I have food to eat that you know not." 33 Therefore the disciples said to one another, "Anyone did not bring him anything to eat, did they?"

34 Jesus said to them, "My food is that I should do the will of the one who sent me, and should finish his work. 35 Say you not that it is yet four months and the harvest comes? Behold, I say to you, lift up your eyes, and see the fields, for they are already white toward harvest. 36 The one reaping receives a reward[d] and gathers fruit unto life eternal, that the one sowing and the one reaping might rejoice together. 37 For in this the saying is true: 'That one is sowing and another reaping.' 38 I sent you to reap what you did not work for; others have worked, and you enter into their works."

39 Now out of the village many of the Samaritans believed in him through the word of the woman testifying: "because he told me all things whatever I did." 40 When therefore the Samaritans came to him, they asked him to continue with them; and he stayed there two days. 41 And many more believed through his word. 42 To the woman they said, "No longer through your word do we believe. For we ourselves have heard, and we know that this is truly the Savior of the world, the Christ."

43 Now after the two days he went out from there into Galilee. 44 For Jesus himself testified that a prophet has no honor in his own country. 45 When therefore he came into Galilee, the Galileans received him, having seen all the great things he had done in Jerusalem during the feast; for they themselves had also gone to the feast.

46 Therefore Jesus came again to Cana of Galilee, where he had made the water wine. And there was a certain court official whose son was sick in Capernaum. 47 He having heard that Jesus had come out of Judea into Galilee, went to him and asked that he would come down and heal his son; for he was about to die. 48 Therefore Jesus said to him, "If no signs and wonders you see, you will never no never believe."

49 The court official said to him, "Sir, come down before my child dies!" 50 Jesus said to him, "Go, your son lives." The man believed the word that Jesus said to him, and went away.

51 Now already as he is going down his servants met him, saying his child lives. 52 Therefore he

asked from them the hour in which he got better. Therefore they said to him, "Yesterday about one p.m. the fever left him." 53 Therefore the father knew that *it was* there in the hour in which Jesus said to him, "Your son lives." And he himself believed, and his whole household. 54 Now this is again the second sign Jesus did having come out of Judea into Galilee.

JOHN FIVE

1 After these things was a feast of the Jews, and Jesus went up to Jerusalem. 2 Now there is in Jerusalem at the Sheep Gate[e] a pool, called in the Hebrew language, Bethesda, having five porches. 3 In these were lying a multitude of the sick, blind, lame, paralyzed, awaiting the moving of the water. 4 For a messenger, at a season, descended into the pool and stirred the water. The person therefore *who* first entered after the stirring of the water was made well from whatever disease he was held by at the time.

5 Now there was a certain man there, himself being in sickness thirty and eight years. 6 Jesus, having seen him lying, and having known that he has been already a long time, said to him, "Do you want to become well?" 7 The sick man answered him, "Sir, I have not a man, that when the water has been stirred, he might put me into the pool; but when I am going another before me descends." 8 Jesus said to him, "Rise, lift up your bed, and walk." 9 And immediately the man became well, and lifted his bed, and walked. And it was Sabbath on that day.

10 Therefore the Jews said to the one having been healed, "Sabbath it is, and it is not lawful for you to lift up your bed." 11 Then he answered them. "The one having made me well, he said to me, 'Lift up your bed and walk.'" 12 Therefore they asked him, "Who is the man, the one having said to you, 'Lift up your bed and walk'?" 13 Now the person who had been healed knew not who it was, for Jesus had withdrawn, a crowd being in the place.

14 After these things Jesus found him in the temple, and said to him, "See, you have become well. Sin no more, that something worse does not happen to you." 15 The man went away and told the Jews that Jesus was the one who had made him well. 16 And because of this the Jews persecuted Jesus, and sought to kill him, because he did these things on a Sabbath. 17 But Jesus responded to them, "My Father is working up to the present moment, and I am working." 18 Because of this, then, the Jews sought the more to kill him, because he not only was breaking the Sabbath, but also he called God his own father, making himself equal with God.

19 Jesus, then, responded and said to them, "I tell you the truth, the Son can do nothing of himself, except anything he might see the Father doing; for whatever he does, these things also the Son in

The Book of John

like manner does. 20 For the Father loves the Son, and shows all things to him that he himself does; and greater works than these he will show him, so that you might marvel. 21 For even as the Father raises the dead and gives life, thus also the Son gives life to whom he will. 22 For the Father from this time judges not even one,[f] but has given all judgment to the Son, 23 that all may honor the Son even as they honor the Father. The one not honoring the Son is not honoring the Father who sent him.

24 "I tell you the truth, that the person hearing my word and believing the One who sent me, has eternal life, and comes not into judgment, but has passed out of death into life.

25 "I tell you the truth, that an hour is coming, and now is, when the dead will hear the voice of the Son of God, and those having heard will live. 26 For as the Father has life-in-himself, so also to the Son he gave life to have in himself, 27 and he gave to him authority to execute judgment, because he is Son of Man. 28 Do not marvel at this, because an hour is coming in which all those in the grave will hear his voice 29 and will come forth: the ones having practiced good, to resurrection of life; the ones habitually doing evil, to resurrection of judgment.[g]

30 "I am not able of myself to do anything. Even as I hear, I judge; and my judgment is just, because I seek not my will, but the will of the One having sent me. 31 If I bear testimony about myself, my testimony is not true. 32 Another it is who is giving testimony about me, and I know that the testimony which he gives is true testimony about me.

33 "You have sent to John and he has borne testimony to the truth. 34 Now I do not receive the testimony from man, but I say these things that you might be saved. 35 He was the burning and shining lamp, and you were willing to rejoice for a season in his light. 36 But I have the testimony greater than that of John. For works that the Father has given me that I should complete them, the same works that I do bear testimony about me, that the Father has sent me.

37 "And the One having sent me, the Father himself, has testified about me. Not at any time have you heard his voice, nor have you seen his form. 38 And his word you do not have abiding in you, because the One he sent, you do not believe him. 39 You all[h] search the Scriptures, because you all think in them to have eternal life; yet they are testifying about me. 40 And you all are not willing to come to me that you may have life.

41 "I do not receive glory from men. 42 But I know you, that the love of God you have not in yourselves. 43 I have come in the name of my Father, and you do not receive me. If another should come in his own name, him you will receive. 44 How are you able to believe, receiving praise from one

another? But the praise that is from the only God you do not seek.

45 "Think not that I will accuse you to the Father. There is one accusing you: Moses, in whom you set your hope. 46 For if you believed Moses you would believe me, for he wrote about me. 47 But if you do not believe his writings, how will you believe my words?"

JOHN SIX

1 After these things Jesus went away over the Sea of Galilee (of Tiberius). 2 Now a great crowd followed him, because they saw the signs which he did on those with sickness. 3 And Jesus went up into the mountain, and there sat with his disciples. 4 Now the Passover was near, the feast of the Jews.

5 Then Jesus, having lifted up his eyes, and having seen that a great crowd is coming to him, said to Philip, "From where may we buy bread that these might eat?" 6 Now this he said testing him; for he knew what he was about to do.

7 Philip responded to him, "Two hundred denarii of bread is not sufficient to them that each one might receive a little." 8 Said to him one of his disciples, Andrew, the brother of Simon Peter, 9 "Here is a little boy who has five barley bread and two small fish; but what are these for so many?"

10 Jesus said, "Make the men recline *to eat.*"[j] Now there was much grass in the place. Therefore the men reclined *to eat*, the number about five thousand. 11 Now Jesus took the bread, and having given thanks, distributed to the disciples and the disciples to those reclining; and likewise of the fish, as much as they desired.

12 Now when they were full, he said to his disciples, "Gather together the fragments remaining, that not anything may be lost." 13 Therefore they gathered together and filled twelve hand-baskets with fragments from the five barley bread which remained to those having eaten.

14 Therefore the men, having seen what sign he had done, said, "This is truly the prophet who is coming into the world." 15 Therefore Jesus, knowing they are about to come and seize him that they may make him king, departed again to the mountain himself alone.

16 Now when it became evening, his disciples went down to the sea, 17 and having entered into a boat, they were going over the sea to Capernaum. And it had already become dark, and Jesus had not come to them. 18 And the sea was agitated by a strong wind blowing.

19 Now having rowed about three miles,[k] they see Jesus walking on the sea and coming near the boat; and they were terrified. 20 But he said to them, "It is I, fear not." 21 Then they were willing to receive him into the boat, and immediately the boat was at the land to which they were going.

22 On the next day, the crowd standing on the other side of the

sea, having previously seen there was no other boat there except one (the one into which his disciples entered), and that Jesus had not entered the boat with his disciples, but his disciples went away alone—23 but other boats came from Tiberius, near the place where they ate bread, the Lord having given thanks—24 therefore when the crowd saw that Jesus is not there, nor his disciples, they themselves entered into the boats, and came to Capernaum, seeking Jesus.

25 And having found him on the other side of the sea, they said to him, "Rabbi, when did you get here?" 26 Jesus answered them and said, "I tell you the truth, you seek me, not because you saw signs, but because you ate of the bread and were filled. 27 Labor not for the food perishing, but for the food enduring unto eternal life, which the Son of Man will give to you, for him the Father sealed, even God."

28 Therefore they said to him, "What may we do, that we might be doing the works of God?" 29 Jesus answered and said to them, "This is the work of God, that you should believe in him whom he sent." 30 Therefore they said to him, "Then what sign do you that we might see and may believe you? What do you work? 31 Our fathers ate the manna in the wilderness, as it is written, 'He gave them bread out of heaven to eat.'"

32 Therefore Jesus said to them, "I tell you the truth, Moses has not given you the bread out of heaven, but my Father gives you the true bread out of heaven. 33 For the bread of God is the one coming out of heaven and giving life to the world." 34 Therefore they said to him, "Sir, always give to us this the bread."[l]

35 Jesus said to them, "I, I am[m] the bread of life. The one coming to me may never no never hunger, and he believing in me shall never no never thirst at any time.

36 "But I said to you that also you have seen me and do not believe. 37 All those the Father gives me will come to me, and the one coming to me I will never no never cast out. 38 For I have come down out of heaven, not that I may do my own will, but the will of him having sent me. 39 Now this is the will of him having sent me, that all that he has given me, I may lose none of it, but may raise it up at the last day. 40 For this is the will of the One sending me, that everyone seeing the Son and believing on him may have eternal life; and I will raise him up at the last day."

41 Therefore the Jews were complaining about him, because he said, "I am the bread having come down out of heaven." 42 And they were saying, "Is this not Jesus, the son of Joseph, of whom we know his father and his mother? How therefore is he saying, 'I have come down out of heaven'?"

43 Jesus answered and said to them, "Do not complain among one another. 44 No one is able to come to me unless the Father, the one having sent me, draws him, and I will raise him up at the last day. 45 It is written in the prophets, 'And they will all be taught of God.' Everyone having heard from the Father and having learned comes to me. 46 Not that anyone has seen the Father, except the one who is from God; he has seen the Father.

47 "I tell you the truth, the one believing has eternal life. 48 I, I am the bread of life. 49 Your fathers ate the manna in the wilderness, and died. 50 This is the bread coming down out of heaven that anyone might eat of it and not die. 51 I, I am the living bread having come down out of heaven. If anyone may eat of this bread he will live forever; and the bread also that I will give is my flesh, which I will give for the life of the world."

52 Therefore the Jews were arguing with one another, saying, "How is he able to give us his flesh to eat?" 53 Therefore Jesus said to them, "I tell you the truth, except you may have eaten the flesh of the Son of Man and may have drunk his blood, you have no life in yourselves. 54 The one eating my flesh and drinking my blood has eternal life, and I will raise him up in the last day. 55 For my flesh truly is food and my blood truly is drink. 56 The one eating my flesh and drinking my blood abides in me and I in him.

57 "As the living Father sent me, and I live because of the Father, also the one feeding on me, even that person will live because of me. 58 This is the bread having come down out of heaven. Not as your fathers ate the manna and died. The one eating this bread will live forever." 59 These things he said in a synagogue, teaching in Capernaum.

60 Many, therefore, of his disciples, having heard said, "This word is hard; who is able to understand it?"

61 But Jesus, knowing in himself that his disciples are complaining about this, said to them, "Does this offend you? 62 What if, then, you should see the Son of Man ascending where he was before?

63 "The Spirit, he is giving life; the flesh profits nothing. The words that I speak to you are spirit, and they are life. 64 But there are of you some who believe not." (For from the beginning Jesus knew who those are not believing, and who it is who will betray him.) 65 And he said, "Because of this I have said to you, that no one is able to come to me except it may have been given to him from the Father."

66 From that *time* many out of his disciples turned back and no longer walked with him. 67 Therefore Jesus said to the Twelve, "Do you also desire to go away?"

68 Simon Peter answered him, "Master, to whom will we go? You have the words of eternal life. 69

And we have believed and have known that you are the holy one of God."ᵐ

70 Jesus answered them. "Did not I choose you, the Twelve, and one of you is a devil?" 71 But he spoke of Judas of Simon Iscariot, one of the Twelve, for he was about to betray him.

JOHN SEVEN

1 After these things Jesus was walking in Galilee; for he did not desire to walk in Judea, because the Jews were seeking to kill him. 2 Now the feast of the Jews, of Tabernacles, was near.

3 Therefore his brethren said to him, "Depart from here, and go into Judea, that also your disciples will see your works that you are doing. 4 For no one does anything in secret, and himself seeks to be in public. If you do these things, show yourself to the world." 5 For not even his brethren were believing in him.

6 Therefore Jesus said to them, "My time has not yet come, but your time is always ready. 7 The world is not able to hate you, but me it hates, because I bear testimony about it, that its works are evil. 8 You go up to the feast. I am not yet going up to the feast, for my time has not yet been fulfilled." 9 And having said these things to them, he remained in Galilee.

10 Now when his brethren had gone up to the feast, then he also went up, not openly, but as in secret. 11 The Jews, then, were seeking him, and said at the feast, "Where is he?" 12 And there was much complaining about him in the crowds. Indeed some said, "He is good"; but others said, "No; on the contrary, he is deceiving the people." 13 However, no one publicly spoke about him, because they were afraid of the Jews.

14 Now, about the middle of the feast, Jesus went up into the temple, and was teaching. 15 Then the Jews were marveling, saying, "How does this one know learning, having never studied?" 16 Therefore Jesus answered them and said, "My teaching is not of myself, but of the One having sent me. 17 If anyone desires to practice his will, he will know about the teaching, whether it is from God, or I speak from myself. 18 The one speaking from himself seeks his own glory; but the one seeking the glory of the One having sent him, he is true and no unrighteousness is in him.

19 "Did not Moses give to you the Law, yet not one of you keeps the Law? Why do you seek to kill me?" 20 The crowd responded, "You have a demon. Who seeks to kill you?" 21 Jesus answered and said to them, "One work I did, and you all marvel 22 because of this.º Moses has given you circumcision—not that it is of Moses, it is of the fathers—and on a Sabbath you circumcise a man. 23 If a man receives circumcision on a Sabbath, that the Law of Moses might not be broken, are you angry with me because I made a man completely well on a

Sabbath? 24 Judge not according to appearance, but judge the righteous judgment."

25 Therefore some of those of Jerusalem said, "Is this not he whom they seek to kill? 26 But look! He speaks freely, and they say nothing to him, not ever. Do those who rule truly know that this is the Christ? 27 But this one we know from where he is; but the Christ, whenever he might come, no one knows from where he is."

28 Jesus cried out, therefore, in the temple, teaching and saying, "You know me, and you know from where I am. And of myself I have not come, but the One having sent me is true, whom you do not know. 29 I know him, because I am from him and he sent me." 30 Therefore they were seeking to take him; but no one laid a hand upon him, because his hour had not yet come.

31 Now many of the crowd believed on him, and said, "The Christ—when he may come—he will not do more signs than this man has done, will he?" 32 The Pharisees heard the crowd's muttering these things about him, and the chief priests and the Pharisees sent temple police,ᵖ that these might seize him. 33 Therefore Jesus said, "Yet a little time I am with you, and I go away to the One having sent me. 34 You will seek me, and will not find me; and where I am you are not able to come."

35 Therefore the Jews said among themselves, "Where is he about to go that we will not find him? Is he about to go to the Dispersed among the Greeks, and to teach the Greeks? 36 What is this word that he said, 'You will seek me and will not find me'; and 'Where I am you are not able to come'?"

37 Now in the last day, the great *day* of the feast, Jesus stood and cried out, saying, "If anyone thirsts, let him come to me and drink. 38 The person believing on me, as the Scripture has said, rivers of living water will flow out of his heart."ᵠ 39 But this he said about the Spirit, whom those having believed on him were about to receive; for the Holy Spirit was not yet given, because Jesus was not yet glorified.

40 Therefore some of the crowd having heard these words, said, "This is truly the prophet." 41 Others said, "This is the Christ." But some said, "Surely the Christ does not come out of Galilee? 42 Has not the Scripture said that out of the seed of David, and from Bethlehem, the village where David was, comes the Christ?" 43 Therefore the crowd was divided because of him. 44 Now some of them wanted to seize him, but no one laid hands on him.

45 Then the temple police returned to the chief priests and Pharisees. And they said to them, "What is the reason you did not bring him?" 46 The temple police responded, "No man ever spoke like this." 47 Then the Pharisees answered them, "Have you not

also been deceived? 48 Not any of the rulers has believed on him, or of the Pharisees, have they? 49 But this crowd, not knowing the Law, they are accursed."

50 Nicodemus (the one having previously come by night to him, being one of them) said to them, 51 "Our Law does not judge a man if it has not first heard from him, and known what he does, does it?" 52 They answered and said to him, "You are not also from Galilee, are you? Search and see that out of Galilee a prophet is not raised." 53 And each went to his house. 8:1 But Jesus went to the Mount of Olives.

JOHN EIGHT

2 Now early in the morning he came again into the temple, and all the people came to him; and having sat down he was teaching them.

3 Now the scribes and the Pharisees brought unto him a woman having been caught in adultery.[r1] And having set her in the midst, 4 they said to him, "Teacher, this woman was caught in the very act, committing adultery. 5 Now in the Law Moses commanded us that such be stoned; you therefore, what say you?" 6 But this they said, testing him, that they might have *some excuse*[2] to accuse him.

But Jesus, having stooped down, with his finger wrote on the ground. 7 Now as they continued asking him, and having raised himself up, he said to them, "The person who is sinless among you, let him throw the first[s] stone at her." 8 And again having stooped down, he wrote on the ground.

9 Now those having heard, they went out one by one, having begun from the eldest; and he was left alone, and the woman being in the midst.[t] 10 Now Jesus having raised up said to her, "Woman, where are *your accusers*? Has no one condemned you?" 11 Then she said, "No one, Sir."[u] Then Jesus said, "Neither do I condemn you; go and sin no more."

12 Then Jesus spoke to them again, saying, "I, I am the light of the world. The person habitually following me will never no never walk in the darkness, but will have the light of life."

13 Therefore the Pharisees said to him, "You testify about yourself; your testimony is not true." 14 Jesus answered and said to them, "Even if I am testifying about myself, my testimony is true because I know from where I came and where I go; but you know not from where I come or where I go.

15 "You judge according to the flesh; I am not judging anyone. 16 And yet if I judge, my judgment is true because I am not alone, but I and the Father having sent me. 17 Also in your Law it has been written the testimony of two men is true. 18 I am the one testifying about myself and the Father having sent me testifies about me."

19 Therefore they said to him, "Where is your Father?" Jesus answered, "You know neither me

nor my Father. If you had known me, also my Father you would have known." 20 These words Jesus spoke in the treasury, teaching in the temple; and no one laid hold of him, for his hour had not yet come.

21 Jesus said to them again, "I am going away, and you will seek me, and in your sin you will die. Where I go you are not able to come." 22 Then the Jews said, "He will not kill himself, will he, because he says, 'Where I go you are not able to come'?"

23 And he said to them, "You are from below; I am from above. You are of this world; I am not of this world. 24 Therefore I said to you, that you will die in your sins; for if you do not believe that I am, you will die in your sins."

25 Therefore they said to him, "You, who are *you*?" Jesus said to them, "What also I am saying to you from the beginning. 26 Many things I have to say and to judge concerning you; but the One having sent me is true, and I, what I have heard from him, these things I say in the world." 27 They understood not that to them he spoke of the Father.

28 Therefore Jesus said to them, "When you shall have lifted up the Son of Man, then you will know that I am, and from myself I do nothing, but as the Father taught me, these things I speak. 29 And the One having sent me is with me. The Father has not left me alone, because I always do the things pleasing to him." 30 As he was speaking many believed in him.

31 Jesus therefore said to those having believed in him, "If you abide in my word, you are truly my disciples. 32 And you will know the truth, and the truth will set you free." 33 They responded to him, "We are Abraham's descendants, and to no one have we been in bondage ever; by what means say you, 'You will become free'?"

34 Jesus answered them, "I tell you the truth, that everyone practicing sin is a slave of sin. 35 But the slave does not abide in the house forever; the son abides forever. 36 If therefore the Son shall set you free, you will be free indeed. 37 I know that you are Abraham's descendants, but you seek to kill me, because my word does not receive a place in you. 38 That which I have seen with the Father, I speak; and you therefore do what you have seen with your father."

39 They answered and said to him, "Our father is Abraham." Jesus said to them, "If Abraham's children you were, the works of Abraham you would do; 40 but now you seek to kill me, a man who has spoken the truth to you that I heard from God. Abraham did not do this. 41 You are doing the works of your father." Then they said to him, "We have not been born of sexual immorality; we have one Father—God."

42 Jesus said to them, "If God were your Father, you would have loved me, for I came forth from

God and am here; for not even of myself have I come, but he sent me.

43 "Why is it you do not understand my speech? Because you are not able to hear my word. 44 You are of your father the devil, and the desires of your father you desire to do. He was a murderer from the beginning, and has not stood in the truth, because there is no truth in him. Whenever he might speak a lie from his own he speaks; for he is a liar and the father of it. 45 But because I speak the truth, you do not believe me. 46 Which of you convicts me concerning sin? If I speak the truth, why is it you do not believe me? 47 The person who is of God hears the words of God; this is why you do not hear, because you are not of God."

48 The Jews responded and said to him, "Do we not rightly say that you are a Samaritan and have a demon?" 49 Jesus answered, "I do not have a demon; but I honor my Father, and you dishonor me. 50 But I do not seek my glory; there is One seeking and judging. 51 I tell you the truth, if anyone keeps my word, he shall never no never see death to eternity."

52 Then said the Jews to him, "Now we know that you have a demon! Abraham died, and the prophets, and you say, 'If anyone keeps my word he shall never no never taste death to eternity.' 53 You are not greater than our father Abraham who died, are you; and the prophets *who* died; who do you make yourself out to be?"

54 Jesus answered, "If I glorify myself my glory is nothing. It is my Father who is glorifying me, of whom you say, 'He is our God.' 55 And you have not known him, but I know him; and if I say that I know him not, I will be like you, a liar. But I know him, and I keep his word. 56 Abraham your father rejoiced in that he should see my day, and he saw and rejoiced."

57 Therefore the Jews said to him, "You are not yet fifty years old, and you have seen Abraham?" 58 Jesus said to them, "I tell you the truth, before Abraham came into existence, I existed." 59 Therefore they took up stones that they might throw at him; but Jesus hid himself, and went out of the temple, going through the midst of them, and so passed by,

JOHN NINE

1 and passing by he saw a man blind from birth. 2 And his disciples asked him, saying, "Rabbi, who sinned, this *man* or his parents, that he should be born blind?" 3 Jesus responded, "Neither this *man* sinned nor his parents, but that the works of God should be made known in him. 4 We must work the works of the One having sent me while it is day; night is coming when no one is able to work. 5 While I may be in the world, I am light of the world."

6 Having said these things, he spit on the ground and made mud out of the spittle, and smeared the

mud on his eyes, 7 and he said to him, "Go, wash in the pool of Siloam" (which translated is "sent"). Therefore he went, and washed, and returned seeing.

8 Therefore the neighbors and those having seen him—that before he was begging—said, "Is this not he who was sitting and begging?" 9 Some said, "It is he." But others were saying, "No, but he is like him." The man kept saying, "I am he." 10 Therefore they said to him, "How then were your eyes opened?" 11 He said, "The man called Jesus made mud, and smeared it on my eyes, and said to me, 'Go to Siloam and wash.' Therefore having gone and having washed I received sight." 12 And they said to him, "Where is he?" He says, "I know not."

13 They bring him to the Pharisees, the one once blind. 14 Now Sabbath was the day in which Jesus had made the mud and opened his eyes. 15 Therefore also the Pharisees asked him again, how he had received sight? Now he said to them, "He put mud on my eyes, and I washed, and I see." 16 Therefore some of the Pharisees said, "This man is not from God, because the Sabbath he does not keep." However, others said, "How is a sinful man able to do such signs?" And there was a division among them.

17 Therefore they said again to the blind man, "What say you about him, because he opened your eyes?" And he said, "He is a prophet." 18 Therefore the Jews did not believe concerning him, that he had been blind and had received sight, until when they called his parents *of* the one having received sight.

19 And they asked them, saying, "This is your son, of whom you say that he was born blind? How then does he now see?" 20 Therefore his parents answered and said, "We know that this is our son, and that he was born blind; 21 but how he now sees we know not, or who opened his eyes we know not. Ask him, he is of age; he will speak concerning himself." 22 These things said his parents, because they feared the Jews; for the Jews had already agreed that if anyone should confess him Christ, he should be put out of the synagogue. 23 Because of this his parents said, "He is of age, ask him."

24 Therefore they called out a second time the man who had been blind, and said to him, "Give glory to God. We know that this man is a sinner." 25 Then he answered. "Whether he is a sinner I know not. One thing I do know. That being blind, now I see." 26 Therefore they said to him, "What did he to you? How opened he your eyes?" 27 He answered them, "I told you already, and you did not listen. Why again do you desire to hear? You do not also desire to become his disciples, do you?"

28 And they slandered him, and said, "You are a disciple of that one, but we are Moses' disciples. 29 We know that God has spoken to

Moses. But this one, we know not from where he is."

30 The man answered and said to them, "In this indeed is a strange thing; that you know not from where he is, yet he opened my eyes! 31 We know that God does not hear sinners, but if anyone is God-fearing, and does his will, he hears. 32 Never from the ages has it been heard that anyone opened the eyes of one having been born blind. 33 If this man were not from God, he would not be able to do anything." 34 They answered and said to him, "You were born entirely in sins, and you teach us?" And they cast him out.

35 Jesus heard that they had cast him out; and having found him, he said, "Do you believe on the Son of God?"[V1] 36 He answered and said, "Who is he, sir, that I might believe on him?" 37 Jesus said to him, "You have both seen him and he is the one speaking with you." 38 Then the man said, "Lord, I believe"; and he worshiped him. 39 And Jesus said, "For judgment I came into this world, that those not seeing might see, and those seeing might become blind."

40 Some of the Pharisees, those who were with him, heard these things, and they said to him, "We are not also blind, are we?" 41 Jesus said to them, "If you were blind, you would not have sin; but now you say, 'We see.' Your sin remains."

JOHN TEN

1 "I tell you the truth, the person not entering in by the door to the sheepfold, but climbing up another way, he is a thief and a robber. 2 But the person entering in by the door is shepherd of the sheep. 3 To him the doorkeeper opens, and the sheep hear his voice; and he calls his own sheep by name, and leads them out. 4 When he has brought out all his own, he goes before them; and the sheep follow him, because they know his voice. 5 But another they will not in any way follow, but will flee from him, because they do not recognize the voice of strangers." 6 This illustration Jesus spoke to them, but they did not know what it was that he was saying to them.

7 Therefore Jesus again said to them, "I tell you the truth, I, I am the door of the sheep. 8 All who ever came before me are thieves and robbers; but the sheep did not hear them. 9 I, I am the door. If anyone enter in by me, he will be saved, and will go in, and will go out, and will find pasture. 10 The thief comes not, except that he might steal and kill and destroy. I came that they might have life, and might have it abundantly.

11 "I, I am the good shepherd. The good shepherd lays down his life for the sheep; 12 and the hired one, not being the shepherd, whose sheep are not his own, sees the wolf coming, and leaves the sheep, and flees—and the wolf takes and scatters them— 13 because he is a hired one and he is not concerned about the sheep.

14 "I, I am the good shepherd; and I know the ones who are mine, and I am known by the ones who are my own. 15 As the Father knows me, I also know the Father. And my life I lay down for the sheep. 16 And other sheep I have, which are not of this fold; those also it is necessary for me to bring, and my voice they will hear; and there will be one flock, one shepherd.

17 "Through this the Father loves me: because I lay down my life that I might take it again. 18 No one takes it from me, but I lay it down of myself. I have authority to lay it down and I have authority to take it again. This command I received from my Father."

19 Again there was division among the Jews, because of these words. 20 And many of them said, "He has a demon and is out of his mind. Why do you listen to him?" 21 Others said, "These words are not those of a demonized person. A demon is not able to open the eyes of the blind, is he?"

22 At this time the feast of Dedication took place in Jerusalem. It was winter, 23 and Jesus was walking in the temple in Solomon's porch. 24 Now the Jews surrounded him, and said to him, "Until when do you hold our soul in suspense? If you are the Christ, tell us plainly."

25 Jesus answered them, "I told you, and you do not believe. The works that I do in my Father's name, these testify about me, 26 but you do not believe, because you are not of my sheep. As I said to you, 27 my sheep hear my voice, and I know them, and they follow me, 28 and I give them life eternal; and never no never will they perish for the age; and never will anyone take them out of my hand. 29 My Father who has given them to me is greater than all; and no one is able to take them out of the Father's hand. 30 I and the Father are one."

31 Therefore again the Jews took up stones that they might stone him. 32 Jesus answered them, "Many good works I have shown you from the Father. Because of which work of these do you stone me?" 33 The Jews answered him, saying, "Concerning a good work we do not stone you, but for slander against God, and because you, being a man, make yourself God."

34 Jesus answered them, "Is it not written in your Law, 'I said, "You are gods"?' 35 If he called them gods, to whom the word of God came—and the Scripture is not able to be broken—36 do you say of him whom the Father sanctified and sent into the world, 'You slander God,' because I said, 'I am the Son of God'? 37 If I do not do the works of my Father, do not believe me; 38 but if I do, even if me you do not believe, believe the works, that you might understand, and might believe that the Father is in me and I in the Father."

39 Therefore they sought again to take him; and he went forth out of their hand, 40 and

departed again beyond the Jordan, to the place where John was at first immersing; and he stayed there. 41 And many came to him, and said, "John indeed did no sign, but all that John said about this man was true." 42 And many believed in him there.

JOHN ELEVEN

1 Now a certain man was sick, Lazarus of Bethany, of the village of Mary and her sister Martha. 2 Mary was the one having anointed the Lord with ointment, and wiped his feet with her hair, whose brother Lazarus was sick. 3 Therefore the sisters sent to him, saying, "Master, behold, he whom you love is sick."

4 Now Jesus having heard, said, "This sickness is not unto death, but for the glory of God, that the Son of God might be glorified by it." 5 (Now Jesus loved Martha, and her sister, and Lazarus.) 6 When, therefore, he heard that he is sick, he then remained two days in the place which he was.

7 Then after this, he says to the disciples, "Let us go into Judea again." 8 The disciples say to him, "Rabbi, just now the Jews were seeking to stone you, and are you going there again?" 9 Jesus answered, "Are there not twelve hours in the day? If anyone walks in the day, he does not stumble, because the light of this world he sees. 10 But if anyone walks in the night, he does stumble, because the light is not in him." 11 These things he said.

And after this he says to them, "Lazarus our friend has fallen asleep, but I go that I might awaken him." 12 Said, therefore, his disciples, "Master, if he has fallen asleep he will get well." 13 However Jesus had spoken of his death; but they thought that he was speaking about the rest of sleep. 14 Then therefore Jesus plainly said to them, "Lazarus has died. 15 And I am glad for your sake, in order that you might believe, that I was not there. But let us go to him." 16 Therefore Thomas, called Didymus, said to the fellow disciples, "Let us also go, that we might die with him."

17 Therefore, having come, Jesus found him already having been in the tomb four days. 18 Now Bethany was near Jerusalem, about one and one-half miles distant. 19 And many of the Jews had come unto Martha and Mary, that they might comfort them concerning their brother.

20 Therefore Martha, when she heard that Jesus is coming, met him; but Mary was sitting in the house. 21 Therefore Martha said to Jesus, "Master, if you had been here, my brother would not have died. 22 But also now I know, that whatever you might ask God, God will give you."

23 Jesus said to her, "Your brother will rise again." 24 Martha says to him, "I know that he will rise again in the resurrection in the last day." 25 Jesus said to her, "I, I am the resurrection and the life. The one believing in me, even if he

should die, he will live. 26 And everyone living and believing in me will never no never die to the age. Believe you this?" 27 She says to him, "Yes, Master. I have believed that you are the Christ, the son of God, the one coming into the world."

28 And having said these things she went away, and secretly called Mary her sister, having said, "The teacher is come and calls you." 29 Now she, when she heard, rises up quickly and comes to him.

30 Now Jesus had not yet come into the village, but was still in the place where Martha had met him. 31 Then the Jews being with her in the house and comforting her, having seen that Mary quickly rose up and went out, followed her, saying she is going to the tomb, that she might weep there.

32 Therefore Mary, when she came where Jesus was, having seen him, fell at his feet, saying to him, "Master, if you had been here, my brother would not have died." 33 Jesus, then, when he saw her weeping, and the Jews having come with her weeping, he was deeply moved in spirit and troubled himself.

34 And he said, "Where have you laid him?" They say to him, "Sir, come and see." 35 Jesus wept. 36 Therefore the Jews said, "Behold how he loved him!" 37 Some of them, however, said, "Was not this one—having opened the eyes of the blind—able to cause that also this one might not have died?"

38 Jesus therefore, again being deeply moved in himself, comes to the tomb. And it was a cave, and a stone was lying against it. 39 Jesus says, "Take away the stone." Says to him the sister of the one having died, Martha, "Master, already he stinks, for it is four days." 40 Jesus says to her, "Said I not to you that if you might believe you will see the glory of God?"

41 Therefore they took away the stone where the dead one was laid. Then Jesus lifted his eyes upwards and said, "Father, I thank you that you have heard me. 42 And I know that you always hear me, but on account of the crowd standing around I said it, that they might believe that you sent me."

43 And having said these things, he cried with a loud voice, "Lazarus, come out!" 44 The one having been dead came out, the feet and the hands being bound with linen bands, and his face bound about with a sweat-cloth.[v2] Jesus says to them, "Unbind him and let him go."

45 Then many of the Jews having come to Mary, and having seen what he did, believed on him. 46 But some of them went to the Pharisees, and told them what Jesus had done. 47 Therefore the chief priests and the Pharisees gathered a council, and said, "What do we? For this man does many signs. 48 If we may let him alone thus, all will believe on him, and the Romans will come, and will take away both our place and the nation."

₄₉ But a certain one of them, Caiaphas, being high priest that year, said to them, "You know nothing at all. ₅₀ Nor do you consider that it is advantageous for us that one man should die for the people, and not that all the nation should perish." ₅₁ Now this he said not from himself; but being high priest that year, he prophesied that Jesus was about to die for the nation; ₅₂ and not for the nation only, but also that the children of God, those having been scattered, he might gather together into one.

₅₃ Therefore from that day they took counsel with one another, that they might kill him. ₅₄ Therefore Jesus no longer walked openly among the Jews, but went from there into the region near the wilderness, to a city called Ephraim, and there he remained with the disciples.

₅₅ Now the Passover of the Jews was near, and many went up to Jerusalem out of the country before the Passover, to purify themselves. ₅₆ Then they were seeking Jesus, and were saying with one another, standing in the temple, "What is your opinion? That he might not come to the feast?" ₅₇ Now the chief priests and the Pharisees directed that if anyone should know where he is, he should make it known, that they might take him.

JOHN TWELVE

₁ Then Jesus, six days before the Passover, came to Bethany, where Lazarus was, who had died, whom Jesus had raised out from the dead. ₂ Therefore they made him a supper there, and Martha served, and Lazarus was one of those reclining *to eat* with him.

₃ Then Mary, having taken about a pound of ointment of nard, very expensive, anointed Jesus' feet, and wiped his feet with her hair; and the house was filled from the fragrance of the ointment.

₄ Says then one of his disciples, Judas of Simon Iscariot,ʷ the one being about to betray him, ₅ "Why was not this ointment sold for three hundred denarii and given to the poor?" ₆ But he said this, not that he cared for the poor, but because he was a thief, and had the moneybag, and took away what was put in. ₇ Therefore Jesus said, "Leave her alone; she has kept it for the day of my embalming.ˣ ₈ For the poor always you have with you, but me you have not always."

₉ Therefore a great crowd of the Jews knew that he was there; and they came not because of Jesus only, but also that they might see Lazarus, whom he had raised out from the dead.

₁₀ And the chief priests took counsel that also Lazarus they might kill, ₁₁ because on account of him many of the Jews were going away and were believing on Jesus.

₁₂ On the next day the large crowd, the one having come to the feast, having heard that Jesus was coming into Jerusalem, ₁₃ took the branches of palm trees and went out to meet him, and were shouting: "Hosanna! Blessed the one coming in the name of the Lord, even the King of Israel!"

14 Then Jesus, having found a young donkey, sat upon it, as it is written, 15 "Fear not, daughter of Zion; behold, your king comes, sitting on a donkey's colt." 16 These things his disciples did not know at first; but when Jesus was glorified, then they remembered that these things were written of him and these things they had been done to him.

17 Bore witness[y] therefore the crowd which was with him when Lazarus he called out of the tomb and raised him out from the dead. 18 For this reason also the crowd met him, because it heard of his having done this sign. 19 Therefore the Pharisees said among themselves, "Do you not see that you gain nothing? Behold, the world has gone after him."

20 Now there were certain Greeks among those coming up that they might worship at the feast. 21 These therefore came to Philip, who was from Bethsaida of Galilee, and they asked him, saying, "Sir, we desire to see Jesus." 22 Philip comes and tells Andrew; Andrew and Philip come and tell Jesus.

23 And Jesus responding to them, saying, "The hour has come that the Son of Man should be glorified. 24 I tell you the truth, unless the seed of wheat, having fallen into the ground, should die, it remains alone; if however it should die, it bears much fruit.

25 "The one loving his life, loses it, and the one hating his life in this world will keep it to life eternal. 26 If anyone serves me, let him follow me; and where I am, there also my servant will be. If anyone serves me, the Father will honor him.

27 "Now my soul has been troubled, and what shall I say? 'Father, save me from this the hour?' But for this reason I came to this the hour! 28 Father, glorify your name." Therefore a voice came out of heaven: "I have both glorified it and will glorify it again." 29 Therefore the crowd, the ones having stood and having heard, said, "There has been thunder." Others said, "A messenger has spoken to him."

30 Jesus responded and said, "This voice has not come because of me, but because of you. 31 Now is the judgment of this world; now the ruler of this world will be cast out. 32 And I, when[z] I am lifted up from the earth, will draw all persons to myself." 33 Now this he said, declaring by what death he was about to die.

34 Then the crowd answered him, "We have heard out of the Law that the Christ remains to the age, and how say you that it is necessary the son of man be lifted up? Who is this son of man?"

35 Therefore Jesus said to them, "Yet a little while the light is with you. Walk while you have the light, that the darkness might not overtake you; and the one walking in darkness knows not where he is going. 36 While you have the light,

believe in the light, that you may become sons of light." These things Jesus spoke, and having gone away, was hidden from them.

37 Although he had done so many signs in their presence, they did not believe in him, 38 that the word of Isaiah the prophet might be fulfilled, that said, "Lord, who has believed our report? And to whom has the arm of the Lord been revealed?" 39 Because of this they were not able to believe, for Isaiah said again: 40 "He has blinded their eyes, and hardened their hearts, that they should not see with their eyes, and understand with their heart, and turn, and I will heal them."

41 These things Isaiah said, because he saw his glory and spoke concerning him. 42 Still however, even many from the rulers believed on him, but because of the Pharisees they confess not, that they might not be put out of the synagogue; 43 for they loved the praise of men more than the praise of God.

44 Then Jesus cried out and said, "The one believing on me, believes not on me but on the one having sent me. 45 And the one acknowledging me acknowledges the one having sent me. 46 I have come as a light into the world, that everyone believing in me may not remain in the darkness. 47 And if anyone hears my words, and does not keep them, I do not judge him; for I came not that I might judge the world, but that I might save the world. 48 The one rejecting me and not receiving my words, has one judging him: the word that I spoke, that will judge him in the last day. 49 For I have not spoken from myself, but the Father himself having sent me, gave me a commandment, what I should say and what I should speak. 50 And I know that his commandment is eternal life. Therefore, I speak. As the Father has said to me, so I speak."

JOHN THIRTEEN

1 Now before the feast of the Passover, Jesus having known that his hour had come that he should depart out of this world to the Father—having loved his own who were in the world, to the end he loved them. 2 And supper taking place (the devil having already put into the heart that he, Judas of Simon Iscariot, should betray him), 3 having known that all things the Father has given him into his hands, and that from God he came out and to God he is going, 4 he rises from the supper, and lays aside the garments, and having taken a towel he girded himself. 5 Afterward he pours water into the basin and began to wash the disciples' feet, and to wipe with the towel with which he was girded.

6 He comes therefore to Simon Peter, who says to him, "Master, do you wash my feet?" 7 Jesus answered and said to him, "What I do you know not now, but you will know after these things." 8 Peter says to him, "May you never no never wash my feet, forever!"

Jesus answered him, "If I do not wash you, you have no portion with me." 9 Simon Peter says to him, "Master, not my feet only but also the hands and the head."

10 Jesus says to him, "the one having been bathed has no need, except his feet to wash, but is wholly clean; and you are clean, but not all." 11 For he knew the one who was betraying him; on account of this he said, "You are not all clean."

12 Therefore, when he had washed their feet, and taken his garments, and having reclined again, he said to them, "Do you know what I have done to you? 13 You call me 'Teacher' and 'Master,' and you say rightly, for I am. 14 If I therefore have washed your feet—the Master and the Teacher—you also ought to wash the feet of one another. 15 For I gave you a pattern, that as I did to you, also you should do. 16 I tell you the truth, a servant is not greater than his master, nor is the one sent greater than the one having sent him. 17 If these things you know, blessed are you if you do them.

18 "I speak not about all of you, I know whom I chose—but that the Scripture might be fulfilled: 'the one eating my bread, lifted up against me his heel.' 19 I am telling you now before it comes to pass, that you should believe when it comes to pass, that I, I am. 20 I tell you the truth, the one receiving whomever I may send receives me; and the one receiving me receives the one having sent me."

21 Having said these things, Jesus was troubled in spirit, and testified and said, "I tell you the truth, one of you will betray me." 22 Then the disciples looked upon one another, in doubt about whom he was speaking. 23 Now there was reclining in Jesus' bosom one out of his disciples, whom Jesus loved. 24 Therefore Simon Peter nods to him, and tells him to ask who, if he will say,[aa] about whom he is speaking.

25 Now he having thus leaned upon Jesus' breast, he says to him, "Master, who is he?" 26 Jesus answered, "He it is to whom I will dip the morsel and I will give." Thereupon himself having dipped the morsel, he takes it and gives it to Judas of Simon Iscariot. 27 And after the morsel, Satan entered into him. Jesus therefore says to him, "What you do, do quickly."

28 Now no one knew, of those reclining *to eat*, why he said this to him. 29 For some thought, inasmuch as Judas had the money box, that Jesus is saying to him, "Buy what things we have need for the feast"; or that he should give something to the poor. 30 Then, having received the morsel, he immediately went out; and it was night.

31 When, therefore, he had gone out, Jesus says, "Now the Son of Man has been glorified, and God has been glorified in him. 32 If God is glorified in him, God will also glorify him in himself, and will

immediately glorify him.

33 "Little children, yet a little while I am with you. You will seek me, and as I said to the Jews, 'Where I go you are not able to come,' so I say to you now.

34 A new commandment I give to you, that you should love one another; as I have loved you, so that also you should love one another. 35 In this all will know that you are my disciples: if love you have among one another."

36 Simon Peter says to him, "Master, where go you?" Jesus answered him, "Where I go you are not able to follow me now; but you will follow me afterward." 37 Peter says to him, "Master, what is the reason I am not able to follow you now? I will lay down my life for you." 38 Jesus answered, "Will you lay down your life for me? I tell you the truth, not at all will[bb] a rooster crow until that you will deny me three times."

JOHN FOURTEEN

1 "Let not your heart be troubled; keep on[cc] believing in God and believe in me. 2 In my Father's house are many abiding places; but if not I would have said that to you. I go to prepare a place for you. 3 And when I should go and prepare a place for you, I am coming again and will receive you to myself; that where I am, you may be also. 4 And where I am going you know, and the way you know."

5 Thomas says to him, "Master, we know not where you are going; how are we able to know the way?" 6 Jesus says to him, "I, I am the way, and the truth, and the life. No one comes to the Father except by means of me. 7 If you had understood me, also my Father you would have perceived; from this present time you understand him and have perceived him."[dd]

8 Philip says to him, "Master, show us the Father, and that is enough for us." 9 Jesus says to him, "I am with you all so long a time and you have not understood me, Philip? The one having perceived me has perceived the Father; how say you, 'Show us the Father?' 10 Believe you not that I am in the Father and the Father is in me? The words that I speak to you I speak not from myself, but the Father dwelling in me does his works. 11 Believe me that I am in the Father and the Father in me; but if not, believe on account of the works themselves.

12 "I tell you the truth, the one believing in me, the works that I do he also will do, and greater than these he will do, because I am going to my Father. 13 And whatever you might ask in my name, this I will do, that the Father might be glorified in the Son. 14 If you ask me anything in my name, I will do it.

15 "If you keep on loving me you will obey my commandments. 16 And I will pray the Father, and a Helper equal to me[ee] he will give you, that he continuously be with you forever, 17 the Spirit of truth,

whom the world is not able to receive, because it does not see or know him; but you know him, because he dwells with you and will be in you. 18 I will not leave you as disciples abandoned by their master;[ff] I am coming to you.

19 "Yet a little while and the world sees me no more, but you see me. Because I live you also will live. 20 In that day you will know that I am in my Father, and you in me, and I in you. 21 The one having my commandments and obeying them, he is the one loving me. And the one loving me will be loved by my Father, and I will love him and I will make myself known to him."

22 Judas (not the Iscariot) says to him, "Master, and what has happened that to us you are about to make yourself known, and not to the world?" 23 Jesus answered and said to him, "If anyone loves me, my word he will keep; and my Father will love him, and we will come to him, and will make our abiding place with him. 24 The one not loving me does not keep my words; and the word that you hear is not mine but the Father's who sent me.

25 "These things I have said to you, abiding with you. 26 But the Helper, the Holy Spirit, whom the Father will send in my name, he will teach you all things, and bring to your remembrance all things that I have said to you.

27 "Peace I leave with you, my peace I give to you; not as the world gives, I give to you. Let not your heart be troubled, nor let it fear. 28 You heard that I said to you, 'I am going away and I am coming back to you.' If you loved me, you would have rejoiced because I am going to the Father, because my Father is greater than me.

29 "And now I have told you before it comes to pass, that when it shall have come to pass, you might believe. 30 I will no longer talk much with you; for the ruler of this world is coming, and in me he has absolutely nothing; 31 but that the world might know that I love the Father, and as the Father gives me command, so I do. Rise up, let us go from here."

JOHN FIFTEEN

1 "I, I am the genuine vine, and my Father is the vinedresser. 2 Every branch in me not bearing fruit, he lifts up; and every one bearing fruit, he cleanses, that it might bear more fruit. 3 You are already clean, on account of the word that I have spoken to you.

4 "Abide in me, and I in you. As the branch is not able to bear fruit of itself if it does not abide in the vine, so you cannot if you do not abide in me. 5 I am the vine, you are the branches. The one abiding in me and I in him, he bears much fruit; because apart from me you are able to do absolutely nothing. 6 If anyone should not abide in me he is cast out as the branch and dried up; and they gather them and into the fire it is cast and burned.

7 "If you abide in me, and my

words abide in you, you shall ask whatever you may wish, and it will come to pass for you. 8 In this my Father is glorified: that you should bear much fruit and become my disciples. 9 As the Father has loved me, I also have loved you. Abide in my love. 10 If my commandments you keep you will abide in my love, as I have kept my Father's commandments and abide in his love. 11 These things I have spoken to you, in order that my joy might abide in you, and your joy might be full.

12 "This is my commandment: that you may love one another as I loved[99] you. 13 Greater love than this no one has: that one might lay down his life for his friends. 14 You are my friends, if you do what I command you.

15 "I no longer call you servants, because the servant knows not what his master is doing. But you I have called friends, because all things that I heard from my Father I have declared to you.

16 "You chose me not, but I chose you, and appointed you, in order that you may go, and may bear fruit, and your fruit may remain, so that whatever you may ask the Father in my name, he may give you. 17 These things I command you, that you may continue to love one another.

18 "If the world hates you, you know that it has hated me before you. 19 If you were of the world, the world its own would love. But because you are not of the world, but I chose you out of the world, on account of this the world hates you. 20 Remember the word that I said to you, 'A servant is not greater than his master.' If they persecuted me they will also persecute you. If my word they kept they will keep yours also. 21 But all these things they will do against you on account of my name, because they have not known the one having sent me.

22 "If I had not come and spoken to them, they would not have had sin. But now they have no excuse for their sin. 23 The one hating me also hates my Father. 24 If I had not done the works among them that no other has done, they would not have had sin; but now they have both seen and have hated both me and my Father. 25 But that the word might be fulfilled having been written in their Law, 'They hated me without cause.'

26 "But when the Helper comes, whom I will send to you from the Father, the Spirit of truth who proceeds from the Father, he will testify about me; 27 and you also will testify, because from the beginning you are with me."

JOHN SIXTEEN

1 "These things I have spoken to you that you might not fall away. 2 They will put you out of the synagogues—yea, an hour is coming that everyone having killed you may think to offer a service to God. 3 And these things they will do because they do not know the Father, nor me. 4 But these things I have said to you, that when the

hour of them might come, you might remember them, that I told you. But these things I did not say to you from the beginning, because I was with you.

5 "But now I am going to the one having sent me, and none of you asks me, 'Where are you going?' 6 But because I have said these things to you, sorrow has filled your heart. 7 But I say the truth to you, it is profitable for you that I should go away. For if I do not go away the Helper will never no never come to you. But if I go I will send him to you.

8 "And having come he will convict the world about sin, and about righteousness, and about judgment. 9 Indeed about sin, because they do not believe in me. 10 And about righteousness, because I go away to the Father and you see me no more. 11 And about judgment, because the ruler of this world has been judged.

12 "Many things I still have to say to you; but you are not able to bear them now. 13 But when he, the Spirit of Truth, comes, he will teach you in all the truth; for he will not speak from himself, but whatever he will hear he will speak; and he will speak to you the things coming. 14 He will glorify me, because he will take and declare to you out of that which is mine. 15 All things, whatever the Father has, are mine; on account of this I said that out of that which is mine he will take and declare to you.

16 "A little and you no longer see me, and again a little and you will see me, because I am going away to the Father." 17 Therefore his disciples said to one another, "What is this that he says to us, 'a little and you do not see me,' and again, 'a little and you will see me' and 'because I am going to the Father?'" 18 Therefore they said, "What is it he says, 'a little?' We do not know what he is saying."

19 Jesus knew that they wanted to ask him, and he said to them, "Do you inquire about this among one another, that I said, 'A little and you do not see me,' and again, 'a little and you will see me'? 20 I tell you the truth, that you will weep and will mourn, but the world will rejoice. You will be grieved, but your grief will turn to joy. 21 The woman, when she is giving birth, has pain, because her hour has come. But when she births the child she no longer remembers the affliction on account of the joy that a person has been born into the world.

22 "And therefore you now indeed have grief. But, again, I will see you, and your heart will rejoice, and no one will take your joy from you. 23 And in that day you will not ask nothing of me. I tell you the truth, whatever you might ask the Father in my name, he will give you. 24 Until now you have asked nothing in my name. Ask and you will receive, that your joy might be full.

25 "These things I have spoken to you in dark sayings; an hour is coming when I will speak to

you no more in dark sayings, but plainly; I will tell you about the Father. 26 In that day you will ask in my name, and I do not say to you that I will ask the Father for you; 27 for the Father himself loves you, because you have loved me, and have believed that I came out from the Father. 28 I came out from the Father, and have come into the world; again, I leave the world and go to the Father."

29 His disciples say to him, "See, now you speak plainly and do not speak dark sayings. 30 Now we know that you know all things, and have no need that anyone should ask you. By this we believe, that you came from God."

31 Jesus answered them, "Now you believe? 32 Observe, an hour is coming and has come when you will be scattered, each to his own place; and you will leave me alone, yet I am not alone, because the Father is with me.

33 "These things I have spoken to you, that in me you might have peace; in the world you have affliction. But be courageous, I have overcome the world."

JOHN SEVENTEEN

1 Jesus spoke these things; and having lifted up his eyes to the heaven, said, "Father, the hour has come. Glorify your Son in order that the Son should glorify you. 2 As you gave him authority over all flesh, that all whom you have given him he might give to them eternal life—3 and this is eternal life, that they should know you, the only genuine God, and Jesus Christ whom you have sent—4 I glorified you on the earth, having completed the work that you have given me that I should do. 5 And now you glorify me, Father, with yourself, with the glory that I had with you before the world existed.

6 "I made known your name to the persons whom you have given me out of the world. They were yours, and you gave them to me, and they have kept your word. 7 Now they have known that all things, whatever you have given me, are of you, 8 because the words that you have given me, I have given them; and they received and truly knew that from you I came out; and they believed that you sent me.

9 "I am praying for them. I do not pray about the world, but about those whom you have given me, for they are yours—10 and all things of mine are yours, and yours mine—and I have been glorified in them.

11 "And I am no longer in the world, but they themselves are in the world, and I am coming to you. Holy Father, keep them in your name, those you have given me, that they should be one, as we. 12 When I was with them I was keeping them in your name, those you have given me. And I kept them, and none of them has perished, except the son of destruction, that the Scripture might be fulfilled. 13 But now I am coming to you, and these things I speak in the world, that they might

have my joy filled abundantly in them.

14 "I have given them your word, and the world hated them, because they are not of the world, even as I am not of the world. 15 I do not ask that you should take them out of the world, but that you should guard them safely from the evil. 16 They are not of the world as I am not of the world. 17 Sanctify them by the truth: your word is truth. 18 As you sent me into the world I also sent them into the world, 19 and for them I sanctify myself, that they might also be sanctified in truth.

20 "And I do not ask only for these, but also for those believing in me through their word, 21 that all might be one—as you Father in me and I in you—in order that they also might be in us, so that the world might believe that you sent me. 22 And the glory that you have given me, I have given them, that they might be one, as we. 23 I in them and you in me that they might be made complete into one, that the world might know that you sent me and loved them, even as you loved me.

24 "Father, those you have given me, I desire that where I am they also might be with me, that they might behold my glory that you gave me because you loved me before the foundation of the world. 25 And the world has not known you, righteous Father, but I have known you, and these have known that you sent me, 26 and I have made known to them your name, and will make known, that the love with which you loved me might be in them, and I in them."

JOHN EIGHTEEN

1 Having said these things, Jesus went out with his disciples beyond the winter-flowing stream[hh] Kidron, where there was a garden, into which he entered, and his disciples.

2 But Judas, who was delivering him up, also knew the place, because Jesus often gathered together there with his disciples. 3 Judas therefore, having received the company and officers from the chief priests and from the Pharisees, comes there with small lanterns and large torches and weapons.

4 Jesus therefore, knowing all things that are coming upon him, having gone forth also said to them, "Who seek you?" 5 They answered him, "Jesus of Nazareth." He says to them, "I, I am he." And also Judas, he who is delivering him up, was standing with them.

6 When therefore he had said to them, "I, I am he," they withdrew backwards and fell to the ground. 7 Therefore he again questioned them, "Who seek you?" And they said, "Jesus of Nazareth." 8 Jesus answered, "I have told you that I, I am he. If therefore you seek me, allow these to go away," 9 that the word might be fulfilled that he had spoken, "Those whom you have given me, I lost not one."

10 Then Simon Peter, having

a sword, drew it and struck the servant of the High Priest, and cut off his right ear; and the servant's name was Malchus. 11 Therefore Jesus said to Peter, "Put the sword into the sheath. The cup which the Father has given me, may I not drink it?"

12 Then the company and the captain and the officers of the Jews took hold of Jesus and bound him; 13 and they led him away to Annas first; for he was father-in-law of Caiaphas, who was High Priest that year. 14 Now Caiaphas was the one having given counsel to the Jews that it is profitable for the one man to die for the people.

15 Now following Jesus were Simon Peter and the other disciple. Now that disciple was known to the High Priest, and he entered with Jesus into the High Priest's courtyard. 16 But Peter stood outside at the door. Therefore the other disciple, the one known to the High Priest, went out and spoke to the doorkeeper, and brought Peter in.

17 Then the servant girl, the doorkeeper, says to Peter, "Are you not also of the disciples of this man?" He says, "I am not." 18 Now the servants and the officers were standing, having made a fire of live coals (for it was cold), and were warming themselves. And Peter was also with them, standing and warming himself.

19 Then the High Priest questioned Jesus about his disciples and about his teaching. 20 Jesus answered him, "I have spoken openly to the world; I always taught in the synagogue and in the temple where the Jews always come together; and I spoke nothing in secret. 21 Why do you question me? Question those having heard what I said to them—behold, they know what I said."

22 Now he having said these things, one of the officers standing by hit Jesus with the palm of his hand, having said, "Thus answer you the High Priest?" 23 Jesus answered him, "If I spoke evil bear witness about the evil; but if rightly, why do you hit me with the palm?" 24 Then Annas sent him bound to Caiaphas the High Priest.

25 But Simon Peter was standing and warming himself. Then they said to him, "Are you not also one of his disciples." He denied and said, "I am not." 26 One of the servants of the High Priest, being kinsman of whom Peter had cut off the ear, says, "Did I not see you in the garden with him?" 27 Then Peter again denied, and immediately a rooster crowed.

28 Then they led Jesus from Caiaphas into the Praetorium;[ii] and it was early. And they did not enter into the Praetorium, that they should not be defiled, but might keep the festival.[jj] 29 Therefore Pilate went out to them, and said, "What accusation bring you against this man?"

30 They answered and said to him, "If he were not doing evil, we would not have delivered him to you." 31 Therefore Pilate said to them, "Take him yourselves and

judge him according to your Law." The Jews said to him, "It is not permitted to us to put anyone to death," 32 that Jesus' word might be fulfilled, that he had spoken, declaring what death he was about to die.

33 Therefore Pilate again entered into the Praetorium, and called Jesus, and said to him, "You are the king of the Jews?" 34 Jesus answered, "You say this of yourself, or did others say to you about me?" 35 Pilate answered, "I am not a Jew, am I? Your nation and the chief priests delivered you to me. What have you done?" 36 Jesus answered, "My kingdom is not of this world. If my kingdom were of this world, my associates would fight that I might not be delivered up to the Jews. But now my kingdom is not from here."

37 Therefore Pilate said to him, "Then you are a king?" Jesus answered, "You say, because I am a king. I have been born for this and for this I have come into the world: that I might bear witness to the truth. Everyone who is of the truth listens to my voice." 38 Pilate says to him, "What is truth?"

And having said this, he again went out to the Jews, and says to them, "I find no guilt in him. 39 Now it is a custom with you that I should release one to you at the Passover. Therefore is it your will that I should release to you the king of the Jews?" 40 Then again they cried out, saying, "Not this one, but Barabbas!" Now Barabbas was a robber.

JOHN NINETEEN

1 Pilate therefore then took Jesus, and had him flogged.kk 2 And the soldiers, having twisted together a crown of thorns, put it on his head, and put around him a purple robe. 3 And they came up to him and said, "Hail King of the Jews!" And they hit him with the palm of their hands.

4 And Pilate again went out and says to them, "Behold, I bring him out to you in order that you might know that I find no guilt in him." 5 Jesus therefore went out wearing the thorny crown and the purple robe; and he says to them, "Behold the man." 6 Therefore when the chief priests and the officers saw him, they cried out, saying, "Crucify! Crucify!" Pilate says to them, "Take him yourselves and crucify. For I find in him no guilt."

7 The Jews answered him, "We have a Law, and according to the Law he ought to die, because he made himself Son of God."

8 Therefore when Pilate heard this word he was more afraid. 9 And he went into the Praetorium again and says to Jesus, "From where are you?" But Jesus did not give him an answer. 10 Therefore Pilate says to him, "Speak you not to me? Do you not know that I have authority to release you, and I have authority to crucify you?" 11 Jesus answered him, "You would have no authority over me at all, if it were not given to you from above. Because of this, the one having delivered me to you has

greater sin."

12 From that time Pilate sought to release him; but Jews cried out, saying, "If this man you release, you are not a Friend of Caesar. Anyone making himself a king speaks against Caesar."

13 Pilate, therefore, having heard these words, brought out Jesus, and sat down upon the judgment seat, at a place called Stone Pavement, but in Aramaic, Gabbatha. 14 Now it was the preparation of the Passover; it was about noon; and he says to the Jews, "Behold your king." 15 They cried out, therefore, "Away with him, crucify him!" Pilate says to them, "Should I crucify your king?" The chief priests answered, "No king we have, except Caesar." 16 Therefore he then delivered him to them that he might be crucified.

Therefore they took Jesus. 17 And bearing the cross himself, he went out to the place called, "Of the Skull," the place which is called in Aramaic, "Golgotha," 18 where they crucified him; and with him two others, on this side and on that side, and Jesus between.

19 Then Pilate wrote a title, and put it on the cross. Now it was written, "Jesus of Nazareth, the King of the Jews." 20 This the title, therefore, many of the Jews read, because the place where Jesus was crucified was near the city; and it was written in Aramaic, in Latin, in Greek. 21 Therefore the chief priests of the Jews said to Pilate, "Write not 'the King of the Jews,' but that he said, 'I am King of the Jews.'" 22 Pilate answered, "What I have written, I have written."

23 Then the soldiers, when they crucified Jesus, took his garments and made four parts, to each soldier a part, and also the tunic. Now the tunic was seamless, woven whole from the top throughout. 24 Therefore they said to one another, "Let us not tear it up, but let us cast lots for it, whose it will be"; in order that the Scripture might be fulfilled that said, "They divided my garments among them, and for my clothing they cast a lot." Therefore, truly, the soldiers did these things.

25 Now his mother had been standing by the cross of Jesus, and his mother's sister, Mary the one of Clopas, and Mary the Magdalene. 26 Jesus therefore, having seen the mother and the disciple standing by, whom he loved, says to *the* mother, "Woman, behold your son." 27 Then he says to the disciple, "Behold your mother." And from that hour the disciple took her to his own place.

28 After these things, Jesus knowing that now all things had been accomplished, in order that the Scripture might be fulfilled, he says, "I thirst." 29 A vessel full of vinegar had been set; a sponge therefore was filled with the vinegar; having put it on a stalk of hyssop, they brought it to his mouth. 30 Therefore, when Jesus took the vinegar, he said, "It is finished." And having bowed his head, he yielded up his spirit.

31 Jews, therefore, because it was Preparation, in order that the bodies might not remain on the cross on the Sabbath—for that particular[ll] Sabbath was the high day—asked Pilate that their legs might be broken and that they might be taken away. 32 Therefore the soldiers came, and indeed broke the legs of the first, and of the other, having been crucified with him. 33 But having come to Jesus, when they saw he was already dead, they did not break his legs, 34 but one of the soldiers pierced his side with a spear, and immediately blood and water came out.

35 And the one having seen has borne testimony; and his testimony is true; and he knows that he is speaking the truth, in order that you also might believe. 36 For these things took place in order that the Scripture might be fulfilled, "Not one bone of him will be broken"; 37 and another Scripture says, "They will look on the one they have pierced."

38 Now after these things, Joseph from Arimathea—being a disciple of Jesus, but hidden through fear of the Jews—asked Pilate that he might take away Jesus' body; and Pilate gave permission. Therefore he came and took away his body.

39 Now Nicodemus also came—the one having come to him by night at the first—bearing a mixture of myrrh and aloes, about seventy-five pounds.[mm] 40 Therefore they took Jesus' body and bound it in linen cloths,[nn] with the spices, as is customary among the Jews, to prepare for burial. 41 Now there was a garden in the place where he was crucified, and in the garden a new tomb, in which no one not yet was laid. 42 There, therefore, on account of the Preparation of the Jews, because the tomb was near, they laid Jesus.

JOHN TWENTY

1 Now the first of the week, Mary the Magdalene comes early to the tomb, it being still dark, and she sees the stone having been removed from the tomb. 2 Then she runs and comes to Simon Peter, and to the other disciple whom Jesus loved, and she says to them, "They have taken away the master out of the tomb, and we do not know where they have laid him."

3 Then Peter and the other disciple went out and came to the tomb. 4 Now the two ran together, and the other disciple ran ahead faster than Peter, and came first to the tomb. 5 And having stooped down, he sees laying there the linen cloths; however he did not enter.

6 Then also comes Simon Peter following him, and he entered the tomb, and sees the linen cloths lying there, 7 and the sweat-cloth[oo] which was upon his head not lying with the linen cloths, but having been folded up by itself in a place.

8 Therefore then entered also the other disciple, the one having

come first to the tomb, and he saw and believed; 9 for they did not yet understand the Scripture, that he must rise out from the dead. 10 The disciples then went away again to their own place.

11 But Mary stood outside at the tomb, weeping. Then as she wept, she stooped down into the tomb, 12 and she sees two messengers, in white, sitting one at the head and one at the feet where Jesus' body had lain. 13 And they say to her, "Woman, why do you weep?" She says to them, "Because they have taken away my master, and I do not know where they have laid him."

14 Having said these things she turned back around. And she sees Jesus standing there and does not know that it is Jesus. 15 Jesus says to her, "Woman, why do you weep? Whom do you seek?" She, thinking that it is the gardener, says to him, "Sir, if you have carried him off, tell me where you have laid him, and I will take him away."

16 Jesus says to her, "Mary." Having turned around she says to him in Aramaic, "Rabonni," which is to say, "Teacher." 17 Jesus says to her, "Do not handle me, for I have not yet ascended to the Father; but go to my brethren and say to them, 'I am ascending to my Father and your Father, and to my God and your God.'"

18 Comes Mary the Magdalene announcing to the disciples, "I have seen the master," and he had said these things to her. 19 Then being evening the same day (the first of the Sabbaths[pp]) and the doors having been shut where the disciples were through the fear of the Jews, Jesus came and stood in the midst, and he says to them, "Peace to you." 20 And having said this, he showed his hands and his sides to them. Then the disciples rejoiced, having seen the Lord.

21 Then Jesus said to them again, "Peace to you. As the Father has sent me forth, I also send you." 22 And having said this he breathed and says to them, "Receive the Holy Spirit. 23 If of any you may forgive the sins, they are forgiven them; if any you may retain, they are retained."

24 But Thomas, one of the Twelve, the one called Didymus, was not with them when Jesus came. 25 Now the other disciples kept saying to him, "We have seen the Master!" But he said to them, "If I do not see in his hands the mark of the nails, and put my finger into the mark of the nails, and put my hand into his side, I will never no never believe."

26 And again after eight days his disciples were inside, and Thomas with them. Comes Jesus, the doors having been shut, and he stood in the midst and said, "Peace to you." 27 Then he says to Thomas, "Bring your finger here and see my hands, and bring your hand and put it into my side, and be not unbelieving but believing." 28 Thomas responded and said to him, "My Lord and my God!" 29

Jesus says to him, "Because you have seen me, you have believed. Blessed are those not having seen yet having believed."

30 And truly now, many other signs did Jesus in the presence of his disciples, which are not written in this book. 31 But these have been written that you might believe that Jesus is the Christ, the Son of God, and that believing you might have life in his name.

JOHN TWENTY-ONE

1 After these things, Jesus revealed himself again to the disciples at the Sea of Tiberius. And he revealed himself in this way.

2 Simon Peter, and Thomas called Didymus, and Nathanael from Cana of Galilee, and the ones of Zebedee, and two others of his disciples, they were together. 3 Simon Peter says to them, "I am going to fish." They say to him, "We also will come with you." They went out and went up into the boat, and in that night caught nothing.

4 Now morning having already come, Jesus stood on the shore. Nevertheless the disciples knew not it is Jesus. 5 Jesus therefore says to them, "Children, you don't have any fish, do you?" They answered him, "No." 6 Then he said to them, "Cast the net to the right side of the boat, and you will find some." Therefore they cast, and they were not able to haul it in from the multitude of the fish.

7 Says therefore the disciple whom Jesus loved, to Peter, "It is the Lord." Therefore Simon Peter, having heard that it is the Lord, put on his outer garment, for he was naked, and he cast himself into the sea. 8 And the other disciples came in the boat, for they were not far from the land, but about 350 feet, dragging the net with the fish.

9 Therefore, when they got onto the land, they see a fire of coals lying, and fish lying on it, and bread. 10 Jesus says to them, "Bring some of the fish that you have now caught." 11 Therefore Simon Peter went up and drew the net to the land, full of large fish, a hundred fifty-three; although there are so many the net was not torn.

12 Jesus says to them, "Come have breakfast." But none of the disciples dared to ask him "Who are you?" knowing that it is the Lord. 13 Comes Jesus and takes the bread and gives it to them, and likewise the fish. 14 This is now the third time Jesus was revealed to the disciples, having been raised out from the dead.

15 Then when they had dined, Jesus says to Simon Peter, "Simon of Jonah, love you me more than these?" He says to him, "Yes Lord, you know that I love you." He says to him, "Feed my lambs."

16 He says to him again a second time, "Simon of Jonah, love you me?" He says to him, "Yes Lord, you know that I love you." He says to him, "Shepherd my sheep."

17 He says to him the third time, "Simon of Jonah, love you

me?" Peter was grieved because he said to him the third time, "Love you me?" And he said to him, "Lord you know all things. You know that I love you." Jesus says to him, "Feed my sheep."

18 "I tell you the truth, when you were younger you put on your belt and walked where you desired. But when you are old you will stretch forth your hands and another will tie you and will carry you where you do not desire." 19 Now this he said signifying by what death he will glorify God.

And having said this, he says to him, "Follow me." 20 Peter, having turned, sees the disciple whom Jesus loved following, who had also reclined at the supper on his breast, and said, "Master, who is it who is betraying you?" 21 Peter, then, having seen, says to Jesus, "Lord, what about this man?" 22 Jesus says to him, "If I desire him to remain until I come, what *is it* to you? You follow me."

23 Therefore this saying went out among the brethren, that the disciple dies not. However, Jesus did not say to him, that he dies not, but, "If I desire him to remain until I come, what to you?" 24 This is the disciple bearing witness about these things, and the one having written these things; and we know that his testimony is true.

25 Now there are also many other things that Jesus did, which if they should be written, every one, I suppose not even the world itself to have space to hold the books to be written.[qq]

The Book of Acts

The Book of Acts is Luke's continuation of his account of the good news, showing the ministry of the Christ through the Holy Spirit, as the Holy Spirit acted through the Twelve, Paul, and other disciples, to take the good news throughout the known world. The Book of Acts was written ca. AD 62–63, during the time Paul was awaiting trial before the Caesar, and reveals selected events between the AD 33 Pentecost and AD 63, when Paul was released from prison.

ACTS ONE

1 Truly the first discourse I produced concerning all things, O Theophilus,[a1] which Jesus began to both do and to teach, 2 until the day, having given instructions to the apostles whom he had chosen by the Holy Spirit, he was taken up, 3 to whom also he presented himself alive after his suffering by many infallible proofs, during forty days being seen by them and speaking the things concerning the kingdom of God.

4 And being gathered together, he commanded them not to leave from Jerusalem, but to await the promise of the Father, "That which you heard of me. 5 Because John truly immersed you with water, but you will be immersed with the Holy Spirit after not many days."

6 Then[a2] those gathered together were asking him, saying, "Lord, if at this time, are you restoring the kingdom to Israel?" 7 He said to them, "It is not yours to know the times or seasons which the Father has placed in his own authority. 8 But you will receive power, the Holy Spirit having come upon you, and you will be witnesses for me, in both Jerusalem, and in all Judea, and Samaria, and to the extremity of the earth."

9 And having said these things, they looking on, he was taken up and a cloud hid him from their eyes. 10 And as their eyes were fixed as he was going into the heaven, also, look, two men stood nearby them in white clothing, 11 who also said, "People, Galileans, why do you stand looking into heaven? This Jesus, having been taken up from you into heaven, will thus come even as you saw him going into heaven."

12 Then they returned to Jerusalem from the mount called Olivet, which is near Jerusalem, a Sabbath day's journey away. 13 And when they had entered into the upper room, they went up where they were staying, both Peter and John, and Jacob and Andrew, Philip and Thomas, Bartholomew and Matthew, Jacob of Alphaeus, and Simon the Zealot, and Judas of Jacob. 14 These all were continuing steadfastly, all together in prayer, with the women, and Mariam the mother of Jesus, and his brethren.

15 And in these days Peter stood up among the brethren,

saying—then was the number of names at the same place about one hundred twenty—16 "People, brethren, it was necessary the Scripture to be fulfilled, which was spoken before by the Holy Spirit, by the mouth of David concerning Judas, the one who was a guide to those having seized Jesus, 17 because he was numbered with us and obtained a share of this ministry. 18 Truly this one then acquired a field out of the wages of unrighteousness, and falling headlong he burst in the middle, and all his inward parts poured out. 19 And it became known to all those living in Jerusalem, so that the field was named in their own language, Akeldama, that is, 'Field of Blood.'

20 "For it is written in the book of Psalms, 'Let his house become desolate,' and 'Let no one live in it,' and 'Let another take his office.' 21 It is necessary, therefore, the men who accompanied us, in all the time that the Lord Jesus came in and went out among us, 22 beginning from John's immersing until the day in which he was taken up from us, one of these to become a witness of his resurrection with us."

23 And they put before them two, Joseph called Barsabbas, who was called Justus, and Matthias. 24 And praying they said, "You Lord search the heart of all. Show which of these two you have chosen, one 25 to take the place of this ministry and apostleship, from which Judas turned aside to go to his own place." 26 And they gave lots for them, and the lot fell on Matthias. And he was numbered with the eleven apostles.

ACTS TWO

1 And with the day of Pentecost fully come, they were all together in the one place. 2 And suddenly came out of heaven a sound like a rushing violent wind, and it filled all the house where they were sitting. 3 And there appeared to them dividing tongues as of fire and sat upon each one of them. 4 And they were all filled with the Holy Spirit, and began to speak in other languages[a3] as the Spirit was giving to them to speak.

5 Now Jews were residing in Jerusalem, devout men from every nation of those under heaven. 6 Now when this sound occurred, the crowd came together and was confused, because each one was hearing them speak his own language.

7 Then they were astonished and were marveling, saying, "Look, are not all these who are speaking Galileans? 8 And how can we each hear our own language in which we were born? 9 Parthians, and Medes, and Elamites; and those inhabiting Mesopotamia, Judea also, and Cappadocia, Pontus, and Asia; 10 both Phrygia and Pamphylia, Egypt and the parts of Libya that are around Cyrene, and those visiting here from Rome, 11 both Jews and proselytes, Cretans and Arabs—we hear them speaking the great things of God in our own languages."

12 Now all were amazed and thoroughly perplexed, saying one to another, "To what purpose is this?" 13 But others, mocking, were saying, "They are full of new wine."

14 But Peter, standing with the eleven, lifted up his voice and declared to them, "Men of Judea and those residing in Jerusalem. All this let it be known to you and give attention to my words. 15 For these are not intoxicated with alcohol as you suppose; for it is about midmorning of the day. 16 But this is that spoken by the prophet Joel:

17 "And will be in the last times, says God, I will pour from my Spirit upon all flesh. And your sons will prophesy and your daughters; and your young men will see visions, and your elders will dream dreams. 18 And even upon my servants and upon my handmaidens in those times, I will pour from my spirit and they will prophecy. 19 And I will show wonders in heaven above, and signs on the earth below: blood and fire and dense smoke. 20 The sun will be turned into darkness, and the moon into blood, before the great and awesome coming day of the Lord. 21 And it shall be everyone, who if they shall call upon the name of the Lord, will be saved.'

22 "Men, Israelites, hear these words. Jesus of Nazareth, a man approved by God to you by mighty works and wonders and signs, which God did by him in your midst, as you yourselves know. 23 Him, by the determinate counsel and foreknowledge of God, delivered by lawless hands, having crucified, you put to death, 24 whom God raised up, loosing the bonds of physical death, inasmuch as it was not possible for him to be held by it.

25 "For David says about him, 'I foresaw the Lord always before me. Because he is at my right hand, so that I may not be shaken. 26 Because of this my heart was joyful and my tongue rejoiced. And now also my flesh will dwell in hope, 27 because you will not abandon my soul in hades, nor will you give up your holy one to see decay. 28 You have made known to me paths of life. You will fill me with joy in your presence.'

29 "Men, brethren, it is right to speak with confidence to you concerning the patriarch David, that he both died and was buried, and his tomb is among us to this day. 30 Being therefore a prophet, and knowing that God swore to him with an oath, the fruit out of his loins to set upon his throne. 31 Having foreseen, he spoke concerning the resurrection of the Christ, that neither was he abandoned into hades, nor his flesh saw decay.

32 "This Jesus God has raised up, whereof all we are witnesses. 33 Therefore, having been exalted to the right hand of God, and having received the promise of the Holy Spirit from the Father, he has poured out this which you are both seeing and hearing.

34 "For David did not ascend

into the heavens, but he himself said, 'The Lord said to my Lord, "Sit at my right hand, 35 until I place your enemies a footstool at your feet."' 36 Assuredly, therefore, let all the house of Israel know that God has made him both Lord and Christ—this Jesus whom you crucified."

37 Now having heard they were deeply moved in their heart. Then they said to Peter and the other apostles, "What shall we do, men, brethren?" 38 Then Peter to them: "Convert,[b] and be immersed, every one of you, in the name of Jesus Christ, for the forgiveness of your sins, and you will receive the gift of the Holy Spirit. 39 For to you is the promise, and to your children, and to all those far away, as many as shall call to oneself our Lord and God."

40 And many other words he earnestly testified, and was exhorting them, saying, "Be saved from this perverse generation." 41 Therefore those indeed receiving his word were immersed. And were added on that day about three thousand souls.

42 Now they were steadfastly continuing in the teaching of the apostles, and in fellowship, the breaking of bread, and the prayers. 43 Then awe was coming upon every soul, and many wonders and signs were happening through the apostles.

44 Now all those having believed were together, the same having all things in common. 45 And their possessions and goods they were selling and dividing them to all, as anyone had need.

46 And continuing steadfastly every day as with one mind in the temple, then at each home breaking bread, they were sharing food with gladness and sincerity of heart, 47 praising God and having favor with all the people. And the Lord kept on adding every day to their number those who were being saved.

ACTS THREE

1 Now Peter and John were going up into the temple at the hour of prayer, about midafternoon. 2 And a certain person, being lame from the womb of his mother, was being carried, whom they placed every day at the gate of the temple called "Beautiful," to beg money from those going into the temple. 3 Who, having seen Peter and John about to enter into the temple, was asking to receive money. 4 Now Peter, intently looking at him, with John, he said, "Look unto us." 5 And he gave attention to them, expecting to receive something from them.

6 But Peter said, "Silver and gold I have none. But this I have to give to you. In the name of Jesus Christ of Nazareth, get up and walk." 7 And taking him by the right hand, he raised him up. Now immediately his feet were strengthened, and his ankles.

8 And leaping up, he stood and began walking. And he entered into the temple with them,

walking and leaping and praising God. 9 And all the people saw him walking and praising God. 10 Now they recognized him, that he was the one sitting for money at the Beautiful gate of the temple. And they were filled with wonder and amazement at what had happened to him.

11 Now he is staying near to Peter and John. All the people, greatly amazed, ran together to them in the porch called "Solomon's." 12 But seeing this, Peter responded to the people, "Men, Israelites, why do you wonder at this? Or why look intently on us, as if by our own power or godliness we have made him to walk? 13 The God of Abraham, the God of Isaac, the God of Jacob—the God of our fathers—has glorified his servant, Jesus, whom you indeed betrayed and disowned in the presence of Pilate, he having judged to release him.

14 "But you denied the holy and righteous One, and demanded a man, a murderer, to be given to you. 15 And the author of life you killed, whom God has raised up out from the dead, whereof we are witnesses. 16 And upon faith in his name, his name has strengthened this person whom you see and know. And the truth that is in him has given to him this perfect wholeness in the presence of all of you.

17 "And now, brethren, I know that you acted in ignorance, as also your rulers. 18 But what God foretold by the mouth of all the prophets, that his Christ should suffer, he has thus fulfilled. 19 Convert, therefore, and turn you to him for the blotting out of your sins, 20 so that times of refreshing may come from the presence of the Lord, and he may send the One appointed to you, Christ Jesus, 21 whom it is necessary heaven indeed to receive, until the times of the restitution of all things, of which God spoke by the mouth of his holy prophets from the age.

22 "Moses indeed said, 'The Lord your God will raise up a prophet to you out from your brethren, like me. Him you will listen to in all things, as much as he may say to you.' 23 Now it will be every soul who, if might not listen to that prophet, will be utterly destroyed out from the people.

24 "And now all the prophets from Samuel, and those after, as many as have spoken, also proclaimed these times. 25 You are the sons of the prophets and of the covenant God made with your fathers, saying to Abraham, 'And in your seed, all the families of the earth will be blessed.' 26 To you first, God, having raised up his servant, sent him, blessing you by turning away each from your wickedness."

ACTS FOUR

1 Now as they were speaking to the people, the priests and the commander of the temple police and the Sadducees came upon them, 2 grieved on account of their

teaching the people and proclaiming in Jesus the resurrection out from the dead. 3 And they laid hands on them and put them into custody until the next day, for it was already evening. 4 But many of those having heard the word believed, and the number of men became about five thousand.

5 Then it happened on the next day, their rulers, and elders, and scribes were gathered together in Jerusalem, 6 and Annas the high priest, and Caiaphas, and John, and Alexander, and as many as were of high priestly descent. 7 And placing them in the middle, they began to ask, "In what power or in what name did you this?"

8 Then Peter, having been filled with the Holy Spirit, said to them, "Rulers of the people and elders. 9 If today we are being judged as to a good work to the infirm man, by what means he has been healed, 10 let it be known to you all and to all the people of Israel, that in the name of Jesus Christ of Nazareth, whom you crucified, whom God raised out from the dead, in him this man stands before you whole. 11 This is the stone having been rejected by you the builders, which has become into the head of the corner. 12 And the salvation is not in any other. For there is not another name under heaven having been given among men by which necessity we are to be saved."

13 Now seeing Peter's confidence, and John's, and having understood that they are uneducated men, and ordinary, they were astonished. Then they perceived that they had been with Jesus. 14 And seeing the man having been healed standing with them, they had nothing to speak against.

15 Now having commanded them to leave the council room, they began to confer with one another, 16 saying, "What shall we do to these men? For that truly a noteworthy sign has happened through them, is evident to all those living in Jerusalem, and we are not able to deny it. 17 But that it might not spread further abroad among the people, let us warn them no longer to speak in this name to no person." 18 And having called them, they commanded them not at all to speak nor to teach in the name of Jesus.

19 But Peter and John responding said to them, "Whether it is right before God to listen to you, rather than God, you must judge. 20 For we are not able, that which we have seen and heard, not to speak."

21 And having threatened them further, they let them go, finding nothing how they might punish them, on account of the people, because all were glorifying God for that having happened. 22 For the man, on whom had happened this sign of healing, was more than forty years of age.

23 Now having been released, they came to their own and made

known to them as much as the chief priests and the elders had said. 24 And having heard, as one they lifted up their voice to God and said, "Sovereign Lord, you made the heaven, and the earth, and the sea, and all that is in them.

25 "Our Father, you spoke by the Holy Spirit through the mouth of your servant David, 'Why did Gentiles rage, and peoples consider vain things? 26 The kings of the earth and the rulers were gathered together themselves to stand against the Lord and against his Christ.' 27 For in truth were gathered together, in this city, against your holy servant Jesus whom you anointed, both Herod and Pontius Pilate, with gentiles and peoples of Israel, 28 to do whatever your hand and purpose had foreordained to happen.

29 "And now, Lord, look upon their threats, and give to your servants with all boldness to speak your word, 30 in that you stretch out your hand for healing, and signs, and wonders to take place, through the name of your holy servant Jesus."

31 And they having prayed, the place in which they were assembled was shaken, and they were all filled with the Holy Spirit, and were speaking the word of God with boldness.

32 And those of the multitude having believed were one in heart and soul, and not one claimed to be his own anything of that which he possessed, but to them were all things in common. 33 And with great ability the apostles of the Lord Jesus were giving testimony of the resurrection; and abundant grace was upon them all.

34 For there was not even anyone in want among them. For as many as owners of lands or houses were selling them, were bringing the profit of what was sold, 35 and were laying at the feet of the apostles; then distribution was made to each just as anyone had need.

36 Now Joseph who was called Barnabas by the apostles (which is translated, 'Son of Encouragement'), a Levite, a Cypriot by birth, 37 selling a field owned by him, brought the money and laid it at the feet of the apostles.

ACTS FIVE

1 Now a certain man named Ananias, with Sapphira his wife, sold a property, 2 and he kept back some of the profits, his wife also being aware, and having brought a certain portion, he laid it at the apostles' feet. 3 But Peter said, "Ananias, what is the reason Satan has filled your heart for you to lie to the Holy Spirit and to keep back from the profit of the land? 4 While it remained, did it not remain to you? And having been sold, was it in your own authority? Why did you decide in your heart this action? You have not lied to men, but to God."

5 Now Ananias, hearing these words, fell down and died. And great fear came upon all those

hearing. 6 Then, getting up, the younger men covered him. And having carried him out, buried him.

7 Now it happened, about three hours later, his wife also, not knowing what had happened, came in. 8 Then Peter asked her, "Tell me, did you sell the land for so much?" And she said, "Yes, for so much." 9 But Peter said to her, "Why did you agree together to test the Lord?" Look, the feet of those who buried your husband are at the door, and they will carry you out."

10 Then she immediately fell down at his feet and breathed her last. Then the young men, coming in, found her dead. And carrying her out, they buried her by her husband. 11 And great fear came upon all the church and upon all those hearing these things.

12 Now by the hands of the apostles signs were happening and many wonders among the people. And they were all by unanimous consent in Solomon's Porch. 13 Now of the others, no one ventured to join them; but the people were praising them.

14 Now, more were added believing on the Lord, multitudes of both men and women, 15 so as even into the streets, to bring out the sick and to put them on cots and mats, that Peter coming, at least the shadow might overshadow some of them. 16 Now the multitude were also coming together from cities surrounding Jerusalem, bringing sick and those being harassed by unclean spirits, who all were healed.

17 But the high priest rose up. And all those with him, being of the sect of the Sadducees, were filled with envy. 18 And they laid hands on the apostles and put them in the public prison. 19 But a messenger of the Lord, opening the doors of the prison during the night, then having brought them out, said, 20 "Go, and standing in the temple speak to the people all the words of this life."

21 Now having heard, they entered at the dawn into the temple and were teaching. Now the high priest and those with him having come, they called together the Council, even all the Sanhedrin of the sons of Israel, and sent to the prison to bring them. 22 And the temple police having come did not find them in the prison. Then returning they reported back, 23 saying, "We found the prison shut, with all security, and the guards standing before the doors. But opening them we found no one inside."

24 Now when they heard these words, both the captain of the temple police and the chief priests were perplexed about them, what this might be. 25 Then, a certain one having come, reported to them, "Look, the men who you put in the prison are in the temple standing and teaching the people." 26 Then leaving, the captain with temple police were bringing them, not with force, for they feared the people lest they might be stoned.

27 Then having brought them, they set them in the Council. And the high priest asked them, 28 saying, "Did we not order you by a charge not to teach in this name? And look, you have filled Jerusalem with your teaching, and you intend to bring upon us the blood of this man."

29 But answering, Peter and the apostles said, "The necessity is to obey God rather than men. 30 The God of our fathers raised up Jesus, whom you killed, having hanged on a tree. 31 Him God exalted by his right hand as leader and savior, to give repentance to Israel and forgiveness of sins. 32 And we are witnesses of these things, and also the Holy Spirit, whom God has given to those obeying him."

33 Then having heard, they were enraged and desired to execute them. 34 But a certain man stood up in the Council, a Pharisee named Gamaliel, a teacher of the Law honored by all the people. He ordered the men to put them out for a short while.

35 Then he said to them, "Men, Israelites, take heed to yourselves with these men, what you are about to do. 36 For before these times Theudas rose up, saying himself to be somebody, to whom a number of men were joined, about four hundred, who was put to death, and all, as many as had been persuaded by him, were dispersed, and it came to nothing.

37 "After this man Judas the Galilean rose up, in the times of the registration, and drew people away after him. And he died, and all, as many as were persuaded by him, were dispersed.

38 "And now I say to you, remove yourselves from these men, and let them alone. Because if it be from men, this plan or this work will be destroyed. 39 But if it is from God, you will not be able to destroy them, lest also you would be found fighting against God."

40 Now they were persuaded by him. And calling in the apostles, having beaten them, they commanded them not to speak in the name of Jesus, and released them.

41 Therefore they indeed left from the presence of the Council, rejoicing that they had been counted worthy to suffer dishonor for the Name. 42 Then every day in the temple and from house to house, they did not stop teaching and proclaiming the good news that Jesus is the Christ.

ACTS SIX

1 Now in these times the disciples are multiplying. The Hellenists Jews began grumbling against the Hebrews, because in the daily ministration their widows were neglected.

2 Then the Twelve called the multitude of the disciples. They said, "It is not well-pleasing for us to neglect the word of God to minister to tables. 3 Therefore, brethren, select men with a good testimony out from yourselves,

seven full of the Spirit and wisdom, whom we will set over this task. 4 Now we will continue steadfastly in the prayer and ministry of the word."

5 And this saying was satisfactory before all the multitude. And they chose Stephen, a man full of faith and the Holy Spirit, and Philip, and Prochorus, and Nicanor, and Timon, and Parmenas, and Nicolas a convert of Antioch, 6 whom they set before the apostles. And praying, they laid their hands on them.

7 And the word of God increased, and the number of the disciples in Jerusalem was exceedingly multiplied. Then a great number of the priests were becoming obedient to the faith.

8 Now Stephen, full of grace and power, was doing wonders and great signs among the people. 9 But certain of those arose out of the synagogue, called "Freedmen," including Cyrenians, and Alexandrians, and those from Cilicia and Asia, disputing with Stephen. 10 And they did not have the ability to stand against the wisdom and the Spirit by whom he was speaking.

11 Then they induced men to say, "We have heard him speaking slanderous words against Moses and God." 12 Then they incited the people and the elders and the scribes, and coming near they took him with great violence and brought him to the Council. 13 They also set false witnesses, saying, "This man does not stop speaking words against the holy place and the Law. 14 For we have heard him saying that Jesus of Nazareth will destroy this place and will change the customs that Moses delivered to us." 15 And looking intently at him, all sitting in the Council saw his face as the face of a messenger *of God.*

ACTS SEVEN

1 Then the high priest said, "If these things are so?" 2 And Stephen was speaking, "Men, brethren, and fathers listen. The God of glory appeared to our father Abraham, being in Mesopotamia, before his living in Haran. 3 And God said to him, 'Go from your country and your relatives, and come into the land which I will show to you.' 4 Then having left from the land of the Chaldeans, Abraham lived in Haran.

"From there, after Abraham's father died, God moved him into this land, in which you now live. 5 And he did not give to him an inheritance in it, not even a footstep. But he promised to give it to him for a possession, and to his descendants after him, there not being to him a child.

6 "But thus spoke God, that his offspring will be a temporary dweller in a strange land, and they will enslave it and they will mistreat it four hundred years. 7 And the nation to which if they will be enslaved, 'I will judge,' God said, 'and after these things they will come out and will serve me in this

place.' 8 And he gave to him the covenant of circumcision. And thus Abraham fathered Isaac and circumcised him on the eighth day, and Isaac Jacob, and Jacob the Twelve patriarchs.

9 "And the patriarchs, being envious of Joseph, sold him into Egypt. But God was with him 10 and rescued him out of all his tribulations, and gave him favor and wisdom before Pharoah, king of Egypt. And he appointed him procurator over Egypt, and over all his house.

11 "Then came a famine upon all of Egypt and Canaan, and great affliction; and our fathers did not find food. 12 Now Jacob, having heard there is grain in Egypt, he sent our fathers first; 13 and on the second time Joseph made himself known to his brothers; and the family of Joseph became known to Pharaoh.

14 "Then Joseph having sent, he summoned Jacob, his father, and all the relatives: in all seventy-five persons. 15 And Jacob went down into Egypt and died, he and our fathers. 16 And they were taken into Shechem and placed in the tomb which Abraham had bought for an amount of silver from the sons of Hamor in Shechem.

17 "Now as the time of the promise that God had promised to Abraham was drawing near, the people increased and multiplied in Egypt, 18 until that there arose another king over Egypt who did not know Joseph, 19 he being deceitful with our people, ill-treating our fathers, making them abandon the infants that they would not continue to live.

20 "In that time Moses was born, and he was beautiful to God, who was brought up three months in the house of his father. 21 Then he, having been exposed, Pharoah's daughter took him, and brought him up a son for herself; 22 and Moses was instructed in all the wisdom of the Egyptians.

"Now he was mighty in his words and deeds. 23 Then when a time of forty years had passed, it came into his mind to visit his brethren, the sons of Israel. 24 And seeing a certain one being wronged, he defended him, and did justice for the one being oppressed, having killed the Egyptian.

25 "Now he assumed his brethren to understand that God by his hand is giving them salvation; but they did not understand. 26 And on the following day, he appeared to those who were quarrelling and urged them to peace, having said, 'Men, you are brothers. So that why wrong you one another?'

27 "But the one mistreating his neighbor pushed him away, saying, 'Who made you a ruler and judge over us? 28 Do you wish to kill me, the same way you killed the Egyptian yesterday?' 29 Then Moses fled at this saying, and came to live in Midian, where he fathered two sons.

30 "And forty years having passed, a messenger appeared to

him in the wilderness of the mountain Sinai, in a flame of fire of a bush. 31 And Moses having seen, wondered at the sight. Then him coming near to consider it, there was the Lord's voice: 32 'I am the God of your fathers: the God of Abraham, and of Isaac, and of Jacob.' Then Moses became terrified, he dared not to observe.

33 "Then the Lord said to him, 'Take the sandal off of your feet, for the place in which you stand is holy ground. 34 Having seen, I saw the affliction of my people in Egypt, and their groaning I have heard, and I have come down to deliver them. And now come, I will send you to Egypt.'

35 "This Moses, whom they refused, having said, 'Who appointed you ruler and judge?'—him whom God sent as ruler and liberator by the hand of the messenger appearing to him in the bush—36 this one led them out of Egypt, having done wonders and signs in the land of Egypt, and in the Red Sea, and in the wilderness forty years.

37 "This is the Moses saying to the sons of Israel, 'A prophet God will raise up for you out from your brethren, like me.' 38 This is the one having been in the public assembly in the wilderness, with the messenger speaking to him in the Mount Sinai, and of our fathers, who received living oracles to give to us, 39 to whom our fathers were not willing to be obedient, but thrust away, and turned back in their hearts to Egypt, 40 saying to Aaron, 'Make us gods who will go before us. As for this Moses, who brought us out from the land of Egypt, we know not what has happened to him.'

41 "And they made a calf in those times and offered a sacrifice to the idol, and they rejoiced in the works of their hands. 42 Then God turned away, and delivered them to worship the host of heaven, as it has been written in the scroll of the prophets: 'Did you not offer slaughtered animals and sacrifices to me in the forty years in the wilderness, O house of Israel? 43 And you took up the tabernacle of Molech, and the star of your god Rhaiphan, the images that you made to worship them. And I will move you beyond Babylon.'

44 "The tabernacle of the testimony was with our fathers in the wilderness, just as the one speaking to Moses had commanded, to make it according to the model that he had seen, 45 and which our fathers brought it, having received it by succession with Joshua in the taking possession of the nations, whom God drove out from the presence of our fathers, until the times of David, 46 who found grace in God's presence and asked to find a dwelling place for the God of Jacob; 47 but Solomon built him a house.

48 "But the Most High does not dwell in that made with hands. As the prophet says, 49 'Heaven is to me a throne, and the earth a footstool of my feet. What kind of

house will you build me,' says the Lord, 'or what is the place of my rest? 50 Has not my hand made all these things?'

51 "Obstinate and uncircumcised in heart and ears, you always resist the Holy Spirit; as your fathers, you also. 52 Which of the prophets did your fathers not persecute? And they killed those who foretold about the coming of the Righteous One, of whom you have become traitors and murderers, 53 who received the Law by the appointment of messengers, and have not kept it."

54 Now hearing these things, they were enraged in their hearts and began gnashing their teeth at him. 55 But he was full of the Holy Spirit, and looking intently into heaven, saw the glory of God, and Jesus standing at the right hand of God. 56 And he said, "Look! I see the heavens opened, and the Son of Man standing at the right hand of God."

57 Then exclaiming in a loud voice, they stopped up their ears and rushed with one accord upon him, 58 and casting him out of the city, they began to stone him. And the witnesses laid aside their clothing at the feet of a young man named Saul.

59 And as they were stoning Stephen, he was calling out and saying, "Lord Jesus, receive my spirit." 60 Then falling on his knees, he cried out in a loud voice, "Lord, do not confirm to them this sin." And having said this, he died.

ACTS EIGHT

1 Now Saul was there approving the murder. Then on that day began a great persecution against the church which was in Jerusalem. Then all were dispersed throughout the lands of Judea and Samaria, except the apostles. 2 Now devout men buried Stephen, and made great lamentation over him. 3 But Saul was ravaging the church, entering their houses, dragging away men and women, delivering them to prison.

4 Then therefore, those having been dispersed, went about preaching the word. 5 Now Philip, having gone to a city of Samaria, was proclaiming to them the Christ. 6 Then the crowds with one accord were giving attention to the things spoken by Philip in their hearing and seeing the signs he was doing. 7 For many of those having unclean spirits, crying in a loud voice, were coming out; and many, being paralyzed and lame, were healed. 8 Then there was great joy in that city.

9 Now a certain man named Simon, who before in the city was practicing magic and astonishing the people of Samaria, saying himself to be someone great, 10 to whom all gave attention from small to great, saying, "This one is the power of God that is called 'great.'"

11 Now they were giving him attention because he had amazed them a long time with the magical arts. 12 But when they believed Philip, preaching the good news concerning the kingdom of God, and the name of Jesus Christ, they

were immersed, both men and women. 13 And Simon himself also believed, and having been immersed, was continuing steadfastly with Philip. Then carefully observing the signs and great miracles, he was amazed.

14 Now the apostles in Jerusalem, having heard that Samaria had received the word of God, they sent to them Peter and John, 15 who having come down, prayed for them that they might receive the Holy Spirit. 16 For not yet was he fallen upon any of them. But they had only been immersed into the name of the Lord Jesus. 17 Then they began to lay their hands upon them, and they received the Holy Spirit.

18 But Simon having seen that through the laying on of the hands of the apostles the Holy Spirit was given, he offered to them money, 19 saying, "Give to me also this authority, that on whom if I might lay the hands, he might receive the Holy Spirit."

20 But Peter said to him, "Your silver, with you, may it be to destruction, because you thought by money the gift of God may be purchased. 21 There is no part to you, nor share, in this matter, for your heart is not right before God. 22 Therefore repent of this your wickedness, and pray earnestly to the Lord, if indeed the intent of your heart will be forgiven. 23 For I see you being in the gall of bitterness and the bond of unrighteousness." 24 Then Simon answering said, "You beseech the Lord on my behalf, so that nothing may come upon me, of which you have spoken."

25 Truly therefore, they earnestly testified, and having spoken the word of the Lord, traveled back to Jerusalem; then to many villages of the Samaritans they were preaching the good news.

26 Now a messenger of the Lord spoke to Philip, saying, "Get up and go toward the south, to the road going down from Jerusalem to Gaza." This is the desert road.

27 And getting up, he went. And look, a man, an Ethiopian, a eunuch, an official of Queen Candace of the Ethiopians, who was over all her treasure, who had come to Jerusalem to worship. 28 He was returning and sitting in his chariot, and he was reading the prophet Isaiah.

29 Then the Spirit said to Philip, "Go near and join yourself to this chariot." 30 Then Philip, having run up, heard him reading Isaiah the prophet, and said, "Do you also understand what you are reading?" 31 And he said, "For how could I be able, if someone will not guide me?" Then he invited Philip to come up and sit with him.

32 Now the passage of the Scripture which he was reading was this. "As a sheep to slaughter he was led, and as a lamb before the one shearing him is silent, so he opens not his mouth. 33 In his humiliation justice was taken away from him. Who will declare his generation? For his life is removed

from the earth."

34 Now responding, the eunuch said to Philip, "I beseech you, concerning whom the prophet says this? Concerning himself, or concerning some other?" 35 Then Philip, having opened his mouth, and beginning from that Scripture, proclaimed the good news to him—Jesus.

36 Then as they were going along the road, they came upon some water. Then says the eunuch, "Look, water. What prevents me to be immersed." 37 Then Philip said, "If you believe out of all the heart, it is permitted." He responded and said, "I believe the Son of God to be Jesus the Christ."

38 And he commanded the chariot to stop. And they both went down into the water, both Philip and the eunuch, and he immersed him. 39 Now when they came up out of the water, the Spirit of the Lord caught up Philip, and the eunuch saw him no more; for he went on his way rejoicing. 40 But Philip was found at Azotus, and passing through, he proclaimed the good news to all towns, until his coming to Caesarea.

ACTS NINE

1 But Saul—still breathing out menace and murder toward the disciples of the Lord—going to the high priest, 2 desired of him letters to Damascus for the synagogues, so that if he found any of that Way, whether men or women, he might bring them bound to Jerusalem.

3 Now in going, it happened as he drew near to Damascus, suddenly a light from heaven flashed around him. 4 And falling on the ground, he heard a voice saying to him, "Saul, Saul. Why do you persecute me?" 5 Then he said, "Who are you, Sir?" Then, "I am Jesus, whom you are persecuting.[c1] 6 But get up and enter into the city, and it will be told to you what you must do."

7 Now the men traveling with him stood speechless, hearing indeed the voice, but seeing no one. 8 Then Saul got up from the ground. But opening his eyes, he could not see. Then leading him by the hand, they brought him to Damascus. 9 And he was three days without sight, and he did neither eat nor drink.

10 Now there was a certain disciple in Damascus named Ananias. And the Lord said to him in a vision, "Ananias." And he said, "I am here, Lord." 11 And the Lord to him, "Get up. Go into the street called Straight, and look in Judas' house for Saul named of Tarsus. For look, he is praying, 12 and he saw a man in a vision named Ananias coming and putting hands on him, that he might see again.

13 But Ananias responded, "Lord, I have heard from many about this man, how many evils he did to your saints in Jerusalem. 14 And he is here with authority from the chief priests to bind all those calling on your name." 15 But the Lord said to him, "Go. Because this man is my chosen vessel to carry my name before the gentiles and

kings and the sons of Israel. 16 For I will show to him how much he must suffer for my name."

17 Then Ananias went, and he entered into the house, and laying hands upon him, he said, "Brother Saul, the Lord has sent me, Jesus, the one having appeared to you on the road by which you were coming, that you may see again and be filled with the Holy Spirit." 18 And immediately fell from his eyes like scales, and he could see again. And getting up he was immersed; 19 and taking food, he was strengthened. Now he was with the disciples in Damascus certain days.

20 And immediately he began proclaiming Jesus in the synagogues, that he is the son of God. 21 Then all hearing were amazed, and were saying, "Is this not the one having wreaked havoc in Jerusalem on those calling upon this name? And for this he had come here, that binding them he might bring them to the chief priest?" 22 But Saul was much the more empowered, and continued to confound the Jews dwelling in Damascus, proving that this is the Christ.

23 Now when many days had passed, the Jews plotted together to kill him. 24 But their plot became known to Saul. Now they were also watching the city gates day and night, so that they might kill him. 25 But his disciples took him by night, they let him down through the wall, lowering him in a basket.

26 Now arriving in Jerusalem, he tried to join the disciples. And all feared him, not believing that he is a disciple. 27 But Barnabas, taking him, brought him to the apostles. And he told them how on the road he had seen the Lord, and that he had spoken to him, and how in Damascus he had spoken openly in the name of Jesus. 28 And he was with them going in and going out in Jerusalem, speaking openly in the name of the Lord.

29 And he was speaking and reasoning with the Hellenist Jews, but they were attempting to kill him. 30 But knowing this, the brethren brought him to Caesarea, and sent him away to Tarsus.

31 Then indeed the church throughout all of Judea, and Galilee, and Samaria had peace, being built up in the faith and going on in the fear of the Lord; and by the exhortation of the Holy Spirit they were multiplied.

32 Now it happened that Peter, passing through all, also went to the saints dwelling in Lydda. 33 Now there he found a certain man named Aeneas, for eight years lying on a padded quilt, who was paralyzed. 34 And Peter said to him, "Aeneas, Jesus Christ heals you. Get up and make your own bed." And immediately he got up. 35 And all those dwelling in Lydda and Sharon saw him, and they turned to the Lord.

36 Now in Joppa there was a disciple named Tabitha, which translated is called Dorcas. She was full of good works and of compassionate acts for the poor

that she continually did. 37 But it happened in those days becoming ill she died. Then they washed her and placed her in an upper room.

38 Now Joppa being near Lydda, the disciples, hearing that Peter is in it, sent two men to him, begging, "Do not delay coming to us." 39 Then getting up, Peter went with them, who having arrived, brought him into the upper room. And all the widows stood by him, wailing and showing him the tunics and clothing that Dorcas had made while she was with them.

40 Then Peter, putting all outside, and getting on his knees, he prayed. And turning to the body he said, "Tabitha, get up." And she opened her eyes, and seeing Peter, she sat up. 41 Then giving her his hand, he helped her stand up. And calling the saints and the widows, he presented her living.

42 Now it became known throughout all of Joppa; and many believed on the Lord. 43 Then it happened he stayed many days in Joppa with a certain Simon, a tanner.

ACTS TEN

1 Now a certain man in Caesarea, named Cornelius, was a centurion of the cohort that is called Italian. 2 He was pious and reverencing God with all his household, doing many compassionate acts to the people and always praying to God. 3 He saw clearly in a vision, at about midafternoon, a messenger of God coming to him and saying to him, "Cornelius."

4 And intently looking at him, and becoming fearful, he said, "What is it sir?" Then he said to him, "Your prayers and your compassionate works have ascended as a memorial before God. 5 And now send men to Joppa and summon Simon, a man who is called Peter. 6 He is a guest with a certain Simon, a tanner, whose house is by the sea. He will tell you what you ought to do."

7 When the messenger speaking to him had left, he called of those attending to him two of his servants and a pious soldier. 8 And telling them all things, he sent them to Joppa.

9 Then the next day, as those are travelling and coming near the city, Peter went up on the roof to pray, about noon. 10 Now he became hungry and wanted to eat. But as they were preparing, he fell into a trance. 11 And he sees heaven opening, and a certain vessel descending, as a great linen cloth, being let down upon the earth by four corners, 12 in which were all the four-footed animals and creeping things of the earth, and birds of heaven.

13 And a voice came to him. "Peter, get up, kill and eat." 14 And Peter said, "By no means, Lord. For never have I eaten anything common or unclean." 15 And a voice came again to him for the second time. "That which God has cleansed, you may not call common." 16 Now this happened three times. And immediately the

vessel was taken up into the heaven.

17 Now while in himself Peter was perplexed, what that vision he had seen might mean, look, the men sent from Cornelius, having asked for the house of Simon, stood at the gate. 18 And having called, they were asking, if Simon who is called Peter was a guest here? 19 And as Peter was considering the vision, the Spirit said to him, "Look, three men are seeking you. 20 But get up, go down, and go with them, doubting nothing, because I have sent them."

21 Then Peter went down to the men who had been sent to him from Cornelius. He said, "Behold I am the one whom you seek. Why are you here?" 22 And they said, "Cornelius, a centurion, a man righteous and fearing God, having a good witness by all the nation of the Jews, was divinely admonished by a holy messenger to send for you to his house and to hear words from you." 23 Therefore, having called them in, he received them as guests. Then on the next day, getting up, he went out with them, and some of the brethren from Joppa went with him.

24 Then on the next day, he entered into Caesarea, and Cornelius was expecting them, having called together his relatives and close friends. 25 Now as Peter was entering, Cornelius met him, falling at his feet, publicly showing him great respect.[c2] 26 But Peter lifted him up, saying, "Get up. I myself am also a man."

27 And talking with him, he entered, and found many gathered together. 28 Then he was saying to them, "You know how unlawful it is for a man, a Jew, to join himself or to come near to a foreigner. To me, however, God has shown not to call man common or unclean. 29 Also therefore I came without objection, being invited. I ask, therefore, for what reason did you invite me?"

30 And Cornelius was saying, "Four days ago, until this hour, I was about midafternoon praying in my house. And behold, a man stood before me in bright clothing, 31 and said, 'Cornelius, your prayer has been heard, and your compassionate works have been remembered before God. 32 Send therefore to Joppa and call for Simon, who is called Peter. He is a guest in the house of Simon, a tanner by the sea.' 33 Therefore, at once I sent to you. You, then, did right to come. Now therefore, we are all present before God to hear all the things commanded you by the Lord."

34 The Peter opened his mouth, saying, "Of a truth I understand that God is not one who is a respecter of persons. 35 But in every nation the one reverencing him and working righteousness is acceptable to him. 36 "The word that he sent to the sons of Israel, proclaiming the good news of peace through Jesus Christ—he is Lord of all— 37 you yourselves know the word having

come through all Judea, having begun from Galilee, after the immersing that John proclaimed.

38 Jesus from Nazareth, how God anointed him with the Holy Spirit, and with power, who went about doing good and healing all those who were oppressed by the devil, because God was with him. 39 And we are witnesses of all things that he did in both the land of the Jews and in Jerusalem. Whom also they put to death, having hanged him on a tree.

40 "This one God raised up on the third day, and gave him to become known, 41 not to all the people, but to witnesses who were chosen beforehand by God; to us who did eat with him and drink with him after his rising out from the dead. 42 And he instructed us to proclaim to the people and to testify fully that he is the one having been appointed by God as judge of living and dead. 43 To him all the prophets bear witness, that everyone believing on him receives forgiveness of sins through his name."

44 Peter still speaking these words, the Holy Spirit fell upon all those hearing the word. 45 And the believers out of the circumcision were amazed, as many as had come with Peter, that also upon the gentiles the gift of the Holy Spirit had been poured out. 46 For they were hearing them speaking in languages and magnifying God.

Then Peter responded, 47 "Is anyone able to hinder the water not to immerse these who have received the Holy Spirit just as we also?" 48 Then he commanded them to be immersed in the name of Jesus Christ. Then they asked him to remain some days.

ACTS ELEVEN

1 Now the apostles and the brethren in Judea heard that also the gentiles had received the Word of God. 2 Then when Peter went up to Jerusalem, those of the circumcision began disputing, 3 saying, "You went to men uncircumcised, and ate with them."

4 Now Peter began to explain to them in order, saying, 5 "I was in the city of Joppa, praying, and I saw in a trance a vision, a certain vessel descending like a great linen sheet, being let down by four corners out of heaven; and it came down until it reached me. 6 Looking intently on it, I observed and I saw the four-footed animals of the earth, and the wild beasts, and the creeping things, and the birds of the air.

7 "Then also I heard a voice saying to me, 'Get up, Peter, kill and eat.' 8 But I said, 'In no way, Lord, because nothing common or unclean has ever entered into my mouth.' 9 But the voice out of heaven answered for a second time, 'What God has cleansed you do not call unclean.'

10 "Now this happened on three times, and all was drawn up again into heaven. 11 And look, immediately three men stood at the house where I was a guest,

having been sent to me from Caesarea. 12 Then the Spirit told me to go with them, not making a distinction. And these six brethren went with me also, and we entered into the man's house. 13 Then he related to us how he had seen the messenger in his house, who stood and said, 'Send forth to Joppa, and send for Simon, who is called Peter, 14 who will speak words to you, by which you will be saved, and all your household.'

15 "And in my beginning to speak, the Holy Spirit fell upon them, even as upon us in the beginning. 16 Then I remembered the word of the Lord, how he had said, 'John truly immersed with water. But you will be immersed with the Holy Spirit.' 17 If then God has given to them the same gift as also to us having believed on the Lord Jesus Christ, how was I able to hinder God?" 18 Then having heard these things, they agreed, and glorified God, saying, "Then also to the gentiles God has given conversion unto life."

19 Those, indeed, therefore, having been dispersed abroad by the tribulation taking place over Stephen, passed through to Phoenicia, and Cyprus, and Antioch, speaking the word to no one except only to the Jews. 20 But some of them were men of Cyprus and Cyrene, who coming into Antioch *of Syria*, were speaking also to the Hellenist Jews, proclaiming the good news: the Lord Jesus Christ. 21 And the hand of the Lord was with them. Then a large number having believed turned to the Lord.

22 Now word of these things concerning them was heard in the ears of the church that was in Jerusalem. And they sent out Barnabas to go as far as Antioch *of Syria*. 23 Who coming and seeing the grace of God, rejoiced and exhorted all to abide in the Lord with deliberate intent of heart, 24 because he was a good man, and full of the Holy Spirit, and of faith. And many people were added to the Lord.

25 He then went out to Tarsus to seek Saul. 26 And having found him, he brought him to Antioch *of Syria*. Then it happened they also came together a whole year with the church and taught many people. Then the disciples were first called in Antioch, "Christians."

27 Now in those times, prophets came down from Jerusalem to Antioch *of Syria*. 28 Then one of them named Agabus stood up. By the Spirit he declared a great famine is about to be over all the world; which came to pass under Claudius. 29 And the disciples, as anyone was prospered, each of them decided, for ministry, to send to the brethren living in Judea. 30 Which also they did, sending to the elders by the hand of Barnabas and Saul.

ACTS TWELVE

1 Now at that time, Herod the King reached out his hands to harm some of those of the church. 2 Then he put to death Jacob, the brother of John, with the sword. 3

Then seeing that it is pleasing to the Jews, he further took Peter also, during the days of Unleavened Bread. 4 And whom, having taken, he put in prison, delivering him to four squads of four soldiers each to guard him, intending after the Passover to bring him out to the people. 5 Indeed, therefore, Peter was kept in the prison. But earnest prayer was being made to God by the church concerning him.

6 When Herod was about to bring him out, that night Peter was sleeping between two soldiers, bound with two chains; also guards before the door were watching the prison. 7 And look, a messenger of the Lord stood by, and a light shone in the prison. Then striking Peter's side he woke him, saying, "Get up quickly." And his chains fell from his hands. 8 Then the messenger said to him, "Put on your belt and sandals." And so he did. And he says to him, "Wrap your cloak around you and follow me."

9 And going out, he was following and did not know that what was happening by means of the messenger was genuine, but he was thinking he saw a vision. 10 Then, passing by a first guard and a second, they came to the iron gate leading into the city, which opened to them by itself. And going out, they went further one street, and the messenger immediately withdrew from him. 11 And Peter, having come to himself, said, "Now I truly know that the Lord sent his messenger to me and took me out of the hand of Herod and all the expectation of the Jewish people."

12 Having considered, he came to Mary's house, mother of John who is called Mark, where many were gathered together and praying. 13 Then he having knocked at the door of the gate, a girl named Rhoda came to answer. 14 And recognizing Peter's voice, from joy she did not open the gate, but running in she announced Peter was standing before the gate. 15 But they said to her, "You are out of your mind." But she kept on insisting it to be so. But they kept saying, "It is his messenger."[d]

16 But Peter kept on knocking. Then opening the gate they saw him and were astonished. 17 Then gesturing to them with his hand to be silent, he told them how the Lord had brought him out of the prison. Then he said, "Go tell Jacob and the brethren these things." And leaving he went to another place.

18 Now when it was day, there was no small commotion among the soldiers, what then has become of Peter. 19 Then Herod was seeking him, and not finding him, examined the guards, then commanded them to be executed. And going down from Judea to Caesarea, he stayed there.

20 Now he had been enraged with the Tyrians and Sidonians. Then with one accord they came to him. And persuading Blastus, who was over the king's bedroom, they were seeking peace—because

their region was being fed by the King's. 21 Then, on the day arranged, Herod, having put on royal clothing and sitting on the judgment seat, made a public address to them. 22 And the people were crying out, "Voice of a god and not of a man!" 23 Then immediately a messenger of the Lord struck him, because he did not give the glory to God. And being eaten by worms, he died.

24 But the word of God continued to grow and to multiply. 25 Then Barnabas and Saul returned, the mission to Jerusalem completed, bringing with them John, the one called Mark.

ACTS THIRTEEN

1 Now there were in Antioch *of Syria*, in the church being there, prophets and teachers: both Barnabas and Simeon, who is called Niger, and Lucius the Cyrenian, also Manaen brought up with Herod the Tetrarch, and Saul.

2 Now as they were ministering to the Lord and fasting, the Holy Spirit said, "Separate now to me Barnabas and Saul for the work to which I have called them." 3 Then having fasted, and having prayed, and having laid the hands on them, they sent them away.

4 Therefore, they indeed having been sent out by the Holy Spirit, went to Seleucia. From that place they sailed to Cyprus. 5 And coming into Salamis, they began proclaiming the word of God in the synagogues of the Jews. Now, they had also John as an assistant.

6 Then passing through all the island, as far as Paphos, they found a man, a certain diviner, a Jewish false prophet, whose name was Bar-Jesus, 7 who was with the Proconsul Sergius Paulus, a discerning man. He called Barnabas and Saul, desiring to hear the word of God.

8 But Elymas the diviner—for thus means his name—was opposing them, seeking to turn the Proconsul away from the faith. 9 Then Saul, that is, Paul, filled with the Holy Spirit, looking intently upon him, 10 said, "O full of all deceit and all mischief, son of the devil, enemy of all righteousness, will you not stop perverting the straight ways of the Lord? 11 And now, look, the hand of the Lord is upon you, and you will be blind, not seeing the sun during a season." Then immediately mist and darkness fell upon him, and going about he was seeking someone to lead him by the hand. 12 Then the Proconsul, having seen what happened, he believed, being astonished at the teaching of the Lord.

13 Then having sailed from Paphos, and those with him, Paul came to Perga of Pamphylia. But John left them, returning to Jerusalem. 14 Now they passed through from Perga, and coming to Antioch of Pisidia, went into the synagogue on the day of the Sabbaths, sitting down. 15 Then after the reading of the Law and of the prophets, the rulers of the synagogue sent to them, saying, "Men, brethren, if there is among

you a word of exhortation toward the people, speak."

16 Then Paul getting up, and making a gesture with his hand, he said, "Men, Israelites, and those fearing God, listen. 17 The God of this people of Israel chose our fathers, and prospered the people in the sojourn in the land of Egypt, and with an uplifted arm brought them out of it. 18 And so for a period of forty years he endured their ways in the wilderness. 19 And after destroying seven nations in the land of Canaan, he distributed their land by lot to them, 20 during four hundred and fifty years. And after these things he gave them judges until Samuel the prophet.

21 "Then they asked for a king, and God gave to them Saul, son of Kish, a man of the tribe of Benjamin, forty years. 22 And having removed him, he raised up David to them as king, to whom he also said, giving this witness, 'I have found David, the son of Jesse, a man according to my heart, who will do all my will.'

23 "God, of this man's offspring, according to promise, has brought to Israel the Savior Jesus, 24 of whom, before his coming, John proclaimed an immersion of repentance to all the people of Israel. 25 While then John was fulfilling his ministry, he was saying, 'Whom do you suppose me to be? I am not he, but look, he comes after me, of whom I am not worthy to untie a sandal on his feet.'

26 "Men, brethren, sons of the family of Abraham, and those among you fearing God, to us the message of this salvation has been sent. 27 For those living in Jerusalem and their rulers, not knowing him and the voices of the prophets read on every Sabbath, condemning him, they fulfilled them. 28 And no reason of death found, they begged Pilate to put him to death. 29 Then when all the things having been written about him were completed, they took him down from the tree, and they put him in a tomb. 30 But God raised him out from the dead, 31 who appeared for many days to those who came with him from Galilee to Jerusalem, who are now witnesses of him to the people.

32 "And to you we proclaim the good news, the promise made to the fathers, 33 this that God has fulfilled to their children, to us, having raised up Jesus. As also has been written in the second psalm: 'You are my son. Today I have begotten you.' 34 Now that he raised him out from the dead, being no more to return to corruption, thus he spoke, 'I will give to you the holy and sure blessings of David.' 35 For this reason also in another he says, 'You will not allow your holy one to see corruption.'

36 "For David, indeed, having served the purpose of God in his own generation, fell asleep and was added to his fathers, and saw corruption. 37 But the one God raised up did not see corruption.

38 "Therefore be it known to

you, men, brethren, that through this one, to you forgiveness of sins is proclaimed. 39 And from all things from which you were not able in the Law of Moses to be justified, in him everyone believing is justified. 40 Be aware, therefore, so that what is said in the prophets might not come upon you: 41 'Observe you despisers, and wonder, and fear, because I am working a work in your times, a work that you would never no never believe, even if one should declare it to you.'"

42 As they were leaving, they were desiring these words be spoken to them on the next Sabbath. 43 Then the synagogue service having ended, many of the Jews, and of the worshiping gentile converts,[e1] followed Paul and Barnabas, who speaking to them kept on persuading them to continue in the grace of God.

44 Then on the next Sabbath, almost all the city gathered together to hear the word of the Lord. 45 But the Jews, seeing the crowds, were filled with jealousy, and began speaking against the things spoken by Paul, slandering. 46 Paul, and also Barnabas, speaking boldly said, "To you it was necessary the word of God first be spoken. But because you reject it, and you judge yourselves unworthy of eternal life, look, we are turning to the gentiles. 47 For so the Lord has commanded us: 'I have set you for a light of the gentiles, for you to be salvation to the uttermost part of the earth.'"

48 Then hearing this, the gentiles were rejoicing and glorifying the word of the Lord, and believed, as many as were ordained to eternal life. 49 Then the word of the Lord was published throughout all the region.

50 But the Jews stirred up the women of high standing, and the leading men of the city, and they excited a persecution against Paul and Barnabas; and they forced them out of their territory. 51 But, shaking off the dust on their feet against them, they went to Iconium. 52 And the disciples were filled with joy and the Holy Spirit.

ACTS FOURTEEN

1 Now it happened in Iconium, they entered together into the synagogue of the Jews, and spoke, so that a great number of both Jews and Greeks believed. 2 But the unbelieving Jewish excited and made evil the souls of the gentiles against the brethren. 3 Therefore, indeed, a long time they remained, speaking boldly for the Lord, the One bearing witness to the word of his grace, giving signs and wonders to be done through their hands.

4 Now the many of the city were divided, and indeed some were with the Jewish, but some with the apostles. 5 But when there was an attempt of both gentiles and Jewish, with their rulers, to injure and to stone them, 6 having become aware, they fled to the cities of Lycaonia, Lystra and Derbe, and the surrounding region. 7 And proclaiming the good

news, there they remained.

8 And a certain man in Lystra, crippled in the feet, was sitting, lame from his mother's womb, who had never walked. 9 This one heard Paul speaking, who, looking intently at him and seeing that he has faith to be healed, 10 said in a loud voice, "Stand upright on your feet." And he jumped up and began to walk. 11 And the crowds seeing what Paul had done, cried out in a loud voice in the Lycaonian speech, saying, "The gods like men have come down to us!" 12 Then they began calling Barnabas Zeus, and Paul Hermes, because he was the chief speaker.

13 And the priest of Zeus, being just outside the city, brought oxen adorned with garlands to the gates, with the crowds desiring to sacrifice. 14 But hearing this, the apostles Barnabas and Paul tore their clothing, rushed out into the crowd, crying out 15 and saying, "Men, why do you these things? We also are men of like nature with you, proclaiming the good news to you, to turn from these vanities to the living God, who made the heaven and the earth and the sea and all things in them. 16 Who in the past generations permitted all the nations to go their ways. 17 And yet he has not left himself without witness, doing good, giving you rains from heaven and fruitful seasons, filling your hearts with food and gladness." 18 And saying these things, they with difficulty restrained the crowds not to sacrifice to them.

19 But Jews came from Antioch *of Pisidia* and Iconium, and persuaded the crowds. And having stoned Paul, they dragged him outside the city, thinking him to be dead. 20 But the disciples surrounding him, getting up, he entered into the city. And on the following day he left with Barnabas to Derby. 21 Then proclaiming the good news to that city, and discipling many, they returned to Lystra, and to Iconium, and to Antioch *of Pisidia*, 22 confirming the souls of the disciples, exhorting them to continue in the faith, and that it is necessary through many tribulations to enter into the kingdom of God.

23 Now having appointed for them elders in every church, having prayed, with fasting, they entrusted them to the Lord in whom they had believed. 24 And passing through Pisidia they came to Pamphylia. 25 And after speaking the word in Perga they went down to Attalia. 26 From there they sailed to Antioch *of Syria*, from where they had been entrusted to the grace of God for the word that they had fulfilled. 27 Then arriving, they gathered together the church, declaring all that God had done with them, and that he had opened to the gentiles a door of faith. 28 Then they stayed a long time with the disciples.

ACTS FIFTEEN

1 And certain ones who came down from Judea were teaching the brethren, "If you are not circumcised according to the

custom of Moses you are not able to be saved." 2 Then, no small dispute and debate by Paul and Barnabas with them having occurred, they appointed Paul and Barnabas to go up, and certain others out of them, to the apostles and elders, to Jerusalem, about this question. 3 Therefore, they indeed having been sent forth by the church, passed through both Phoenicia and Samaria, telling in full the conversion of the gentiles, and they were bringing great joy to all the brethren.

4 Then arriving at Jerusalem, they were welcomed by the church and the apostles and the elders. Then they declared all that God had done with them. 5 Now certain of those of the party of the Pharisees who believed, rose up, saying, "It is necessary to circumcise them, then to command to keep the Law of Moses." 6 Then the apostles and the elders gathered together to take care of this matter.

7 Now much discussion having occurred, Peter standing up said to them, "Men, brethren, you know that from early times, God chose among you through my mouth the gentiles to hear the word of the good news, and to believe. 8 And God, knowing the heart, bore witness in them, giving them the Holy Spirit, as also to us, 9 and he made not one distinction between us and them, by faith having cleansed their hearts. 10 Now therefore, why are you putting God to the test, to put a yoke upon the neck of the disciples, that neither our fathers, nor we, have been able to bear? 11 But through the grace of Lord Jesus Christ, to be saved, we believe in the same manner as they also."

12 Now all the many kept silent, and were listening to Barnabas and Paul telling what God had done, signs and wonders among the gentiles through them.

13 Now after, they were silent. Jacob responded, saying, "Men, brethren, hear me. 14 Simon has said how first God looked with mercy, to take out of the gentiles a people for his name. 15 And with this the words of the prophets agree. As it is written: 16 'After these things I will return and will build again the tabernacle of David which has fallen in ruins, and the ruins of it I will build again, and will set it upright, 17 so that the remnant of men may seek out the Lord, and all the peoples upon whom my name has been called, says the Lord, doing these things' 18 known from eternity. [e2]

19 "Therefore I judge to trouble not those who from the gentiles are turning to God, 20 but to send word to them by letter to abstain from the pollutions of idols, and sexual immorality, and that which is strangled, and from blood. 21 For Moses, from generations of old, has in every city those preaching him in the synagogues, being read on every Sabbath."

22 Then it seemed good to the apostles and to the elders, with all the church, having chosen men out

from them, to send to Antioch *of Syria* with Paul and Barnabas, Judas called Barsabbas, and Silas, leading men among the brethren, 23 having written by their hand:

"The apostles and the elders, brethren, to those in Antioch and Syria and Cilicia, brethren among the gentiles, Greeting.

24 "Because now we have heard that some from us going out troubled you by words, upsetting your minds, saying to be circumcised and keep the Law, to whom we had not given command, 25 it seemed good to us, having come with one mind, having chosen men to send to you with our beloved Barnabas and Paul, 26 men having committed their lives for the name of our Lord Jesus Christ.

27 "Therefore we have sent Judas and Silas, and they by speech are telling you the same things. 28 For it seemed good to the Holy Spirit and to us, to lay no more burden upon you, except these necessary things: 29 to abstain from whatever is sacrificed to an idol, and from blood, and from what is strangled, and from sexual immorality. Keeping yourselves from these, you will do well. Be well."

30 They therefore, indeed, having been sent, went to Antioch *of Syria*. And gathering the many, they delivered the letter. 31 Now having read, they rejoiced at the encouragement. 32 Both Judas and Silas, themselves also being prophets, through speech much exhorted and strengthened the brethren. 33 Continuing for a time, they were sent away in peace from the brethren to those having sent them. [34ᶠ] 35 But Paul and Barnabas stayed in Antioch *of Syria*, teaching and preaching, with many others also, the word of the Lord.

36 Now after some days, Paul said to Barnabas, "Truly, let us go back and look after the brethren in every city in which we declared the word of the Lord, how they are." 37 Now Barnabas decided to also take John called Mark. 38 But Paul thought suitable not to take along the one having left from them from Pamphylia and not going with them to the work. 39 But a sharp disagreement arose, so that they separated from one another. And Barnabas, taking Mark, sailed to Cyprus. 40 But Paul chose Silas, and left, being commended to the grace of the Lord by the brethren. 41 Then he was passing through Syria and Cilicia, confirming the churches.

ACTS SIXTEEN

1 Then he also came to Derbe and to Lystra. And behold, a certain disciple was there named Timothy, the son of a believing Jewish woman, but his father a Greek, 2 who bore honorable testimony by the brethren in Lystra and Iconium. 3 This one Paul wanted to go out with him, and taking him he circumcised him, on account of the Jews being in those parts. For they all knew that his father was a Greek.

4 Then, as they were passing through the cities, they charged them to keep the decisions decided by the apostles and elders who were in Jerusalem. 5 Truly, therefore, the churches were strengthened in the faith, and increased in number every day.

6 Then passing through Phrygia and the Galatian region, the Holy Spirit having forbid them to speak the word in Asia, 7 then coming down to Mysia they tried to go into Bithynia, and the Spirit of Jesus did not permit them. 8 Then passing by Mysia they came down to Troas.

9 And a vision appeared to Paul during the night, a certain man of Macedonia was standing and imploring him and saying, "Passing over into Macedonia, help us." 10 Now when he had seen the vision, we immediately desired to go into Macedonia, concluding that God had called us to proclaim the good news to them.

11 Then sailing from Troas, we took a straight course to Samothrace. Then the next day to Neapolis, 12 and from there to Philippi, which is a leading city of the region of Macedonia, a colony. Now we remained in this city for some days. 13 Then on the day of the Sabbaths, we went out, outside the city gate, where we supposed there was to be prayer by a river. And sitting down, we spoke to the women having gathered.

14 And a certain woman named Lydia, a seller of purple cloth, of the city of Thyatira, worshiping God, was listening, whom the Lord opened her heart to give attention to the things spoken by Paul. 15 Then when she was immersed, and her household, she implored, saying, "If you have judged me to be faithful to the Lord, come into my house and abide." And she persuaded us.

16 Now it happened, in our going to the place of prayer, a certain girl having a spirit of Python, met us; who much gain was bringing her masters by fortune-telling. 17 This one, following Paul and us, was calling aloud, saying, "These men are servants of the God, the Most High, who proclaim to you the way of salvation." 18 Then this she continued for many days. Then Paul became wearied, and turning to the spirit he said, "I command you in the name of Jesus Christ to come out of her." And it came out the same hour.

19 Now her masters, seeing that the hope of their profit was gone, seizing Paul and Silas, they dragged them into the marketplace before the rulers. 20 And bringing them to the magistrates, they said, "These men greatly disturb our city, being Jews, 21 and proclaim customs it is not lawful for us to accept nor practice, being Romans."

22 And the crowd rose up together against them, and the magistrates, having torn their clothing, commanded they be beaten with rods. 23 Then having

given them many blows, they cast them into prison, charging the jailor to keep them securely, 24 who having received such an order, threw them into the inner prison, and fastened their feet in the stocks.

25 Now about midnight, Paul and Silas were praying and singing praises to God. Now the prisoners were listening to them. 26 Then suddenly there was a great earthquake, so that the foundations of the prison were shaken. Then immediately the doors of all were opened, and the chains of all were loosened. 27 Then the jailor having been awakened, and seeing the doors of the prison opened, drawing his sword, he was about to kill himself, supposing the prisoners to have escaped. 28 But Paul called out in a loud voice, saying, "Do no harm to yourself, for we are all here."

29 Then having called for lights, he sprang in, and being terrified, he fell down before Paul and Silas. 30 And bringing them out he said, "Sirs, what is necessary to do that I may be saved?" 31 And they said, "Believe on the Lord Jesus, and you will be saved, you and your household." 32 And they spoke to him the word of the Lord, and with all those in his house. 33 And taking them in that hour of the night, he washed the wounds from them; and he was immersed, he and his household immediately. 34 Then bringing them into the house he laid a table for them, and rejoiced with all his household having believed in God.

35 Now day having arrived, the magistrates sent the officers, saying, "Release those men." 36 Now the jailor told these words to Paul: having sent the officers, that you may be let go. Now therefore leaving, depart in peace. 37 But Paul was saying to them, "Having publicly beaten us, uncondemned men, being Romans, they threw us into prison, and now secretly do they throw us out? No! For instead coming themselves, let them bring us out."

38 Then to the officers the sergeants told these words. Now they were afraid, hearing that they are Romans. 39 And coming, they appealed to them, and brought them out, and asked them to go out of the city. 40 Then leaving out of the prison, they came to Lydia. And having seen them, they exhorted the brethren and left.

ACTS SEVENTEEN

1 Then passing through Amphipolis and Apollonia, they came to Thessalonica, where was a synagogue of the Jews. 2 Now according to the custom with Paul, he went in to them, and for three Sabbaths he discussed with them from the Scriptures, 3 showing and setting before them that it was necessary the Christ to have suffered and to have risen out from among the dead; and that this Jesus is the Christ whom I preach to you. 4 And some of them were persuaded and joined themselves to Paul and to Silas, with a great many worshiping Greeks, and of the leading women not a few.

5 Then the Jews became envious, and taking certain wicked men idle in the marketplace, and raising a mob, they raised a disturbance in the city. And they suddenly attacked Jason's house, seeking to bring them out to the people. 6 But not finding them, they violently took Jason and certain brethren before the city leaders, shouting, "The ones the world unsettling, these are come here also, 7 whom Jason has welcomed. And all these things are opposed to the decrees of Caesar, saying Jesus to be another king." 8 Then they agitated the crowd. And the city leaders hearing these things, 9 and taking security from Jason and the rest, they let them go.

10 And the brethren immediately sent both Paul and Silas away by night to Berea, who having arrived, went into the synagogue of the Jews. 11 Now these were more noble-minded than those in Thessalonica, who received the word with all readiness, every day examining the Scriptures, if these things were so. 12 Therefore many of them truly believed, and of the prominent Greek women and men not a few.

13 But when those Jews from Thessalonica knew that also in Berea the word of God was proclaimed by Paul, they came there also, agitating and disturbing the crowds.

14 Now immediately the brethren sent Paul away to go to the sea. But both Silas and Timothy remained there. 15 Then those responsible for Paul brought him to Athens. And, receiving a command for Silas and Timothy to come to him as soon as possible, they left.

16 Now in Athens, as Paul was waiting for them, his spirit in him was provoked, seeing the city to be full of idols. 17 Therefore, truly, he continued to discourse in the synagogue with the Jews and those worshiping, and in the marketplace on every day with those whom he happened to meet.

18 Then also some of the Epicureans and Stoics, philosophers, encountered him. And some were saying, "What does this 'babbler' wish to say?" But others, "He seems to proclaim foreign gods," because he was proclaiming the good news of Jesus and the resurrection.

19 Then taking hold of him they took him to the Ares Hill, saying, "Are we able to know what is this new thing which you are teaching? 20 For some novel things you are bringing to our ears. Therefore we are willing to know what these things mean."

21 Now all the Athenians and the resident foreigners spend their time in nothing else than to say something and hear something new.

22 Then Paul stood in the midst of the Ares Hill, saying, "Men, Athenians, I see in all things you are religiously disposed. 23 For passing through and seeing the

objects of your worship, I discovered an altar on which was inscribed, 'To An Unknown God.' Whom therefore not knowing you worship, him I proclaim to you.

24 "The God having made the world and all the things that are in it, he of heaven and earth being Lord, resides not in hand-made temples, 25 nor by men's hands is he served, as needing anything, himself the one giving to all life and breath and all. 26 And he made of one every nation of humankind to live upon all the face of the earth, having determined and set in order seasons and limits of their dwelling place, 27 to seek God, if perhaps truly they might feel their way to him, and might find him—for truly he is not far from each of us. 28 For in him we live and move and exist. As also some of the poets among you have said: 'For of him also we are offspring.'

29 "Therefore, being offspring of God, we ought not regard a sculpture of God of gold or silver or stone, of the craft and imagination of man, to be like deity. 30 Truly, therefore, the times of ignorance God bore with. Now he commands all persons everywhere to convert, 31 because he set a day in which he is about to judge the world in righteousness, by a man whom he appointed, having given assurance to all, by raising him out from the dead."

32 Now having heard of a resurrection of the dead, some truly began to mock him. But some said, "We will hear you about this again also." 33 Then Paul left them. 34 But some persons, joining themselves to him, believed; among whom also Dionysius the Areopagite, and a woman named Damaris, and others with them.

ACTS EIGHTEEN

1 After these things, having left out of Athens, he came to Corinth. 2 And he found a certain Jew named Aquila, of Pontus by birth, having lately come from Italy, and Priscilla his wife—because Claudius had commanded the Jews to leave Rome—he came to them. 3 And because they were of the same occupation he stayed with them and worked; for they were tentmakers by trade.

4 Then he was reasoning in the synagogue on every Sabbath, persuading both Jews and Greeks. 5 Now when both Silas and Timothy came down from Macedonia, Paul was pressed with the word, earnestly bearing witness to the Jews the Christ to be Jesus. 6 But they opposed him and slandered him, so he shook out his clothing and said to them, "Your blood be on your head. I am clean. From now on I will go to the gentiles." 7 And leaving from there, he came to the house of a certain one worshiping God, named Titius Justus, whose house was next to the synagogue.

8 Now Crispus, the ruler of the synagogue, believed in the Lord, with all his household. And many of the Corinthians hearing believed and were immersed. 9 Now the Lord said to Paul in the night, in a

vision, "Fear not, but keep on speaking, and do not be silent 10 for this reason: I am with you; and no one will lay a hand on you to harm you for this reason: there are to me many people in this city." 11 Now he continued a year and six months, teaching among them the word of God.

12 Now Gallio being Proconsul of Achaia, the Jews rose up against Paul with one accord, and led him to the judgment seat, 13 now saying, "Against the law, this man earnestly persuades men to worship God." 14 Then Paul, about to say something, Gallio said to the Jews, "Truly if this was some unrighteousness or evil crime, O Jews, I would have born patiently with you according to reason. 15 But if it is a dispute about a word, and names, and according to your law, you will see to it yourselves. I choose not to be a judge of these things." 16 And he drove them from the judgment seat. 17 Then all having taken hold of Sosthenes, the ruler of the synagogue, began beating him before the judgment seat. And nothing about these things mattered to Gallio.

18 Now Paul, after staying many more days, then taking leave of the brethren, sailed to Syria, and with him Priscilla and Aquila. Paul had shaved his head in Cenchrea, for he had taken a vow. 19 Then they came to Ephesus, and he left them there. Now Paul himself went into the synagogue and reasoned with the Jews. 20 Then they entreated him to remain a longer time, and he did not consent, 21 but leaving he said, "I will return again to you, God willing," sailing from Ephesus, 22 and landing at Caesarea. Then having greeted the church, he went to Antioch *of Syria*. 23 And after staying some time, he left, passing successively through the Galatian region and Phrygia, strengthening all the disciples.

24 Now a certain Jew named Apollos, born in Alexandria, an eloquent man, came to Ephesus, being able in the Scriptures. 25 He was taught in the way of the Lord. And being zealous in spirit, he was speaking and was earnestly teaching the things concerning Jesus, knowing only John's immersing. 26 He then began to speak boldly in the synagogue. Now Priscilla and Aquila having heard him, they took him and more exactly expounded to him the way of God. 27 He then deciding to pass through into Achaia, having been encouraged, the brethren wrote to the disciples to welcome him, who when arriving, greatly helped those having believed through grace. 28 For he powerfully disputed the Jews publicly, showing according to the Scriptures Jesus to be the Christ.

ACTS NINETEEN

1 Now it happened while Apollos was in Corinth, Paul passed through the inland parts to come to Ephesus. And finding certain disciples, 2 he said to them, "If you did receive the Holy Spirit having believed?" Then they said to him, "We did not even hear that there is

a Holy Spirit." 3 Then he said, "Into what then were you immersed?" And they said, "Into John's immersing." 4 Then said Paul, "John immersed an immersion of repentance, telling the people they should believe in the one coming after him, that is, in Jesus."

5 Then having heard, they were immersed in the name of the Lord Jesus. 6 And Paul, laying hands on them, the Holy Spirit came upon them. Then they were speaking in foreign languages and prophesying. 7 Now there were in all about twelve men.

8 Now entering into the synagogue, he was boldly speaking, for three months reasoning and persuading about the kingdom of God. 9 But when some were hardened and were unbelieving, speaking evil of the Way before the many, he left them, separating the disciples, daily publicly teaching in the lecture hall of Tyrannus. 10 This then continued for two years, so that all those living in Asia heard the Word of the Lord, both Jews and Greeks.

11 Then God was mightily working not ordinary works through Paul's hands, 12 even so that to the ill his handkerchiefs or aprons were brought from his skin, and the diseases left them; also evil spirits left.

13 But also some of the itinerant Jews, exorcists, tried to name over those having evil spirits the name of the Lord Jesus, saying, "I adjure you by Jesus whom Paul proclaims." 14 Now there were certain of Sceva (a Jew, a chief priest), sevens sons who are doing this. 15 But the evil spirit responding said to them, "Jesus I know; and Paul I recognize; but you, who are you?" 16 Then the man in whom was the evil spirit assaulted them, overpowering them, overcoming them so that nude and wounded they ran out of that house.

17 Now this became known to all, both Jews and Greeks, living in Ephesus. And fear came upon all, and the name of the Lord Jesus was praised. 18 Then many of those having believed were coming, confessing, and declaring their works. 19 Then many of those practicing the black arts, bringing their books, burned them before all. And they reckoned the prices of them and found it to be five thousand pieces of silver. 20 Thus with the Lord's power the word continued to increase and prevail.

21 Now after these things had taken place, Paul purposed by the Spirit to pass through Macedonia and Achaia, then go to Jerusalem, saying, "After having been there, it is necessary for me to also see Rome." 22 Then sending into Macedonia two of those serving him, Timothy and Erastus, he stayed for a time in Asia.

23 Now it happened at that same time not a small commotion concerning the Way. 24 For a certain man named Demetrius, a worker in silver, was making silver shrines of Artemis, which was -

bringing to the artisans no little business. 25 Then gathering the workmen in such things, he said, "Men, you know that from this business is our prosperity. 26 And you see and hear that not only in Ephesus, but almost all of Asia this Paul has persuaded a great many people who have turned away, saying that they are not gods which are made by hands. 27 But not only this is a danger to us, refuting the business to come, but also the temple of the great goddess Artemis accounted for nothing, and also her glory to be cast down, whom all Asia and the world worship."

28 Then having heard, and becoming full of indignation, they were crying out, saying, "Great is Artemis of the Ephesians!" 29 And the whole city was filled with an uproar. And with one accord they rushed to the theater, seizing Gaius and Aristarchus, Macedonians, fellow travelers with Paul. 30 But Paul, deciding to go in to the people, the disciples would not let him. 31 Then also some of the Asiarchs, being his friends, sent to him, urging him not to venture himself into the theater. 32 Truly others some thing were crying out; for the public assembly was confused, and most did not know for what cause they had come together.

33 Now out of the crowd the Jews together thrust forward Alexander. And Alexander, having beckoned with the hand, was wanting to make a defense to the people. 34 But knowing that he is a Jew, there was one cry from all, continuing about two hours crying out, "Great is Artemis of the Ephesians!"

35 Then the clerk, having calmed the crowd, says, "Men, Ephesians, for what man is there who knows not the city of the Ephesians as being the temple warden of the great Artemis, and of that fallen from the sky? 36 Therefore these things being indisputable, it is necessary for you to be calm, and to do nothing rashly. 37 For you brought these men, neither sacrilegious nor slandering our goddess.

38 "If therefore truly Demetrius and the artisans with him have a matter against anyone, courts are conducted, and there are Proconsuls; let them accuse one another. 39 But if anything more than this you demand, it will be determined in the lawful public assembly. 40 For we are in danger of being accused of an insurrection for this day, there being not one cause for which we are able to give a reason for this public tumult." 41 And having said these things, he dismissed the public assembly.

ACTS TWENTY

1 Now after the uproar had ended, Paul called the disciples, and encouraged them, and saying farewell, left to go to Macedonia. 2 Then passing through those regions, and exhorting them with many words, he came to Greece. 3 He continued three months. A conspiracy was made against him by the Jews. He being about to sail

into Syria, he decided to return through Macedonia.

4 Now Sopater Phyrrus, a Berean, went with him; and of the Thessalonians, Aristarchus and Secundus; and Gaius of Derbe and Timothy; and the Asians, Tychicus and Trophimus. 5 But these having gone ahead waited for us in Troas. 6 Then we sailed away from Philippi after the days of Unleavened, and we came to them at Troas in five days, where we stayed seven days.

7 Then at the first day of the week, as we came together to break bread, Paul spoke with them, intending to leave the next day. He continued speaking until midnight.

8 Now there were many lamps in the upper room where we were gathered. 9 And a certain man named Eutychus was sitting by the window, overcome by deep sleep as Paul spoke at length. Having been overcome by the sleep, he fell down from the third story; and was taken up dead. 10 But Paul, having went down, took him in his arms and embraced him, saying, "Do not lament, for his life is in him." 11 Then he went up, and they broke bread, and ate, and having spoken for a long time, until daybreak, he left. 12 Now they brought the young man alive, and were not a little comforted.

13 But we, having gone ahead to the ship, sailed to Assos, there to pick up Paul. For so he had arranged, intending to go on foot. 14 Then he met us at Assos and we picked him up; and we came to Mitylene. 15 From there we sailed away, arriving on the next day opposite Chios. Then the next day we came to Samos. Then the following day we came to Miletus. 16 For Paul had decided to sail past Ephesus, so that he might not spend time in Asia. For he hurried, if it was possible for him to be in Jerusalem on the Day of Pentecost.

17 Then from Miletus he sent to Ephesus, calling for the elders of the church. 18 Then when they had come to him, he said to them, "You know from the first day on which I arrived in Asia, how I was with you the entire time, 19 serving the Lord with all humility, and tears, and trials coming upon me by the schemes of the Jews. 20 How in nothing did I hesitate not to declare that which was profitable to you, and to teach you publicly and from house to house, 21 repeatedly testifying to both Jews and to Greeks, repentance toward God and of faith in our Lord Jesus Christ.

22 "And now, look, I go bound in the Spirit to Jerusalem, not knowing what will happen to me there, 23 except that the Holy Spirit in every city repeatedly testifies to me, saying that bonds and tribulations await me. 24 But I do not say I make my life dear to myself, so as to complete my course and the ministry I received from the Lord Jesus, to earnestly testify of the good news of the grace of God.

25 "Now, look, I know that never again will you see my face,

among whom you all I have gone about preaching the kingdom. 26 Therefore, I testify to you in this day, that I am clean of the blood of all. 27 For I have not hesitated from not declaring all the counsel of God to you. 28 Attend to yourselves and to all the flock among which the Holy Spirit has set you as overseers, to shepherd the church of God which he acquired through his own blood.

29 "I know that after I leave, fierce wolves will come in among you, not sparing the flock. 30 And out from your own selves men will rise up speaking perverse things, to draw away disciples after them. 31 Therefore be mindful, remembering that three years, night and day, I did not cease with tears warning each one.

32 "And now, I entrust you to God and to the word of his grace, able to build and to give you an inheritance among all those having been sanctified. 33 I did not wrongfully desire any person's silver or gold or clothing. 34 You yourselves know that my needs and those with me, these hands served. 35 In all things I plainly taught you that by thus laboring it is necessary to help those who are weak, and also to remember the words of the Lord Jesus, how he himself said, 'It is more blessed to give than to receive.'"

36 And having said these things, bowing his knees, with all of them he prayed. 37 Then there was much weeping among all. And falling upon Paul's neck they were kissing him, 38 especially distressed over the word that he had spoken, that no more are they about to see his face. Then they accompanied him to the ship.

ACTS TWENTY-ONE

1 Then after, it happened our sailing, drawing away from them, sailing a direct course, we came to Cos, and the next day to Rhodes, and from there to Patara. 2 And finding a ship passing over to Phoenicia, going on board, we set sail. 3 Then, sighting Cypress, and leaving it on the left, we kept sailing to Syria and landed at Tyre; for there the ship unloaded its merchandise.

4 Then seeking out the disciples, we stayed there seven days. They kept on saying to Paul through the Spirit not to go up to Jerusalem. 5 Then after we had completed the days, leaving, we traveled. All joined us, with wives and children, as far as outside the city. And on the shore bending the knees, we prayed, 6 and said farewell to one another. Then we went into the ship, and they returned to their own.

7 Then the voyage from Tyre being completed, we came down to Ptolemais, and greeting the brethren, we stayed with them one day. 8 Then we left on the next day and came to Caesarea, and entered the house of Philip the evangelist, he of the seven, and stayed with him. 9 Now this man had four daughters, virgins, prophesying.

10 Then continuing there many days, a certain one came down from Judea, a prophet named Agabus. 11 And having come, he took Paul's belt, bound his feet and hands, and said, "Thus says the Holy Spirit, 'The man whose belt this is, in this way the Jews in Jerusalem will bind and will deliver him into the hands of the gentiles.'" 12 Then when we heard those things, both we and those in that place exhorted him not to go up to Jerusalem.

13 Then Paul responded. "What are you doing, weeping and breaking my heart? For I am ready not only to be bound, but also to die at Jerusalem, for the name of the Lord Jesus." 14 Then, not having persuaded him, we were silent, saying, "The Lord's will be done." 15 Now after these days, we packed the baggage and began our way to Jerusalem. 16 Then also disciples from Caesarea came with us, bringing one with whom we would lodge, Mnason of Cyprus, a disciple from the beginning.

17 Now arriving at Jerusalem, the brethren gladly received us. 18 Then on the next day, Paul went with us to Jacob, and all the elders were present. 19 And after greeting them, he told one by one the things God had done among the gentiles through his ministry. 20 Then those hearing glorified God.

Then they said to him, "You see, brother, how many thousands there are among the Jews who have believed, and all are zealous for the Law. 21 Now they have been told about you, that you teach all those Jews among the gentiles to depart from Moses, telling them not to circumcise the children, nor to live according to the customs. 22 What then to do? Assuredly they will hear that you have come.

23 "This therefore you do what we say to you. There are with us four men having on themselves a vow. 24 Take these men, be purified with them, and bear expense for them, so that they will shave their head, and all will know that of which they have been told about you is nothing: you follow the rule keeping the Law. 25 Now about those of the gentiles having believed, we wrote, giving our judgment, for them to 'avoid the things both sacrificed to idols, and blood, and what is strangled, and sexual immorality.'"

26 Then Paul took the men on the following day, having been purified with them, entering into the temple, announced fulfillment of the days of the purification, until that offering was offered for each one of them.

27 Now when the seven days were about to be completed, Jews from Asia, seeing Paul in the temple, excited all the crowd and laid hands upon him, 28 crying out, "Men, Israelites, help! This is the man who teaches all those everywhere against the people and the Law and this place. And he has brought Greeks into the temple and defiled this holy place." 29 For they had before seen Trophimus the Ephesian in the city with him,

and whom they assumed Paul had brought into the temple.

30 Then the whole city was agitated, and the people ran together. And seizing Paul they dragged him outside the temple, and immediately the doors were shut. 31 Now as they were seeking to kill him, information came to the commander of the cohort, that all Jerusalem was in an uproar, 32 who immediately ran down upon them with soldiers and centurions. And seeing the commander and the soldiers, they stopped beating Paul.

33 Then coming near, the commander took him, and commanded him to be bound with two chains, and began to ask who he might be and what it is he has been doing. 34 But others in the crowd were crying out one thing or another. Now, not being able to discern the facts through the uproar, he ordered him to be brought into the barracks. 35 Now when he came to the stairs, it happened he was carried by the soldiers, because of the violence of the crowd. 36 For the crowd of people were following, crying out, "Away with him!"

37 Then about to be brought into the barracks, Paul said to the commander, "Is it allowed to me to say something to you?" Then the commander was saying, "You know Greek? 38 Then you are not the Egyptian who stirred up sedition before these times and led four thousand men of the assassins out into the wilderness?"

39 Then Paul said, "I am truly a Jew, a man of Tarsus of Cilicia, a citizen of a not insignificant city. Now I implore you, allow me to speak to the people." 40 Then permitting him, Paul stood on the stairs and made a sign with the hand to the people. Then there was great silence, and he spoke to them in the Hebrew language, saying:

ACTS TWENTY-TWO

1 "Men, brethren, and fathers, now hear my defense to you." 2 Then hearing that he was addressing them in the Hebrew language, they became more quiet. And he says, 3 "I am a man, a Jew, born in Tarsus of Cilicia, but educated in this city at the feet of Gamaliel, being instructed exactly according to the Law of our fathers, being zealous for God, even as all you are this day. 4 Who this Way persecuted as far as death, binding and betraying to prisons both men and women, 5 as also the high priest bears witness to me, and all the elders, from whom I received letters to the brethren. I was on my way to Damascus to bring also those there, being bound, to Jerusalem, in order they might be punished.

6 "But it happened to me as I traveled and drew near to Damascus, about noon, suddenly out of heaven flashed a great light around me. 7 Then I fell to the ground and heard a voice saying to me, 'Saul, Saul, why do you persecute me?' 8 They I answered, 'Who are you Sir?' Then he said to

me, 'I am Jesus of Nazareth, whom you are persecuting.' 9 Now those with me saw the light. But they did not hear the voice of the one speaking to me. 10 Then I said, 'What shall I do, Lord?' Now the Lord said to me, 'Get up, go to Damascus, and there you will be told about all things that it has been appointed you to do.'

11 "Now while I could not see for the glory of that light, I being led by the hand by those who were with me, came to Damascus. 12 Then a certain Ananias, a devout man according to the Law, borne witness to by all Jews living there, 13 came to me and stood by me and said to me, 'Brother Saul, receive your sight.' And the same hour I saw him. 14 And he said, 'The God of our fathers has appointed you to know his will, and to see the Righteous One, and to hear the voice out of his mouth, 15 because you will be a witness for him to all men of what you have seen and heard. 16 And now why delay? Get up, be immersed and wash away your sins, calling on his name.'

17 "Then it happened to me, having returned to Jerusalem, and my praying in the temple, I fell into an ecstasy 18 and saw him saying to me, 'Make haste and go away quickly out of Jerusalem, because they will not receive your testimony about me.' 19 And I said, 'Lord, they know that I was imprisoning and beating in each of those synagogues those believing on you. 20 And when the blood of Stephen was poured out, your witness, I myself also was nearby and approving, and keeping the clothing of those killing him.' 21 And he said to me, 'Go, for I will send you far away to the gentiles.'"

22 Now they were listening to him until this word. And they cried out with a loud voice, saying, "Away from the earth with such! For he is not fit to live!" 23 Then they were crying out, and throwing off their clothes, and throwing dust into the air. 24 The commander ordered him to be brought into the barracks, instructing him to be examined by flogging, so he might know why they were crying out against him.

25 But as he stretched him out with the thongs, Paul said to the centurion nearby, "Is it lawful for you to flog a man, a Roman, uncondemned?" 26 Then hearing this, the centurion went to the commander, reported it, saying, "What are you going to do? For this man is a Roman."

27 Then coming near, the commander said to him, "Tell me, are you a Roman?" And he said, "Yes." 28 Then the commander said, "With a great sum I bought this citizenship." But Paul said, "But I was so born." 29 Immediately those about to examine him left, and the commander also was afraid, knowing he is a Roman, and because he had bound him.

30 Now the next day, wanting to know with certainty why he is accused by the Jews, he unbound him and commanded the chief priest and all the council to meet

with him. And bringing Paul, he set him among them.

ACTS TWENTY-THREE

1 Then Paul, looking intently at the council, said, "Men, brethren, I in all good conscience have lived as a good citizen of God up to this day." 2 Then the high priest, Ananias, told those nearby to hit him on his mouth. 3 Then Paul said to him, "God is about to hit you, whitewashed wall! And do you sit judging me according to the Law, and violate the Law, commanding me to be struck?" 4 Now those nearby said, "Do you reproach the high priest of God?" 5 Then Paul said, "I did not know, brethren, that he is high priest. For it is written, 'You shall not speak evil of the ruler of the people.'"

6 Then Paul, knowing that the one part is Sadducees but the other Pharisees, exclaimed to the council, "Men, brethren, I am the son of a Pharisee. I am judged concerning the hope and resurrection of the dead." 7 Then him saying this, a dispute began between the Pharisees and Sadducees, and the crowd was divided. 8 For truly Sadducees say there is no resurrection, no messenger (no spirit). But Pharisees confess both.

9 Then began a great clamor, and some of the scribes rose up, of the party of the Pharisees, disputing earnestly, saying, "Nothing evil we find in this man. Now what if a spirit has spoken to him, or a messenger?" 10 Then a great dissension began. The commander, fearing lest Paul be torn to pieces by them, commanded the soldiers to go down and take him by force from their midst, then bring him into the barracks.

11 Now the following night, the Lord stood near him, saying, "Have courage. For as you have repeatedly testified about me in Jerusalem, so it is necessary you also testify in Rome."

12 Now when it was day, the Jews, having made a conspiracy, placed themselves under an oath, saying neither to eat nor to drink until that they might kill Paul. 13 Now there were more than forty having made this oath. 14 They came to the chief priests and elders, saying, "We have bound ourselves with an oath, to eat nothing, until that we should kill Paul. 15 Now therefore, you make known to the commander, along with the council, that he might bring him to you, to examine the things about him more accurately. We then, before he comes near, are ready to kill him."

16 But hearing of this ambush, Paul's nephew, his sister's son, came near and entered the barracks, telling Paul. 17 Then Paul called to himself one of the centurions, saying, "Take this young man to the commander, for he has something to report to him." 18 Therefore indeed, the one taking him brought him to the commander, and he said, "The prisoner Paul called to me, asking me to lead this young man to you."

19 Then holding his hand, the commander, withdrawing to a private place, asked, "What is it you have to report to me?"

20 Then he said, "The Jews have agreed to ask you that tomorrow you might bring Paul into the council, as though something more accurately to ask about him. 21 You therefore should not be persuaded by them. For they lie in wait for him, more than forty men, who took an oath neither to eat nor to drink until that they have killed him. And now they are ready, waiting for your order." 22 Therefore then, the commander released the young man, instructing him, "Tell no one of this you made known to me."

23 And calling a certain two of the centurions, he said, "Prepare two hundred soldiers, in order they might go as far as Caesarea, and seventy horsemen, and two hundred spearmen, for the third hour of the night. 24 Provide horses for Paul to ride, that they may bring him safely to Felix the procurator."

25 He wrote a letter, having this form: 26 Claudius Lysias, to the most excellent procurator Felix, greetings. 27 This man, having been seized by the Jews, and about to be killed by them, I came with soldiers and rescued him, having learned he is a Roman. 28 Determining then to know the crime of which they were accusing him, I took him to their council; 29 I discovered he was accused about questions of their Law, but no accusation worthy of death or of chains. 30 Then I was told of a conspiracy that would be against the man. I at once sent him to you, instructing also the accusers to speak these things against him before you.

31 Therefore the soldiers indeed did as ordered, taking Paul and bringing him by night to Antipatris. 32 Then on the next day, after committing the horsemen go with him, they returned to the barracks. 33 Those entered into Caesarea, and delivering the letter to the procurator, also presented Paul to him. 34 Then having read it, and asking from what province he is, and learning that he is from Cilicia, 35 said, "I will fully hear you, when also your accusers may arrive." He commanded him to be guarded in the praetorium of Herod.

ACTS TWENTY-FOUR

1 Then, after five days, the high priest Ananias came down, with some elders and a certain advocate Tertullus, who made to the governor their accusations against Paul. 2 Then being called, Tertullus began to accuse him, saying,

"Much peace we have on account of you, and reforms are happening to this nation through your prudence. 3 In every way and everywhere we embrace these things, most noble Felix, with all gratitude. 4 However, in order not to delay you any longer, I beg your courtesy to hear us in a few words. 5 For we have discovered this man to be a pestilence, and exciting sedition among all the Jews in the world, and a leader of the sect of the Nazarenes, 6a who also tried to profane the temple, and whom we seized. [6b, 7, 8a ⁹]

8b "From him you will be able yourself, having examined him about all these things, to know what we accuse him." 9 Then the Jews agreed together, affirming these things were so.

10 Then Paul answered when the governor made a sign to him to speak. "Knowing that for many years you have been a judge to this nation, I cheerfully make a defense to the things concerning myself. 11 You are able to know that not more than twelve days have passed from when I went up to worship in Jerusalem. 12 And neither in the temple did they find me discussing anything with anyone, or making a disturbance of a crowd, nor in the synagogues, nor in the city.

13 "Nor are they able to prove to you any of the things of which they now accuse me. 14 But I confess this to you, that according to the way they call a sect, so I serve the God of our fathers, believing all things throughout the Law and that have been written in the prophets, 15 having in God a hope which they themselves also await: there is about to be a resurrection of both just and unjust. 16 In this also I myself strive to have a conscience without offence toward God and men, through all things.

17 "Now after many years, I came to bring alms and offerings to my country, 18 in which they found me purified in the temple, not with a crowd, nor in tumult. But some Jews from Asia, 19 who ought to appear before you and make accusation, if they may have anything against me. 20 Otherwise, let these themselves say they found any unrighteousness when I stood before the council, 21 than about this one statement which I cried out standing among them, 'concerning the resurrection of the dead I am judged this day by you.'"

22 But Felix, having an accurate knowledge of the things concerning the Way, put them off, saying, "When Lysias the commander may come, I will examine the things respecting you." 23 Then he commanded the centurion to keep him, to have liberty, and not to forbid his own to minister to him.

24 Then after some days, he came with Drusilla, his wife, who was Jewish. And he sent for Paul and heard him concerning the faith in Jesus Christ. 25 Then he conversed about righteousness and self-control and the coming judgment. Becoming frightened, Felix responded, "For the present moment go away. Then when I have a suitable time I will call for you." 26 Also at the same time he was hoping that Paul would give him something useful. Therefore, also, often, sending for Paul, he conversed with him. 27 But after two years were completed Felix received his successor Porcius

Festus. Then desiring to gain favor with the Jews, Felix left Paul bound.

ACTS TWENTY-FIVE

1 Therefore Festus arrived in the province. After three days he went up to Jerusalem from Caesarea. 2 Then the chief priests and the leaders of the Jews made their accusations against Paul. And they were urging him, 3 begging a favor against him, that he may send for him to Jerusalem, forming an ambush to kill him on the way. 4 Then indeed Festus responded, "Paul is to be kept in Caesarea." But he himself is ready to quickly leave. 5 "Therefore those among you," he said, "in authority, go down also. If there is anything wrong in the man, let them accuse him."

6 Now having spent with them not more than eight or ten days, he returned to Caesarea. On the next day, sitting on the judgment seat, he commanded Paul to be brought. 7 Then when he was present, the Jews who came down from Jerusalem stood around him, bringing many and weighty charges, which they were not able to prove.

8 Paul made his defense. "Neither against the Law of the Jews, nor against the temple, nor against Caesar, have I sinned in anything." 9 But Festus, desiring to lay a favor on the Jews, responding to Paul, saying, "Are you willing to go up to Jerusalem and there be judged before me concerning these things?"

10 Then Paul said, "I am standing before the judgment seat of Caesar, where I ought to be judged. Toward the Jews I have done nothing wrong, as also you know very well. 11 Truly if I have done anything wrong and deserving of death I do not refuse to die. But if there is nothing of which they accuse me, no one can hand me over to them. I appeal to Caesar." 12 Then Festus, having spoken with the council, responded, "You have appealed to Caesar, to Caesar you will go."

13 Now some days having passed, Agrippa the king and Bernice came down to Caesarea, greeting Festus. 14 Now as they stayed there many days, Festus set before the king the things about Paul, saying, "There is a certain man left by Felix a prisoner, 15 concerning whom, my being in Jerusalem, the chief priests and the elders of the Jews made accusations, begging judgment against him, 16 to whom I responded is it not customary with Romans to hand over any person before that one accused may face his accusers, and may have the opportunity of defense concerning the accusation.

17 "Therefore, making no delay coming here, the next day sitting on the judgment seat, I commanded the man to be brought, 18 concerning whom the accusers, having stood, brought no charge of wrong doing, which I was expecting. 19 But they had against him certain questions concerning their own religion, and

concerning a certain Jesus, who having been dead, Paul was affirming to be alive. 20 Now being perplexed concerning this inquiry, I asked if he was willing to go to Jerusalem and there be judged concerning these things. 21 But Paul, calling himself to be kept for the Emperor's decision, I commanded him to be kept until that I might send him to Caesar." 22 Then Agrippa said to Festus, "I have also been desirous myself to hear the man." He says, "Tomorrow you will hear him."

23 Therefore on the next day, Agrippa and Bernice having arrived with much splendor, and entering into the audience room, with both military officers and men of prominence in the city, and Festus having given command, Paul was brought. 24 And Festus said, "King Agrippa, and all the people present with us, you see this one, concerning whom all the multitude of the Jews applied to me, in both Jerusalem and here, crying out that he ought not to live no more. 25 But I understood him to have done nothing worthy of his death. But he having appealed to the Emperor, I determined to send him. 26 Now concerning him, I have nothing definite to write to my Lord. Therefore I brought him before you all, and especially before you, King Agrippa, so that an examination having taken place, I might have something to write. 27 For it seems irrational to me sending a prisoner without also accusations to declare against him."

ACTS TWENTY-SIX

1 The Agrippa said to Paul, "It is permitted you to speak for yourself." Then Paul, having stretched out the hand, began his defense. 2 "Concerning all which I am accused by Jews, King Agrippa, I count myself blessed before you, on this day about to defend myself, 3 you being especially knowing of all the customs of the Jews, and also disputes. Therefore I request you patiently hear me.

4 "Truly then the manner of my life from youth, from the first, was among my nation, also in Jerusalem, know all Jews, 5 knowing me before from the first, if they wish to testify, that according to the strictest sect of our religion, I lived as a Pharisee. 6 And now for the hope of the promise made by God to our fathers I stand, being judged, 7 for which our twelve tribes in earnestness, night and day serving, hope to attain. Concerning which hope I am accused by the Jews, O king. 8 Why is it considered unbelievable to you if God raises the dead?

9 "Therefore, truly, I thought in myself I ought to do much against the name of Jesus, 10 which also I did in Jerusalem; then also I confined in prisons many of the saints, receiving authority from the chief priests. When they were put to death I voiced my assent against them. 11 And in all the synagogues often punishing them, I was compelling them to revile God. Then being vehemently

furious against them I continued to persecute them, even as far as to foreign cities.

12 "Then when travelling to Damascus with authority and commission of the chief priests, 13 at mid-day on the road I saw, O king, from heaven above, the brightness of the sun, a light shining around me and those travelling with me. 14 All of us fell down to the ground. I heard a voice saying to me in the Hebrew language, 'Saul, Saul, why do you persecute me? It is hard for you to kick against the goads.'

15 "Then I said, 'Who are you Sir?' And the Lord said, 'I am Jesus, whom you are persecuting. 16 But get up and stand on your feet. For this purpose I have appeared to you: to appoint you a servant and a witness of that which you have both seen of me, then of that I will show to you, 17 delivering you out from the people and out from the gentiles to whom I am sending you 18 to open their eyes, that they might turn from darkness to light, and from the authority of Satan to God, that they may receive forgiveness of sins and an inheritance among those who have been sanctified by faith that is in me.'

19 "Whereupon, O King Agrippa, I was not disobedient to the heavenly vision, 20 but first to those in Damascus, and all in Jerusalem, and the region of Judea, and to the gentiles, I kept on declaring to convert and to turn to God, habitually doing works suitable to repentance.

21 "On account of these things the Jews seized me as I was in the temple; they were trying to kill me. 22 Therefore, having received help from God unto this day, I have stood bearing witness to both small and great, saying nothing other than what both the prophets said was about to happen, and Moses: 23 that the Christ would suffer. As first out of resurrection from the dead ones, he is about to preach light to both our people and to the gentiles."

24 Now of the things he said in his defense, Festus in a loud voice said, "Paul, you are out of your mind! Your much learning turns you to madness." 25 But Paul said, "No, I am not out of my mind, most excellent Festus, but of truth and of sound mind I speak every word. 26 For concerning these things the king understands, to whom also being bold I speak. For not any of these things are hidden from him. For I am persuaded no not one of these things is done in a corner. 27 King Agrippa, believe you the prophets? I know that you believe."

28 Now Agrippa said to Paul, "With so little do you persuade me to be made a Christian?" 29 And Paul said, "I would wish to God, both in little and in much, not only you but also all those hearing me this day to become such as I also am, except these bonds."

30 Then the king got up, and the procurator, and Bernice, and those sitting with them. 31

Withdrawing, they began speaking to one another, saying, "This man is doing nothing worthy of bonds or of death." 32 Then Agrippa said to Festus, "This man could have been set at liberty if he had not appealed to Caesar."

ACTS TWENTY-SEVEN

1 Now when our sailing to Italy was chosen, they delivered both Paul and certain other prisoners to a centurion named Julius, of the Augustus cohort. 2 Then boarding a ship of Adramyttium, about to sail to the along-the-way places in Asia, we set sail. Aristarchus, a Macedonian of Thessalonica, was with us. 3 Then the next day we made port at Sidon. Then Julius, having treated Paul kindly, allowed him to go to his friends to receive care. 4 From there, putting out to sea, we sailed under the shelter of Cyprus, because of the winds being contrary.

5 And then sailing along Cilicia and Pamphylia, we landed at Myra of Lycia. 6 And there the centurion found a ship of Alexandria sailing to Italy. He entered us into it. 7 Now for many days, sailing slowly and with difficulty, we came near Cnidus. The wind not permitting us, we sailed under the shelter of Crete, near Salmone. 8 With difficulty and sailing near it, we came to a certain place called "Fair Havens," to which nearby was Lasea city.

9 Now enough time passed, and the voyage already dangerous (the Day of Atonement already past), Paul was exhorting them, 10 saying to them, "Men. I understand that the voyage is about to be with damage and much loss, not only of the cargo and of the ship, but also our lives." 11 But the centurion was persuaded by the pilot and ship owner, rather than the things spoken by Paul. 12 Now as the harbor was unsuitable to spend the winter, the majority, looking toward the southwest and toward the northwest, reached a decision to set sail from there, if somehow that they may be able to attain to Phoenix, a harbor of Crete, to winter there.

13 Now a south wind blowing gently, they thought they had achieved their purpose. Then taking up, they began sailing near Crete. 14 But not long after there came down from there a violent wind called Euroclydon. 15 Then the ship being caught, and not able to bear up against the wind, we put the ship into the wind to be driven along. 16 Then having sheltered under a certain island called Cauda, we were able, with difficulty, to gain control of the ship's boat, 17 which raising up, they made use of helps, girding the ship across the keel and deck. Then fearing lest they should fall into the sandbank, they lowered the mast, in this manner being driven along.

18 Now we being violently storm-tossed, on the next day they prepare to cast out the ship's load, 19 and on the third day, by their own hands, they cast away the

ship's equipment. 20 Then neither sun nor stars showing for many days, and no small tempest pressing upon us, from then on all hope of our deliverance was abandoned. 21 There was also much time without food.

At that time Paul stood up in the midst of them, saying, "Truly it was right, O men, giving attention to me, not to have set sail from Crete, than to have gained this damage and loss. 22 And now I exhort you to be of good cheer. For loss of life there will be none from you, only the ship. 23 For this night, of God whose I am and whom I serve, a messenger stood by me, 24 saying, 'fear not, Paul, it is necessary you stand before Caesar. And look, God has given to you all those sailing with you.' 25 Therefore be of good cheer, men. For I believe God, that thus it will be according to the way it was said to me. 26 But it is necessary we be cast upon a certain island."

27 The1n when the fourteenth night had come, we being driven about the Adriatic, toward the middle of the night, the sailors suspected that they were drawing near to some land. 28 And testing the depth of the water, they found twenty fathoms. Then a little farther and again testing the depth of the water, they found fifteen fathoms. 29 Then fearing lest we might fall somewhere on rocky places, four anchors were cast out of the stern; and they were praying for day to come.

30 Then some sailors sought to escape out of the ship, and let down the ship's boat into the sea, under pretense, as being about to cast out bow anchors. 31 Paul said to the centurion and to the soldiers, if these do not remain in the ship, you are not able to be saved. 32 Then the soldiers cut the ropes of the ship's boat and allowed her to fall away. 33 Then until day was dawning Paul kept on urging all to partake of food, saying, "Today is the fourteenth day which you continue waiting without eating, having taken nothing. 34 Therefore, I exhort you to take food. For this is for your deliverance. For not one of you, a hair of the head will be lost."

35 Then having said those things, and taking bread, he gave thanks to God before all. And breaking it he began to eat. 36 Then having been cheered, all also took food. 37 Then we were all the souls in the ship, two hundred seventy-six. 38 Then, having been filled with food, they began to lighten the ship, casting the wheat into the sea. 39 Now when it was day, they did not recognize the land, but they noticed a certain bay, having a coast on which they decided, if they were able, to drive the ship.

40 And cutting the anchors, leaving them in the sea, at the same time they loosened the ropes of the rudders. And hoisting the foresail to the blowing wind, they began bringing the ship toward the coast. 41 But falling into a place between two currents, they ran the ship aground. And truly the bow

sticking firm it remained unmovable. And the stern was being broken by the violence of the waves.

42 Now of the soldiers, the decision was that they should kill the prisoners, lest any swimming away should escape. 43 But the centurion, desiring to save Paul, prevented them from their purpose. Then he commanded those being able to swim to let themselves down from the ship to go out on the land, 44 and the rest, indeed some on boards, then some on things from the ship. And thereby it happened that all were brought safely to the land.

ACTS TWENTY-EIGHT

1 And having been delivered, then we learned that the island is called Malta. 2 And the barbarians were showing us no ordinary kindness. For having kindled a fire, they received all of us because of the coming rain and because of the cold. 3 Now Paul gathered together many sticks and laid them on the fire. A viper came out from the heat, fastening on Paul's hand. 4 Now when the barbarians saw the beast suspended from his hand, they said to one another, "Assuredly this man is a murderer, who having been saved from the sea, justice has not permitted to live."

5 Then, indeed, he shook off the creature into the fire, suffering no injury. 6 But they were expecting he was about to become swollen, or to suddenly fall down dead. Now they expected a long time. And seeing nothing hurtful happening to him, they changed their mind and declared him to be a god.

7 Now around that place were fields of the chief of the island, named Publius, who courteously received us three days as guests. 8 Then it happened Publius' father was lying oppressed with fevers and dysentery, to whom Paul, entering and praying, laying his hands on him, healed him. 9 Then this having happened, also the rest in the island who had illness came and were healed. 10 These also honored us with many honors, and on setting sail they gave us the things for our needs.

11 Then after three months we sailed in a ship having wintered in the island, Alexandrian, with an ensign of Castor and Pollux. 12 And putting in at Syracuse, we remained three days. 13 From there, taking up the anchors round about, we arrived at Rhegium. And after one day a southwest wind sprang up, the second day we came to Puteoli, 14 where finding some brethren, we were invited to stay with them seven days. And so we came to Rome.

15 From there the brethren, having heard things concerning us, came out to meet us as far as the market of Appius and Three Taverns. Whom Paul, seeing, took courage, giving thanks to God. 16 Now when we came to Rome,[h] Paul was allowed to stay by himself, with the soldier guarding him.

17 Then it happened after three days he called together those who were leaders of the Jews. Then them coming together, he said to them, "Men, brethren, I have done nothing against the people or the customs of our fathers. I was delivered from Jerusalem a prisoner into the hands of the Romans, 18 who having examined me, were wanting to let me go, because not one cause of death existed in me. 19 But because the Jews contradicted, I was compelled to appeal to Caesar—not as having anything to accuse my nation. 20 Therefore, for this cause, I have called for to see you and to speak to you. On account of the hope of Israel I have this chain hung around me."

21 And to him they said, "We received neither letters from Judea concerning you, nor have any of the brethren arriving made known or said anything evil concerning you. 22 But we think it appropriate to hear from you what you think, for truly concerning this sect it is known to us that it is spoken against everywhere." 23 Then appointing him a day, many came to him at the house, to whom he expounded, testifying to the kingdom of God, persuading them concerning Jesus from both the Law of Moses and the prophets, from morning to evening.

24 And truly some were persuaded of the things he spoke; but some refused to believe. 25 Then disagreeing with one another, they began leaving; Paul said one statement: "Rightly the Holy Spirit spoke through Isaiah the prophet to your fathers, 26 saying, 'Go to this people and say, in hearing you will hear and not understand, and in seeing you will see and no not perceive. 27 For the heart of this people has become dull, and with the ears they hear with difficulty, and their eyes they have shut, lest ever they should see with the eyes and they should hear with the ears and should understand with the heart, and should turn, and I will heal them.' 28 Therefore, be it known to you, that to the gentiles has been sent this salvation of God; and they will listen." [29^j]

30 Then he remained two whole years in his own rented house, and welcomed all coming to him, 31 proclaiming the kingdom of God and teaching the things concerning the Lord Jesus Christ with all boldness, no one hindering.

The Book of Romans

The Book of Romans is Paul's introduction of himself and his doctrine to the local church in Rome, Italy, which he planned to visit after his ca. AD 58 visit to Jerusalem. The book was written ca. AD 58 at Corinth, Greece, at the end of Paul's third missionary journey, before Paul went to Jerusalem and was arrested. Paul was not unknown to many in the Roman church, 16:1–16, but he had not founded the church in Rome. The Book of Romans is sixth in the order of Paul's letters, after 1 Thessalonians, Galatians, 2 Thessalonians, 1 and 2 Corinthians.

ROMANS ONE

1 Paul, servant of Christ Jesus, called apostle, having been set apart for the good news of God, 2 which he proclaimed beforehand through his prophets in the holy scriptures 3 concerning his Son, who was born out of the offspring of David according to flesh, 4 being declared Son of God in power according to *his* spirit[a1] of holiness by resurrection from the dead, Jesus Christ our Lord. 5 Through whom we received grace and apostleship unto obedience of faith among all the gentiles on behalf of his name, 6 among whom you are also called of Jesus Christ.

7 To all those who are in Rome, beloved of God, called saints, grace to you and peace from God our Father and our Lord Jesus Christ.

8 First, truly, I thank my God through Jesus Christ for all of you, because your faith is being proclaimed in all the world. 9 For my witness is God—whom I serve in my spirit in the good news of his Son—how constantly I make mention of you 10 at all times in my prayers, asking if by what means now at last by the will of God I will be prospered to come to you. 11 For I earnestly desire to see you, that I might impart to you some spiritual benefit, to your strengthening, 12 and that is to be encouraged with you, through the faith in one another, both yours and mine.

13 Now I do not want you to be unknowing, brethren, that often I purposed to come to you but was prevented, up to this time, that some fruit I might also have among you, even as among the other gentiles. 14 Both to Greeks and to barbarians, both to wise and to foolish, I am a debtor. 15 So accordingly I am willing also to you in Rome to proclaim the good news.

16 For I am not reluctant concerning the good news. For it is the power of God unto salvation to all believing, both to Jewish first and to Greek. 17 For the righteousness of God is revealed in it, by faith to faith, as it was written, "And the righteous will live by faith."

18 For the wrath of God from heaven is revealed upon all ungodliness and unrighteousness of humankind, by unrighteousness

suppressing the truth, 19 because the known of God is revealed in them, for God has revealed it to them. 20 For that which cannot be seen visibly of him are perceived, being understood from the creation of the world by the things made, both his eternal power and deity, for them to be without excuse.

21 For having known God, they did not glorify him as God, or were thankful, but were without real wisdom in their reasonings, and their foolish heart was darkened. 22 Asserting themselves wise they acted as fools, 23 and they exchanged the glory of the incorruptible God for the likeness of an image of corruptible man, and birds, and quadrupeds, and creeping things.

24 Therefore, God delivered them in the appetites of their hearts for unnatural pollution, to abuse their bodies with themselves. 25 They changed the truth of God into a lie, and worshiped and served the created thing contrary to the One who created it, who is blessed to the ages, amen.

26 Because of this God delivered them to disgraceful passions. For even their females exchanged the natural use into that opposed to nature. 27 Then in the same manner also the males quit the natural use of the female, lusting in their appetite for one another, males with males practicing the obscenity, and receiving in full in themselves the inevitable recompense of their error.

28 And because they did not judge it fit and proper to know God, God delivered them to an undiscerning mind to do abominable things, 29 being filled with all unrighteousness, malevolence,[a2] covetousness, being evil, filled with envy, murder, strife, deceit, malignity, a whisperer, 30 a slanderer, haters of God, insolent persecutors, arrogant, a boaster, an inventor of evil, disobedient to parents, 31 unreasonable, untrustworthy, unloving to family, unmerciful. 32 Who having known the legal rights of God, that those doing such things are deserving of death, not only are doing them, but also approving those practicing them.

ROMANS TWO

1 You are therefore without excuse, O man, each who is judging. For in that which you judge the other, you the one judging are judging yourself guilty for doing the same things. 2 But we know that the judgment of God is according to truth, upon those habitually doing such things.

3 But do you reckon, O man, the one judging those doing things, you also doing them, that you will escape the judgment of God? 4 Or do you despise the riches of his kindness, and the restraint, and the patience with people, not understanding that the goodness of God leads you to repentance? 5 But according to your stubborn and unrepentant

heart, you are laying up to yourself wrath in the day of wrath and revelation of the righteous judgment of God—6 who will give to each according to their works.

7 Truly to those accordingly patient in good work, who are seeking glory and honor and incorruptibility: eternal life. 8 But to those out of self-interest and disbelieving the truth, but assenting to unrighteousness: wrath and indignation, 9 tribulation and great distress, upon every soul of man working evil, both of Jewish first, and also of Greek. 10 But glory and honor and peace to all doing good, to both Jewish first, and to Greek. 11 For there is not at all favoritism with God.

12 For as many as sinned without Law also without Law will perish. And as many as with Law sinned according to Law will be judged. 13 For not the hearers of Law are righteous with God, but doers of Law will be justified. 14 For when gentiles not having Law by nature do the things of the Law, these not having Law are to themselves a law, 15 who show the work of the Law written in their hearts, their conscience testifying, and between one another the reckoning accusing or else defending, 16 in that day when God will judge the secrets of men, according to my good news, by Christ Jesus.[b]

17 But if you[c] are named a Jew—and rest in the Law, and glory in God, 18 and know the will, and prove things that are different—being instructed out of the Law, 19 are persuaded you yourself are a guide of the blind, a light to those in darkness, 20 instructor of the unwise, a teacher of infants, having the embodiment of knowledge and of the truth in the Law; 21 you therefore teaching another, do you not teach yourself? You preaching not to steal, do you steal? 22 You saying not to commit adultery, do you commit adultery? You abhorring idols, do you commit sacrilege? 23 You who glory in Law, through breaking the Law you dishonor God? 24 God's name through you is slandered among the gentiles, as it was written.

25 Truly circumcision is profit if you do the Law. But if you are a transgressor of Law, your circumcision has become uncircumcision. 26 Therefore, if the uncircumcision observes the precepts of the Law, will not his uncircumcision be reckoned for circumcision? 27 And those by nature uncircumcision, the Law fulfilling, will judge you who with the letter and circumcision are breaking the Law. 28 For not the one in the outward is Jewish, neither the one in the outward in flesh is circumcision, 29 but he who in the inward is Jewish, and circumcision of heart in spirit not in letter; of whom the praise is not of men but of God.

ROMANS THREE

1 What, therefore, the advantage of the Jewish? Or what the profit of the circumcision? 2

Much in every way. First, truly, for that the oracles of God were committed in trust to them. 3 For what if some disbelieved? Should their unbelief render useless the faithfulness of God? 4 Never may it be!

Now God be true but every person a liar, as was written, "That you might be justified in your words and will prevail in your being judged." 5 But if our unrighteousness declares God's righteousness, what shall we say? Is God unrighteous inflicting the wrath? I speak according to humankind. 6 Never may it be! Else how will God judge the world? 7 But if the truth of God abounded in my lie to his glory, why yet am I also judged as though a sinner? 8 And not as slandered, and as some affirm us to say, "Let us do evil that good may come?" Their condemnation is just.

9 What then? Are we better? Not at all. For we previously accused both Jews and Greeks, all to be under sin. 10 As it was written, none is righteous, not one. 11 None is understanding. None is seeking God. 12 They all turned away. Together they became vile.

None is practicing good: there is not so much as one. 13 Their voice box: a grave opening; with their tongues always deceiving. Under their lips: venom of vipers; 14 of whom the mouth is full of bitterness and imprecation. 15 Their feet: swift to shed blood. 16 Their paths: ruin and misery; 17 and the way leading to peace they have not known. 18 There is not fear of God before their eyes.

19 Now we know that as much as the Law is saying, it says to those with the Law, so that every mouth might be stopped and all the world might be under judgment to God. 20 For this reason not any flesh will be justified before him by works of the Law; for through the Law is knowledge of sin.

21 But now, apart from Law, God's righteousness is revealed, being testified by the Law and the prophets, 22 namely God's righteousness through the faithfulness of Jesus Christ toward all[d] those believing. For there is no distinction, 23 for all have sinned and come short of God's glory, 24 being freely justified by his grace through the redemption that is by Christ Jesus. 25 Whom God set forth publicly as a propitiation, through faith in his blood, for declaring his righteousness—because of the passing over of the sins that are past because of the temporary long-suffering of God— 26 through setting forth publicly God's righteousness in the present time, for him to be just and justifying the one having faith in Jesus.

27 Where then the boasting? It is excluded. By what law? That of works? No, but by a law of faith. 28 For[e] we reckon a person to be justified by faith without works of Law. 29 Or *is he* the God of Jewish only, not also of gentiles? Yes, also of gentiles. 30 Indeed one God,

who will justify circumcision by faith and uncircumcision through the faith. 31 Then do we render Law useless through the faith? Never may it be! On the contrary we confirm Law.

ROMANS FOUR

1 What then shall we say Abraham, our father according to flesh, to have found?[f] 2 For if Abraham was justified from works he has something to glory, but not toward God. 3 For the Scripture says what? That Abraham believed God and it was reckoned to him for righteousness. 4 Now to the one working the wage is not reckoned according to grace but according to what is owed. 5 But to the one not working, but believing on the one justifying the ungodly, his faith is reckoned for righteousness.

6 Just as also David affirms the blessedness of the person to whom God reckons righteousness without works: 7 "Blessed those forgiven their lawlessness and whose sins are covered, 8 blessed the person to whom the Lord will never no never reckon sin." 9 This blessing then, on the circumcision or also on the uncircumcision? For we are saying that to Abraham the faith was reckoned as righteousness. 10 How then was it reckoned? Being in circumcision or in uncircumcision? Not in circumcision but in uncircumcision.

11 And he received the sign of circumcision as proof of the righteousness of the faith during the uncircumcision, for him to be the father of all those believing during uncircumcision, to them also to be reckoned the righteousness. 12 And father of those circumcised—not of only circumcised, but also those living in the example of the faith of Abraham our father during uncircumcision.

13 For not through Law was the promise to Abraham or his descendants to be heir of the world, but through righteousness of faith. 14 For if those of Law are heirs, faith is made empty and the promise rendered ineffective. 15 For Law produces wrath. Now where there is no Law, also no transgression: 16 therefore this is of faith so that it is according to grace.

For it is certain the promise is to all the offspring: not to that of the Law only, but also those of Abraham's faith, who is father of us all. 17 As it was written, "I have made you a father of many nations," in the presence of God whom he believed, the one giving life to the dead and calling the thing not existing into existence.

18 Who contrary to hope, in hope believed, for him to become father of many nations, according to that which was declared, "So your offspring will be." 19 And not being weak in the faith, considering his body is now impotent[g], being about one hundred years, and the deadness of Sarah's womb. 20 But with respect to the promise of God he did not waver through unbelief, but was strengthened in faith,

having given glory to God, 21 and being fully persuaded that what has been promised he is also able to do. 22 And accordingly it was reckoned to him for righteousness.

23 Now it was not written on account of him alone that it was reckoned to him, 24 but also on account of us, to whom it is about to be reckoned, to those believing on the one having raised Jesus our Lord out from the dead ones, 25 who was delivered because of our sins, and was raised for our justification.

ROMANS FIVE

1 Therefore, having been justified by faith, we have peace with God through our Lord Jesus Christ, 2 through whom also we have access[h] into this grace in which we stand. And we glory in hope of the glory of God. 3 Not only now, but also we glory in afflictions, knowing that afflictions produce endurance. 4 Then also endurance, character; then also character, hope. 5 Then also hope does not disappoint, because God's love has poured out into our hearts through the Holy Spirit, the one who was given to us.

6 For yet Christ, we still being wretched, died for the godless at a proper season. 7 For scarcely on behalf of the righteous will anyone die. On behalf of the good perhaps anyone would even venture to die. 8 But God declares his love for us, that we still being sinners, Christ died on our behalf. 9 All the more therefore, now having been declared righteous in his blood, we will be delivered because of him from the wrath.

10 For if being enemies we were reconciled to God through the death of his son, all the more having been reconciled we shall be delivered by his life. 11 And not only that, but also we are rejoicing in God through our Lord Jesus Christ, through whom now we have received the reconciliation 12 on account of this: just as through one person sin came into the world, and through sin the death, also in this manner the death came upon all persons, in that all sinned.

13 For continually until the times of the Law sin was in the world. But sin is not imputed there not being Law. 14 Nevertheless death reigned from Adam unto Moses, even over those not having sinned in the same manner of Adam's transgression, who is a prototype of the one coming.

15 But as not as the wrongdoing, so also the undeserved gift. For if in the wrongdoing of the one the many died, all the more God's grace, and the gift by grace which is of one man, Jesus Christ, unto the many did superabound. 16 And the gift is not for the sake of one having sinned, for truly the judgment of one was unto condemnation, but the undeserved gift is because of many trespasses, unto justification.

17 For if in the one trespass death reigned through the one, *Adam*, all the more that the superabundance of grace, and

receiving of the gift of righteousness, will reign within life through the one, Jesus Christ.

18 Then therefore, so as on account of one trespass to all persons unto condemnation, thus also on account of one act of obedience to all persons to justification of life. 19 For just as through the disobedience of the one person the many were made sinners, so also through the obedience of the one the many will be made righteous.

20 Now Law entered so that the trespass might abound. But where sin abounded, grace superabounded, 21 so that just as the sin reigned in death, so also the grace might reign through righteousness to eternal life through Jesus Christ our Lord.

ROMANS SIX

1 What then will we say? Shall we persevere in sin that grace may abound? 2 Never may it be! We who died to sin, in what way shall we still live in it? 3 Or do you not understand that as many as were immersed into Christ Jesus were immersed into his death? 4 Therefore we were buried together with him by immersion into death, so that just as Christ was raised up out from the dead for the sake of the Father's glory, so also we should live in newness of life.

5 For if we have become in the likeness of his death, assuredly also we will be of the resurrection. 6 We are knowing this: that our old self was crucified together with him, so that the body of sin might be made ineffective, that no longer are we enslaved to sin. 7 For the one having died has been justified from sin.

8 But if we died with Christ, we also believe that we will live with him, 9 knowing that Christ, having been raised up out from the dead, dies no more; death no more has authority over him. 10 For that he died, he died to sin once for all. But that he lives, he lives to God. 11 So also you reckon yourselves to be dead indeed to sin, but living to God in Christ Jesus.[i]

12 Therefore, do not let sin rule in your mortal body, for obedience to its desires. 13 Neither present your members to sin as instruments of unrighteousness, but present yourselves to God as living out from the dead, and your members as instruments of righteousness to God. 14 For sin will not have authority over you, because you are not under Law but under grace.

15 What therefore? Should we sin because we are not under Law but under grace? Never may it be! 16 Do you not know that to whom you present yourselves as slaves for obedience, slaves you are to him whom you obey, whether of sin to death or of obedience to righteousness? 17 Now thanks to God that you were being slaves of sin, but now you have been obeying from the heart that form of instruction into which you were delivered. 18 Now having been set free from sin, you have become

servants to righteousness.

19 I speak in the manner of humankind because of the weakness of your flesh. For just as you presented your members in slavery to moral uncleanness and to lawlessness unto lawlessness, so now present your members in slavery to righteousness unto holiness.

20 For when you were slaves of sin, you were free from righteousness. 21 Therefore, what fruit had you then in that for which you are now ashamed? For the result of those things is death. 22 But now you have been freed from sin. Now having become servants to God you have your fruit unto holiness. 23 For the wages of sin is death; but God's gift is eternal life in Christ Jesus our Lord.

ROMANS SEVEN

1 Or do you not understand, brethren (for I speak to those knowing the Law), that the Law has authority over the person during his life? 2 For the married woman is legally obligated to the living husband. But if the husband should die she is separated from the law of the husband. 3 Therefore, then, the husband living, she will be called an adulteress if she may be with another man. But if the husband should die she is free from the law, her not being an adulteress having been with another man.

4 Thus, my brethren, you also have been put to death to the Law through the body of Christ, for you belong to another, to the one having been raised out from the dead, so that we may bear fruit to God. 5 For when we were in the flesh, the passions of sins that *are* through the Law were working in our members to bring forth fruit to death. 6 But now we have been separated from the Law, having died to that which we were legally obligated, for us to serve in newness of spirit and not in oldness of letter.

7 What then shall we say? The Law *is* sin? Never may it be! But I did not know sin if not by the Law. For that is, I had not known wrongful desire if the Law had not said "You will not wrongfully desire." 8 But sin taking opportunity through the commandment, it produced in me all manner of wrongful desire: for without the Law sin is dead. 9 Now I was alive when without Law. But the commandment having come, the sin lived again and I died. 10 And I discovered the commandment that *was* to life, this *was* to death. 11 For the sin, having taken opportunity through the commandment, completely deceived me, and through it put me to death. 12 So that truly the Law is holy, and the commandment holy and righteous and good.

13 Therefore that *which is* good, to me has become death? Never may it be! But sin, so that it might be seen to be sin, through that which is good to me, is producing death, so that sin through the commandment might

be more exceedingly sinful. 14 For we know that the Law is spiritual, but I am fleshly, being sold under sin.

15 For what I do, I do not approve: for not what I want, this I am doing; yea, what I hate, this I practice. 16 Now if that which I do not want, this I practice, then I am agreeing to the Law, that is it good.

17 Now on the contrary I am no longer doing it, but the sin dwelling in me. 18 For I know that there resides nothing in me—that is, in my flesh—in itself good. For to desire is present with me, but to be doing the good, not.[j] 19 For that good I desire, I do not practice, but the evil I do not want, this I am doing. 20 But if what I am not desiring, this I do, it is no longer I who am doing it, but sin residing in me.

21 So I discover this law: that I desiring to do good, that evil is present with me. 22 For I delight in the law of God, according to the inner person. 23 But I see another law in my members, opposing the law of my mind, and making me captive to the law of sin existing in my members. 24 I am a miserable man! Who will rescue me out of the body of this death?

25 Now thanks be to God through Jesus Christ our Lord! So then, I myself truly with the mind serve God's law, but the flesh the law of sin.

ROMANS EIGHT

1 Therefore now there is not even one condemnatory judgment to those in Christ Jesus.[k] 2 For the law of the Spirit of life in Christ Jesus has made you free from the law of sin and of death. 3 For the impotent law, in that it was weak through the flesh, God having sent his Son in likeness of sinful flesh, and concerning sin, condemned sin in the flesh, 4 so that the righteousness of the Law may be fulfilled in us, not according to the manner of flesh, but according to spirit.

5 For those being according to flesh, are mindful of things of the flesh. But those according to spirit things of the Spirit. 6 For the will of the flesh, death; but the will of the Spirit, life and peace, 7 because the will of the flesh is hatred toward God, for it does not submit to the law of God, for it is not able. 8 Now the ones being in the flesh are not able to please God.

9 But you are not in flesh but in spirit, assuming God's Spirit resides in you. But if anyone has not Christ's Spirit, he is not of him. 10 But if Christ is in you, truly the body is dead on account of sin, but the spirit is living on account of righteousness. 11 But if the Spirit of the one having raised up Jesus out from the dead resides in you, the one having raised up Christ Jesus out from the dead will also give life to your mortal body, on account of his Spirit dwelling in you.

12 So then, brethren, we are not debtors to the flesh to live according to flesh. 13 For if you live according to flesh, you are

destined to die. But if by spirit you put to death the acts of the body, you will live. 14 For as many as are led by God's Spirit, these are God's sons. 15 For you have not received a slavish spirit once more to fear, but you have received a spirit of adoption by which we cry out "Abba! Father!" 16 The Spirit himself bears witness with our spirit that we are children of God. 17 Now if children, also heirs, truly heirs of God, now joint-heirs of Christ, seeing that we suffer together so that also we may be glorified together.

18 For I reckon that the sufferings of the present time are not comparable to the coming glory to be revealed to us. 19 For the earnest expectation of the creation waits the revealing of the sons of God. 20 For the creation was subjected to futility, not willingly, but according to the one having subjected it, in expectation 21 that also the creation itself will be freed from the slavery of corruption into the freedom of the glory of God's children.

22 For we know that all the creation groans together and is in pain together until now. 23 And not only, but also ourselves, having the firstfruit of the Spirit, we ourselves also in ourselves are distressed, waiting adoption—the redemption of our body. 24 For in this expectation we were saved. But seeing expectation is not expectation. For what any one sees, does he expect? 25 But if what we do not see we expect, we wait through patience.

26 Now also in the same manner, the Spirit assists our weakness. For the things we should pray for as is necessary, we do not know, but the Spirit himself intercedes on our behalf with unutterable groanings. 27 Now the one searching hearts knows what is the will of the Spirit, because according to God he intercedes for the saints.

28 Now we know that to those loving God, all things work together for good, to those being called according to his purpose. 29 For those whom he foreknew, also he decreed beforehand to conform to the image of his Son, for him to be firstborn among many brethren. 30 Now those he decreed beforehand, these also he called; and whom he called, these also he justified. Now whom he justified, these also he glorified.

31 What then will we say to these things? If God is for us, who is against us? 32 He who truly spared not his own Son, but for all of us gave him up, how not also with him, will he give us all things? 33 Who will bring an accusation against God's elect? God is the one justifying. 34 Who is the one condemning? Christ Jesus is the one having died, now rather being raised up, who is at the right hand of God, and who is interceding for us.

35 Who will separate us from Christ's love? Tribulation, or great distress, or persecution, or famine, or nakedness, or danger, or sword? 36 As has been written, "For

your sake we are put to death all the day, we have been reckoned as sheep for slaughter." 37 But in all these we more than conquer through the one having loved us. 38 For I am persuaded that neither death, nor life, nor messengers, nor rulers, nor present, nor future, nor powers, 39 nor height, nor depth, nor any other created thing, will be able to separate us from God's love in Christ Jesus our Lord.

ROMANS NINE

1 I speak truth in Christ, I am not lying, my conscience testifying with me in the Holy Spirit, 2 that my sorrow is great and unceasing in my heart. 3 I could earnestly wish myself to be accursed, separated from Christ for my brethren, my kinsmen according to flesh, 4 those who are Israelites, of whom the adoption as sons, and the glory, and the covenants, and the law-giving, and the promises. 5 Of whom the Fathers, and out of whom is Christ according to the flesh, God being over all, blessed to the ages, amen.

6 But not as though the Word of God has failed. For not all who are out of Israel are these Israel. 7 Nor because they are offspring of Abraham are all children, but "In Isaac your offspring will be called." 8 That is, not the children of the flesh that are children of God, but the children of the promise are reckoned as offspring. 9 For of the promise the word is this, "According to this time I will come, and there will be to Sarah a son."

10 Now not only *Sarah*, but also Rebecca, from one conception by Isaac our father. 11 For not yet being born, not having done anything good or evil, so that election according to the purpose of God might remain. 12 Not of works but of the one calling it was said to her, "The older will serve the younger."[1] 13 As it has been written, "Jacob I loved, but Esau I hated."

14 What then will we say? Is there not injustice with God? Never may it be! 15 For to Moses he says, "I will show mercy to whom I may show mercy," and "I will have compassion on whom I may have compassion." 16 So then, not of the willing, nor of the running, but of God showing mercy. 17 For the Scripture says to Pharaoh, "For this therefore I have raised you up, so that I may show with you my power, and that my name may be declared in all the earth." 18 So then to whom he wills, he shows mercy, but to whom he wills, he hardens.

19 Certainly you will say to me, "Why still does he find fault? For who is resisting his purpose?" 20 O man, yes indeed, who are you disputing God? Should the thing formed say to the one molding, "Why have you made me like this?" 21 Or does the potter not have authority over the clay, out of the same lump to make one truly a vessel unto honor, but one unto dishonor?

22 Now what if God, desiring to show his wrath and to make known his power, endured with

much patience vessels of wrath prepared for destruction, 23 even so that he may make known the riches of his glory upon vessels of mercy that he prepared beforehand for glory, 24 even whom he has called, not only us out from Jewish, but also out from gentiles?

25 As also in Hosea he says, "I will call those not my people, my people, and her not being loved, being loved. 26 And it will be in the place where it was said to them, 'You are not my people,' there they will be called 'sons of the living God.'"

27 Also Isaiah cries out on account of Israel, "Though the number of the sons of Israel may be as the sand of the sea, the remnant will be saved. 28 For the word he performs and decrees the Lord will do on the earth."[12] 29 And as Isaiah foretold, "If the Lord of Hosts had not left us offspring, we would have become like Sodom, and we would have been made like Gomorrah."

30 What then will we say? That the gentiles not pursuing righteousness, have attained righteousness, now righteousness that is by faith? 31 But Israel, pursuing a law of righteousness, did not attain to a law? 32 On account of why? Because not by faith but as by works. They stumbled on the stone of stumbling, 33 as it has been written, "Look, I lay in Zion a stone of stumbling and a rock of offense," and "the one believing on him never will be made ashamed."

ROMANS TEN

1 Brethren, truly the good intent of my heart and the prayer to God on their behalf is for salvation. 2 For I bear witness to them, that they have zeal for God, but not according to knowledge. 3 For not knowing the righteousness of God, and striving to establish their own righteousness, they have not submitted to the righteousness of God. 4 For Christ is the completion of law—to all believing unto righteousness.

5 For Moses writes the righteousness that is of the Law: "the person doing will live by them." 6 But the righteousness of faith speaks thusly: "you should not say in your heart, 'Who will ascend into heaven?' (that is, to bring Christ down), 7 or, 'Who will descend into the abyss?'" (that is, to bring Christ up out from the dead). 8 But what says it? "The word is at hand, in your mouth and in your heart," that is, the word of faith which we proclaim: 9 that if you confess[m] with your mouth, "Lord Jesus," and believe in your heart that him God raised out from *the* dead, you will be saved. 10 For by the heart it is believed unto righteousness and by the mouth it is confessed unto salvation.

11 For the scripture says, "All believing on him will not be put to shame." 12 For there is no distinction between Jewish and Greek, for the same Lord of all is rich toward all those calling him. 13 For all that may call upon the

Lord's name will be saved. 14 How then may they call on whom they have not believed? Now how may they believe of whom they have not heard? Now how may they hear without proclaiming? 15 Now how may they proclaim if they might not be sent? As it has been written, "How beautiful the feet of those proclaiming good news of good things!"

16 But not all obeyed the good news. For Isaiah says, "Lord, who has believed our report?" 17 So faith from hearing and hearing through a word about Christ. 18 But I ask, is it possible they did not hear? Yes indeed, their voice has gone out into all the earth, and their words to the remotest regions of the inhabited earth.

19 But I ask, is it possible Israel did not know? First Moses says, "I will provoke you to jealousy by those not a nation; I will provoke you to anger by a nation without understanding." 20 Now Isaiah is very bold and says, "I was found by those not seeking for me; I was revealed to those not asking for me." 21 But toward Israel he says, "All the day I have stretched forward my hands to a people disbelieving and disobeying."

ROMANS ELEVEN

1 I ask then, did God not reject his people? Never may it be! For I also am an Israelite, out of Abraham's offspring, of Benjamin's tribe. 2 God did not reject his people whom he foreknew. Or know you not by Elijah what the Scripture says, how he intercedes with God against Israel: 3 "Lord, they have killed your prophets, they have razed your altars, and I alone remain, and they are seeking my life." 4 But what is the reply saying to him? "I have reserved to myself seven thousand men who have not bent the knee to Baal."

5 Thus then, also in the present time, there has been a remnant according to the election of grace. 6 If now by grace, no longer from works. For otherwise grace no more would be grace. [n]

7 What then? What Israel is striving after, this it has not acquired—but the elect acquired. Now the rest were hardened. 8 As it has been written, "God gave them a spirit of dullness—eyes not to see and ears not to hear," unto the today of this day. 9 And David is saying: "Let their table be for a snare, and for a trap, and for a stumbling block, and for a retribution to them. 10 Let their eyes be darkened to not see, and their backs continually bowed low."

11 I ask then, did they not stumble that they might fall? Never may it be! But in their trespass there *is* salvation to the gentiles, so as to provoke them to emulation. 12 But if their trespass *is* the riches of the world, and their failure *is* the riches of the gentiles, how much more their fullness?

13 Now to you, the gentiles, I am speaking. Inasmuch as, truly, I am apostle of gentiles, I exalt my ministry, 14 if in some way I shall

provoke to emulation my flesh and shall save some of them. 15 For if their rejection is a reconciliation of the world, what the acceptance if not life out from the dead?

16 Now if the firstfruit is holy, also the whole. And if the root is holy, also the branches. 17 But if some of the branches were broken off, now you, being a wild olive tree, were grafted in among them, and have become a joint partaker of the fatness of the root of the olive tree. 18 Do not boast against the branches; but if you boast against them, you do not bear the root but the root you. 19 Then you will say, "Branches were broken off that I might be grafted in." 20 Well said. By their unbelief they were broken off. But you by faith stand. Be not high-minded but fear. 21 For if God did not spare the branches according to nature, [not at all°] neither you will he spare.

22 See, therefore, the kindness and severity of God. Truly upon those having fallen, severity. But upon you, kindness, if you might continue in the kindness, for otherwise you also will be cut off. 23 Now even they, if they do not continue in unbelief, will be grafted in. For God is able again to graft them in. 24 For if you were cut off out of a wild olive tree according to nature, and contrary to nature were grafted into a good olive tree, how much more these who *are* according to nature, will be grafted into their own olive tree?

25 For I do not want you to be ignorant, brethren, of this mystery (that you may not be wise in yourselves), that a hardening has happened in part to Israel, until that the fullness of the gentiles may come in, 26 and so all Israel will be saved, even as has been written, "The Deliverer will come out of Zion, he will put away ungodliness from Jacob. 27 And this to them *is* the covenant from me, when I may take away their sins."

28 Truly as regards the good news they are enemies on account of you all, but beloved as regards the election, on account of the fathers. 29 For without regret the spiritual gifts and the call of God. 30 For just as you all once were disobedient to God, but now those of the disobedience have been shown mercy, 31 so also these now have been disobedient for your mercy, in order that they also now might have mercy. 32 For God has imprisoned all in disobedience, in order that he might have mercy to all.

33 O the depth of riches, both of wisdom and knowledge of God! How inscrutable his judgments and untraceable his ways. 34 For who has known the mind of the Lord, or who has been his counselor? 35 Or who has given first to him and it will be repaid to him? 36 Because from him, and through him, and unto him, the all. To him the glory to the ages. Amen.

ROMANS TWELVE

1 Therefore I exhort you, brethren, through the compassions of God, to present yourselves a living offering, holy, well-pleasing

to God, which is your reasonable service. 2 And do not be conformed to this age, but be transformed by the renewing of the mind, for you all to discern what is the will of God, the good and well-pleasing and complete.

3 For I am saying through the grace that was given to me, to all being with you, not to be thinking too highly above than you ought to think, but to think in order to be of sound mind, to each as God has distributed a measure of faith. 4 For just as in one body we have many members, but all members have not the same function, 5 so we the many are one body in Christ, and members each one of one another, 6 and having various gifts according to the grace that was given to us.

If any prophecy, according to the proportion of the faith. 7 If any serve, in the service. If any the teaching, in the teaching. 8 If any the exhorting, in the exhortation. If any giving, in faithfulness. Those ruling, with diligence. Those showing mercy, with cheerfulness. 9 The love without pretense: detesting the evil, adhering to the good. 10 In brotherly love, tender affection to one another, in the honor, mutually respecting one another. 11 In diligence, not lazy, being fervent in spirit, serving the Lord, 12 rejoicing in confident assurance, being patient in afflictions. If in prayer, being steadfast. 13 Distributing to the needs of the saints, pursuing kindness to strangers.

14 Bless the ones persecuting you. Bless and do not wish anyone evil. 15 Rejoice with those rejoicing, lament with those lamenting. 16 Have the same regard toward one another, not regarding the high *things* but led by the lowly *things*. Be not wise in your own estimation. 17 To no one repaying evil for evil, providing good deeds in the sight of all persons.

18 If possible from you, living in peace with all persons, 19 never avenging yourselves, beloved. Rather, give place to wrath; for it has been written, "For vengeance is mine, I will avenge," says the Lord. 20 But if your enemy might hunger, provide him food, if he may thirst, give him drink. For these things doing, you will heap up burning coals of fire on his head. 21 Be not overcome by the evil, but overcome the evil with the good.

ROMANS THIRTEEN

1 Let every soul place themselves in submission to the authorities being higher. For there is no authority except by God, and those existing having been appointed by God. 2 Accordingly, the one opposing the authority is standing against God's ordinance; and those standing against will receive judgment on themselves. 3 For the rulers are not a terror to good works but to evil. But do you desire not to fear the authority? Do the good and you will have approval from him.

4 For he is God's servant to you for the good. But if you do evil,

be afraid, for he bears the sword not in vain. For he is a servant of God, an avenger for wrath to the one doing evil. 5 Therefore, *it is* necessary to be in submission, not only for the sake of the wrath, but also on account of the conscience.

6 For because of this, you also pay taxes. For they are God's servants, continually insisting upon this very thing. 7 Give to all their service: to whom the tax, the tax; to whom the tribute, the tribute; to whom the respect, the respect; to whom the honor, the honor.

8 To no one owe nothing, except to love one another. For the one loving the other has fulfilled the Law. 9 For you will not commit adultery, you will not murder, you will not steal, you will not wrongly desire, and if any other commandment in the word it is summarized in this, "You will love your neighbor as yourself." 10 Love to the neighbor does not do evil, therefore love fulfills the Law.

11 And knowing this the season, that *it is* the hour for you already to awaken out of sleep. For nearer now *is* our salvation than when we first believed. 12 The night is far spent, but the day approaches. Therefore we should renounce the works of darkness, we should put on the armor of light. 13 As in daytime, we should live our manner of life respectably, not in riotous conduct and drunkenness, not in unlawful cohabitation and excessive pleasure, not in strife and envy. 14 But put on the Lord Jesus Christ, and of the flesh make no provision for your wrong desires.

ROMANS FOURTEEN

1 But the one being weak in the faith, receive, not for judgment of opinions. 2 Truly, one believes to eat all, but the one being weak eats plants. 3 The one eating, let him not despise the one not eating. But the one not eating, let him not judge the one eating; for God has received him. 4 Who are you judging another's domestic servant? To his own master he stands or falls. But he will not fall, for the Lord is able to cause him to stand.

5 For truly, one judges *one* day above *another* day, but *another one* judges every day *the same: let* each in his own mind *be* fully persuaded. 6 The one keeping the day, to the Lord keeps it. [ᵖ] The one eating, to the Lord eats, for he gives thanks to God. And the one not eating, to the Lord he does not eat, and he gives thanks to God. 7 For none of us lives to himself, and none *of us* dies to himself. 8 And for both we should live: to the Lord we live; and if we should die, to the Lord we die. And if therefore we should live, and if we should die, the Lord's we are. 9 For unto this Christ died and lived again, that he should rule over both dead and living.

10 But you, why do you judge your brother? Or also you, why do you despise your brother? For we all will stand before the judgment seat of God.ᑫ 11 For it has been written, "I live," says the Lord,

"that to me every knee will bow, and every tongue will confess," to God. 12 So then, each of us will give a word concerning himself to God.

13 No more, therefore, should we judge one another. But rather choose this: not to set an occasion for sinning before a brother, or a cause of offense. 14 I know and I am persuaded in the Lord Jesus, that nothing is unclean of itself, except to him reckoning something to be unclean: to that one it is unclean. 15 For if for the sake of food your brother is offended, then you are no longer conducting your life according to love. Do not ruin[r] that one with your food, for whom Christ died. 16 Therefore, do not let your good be slandered.

17 For the kingdom of God is not eating and drinking, but righteousness and peace and joy in the Holy Spirit. 18 For the one serving Christ in these things *is* well-pleasing to God and accepted by men. 19 So then, we should pursue the *things* of peace and the *things* for spiritual profit, with respect to one another. 20 Do not because of food destroy the work of God. Truly all *is* clean, but harmful to the person eating with offence. 21 *It is* good to not eat meat, neither to drink wine, nor *that* in which your brother stumbles.[s] 22 The faith that you have, keep to yourself before God. Blessed the one not judging himself in what he approves. 23 But the one doubting, if he eats, has been condemned, because not of faith. Now all that is not of faith is sin.

ROMANS FIFTEEN

1 Also we are obligated, we the strong, to bear the scruples of the weak, and not to please ourselves. 2 Let each of us please the neighbor for the good, for spiritual profit. 3 For even Christ did not please himself, but as it has been written, "The slander of those reproaching you have fallen on me."

4 For all that has been written, was written for our instruction, so that through the endurance of circumstances and through the encouragement of the scriptures we might have hope.

5 Now the God of the endurance and the encouragement, may he give you to be of the same mind with one another, according to Christ Jesus, 6 so that with unanimous consent, with one mouth, you may glorify the God and Father of our Lord Jesus Christ. 7 Therefore, receive one another, as also Christ received you, unto the glory of God.

8 For I say Christ to have become a minister of the circumcision for God's truth, in order to affirm the promises to the fathers; 9 and the gentiles, for mercy, to glorify God, as was written, "Because of this I will praise you among gentiles, and to your name I will sing." 10 And again it says, "Rejoice all you gentiles, with his people." 11 And again, "Praise the Lord all the gentiles, and praise him all the peoples." 12 And again, Isaiah says, "There will

be the root of Jesse, and the one arising to rule gentiles. In him gentiles will hope." 13 Now may the God of hope fill you with all joy and peace in the believing, for you to superabound in the hope, in the power, of the Holy Spirit.

14 Now I am persuaded, my brethren (I myself also concerning you), that also yourselves are full of goodness, being filled with all the knowledge, being able also to warn one another. 15 But I have written more boldly to you in some measure, as reminding you, because of the grace that was given to me by God, 16 for me to be a minister of Jesus Christ to the gentiles, administering the gospel of God, so that the offering of the gentiles may be acceptable, being sanctified by the Holy Spirit.

17 Therefore I have the boasting in Christ Jesus, in that pertaining to God. 18 For I will not dare to speak of anything except what Christ has accomplished through me to obedience of the gentiles—in word and deed, 19 by the power of signs and wonders, by the power of God's Spirit—so as in me from Jerusalem and round about unto Illyricum, to have fully *declared* the good news of Christ; 20 thus now aspiring to proclaim the good news where Christ has not been named, so that I may not build upon another's foundation. 21 But as was written, "to whom it was not made known concerning him" and "those that have not heard will understand." 22 And therefore I have been hindered much to come to you.

23 But now no longer having a place in these regions, but a having a great desire to come to you for many years, 24 whenever I may go to Spain, I hope before passing through to see you, and by you to be brought on my way there, if first of you all I might enjoy your company for a while. 25 But now I am going to Jerusalem, ministering to the saints. 26 For Macedonia and Achaia were resolved to make a certain contribution for the poor among the saints in Jerusalem.

27 For they were resolved and indebted they are to them. For if their spiritual things the gentiles have shared in, they ought also in the material things to minister to them. 28 This therefore having completed and having delivered to them this fruit, I will depart through you into Spain. 29 Now I know when coming to you I will come in the fullness of Christ's blessing.

30 Now I call upon you, brethren, by our Lord Jesus Christ and by the love of the Spirit, to strive together with me in the prayers for me to God, 31 so that I might be delivered from those disbelieving in Judea; and my ministry, which is in Jerusalem, may be acceptable to the saints, 32 so that in joy, having come to you by God's will, I may be refreshed with you. 33 Now the God of peace abide with all of you. Amen.

ROMANS SIXTEEN

1 Now I commend to you Phoebe, our sister, being also a deacon of the church in Cenchrea,

2 that you may receive her in the Lord, as is proper of the saints, and you might stand by her in whatever matter she may have need of you. For also she has been a patron of many, and of me myself.

3 Greet Prisca and Aquila, my fellow-workers in Christ Jesus 4 (who for my life stuck out their neck, whom not only I thank, but all the churches of the gentiles), 5 and the church at their house. Greet Epenetus, my beloved, who is a firstfruit of Asia for Christ.

6 Greet Mary, who wearied herself with much labor for you. 7 Greet Andronicus and Junias, my kinsmen and fellow prisoners with me, who are well-thought-of among the apostles, who also were before me in Christ. 8 Greet Ampliatus, my beloved in the Lord.

9 Greet Urbanus, our fellow-worker in Christ, and Stachys my beloved. 10 Greet Apelles, the proven in Christ. Greet those of Aristobulus. 11 Greet Herodion, my kinsmen. Greet those of Narcissus being in the Lord.

12 Greet Tryphena and Tryphosa, the ones wearied with labor in the Lord. Greet Persis the beloved, who labored much in the Lord. 13 Greet Rufus, the chosen of the Lord, and the mother of him and of me. 14 Greet Asyncritus, Phlegon, Hermes, Patrobas, Hermas, and the brethren with them.

15 Greet Philologus and Julia, Nerus and his sister, and Olympas and all the saints with them. 16 Greet one another with a token of holy love and friendship. All the churches of Christ greet you.

17 Now I admonish you, brethren, give attention to those causing separation and stumbling contrary to the teaching that you have learned, and turn aside from them; 18 for such do not serve our Lord Christ but their own stomach. And by eloquent words and fair speeches they deceive the hearts of the harmless. 19 For your obedience has reached all. Over you, therefore, I rejoice. But I desire you truly to be wise to the good, innocent to the evil. 20 Now the God of peace will crush Satan under your feet shortly. The grace of our Lord Jesus Christ be with you.

21 Timothy greets you, my fellow-worker; also Lucius and Jason, and Sosipater, my kinsmen. 22 I Tertius, the one who wrote down this letter, greet you in the Lord. 23 My host Gaius greets you, and all of the church. Erastus, the steward of the city, greets you, and Quartus, the brother. 24 The grace of our Lord Jesus Christ be with you all, truly.[t]

25 Now to him being able to strengthen you, according to my good news and the proclaiming of Jesus Christ, according to the revelation of the mystery, in times of the ages having been kept in silence, 26 but now revealed, that is through the prophetic scriptures, according to the command of the eternal God, unto obedience of faith, being made known to all the

gentiles, 27 God only wise, through Jesus Christ, which is the glory to the ages,ᵘ truly.

The Book of First Corinthians

The Book of First Corinthians was written ca. AD 57, from Ephesus, in the third year of Paul's third missionary journey (AD 54–58). The book is partly a response to a prior letter to Paul from the Corinthians, 5:9; 7:1, partly to address troubling issues reported to Paul by those of Chloe (i.e., of her household), 1:11, and to address issues Paul had heard from others, 5:1. Many doctrinal issues and things of the practical Christian life are addressed in this letter.

FIRST CORINTHIANS ONE

1 Paul, appointed apostle of Christ Jesus by God's will, and Sosthenes the brother. 2 To the church of God being in Corinth, the ones sanctified in Christ Jesus, called saints together with all those calling on the name of our Lord Jesus Christ in every place, theirs and ours. 3 Grace to you, and peace, from God our Father and Lord Jesus Christ.

4 I thank my God at all times concerning you, for the grace of God that was given you in Christ Jesus, 5 so that in everything you have been enriched in him in all speech and all knowledge, 6 even as the testimony of the Christ has been confirmed in you, 7 even as not to be lacking in not one gift, expecting the revelation of our Lord Jesus Christ, 8 who also will preserve you unaccused to the end in the day of our Lord Jesus Christ. 9 God is faithful, by whom you were called into fellowship with his son Jesus Christ our Lord.

10 Now I exhort you, brethren, for the sake of the name of our Lord Jesus Christ, that you all speak the same, and there not be among you factions, but you be fit together in the same mind and in the same will. 11 For it was told to me about you, my brethren, by those of Chloe, that there are quarrels among you.

12 Now I mean this: that each of you says, "Truly I am of Paul," but "I of Apollos," but "I of Cephas," but "I of Christ." 13 Has Christ been divided? Paul was not crucified for you, was he? Or were you immersed into the name of Paul? 14 I thank God that I immersed no one of you, except Crispus and Gaius, 15 so that no one may say that you were immersed into my name. 16 But I also immersed the household of Stephanus. As to the rest, I do not know whether any other I immersed.

17 For Christ did not send me to immerse, but to proclaim the good news, not in the wisdom of discourse, that the cross of Christ may not be emptied. 18 For truly to those who are perishing the word of the cross is absurd; but to those being saved, to us it is the power of God. 19 For it was written, "I will ruin the wisdom of the wise, and the discernment of the discerning I will make void."

20 Where the wise? Where the scribe? Where the debater of this

the age? Has not God made foolish the wisdom of the world? 21 For since indeed in God's wisdom the world did not know God through the wisdom, God was pleased through the absurdity of the preaching to save those believing.

22 And inasmuch as Jews are seeking signs and Greeks are striving for wisdom, 23 but we preach Christ having been crucified—truly to the Jewish a scandal, but to gentiles absurd. 24 But to those who are the called, both Jews and Greeks, Christ is God's power and God's wisdom, 25 because the absurdity of God is wiser than men, and the weakness of God stronger than men.

26 For consider your calling, brethren, that not many wise according to flesh, not many powerful, not many of high rank. 27 But God has chosen the absurd things of the world that he might confound the wise; and God chose the weak of the world that he might confound the strong. 28 And the ignoble of the world, and that scorned, God chose, and things not being, that things being he might cause to cease, 29 so that all flesh might not boast before God.

30 But from him you are in Christ Jesus, who has been made wisdom unto us from God, righteousness, and also sanctification, and redemption, 31 in order that, as it was written, "The one boasting, in the Lord let him boast."

FIRST CORINTHIANS TWO

1 And I, having come to you, brethren, did not come by virtue of superior discourse, or wisdom, preaching to you the testimony[a] of God. 2 For I decided not to know anything among you except Jesus Christ, and him having been crucified. 3 And I was with you in weakness, and in fear, and in much trembling. 4 And my speech and my preaching *were* not in persuasive words of wisdom, but in demonstration of spirit and of power, 5 so that your faith might not be in wisdom of men, but in God's power.

6 Now we speak wisdom among the mature, but not the wisdom of this age, nor of the rulers of this age, who are coming to nothing. 7 But we speak God's hidden wisdom,[b] having been hidden, which God foreordained before the ages of the ages for our glory, 8 which not one of the rulers of this age has known. For if they had known, the Lord of glory they would not have crucified. 9 But as it was written, "What eye has not seen, and ear has not heard, and has not entered into the heart of man, all that God has prepared for those loving him." 10 Now to us God has revealed *these things* through the Spirit.

For the Spirit searches all things, even the depths of God. 11 For who among men knows the things of the man, except the spirit of the man that is within him? And so the things of God no one knows except the Spirit of God. 12 Now we have received not the spirit of the world but the Spirit who is from

God, that we might know the things having been given to us by God, 13 which also we speak, taught not by words of human wisdom, but taught in spirit,[c] with spiritual comparing spiritual.

14 But a[d] natural person does not accept things of the Spirit of God, for they are absurd to him, and he is not able to know them, because they are discerned spiritually. 15 But the spiritual, he himself discerns all, but by none is discerned. 16 For who has known the Lord's mind? Who will teach him? But we have Christ's mind.

FIRST CORINTHIANS THREE

1 And I, brethren, was not able to speak to you as to spiritual, but as to fleshly, as to babies in Christ. 2 I gave you milk to drink, not food for chewing,[e] for you all were not yet able. But now you are still not able, 3 for you are still fleshly. For whereas envy and strife *are* among you, are you not fleshly, and are behaving according to humankind? 4 For when this one might say, "Truly I am of Paul," but another "I am of Apollos," are you not fleshly?

5 What[f] then is Apollos? And what is Paul? Servants through whom you believed, and to each as the Lord has given. 6 I planted, Apollos watered, but God kept it growing. 7 So neither the one planting is anything, nor the one watering, but only the one, God, giving growth. 8 Now the one planting and the one watering are one, but each will receive his own reward, according to his own labor.

9 For of God we are fellow workers. You are God's field; you are God's building.

10 According to the grace of God having been given to me, as a wise master builder, I have laid the foundation. But another is building upon it. But let each one discern how he builds. 11 For other foundation no one is able to lay on the one already having been laid, which is Jesus Christ.

12 Now if anyone builds upon the foundation *with* gold, silver, precious stones, wood, hay, straw, 13 the work of each will become known, for the day will fully declare it, because in fire it is revealed. And the work of each, of what kind it is, the fire will examine. 14 If the work of this one which he built will remain, he will receive a reward. 15 If the work of this one will be burned up, he will suffer loss—but he himself will be saved; but so as through fire.

16 Do you not know that you yourselves are the temple of God, and the Spirit of God dwells in you? 17 If anyone defiles the temple of God, God will bring him to a worse state. For God's temple is holy, which you are.

18 Let no person deceive himself. If anyone thinks in his time to be wise among you, let him become foolish, so that he may become wise. 19 For the wisdom of this world is foolishness in the sight of God. For it was written, "He is catching the wise in their cunning." 20 And again, "The Lord knows the thoughts of the wise, and they are

fruitless." 21 Therefore, let none boast in humankind. For all things are yours, 22 whether Paul, or Apollos, or Cephas, or *the* world, or life, or death, or present, or coming—all yours, 23 and you of Christ and Christ of God.

FIRST CORINTHIANS FOUR

1 In this manner a person is to esteem us as ministers of Christ and stewards of God's previously hidden things.[91] 2 But now it is expected in the stewards that each may be found faithful. 3 But to me it is the least that I should be judged by you, or by a day in court. But also I do not judge myself. 4 For I am not aware of anything against myself; but I am not justified by this. To the contrary, the one judging me is the Lord. 5 Accordingly, do not judge anything before the time, until the Lord may have come, and who will shine light upon the hidden things[92] of darkness, and will reveal the intentions of the hearts. And then the praise will come to each from God.

6 Now these things, brethren, I have applied to myself and Apollos on account of you, so that in us you may learn not *to go* beyond what has been written, that not one above the other you be puffed up against the other. 7 For who makes you differ one from another? But what do you have which you did not receive? Now if also you did receive, why do you boast as not receiving?

8 Even now you have abundance. Even now you have become rich. Apart from us you reigned; and I wish you really did reign, so that also we might reign with you. 9 For I think God has set forth us apostles last, as appointed to death, because we have become a public show to the world, also to messengers and to men. 10 We? Fools on account of Christ. But you? Wise in Christ. We *are* weak, but you *are* strong; you *are* honored, but we *are* without honor.[93]

11 Continually until the present hour, we also hunger and thirst, and are poorly clothed, and are mistreated, and have no fixed home, 12 and we are laboring, working with our own hands. Being reviled, we bless. Being persecuted, we endure. 13 Being reproached, we exhort. We have become as outcasts of the earth, of all scum until now.

14 I do not write these things shaming you, but as my beloved children admonishing you. 15 For if you might have ten thousand teachers in Christ, yet not many fathers. For in Christ Jesus through the good news I have fathered you. 16 Therefore I exhort you, become a follower of me. 17 On account of this I sent Timothy to you, who is my child, beloved and faithful in the Lord, who will remind you of my ways that are in Christ Jesus, as everywhere in every church I teach.

18 As to me not coming now to you, some have become puffed up. 19 But shortly I will come to you, if the Lord wills, and I will not

know the speech of those being puffed up, but the power. 20 For the kingdom of God is not in word, but in power. 21 What desire you? I might come to you with a rod? Or in love and a spirit of gentleness in strength?

FIRST CORINTHIANS FIVE

1 Everywhere is reported among you sexual immorality, and such sexual immorality as not even among the nations, so as to have the father's wife. 2 And you are puffed up, and have not rather lamented, so that you might take out from among you the one having done this act. 3 For I truly, as being absent in body, now being present in spirit, have even now judged as being present, the one having done this—4 you gathered together in the name of our Lord Jesus, and me in spirit with the power of our Lord Jesus—5 to deliver such a one to Satan for destruction of the flesh, so that the spirit may be saved in the day of the Lord.

6 Your boasting *is* not good. Do you not know a little leaven all the lump leavens? 7 Purge the old leaven that you may be a new lump, even as you are unleavened. For also our Passover lamb has been sacrificed, Christ, 8 so that we may celebrate the feast, not with old leaven, not with leaven of wickedness and malice, but with unleavened of purity and of truth.

9 I wrote to you in the letter not to associate with the sexually immoral—10 not with all the sexually immoral of this world, or the covetous and extortioners, or idolators, since in that case you would need to go out of the world.

11 But now, I have written to you not to keep company if anyone named a brother might be sexually immoral, or covetous, or an idolator, or verbally abusive, or a drunkard, or extortioner: with such a one not even to eat. 12 For what *is it* to me to judge those outside? Do you not judge those within? 13 But those outside God will judge. Remove that evil away from yourselves.

FIRST CORINTHIANS SIX

1 Is anyone of you so bold, having a matter against the other, to judge before the unrighteous, and not before the saints? 2 Or know you not that the saints will judge the world? And if by you the world is judged, are you unworthy of the least judgments? 3 Know you not that we will judge messengers? Much more pertaining to this life. 4 So truly pertaining to this life, if you have judgments, do you set as judges the ones scorned by the church?

5 I say this to shame you all. So is there not among you no one wise, who will be able to judge as a mediator his brethren? 6 Instead, brother judging with brother, and this before unbelievers. 7 Truly already, therefore, it is in every way a failure for you, that you have lawsuits with one another. On account of this, why not rather be wronged? On account of this, why not rather be cheated? 8 But you wrong and cheat, and these things

to brethren!

9 Or know you not unrighteous ones will not inherit God's Kingdom? Be not led astray. Not sexually immoral, nor idolators, nor adulterers, nor effeminate with other males,[h] nor homosexuals, 10 nor thieves, nor those greedy for what others have, nor drunkards, nor verbal abusers, nor extortioners, will inherit God's Kingdom. 11 And certain of you were these. But you were washed, but you were sanctified, but you were justified, in the name of our Lord Jesus Christ and by the Spirit of our God.

12 All is lawful to me, but not all is profitable. All is lawful, but I will not be ruled by any certain thing. 13 Meats for the belly and the belly for meats, but God will do away with both this and that. But the body *is* not for sexual immorality but for the Lord, and the Lord for the body. 14 Now God both the Lord has raised and us will raise, by his power.

15 Know you not that your bodies are members of Christ? Taking up, then, the members of the Christ, shall I make *them* members of a prostitute? Never may it be! 16 Or know you not that the one joining to the prostitute is one body? For it says the two will become into one flesh. 17 But the one joining to the Lord is one spirit.

18 Run away from sexual immorality. Every act of sinning, whatever if a person might do, is outside the body. But the one committing unlawful sexual intercourse[i] commits an act of sinning against his own body. 19 Or know you not that your body is a temple of the Holy Spirit in you, whom you have from God? And you are not your own, 20 for you were bought with a price. Therefore by all means glorify God in your body.[j]

FIRST CORINTHIANS SEVEN

1 Now about those things of which you wrote. What is good is a man not to be involved with a woman. 2 But for the sake of sexual immorality, each man have his wife, and each woman have her own husband. 3 The husband to the wife fulfil the duty; now in the same manner also the wife to the husband. 4 The wife has not authority over her own body, but the husband; now in the same manner also, the husband has not authority over his own body, but the wife.

5 Do not deprive one another, except by agreement for a season, that you might be free for prayer. And again be the same as before, so that Satan may not tempt you on account of the lack of your strength. 6 Now I say this as counsel,[k1] not as commandment. 7 Now I wish all persons also to be as myself. But each has his own gift from God. Truly one has this, but one that.

8 Now I say to the unmarried and to the widows, it is good for them if they may remain even as I am. 9 But if they do not have strength, let them marry. For it is better to marry than to burn. 10

Now to those being married I give this command—not me but the Lord—a wife is not to be severed from a husband; 11 but and if she may have separated, let her continue unmarried, or to the husband be reconciled; and a husband is not to send away a wife.

12 Now to the rest I say—I not the Lord[k2]—if any brother has an unbelieving wife, and she assents to abide with him, do not put her away. 13 And if any woman has an unbelieving husband, and he assents to abide with her, do not put away the husband. 14 For the unbelieving husband is made clean by the wife, and the unbelieving wife is made clean by the husband; otherwise your children are unclean, but now they are made clean.

15 But if the unbeliever puts away, they put themselves away. The brother or the sister is not bound in this kind. But God has called you into peace. 16 For how know you, wife, if you will save the husband? Or how know you, husband, if you will save the wife?

17 If to each one as may be—as the Lord has distributed, to each as God has called—so let him conduct the manner of life. And in this manner in the churches I order all. 18 Was anyone called having been circumcised? He is not to be uncircumcised. Was anyone called in uncircumcision? He is not to be circumcised. 19 Circumcision is nothing and uncircumcision is nothing, but observing God's commandments. 20 Each in the calling in which he was called, in this he is to abide.

21 Were you a slave when called? It is not to be a concern to you. But if also you are able to become free, rather more make the most of it. 22 For one having been called in the Lord as a slave is the Lord's freedman. In the same way the one having been called free is Christ's slave. 23 You were bought with a price; do not let[l] yourselves become slaves of men. 24 Each in that he was called, in that abide with God.

25 Now concerning virgin women of marriageable age.[m] I do not have a commandment of the Lord, but I give my judgment as having received mercy from the Lord to be worthy of trust. 26 Therefore this custom is good: on account of the necessity at hand, that it is good for a man to remain in the same manner. 27 Have you been bound to a wife? Do not seek to be separated. Are you free from a wife? Do not seek a wife. 28 But if also you may have married you did not commit an act of sinning. And if you may have married the virgin woman of marriageable age, she did not commit an act of sinning. But these will have afflictions in the flesh.

Now I am treating you with kindness. 29 Now this I say brethren, the season is full of distress.[n] And from now on those having wives should be as none having; 30 and those lamenting as not lamenting; and those rejoicing as not rejoicing; and those buying as not possessing; 31 and those making use of the world as not abusing. For the external form° of this world is perishing.

32 Now I wish you to be without undue concerns. The unmarried person cares for the things of the Lord, how he may please the Lord. 33 But the married cares for the things of the world, how he may please the wife, 34 and is divided. And the unmarried woman, and the virgin of marriageable age, cares for the things of the Lord, and that she may be holy in the body and in the spirit. But the married cares for the things of the world, how she may please the husband. 35 Now this I say for the benefit of you yourselves. Not, I say, that I might impose upon you what you do not desire, but for what is appropriate and devoted to the Lord without distraction.

36 But if anyone supposes *himself* to be behaving indecently against his virgin of marriageable age—if she is past the usual age for marriage, and so it ought to be—what he wills let him do, he does not commit an act of sinning, let them marry. 37 But he who stands steadfast in his heart, not having necessity, but ruling over his own will, and has discerned this in his own heart to keep himself unmarried,p he will do well. 38 So also the one marrying his own virgin does well; and the one not marrying will do better.

39 A wife is bound for as long a time as her husband may live. But if the husband may have died, she is free to be married to whom she decides, only in the Lord. 40 But she is blessed if she might live as according to my opinion. Now I think I also have God's Spirit.

FIRST CORINTHIANS EIGHT

1 Now about the sacrifices of idols. Concerning this, we know we have all knowledge; knowledge puffs up, but love builds up. 2 If anyone imagines to have known everything, he does not yet know as it is necessary to know. 3 But if anyone loves God he is known by him.

4 Therefore, about the eating of the sacrifices of idols, we know this: an idol is nothing in the world, because there is no God except One. 5 For even if indeed there are gods spoken of—whether in heaven or on earth, as indeed there are many gods and many lords—6 but to us *there is* one God, the Father, of whom *are* all things, and we for him, and one Lord, Jesus Christ, through whom *are* all things, and we through him.

7 But this knowledge *is* not in all. But some by custom unto now eat of the idol as a thing offered to an idol. And their conscious being weak it is defiled. 8 But food will not commend us to God. Neither do we come short if we should not eat, nor do we have an advantage if we should not eat. 9 But watch out, lest in some way this your authority becomes an occasion for sinning to those being weak.

10 For if any might see you having knowledge, eating in an idol's temple, his conscience being weak will not be built up in order to eat the things sacrificed to idols. For the one being weak 11 is destroyed through your knowledge—the brother for whom Christ died. 12 But in this manner sinning against the brethren and wounding their weak conscious, you sin against Christ. 13 Therefore, if food offends my brother, never no never may I eat meat to the age, so that I may not offend my brother.

FIRST CORINTHIANS NINE

1 Am I not free? Am I not an apostle? Have I not seen Jesus our Lord? Are you not my workmanship in the Lord? 2 If to others I am not an apostle, yet at least I am to you. For you are the seal of my apostleship in the Lord.

3 My defense to those judging me is this. 4 Is it possible[q] we have no authority to eat and to drink? 5 Is it possible we have no authority to take a sister, a wife, as companions, as also the other apostles, and the brothers of the Lord, and Cephas?? 6 Or do only I and Barnabas have no authority to work or not?[r]

7 Who at any time wages war at his own expense? Who plants a vineyard and does not eat its fruit? Or who shepherds a flock and does not drink from the milk of the flock? 8 Do I not say these things according to humankind? Or does not the Law also say these things? 9 For in the Law of Moses it has been written, "You shall not muzzle an oxen treading out grain." Does God care only for the oxen? 10 Or is he speaking by all means for our sake? For our sake. For it was written because the one plowing ought to plow in expectation to partake, also the one threshing in *the same* expectation.

11 If we among you have sown spiritual, *is it* too much if we from you will reap material? 12 If others of authority over you partake, not we more? But we did not use this authority. Rather, we bear all things, so that we might not give any hindrance to the good news of Christ. 13 Know you not that those working in the temple, eat that of the temple? Those serving at the altar partake in the altar? 14 And so the Lord has ordained to those proclaiming the good news, to live from the good news. 15 But I have not used any of these.

Now I have not written these things that thus it should be with me. For better rather me to die before anyone will make my boasting empty. 16 For if I proclaim the good news, there is to me no boasting; for I am compelled; for woe be to me if I should not preach the good news. 17 For if I do this willingly, I have a reward. But if unwillingly, a responsibility has been entrusted to me. 18 What then is my reward? That in proclaiming the good news without charge I may present the good news so as to not abuse my authority in the good news.

19 For being free from all, to all I myself become a servant, so that I may gain the more. 20 And I became to the Jewish, as a Jew, so that I might gain Jewish. To those under Law, as under Law, not being myself under Law, so that I might gain those under Law. 21 To those outside Law, as outside Law—not being outside God's law but under law to Christ—so that I might gain those outside Law. 22 I became to the weak, weak, that the weak I might gain. To all these things I have become all, so that by all means I might save some. 23 Now I do all for the sake of the good news, that I might become a joint partaker with it.

24 Know you not that those in a stadium running, truly all run, but one receives the prize? Thus run that you might receive. 25 Now everyone contending is self-controlled in all things—they truly then that a corruptible crown they may receive, but we an incorruptible. 26 Indeed now I thus run, as not uncertainly. So I box, as not beating air. 27 But I mortify my body and bring it into subjection, lest having preached to others, I might be disapproved.

FIRST CORINTHIANS TEN

1 For I do not want you to be ignorant, brethren, that our fathers were all under the cloud, and all passed through the sea. 2 And all were immersed with respect to Moses, in the cloud and in the sea. 3 And all ate the same spiritual food. 4 And all drank the same spiritual drink. For they were drinking from the spiritual rock accompanying *them;* but the rock was Christ.

5 But with respect to many of them God was not well-pleased, for they were overthrown in the wilderness. 6 Now these things have become types to us, in order we may not become someone who desires evil things, as they desired. 7 Neither are you to be idolators, as some of them, as it was written, "the people sat to eat and to drink and stood to play."

8 Neither should we commit sexual immorality as some of them did commit sexual immorality, and in one day twenty-three thousand fell. 9 Neither should we put the Christ to the test, as some of them tested, and by serpents perished. 10 Neither are you to murmur, as some of them murmured, and perished by the destroyer.

11 Now these things happened to them as types and were written to warn us, to whom the ends of the ages have arrived. 12 Therefore the one thinking to stand, let him consider lest he fall. 13 No temptation has taken hold of you except as is common to humankind, but God is faithful who will not allow you to be tempted beyond what you are able, but will cause with the temptation also the escape, to be able to endure.

14 Therefore by all means, my beloved, run from idolatry. 15 I speak as to the discerning. Discern for yourselves what I say. 16 The cup of blessing which we bless, is

it not participation in the blood of Christ? The bread which we break, is it not participation in the body of Christ? 17 Because one bread we the many are one body. For all share in the one bread.

18 Observe Israel according to the flesh. Are not those eating the sacrifices participants in the altar? 19 What then do I say? That whatever is offered to an idol is anything? Or that an idol is anything? 20 Rather that whatever the gentiles sacrifice, *it is* to demons and not to God they sacrifice. Now I do not desire you to be participants with demons. 21 You are not able to drink the cup of the Lord and the cup of demons. You are not able to partake of the table of the Lord and the table of demons. 22 Or are we provoking the Lord to jealousy? Are we stronger than he?

23 All things are possible, but not all things benefit. All things are possible, but not all things build up. 24 Let no one seek after his own, but that of another. 25 All being sold in the meat market, eat, inquiring nothing on account of conscience, 26 for of the Lord the earth and its fullness.

27 If someone of the unbelieving invites you and you decide to go, eat all setting before you, inquiring nothing on account of conscience. 28 But if someone might say to you, "This is offered to an idol," do not eat, for the sake of he having disclosed it, and the conscience.[s1] 29 Now conscience, I am saying, not your own but that of the other. For what purpose to judge my freedom by another's conscience? 30 If I in thankfulness partake, why am I slandered for that which I give thanks?

31 Therefore if you eat, or drink, or something you do, do all things to the glory of God. 32 And you do not give offense to Jews and Greeks and to the church of God, 33 as I also please all in all things, not seeking the profit of myself, but that of the many, that they might be saved. 11:1 Be followers of me, as I also of Christ.[s2]

FIRST CORINTHIANS ELEVEN

11:2 Now I praise you that in all things you have remembered me, and you are keeping the doctrines just as I declared to you.

3 Now I desire you to know that of every man the head is Christ, but the husband head of a wife; but of the Christ, God. 4 Every man praying or prophesying, having *something* on his head, dishonors his head. 5 Now every woman praying or prophesying with her head uncovered, dishonors her head—for it is one and the same as having her hair cut off. 6 For if a woman covers not her head, let her also cut her hair. Now if it is indecent[t] to a woman to cut the hair or shave the head, let her cover her head.

7 For a man truly ought never to cover the head, being the image and glory of God. But the woman is the glory of man. 8 For man is not of woman but woman of man.

9 For truly man was not created on account of the woman, but woman on account of the man. 10 On account of this the woman ought to have *an emblem of* authority on the head, on account of the messengers.

11 However, woman *is* not without man and man *is* not without woman, in the Lord. 12 For just as the woman *is* of the man, so also the man *is* through the woman; but all *is* from God. 13 In you yourselves judge: is it proper for an uncovered woman to pray to God? 14 Does not even the natural order itself teach you that a man truly, if he has long hair, it is a dishonor to him, 15 but if a woman has long hair, to her it is glory? Because the long hair is given to her in place of a covering. 16 Now if anyone thinks to be contentious, we have no such practice, nor the churches of God.

17 Now in declaring this I do not praise you, because you meet together not for the better but for the worse. 18 First truly, you meeting in public assembly, I hear there to be divisions among you, and in part I believe it. 19 For also it is necessary there to be factions among you, in order that also those approved should be revealed among you.

20 Therefore of you meeting together in one place, it is not to eat a Lord's supper. 21 For one takes first his own supper in the eating, and this *one* truly is hungry, but that *one* is drunken. 22 For is it possible you do not have houses in which to eat and drink? Or do you despise the church of God and put to shame those having nothing? What might I say to you? Might I praise you in this? No praise!

23 For I received from the Lord, and which I delivered to you, that the Lord Jesus in the night when he was delivered up, took bread, 24 and having given thanks, and having broke it, said, "This is my body, which *is* for you, this do in remembrance of me."ᵘ 25 And in like manner the cup after the supper, saying, "This cup is the new covenant in my blood. This do as often as if you might drink, in remembrance of me." 26 For as often as if you might eat this bread and might drink the cup, you proclaim the death of the Lord until that he should come.

27 Whoever, therefore, may eat the bread or may drink the cup of the Lord irreverently, will be held guilty of the body and of the blood of the Lord. 28 But a person is to examine himself, and in this manner let him eat from the bread and let him drink from the cup. 29 For the *one* eating and drinking *irreverently*, judgment on himself eats and drinks, not distinguishing the body. 30 On account of these things many among you *are* weak and infirm, and many are fallen asleep.

31 Now if we ourselves were discerning, we would not be judged. 32 But being judged by the Lord we are chastised, so that we may not be condemned with the

world. 33 So then, my brethren, meeting together in order to eat, wait for one another. 34 If any person is hungry let him eat at home, so that you may not meet together for judgment. Now the other things, according as I may come, I will set in order.

FIRST CORINTHIANS TWELVE

1 Now about spiritual things. Brethren, I do not desire you to be in error. 2 You know that when you were pagans to the voiceless idols, even as you were led along you were going astray. 3 Therefore I declare to you that no one speaking by God's Spirit says, "Jesus *is* accursed"; and no one is able to say, "Jesus *is* Lord," if not by the Holy Spirit.

4 Now there are distributions of gifts, but the same Spirit. 5 And there are distributions of ministries, but the same Lord. 6 And there are distributions of activities, but the same God is working all things in all persons. 7 Now to each is given the manifestation of the Spirit for the common benefit.

8 For truly to one because of the Spirit is given a word of wisdom. Now to another a word of knowledge according to the same Spirit. 9 And to a different one, faith, by the same Spirit. Now to another one gifts of healing in that one Spirit. 10 Now to another working of miracles. Now to another prophecy. Now to another distinguishing of spirits. To a different one, kinds of languages. Now to another, translating of languages. 11 Now *in* all these things works the one and the same Spirit, distributing to each individually as he wills.

12 For even as the body is one and has many members, but all the members of the body, being many, are one body, so also Christ. 13 For also by one Spirit we all were immersed into one body, whether Jewish or Greek, whether slaves or free. And we all were given to drink in spirit.

14 For also the body is not one member but many. 15 If the foot might say, "Because I am not a hand I am not of the body," it is not, contrary to this, not of the body. 16 And if the ear might say, "Because I am not an eye I am not of the body," it is not, contrary to this, not of the body. 17 If all the body an eye, where the hearing? If all the body hearing, where the sense of smell? 18 But now God has assigned the members a place, each one of them in the body, even as he willed.

19 Now if all were one member, where the body? 20 But now, truly, many members but one body. 21 And the eye is not able to say to the hand, "I have no need of you." Or again the head to the feet, "I have no need of you." 22 But much rather, those members of the body appearing to be weaker are necessary. 23 And those of the body we think to be without honor, these we bestow abundant honor, and our unattractive have abundant propriety; 24 and our attractive

have no such necessity.

But God has composed the body, to those lacking having given abundant honor, 25 in order that there may not be division in the body, but the members may take care for the sake of one another. 26 And if one member suffers, all the members suffer; if one member is honored, all the members rejoice. 27 Now Christ's body you are, and members in part. 28 And truly God has appointed that one in the church: first apostles, secondly prophets, third teachers, then powers, then healing gifts, helps, governance, kinds of languages. 29 Not all apostles, not all prophets, not all teachers, not all powers, 30 not all have healing gifts, not all speak in languages, not all translate. 31 But desire zealously the greater gifts, and further according to a far better way I teach to you all.

FIRST CORINTHIANS THIRTEEN

1 If in the languages of humankind I speak, and of messengers, but do not have love, I have become loud brass or clanging cymbal. 2 And if I might prophecy and perceive all the hidden and all the knowledge, and if I might have all the faith so as to remove from its place mountains, but have not love, I am nothing. 3 And if I might divide to the poor all my possessions, and if I might deliver up my body in order that I might boast, but do not have love, I profit nothing.

4 This love is patient with people, is willing to help. This love is not moved with envy. This love is not boastful, not puffed up, 5 does not behave in an unbecoming manner, does not strive to seek things of itself, is not roused to anger, is not occupied with wrongs, 6 does not have joy during unrighteousness but rejoices together in the truth. 7 Covers all, believes all, hopes all, suffers all.

8 This love never fails. But if prophesies, they will end; if languages, they will cease; if knowledge it will end. 9 For we know of part, and of part we prophesy. 10 But when the completeness may come, the of part will end. 11 When I was a child, I was speaking as a child, I was thinking as a child, I was reasoning as a child. When I became an adult I put an end to childish things. 12 For we see presently through an imperfect image because of obscurity, but then face to face. Presently I know of part, but then I will fully know as also I have been fully known. 13 But now these three things, faith, hope, love, continue. But love is the greatest of these. 14:1 Pursue this love.ᵛ

FIRST CORINTHIANS FOURTEEN

Now desire zealously the spirituals, but more in order that you might prophesy. 2 For the one speaking a language speaks not to human beings but to God because no one understands,ʷ but in spirit he speaks things hidden.ˣ 3 But the one prophesying to human beings speaks instruction, and exhortation, and encouragement. 4 The one speaking in a language builds up himself. But the one prophesying builds up the church.

5 Now I wish you all to speak in languages, but more that you might prophesy: now greater the one prophesying than the one speaking in languages, unless he should translate so that the church might receive profit. 6 But now brethren, if I might come to you speaking in languages, what will I profit you, except I might speak to you either with revelation, or with knowledge, or with prophecy, or with teaching?

7 Even the lifeless things giving a sound, whether pipe or lyre, if they do not give distinction to the sounds, how will the piping or the lyre's playing be understood? 8 For also if a trumpet gives an uncertain sound, who will make himself ready for war? 9 So also you, if with the language you give speech not understandable, how will it be known what you are speaking? For you will be speaking into air.

10 If, it may be, there are so many kinds of languages in the world, and none without meaning. 11 If, therefore, I do not know the significance of the sound, I will be a foreigner to the one speaking, and to me the one speaking a foreigner. 12 So you also, inasmuch as you zealously desire spirituals, for the building up of the church strive that you may have more than enough. 13 Therefore, the one speaking in a language, let him pray that he might translate.

14 For if I pray in a language, my spirit prays, but my understanding is unfruitful. 15 What then is it? I will pray in spirit, but I will pray also with the understanding. I will sing in spirit, but I will sing also with the understanding. 16 For otherwise, if you bless in spirit, the one filling the place of the uninstructed, how will he declare the "amen" at the time of your thanksgiving, since he does not know what you are saying? 17 For you truly are giving good thanksgiving, but the other is not built up.

18 I thank God, more than all of you I speak in languages. 19 But in church I desire to speak five words with my understanding, in order that I may also instruct others, rather than ten thousand words with a language.

20 Brethren, do not be children in your understanding. Yet in the evil be little children. But in your thinking be mature. 21 Because it has been written in the law, "With other languages and with other lips I will speak to this people, and not even in this manner will they listen to me," says the Lord. 22 So then the languages are for a sign, not to those believing, but to the unbelieving. But prophecy not to the unbelieving, but to the believing.

23 If therefore the whole church itself meets together, and all might speak in languages, but uninstructed persons come in, or unbelievers, will they not say that you all are incoherent? 24 But if all

prophesy, then should come in some unbeliever or uninstructed, he is convicted by all, he is judged by all, 25 the secrets of his heart become revealed. And thus falling on his face he will worship God, declaring that truly God is among you.

26 What then is it, brethren? When you may meet together, each individual has a song, has a teaching, has a language, has a translation. Let all things be done to edify. 27 If anyone speaks in a language, let the rule be two, or the most three, and in turn, and one translate. 28 But if there is not a translator, keep silence in the church, but speak to himself and to God.

29 Now prophets, let two or three speak and let the others examine. 30 But if a revelation might have been made to another sitting by, let the first be silent. 31 For you are able one by one all to prophesy, so that all may learn and all may be encouraged. 32 And spirits of prophets are in submission to prophets. 33 For he is not the God of confusion, but of peace.

As in all the churches of the saints, 34 the women in the churches, let them be silent. For it is not permitted to them to speak, but to be in submission, as also the law says. 35 But if they desire to learn anything, at home let them ask their own husbands. For it is inappropriate for a woman to speak in church. 36 Or has the Word of God come forth from you? Or to you only has it come? 37 If anyone thinks himself to be a prophet, or spiritual, let him recognize these I write to you are commands of the Lord. 38 But if anyone has no discernment, let him be ignored.

39 So, my brethren, zealously desire to prophecy, and to speak with languages do not restrain; 40 but all things be decently and with good order.

FIRST CORINTHIANS FIFTEEN

1 Now I made known to you, brethren, the good news that I proclaimed to you, which you also received, in which also you continue, 2 by which also you are being delivered, in what words I proclaimed to you, if no doubt you hold fast, except that you had believed in vain.

3 For I have declared to you foremost with respect to what I also received, that Christ died for our sins according to the scriptures, 4 and that he was buried, and that he was raised the third day according to the scriptures, 5 and that he was seen[y] by Cephas, then by the Twelve. 6 Afterwards he was seen by more than five hundred brethren at once, out of whom the more live until this present time, but part have become asleep. 7 Then he was seen by Jacob, then by all the apostles.

8 Now last of all, as it were not born at the right time, he was seen also by me. 9 For I am the least of the apostles, who am not fit to be

named[z] an apostle, because I persecuted the church of God. 10 But by God's grace I am what I am; and his grace toward me has not been fruitless. But more abundantly than them all I labored—but not I but God's grace that *was* with me. 11 Therefore, whether I or they, thus we proclaim and thus you believed.

12 Now if Christ is proclaimed, that he has been raised out from dead ones, how say some among you that there is not a resurrection of dead ones? 13 But if there is not a resurrection of dead ones, neither has Christ been raised. 14 Now if Christ has not been raised, then our proclamation is meaningless—your faith is also meaningless. 15 Then also we are found false witnesses of God, because we have testified concerning God that he raised up the Christ, who if he has not raised up then the dead ones are not raised.

16 For if dead ones are not raised, neither has Christ been raised, 17 Now if Christ has not been raised, then your faith is empty; you are still in your sins. 18 Then also those becoming asleep in Christ have perished. 19 If in this life, in Christ we are having hope, only, we are more than all humankind worthy of pity.

20 But now Christ has been raised out from dead ones, firstfruit of those becoming asleep. 21 For since death by a man, also resurrection of dead ones by a man. 22 For as in Adam all die, so also in Christ all will be made alive. 23 But each in their own order: *the* firstfruit Christ, then those of Christ at his coming, 24 then the end, when he shall deliver up the kingdom to the God and Father, when he shall put an end to all dominion and all authority and power.

25 For he must rule until that he shall have placed all the enemies under his feet. 26 Death is the last enemy to be put to an end. 27 For all things he has subjected under his feet. But when it may be said that all things have been placed in subjection, it is evident that the one having placed all things in subjection to him is excepted. 28 Now when all things shall have been placed in subjection to him, then also himself the Son will be placed in subjection to the one having placed all things in subjection to him, so that God may be all in all.

29 For then what will they do who are immersed in place of the dead ones? If the dead ones are not raised at all, why also are they immersed in place of them?

30 Why also are we in danger every hour? 31 I affirm by my boasting in you, brethren, which I have in Christ Jesus our Lord, every day I die. 32 If according to man I fought wild beasts in Ephesus, what to me the profit? If dead ones are not raised, let us eat and let us drink, for tomorrow we die. 33 Do not be misled. Evil conversations will corrupt virtuous character. 34 Sober up righteously

and stop sinning. For some are willfully ignorant of God—to your shame I speak.

35 But someone will say, "How are the dead ones raised? But with what body do they come?" 36 You fool! What you sow does not come to life unless it dies. 37 And what you sow, that will not be the body you sow, but bare grain, if it may be of wheat, or some of the others. 38 But God gives it a body as he has willed, and to each of the seeds its own body.

39 Not all flesh *is* the same flesh, but truly one of humankind, but another flesh of beasts, but another flesh of birds, but another of fish, 40 and heavenly bodies, and earthly bodies. But truly, one of heavenly glory, but that of earthly different. 41 One glory of sun, and another glory of moon, and another glory of stars; for star from star differs in glory.

42 And in this manner the resurrection of the dead ones. It is sown in decay, it is raised in incorruption. 43 It is sown in dishonor, it is raised in glory. It is sown in weakness, it is raised in power. 44 It is sown a natural body, it is raised a spiritual body. If there is a natural body, there is also spiritual.

45 And so it has been written, "Came into existence the first man Adam for a living soul," the last Adam for a life-giving spirit. 46 But not first the spiritual but the natural, then the spiritual. 47 The first man from earth, made of earth, the second man from heaven. 48 As the one made of earth, so also those made of earth. And as the heavenly, so also those of heaven. 49 And as we have borne the image of the earthly, we will also bear the image of the heavenly.

50 Now this I say, brethren, that flesh and blood is not able to inherit the kingdom of God, nor the decay inherit the incorruption. 51 Behold, something hidden I tell to you. We will not all sleep, but we will all be changed, 52 in an instant, in the twinkling of an eye, at the last trumpet. For the trumpet will announce, and the dead ones will be raised incorruptible, and we will be transformed. 53 For it is necessary this the corruptible to put on incorruption, and this the mortal to put on immortality.

54 Now when this the corruptible shall have put on incorruptible, and this the mortal shall have put on immortality, then will come to pass the word having been written, "Death has been swallowed up in victory." 55 Where of you, Death, the victory? Where of you, Death, the sting? 56 Now the sting of death, the sin; now the power of sin, the law. 57 But thanks to God, the one giving us victory through our Lord Jesus Christ.

58 Therefore, my beloved brethren, be steadfast, unmovable, always abounding in the work of the Lord, knowing that your labor is not in vain in the Lord.

FIRST CORINTHIANS SIXTEEN

1 Now concerning the

collection which is for the saints. As I have appointed the churches of Galatia, so also you are to do. 2 Every first of the seven *days*, each of you put beside him, storing up what if you may be successful[aa] *in the collection*, so that not when I may come then there should be collections. 3 Now when I might arrive, whoever if you might approve, these I will send with letters to carry your benevolence to Jerusalem. 4 Now if it is suitable for I also to go, they will go with me.

5 Now I will come to you when I may go through Macedonia, for I am going through Macedonia. 6 But with you perhaps I will stay, or even I will winter, so that you might help me wherever if I may go. 7 For I do not want to see you now in passing, for I hope to remain with you a certain amount of time, if the Lord permits. 8 But I will remain in Ephesus until Pentecost. 9 For a great and effective door has opened to me; and many opposing.

10 Now if Timothy comes, see that he might be with you without fear. For he is doing the work of the Lord, as also I. 11 Therefore no one should treat him scornfully. But help him in peace, so that he might come to me. For I am expecting him with the brethren.

12 Now concerning Apollos the brother, I much encouraged him that he might go to you with the brethren, and his desire was not at all that now he might come; but he will come whenever he may have opportunity.

13 You all be mindful, stand fast in the faith, act like adults, grow strong. 14 Let all you do be done in love. 15 Now I encourage you, brethren, you know the house of Stephanus, that it is the firstfruit of Achaia, and they have devoted themselves to service to the saints, 16 that you also be submitted to such as these, and to all, working together and laboring. 17 But I rejoice at the coming of Stephanus, and Fortunatus, and Achaicus, because these have supplied your need. 18 For they refreshed my spirit and yours. Therefore know such as these.

19 The churches of Asia greet you all. Aquila and Prisca heartily greet you all in the Lord, with the church at their house. 20 All the brethren greet you. You all greet one another with a holy kiss. 21 The greeting of Paul with my own hand. 22 If anyone does not love the Lord, let him be accursed. Our Lord has come. 23 The grace of the Lord Jesus be with you. 24 My love with you all in Christ Jesus, truly.

The Book of Second Corinthians

The Book of Second Corinthians was written ca. AD 57, in the third year of Paul's third missionary journey (AD 54–58), as a response to a letter the Corinthian church had written to Paul, in response to his 1 Corinthians letter. The letter was written in Macedonia, 2:12–13; 7:5–9, after the "Great is Artemis of the Ephesians!" riot, Acts 19:28ff. The first letter had apparently stirred up rebellion among some and revealed serious issues in that local church. Second Corinthians is essentially Paul's defense of his apostolic authority to correct doctrinal and practical issues affecting the church. Among the issues Paul addresses is the attitude and motivation to participate in a voluntary monetary collection intended for the suffering brethren in Jerusalem. Paul addresses issues affecting Christian values and practices throughout the New Testament church age, giving the book continuing value for the local New Testament church.

SECOND CORINTHIANS ONE

1 Paul, apostle of Christ Jesus by God's will, and Timothy the brother. To the church of God that is in Corinth, with all the saints that are in all Achaia.

2 Grace to you and peace from God our Father and Lord Jesus Christ.

3 Worthy of praise the God and Father of our Lord Jesus Christ, the Father of the mercies and God of all encouragement.ª 4 The one encouraging us during all our affliction, in order that we are to be able to encourage those in every affliction, through the encouragement with which we ourselves are encouraged by God.

5 Because as the sufferings of the Christ superabound toward us, to such a degree also through the Christ our encouragement. 6 But if we are oppressed *it is* for the sake of your encouragement and salvation. If we are encouraged *it is* for the sake of your encouragement working in endurance of the same sufferings that also we experience. 7 And our hope for you is unfailing, knowing that just as you are partners of the sufferings, so also of the encouragement.

8 For we do not want you to be ignorant, brethren, concerning our affliction that took place in Asia. That we were oppressed more exceedingly beyond our ability, so as for us to utterly despair even to live. 9 But we in ourselves had the sentence of death, so that we should not have confidence in ourselves but in God, the one raising the dead ones. 10 Who out of so great a death did deliver us, and will deliver us. In whom we have hope that also still he will deliver us, 11 you also working together for our sake by prayer, so that by many persons, for the gift of grace toward us through many, thanks might be given for us.

12 For this is our boast, the testimony of our conscience, that in God's holiness and purity, not in

fleshly wisdom, but in God's grace, we have conducted ourselves in the world, but abundantly toward you all. 13 For no other we write to you other than what you read, that you also are aware.[b] Now I hope that you will understand until the end, 14 as also you have understood us in part, so that boasting of you, even as we are, you also are ours in the day of our Lord Jesus.

15 And with this confidence I previously intended to come to you, so that you might have a second blessing, 16 and through you to pass through into Macedonia, and again from Macedonia to come to you, and by you to be helped forward to Judea. 17 Therefore thus intending, was I perhaps being shallow-minded?[c] Or what I intend, I intend according to flesh, so that with me there might be "Yes, yes," and "No, no?"

18 But God *is* faithful, that our word to you was not "Yes" and "No." 19 For the Son of God, Christ Jesus, the one among you having been proclaimed by us, by me and Silas and Timothy, was not "Yes" and "No," but has always been "Yes" in him. 20 For as many promises in God, in him the "Yes." Therefore also through him the "Amen" to God, for glory through us. 21 Now the one securing us with you in Christ, and anointed us, *is* God, 22 the one who also sealed us and gave us the Spirit as guarantor[d] in our hearts.

23 Now I call God as witness against my soul, that sparing you I have not yet come to Corinth. 24 Not that we are lord over your faith, but are fellow workers of the joy with you. For you stand firm in the faith.

SECOND CORINTHIANS TWO

1 For this I decided in myself, not to come to you again in sorrow. 2 For if I again give you sorrow, who is giving me joy, if not the one given sorrow by me? 3 And I wrote this same thing, so that having come I might not have sorrow from those of whom I ought to have joy, trusting in you all that my joy is of you all.

4 For out of much affliction and anguish of heart I wrote to you all through many tears, not that you might be sorrowed, but that you may know the love that I have more abundantly toward you all. 5 But if anyone has given sorrow, he has not sorrowed me, but in part (that I may not be too severe) all you.

6 Sufficient to such a one this the punishment which is by the many, 7 so that on the contrary, rather, for you to forgive and encourage, lest, perhaps, such a one might be swallowed up by more abundant sorrow. 8 Therefore I encourage you to confirm love toward him.

9 Truly, for this also I wrote, so that I might know your character,[e] if you all are obedient to everything. 10 Now to whomever anything you forgive, I also. For also I, to whom I forgave, if

anything I forgave, for your sake in the presence of Christ, 11 so that we may not be taken advantage of by Satan. For we are not ignorant of his ways.[f]

12 Now I came to Troas for the good news of Christ, and a door opening to me in the Lord, 13 I did not have rest in my spirit, because not finding Titus my brother. But bidding them farewell, I went out to Macedonia.

14 But thanks be unto God, the one always leading us in triumph in Christ, and the sweet odor of the knowledge of him revealed through us in every place. 15 For of Christ we are a pleasing odor to God in those being saved and in those not being saved.[g] 16 Truly to one an odor from death to death, but to one an odor from life to life. And toward these things who is sufficient? 17 For we are not, like the many, professing the word of God for personal gain.[h]

SECOND CORINTHIANS THREE

1 Do we once more undertake to commend ourselves? Or perhaps like some we need letters of commendation to you, or from you? 2 You are our letter, having been written in our hearts, known and read by all persons. 3 Because you are revealed as a letter of Christ, to whom we ministered, not written in ink but by the Spirit of the living God, not on tablets of stone but on tablets of human hearts.

4 Now so great confidence we have through the Christ toward God. 5 Not that we are sufficient from ourselves to reckon anything as from ourselves. But our sufficiency is of God, 6 who also has made us sufficient as ministers of a new covenant, not of letter but of spirit. For the letter kills, but spirit gives life.[i]

7 Now if the ministry of death, having been engraved in letters on stone came with glory—so that the sons of Israel were not able to gaze intently with respect to the face of Moses, on account of the glory of his face, which is fading— 8 how not more the ministry of the Spirit will be in glory? 9 For if by the ministry of condemnation glory, much more abounds the ministry of righteousness in glory.

10 For also, that having been glorified has not been glorified in this respect, on account of the surpassing glory. 11 For if that which is fading away on account of glory, much more that continuing in glory. 12 Having therefore such hope, we use great boldness, 13 and not as Moses putting a veil over his face, so that the sons of Israel could not gaze intently with respect to the ending of that fading away.

14 But their minds were hardened, for until the today of this day the same veil remains during the reading of the Old covenant, not being removed, which in Christ is being removed. 15 But unto this day, when Moses might be read, there lies a veil over their heart, 16 except when one may have turned toward the Lord

the veil is taken away.

17 Now the Lord is the spirit. Now where the Lord's spirit—freedom.[j] 18 Now we all with face unveiled, see as in a mirror the Lord's glory, the same image being transformed because of glory into glory, even as from the Lord's spirit.

SECOND CORINTHIANS FOUR

1 On account of this, having this the ministry, as we were given mercy we do not lose courage. 2 But we have rejected the hidden things of disgraceful conduct, not conducting our life by unscrupulous means nor adulterating the word of God, but by the revealing of the truth, presenting ourselves as worthy toward every person in the presence of God. 3 But if also our good news is hidden to those who are not being saved, it is hidden 4 with respect to whom the god of this age has blinded the understanding of those unbelieving, with the result the illumination of the good news of the glory of Christ—who is the very image of God—does not clearly appear.[k]

5 For not ourselves do we proclaim, but Lord Jesus Christ, now ourselves your servants for the sake of Jesus. 6 For God said out of darkness light will give light, who has given light in our hearts for illumination of the knowledge of the glory of God in the face of Jesus Christ.

7 Now we have this treasure in frail vessels, that the excellence of the power may be from God and not from us. 8 In all being oppressed but not constrained, doubting but not despairing, 9 being persecuted but not forsaken, being cast down but not ruined, 10 at all times bearing the death of Jesus in the body, so that also the life of Jesus should be revealed in the body. 11 For at all times we the living are being delivered to death for the sake of Jesus, so that also the life of Jesus may be revealed in our mortal flesh. 12 So then, death works in us, but life in you.

13 But we have the same spirit of faith according to that which was written. "I believed, therefore I have spoken"; and we believe and also speak, 14 knowing that the one having raised up the Lord Jesus, also us through Jesus will raise up and will present *us* with you. 15 For all things are for your sake, so that the grace having abounded for the sake of many, the thanksgiving may superabound to the glory of God. 16 Therefore we do not lose courage.

But also if our outward person is perishing, yet our inner *person* is daily being renewed. 17 For our momentary affliction is easy to bear, because producing for us, abundance to abundance, an eternal weight of glory. 18 We are not attending things seen, but things not seen. For things seen endure for a while, but things not seen *are* endless.

SECOND CORINTHIANS FIVE

1 For we know that if our earthly house, the tent, may be dissolved, we have a building from God, a house not made with hands, perpetual[l] in the heavens. 2 For also in this we groan, longing to be clothed with our dwelling which is from heaven, 3 if also truly we will be found having been clothed, not naked. 4 For also, being in the tent, we groan, being oppressed, because we do not desire to be unclothed but to be clothed, that the mortal may be swallowed up through the life. 5 Now the one having made us for this very *thing* is God, having given to us the guarantee of the Spirit.

6 Therefore, we are at all times confident and knowing that being at home in the body, we are absent from the Lord; 7 for we conduct our life by faith not by sight. 8 Now we are full of confidence and are pleased, rather, to be absent away from the body and to be at home with the Lord. 9 Therefore, also, we aspire to be well-pleasing to him, whether being at home or being away. 10 For it is necessary all of us to be known before the judgment seat of the Christ, that each may receive according to what was done in the body, whether good or evil.

11 Therefore, knowing the fear of the Lord, we persuade others; but to God we have been made known. Now I expect also to have been made known in your consciences. 12 We are not again commending ourselves to you, but are giving to you an occasion of boasting on our behalf, so that you all may have against those boasting in appearance and not in the heart. 13 For if we have been beside ourselves it is to God. If we are in our right mind it is for you. 14 For the love of the Christ compels us, we judging this: that one did die for the sake of all, therefore the all have died. 15 And he did die for all, that those living should no longer live to themselves, but to the one dying for them and being raised.

16 Therefore from now we know no one according to flesh. Even if we did know Christ according to flesh—but now no more do we know. 17 Therefore if anyone *is* in Christ—a new creation *he is*, the old things are past, look, the new is here, 18 and all from God, the one who did reconcile us to himself through Christ, and did give to us the ministry of reconciliation: 19 how that God was by[m] Christ reconciling the world to himself, not imputing to them their wrongdoing, and having appointed to us the word of reconciliation.

20 Therefore, for Christ we are ambassadors, as if God is exhorting[n] through us. We implore you on behalf of Christ, you be reconciled to God. 21 The one not having known sin, God made to be sin for us, so that we might become the righteousness of God in him.[o]

SECOND CORINTHIANS SIX

1 Now working together *with God* we also exhort you not in uselessness to have received the grace of God. 2 For he says, "In an

acceptable season I heard you, and in a day of salvation I helped you." Look, now *is the* acceptable season; look, now *is the* day of salvation.

3 We are not giving even one offense to any, so that the ministry may not be blamed. 4 But in everything we are presenting ourselves as God's servants: in much endurance in afflictions, in distresses without, in distresses within, 5 in beatings, in imprisonments, in strife, in labors, in sleeplessness, in want of food, 6 in purity, in knowledge, in patience, in kindness, in the Holy Spirit, in unfeigned love, 7 in the word of truth, in the power of God, using the instruments of righteousness for the right hand and for the left, 8 through glory and dishonor, through infamy and fame, as deceivers and yet true, 9 as not known yet well-known, as dying and look, we live, as being chastised and not put to death, 10 as being sorrowful but always rejoicing, as helplessly poor but abundantly supplied, as having nothing and possessing all.

11 Our mouth has been opened to you Corinthians, our heart enlarged. 12 You are not constrained by us, but you are restrained in your affections *to us*. 13 Now in return, the same *affections*—I speak as to children—be enlarged also in you *to us*.[p]

14 Do not become unequally yoked with the ones without faith. For what partnership righteousness and lawlessness? Or what fellowship light with darkness? 15 Now what agreement Christ with Belial? Or what part to a believer with *the ones* of no faith? 16 Now what agreement God's temple with idols? For we are God's living temple, as God has said, "I will reside in them and will live among *them*. And I will be their God and they will be to me a people."

17 Therefore, "come out from their midst and be separate," says the Lord, "and do not touch unclean, and I will gather[q] you. 18 And I will be to you for a father, and you will be to me for sons and daughters," says the Lord Almighty.

SECOND CORINTHIANS SEVEN

1 Therefore, having these promises, beloved, may we[r] cleanse ourselves from every defilement of flesh and spirit, completing our sanctification in the fear of God. 2 Receive us. We have wronged no one, we have corrupted no one, we have defrauded no one. 3 I do not speak to condemn. For I said before that you are in our hearts, to die together and to live together. 4 Great *is* my confidence toward you. Great *is* my boasting concerning you. I have been filled with encouragement, I superabound with joy against all our affliction.

5 And even our coming into Macedonia, our flesh had no rest. But in all we are being afflicted; battles without, fears within. 6 But the one—God—comforting the

lowly comforted us by the coming of Titus.

7 Now not only by his arrival, but also by the comfort with which he had been comforted by all of you, telling to us your strong affection, your lamentation, your zeal for me, so as for me the more to rejoice. 8 Because if also I did grieve you in the letter, I do not regret, though also I did regret, because I perceive that the letter, if even for an hour, grieved you. 9 Now I rejoice—not because you were grieved, but because you had been grieved unto repentance. For you were grieved according to God, so that in nothing you might suffer loss through us.

10 For *to be* grieved according to God works repentance to salvation without regret, but the grief of the world produces death. 11 For look, this same thing, to have been grieved according to God, how much *it* worked diligence in you, but also a response, but also indignation, but also fear, but also earnest desire, but also zeal, but also punishment! In everything you presented yourselves to be innocent in this matter. 12 So even if I wrote to you, *it was* not for the sake of the one having done wrong, nor for the sake of the one having suffered wrong, but for the sake of your diligence to be revealed, which concerns us toward you before God.

13 Because of this, we have been comforted. Now during our comfort, more abundantly we rejoiced at the joy of Titus, because his spirit has been refreshed by all of you. 14 For if anything I have boasted to him about you, I was not shamed, but as all things we have in truth spoken to you, so also our boasting to Titus became truth. 15 And his affections toward you are abundantly more, remembering the obedience of all of you, how that with fear and trembling you received him. 16 I rejoice, because in everything I am confident in you.

SECOND CORINTHIANS EIGHT

1 Now, we make known to you, brothers, the grace of God given in the churches of Macedonia, 2 that in much proof of affliction, the overflowing of their joy, and their deep helpless poverty,^{s} superabounded to the riches of their faithful benevolence.^{t}

3 Because I testify, according to ability and beyond ability, of their own accord, 4 with much encouragement asking of us the grace and the fellowship of the ministry toward the saints.^{u} 5 And not as we had hoped, but first they gave themselves to the Lord, and then to us, by God's will, 6 so that we exhorted Titus, that as he had begun, so also he might finish with you also this grace. 7 But even as in all you superabound—in faith, in speech, and knowledge, and all diligence, and in our love to you— that also in this grace you might superabound. 8 I do not speak as a command, but by means of the diligence of others also proving

your love is sincere.

9 For you know the grace of our Lord Jesus Christ, that for your sake he became helplessly poor, although he was rich, so that you through that helpless poverty might become rich. 10 And I give my opinion in this matter. For you this is advantageous, who not only to act, but also to will, did begin from last year. 11 But now also the doing complete, so that just as the readiness of the will, so also to complete, out of that which you have.

12 For if the readiness is present, it is acceptable, according as if he might have, not according as he does not have. 13 For that not for others *there is* rest but for you affliction, but of equity. 14 In the present time, your abundance to the ones of those in need, so that also their abundance may be for your need, so that there may be equity. 15 As it is written, "he with much had no surplus, and he with little had no lack."

16 But thanks to God, the one giving the same diligence for you in the heart of Titus. 17 For truly he accepted our exhortation, but being very diligent, on his own accord he has gone out to you. 18 Now we have sent with him the brother whose praise because of the good news *is* throughout all of the churches. 19 Not only now, but also having been appointed our fellow traveler by the churches, with this grace that is being ministered by us, toward the glory of the same Lord, and our readiness, 20 to avoid this: lest anyone might blame us in this bountiful offering being ministered by us. 21 For we are taking care for what is a noble work, not only before the Lord but also before men.

22 Now we sent with them our brother, whom we have proven often in much to be diligent, but now more diligent with more confidence that is toward you, 23 whether concerning Titus, my partner and for you a fellow worker, whether our brothers, messengers of the churches, the glory of Christ. 24 Therefore, show to them before the churches proof of your love and of our boasting about you.

SECOND CORINTHIANS NINE

1 For truly concerning the ministry that *is* for the saints, it is superfluous for me to write to you. 2 For I know your readiness, which about you I boast to the Macedonians, that Achaia has made ready from last year, and that your zeal has stimulated the many.

3 Now I have sent the brothers, that our boasting about you may not be empty in this matter, that as I have been saying, you may be ready. 4 Lest if Macedonians might come with me and discover you are not ready we might be put to shame—to say nothing of you—in this confidence. 5 Therefore, I reckoned as necessary to encourage the brothers that they might go before *me* to you, and make ready your

blessing promised beforehand, thus to be prepared as a blessing, and not as though extorted [v1] by us from you.

6 Now this, the one sowing sparingly, sparingly also will reap, and the one sowing in blessing, in blessing also will reap—7 each as he resolves in the heart, not out of regret or out of unwillingness, for God loves a glad giver.[v2] 8 Now God is able all grace to superabound to you, so that in all, at all times, having all necessities, you may superabound in every good work. 9 As it has been written, "He has distributed bountifully, he has given to the poor, his righteousness continues to the age."

10 Now the one supplying more seed to him sowing, and bread for food, will generously supply and will increase your seed for sowing, and will increase the rewards[v3] of righteousness, 11 in all *ways* abundantly supplying you all, benevolently to all, which produces through us thanksgiving to God.

12 For the ministry of this service is not only supplying abundantly the needs of the saints, but is also superabounding to God through many thanksgivings, 13 through the proof of this service, they glorifying God upon the obedience of your confession in the good news of Christ, and benevolence of the fellowship toward them and toward all. 14 Their prayers also are for you, a longing for you on account of the exceeding grace of God upon you.

15 Thanks to God for his ineffable[w] gift.

SECOND CORINTHIANS TEN

1 Now I myself, Paul, encourage you by the gentle strength[x] and virtue[y] of Christ—who as to *my* appearance among you am truly humble, but being absent am bold toward you. 2 Now I ask you, not being present, to be bold with the confidence with which I reckon to act boldly toward some reckoning us as living according to flesh. 3 For living in flesh, not according to flesh, we have conflicts. 4 For the weapons of our trials are not fleshly but God empowered for *the* destruction of strongholds, 5 demolishing counsel and every proud adversary lifting up against the knowledge of God, and taking captive every thought into the obedience of Christ, 6 and in having readiness to punish all active disobedience, when your obedience might have been fulfilled.

7 You are looking according to the external. If anyone is persuaded in himself to be of Christ, let him reckon this again within himself, that as he *is* of Christ, so also we. 8 For even if I should boast more here about our authority, which the Lord has given us for building and not for your destruction, I will not be made ashamed, 9 that I may not seem as if to terrify you through the letters. 10 Because the letters, they say, truly *are* not to be made light of, and *are* strong; but the presence of the body *is* weak, and the

speech contemptible. 11 Let such a one reckon this, that such as we are in word by letters, being absent, such also we are in action being present.

12 For we dare not to judge or to compare ourselves with some commending themselves. But these by themselves measuring themselves, and comparing themselves with themselves, do not understand. 13 But we will not boast against things without measure, but according to the measure of the portion God has assigned to us, a measure to also reach as far as you.

14 For not as though not coming to you, we are extending ourselves. For also as far as you we came in the good news of Christ, 15 not to things without measure, boasting in others labors, but having hope, increasing your faith, to be enlarged among you according to our portion, to overflowing. 16 That so as beyond you to proclaim the good news, not ready to boast in these things in another's portion. 17 But the one boasting, in the Lord let him boast. 18 For not the one himself commending, is this one approved, but the one whom the Lord commends.

SECOND CORINTHIANS ELEVEN

1 Oh that you would endure a little in my foolishness (but also you do endure me). 2 I am zealous for you with God's jealousy. For I have married[z] you to one husband, a virgin pure to be presented to Christ. 3 But I fear lest by some means as the serpent seduced Eve in his cunning, your minds might be subverted from the simplicity and the purity in Christ.

4 For truly if the one coming proclaims another Jesus, whom we did not proclaim, or you receive a different spirit which you did not receive, or different good news which you did not accept—you have endured it very well![aa] 5 For I reckon in not one thing to be behind those worthy messengers.[bb] 6 But if plain in speech, yet not in knowledge, but in all I have been revealed in all things to you.

7 Perhaps I committed offense, humbling myself so that you might be exalted, because I freely proclaimed God's good news to you? 8 I robbed other churches, having received wages for the ministry to you. 9 And being present with you, and suffering need, I did not burden any person, for the brothers having come from Macedonia abundantly supplied my need; and in all toward you I kept and will keep myself not burdensome.

10 Christ's truth is in me; that this my boasting will not be silenced in the regions of Achaia. 11 On account of why? Because I do not love you? God knows!

12 But what I do, also I will do, in order that I might remove the opportunity, of those desiring an opportunity, that in what they are boasting they might be found even as also we. 13 For such *are* false messengers, deceitful workers,

changing their outward form[cc] *to seem* as apostles of Christ; 14 and no wonder. For Satan himself changes his outward form *to seem* as a messenger of light. 15 Not surprising therefore, if also his servants change their outward form *to seem* as servants of righteousness, whose end will be according to their works.

16 Again I say, no one should think me to be foolish. But if otherwise, receive me even as foolish, that I also may boast a little. 17 What I am saying, not according to the Lord I am saying, but as in foolishness, in this the confidence of boasting. 18 Since many boast according to the flesh, I also will boast. 19 For gladly you patiently bear with the foolish, you being wise. 20 For you bear it if any enslave you, if any devour you, if anyone takes, if any exalts himself, if any hit you in your face.

21 I speak by way of dishonor, how that we have been too weak! But in whatever any might be bold—because as a fool I speak—I also am bold. 22 Are they Hebrews? I also. Are they Israelites? I also. Are they offspring of Abraham? I also.

23 Are they servants of Christ? I speak for the sake of foolishness: I, in wearisome toil abundantly, in imprisonments abundantly, in wounds abundantly, in exposure to death many times. 24 From the Jews five times I received forty less one. 25 Three times I was beaten with rods, once I was stoned, three times I was shipwrecked, a day and night I spent in the deep sea.

26 In journeys often, in dangers of rivers, in dangers of robbers, in dangers from my kin, in dangers from gentiles, in dangers in city, in dangers in wilderness, in dangers on the sea, in dangers among false brethren, 27 in wearisome toil and everyday labor, without sleep often, in hunger and thirst, in want of food often, in cold and without decent clothing.

28 Apart from these things, the pressure on me every day, the concern for all the churches. 29 Who is faint of heart and I am not faint of heart? Who is offended and I not indignant? 30 If necessary to boast, I will boast in my weakness. 31 The God and Father of the Lord Jesus knows, the one blessed to the ages, that I am not lying. 32 In Damascus, the Ethnarch under Aretas the king was guarding the city of Damascus to seize me. 33 But I was let down in a basket through a window in the wall, and I escaped his hands.

SECOND CORINTHIANS TWELVE

1 To boast is necessary, truly not beneficial. But I will continue with visions and revelations of the Lord. 2 I have known a man in Christ, fourteen years earlier—whether in body I know not or out of the body I know not; God knows—this person being caught up into the third heaven. 3 And I have known such a man—whether in body or out of the body I know not; God knows—4 that he was caught up into paradise and he heard words not possible or lawful

to be spoken—not permissible to man to speak. 5 Concerning such a person I will boast. But concerning myself I will not boast, except in the weaknesses.

6 For if I might desire to boast, I will not be foolish. For I will speak the truth. But I forbear, lest any should reckon to me more than what he sees in me or hears of me, 7 and the excellence of the revelations. Therefore, in order that I may not be exalted, *there* was given to me a thorn in the flesh, a messenger of Satan, that he might mistreat me, so that I may not be exalted.

8 For this, I called upon the Lord three times, that it might be removed from me. 9 And he said to me, "My grace suffices you, for the power is perfected in weakness." Most gladly, therefore, rather will I boast in my weaknesses, so that the power of the Christ may rest upon me. 10 Accordingly, I am pleased in weaknesses, in injuries, in afflictions, in persecutions, and great distresses for Christ. For when I might be without strength, then I am strong.

11 I have become a fool: you compelled me. For I ought to be commended by you. For in no way was I inferior to those most worthy messengers,[dd] even though I am nothing. 12 Truly the signs of the one sent by God[ee] were performed among you in all long suffering, both in signs, and wonders, and miracles. 13 For what is it that you were inferior above the rest *of the* churches, if not that I myself did not burden you? Forgive me this injustice!

14 Look, this third time, I am ready to come to you, and I will not burden you. For I do not seek what is yours, but you. For the children ought not to keep in store goods for the parents, but the parents for the children. 15 Now I most gladly will spend, and will be entirely expended, for your souls. If loving you more abundantly, am I less loved? 16 But so it is, I did not burden you, but being clever I took you by ingenuity. 17 Not any of whom I have sent to you—by him did I take advantage of you? 18 I encouraged Titus, and sent with him the brother. Titus did not take advantage of you, *did he*? Did we not conduct ourselves in the same spirit? Did we not in the same example?

19 Until now are you thinking that to you we are making a defense? Before God in Christ we speak now all things, beloved, for your spiritual growth. 20 For I fear lest in some manner, having come, I may not find you such as I desire, and I might be found by you such as you do not wish. Lest perhaps strife, jealousy, anger, rivalry, slander, hurtful gossip, arrogance, disorder; 21 lest again me having come, my God may humble me as to you, and I should mourn many of those already sinning, and not having repented of the moral uncleanness and sexual immorality and wantonness that they have practiced.

SECOND CORINTHIANS THIRTEEN

1 This third time: I am coming to you. In the mouth of two or three witnesses every word will be confirmed. 2 I have forewarned, as being present the second time; and now being absent I forewarn those having already sinned, and all the others, that if I come to the *same* again I will not spare, 3 inasmuch as you seek a proof in me speaking of Christ, who toward you is not weak but powerful among you. 4 For also he was crucified in weakness, but he lives by God's power. For also we are weak in him, but toward you we will live with him by God's power.

5 Examine yourselves if you are in the faith; put yourselves to the proof. Or do you not yourselves really know that Jesus Christ is in you, unless you are without proof? 6 Now I hope that you will know that we are not without proof. 7 Now we pray to God you do not do even one thing wrong, not that we may appear approved, but that you may do what is right, though we may appear as without proof. 8 For we cannot do against the truth, but for the truth.

9 For we rejoice when we might be weak but you may be strong. This also: we are praying for your complete readiness.ff 10 Therefore, on account of these things, I write being absent, so that being present I may not treat you severely, according to the authority that the Lord has given me for building and not for destruction.

11 But now, brothers, rejoice! Be such as you should be; be encouraged, the same mindset, be at peace. And the God of love and peace will be among you. 12 Greet one another with a holy kiss. 13 All the saints greet you. 14 The grace of the Lord Jesus Christ, and the love of God, and the fellowship of the Holy Spirit be with you all. [99]

The Book of Galatians

The Book of Galatians was written to the churches Paul had established on his first missionary journey in the Roman Imperial province of Galatia: Antioch of Pisidia, Iconium, Lystra, and Derbe of Lycaonia. The dating is controversial, as some believe Galatians is the first of Paul's letters. My view is flexible. If written at Antioch of Syria, then ca. AD 50–51. If written at Corinth, then 1 Thessalonians, Galatians, 2 Thessalonians, ca. AD 51–53. The Book of Galatians is both a defense of Paul's authority and an apologetic against the doctrine expressed in Acts 15:1. In this letter Paul is not creating doctrine, he is explaining doctrine previously given to the Galatians to counter the false doctrine that, "faith in Christ plus obedience to the Law of Moses," is necessary to complete salvation. That heresy continues today in some pseudo-Christian groups requiring obedience to some parts of the Mosaic Law in order to be a complete or completed Christian.

GALATIANS ONE

1 Paul, apostle, not from men, also not by means of man, but by means of Jesus Christ and God Father, the one having raised him out from the dead ones; 2 and all the brethren with me. To the churches of Galatia.

3 Grace to you, and peace, from God our Father and the Lord Jesus Christ, 4 the one having given himself for our sins, in order that he might deliver us out of the present evil age, according to the will of our God and Father, 5 to whom the glory to the ages of the ages, truly.[a1]

6 I am astonished that so quickly you have turned away from the one having called you in the grace of Christ, to a different good news, 7 which is not another of the same kind; but there are some who are troubling you and desiring to pervert the good news of Christ.

8 But even if we or a messenger out of heaven might proclaim[a2] to you contrary to what we did proclaim to you, let him be accursed. 9 Just as we have forewarned, even now again I say, if any person is proclaiming to you contrary to what you received, let him be accursed. 10 For now do I gain the favor of men, or God? Or do I seek to please men? For if yet I were pleasing men I would not be a servant of Christ.

11 For I declare to you, brethren, the good news proclaimed by me, that it is not according to man. 12 For I did not receive it from man, nor was I taught but by means of revelation from Jesus Christ.

13 For you understand my former way of life in Judaism, that I was excessively persecuting the church of God and was destroying it. 14 And I was advancing in Judaism beyond many contemporaries in my own people, being more abundantly zealous of the traditions of my fathers. 15 But when it pleased the One[b] having

separated me from my mother's womb, and having called me by his grace, 16 to reveal his Son in me, that I might proclaim him among the gentiles, I did not immediately consult with flesh and blood, 17 nor did I go up to Jerusalem to those who were apostles before me, but I went away into Arabia, and again returned to Damascus.

18 Then after three years, I went up to Jerusalem to become acquainted with Cephas; and I stayed with him fifteen days. 19 But of the other apostles I saw none; except I saw Jacob the brother of the Lord. 20 Now in what I write to you, look, before God I do not lie.

21 Then I went into the regions of Syria and Cilicia. 22 At that time I was unknown by face to the churches of Judea that are in Christ. 23 But they were only hearing that, "The one formerly persecuting us is now proclaiming the faith which he was at one time destroying." 24 And they were glorifying God in me.

GALATIANS TWO

1 Then, after fourteen years, again I went up to Jerusalem, with Barnabas, also taking along Titus. 2 Now, I went up according to what had been revealed to me, and I set before them the good news that I proclaim among the gentiles—but privately to those esteemed—lest in vain I might be running or have run.

3 But not even Titus, who was with me, being Greek, was compelled to be circumcised, 4 and that because of the false brethren brought in secretly, who came in privately to spy out our freedom that we have in Christ Jesus, in order they will enslave us, 5 to whom not even for an hour did we yield in submission, so that the truth of the good news might continue with you.

6 Now of those esteemed to be someone—of what sort at one time or another to me it does not make a difference, for God does not accept the person of any man—to me the esteemed added nothing. 7 But on the contrary, they having seen I had been entrusted with the good news of the uncircumcision, just as Peter of the circumcision—8 for the one having worked in Peter to apostleship of the circumcision did also in me to the gentiles—9 and having known the grace given to me, Jacob and Cephas and John, those esteemed to be pillars, gave right hands to me and Barnabas, of fellowship, that we to the gentiles, but they to the circumcision. 10 Only that we may remember concerning the poor. Which also I was eager to do the same thing.

11 But when Peter came to Antioch[c] *of Syria* I opposed him face to face, because he was worthy of blame. 12 For before certain ones came from Jacob he was eating with the gentiles. But when they came, he drew back and separated himself, being afraid of those of the circumcision. 13 And with him also the rest of the Jews played the hypocrite, so that even Barnabas was led astray by

their hypocrisy. 14 But when I saw that they were not behaving correctly according to the truth of the good news, I said to Peter in front of all, "If you, being a Jew, live like a Gentile and not like a Jew, why do you compel the gentiles to Judaize?"

15 We, by birth Jews, and not of sinful gentiles, 16 and knowing a person is not justified by works of the Law, only through the faith of Jesus Christ, even we in Christ Jesus have believed that we may be justified in the faith of Christ, and not by works of the Law. Because by works of the Law not any flesh will be justified. 17 But if seeking to be justified in Christ, we ourselves are also found to be sinners, then is Christ a servant of sin? Never may it be! 18 For if that which I destroyed, I build those things again, I declare myself a transgressor.

19 For I through the Law, to the Law died, that I may live to God. 20 I have been crucified with Christ. Now I live—no longer I but Christ lives in me. But now that which I live in the flesh, in faith I live—and that from the Son of God, the one having loved me and having given himself for me. 21 I do not set aside the grace of God. For if righteousness is through the Law, then Christ died for no reason.

GALATIANS THREE

1 Oh foolish Galatians! Who has cast an evil eye on you, before whose eyes Jesus Christ was set forth as having been crucified?[d] 2 This only I desire to learn from you: did you receive the Spirit by works of the Law or by hearing out of faith? 3 Are you so foolish? Having begun in the Spirit are you now being perfected in the flesh? 4 Did you suffer so much to no purpose? If it really was to no purpose?

5 The one, then, supplying to you the Spirit and doing mighty works among you—out of works of the Law or hearing out of faith? 6 Even as Abraham believed God and it was accounted to him as righteousness. 7 Know then that those of faith, these are sons of Abraham. 8 Having foreseen, then, the Scripture that justifies the gentiles by faith, God foretold the good news to Abraham: "in you all the peoples will be blessed."[e] 9 So then those of faith are blessed together with the believing Abraham.

10 For as many as are of works of Law are under a curse. For it is written, "Cursed is everyone who does not persevere in all things that have been written in the book of the Law, to do them." 11 Now, that by the Law no one is righteous with God, is evident, because "The righteous will live by faith." 12 Now, the Law is not out of faith, but the one having done these things will live by them. 13 Christ redeemed us out of the curse of the Law, having become for us a curse, for it has been written, "Everyone hanging on a tree is cursed." 14 So that to the nations the blessing of Abraham may come by Jesus Christ, so that through faith we

may receive the promise of the Spirit.

15 Brethren, I am speaking according to man. Even man's covenant, having been confirmed, no one voids or supplements. 16 Now to Abraham the promises were spoken, and to his seed. It does not say, "and to seeds," as of many, but as of one, "and to your seed," who is Christ. 17 This now I say. The covenant previously confirmed by God, the Law having come four hundred and thirty years after does not cancel so as to render ineffective the promise.

18 For if by Law the inheritance, no longer by a promise. But God has bestowed it to Abraham through a promise. 19 Why then the Law? It was added on account of transgressions (until that seed should have come to whom the promise had been made), having been commanded through messengers by the hand of a mediator.

20 Now, a mediator is not of one, but God is one. 21 Is the Law, therefore, against the promises of God? Never may it be! For if a Law had been given able to give life, truly from out of the Law there would have been righteousness. 22 But the Scripture included the whole under sin, so that the promise by faith of Jesus Christ may be given to those believing.

23 Now before faith came we were being guarded under the Law, enclosed until the faith about to be revealed. 24 So that the Law became our guardian[f1] unto Christ, so that by faith we may be justified. 25 But faith having come we are no longer under a guardian.

26 For you are all sons of God through the faith in Christ Jesus. 27 For as many as were immersed into Christ have put on Christ. 28 There is not Jew nor Greek, there is not slave nor free, there is not male nor female—for you all are one in Christ Jesus. 29 Now if you are Christ's, then you are Abraham's seed, heirs according to the promise.

GALATIANS FOUR

1 Now I say, for as long a time the heir is a child, being owner of everything, he differs not from a servant. 2 But he is under guardians and overseers, until the day appointed by his father. 3 So also we, when we were children, were dependent under the principles of the world.

4 But when the fullness of the time had come, God sent forth his Son, having been born of a woman, having been born under the Law, 5 that he may redeem those under the Law, so that we may receive the adoption as sons. 6 Now because you are sons, God sent forth the Spirit of his Son into our hearts, crying out, "Abba, Father." 7 So you are no longer a servant, but a son; if now a son, also an heir through God.[f2]

8 But truly at that time not knowing God, you were in bondage to those by nature not being gods. 9 But now, having known God—but rather, having

been known by God—how is it you turn again to the weak and impoverished principles, to which you again desire to be subjected anew? 10 You observe times, and months, and seasons, and years. 11 I fear for you, lest somehow I have labored for you to no purpose. 12 I implore you, become as I am, because I also am as you, brethren. In nothing have you wronged me.

13 Now you know that in weakness of the flesh I proclaimed the good news to you at the first. 14 And your trial with my flesh you did not despise, did not reject with contempt, but as a messenger of God you received me, as Christ Jesus. 15 What has become of your blessedness?[9] For I bear witness to you that, if you had been able, you would have dug out your eyes and given them to me.

16 So have I become your enemy, speaking truth to you? 17 They are zealous for you—not well, but to exclude you. They desire that you might be zealous for them. 18 Now, it is good to be zealous in a right thing at all times, and not only in my being present with you. 19 My children, of whom I am again in birthing pains until the image of Christ shall be formed in you. 20 Truly I desired to be present with you now and to change my tone of voice, because I am in doubt as to you.

21 Tell me, those desiring to be under the Law, do you not listen to the Law? 22 For it has been written that Abraham had two sons: one of the servant and one of the freeborn. 23 But truly, the one of the servant was born according to the flesh, but the one of the freeborn through the promise. 24 Which things are allegorized. For these are the two covenants: truly one from Mount Sinai unto begetting servitude, which is Hagar. 25 And Hagar is Mount Sinai in Arabia; now she corresponds to the present Jerusalem, for she is in servitude with her children. 26 But the Jerusalem above is freeborn, who is mother of us all. 27 For it has been written: "Rejoice, you barren, the one not bearing children. Break forth and call aloud, the one not in birth pains. Because many are the children of the desolate, more than of her having the husband."

28 Now you, brethren, like Isaac, are children of promise. 29 But, just as the one born according to the flesh was persecuting the one according to spirit, so also now. 30 But what says the Scripture? "Cast out the servant and her son. For it is not possible the son of the servant will inherit with the son of the freeborn." 31 So then, brethren, we are not children of the servant, but of the freeborn.

GALATIANS FIVE

1 In freedom Christ has made us free. Stand firm, then, and do not again subject yourselves in a yoke of servitude. 2 Pay attention. I Paul say to you that if you shall become circumcised, Christ will profit you nothing. 3 Now I give witness again to every person that

being circumcised one is a debtor to keep all the Law. 4 You are alienated from Christ, whosoever by the Law are being justified; from grace you have fallen away. 5 For we by the Spirit by faith eagerly await the hope of righteousness. 6 For in Christ Jesus neither circumcision has any value, nor uncircumcision, but only faith working through love.

7 You were running well. Who hindered you, not to obey the truth? 8 This persuasion is not of the one calling you. 9 A little leaven leavens the whole lump. 10 I am confident for you in the Lord, that you will have no other mind. But the one troubling you will bear the judgment, whoever he might be.

11 Now, brethren, if circumcision I still proclaim, why am I still persecuted? Then the offense of the cross has been rendered ineffective. 12 Would that those unsettling you would separate themselves from you.[h]

13 For you were called to freedom, brethren, but not the freedom for an opportunity to the flesh. But through love serve one another. 14 For in one word all Law is fulfilled in this: you shall love your neighbor as yourself. 15 But if you bite and devour one another, take heed lest by one another you may be consumed.

16 Now I say, conduct your manner of life according to the Spirit, and the strong desire of the flesh you may not at all fulfill. 17 For the flesh strongly desires against the Spirit, and the Spirit against the flesh. For these are opposed to one another, so that you might not desire those things you should do. 18 But if you are led by the Spirit, you are not under the Law.

19 Now, the works of the flesh are plain, which are sexual immorality, moral impurity, a shameless love of sin, 20 idolatry, sorcery, enmities, strife, envies, outbursts of anger, personal ambition and partisan rivalry, division, factions, 21 embittered resentment, drunkenness, debauchery, and things like these, of which I forewarn you, even as I warned before, that those habitually doing such things will not inherit God's kingdom.

22 But the fruit of the Spirit is, godly love, joy, peace, patience, kindness, generousness, faithfulness, 23 gentleness in strength,[i] chaste; against such things there is no Law.

24 Now those of Christ Jesus have crucified the flesh with the passions and strong desires. 25 If we live by the Spirit, by the Spirit we will also conduct our manner of life. 26 We should not become boastful, provoking one another, envying one another.

GALATIANS SIX

1 Brethren, even if someone should be detected[j] in some wrongdoing, you, the spiritual ones, restore such a one in a spirit of strength and gentleness, giving attention to yourself, lest you also be tempted. 2 Bear you one another's burdens, and thereby

you will fulfill the Law of Christ. 3 For if any considers himself to be something, being nothing he deceives himself. 4 But each consider their own work, and then as to their self alone the boasting they will have, and not as to another. 5 For each will bear his own load. 6 Now, the one who is being taught in the word, share in all good things with the one teaching.

7 Do not be lead astray: God is not mocked. For whatever if a man might sow, that also he will reap. 8 For the one sowing in his flesh, from the flesh will reap corruption. But the one sowing in the spirit,[k] from the Spirit will reap eternal life.

9 Now in doing well, we should not be slothful; for in due season we will reap, not giving up. 10 So then, as we have opportunity, we should work good toward all, but especially toward the household of the faith.

11 See in how large letters I have written to you with my own hand.

12 As many as desire to make a fair appearance in the flesh, these compel you to be circumcised—only that for the cross of Christ Jesus they may not be persecuted. 13 For not even those who are themselves circumcised keep the Law, but they desire you to be circumcised, so that they may boast in your flesh.

14 But for myself, never may it be to boast, except in the cross of our Lord Jesus Christ, through which the world has been crucified to me, and I to the world. 15 For neither circumcision is anything, nor uncircumcision; but a new creation.

16 And as many who by this rule will conduct their manner of life, peace upon them, and mercy; and mercy upon the Israel of God.

17 Henceforth let none give troubles to me. For I bear the marks of Jesus on my body. 18 The grace of our Lord Jesus Christ be with your spirit, brethren. Amen.

The Book of Ephesians

The Book of Ephesians was written from Rome, Italy, during Paul's first Roman imprisonment, ca. AD 61–63. The letter is in some ways a follow-up to Acts 20:17-38, Paul's meeting with the Ephesian elders, ca. AD 58. The purpose of the letter is advanced instruction for advanced Christians. Paul is building them up (cf. Acts 20:32) by teaching them the "meat" of Christianity: the decrees and doctrines underlying their salvation, the mystery of the New Testament church, the practice of their faith, and the administration of the local church. One of the more notable features of the letter are the fourteen ministries of the Holy Spirit in the local church (1:13, 14, 17; 2:18, 22; 3:5, 16; 4:3, 4, 30; 5:9, 18; 6:17, 18).

EPHESIANS ONE

1 Paul, apostle of Christ Jesus through God's will. To the saints that are in Ephesus, even *the* faithful in Christ Jesus. 2 Grace to you, and peace, from God our Father, and Lord Jesus Christ.

3 Worthy of praise is the God and Father of our Lord Jesus Christ, the One having blessed us with every spiritual blessing in the heavenly realms in Christ, 4 even as he chose us in him before the beginning of the universe,[a] for us to be holy and without blemish[b] in his presence.

In love 5 he predestined us for sonship[c] to himself through Jesus Christ, according to the good pleasure of his will, 6 to praise and glory of his grace.

Who made us accepted in the Beloved, 7 in whom we have the redemption through his blood, the forgiveness of trespasses, according to the riches of his grace, 8 which he caused to abound unto us in all wisdom and prudence.

9 He has made known to us the hidden *things*[d] of his will, according to his pleasure which he purposed in himself 10 for the dispensation of the fullness of the times: to gather together all the things in Christ, the things in the heavens and the things upon the earth 11 in him.

In whom also we were made his heirs and his inheritance,[e] having been predestined according to the purpose of the One, all things working according to the counsel of his will. 12 For us, the ones having first trusted in the Christ, to be for praise of his glory. 13 In whom also you have heard the word of the truth, the good news of your salvation. In whom also having believed you were sealed by[f] the Holy Spirit of promise, 14 who is the guarantor[g] of our inheritance to redemption of the purchased possession, to praise his glory.

15 Because of this I also, having heard of the faith among you in the Lord Jesus Christ, and the love toward all the saints, 16 do not stop giving thanks for you, making mention in my prayers. 17

That the God of our Lord Jesus Christ, the glorious Father, may give to you a spirit of wisdom and revelation in knowledge of him, 18 the eyes of your heart being given understanding, in order for you to know what is the hope of his calling, what are the glorious riches of his inheritance in the saints, 19 and what is the surpassing greatness of his power toward us, the ones believing according to the mighty working of his strength, 20 which he worked in the Christ having raised him out from the dead.

And he seated him at his right hand in the heavenly realms, 21 far above all rule and authority and power and lordship, and every name being named, not only in this age, but also in the coming. 22 And he subjected all things under his feet, and gave him headship over all things for the church, 23 which is his body, the fullness of the One filling all things in all things.

EPHESIANS TWO

1 And you being dead in your trespasses and your sins

2 (in which you formerly walked according to the age of this world, according to the ruler who rules the lower spirit world,[h] that spirit now working in the sons of disobedience; 3 among whom also we all once conducted ourselves in the lusts of our flesh, doing the desires of the flesh and the mind, and were by nature children of wrath, as even the rest),

4 but God being rich in mercy, because of his great love with which he loved us, 5 even we being dead in trespasses, made us alive together with Christ—by grace you are having been saved[i]—6 and raised us together and seated us together in the heavenly places in Christ Jesus, 7 in order that he might show in the coming ages the exceeding riches of his grace in kindness toward us in Christ Jesus.

8 For by grace you are having been saved,[i] through faith, and that not of yourselves. Of God the gift, 9 not from works, so that no one should boast. 10 For we are his workmanship, having been created in Christ Jesus for good works, which God previously prepared in order that we should conduct our manner of life in them.

11 Therefore, call to mind that in past time you, the gentiles in flesh, the ones called uncircumcision by that called circumcision (in the flesh, made by hands)—12 that you were at that time separate from Christ, estranged from the community of Israel, and strangers to the covenants of the promise, not having hope, and without God in the world. 13 But now in Christ Jesus you, the ones once being far off, have become near by the blood of the Christ.

14 For he is our peace, the One making both one, and breaking down the barrier of the fence—the hostility—15 in his flesh voiding the Law of the commandments in ordinances, so that the two he should create in

himself into one new man, making peace. 16 And he should restore both in one body to God through the cross, by it putting to death the hostility. 17 And coming he proclaimed the good news: peace to you, the ones far off, and peace to those near. 18 For through him we both have the access by one Spirit to the Father.

19 So then you are no longer strangers and wandering, but are fellow citizens of the saints and of the household of God, 20 having been built upon the foundation of the apostles and prophets, the foundation cornerstone being Jesus Christ himself, 21 in whom the whole building, being joined together, is growing into a holy temple in the Lord, 22 in whom also you all are being built together for a habitation of God in the Spirit.[j]

EPHESIANS THREE

1 For this reason, I Paul, the prisoner of Christ Jesus for you gentiles—2 if indeed you have heard the dispensation of the grace of God that has been given to me toward you. 3 That by revelation he made known to me the hidden *things*, even as I had written before in brief, 4 by which you reading are able to understand my comprehension in the hidden *things* of Christ.

5 Which in other generations was not revealed to the sons of men, as now it has been supranaturally revealed to his holy apostles and prophets by the Spirit: 6 the gentiles are joint-heirs, and united in one body, and joint-partakers of the promise in Christ Jesus, through the good news; 7 of which I became a servant, according to the gift of the grace of God, given to me according to the working of his power.

8 To me, less than the least of all saints, was given this grace: to proclaim to the gentiles the unsearchable riches of the Christ; 9 and to enlighten all what is the dispensation of the hidden *things*, which was concealed from the ages in God, the One who created all things, 10 in order that now should be made known to the rulers and the authorities in the heavenly realms, through the church, the diverse wisdom of God, 11 according to the purpose of the ages, which he accomplished in Christ Jesus our Lord.

12 In whom we have boldness to speak and approach in confidence through faith in him. 13 Therefore I desire you do not become discouraged at my tribulations for you, which is your glory.

14 For this reason I bend my knees in reverence to the Father of our Lord Jesus Christ, 15 from whom his whole family in the heavens and on earth is named, 16 that he might give you according to the riches of his glory, with power to be strengthened through his Spirit in the inner man, 17 the Christ to take up residence through faith in your hearts, in love becoming rooted and grounded, 18 so that you should be fully able to comprehend, with all the saints,

what is the breadth and width and height and depth—19 to know then the love of Christ which surpasses knowledge, so that you may be filled unto all the fullness of God.

20 Now to the One who is able above all things to do more than we ask or think, according to the power working in us, 21 to him the glory in the church and in Christ Jesus, to all the generations of the age of the ages, truly.

EPHESIANS FOUR

1 I, therefore, the prisoner of the Lord, admonish you to conduct your life worthy of the calling to which you were called, 2 with all humility, without arrogance but delighting to serve, with patience toward others, bearing patiently one another in love, 3 being diligent to keep the unity of the Spirit in the bond of peace—4 one body and one Spirit, just as also you were called into one hope of your calling; 5 one Lord, one faith, one immersing; 6 one God and Father of all, who is over all and through all, and in all.

7 But to each of us has been given the grace according to the measure of the gift of Christ. 8 Therefore it says, "Having ascended on high, he led captive captivity, and gave gifts to men." 9 Now that he ascended, what does it imply but that he also descended into the lower parts of the earth? 10 The One having descended, the same is also the One having ascended above all the heavens, so that he should fill all.

11 And he indeed gave some apostles, but some prophets, but some evangelists, but some shepherd-teachers, 12 for the maturing of the saints for the work of service for building up of the body of Christ, 13 until we all should attain to the unity of the faith and of the knowledge of the Son of God, unto a mature person, to the measure of maturity in the fullness of Christ, 14 so that we should no longer be babies, fluctuating and carried here and there by every empty doctrine being taught by the trickery of men in craftiness, for the purpose of deceit.

15 But being truthful with love, we should grow up unto him in all things, who is the head, Christ, 16 from whom all the body—being joined together and united together by means of every supporting connection—according to the working of the measure of each individual part, the growth of the body it makes in itself to building up itself in love.

17 This therefore I say and testify in the Lord. You are no longer to conduct your manner of life[k] as also the gentiles are conducting their manner of life: in the futility of their mind, 18 their understanding darkened, being separated from the life of God through the ignorance that is in them, through the hardness of their heart. 19 Who being insensible to shame, have given themselves up to perversion, to work moral uncleanness with all insatiable desire.

20 But you do not in this way know Christ—21 if indeed him you have heard, and in him have been taught, just as is the truth in Jesus. 22 You are to renounce concerning the former way of life, the old man, which is corrupted according to its deceitful desires, 23 to be renewed now in the spirit of your mind, 24 and put on the new man, having been created according to God in righteousness and holiness of the truth.

25 Therefore, having renounced lying, let each one speak the truth with his neighbor, because we are members of one another. 26 When you are angry, take care that you do not sin. Do not let the sun go down upon your violent, seething, exasperated anger.[l] 27 Neither give opportunity to the devil. 28 The one stealing, let him no longer steal, but rather let him toil, working with his own hands what is good, so that he might impart something to the one in need.

29 Do not let any corrupt word out of your mouth, but any that is good for needful building up, so that it may give grace to those hearing. 30 And do not grieve the Holy Spirit of God, by whom you have been sealed for the day of redemption. 31 All bitterness, and rage, and anger, and controversy, and slander remove these from yourselves, along with all wickedness. 32 Instead be kind to one another, full of compassion, forgiving each other, as also God in Christ forgave you.

EPHESIANS FIVE

1 Be therefore followers of God, as beloved children, 2 and conduct your life in love, just as also Christ loved us and gave up himself for us, an offering and a sacrifice for a sweet aroma to God.

3 Now sexual immorality, and all impurity, or greediness,[m] let it not even be named among you, even as is proper in saints, 4 and shameful conduct, and foolish talking, or coarse joking, which are not fitting; but rather thankful speech.

5 For this you know, understanding that any who prostitute themselves sexually,[n] or an immoral person, or a covetous person (who is an idolater), has no inheritance in the kingdom of Christ and God. 6 Let none deceive you with empty words. For through these things comes the wrath of God upon the sons of disobedience. 7 Therefore, do not be partakers with them.

8 For you were at one time darkness—but now light in the Lord. Conduct yourselves as children of light. 9 For the fruit of the light consists in all goodness and righteousness and truth, 10 discovering what is well-pleasing to the Lord.

11 And do not participate in the unprofitable works of darkness, but rather also rebuke them. 12 For the things being done in secret by them, it is even shameful to speak. 13 But everything that is exposed becomes revealed by the light, for

everything shown openly is light. 14 Therefore it says, "Awake, you sleeping one, and rise up out from the dead, and the Christ will give you light."

15 Carefully take heed, then, how you conduct your life, not as unwise, but with wisdom, 16 redeeming the time because the times are morally, spiritually evil. 17 Because of this, do not be unwise, but understand what is the will of the Lord.

18 And do not be intoxicated with wine, in which there is dissipation, instead keep on being filled by the Spirit, 19 speaking to one another in psalms and hymns and spiritual songs, singing and making music in your heart to the Lord, 20 giving thanks at all times for all things in the name of our Lord Jesus Christ to the God and Father.

21 Submit yourselves to one another in reverence and awe of Christ. 22 The wives to their own husbands, as to the Lord, 23 because the husband is head of the wife, even as Christ is head of the church, he himself the Savior of the body. 24 But even as the church is in submission to Christ, even so the wives to their husbands in all things.

25 The husbands are to love their wives, even just as Christ loved the church and gave up himself for her, 26 so that he might sanctify her, having cleansed her by the washing of water with the Word, 27 in order that he should present to himself the church in glory, not having spot or wrinkle or any of such things, but that it should be holy and without blemish.

28 Even so husbands are obligated to love their wives as their own bodies. The one loving his wife loves himself. 29 For no one, at any time, hated his flesh, but he nurtures it and nourishes it, even as Christ the church, 30 because we are members of his body, [out of his flesh and out of his bones°]. 31 Because of this, a man will leave his father and mother and be joined to his wife, and the two will become one flesh.

32 This mystery is great, but I speak in reference to Christ and the church. 33 But you also, each in particular, so love his wife as himself, and the wife that she may respect and reverence the husband.

EPHESIANS SIX

1 Children, obey your parents in the Lord, for this is right. 2 Honor your father and mother, which is the first commandment with a promise, 3 that it may be well with you, and you will be long-lived upon the earth.

4 And fathers, do not provoke your children to anger, irritation, or resentment but bring them up in godly training and encouraging reproof of the Lord.

5 Slaves, obey your masters according to the flesh with respectful fear and reverence, in sincerity of your heart, as to Christ, 6 not for the sake of appearance

only, as those who please men, but as the servants of Christ, doing the will of God from the heart, 7 with goodwill serving as to the Lord and not to men, 8 knowing that each one, for whatever good he should do, this he will receive again from the Lord, whether slave or free.

9 And masters, do the same to them, giving up threatening, knowing that also the Master of them and of you is in the heavens, and he does not show favoritism.

10 From now on, be strong in the Lord and in his powerful strength. 11 Put on the complete armor of God, for you to be able to stand against the methods of the devil. 12 Because our struggle is not against blood and flesh, but against the rulers, against the authorities, against the lords of the darkness of this world, against the spiritual things of evil in the heavenly realms.

13 Because of these things, take up the complete armor of God, so that you may be able to resist in the evil day, and having done all things, to stand. 14 Stand, therefore, having your loins encircled with truth, and having put on the breastplate of righteousness, 15 and having shod your feet with the firm footing of the good news of peace, 16 with all taking up the shield of faith, with which you will be able to quench all the flaming arrows of the evil one. 17 And take the helmet of salvation, and the sword of the Spirit, which is the Word of God, 18 with all prayer and petition, praying in every season in the Spirit, and to that end, attentive with all perseverance and petition for all the saints, 19 and for me, that to me may be given speech in opening my mouth, by freely speaking to make known the mystery of the good news, 20 for which I am an ambassador with a chain, that in it I may be without constraint, as I ought to speak.

21 Now, that you may also know the things concerning me, what I am doing, Tychicus will make known to you, the beloved brother and faithful servant in the Lord, 22 whom I have sent to you for this very purpose, that you might know the things concerning us, and he may encourage your hearts.

23 Peace to the brethren and love with faith from God Father and Lord Jesus Christ. 24 Grace be with all those loving our Lord Jesus Christ in incorruptibility.

The Book of Philippians

The Book of Philippians was written from Rome, Italy, during Paul's first Roman imprisonment, ca. AD 61–63. Philippians is a friendship letter, written to people with whom Paul had a close relationship. No letter from Paul is free from instruction in doctrine and practice, but the focus of this letter is friendship and fellowship. His purpose was to strengthen the Philippian's relationship in Christ, as sufficient to do and endure through whatever God might require of his saved people. The theme is confidence in Christ in the midst of affliction.

PHILIPPIANS ONE

1 Paul and Timothy, servants of Christ Jesus, to all the saints in Christ Jesus there in Philippi with overseers[a] and deacons. 2 Grace to you and peace from God our Father, and Lord Jesus Christ.

3 I give thanks to my God upon every remembrance of you, 4 always in my every petition for all of you, making the petition with joy 5 for your participation in the good news from the first day until now, 6 being persuaded of this very thing, that the One having begun a good work in you will complete it until the day of Christ Jesus. 7 Accordingly, it is right for me to have this opinion about all of you, because I have you in my heart. In both my imprisonment and in the defense and confirmation of the good news, you are all partners with me of grace.

8 For God is my witness how I long after all of you in the affection of Christ Jesus. 9 And this I pray, that your love yet more and more may superabound in knowledge and all discernment, 10 for you to discern the things that are excellent, so that you may be pure and not taking or giving offense unto the day of Christ, 11 being filled with the fruit of righteousness that is because of Jesus Christ, to the glory and praise of God.

12 Now I want you to know, brethren, that the things concerning me have really served to the advancement of the good news, 13 so my imprisonment in Christ has become apparent to all the palace guard, and to all the rest. 14 And many of the brethren, trusting in the Lord by my imprisonment, dare fearlessly to abundantly speak the Word of God—15 indeed, some even from envy and strife, but some from goodwill, are proclaiming Christ; 16 the latter truly out of love, knowing that I am set for the defense of the good news; 17 but the former out of selfish ambition are proclaiming Christ, not sincerely, supposing to add trouble to my imprisonment.

18 What then? Except that in all ways, whether in appearance or in truth, Christ is proclaimed. And in this I rejoice. Yes, and I will rejoice. 19 For I know that this will turn out for me to deliverance[b] through your prayer and help, by the Spirit of Jesus Christ, 20 according to the earnest expectation and my hope that in nothing will I be put to shame, but

in all boldness, as always also now, Christ will be magnified in my body, whether by life or by death.

21 For me, to live *is* Christ and to die *is* gain. 22 And if to live in the flesh, this to me is fruitful work. And what I shall choose I know not. 23 I am constrained between the two, having the desire to depart and to be with Christ, for that is much better; 24 but to remain in the flesh is necessary for your sake. 25 And being persuaded of this, I know that I will remain and will continue with all of you for your progress and joy of the faith, 26 so that your boasting may abound to Christ Jesus in me through my coming again to you.

27 Only conduct yourselves worthy of the good news of Christ, so that whether I come and see you, or being absent, I may hear the things concerning you, that you are standing firm in one spirit, with one mind striving together for the faith of the good news, 28 and not being intimidated[c] in nothing by those opposing, which is to them proof of destruction; but to you of salvation, and this from God.

29 Because to you is given for sake of Christ, not only to believe in him, but also to suffer for him, 30 experiencing the same conflict such as you saw in me and now hear of in me.

PHILIPPIANS TWO

1 If, therefore, any encouragement in Christ, if any comfort of love, if any fellowship of spirit, if any affections and compassions, 2 fill my joy so that you may have the same mindset, having the same love, joined together in soul, minding the same thing, 3 not according to self-interest or according to empty pride, but in humility regarding one another as superior to themselves, 4 each not giving attention to the things of themselves, but each also the things of others.

5 Let this mindset be in you that was also in Christ Jesus, 6 who existing in the essential nature of God, did not regard equality with God for his own advantage, 7 but emptied himself, having taken on his own initiative and power the essential nature of a servant, being in the likeness of men, 8 and having been found in the physical form of men, he humbled himself, becoming obedient to death, even the death of the cross. 9 And therefore God highly exalted him, and gave to him the name above every name, 10 that at the name of Jesus every knee should bow, in the heavens and on earth and under earth, 11 and every tongue should confess that Jesus Christ is Lord, to the glory of God the Father.

12 Therefore, my beloved, even as you have always obeyed, not only in my presence, but now much more in my absence, work out your own salvation with fear and trembling. 13 For God is the One working in you both to will and to work according to his good pleasure.

14 Do all things without grumbling and contention, 15 so that you may be blameless and undefiled, children of God, without blemish in the midst of a generation wicked and perverted, among whom you shine as lights in the world, 16 holding onto the Word of life, that I may boast in the day of Christ that not in vain did I run, nor in vain toil. 17 But even if I am poured out on the sacrifice and service of your faith, I am glad and rejoice with you all. 18 And likewise you also be glad and rejoice with me.

19 But I hope in the Lord Jesus to soon send Timothy to you, that I may be encouraged knowing the things about you. 20 For I have no one like-minded, who will sincerely care for the things about you. 21 For all others are seeking their own things, not the things of Christ Jesus. 22 But you know how he has proved himself true, that as a father with a child he has served with me in the good news. 23 Therefore, I truly hope to send him immediately, when I shall know the things concerning me. 24 Now, I am persuaded in the Lord that also I myself will soon come.

25 Now I thought it necessary, Epaphroditus my brother and fellow worker and fellow soldier, now your messenger and minister to my needs, to send him to you, 26 since he was longing after you all, to see you face to face, and was depressed because you heard he was ill. 27 And truly he was ill, near to death, but God had mercy on him; but not on him alone, but also on me, that I should not have sorrow upon sorrow.

28 Therefore I have been diligent to send him, that in seeing him again you may rejoice. 29 Therefore, receive him in the Lord with all joy, and hold such in honor. 30 Because for the sake of the work of Christ he came near unto death, disregarding his life so that he might complete your lack of ministry toward me.

PHILIPPIANS THREE

1 As to the rest, my brethren, rejoice in the Lord. To write the same things to you, truly to me is not tedious, but for you is safe.

2 Discern[d] the dogs. Discern the evil workers. Discern the mutilators. 3 For we are the circumcision, those by God's Spirit serving[e] and glorying in Christ Jesus, and not putting trust in the flesh; 4 though indeed I have trust even in the flesh. If any other supposes to have trust in the flesh, I more—5 circumcision on the eighth day; of the nation Israel; of the tribe of Benjamin; a Hebrew of Hebrews; according to the Law a Pharisee; 6 according to zeal persecuting the church; according to righteousness which is in the Law becoming blameless.

7 But whatever things were of value to me, these things I regard, because of Christ, as having no value.[f] 8 But even more, I also count all things to have no value, because of the superior knowledge of Christ Jesus my Lord, because of whom I have valued all things as

lost, and esteem them worthless,⁹ that I may gain Christ 9 and be found in him, not having my own righteousness, which is from *the* Law, but through the faithfulness of Christ, the righteousness from God on the basis of faith; 10 to know him, and the power of his resurrection, and the fellowship of his sufferings, being conformed to his death, 11 if by any means I may attain to the resurrection from the dead. 12 Not that I have already obtained, or already reached the goal. But I am pursuing, if also I may lay hold of that for which also I was laid hold of by Christ Jesus.

13 Brethren, I do not consider myself to have laid hold. But one thing: truly forgetting the things behind, now reaching to things forward, 14 I pursue toward the goal for the prize of the heavenly calling of God in Christ Jesus. 15 Therefore, as many as are mature should be of this mindset; and if you are differently minded in anything, even this God will reveal to you. 16 Nevertheless, in that which we have attained, by the same to conduct our manner of life.

17 With others be followers of me, brethren, and give attention to those so living, as you have us for a pattern to be followed. 18 For many are conducting their lives— of whom often I have told you, and now even weeping I say—as enemies of the cross of Christ, 19 whose end is ruin, whose god is the belly, and glory in their shame, minding those earthly things. 20 For our citizenship exists in the heavens, from where we also await a Savior, the Lord Jesus Christ, 21 who will transform our body of humiliation, to be conformed to the body of his glory, according to his efficient ability even to subdue all things to himself.

PHILIPPIANS FOUR

1 Therefore my brethren, beloved and longed for, my joy and crown, persevere in this manner in the Lord, beloved. 2 Euodia I exhort and Syntyche I exhort: be of the same mindset in the Lord. 3 Yes, I ask you also, true fellow laborer, aid these women, who labored together with me in the good news, also with Clement and the rest of the fellow laborers, whose names are in the book of life.

4 Rejoice in the Lord always. Again I say, rejoice! 5 Let your clemency be known to all men: the Lord is near. 6 Be anxious about not even one thing or person,ʰ but in everything by prayer and petition on behalf of yourself and others, with thanksgiving, make your requests known to God. 7 And the peace of God surpassing all understanding will guard your hearts and your minds in Christ Jesus.

8 As to the rest, brethren, whatever is truthful, whatever reputable, whatever just, whatever pure, whatever acceptable, whatever of good report—if any virtue and if any praiseworthy— think on these things. 9 What also you have learned, and have received, and have heard, and

have seen in me, practice these things. And the God of peace will be with you.

10 Now I rejoiced greatly in the Lord, because you have again caused your caring for me to flourish. In which also you were mindful, but were lacking opportunity. 11 Not that I speak of being in need. For I have learned in that which I am to be satisfied. 12 And I know how to be low, and I know how to have more than enough. In everything and in all things I have learned also to be filled and to be hungry, and to have more than enough and to suffer need. 13 *In* all things I have strength in the One strengthening me.[i] 14 Nevertheless you did well, participating with me in my troubles.

15 Now you also know, Philippians, that in the beginning of the good news, when I went out from Macedonia, not one church had communicated with me concerning giving and receiving, but you only. 16 Because even in Thessalonica, both once and twice, you sent for my needs. 17 Not that I seek after the gift, but I seek after the fruit abounding to your account. 18 But I have all things and abound. I am full, having received from Epaphroditus the things from you, a sweet-smelling odor, a sacrifice acceptable and well-pleasing to God. 19 And my God will supply all your needs, according to his riches in glory in Christ Jesus.

20 Now to our God and Father, glory to the ages of the ages. Amen. 21 Greet every saint in Christ Jesus. The brethren with me greet you. 22 All the saints greet you, but especially those from Caesar's household. 23 The grace of the Lord Jesus Christ be with your spirit.

The Book of Colossians

The Book of Colossians was written ca. AD 62 from Rome, Italy, during Paul's first Roman imprisonment. Paul had never meet these people or ministered in the tri-city region of Colossae, Laodicea, Hierapolis. The occasion for the letter was apparently news from Epaphras (4:12), a member of the Colossian church (and founding member, 1:7?), that Jewish and gentile religionists were influencing doctrine and practice in the church at Colossae. The letter was carried by Tychicus and Onesimus (a slave returning to his master Philemon), Colossians 4:7, 9. The theme is freedom in Christ from the things of the world.

COLOSSIANS ONE

1 Paul, apostle of Christ Jesus through God's will, and Timothy the brother, 2 to the saints in Colossae, who[a1] are faithful brothers and sisters[a2] in Christ. Grace to you and peace from God our Father.

3 We are always giving thanks God, the Father of our Lord Jesus Christ,[b] at all times praying for you, 4 having heard of your faith in Christ Jesus and the love which you show toward all the saints 5 on account of the hope laid up for you in the heavens; which you heard of before in the word of the truth of the good news, 6 which has come to you, just as also in all the world it is bearing fruit and increasing, just as also among you, from the day you heard and came to know the grace of God in truth, 7 just as you learned from Epaphras, our beloved fellow-servant, who is faithful for you, a servant of Christ, 8 and the one who informed us of your love in spirit.

9 That is why we also, from the day we heard, have not ceased constantly praying for you, and always asking that you may be filled with the knowledge of his will in all wisdom and spiritual understanding 10 to behave[c] worthily of the Lord, pleasing in every way, bearing fruit in every good work, and increasing in the knowledge of God, 11 being empowered with all power according to his glorious power for all endurance and patience.

With joy 12 giving thanks to the Father, the one having qualified us for the share of the inheritance of the saints in the light, 13 he who has delivered us out of the authority of darkness and has transferred us into the kingdom of the Son of his love, 14 in whom we have redemption, the forgiveness of sins.[d]

15 He is the image of the invisible God, the firstborn of all creation, 16 because in him all things were created in the heavens and on the earth, the visible and the invisible, whether thrones or dominions or rulers or authorities— all things stand created[e] through him and for him.

17 He himself is before all things, and all things hold together in him; 18 and he is the head of the body, the church. He is the beginning, firstborn from the dead,

in order that he might be in all things ever preeminent. 19 Because in him God was well-pleased to have all his fullness dwell, 20 and through him to reconcile all things to him, making peace by the blood of his cross (through him), whether the things on the earth or the things in the heavens.

21 And you, who were at one time alienated and enemies in the mind in the works that are evil, 22 now he has reconciled in the body of his flesh though his death, to present you holy and without blemish and unaccused before him, 23 provided you habitually persevere in the faith, established and steadfast and not shifting from the hope of the good news, which you heard proclaimed in all creation under heaven, of which I Paul became a servant.

24 Now I rejoice in my sufferings for your sake, and I make good what is lacking of the afflictions for Christ in my flesh for the sake of his body, which is the church, 25 of which I became a servant according to the commission of God which he gave me toward you to declare fully the Word of God, 26 the secret which was hidden from the ages and from the generations but is now revealed to his saints, 27 to whom God desired to make known what is the wealth of the glory of the hidden *things*[f1] among the peoples, which is, Christ in you, the hope of glory, 28 whom we preach, warning every person and teaching every person, in all wisdom, in order that we might present every person complete in Christ. 29 For this also I constantly labor, always persevering according to his energy operating effectively in me, empowering me.

COLOSSIANS TWO

1 For I want you to know how great a struggle I am having on your behalf, and those in Laodicea, and as many as have not seen my face in the flesh, 2 that their hearts might be encouraged, being united in love, and for all riches of complete understanding, for knowledge of the hidden *things* of God—of Christ [f2] —3 in whom all the treasures of wisdom and knowledge are hidden. 4 These things I say that no one may deceive you by persuasive speech. 5 For though I am absent in flesh, yet in spirit I am with you, rejoicing and seeing your orderly life, and the steadfastness of your faith in Christ.

6 So then, just as you accepted Christ Jesus the Lord, conduct your life in him, 7 rooted and being built up in him and confirmed in the faith, just as you were taught, abounding richly in thanksgiving.

8 Beware lest any person will rob[g] you of the riches of Christ through philosophy and empty deceit derived from the tradition of humankind, according to the elemental principles of the world, and not in accordance with Christ. 9 For in him dwells all the fullness of the deity in bodily form, 10 and in him you are filled, who is the head of all rule and authority.

11 In him also you were circumcised with a circumcision not made with hands in the stripping off of the body of the flesh by the circumcision of the Christ, 12 having been buried with him in immersion, in whom also you were raised with him through your faith in the effective power exercised by God,[h] who raised him from the dead.

13 And you, when you were dead in your sins and in the uncircumcision of your flesh, he made you alive with him, having forgiven us all our sins. 14 He cancelled the bond that testified against us[i] with its decrees, which was opposed to us, and has taken it away by nailing it to the cross. 15 He stripped away the power of the rulers and authorities, publicly shaming them, leading them in his triumph.

16 Therefore let no person pass judgment on you in regard to food and drink, or a holy day or new moon or sabbaths, 17 which are a shadow of the things that were to come, but the reality is Christ. 18 Let no one disqualify you, taking pleasure in humility and worship of the *celestial messengers*[j1] (which he has seen, prying into?[j2]), conceited without cause by his mind of flesh, 19 and not holding onto the head, from whom the whole body, supplied and held together by its joints and ligaments, grows with the growth of God.

20 If, as is true, you have died with Christ and thus were freed from the elemental principles of the world, why do you subject yourself to regulations as though living in the world? 21 Do not handle, neither taste, nor touch— 22 things which are all destined for destruction in being used—in accordance with the precepts and teachings of humankind. 23 Such things indeed may seem wise in self-chosen worship and humility and ascetic discipline; they are not of any value whatsoever against satisfying the flesh.

COLOSSIANS THREE

1 If then you have been raised with Christ, seek the things above, where Christ is, sitting at the right hand of God. 2 Constantly fix your thoughts on[k] what is above, not what is on the earth. 3 For you died, and so your life has been hidden with Christ in God. 4 Whenever Christ—your life—may be revealed, then also you along with him will be revealed in glory.

5 Therefore put to death the on-the-earth members: sexual immorality, moral uncleanness, sensual craving, debased passion, and the craving to have more, which is idolatry, 6 on account of which God's wrath is coming on the sons of disobedience,[l] 7 in which you also conducted yourself once, living in that way.

8 But now also put off all this: chronic anger, angry outbursts, malicious spite, abusive language, obscene speech out of your mouth. 9 Do not lie to one another, because you have put off the old nature, with its conduct, 10 and

have put on the new, which is constantly being renewed in knowledge, in conformity with the image of its creator, 11 where there is not Greek and Jew, circumcision and uncircumcision, Barbarian, Scythian, slave, free; but Christ the all and in all.

12 Clothe yourselves therefore, as God's chosen, holy and loved by him, with a compassionate heart, kindness, humility, gentleness, long-suffering; 13 be tolerant of one another, and be forgiving each other. If, as does happen, anyone has cause for complaint against another, even as also the Lord has forgiven you, so you also; 14 but in addition to all these, add love, which is the bond that perfects, 15 and let the peace of God[m] rule in your hearts, to which also you were called as one body; and make it your habit to be thankful. 16 Let the word of Christ live in you richly, teaching and admonishing each other in all wisdom, singing with psalms, hymns, spiritual songs in thankfulness in your hearts to God.[n] 17 And everything that you might do in word or in deed, do all in the name of Lord Jesus, as you give thanks to God the Father through him.

18 Wives, be subject to your husbands, as is appropriate in the Lord. 19 Husbands, keep on loving your wives, and do not become embittered toward them. 20 Children, obey the parents in all things, for such behavior is proper in the Lord.[o] 21 Fathers, do not antagonize[p] your children, in order that they may not become discouraged. 22 Slaves, obey in all things earthly masters, not with external appearances, to please people, but with sincerity of heart, because you reverence the Lord.[q]

23 Whatever you are doing, work at it with enthusiasm,[r] as to the Lord and not to men, 24 knowing that from the Lord you will receive the reward of the inheritance; you serve the Lord Christ. 25 For the person doing wrong will be repaid for the wrong he did; and there is no partiality.

COLOSSIANS FOUR

1 Masters, treat your slaves justly and fairly, knowing that you also have a Master in heaven.[s]

2 Persist in prayer, being watchful in it with thanksgiving, 3 praying at the same time on our behalf, that God may open to us a door for the message, to speak the hidden *things* of Christ, on account of which also I am in prison, 4 that I should make it known, as it is my duty to speak.

5 Conduct yourselves with wisdom toward those outside, making the most of every opportunity.[t] 6 Let your speech be with grace, seasoned with salt, so that you may know in what way to answer each person.

7 Tychicus will make known to you all my circumstances. He is a beloved brother and faithful servant, and serving with me in the Lord. 8 I have sent him to you for this very purpose, that you may know how we are, and he might

encourage your hearts; 9 with Onesimus, the faithful and beloved brother, who is one of you. All the things here they will make known to you.

10 Aristarchus, my fellow prisoner greets you; and Mark, Barnabas' cousin (concerning whom you have received instructions; if he comes to you, welcome him); 11 also Jesus, who is called Justus. These are the only ones of the circumcision who are fellow workers for the kingdom of God; they have been a comfort to me.

12 Epaphras, who is one of you, greets you. He is a servant of Jesus Christ, constantly striving for you in prayers, that you might stand mature and fully assured in all the will of God. 13 For I bear him witness that he has labored much for you, and those in Laodicea, and those in Hierapolis. 14 Luke the beloved physician greets you, and Demas. 15 Greet the brethren in Laodicea, also Nympha and the church in her house.

16 And when the letter has been read among you, cause it to be read also in the Laodicean church, and you read the one from Laodicea. 17 And say to Archippus, "Pay attention to the ministry that you have received in the Lord, that you should fulfill it."

18 This greeting is in my own hand—Paul. Remember my imprisonment. Grace be with you.

The Book of First Thessalonians

The Book of First Thessalonians was the first of Paul's extant letters, written ca. AD 50–51. The letter was probably written from Corinth. In this book we see in initial form doctrines expressed more fully in later letters. The book is about how to live the Christian life. The doctrines in 1 Thessalonians are sin, the Savior, salvation, experiential sanctification, repentance, and eschatology. The Thessalonians were well instructed believers needing only time and experience to develop the consistency in doctrine and practice that would establish them in the faith.

FIRST THESSALONIANS ONE

1 Paul and Silas[a1] and Timothy, to the church of Thessalonians in God Father and Lord Jesus Christ. Grace to you and peace.[a2]

2 We give thanks to God always concerning all of you, making mention in our prayers, 3 at every opportunity[b1] remembering how your faith works, and your love labors, and your perseverance in the hope[b2] of our Lord Jesus Christ, in the presence of our God and Father, 4 knowing beloved brethren your election by God, 5 because our good news came not to you only in word, but also in power and in the Holy Spirit and much conviction, just as you know what we were among you for your benefit.

6 And you became followers of us, and of the Lord, receiving the word in much tribulation, with joy of the Holy Spirit, 7 so as you became an example to all the ones in Macedonia believing, and in Achaia. 8 Because from you the word of the Lord has been proclaimed, not only in Macedonia and Achaia, but in every place your faith toward God has gone out, so as there is no need to have us to say anything. 9 Because they themselves declare about us what entrance we had with you, and how you turned to God from idols to serve the living and true God, 10 and to await his Son from the heavens, whom he raised out from the dead, Jesus, the one delivering us from the coming wrath.

FIRST THESSALONIANS TWO

1 For you yourselves know, brethren, that our coming to you has not been in vain. 2 But, just as you know, we having previously suffered and been mistreated in Philippi, we were bold in our God to speak to you the good news of God, in much conflict. 3 Because our exhortation is not of error, nor of impurity, nor in deceit. 4 But just as we have been proven worthy by God to be entrusted with the good news, so we speak, not as pleasing men, but God, the one examining our hearts.

5 Because not at any time were we with a word of flattery, just as you know, not with a pretense for greed—God is witness. 6 Not seeking glory from men: not from you; not from

others.

We could have been burdensome as Christ's apostles, 7 but we were gentle in your midst, as a nursing mother might cherish her own children. 8 So, being affectionate toward you, we were pleased to have imparted to you not only the good news of God, but also our own lives, because you have become beloved to us.

9 Because you remember, brethren, our labor and toil—working night and day so as not to burden any one of you—we proclaimed to you the good news of God. 10 You and God are witnesses, how holily and righteously and blamelessly we were toward those believing. 11 Even as you know, each one of you, as a father his own children, 12 encouraging you and comforting and solemnly charging you[c] to live lives worthy of God who calls you into his kingdom and glory.

13 And because of this we also give thanks to God at every opportunity that, having received the word of God, hearing it from us, you accepted it not as the word of men, but even as it truly is, the word of God, which is constantly working in you who believe. 14 Because you, brethren, became followers of the churches of God that are in Judea in Christ Jesus. For you also suffered the same as them, from your own countrymen, as they also from the Jews. 15 Who, both the Lord Jesus having killed, and their own prophets, and having persecuted us, and not pleasing God, and set against all men, 16 hindering us to speak to the gentiles that they might be saved, so as to always fill up their sins. Now has come upon them the wrath to the end.

17 But we, brethren, having been bereaved of you for a short time, in face not in heart, were exceedingly eager, with great desire, to see your face. 18 For this reason we intended to come to you—truly I Paul, both once and twice—and Satan hindered us. 19 Because who is our hope or joy or crown of rejoicing? Is it not even you before our Lord Jesus at his coming? 20 Because you are our glory and joy!

FIRST THESSALONIANS THREE

1 Therefore, no longer restraining the impulse,[d] we thought it good to be left behind alone in Athens, 2 and we sent Timothy, our brother and fellow worker[e] of God in the good news of Christ, to strengthen and to encourage you to benefit your faith, 3 that no one be disturbed in these tribulations. Because you know yourselves that for this we are destined.

4 For even when we were with you, we forewarned you that we are about to suffer affliction; and you know how also it did come to pass. 5 Because of this I also, no longer enduring, sent in order to know your faith, lest in some way the one tempting you had tempted, and our labor would be in vain.

6 But now Timothy has come to us from you. He has brought good news to us of your faith and love, and that you always remember us well, longing to see us, just as also we you. 7 On account of this we were encouraged, brethren, as to you, in all our distress and tribulation, through your faith. 8 Because now we live if you are standing firm in the Lord. 9 For what thanksgiving are we able to give to God about you, in return for all the joy that we rejoice because of you before our God 10 night and day, earnestly imploring for us to see your face and to supply the things lacking in your faith?

11 Now our God and Father himself and our Lord Jesus Christ direct our way to you. 12 And the Lord make you to increase, and to abound in love toward one another, and toward all, just as also we toward you, 13 so he may strengthen your hearts blameless in holiness before our God and Father at the coming of our Lord Jesus Christ with all his saints.

FIRST THESSALONIANS FOUR

1 As to the rest[f] then, brethren, we implore and exhort you in the Lord Jesus that, just as you received from us the manner in which you ought to live your life and to please God, and just as you are living your life, so you should even more. 2 Because you know what instructions we gave you through the Lord Jesus.

3 For this is the will of God, your sanctification: you are to abstain from sexual immorality. 4 Each of you is to know how to control his or her sexuality[g] in holiness and honor: 5 not in the passion of lust, as also the peoples[h] not knowing God; 6 not to overstep the limits in the matter of his brother. Because the Lord is avenging concerning all these things, just as also we told you before, and repeatedly exhorted. 7 For God has not called us to moral impurity, but to holiness. 8 The result is, the one rejecting this despises not man but God, the one also giving his Holy Spirit to you.

9 Now about brotherly love, you have no need for me to write to you, for you yourselves are taught by God to love one another. 10 And you are doing this toward all the brethren, all the ones in Macedonia. But we exhort you, brethren, to abound much more, 11 and to aspire to live quietly, and to attend to your own, and to work with your own hands, just as we commanded you, 12 so that your manner of living may be respectable toward those outside, and you may not have need of anything.

13 Now we do not want you to be ignorant, brethren, about those having fallen asleep, so that you should not be grieved, even just as the rest—those not having hope. 14 Because if we believe that Jesus died and rose again, so also God will bring with him those having fallen asleep through Jesus.

15 For this we declare to you by the word of the Lord, that we

the living remaining unto the coming of the Lord, shall never no never precede those having fallen asleep. 16 Because the Lord himself, by a loud command, by the voice of an archangel, and by the trumpet of God, will descend from heaven, and the dead in Christ will rise first. 17 Then we the living remaining, together with them, will be caught up in the clouds for the meeting of the Lord in the air. And so always with the Lord we will be. 18 Therefore, encourage one another with these words.

FIRST THESSALONIANS FIVE

1 Now about the times and the seasons, brethren, you have no need to be written to you. 2 Because yourselves fully know that the day of the Lord, as a thief in the night, in this manner comes. 3 For when they might say, "Peace and security," then unexpected destruction comes upon them, just as to her having the labor pains in the womb; and never no never might they escape.

4 But you, brethren, are not in darkness, that the day may come upon you like a thief. 5 Because you all are sons of light, and sons of day. We are not of night, nor of darkness.

6 So then we should not sleep as others, but we should give attention and we should be sober-minded. 7 Because those sleeping, by night sleep; and those becoming drunk, by night get drunk. 8 But we, being of the day, should be sober-minded, having put on the breastplate of faith and love, and the helmet, the hope of salvation. 9 Because God has not appointed us for wrath, but for obtaining deliverance[j] through our Lord Jesus Christ, 10 the one having died for us, so that whether we might watch or we might sleep, we may live together with him. 11 Therefore encourage one another, and build up one another, just as also you are doing.

12 Now we implore you, brethren, to know those laboring among you, and set over you in the Lord and exhort you, 13 and to regard them more abundantly in love, on account of their work. 14 Now we exhort you, brethren, to admonish the disorderly, encourage the fainthearted, support the weak, be long-suffering toward all.

15 See that no one to anyone has repaid evil for evil, but always pursue the good toward one another, and toward all; 16 rejoice always; 17 pray every time an opportunity presents itself; 18 in everything give thanks: for this is the will of God in Christ Jesus toward you. 19 Do not hinder[j] the Spirit. 20 Do not reject prophecies, 21 but prove all things to be worthy, or not. Hold fast to the good. 22 Abstain from every form of evil.

23 Now, may the God of peace himself completely sanctify you, and your whole spirit and soul and body be kept blameless with respect to the coming of the Lord Jesus Christ. 24 The one calling you is faithful, who also will do it. 25

Brethren, pray for us. 26 Greet all the brethren with a holy kiss. 27 I charge you by the Lord, this letter to be read to all the brethren. 28 The grace of our Lord Jesus Christ be with you.

The Book of Second Thessalonians

The Book of Second Thessalonians was written ca. AD 51–52. The letter was probably written from Corinth. The occasion for the letter was doctrinal error concerning the relationship between the rapture of the New Testament church (2:1–2) and the coming man of sin (2:3–4). Some person, whether in person or by letter supposedly from Paul, by false revelation had told the Thessalonians the rapture had come, they missed it, and their ongoing persecutions were proof they were in the times of the man of sin. Paul also encourages believers in the midst of persecution, chapter 1, and gives counsel on some practical issues of living the Christian life, chapter 3.

SECOND THESSALONIANS ONE

1 Paul and Silas[a] and Timothy, to the church of the Thessalonians in God our Father and the Lord Jesus Christ. 2 Grace to you, and peace from God our Father and Lord Jesus Christ.

3 We are obligated to always thank God concerning you, brethren, even as is suitable, because your faith is flourishing, and the love of each of you to one another abounds. 4 Accordingly, we ourselves boast in you in the churches of God, about your perseverance and faith in all your persecutions, and in the tribulations that you are patiently bearing, 5 proof of the righteous judgment of God. For you have been counted worthy of the kingdom of God, for which you also suffer, 6 for it is righteous with God to repay with affliction those afflicting you.

7 And to you being afflicted, rest with us at the revealing of the Lord Jesus Christ from heaven with his mighty messengers, 8 in a flame of fire inflicting vengeance on those not knowing God and on those not obeying the good news of our Lord Jesus. 9 These will suffer the penalty of eternal ruin[b] away from the presence of the Lord and from the glory of his power, 10 when he shall come to be glorified in his saints, and to be admired among all those having believed, because our testimony to you was believed in that day.

11 For which also we pray always concerning you, that our God may reckon you worthy of the calling, and he may fulfill every good pleasure of goodness and the work of the faith with power, 12 so that the name of our Lord Jesus may be glorified in you, and you in him, according to the grace of our God and Lord Jesus Christ.

SECOND THESSALONIANS TWO

1 Now we implore you brethren, by the coming of our Lord Jesus Christ and our gathering together unto him, 2 for you not quickly to be wavering in mind nor be disturbed, neither by spirit, nor by word, nor by letter, as if by us, as though the day of the Lord is present.[c]

3 No one should deceive you in any way, because not until the

departure[d] shall have come first, and the man of lawlessness shall have been revealed—the son of destruction, 4 the one opposing and exalting himself above every (so-called) god or object of worship—so as to sit down in the temple of God, showing himself that he is God.

5 Do you not remember that, still being with you, I was saying these things to you? 6 And now that *which is* restraining you know, for him to be revealed in his time. 7 For the mystery of lawlessness is already at work, only the one is restraining at present until he might be out of the midst.

8 And then the lawless one will be revealed, whom the Lord Jesus will publicly execute with the breath of his mouth and will put an end to him by the appearance of his coming; 9 him whose coming is according to the working of Satan in every power, and with signs, and in wonders of falsehood, 10 and in every deceit of unrighteousness unto those perishing against the love of the truth they do not receive in order for them to be saved. 11 And on account of this, God will send to them a work of delusion for them to believe what is false, 12 in order that all those not having believed the truth, but delighting in unrighteousness, should be judged.

13 And we ought to give thanks to God always concerning you, brethren beloved by the Lord, because God did choose you from the beginning to salvation,[e] in sanctification of the Spirit, and by belief of the truth. 14 To this also he called you through our good news, to obtain the glory of our Lord Jesus Christ. 15 So then, brethren, stand firm and hold fast to the teachings that you were taught, whether by word or by letter from us.

16 Now our Lord Jesus Christ himself, and our God and Father, the one having loved us and given us eternal comfort and good hope by grace, 17 may he encourage your hearts and strengthen them in every work and good word.

SECOND THESSALONIANS THREE

1 For the rest, brethren, pray for us, that the word of the Lord may spread quickly and may be glorified, just as also with you. 2 And that we may be delivered from perverse and evil men; for not all are of the faith. 3 Now faithful is the Lord, who will strengthen and keep you from the evil.

4 Now we are persuaded in the Lord as to you, that the things we command, you are both doing and you will do. 5 Now may the Lord direct your hearts into the love of God and into the steadfastness of Christ.

6 Now we command you, brethren, in the name of our Lord Jesus Christ, you are to withdraw from every brother living disorderly and not according to the teaching that you received from us. 7 Because you yourselves know how you ought to follow our example,

because we were not disorderly among you, 8 nor did we freely eat bread from anyone, but in labor and hardship, working night and day, to not be a burden to any of you. 9 Not that we do not have the right, but that we may offer ourselves as a model to you, for you to follow our example.

10 For even when we were with you this we commanded you: that if anyone is not willing to work, neither let him eat. 11 Because we hear some are living disorderly among you, not working at all, but being busybodies. 12 Now to such we warn and exhort by our Lord Jesus Christ, so that working with quietness they may eat their own bread.

13 Now you, brethren, should not grow weary in well-doing. 14 And if anyone does not obey our word through this letter, take notice of this one not to keep company with him, so that he may be ashamed. 15 And yet, do not esteem him an enemy, but admonish him as a brother.

16 Now may the Lord of peace himself give you peace through everything in every way. The Lord be with all of you. 17 This greeting is in my own hand, "Paul," which is the sign in every letter. In this manner I write. 18 The grace of our Lord Jesus Christ be with all of you.

The Book of First Timothy

The Book of First Timothy was written ca. AD 66–67. Paul was released from his first Roman imprisonment ca. AD 63. Between AD 63 and AD 66 he made promised visits, and I believe traveled into Spain. Paul was in Macedonia when he wrote this letter. The occasion was a previous conversation, see 1:3. Essentially the letter tells Timothy how to be a pastor of a local New Testament church, instructing Timothy on both the positive and negative aspects of the work.

FIRST TIMOTHY ONE

1 Paul, apostle of Christ Jesus according to the command of God our Savior and of Christ Jesus our hope, 2 to Timothy, a true child in the faith: grace, mercy, peace from God Father and Christ Jesus our Lord.

3 Just as I urged you to remain in Ephesus—I going to Macedonia[a]—so that you may warn certain not to teach different,[b] 4 nor to give heed to myths and endless genealogies, which bring endless arguments, rather than the administration of God's purpose,[c] which is by faith.

5 Now the goal of instruction is love out of a pure heart and good conscience and sincere faith. 6 From which some, having wrong goals, have turned aside to empty conversation, 7 desiring to be teachers of the Law, not understanding neither what they are saying, nor concerning that which they confidently affirm.

8 Now we know that the Law is good, if one uses it lawfully, 9 knowing this, that the Law is not made for a righteous one, but for the lawless, and disobedient to authority, the godless and sinful, the unholy and profane, the ones abusing fathers and mothers,[d] for man-slayers, 10 the sexually immoral, homosexuals, enslavers, liars, perjurers, and if any other thing opposed to sound teaching, 11 according to the good news of the glory of the blessed God, with which I have been entrusted.

12 I am thankful for the one giving me strength, Christ Jesus our Lord, that he reckoned me faithful, appointing me to serve, 13 formerly being a reviler, and a persecutor, and insolent. But I was shown mercy (because being ignorant I did it in unbelief), 14 the exceedingly abundant grace of our Lord, with faith and love that are in Christ Jesus.

15 Faithful is the saying and worthy of complete acceptance, that Christ Jesus came into the world to save sinners, of whom I am first. 16 But on account of this I was shown mercy: that first in me Jesus Christ might reveal unlimited patience, as a pattern for those about to believe on him to life eternal. 17 Now to the king of the ages, the incorruptible,[e] invisible, only God be honor and glory to the ages of the ages. Amen.

18 This charge I entrust to

you, my child Timothy, according to the prophecies previously made about you, that with respect to them you may war the good warfare, 19 holding faith and a good conscience, which some having cast away, concerning the faith, are shipwrecked, 20 among whom are Hymenaeus and Alexander, whom I have delivered to Satan that they may be disciplined not to speak slanders.

FIRST TIMOTHY TWO

1 Therefore I desire, first of all, petitions be made—prayers, intercessions, thanksgivings—on behalf of all persons, 2 for kings and all those being in authority, so that we may lead a tranquil and undisturbed life, in all godliness and decency. 3 This is good and acceptable before our Savior, God, 4 who would have all persons to be saved and to come to the full knowledge of the truth.

5 For one God, and one mediator of God and men, the man Christ Jesus, 6 the one having given himself as a ransom for all, the testimony in its appointed time, 7 for which I was appointed herald and apostle—I am speaking the truth, I do not lie—a teacher of the gentiles in faith and truth. 8 Therefore I desire the people in every place to pray, lifting up holy hands without anger and contention.

9 In the same manner also women, respectable in clothing, with modesty and moderation, should adorn themselves not with fashionable hairstyles,[f] or gold, or pearls, or expensive clothing, 10 but with what is proper to women professing fear of God, through good works. 11 Let a woman learn in quietness in all submissiveness. 12 But I do not permit a woman to teach, nor to use authority over a man, but to be in quietness. 13 For Adam was first formed, then Eve. 14 And Adam was not deceived, but the woman having been deceived came into transgression. 15 But she will be delivered through childbearing,[g] if they abide in faith and love and holiness, with moderation of her desires.

FIRST TIMOTHY THREE

1 Trustworthy this saying: if anyone aspires to the office of overseer, he desires an honorable work. 2 Therefore the overseer must be above reproach, to be a one-wife kind of husband,[h] circumspect, self-restrained, orderly, hospitable, apt to teach, 3 not abusing wine, not contentious, but appropriate, not quarrelsome, not a lover of money, 4 ruling his own home well, having children in subjection, with all respect.

5 But if one knows not how to rule his own home, how will he care for the church of God? 6 Not newly saved or instructed, so that not lifted up with pride with the result that he might fall into the condemnation of the devil. 7 Now he must also have a good testimony from those outside, so that he might not fall into disgrace and the schemes of the devil.

8 In the same manner deacons *are to be* respectable, not

speaking deceitfully, not given to much wine, not eager for gain, 9 holding to the mystery of the faith with a pure conscience. 10 And these, now let them first be examined, then let them serve, being unaccused. 11 In the same manner women must be reputable, not slanderers, self-controlled, faithful in all things.

12 Let deacons be one-wife kind of husbands, ruling their children well and their own homes. 13 For those having served well gain a good standing for themselves, and great boldness in the faith that is in Christ Jesus.

14 I write these things to you, hoping to come to you in a short time. 15 But if I should delay, so that you may know how one must conduct oneself in the household of God, which is the church of the living God, the pillar and support of the truth. 16 And confessedly, great is the mystery of godliness: who was revealed in flesh, justified in spirit, seen by messengers, proclaimed among multitudes, believed on in the world, taken up in glory.

FIRST TIMOTHY FOUR

1 But the Spirit distinctly says that in latter times, some will forsake the faith, assenting to deceitful spirits and teachings of demons, 2 in hypocrisy of liars, their own conscience having been hardened, 3 forbidding to marry, to abstain from foods that God created for partaking with thanksgiving by the faithful and those knowing the truth. 4 For every creature of God is good, and nothing is to be rejected, being received with thanksgiving, 5 for it is cleansed by the Word of God and prayer.

6 Bringing these things before the brethren, you will be a good servant of Christ Jesus, becoming skilled in the words of the faith and of the good teaching that you have carefully attended. 7 But refuse profane and silly fables.

Rather, train yourself to godliness. 8 For bodily exercise is of a little profit, but godliness is profitable for everything, having a promise of the present life and of the coming. 9 Trustworthy the saying and worthy of full acceptance. 10 For this we are weary with toil and fight, because we have hope upon the living God, who is the Savior of all persons, especially of believers.

11 Command these things and teach. 12 Let no one despise your youth, but be a pattern for the believers in speech, in conduct, in love, in faith, in purity. 13 Until I come, give heed to the public reading of Scripture, to exhortation, to teaching. 14 Do not neglect the gift in you, which was given to you through prophecy, with laying on of the hands of the elders. 15 These things ponder, be committed to them, so that your progress may be evident to all. 16 Give heed to yourself and to the teaching. Continue in them, for doing this, you will deliver both yourself and those hearing you.

FIRST TIMOTHY FIVE

1 Do not rebuke an elder, but exhort him as a father, younger men as brethren, 2 elder women as mothers, younger women as sisters—in all purity.

3 Honor widows—those genuinely widows. 4 But if any widow has children or descendants, let them learn first to respect and honor their own household, and return to the parents *the good they received as children*. For these things are pleasing before God.

5 Now she who is genuinely a widow, and being left alone, has hope in God, and continues in supplications and prayers night and day. 6 But she living in self-indulgence, though living has died.

7 And these things command, so that they may be free from blame or reproach. 8 Now if anyone does not provide for his own and especially his household, he has denied the faith, and he is worse than an unbeliever.

9 Do not enroll a widow less than sixty years, having been a one-husband kind of wife,j 10 having borne witness with good works, if she has raised up children, if she has practiced hospitality toward strangers, if she has washed saint's feet, if she has relieved those distressed, if she has been devoted to every good work.

11 But younger widows refuse: for when they desire for a life of luxury and festivity they may neglect Christ—for which they desire to marry—12 incurring judgment because they have not kept the first faith. 13 And at the same time also they learn to be idle, going about house to house. Then not only idle but also gossips and meddlers, speaking things not being proper.

14 Therefore I want the younger *widows* to marry, to bear children, to manage their households, to not give an occasion to the adversary for reproach. 15 For already some have turned aside after Satan.

16 If any believing has widows let them give aid to them, and not let the church be burdened, so that to those genuine widows it may give aid to them.

17 The elders ruling well, count worthy of double honor, especially those laboring in the word and teaching. 18 For the Scripture says, "You shall not muzzle an ox treading out grain," and "Worthy the workman of his wages."

19 Against an elder do not receive an accusation, unless upon two or three witnesses. 20 But those continually sinning, before all rebuke, so that also the rest might have fear.

21 I earnestly affirm before God and Christ Jesus and the elect messengers that these things you should keep, without partiality, doing nothing out of partiality. 22 Lay hands on no one hastily, nor share in the sins of others. Keep yourself blameless.

23 No longer drink water, but use a little wine, because of your

stomach and frequent illness.

24 Of some persons the sins are apparent, going before them to judgment. But of some they also appear later. 25 In the same manner also, good works are known before all, and even those otherwise are not able to be concealed.

FIRST TIMOTHY SIX

1 As many as are under a yoke as slaves, let them regard their own masters worthy of all honor, so that the name of God and the teaching may not be slandered. 2 Now those having believing masters, let them not despise them because they are brethren, but rather serve them because they are believers and beloved, who benefit by good service. These things teach and exhort.

3 If anyone teaches a different doctrine and does not draw near to the sound words of our Lord Jesus Christ and the teaching according to godliness, 4 he is lifted up with pride, knowing nothing, but adoring about disputing, and strife about words, out of which come envy, love of strife, slander, evil suspicions, 5 unprofitable disputes among persons of perverse minds, and defrauding themselves of the truth, thinking godliness is a means of gain. [k]

6 But godliness with contentment is great gain. 7 For we brought nothing into the world, because we are not able to carry out anything. 8 But having foods and coverings, with these we will be content. 9 But those desiring to be rich fall into temptation and a trap, and many foolish and hurtful desires, which cause people to sink into ruin and loss. 10 The love of money is a root for all kinds of evils, which some coveting have been led astray away from the faith, and themselves pierced by many sorrows.

11 But you, O man of God, run from these things and pursue righteousness, godliness, faith, love, patience with things and circumstances,[l] gentleness in strength.[m] 12 Fight the good fight of the faith. Lay hold of the eternal life, to which you were called, and also did confess the good confession before many witnesses.

13 I charge you before God, the One giving life to all things, and Christ Jesus, the One having testified before Pontius Pilate the good confession, 14 you keep the commandment without spot, free from blame or reproach, until the appearing of our Lord Jesus Christ, 15 which in their own times he will display. The blessed and only Sovereign, the King of those being kings, and Lord of those being Lords, 16 the one alone having immortality, in light dwelling unapproachable, whom no one of humankind has seen, nor is able to see, to whom be honor and eternal dominion. Amen.

17 To the rich in the present age, instruct not to be arrogant, not to have hope in the uncertainty of riches, but on God, the One

providing us richly all things for enjoying, 18 to be rich to do good works, to be bountiful, ready to give, 19 laying up in store for themselves a good foundation for the future, so that they may take hold of that which is genuinely life.

20 O Timothy, guard the trust committed to you, avoiding the profane, empty speaking, and contrary doctrine—falsely called knowledge—21 which some professing have deviated from the faith. Grace among you all.

The Book of Second Timothy

The Book of Second Timothy was written ca. AD 68, from Rome, Italy, during Paul's second Roman imprisonment. The occasion of the book is a farewell letter; Paul expects he will be executed for Christ's sake, 4:6–8. The purpose of the book is to encourage a discouraged pastor, 1:8, 12.

SECOND TIMOTHY ONE

1 Paul, apostle of Christ Jesus by the will of God, according to the promise of life in Christ Jesus. 2 To Timothy, beloved child. Grace, mercy, peace from God Father and Christ Jesus our Lord.

3 I am thankful to God, whom I serve from my forefathers with a pure conscience, as continually I have remembrance of you in my prayers, night and day, 4 desiring earnestly to see you, remembering your tears, so that I might be filled with joy, 5 taking remembrance of the genuine faith in you, which first was in your grandmother Lois, and in your mother Eunice, and that I am persuaded is also in you.

6 For this reason I remind you to revive the gift of God which is in you by the laying on of my hands. 7 For God has not given us a spirit of cowardice, but of strength, and of love, and of self-discipline.

8 Therefore you should not be ashamed of our Lord's testimony, nor of me his prisoner, but suffer together for the good news, according to God's strength, 9 the One having saved us, and having called us with a holy calling, not according to our works, but according to his own purpose and grace, having been given us in Christ Jesus before time eternal, 10 now revealed by the appearing of our Savior, Christ Jesus, having truly put an end to death, now bringing to light life and incorruptibility[a] through the good news, 11 to which I was appointed a herald, and an apostle, and a teacher.

12 And for this reason I suffer these things. But I am not ashamed. For I know whom I have believed, and I am persuaded that he is able to guard for that day what has been committed to me.

13 Hold to the form of sound words, which you did hear from me, in the faith and love that are in Christ Jesus. 14 The good committed to you, guard through the Holy Spirit, the one dwelling in us.

15 This you know, that all those in Asia turned from me, among whom are Phygelus and Hermogenes. 16 May the Lord grant mercy to the household of Onesiphorus, because he often relieved my distress, and was not ashamed of my chains. 17 But arriving in Rome, he promptly sought me and found me. 18 May the Lord give him to find mercy from the Lord in that day. And how much he served in Ephesus you know.

SECOND TIMOTHY TWO

1 You, therefore, my child, be strong in the grace that is in Christ Jesus. 2 And those things you have heard from me among many witnesses, these commit to faithful persons, such as will be competent to teach others also.

3 Share in suffering as a good soldier of Christ Jesus. 4 No one serving as a soldier entangles himself in the affairs of this life, that he may please his commander. 5 But also if someone competes, he is not crowned unless he has competed lawfully. 6 It is necessary the hardworking farmer have the first share of the crops. 7 Consider the things I am saying, for the Lord will give you understanding in all things.

8 Remember Jesus Christ, raised out from the dead, out of David's offspring, according to my good news, 9 in which I suffer affliction, unto imprisonment as an evildoer. But the Word of God is not bound. 10 Because of this, I endure all things for the sake of the elect, so that they also may obtain salvation in Christ Jesus, with eternal glory.

11 Trustworthy this saying: for if we have died with him, also we will live with him. 12 If we endure, also we will reign with him. If we will deny, he also will deny us. 13 If we are faithless, he remains faithful; for he is not able to deny himself.

14 These things you remind, earnestly exhorting before God not to argue about trifles, for there is nothing profitable in the subversion of those hearing. 15 Be eager to present yourself to God as one commended: a workman irreproachable, skillfully teaching[b] the word of truth.

16 But avoid profane, senseless speaking, for they will lead on to more ungodliness, 17 and their speech like gangrene will spread, among whom are Hymenaeus and Philetus, 18 who about the truth have erred, saying the resurrection has already happened; and thereby they are undermining the faith of some. 19 Nevertheless, God's immovable foundation stands, having this inscription: "the Lord knows those who are his." And let every person naming the name of the Lord depart from iniquity.

20 Now in a great house, there are not only vessels golden and silver, but also wooden and earthen. And some truly unto honor, but some unto dishonor. 21 If therefore anyone may have cleansed himself from these, he will be a vessel for honor, having been sanctified, useful to the Master, having been prepared for every good work.

22 Now flee youthful desires, but pursue righteousness, faith, love, peace, along with those calling on the Lord out of a pure heart. 23 But refuse foolish and ignorant arguments, knowing they generate quarrels. 24 Now the servant of the Lord must not quarrel, but to be gentle toward all, apt to teach, patient, 25 in gentleness with strength

disciplining those opposing themselves, supposing God may give them repentance unto knowledge of truth, 26 and they might awaken out of the snare of the devil, having been captured by him to do his will.

SECOND TIMOTHY THREE

1 But know this, that in the last times difficult seasons will be present. 2 For people will be lovers of self, lovers of money, boastful, proud, slandering, disobedient to parents, ungrateful, unholy, 3 without family love, implacable, false accusers, unable to govern their appetites, not gentle, without love of good, 4 betrayers, out of control, lifted up with pride, lovers of pleasure rather than lovers of God, 5 having a form of godliness but denying the power. And from these turn away.

6 For out of this kind of person are those entering into households and taking captive immature women, heaped up with sins, led along by various strong desires, 7 always learning and never being able to come to a knowledge of the truth.

8 Just as Jannes and Jambres resisted Moses, so also these resist the truth, morally depraved persons in understanding, worthless regarding the faith. 9 But they will not progress any further, for their lack of understanding will be plain to all, as also that of those others became.

10 But you have carefully attended my teaching, manner of life, purpose, faith, patience with people, love, patience with circumstances, 11 persecutions, sufferings such as happened to me in Antioch *of Pisidia*, in Iconium, in Lystra; what manner of persecutions I endured! And yet out of all the Lord delivered me. 12 And all also desiring to live piously in Christ Jesus will be persecuted. 13 But evil men and deceivers will increase to worse, deceiving and being deceived.

14 But you, abide in the things you have learned and have been assured of, knowing from whom you learned them. 15 And that from childhood you have known the sacred writings able to make you wise unto salvation through faith in Christ Jesus. 16 Every scripture is God-breathed, and profitable for teaching, for conviction, for correction, for training in righteousness, 17 so that the person who is of God may be competent, completely equipped to every good work.

SECOND TIMOTHY FOUR

1 I earnestly bear witness before God and Christ Jesus—the one about to judge the living and the dead, and by his appearing and his kingdom—2 proclaim the word, be prepared for any opportunity convenient or inconvenient. Convict, rebuke, exhort with all patience and instruction.

3 For there will be a time when they will not listen to sound teaching, but having an itching ear they will gather teachers for themselves according to their own

desires, 4 and truly they will turn away from the truth, and turn aside to myths. 5 But you, be circumspect in all things, endure afflictions, do the work of an evangelist, thoroughly accomplish your ministry.

6 For I am even now pouring out my strength and life, and the time of my death is come. 7 I have fought the good fight, I have completed the race, I have kept the faith. 8 Finally, the crown of righteousness is in store for me, which the Lord, the righteous judge, will give to me in that day. Not only to me, but also to all those loving his appearance.

9 Be diligent to come to me quickly. 10 For Demas has deserted, having loved the present age, and he is gone to Thessalonica; Crescens to Galatia, Titus to Dalmatia. 11 Luke only is with me. Take Mark and bring him with you, for he is useful for the ministry. 12 But Tychicus I have sent to Ephesus.

13 The cloak I left in Troas with Carpus, upon coming, bring; and the books, especially the parchments. 14 Alexander the coppersmith did great harm to me. The Lord will repay him according to his works. 15 You also beware of him, for he has strongly opposed our message.

16 At my first defense no one was present with me, but all left me. May it not be reckoned to them. 17 Now the Lord stood by me and strengthened me, so that through me the proclamation would be fully accomplished, and all the gentiles should hear. And I was delivered out of the mouth of the lion. 18 The Lord—to whom the glory unto the ages of the ages—will deliver me from every evil work and will deliver me into his heavenly kingdom. Amen.

19 Greet Prisca and Aquila, and the house of Onesiphorus. 20 Erastus remained in Corinth, but Trophimus I left ill in Miletus. 21 Be diligent to come before winter. Eubulus greets you, and Pudens, and Linus, and Claudia, and all the brethren. 22 The Lord be with your spirit. Grace with you all.

The Book of Titus

The Book of Titus was written ca. AD 66–67. The occasion was a previous event, 1:5. The purpose was instructing a local church planter. Local churches had developed from Paul's initial visit, ca. AD 61–62, Acts 27:7–13. These churches needed organizational structure, 1:5, and guidance-exhortation in practical Christian living away from worldliness, 1:10ff.

TITUS ONE

1 Paul, servant of God and apostle of Jesus Christ, according to[a] the faith of the elect of God, and knowledge of the truth which is according to godliness, 2 in hope of eternal life, which God who cannot lie promised before times eternal; 3 now revealed in his own seasons, in his word, in the proclamation with which I have been entrusted, according to the commandment of our Savior, God.

4 To Titus, true child according to the common faith: grace and peace from God Father and Christ Jesus the Savior.

5 On account of this, I left you in Crete: so that the things lacking you might set in order. And you should appoint elders in every town, as I directed you: 6 if anyone is unaccused, a one-wife kind of husband,[b] having believing children, not under accusation of debauchery or rebellion. 7 For the overseer ought to be unaccused as God's administrator: not arrogant, not prone to anger, not abusing wine, not contentious, not desiring dishonorable gain, 8 but hospitable, a lover of good, of sound mind, living rightly, holy, self-disciplined, 9 firmly holding—according to the teaching—the faithful word, that he may be able both to encourage with sound instruction, and convict those contradicting.

10 For there are many disorderly, empty talkers, and deceivers, especially those of the circumcision, 11 whom it is necessary to silence, who subvert whole households, teaching things they ought not, for the sake of dishonorable gain. 12 One of them said, their own prophet, "Cretans are always liars, evil beasts, lazy gluttons." 13 This testimony is true. For this reason severely rebuke them, so they may be sound in the faith, 14 not paying attention to Jewish myths and commandments of men, turning away from the truth.

15 All things are pure to the pure. But to those defiled and unbelieving, nothing is pure, but both mind and conscience are defiled. 16 They profess to know God, but in works they deny him, being disgusting and deliberately disobedient, and worthless for any good work.

TITUS TWO

1 But you speak the things that are proper to sound doctrine.

2 Elderly men are to be sober-minded, dignified, discrete, firm in faith, in love, in patience. 3 Elderly

women in the same manner, in behavior not slanderers, not dependent upon much wine, teachers of what is good, 4 so that they may train the young women to be lovers of their husbands, loving their children, 5 discrete, modest, managing their homes, kind, under authority to her own husband, so that the Word of God might not be spoken of as evil. 6 The younger persons, in the same manner, exhort to be discrete.

7 In all things present yourself as a pattern of good works. In the teaching integrity, dignity, 8 sound speech, irreprehensible, so that the one who is of the contrary may be put to shame, having nothing evil to say about us.

9 Servants[c] are to be under the authority to their own masters, in everything to be well-pleasing, not disobedient, 10 not keeping that belonging to another, but showing all good faith, so that the doctrine of God our Savior they may honor in all things.

11 For the grace of God has appeared, bringing salvation to all persons, 12 instructing us that, having renounced ungodliness and worldly desires, we might live discreet and righteous and godly lives in the present age, 13 expecting the blessed hope and appearing of the glory of the great God and our Savior, Christ Jesus, 14 who gave himself for us, that he might redeem us from all lawlessness, and might purify his treasured people, zealous of good works.

15 These things speak and exhort, and rebuke with all authority. Let no one despise you.

TITUS THREE

1 Remind them to be in submission to ruling authorities, to be obedient; to be prepared to every good work. 2 To speak evil of none, to be peaceable, yielding, showing gentle strength toward all persons.

3 For we ourselves also were once foolish, disobedient, having been deceived, serving desires and various physical pleasures, living in malice and envy, hateful, hating one another.

4 But when the kindness and the benevolence of our Savior God appeared, 5 not from works in righteousness that we did, but according to his mercy, he saved us through washing of regeneration and renewing of the Holy Spirit, 6 whom he poured out on us richly through Jesus Christ, our Savior, 7 so that we should become righteous by that grace, heirs according to the expectation of life eternal.

8 Trustworthy is the saying, and concerning these things I desire you to strongly affirm, so that they—those believing God—might be careful to practice good works. These things are excellent and profitable to people.

9 But foolish debates and genealogies and arguments and quarrels about the Law, avoid. For they are unprofitable and fruitless. 10 A divisive person, after

admonishing once and twice, reject, 11 knowing that such a person is subversive, and is sinning, being self-condemned.

12 When I might send Artemas to you, or Tychicus, be diligent to come to me into Nicopolis; for there I have chosen to winter. 13 Diligently help Zenas the lawyer and Apollos on their way, so that nothing to them may be lacking.

14 Now, let our own also learn to practice good works for necessary needs, so that they may not be unfruitful. 15 All those with me greet you. You greet those loving us in the faith. Grace with all of you.

The Book of Philemon

The Book of Philemon was written AD 61–62 from Rome, Italy, toward the end of Paul's first Roman imprisonment. The occasion was the return of Onesimus, a slave who had run away from his master Philemon to Rome, Italy, met Paul, and been saved. Philemon lived in Colossae, Colossians 4:7–9, cf. Colossians 4:17 with Philemon 2. The purpose of the letter was to introduce Onesimus the slave as now a brother in Christ.

1 Paul, prisoner of Christ Jesus, and Timothy the brother, to Philemon the beloved and our fellow laborer, 2 and to Apphia the sister,[a] and to Archippus our fellow soldier, and to the church in your house. 3 Grace to you and peace from God our Father and Lord Jesus Christ.

4 I thank my God, always making mention of you during my prayers, (5 hearing of your love and the faith that you have toward the Lord Jesus and to all the saints), 6 that the fellowship of your faith may be effective in full knowledge of every good in us, in Christ. 7 For I have much joy and comfort from your love, because the hearts of the saints have been refreshed through you brother.

8 Therefore having much boldness in Christ to direct you to what is proper—9 rather because of love I implore you (as being Paul, an old man, but now also of Christ Jesus, a prisoner)—10 I implore you for my child whom I fathered in these chains, Onesimus, 11 the one once useless to you, but now to you and to me useful.

12 Whom I have sent again to you, even him.[b] This one is my heart. 13 Whom I was inclined to keep with me, so that on your behalf he might serve me in the bonds of the good news. 14 But without your consent I was not willing to do as I desired, so that your good may not be compelled but uncompelled. 15 For perhaps because of this he was severed for a time, that you might receive him forever, 16 no longer as a slave but beyond a slave, a beloved brother, especially to me, but how much rather to you, both in the flesh and in the Lord.

17 If me, therefore, you consider a companion, receive him as me. 18 But if anything he wronged you or owes, charge this to me. 19 I, Paul, have written with my own hand. I will repay. Not that I might say to you that you also owe yourself to me. 20 Yes, brother, may I have profit from you in the Lord; refresh my heart in Christ.

21 Relying upon your obedience I have written to you, knowing that you will do also more than I say. 22 Now at the same time also make ready for me a guest room, for I hope that through your prayers I shall be granted to you. 23 Epaphras greets you, my fellow prisoner in Christ Jesus; 24 my fellow laborers Mark, Aristarchus,

Demas, Luke. 25 The grace[c] of the Lord Jesus Christ with your spirit.[d]

The Book of Hebrews

The Book of Hebrews was written by an unknown author to an unknown audience, ca. AD 68–69. The oldest and most reliable title given to the letter is "To Hebrews." The letter alternates between doctrinal argument and exhortation. Examples of the latter are 2:1–4; 3:7–4:13; 5:11–6:20; 10:26–39; 12:15–29. Those passages may be removed without affecting the doctrinal arguments. The book may also be divided into two broad sections: doctrinal, 1:1–10:18; practical, 10:19–13:25. The main arguments of the letter might be summarized as "Christ is superior to Judaism," and "Persevere in the faith by means of faith."

HEBREWS ONE[t]

1 God in the past having spoken to the fathers by[a1] the prophets in many parts and in many ways, 2 in these last times has spoken to us in Son,[a2] whom he placed as heir of all things, through whom he also made the ages, 3 who being the shining of his glory and his exact[b1] essence,[b2] governing all things by his powerful word, having made purification of sins, sat down at the right hand of the Majesty on high, 4 being as much greater than the messengers as the name he has inherited is much more excellent to theirs.

5 For to which of the messengers did he ever say, "You are my son, today have I begotten you?" And again, "I will be unto him a father, and he will be unto me a son?" 6 Then again,[c] when he brought the firstborn into the world, he says, "And let all God's messengers worship him."

7 And, indeed, concerning the messengers, he says, "He makes winds his messengers, and a flame of fire his servants." 8 But unto the Son, "Your throne, O God—to the age of the age,"[d] and "the scepter of your kingdom is the scepter of righteousness." 9 You have loved righteousness and have hated lawlessness. Because of this God, your God, has anointed you with oil of exuberant joy[e] more than your companions.

10 And you at the beginning Lord, laid the foundation of the earth, and the works of your hands are the heavens. 11 They will perish. But you remain, and all, like a garment, will grow old, 12 and like a cloak you will fold them up, and like a garment they will be changed. But you are the same, and your years will never no never end.

13 But to which of the messengers did he ever say, "Sit at my right hand until I should place your enemies as a footstool for your feet." 14 As you know, they are all ministering spirits, sent forth for service on account of those about to inherit salvation.

HEBREWS TWO

1 On account of this, it is necessary we abundantly pay attention to those things we have

heard, that we should not at times transgress.^f1 2 For if the word having been spoken by the messengers was trustworthy, and every transgression and disobedience received a just punishment, 3 how will we escape having neglected so great a salvation, which spoken by the Lord received a beginning, confirmed to us by those who heard, 4 God bearing witness by signs and wonders and various miracles and distributions of the Holy Spirit, according to his will?

5 For he did not place in submission to messengers the world that is coming, of which we are speaking. 6 But someone somewhere has testified, saying, "What is man, that you are mindful of him, or Son of Man, that you regard him?" 7 You made him, a certain one,^f2 a little lower than messengers; with glory and honor you crowned him; 8 all things you have placed in submission under his feet. (For in subjecting to him all things, he left nothing to him not in submission.) But at present, we do not yet see all things submitting to him. 9 Who, however, this one, we see having been made a little lower than messengers, Jesus, through the suffering of death, having been crowned with glory and honor, so that by God's grace he might for all taste death.

10 For it was proper to him—for whom all things and by whom all things—having brought many sons to glory, the originator and leader^g of their salvation through sufferings to make fully qualified.^h 11 Because both the one sanctifying and those being sanctified—all of one; for which reason he is not ashamed to call them brethren, 12 saying, "I will declare your name to my brethren. Among the congregation I will sing your praises." 13 And again, "I will trust on him." And again, "Look, I and the children whom God has given to me."

14 Since, therefore, the children have partaken of blood and of flesh, also he in like manner shared in the same things, so that through death he might render ineffective^i the one holding the power of death, that is, the Devil, 15 and should set free those who through fear of death throughout all their life were bound to slavery.

16 For in truth he helps not messengers, but the offspring of Abraham he helps. 17 Wherefore he ought in all things to be made like his brethren, so that he might become a merciful and faithful high priest in things with God, in order to make propitiation for the sins of the people. 18 For in that he himself has suffered, having been tempted, he is able to help those being tempted.

HEBREWS THREE

1 Whereupon holy brethren, participants of the heavenly call, consider the apostle and high priest of our confession, Jesus, 2 being faithful to the One who appointed him, as also Moses in all his house. 3 For he has been counted worthy of greater glory

than Moses, by so much as the one having built the house has greater honor than the house. 4 For every house is built by someone, but the one having built all is God. 5 And Moses was indeed faithful in all his house, as a servant, unto a testimony of the things that would be spoken. 6 But Christ as a son over his house, whose house we are, if the confidence and the boast of hope we should hold fast [ʲ].

7 Therefore, even as the Holy Spirit is saying, "Today if you should hear his voice, 8 do not harden your hearts, as in the provocation, in the day of testing in the wilderness, 9 where your fathers tested me to prove me, and saw my works forty years. 10 Therefore I was angry with that generation, and I said, 'They always go astray in their heart, and they have not known my ways.' 11 So I declared an oath in my wrath, 'They shall not enter into my rest.'"

12 Be aware, brethren, lest ever there will be in any of you an evil heart of unbelief in withdrawing from the living God. 13 But encourage each other every day, as long as it is called today, so that none of you may be hardened by the deceitfulness of sin. 14 For we have become participants of Christ, if indeed we should hold firm our confidence from the beginning unto the end. 15 As it is said, "Today, if his voice you should hear, do not harden your hearts, as in the provocation."

16 For who having heard, provoked? But not all those coming out of Egypt through Moses. 17 But with whom was he angry forty years, if not with those who sinned, whose corpses fell in the wilderness? 18 But with whom did he take an oath they shall not enter into his rest, if not with those disbelieving? 19 So we see that they were not able to enter in because of unbelief.

HEBREWS FOUR

1 Should we not fear, therefore, the promise to enter into his rest remaining, that any of you should seem to fall short? 2 For we also are those having heard the good news, just as they did. But the word they heard did not profit them, not being joined with the faith of those having heard. 3 For we—those having believed—enter into the rest. As he has said, "So I declared an oath in my wrath, 'They shall not enter into my rest.'" And yet the works have been completed from the foundation of the world.

4 For he has spoken somewhere about the seventh day in this manner, "And God rested on the seventh day from all his works." 5 And in this again, "They shall not enter into my rest." 6 Since, therefore, it remains some to enter into it, and those before receiving the good news did not enter in through disbelief, 7 he again appoints a certain day, "Today," in David, saying after so long a time, just as it has been said, "Today, if you will hear his voice, do not harden your hearts."

8 For if Joshua had given rest

to them, he would not have spoken about another after that day. 9 So then there remains a sabbath-keeping[k] for the people of God. 10 For the one having entered into his rest, also he rested from his works, as God from his own. 11 We should therefore be earnest to enter into that rest, so that no one should fall in the same example of willful unbelief.

12 For the Word of God is living and working, and sharper than any two-edged sword, even piercing through as far as the division of soul and spirit, of joints and also marrows, and able to discern the thoughts and intentions of the heart. 13 And there is no creature hidden before him, but all things are revealed and exposed to the eyes of him to whom we give account.

14 Having, therefore, a great high priest, having passed through the heavens, Jesus, the Son of God, we should hold fast our confession. 15 For we do not have a high priest unable to have compassion on our weaknesses, but one having been tempted in all things the same way, without sin. 16 We should come, therefore, with confidence to the throne of grace, so that we may receive mercy and may find grace for help in time of need.

HEBREWS FIVE

1 For every high priest, being taken from among the people, is appointed on behalf of the people in things for God, that he should offer both gifts and sacrifices for sin, 2 being able to deal gently with those lacking discernment and going astray, because he himself also is encompassed by weakness. 3 And because of this he is obligated, just as for the people, so also for himself, to offer for sins. 4 And no one takes upon himself this honor, but is called by God, just as also Aaron.

5 So also Christ did not glorify himself to become a high priest, but the One having said to him, "You are my son, today I have begotten you." 6 Just as also in another place he says, "You: a priest for the age according to the order of Melchizedek."

7 Who in the times of his flesh, both prayers and supplications, to the One being able to deliver him from death, with loud crying and tears, he offered and was heard, because of reverence. 8 Although being a son, he learned obedience from the things he suffered.[l] 9 And having become fully qualified,[m] he became to all those obeying him the source of eternal salvation, 10 having been named by God a high priest, according to the order of Melchizedek.

11 Concerning this I have much to say, and difficult in explanation to speak, because you have become dull in the hearing. 12 For you ought even to be teachers by this time; you again have need of one to teach you the principles of the first declarations of God, and you have become those in need of milk, not of solid food. 13 For any partaking milk is not skilled in the

word of righteousness; for he is an infant. 14 But for the mature food is solid—the ones who on account of practice have trained the senses to possess the discernment of both good and evil.

HEBREWS SIX

1 Therefore, leaving the first teaching of the Christ, we should go on to maturity, not laying again a foundation of repentance from dead works, and faith in God, 2 teaching about immersions,ⁿ and of laying on of hands, of resurrection of the dead, and of eternal judgment. 3 And this we will do, if God permits.

4 For it is impossible to those having been once enlightened, and having tasted of the heavenly gift, and having become partakers of the Holy Spirit, 5 and having tasted of God's Word, and the powers of the coming age, 6 and then having fallen away, again to restore to repentance, crucifying afresh in themselves the Son of God, and publicly shaming him.

7 For the earth, having drunk in the rain that is often coming upon it, and bearing plants useful to those for whom it is also cultivated, shares blessing from God. 8 But when it brings forth thorns and thistles it is worthless, and near to a curse, whose end is for burning.

9 But we are persuaded, beloved, better concerning you, and accompanying salvation, even if we speak in this manner. 10 For God is not unjust to forget your work and the love that you have shown for his name, having ministered to the saints and still ministering. 11 But we desire each of you to show the same diligence to the certainty of the hope until the end, 12 so that you may not be sluggish, but imitators of those who on account of faith and patience are inheriting the promises.

13 For God having promised to Abraham, because from no one he had greater to swear, he swore from himself, 14 saying, "if assuredly blessing I will bless you and multiplying I will multiply you." 15 And so waiting patiently, he obtained the promise.

16 For men swear by one greater, and the oath for confirmation is an end of all their controversy. 17 In which God, more abundantly desiring to show to the heirs of the promise the unchangeableness of his purpose, mediated by an oath, 18 so that by two unchangeable things, in which it is impossible for God to lie, we should have strong encouragement, having fled for refuge, to take hold of the hope being set before us. 19 Which we have as an anchor of the soul, both immovable and fixed, and entering into that within the veil, 20 where the forerunner has entered for us, Jesus, according to the order of Melchizedek, having become a high priest to the age.º

HEBREWS SEVEN

1 For this Melchizedek (of Salem, king; of God Most High,

priest), having met Abraham returning from the slaughter of the kings, and having blessed him—2 to whom a tenth of all Abraham shared, truly first translated "King of Righteousness," and then also "King of Salem," which is "King of peace"—3 without father, without mother, without genealogy, having neither beginning of days nor end of life, but having been made very much like the Son of God, he remains a priest continually.

4 Now consider how great this one, to whom Abraham, the patriarch, gave a tenth out of the best spoils. 5 And truly those out of the sons of Levi receiving the priestly office, have a commandment to take a tenth from the people according to the Law, that is, from their brethren, although having come out of the loin of Abraham. 6 But the one not descended from them has received a tenth from Abraham, and has blessed the one having the promises. 7 Now apart from all contradiction the inferior is blessed by the superior. 8 And here truly dying men receive tenths; but in that place it is testified that he lives. 9 And so (to speak a word), through Abraham also, Levi, the ones receiving tenths, paid the tenth. 10 For he was still in the loin of his father when Melchizedek met him.

11 Truly then, if perfection[p] were by the Levitical priesthood—for under it the people had received the Law—what need was there, according to the order of Melchizedek, another priest to arise, and not to be called according to the order of Aaron? 12 Namely, the priesthood being changed, from necessity a change of Law also occurs.

13 For concerning whom these things are said, he belonged to another tribe, from which none has served at the altar. 14 For it is well-known that our Lord has sprung out of Judah, a tribe for which, concerning priests, Moses said nothing. 15 And it is yet more abundantly evident another priest rises according to the likeness of Melchizedek, 16 who has not been made according to a Law of fleshly commandment, but according to the power of a life indissoluble.[q] 17 For it is testified, "You: a priest to the age, according to the order of Melchizedek."

18 For truly there is an annulment of the preceding commandment because of its imperfection and unprofitableness. 19 For the Law perfected nothing. Now *there is the* introduction of a better hope, by which we draw near to God. 20 And inasmuch as not apart from an oath—for truly others became priests apart from an oath, 21 but this one with an oath—through the One saying to him, "The Lord has sworn and will not change his mind, 'You are a priest to the age.'" 22 And by so much Jesus has become the guarantor of a better covenant.

23 And truly, those many being made priests, through death are prevented from continuing. 24 But through his abiding to the age,

he holds an unchangeable priesthood. 25 Wherefore also, he is able to forever save all those drawing near to God through him, always living to intercede for them.

26 For truly such a high priest also was fitting for us, holy, blameless, undefiled, having been separated from sinners, and having become higher than the heavens, 27 who has no need every day, as the high priests, first to offer up sacrifices for his own sins, then for those of the people; for this he did once for all, having offered up himself. 28 For the Law appoints men having weakness as high priests. But the word of the oath which was after the Law, a Son to the age always fully qualified.[r1]

HEBREWS EIGHT

1 Now, the principle thing of such things we are speaking? We have a high priest who sat down at the right hand of the throne of the Majesty in the heavens, 2 in the holy places a priest, and in the true tabernacle, which the Lord has pitched,[r2] not man.

3 For every high priest is set in place for offering both gifts and sacrifices. Whereupon it was necessary for this one also to have something that he should offer. 4 Truly, then, if he were on earth he would not even be a priest, there being those offering the gifts according to the Law, 5 who serve a representation and foreshadowing[s] of the heavenly— as Moses was divinely instructed, being about to complete the tabernacle. For he says, "See to it you will make all things according to the pattern that was shown you on the mountain." 6 But he has received a better ministry, as much as he is also mediator of a better covenant, upon which better promises have been established.

7 For if that first had been without fault, a place for a second would not have been sought. 8 For finding fault with them, he says, "Behold, times are coming," says the Lord, "and I will put into effect with the house of Israel and the house of Judah a new covenant, 9 not according to the covenant that I made with their fathers, in the day I took them by my hand to lead them out of the land of Egypt. Because they did not continue in my covenant I did not regard them," says the Lord.

10 "For this is the covenant that I will make with the house of Israel, after those times," says the Lord, "putting my laws into their mind, and I will inscribe them upon their hearts. And I will be to them for God, and they will be to me for people. 11 And no, they should not teach each his neighbor, and each his brother, saying, 'Know the Lord,' because all will know me, from least to greatest of them, 12 because I will be merciful toward their iniquities and their sins; and their sins I shall never no never further remember."

13 In the saying, "New," he has rendered obsolete the first, that now growing old and aging, is near vanishing.

HEBREWS NINE

1 Therefore, truly, even the first had regulations of worship and an earthly sanctuary. 2 For a tabernacle was prepared, the first, which is called holy, in which were both the lampstand and the table and the presentation of the bread. 3 But after the second veil a tabernacle called the holy of holies, 4 having the golden censer of incense, and the ark of the covenant, every part covered with gold, in which the golden jar having the manna, and the staff of Aaron that budded, and the tablets of the covenant; 5 also above it cherubim of glory overshadowing the mercy seat—concerning which now not to speak in detail.

6 Now these things having been prepared, truly into the first tabernacle the priests enter constantly, performing the sacred rites. 7 But into the second the high priest, only once in the year, not without blood, which he offers for himself and the errors[t] of the people. 8 By this the Holy Spirit signified the way had not yet been revealed into the holy places, the first tabernacle still standing. 9 Which is an illustration for the present time, in which both gifts and sacrifices are offered, which are not able to fully cleanse the conscience of the one worshiping, 10 only in foods and drinks and various washings, ordinances of the flesh until the time of reformation being imposed.

11 But when Christ appeared as high priest of the good things having now come, through the greater and more perfect tabernacle not made by hands, that is, not of this creation, 12 nor by the blood of goats and young bullocks, but through his own blood entered once for all into the holies, having obtained eternal redemption. 13 For if the blood of goats and bullocks, and ashes of a heifer, sprinkling those defiled, sanctify for the purification of the flesh, 14 how much more the blood of Christ, who through the eternal Spirit offered himself without blemish to God, will purify our conscience from dead works, in order to serve the living God?

15 And because of this, he is mediator of a new covenant, so that death having come, for redemption of the transgressions under the first covenant, those having been called might receive the promise of the eternal inheritance. 16 For where there is a covenant, the death of the one having made it is necessary to establish it. 17 For a covenant is affirmed after death, because it is not in force when the one having made it is living.

18 Wherefore neither the first has been dedicated apart from blood. 19 For Moses having spoken of every commandment according to the Law to all the people, having taken the blood of young bullocks and of goats, with water and scarlet wool and hyssop, he sprinkled both the book itself and all the people, 20 saying, "This by the blood of the covenant, which God commanded unto you." 21 And

then the tabernacle, and all the vessels of the service, he in the same manner sprinkled with blood. 22 And almost all things are purified with blood, according to the Law, and apart from blood-shedding there is not forgiveness.

23 Truly it was necessary the representations[u] of the things in the heavens, with these to be purified, but the heavenly things themselves with better sacrifices than these. 24 For Christ has not entered into holies made by hands, illustrations of the true, but into heaven itself, to appear in the presence of God for us, 25 nor that many times he should offer himself, just as the high priest enters into the holies every year with blood of another. 26 Otherwise it was necessary for him to have suffered many times from the foundation of the world. But now, once in the culmination of the age, he has been revealed for putting away sin by the sacrifice of himself. 27 And inasmuch as it awaits for men to die once, then after that judgment, 28 so also Christ, having been offered once in order to bear the sins of many, for a second time, apart from sin, will appear to those awaiting him for deliverance.

HEBREWS TEN

1 For the Law having a representation[v] of the coming good things, not itself the reality of those things, each year with the same sacrifices, which they continually offer, is never able to complete[w] those drawing near. 2 Otherwise, would they not have ceased being offered, because no longer having awareness of sins, those worshiping have been cleansed once for all? 3 But in these a commemoration of sins every year—4 impossible for the blood of bulls and of goats to remove sins.

5 Therefore, coming into the world, he says, "Sacrifice and offering you have not desired; but you have prepared me a body. 6 Whole burnt offerings and for sin did not please you. 7 Then I said, 'Look, I have come, in the volume of the book it is written of me to do your will, God.'" 8 Previously saying, "Sacrifice, and offering, and whole burnt offerings, and for sin you did not desire, nor have pleased you, which are offered according to the Law," 9 then he said, "Look, I have come to do your will," he removes the first that the second he may establish.

10 By that will we were and are sanctified through the offering of the body of Jesus Christ once for all. 11 And truly every priest stands every day serving and frequently offering the same sacrifices which are never able to completely take away sins. 12 But this one, having offered one sacrifice for sins in perpetuity, sat down at the right hand of God, 13 hence forward expecting until his enemies may be placed as a footstool for his feet. 14 For by one offering he has completed continually[x] those being sanctified.

15 In addition to all this, the Holy Spirit witnesses to us, for after he had said before, 16 "This is

the covenant that I will make with them after those times," says the Lord, "putting my laws into their hearts and into their minds I will inscribe them," 17 and, "their sins and their lawlessness I will not at all remember." 18 Now where there is forgiveness of these there is no longer an offering for sin.

19 Therefore, brethren, having confidence for entering the holy places by the blood of Jesus, 20 a way new and active which he opened for us through the veil, that is, his flesh, 21 and a great priest over the house of God, 22 we should approach with an upright heart in full assurance of faith, having hearts sprinkled from an evil conscience and the body bathed in pure water.

23 We should hold fast to the confession of our hope, firmly. For the one having promised is faithful. 24 And we should consider one another, to stir up to love and to good works, 25 not deserting the assembling of ourselves together as the custom with some, but being encouraging—and so much more as you see the day drawing near.

26 For if we intentionally commit acts of sinning after receiving the knowledge of the truth, a sacrifice no longer remains for sins, 27 but a certain fearful expectation of judgment, and of fire and fury about to consume the adversaries. 28 Anyone having set aside Moses' Law, he dies without mercies on the basis of two or three witnesses. 29 How much worse punishment, think you, will he deserve, the one trampling underfoot the Son of God, and having regarded as unconsecrated the blood of the covenant by which he was sanctified, and having despised the Spirit of grace? 30 For we know the one having said, "Vengeance is mine, I will repay," and again, "The Lord will judge his people." 31 It is a fearful thing to fall into the living God's hands.

32 But remember the former times in which, having been enlightened, you endured a great conflict of sufferings, 33 this indeed by abusive language and tribulation, being scorned publicly, and this by becoming fellow partakers with others. 34 For also with the prisoners you sympathized, and the robbery of your possessions you accepted with joy, knowing you have a better possession, and abiding.

35 Therefore, do not lose your confidence, which has a great reward. 36 For you have need of perseverance, so that, having done the will of God, you may receive the promise. 37 "For yet a little while, the one coming will come, and will not delay. 38 But my righteous one will live by faith; and if he might withdraw, my soul does not take pleasure in him." 39 But we are not of those withdrawing to destruction, but of faith to preserving of the soul.

HEBREWS ELEVEN

1 Now faith is the title deed[y] of the things of which we are assured, the objective evidence[z] of

the things not yet seen. 2 For in this the ancestors bore honorable testimony.

3 By faith we understand the universe was set in order by God's Word, so that which is seen was not made from things that are visible.

4 By faith Abel offered to God a more excellent sacrifice than Cain, through which he bore testimony to be righteous, God bearing witness to his gifts, and through it, having died, still he speaks.

5 By faith Enoch was translated[aa] not to see death, and he was not found, because God had translated him. For before his translation he was testified to have pleased God.

6 Now without faith—impossible to please. For the one approaching God needs to believe that he exists; and to those earnestly seeking him he becomes a rewarder.

7 By faith Noah, having been divinely warned concerning things not yet seen, being moved with fear, prepared an ark for deliverance of his household, by which he condemned the world, and became heir of the righteousness that is according to faith.

8 By faith, being called, Abraham obeyed to go out into a place that he was certain to receive for an inheritance, and went out not knowing where he is going. 9 By faith he lived as a stranger in the land of the promise, as a foreign country, dwelling in tents with Isaac and Jacob, the joint heirs of the same promise. 10 For he expected the city having foundations, of which the builder and designer is God.

11 By faith also, Sarah herself received ability for conception of offspring, even contrary to the season of her age, since she considered the One having promised faithful. 12 Therefore also from one man were born—and his body impotent—as the stars of heaven in multitude, countless as the sand by the shore of the sea.

13 These all died in faith, not having received the promises, but having seen them from afar, and having embraced them, and having publicly confessed they are on the earth as foreigners and expatriates.[bb] 14 For those saying such things make known that their native country they are seeking. 15 And, if truly they were mindful from where they came out, they would have had opportunity to return. 16 But now they reach out to a better, that is, a heavenly one. Therefore God is not ashamed of them, to be named their God. For he has prepared a city for them.

17 By faith Abraham offered Isaac as a sacrifice to God. Being tested, he was offering even his only begotten son; the one having received the promises, 18 to whom it was said, "In Isaac your offspring will be called," 19 having reckoned that God was able to raise even out from the dead, from where him also in a figure he received.

20 By faith also, concerning things to come, Isaac blessed Jacob and Esau. 21 By faith Jacob, dying, blessed each of the sons of Joseph, and worshiped on the top of his staff. 22 By faith Joseph, dying, made mention of the exodus of the sons of Israel, and gave instructions about his bones.

23 By faith Moses, having been born, was hidden three months by his parents, because they saw the little child was beautiful, and they did not fear the commandment of the king. 24 By faith Moses, having become full-grown, refused to be named son of Pharaoh's daughter, 25 having chosen rather to suffer affliction with the people of God than to have the pleasure of sin for a season, 26 esteeming of greater wealth than the treasures of Egypt the reproach of the Christ. For he was looking to the reward.

27 By faith he left Egypt, not fearing the anger of the king, for he endured as seeing the invisible One. 28 By faith he kept the Passover and the sprinkling of the blood, so that the one slaying the firstborn would not touch them. 29 By faith they passed through the Red Sea, as though dry land, which the Egyptians, having attempted, were drowned.

30 By faith the walls of Jericho fell, having been encircled for seven days. 31 By faith Rahab the prostitute did not perish with those who disbelieved, having received the scouts with peace.

32 And what more shall I say? For the time will fail me telling of Gideon, Barak, Samson, Jephthah, David also, and Samuel, and the prophets, 33 who by faith subdued kingdoms, worked justice, obtained promises, shut the mouths of lions, 34 quenched the power of fire, escaped the edge of the sword, were strengthened from weakness, became mighty in war, routed armies of foreigners. 35 Women received by resurrection their dead.

But others were tortured, not accepting deliverance, so that they might obtain a better resurrection. 36 But others received trials of mockings and of scourgings, and in addition of chains and imprisonment. 37 They were stoned, they were sawn in two, they were executed by the sword, they wandered in sheepskins, in goats' skins, being destitute, being oppressed, being mistreated, 38 of whom the world was not worthy. In deserts wandering, and mountains, and caves, and holes of the earth.

39 And all these, having born testimony through the faith, did not receive the promise, 40 God having provided something better for us, so that apart from us they should not be made complete.

HEBREWS TWELVE

1 And consequently we, having so great a cloud of witnesses surrounding us, putting off every encumbrance, and sin that so easily troubles us, should run the race lying before us with perseverance, 2 looking to the

originator and completer of our faith, Jesus, who in the presence of the joy lying before him, endured the cross, despising its shame, and sat down at the right hand of the throne of God. 3 For repeatedly consider the One having endured such great reproach from sinners against himself, so that you will not become weary, your souls losing hope.

4 You have not yet resisted unto blood in your conflict against sin, 5 and you have forgotten the exhortation that speaks to you as to sons, "My son, do not lightly regard the chastisement of the Lord, nor lose hope when reproved by him." 6 For whom he loves he chastises, and he corrects every son whom he receives.

7 For this reason endure chastisement: God is treating you as sons. For what son *is there* whom a father does not chastise? 8 But if you are without chastisement, of which all become partakers, then you are illegitimate and not sons. 9 So then, truly, we have had chastisers, our fathers of the flesh, and we respected them. Shall we not much more be in submission to the Father of spirits, and shall live?

10 For truly, for a few days, they were chastising us according to that seeming good to them; but he for our advantage, in order to share his holiness. 11 Now all chastisement, truly, to those experiencing it, seems not to be of joy, but of sorrow. But afterward, a wholesome result; to those by it having been trained, it yields righteousness. 12 Therefore, strengthen the weary hands and the feeble knees, 13 and make straight paths for your feet, so that the lame should not be turned aside but rather should be healed.

14 Pursue peace with all, and holiness, without which no one will perceive[cc] the Lord, 15 being watchful lest any be failing of the grace of God, lest any root of bitterness springing up should trouble you, and by this the many might be defiled; 16 lest any fornicator, or profane person, as Esau, who for one meal sold his birthright. 17 For you know that even afterward, desiring to inherit the blessing, he was rejected; for he did not find a place of repentance,[dd] although earnestly sought, with tears.

18 For you have not come to that which was touched, and burning with fire, and to darkness, and to gloom, and to storm, 19 and to the sound of a trumpet, and to a voice of words, which those hearing begged the word not to be addressed to them, 20 for they could not bear up under that commanded, "If even a beast should touch the mountain, it shall be stoned." 21 And so terrifying was the thing they saw, Moses said, "I am greatly afraid and trembling."

22 But you have come to Mount Zion, even to the city of the living God, and to the heavenly Jerusalem, and to ten thousands of God's messengers, 23 to the festal

public assembly, and to the called-out assembly of the firstborn enrolled in the heavens, and to God the judge of all, and to the spirits of the righteous having been made perfect, 24 and to the mediator of a new covenant, to Jesus, and to the blood of sprinkling speaking better things than that of Abel.

25 Take heed lest you refuse the One speaking. For if they did not escape on earth, having refused the One divinely warning, much less we turning away from the One from the heavens, 26 whose voice shook the earth at that time. But now he has announced, saying, "I will yet once shake not only the earth but also heaven." 27 Now, this "yet once," signifies the removing of the things being shaken, as of things having been created, so that the things not being shaken should remain. 28 Therefore, receiving a kingdom not to be shaken, we may have grace, by which we may serve acceptably to God, with reverence and awe. 29 For also our God is a consuming fire.

HEBREWS THIRTEEN

1 Let brotherly love continue.

2 Remember hospitality to strangers, for on account of this some have entertained messengers unaware.

3 Remember the prisoners as though in bonds with them, of those ill-treated, as also yourselves being in the body.

4 Marriage is to be honored by all, and the marriage bed undefiled, for the sexually immoral and adulterers God will judge.

5 The manner of life, without covetousness, being content with the present. For he has said, "Never no never will I leave you, never no never will I forsake you." 6 So we are confident to say, "My helper is the Lord, and I will not be afraid. What shall man do to me?"

7 Remember those leading you, who spoke to you the Word of God, of whom, considering the result of their way of life, imitate the faith.

8 Jesus Christ the same yesterday and today, and to the ages.

9 Do not be carried away by strange and diverse teachings. For it is good the heart be preserved by grace, not foods, in which those so living were not profited.

10 We have an altar, from which those serving in the tabernacle have no authority to eat. 11 For the high priest brings the blood of animals for sin into the holy places. Those bodies are burned outside the camp. 12 Therefore also Jesus, so that he might sanctify the people by his own blood, suffered outside the camp. 13 Therefore we should go out to him outside the camp, bearing his reproach.

14 For we do not have here an abiding city, but we seek the Coming One. 15 Therefore, through him, we should offer the sacrifice of praise through everything to God, which is the fruit of our lips

confessing his name. 16 And of doing good and of sharing, do not be forgetful. God is well pleased with such sacrifices.

17 Obey those leading you, and be submissive. For they are watchful over your souls, as those who will give an account, that they might do this with joy, and not groaning—which for you would be unprofitable.

18 Pray for us. For we are persuaded that we have a good conscience, in all things desiring to conduct ourselves well. 19 Now I vigorously exhort you to do this, so that I might be restored to you more quickly.

20 Now the God of peace, having brought out from the dead the great Shepherd of the sheep by the blood of the eternal covenant, Jesus our Lord, 21 equip you in everything good in order to do his will, working in us that which is well pleasing before him, through Jesus Christ, to whom the glory to the ages of the ages. Amen.

22 Now I exhort you, brethren, bear with this word of exhortation. For I have written to you in only a few words.

23 You know Timothy our brother has been released, with whom, if he should come sooner, I will see you.

24 Greet all those leading you, and all the saints. You greet those from Italy. 25 Grace with all of you. Amen.

The Book of James

The Book of James, i.e., of Jacob,‡ was written ca. AD 44, after Matthew's Gospel was published (ca. AD 42), and after Cornelius (Acts 10) was saved (ca. AD 40–43), but before the Council of Jerusalem (Acts 15, ca. AD 50). The style is similar to the Old Testament wisdom literature: a series of wise sayings on certain subjects. James' concern was the Christian's obedience to God's moral values. James' doctrine is genuine faith produces godly works. The book might be summarized as "Practical preaching from Pastor James on Christian character and Christian duty."

JAMES ONE

1 Jacob, of God and of Lord Jesus Christ, servant. To the twelve tribes that are in the diaspora, greeting.

2 My brethren, reckon all joy whenever you may encounter various trials, 3 knowing that the testing of your faith produces perseverance. 4 Now let the perseverance complete its work, in order that you may be mature and complete, lacking in not one thing.

5 But if, as may be the case, anyone of you lacks wisdom, let him ask from God who gives unconditionally to all and does not reproach, and wisdom will be given to him. 6 But let him ask in faith, doubting nothing. For the person doubting is like a sea wave driven and tossed by the wind. 7 To be sure, let not such a person suppose that he will receive anything from the Lord; 8 he is double-minded, unstable in all his ways.

9 And let the brother, the one who is humble, glory in his exaltation; 10 but he who is rich, in his humiliation, because as a flower of the grass he will pass away. 11 For the sun rises with its scorching heat and then dries up the grass, and its flower falls, and its beautiful appearance perishes; thus also the rich in his pursuits will wither.

12 Blessed the person who endures a trial, because having been proved, that person will receive the crown of life, which the Lord promised to those that love him.

13 Let no one when being tempted say, "From God I am tempted." For God is incapable of being tempted by evil, and he tempts no one. 14 But each is tempted being drawn away and enticed by his own strong desire. 15 Then strong desire having conceived gives birth to sin; and sin being fully grown gives birth to death.

16 Be not deceived, my beloved brethren. 17 Every good giving[a] and every perfect gift is from above, coming down from the Father of lights, with whom there is no variation or shadow of turning. 18 Having willed he brought us forth by the word of truth, for us to be a type of firstfruit from among his creatures.

19 Know this my beloved brethren: let every person also be swift to hear, slow to speak, slow to anger; 20 for man's anger does not produce God's righteousness. 21 Therefore having laid aside all moral filthiness and overflowing of wickedness, in meekness receive the engrafted word that is able to save your souls.

22 And be doers of the word, and not merely hearers, deceiving yourselves. 23 Because if any person is a hearer of the word and not a doer, this one is like a man considering his natural face in a mirror; 24 for he considered himself, and has gone away, and immediately did forget what sort *of person* he was. 25 But the one having looked into the perfect law, that of freedom, and having continued in it, being not a forgetful hearer, but one who does the work, this one will be blessed in his doing.

26 If anyone among you considers himself to be religious, yet not controlling his speech, but deceiving his heart, this one's religion is empty. 27 Religion pure and undefiled before the God and Father is this: to visit orphans and widows in their distress; to keep oneself unblemished from the world.

JAMES TWO

1 My brethren, have the faith of our Lord Jesus Christ, the one of glory, without partiality.[b] 2 For if there may come into your congregation[c] a man with a gold ring, in fine clothing, and there may also come in a poor man in filthy clothing; 3 and you may have looked upon the one wearing the fine clothing, and may have said, "You sit here in this good place," and to the poor may have said, "You stand there or sit under my footstool"; 4 do you not then make a distinction in yourselves and become judges with evil thoughts?

5 Listen, my beloved brethren. Did not God choose the poor of this world, rich in faith,[d] and heirs of the kingdom that he has promised to those who love him? 6 But you dishonored the poor. Do not the rich harshly oppress you, and they drag you to judgment seats? 7 Do they not slander the good name, the one having been called upon you?[e]

8 If you truly fulfill *the* royal Law according to the Scripture, "You shall love your neighbor as yourself," you do well; 9 but if you practice partiality you commit sin, being convicted by the Law as transgressors. 10 For whoever may keep the whole Law, but in one point may fail in that duty, he has become guilty of all. 11 For the One having said, "You may not commit adultery," also said, "You may not murder."[f] Now if you do not commit adultery, but you commit murder, you have become a transgressor of *God's* Law. 12 Speak and live as people who will be judged by the law of freedom. 13 For judgment is without mercy to anyone not having shown mercy. Mercy triumphs over judgment.

14 What is the advantage my brethren, if someone is saying, "I have faith," but does not have works? That kind of faith⁹¹ is not able to save him, is it? 15 If a brother or sister be poorly clothed and in need of daily food, 16 and anyone from among your community says to them, "Go away in peace, be warmed and be filled," but you do not give them the things needed for the body, what is the advantage?

17 So also the faith, except it may have works, by itself is dead.⁹² 18 But someone may say, "You have faith, and I have works." Show me your faith without the works, and I will show you my faith from my works. 19 You believe that God is one; you do well. Even the demons believe, and shudder.

20 But do you wish to know, O empty person, that the kind of faith without works is dead? 21 Abraham our father, wasn't he declared righteous by means of works, when he offered his son Isaac on the altar? 22 You perceive that his faith was working together with his works, and by the works the faith was complete 23 and the Scripture was fulfilled which says, "And Abraham believed God, and it was imputed to him for righteousness." And he was called the friend of God. 24 You perceive that a person is declared righteous by works, and not mere faith.

25 And in like manner also was not Rahab the prostitute declared righteous by works, having received the messengers and sent them out by another way? 26 For just as the body without spirit is dead, so also the kind of faith ʰ without works is dead.

JAMES THREE

1 My brethren, let not many of you become teachers, knowing that we will receive a harsher punishment. 2 For we all sin in many ways.

If anyone does not sin in speech, this is a mature person, able also to control ⁱ the whole body. 3 Now we put bridles in horses' mouths for them to obey us, and we direct their whole body. 4 Think also of ships, although so large and driven by fierce winds, are steered by a very small rudder, wherever the will of the pilot decides.

5 Likewise the tongue is a little member and yet boasts important things. Think on how a small fire ignites a large forest. 6 And the tongue is a fire. The tongue appoints itself ʲ among our members as a world of unrighteousness, that defiles our whole being, and sets on fire the course of one's life, and is set on fire by Gehenna.

7 For every kind, of both animals and birds, of both creeping creatures and creatures of the sea, is tame and has been tamed by humankind. 8 But no person is able to tame the tongue—a restless evil full of deadly poison. 9 With it we speak well of our God and Father, and with it we wish men evil, who have been made according to

God's likeness. 10 Out from the same mouth blessing and cursing come forth.

My brethren, these things ought not to be so. 11 A spring doesn't pour out of the same opening fresh and bitter, does it? 12 My brethren, a fig tree is not able to produce olives, nor a grapevine figs; neither can salt water produce fresh.

13 Who is wise and understanding among you? Let him show his works by good conduct in humble wisdom. 14 But if you harbor bitter envy and self-interest in your hearts, do not boast and lie against the truth. 15 This is not the wisdom from above coming down, but is earthly, natural, demon-like.

16 For where envy and self-interest are there is confusion and every evil practice.ᵏ 17 But wisdom from above is first pure, then peaceful, gentle, willing to yield, full of mercy and good fruits, impartial, without hypocrisy—18 and the fruit of righteousness is sown in peace for those making peace.

JAMES FOUR

1 From what source are wars and battles among you? Is it not from this—from your pleasures that wage war in your body's members? 2 You want and have not; so you murder. And you are envious and cannot obtain; so you fight and war. You do not have because you do not ask. 3 You ask and do not receive because you wrongly ask so that you might expend it on your pleasures.

4 Adulterers and adulteresses! Do you not know that the friendship of the world is enmity toward God? Whoever if, therefore, is willing to be a friend of the world makes himself an enemy of God. 5 Or think you that the Scripture says in vain: "he jealously longs for the spiritˡ he has caused to dwell in us, 6 but he gives greater grace?" Therefore he says: "God opposes the proud, but gives grace to the humble."

7 Be subject, then, to God.ᵐ Stand against the devil and then he will flee away from you. 8 Draw near to God and he will draw near to you. Cleanse your hands, sinners, and purify your hearts, you double-minded. 9 Be afflicted and mourn and weep. Change your laughter to mourning and your joy to gloom. 10 Humble yourselves in the Lord's presence, and he will exalt you.

11 Brethren, do not speak against one another. The person speaking against his brother or judging his brother speaks against the Law and judges the Law. But if one judges the Law, one is not a doer of the Law but a judge. 12 One is lawgiver and judge, the One who is able to save and to destroy. But you, who are you to judge a neighbor?

13 Come now, you who say, "Today or tomorrow we will go into this or that city, and will spend there a year, and do business, and make a profit." 14 You who do not

know what tomorrow will bring, what is your life? You are just a vapor that appears for a little while then also disappears. 15 Instead of saying this you should say, "If the Lord should will, then we shall both live and do this or that." 16 As it is you boast in your arrogance: every such kind of boasting is evil. 17 So, for the person who knows the right thing to do and who does not do it, to him it is sin.

JAMES FIVE

1 Come now, you rich, burst into weeping,[n] howling with grief for your miseries that are coming upon you! 2 Your wealth has rotted and your garments are moth-eaten. 3 Your gold and silver are corroded throughout, and their corrosion will be for a testimony against you, and will eat your flesh as fire. You have laid up treasure in the last times. 4 Behold, the wage of the workers who reaped your fields, that has been withheld by you, cries out, and the cries of those who reaped have entered into the ears of the Lord of Hosts. 5 You have lived in pleasure upon the earth, and self-indulgence; you fattened your hearts in a day of slaughter. 6 You have condemned, you have murdered the righteous; they offer you no resistance.

7 Be patient, therefore, brethren, until the coming of the Lord. Behold, the farmer waits for the precious fruit of the land, being patient with the land until it may receive the early and latter rain. 8 You too have patience. Strengthen your hearts, because the coming of the Lord is drawing near.

9 Brethren, do not continue to grumble against one another, that you may not be judged. Behold, the Judge stands before the doors. 10 Brethren, take as an example of suffering evil and patience, the prophets, who spoke in the name of the Lord. 11 Behold, we call blessed those having endured. You have heard of Job's perseverance and you saw the Lord's intended outcome; that the Lord is full of tender mercy and compassionate.

12 Above all, my brethren, do not swear, neither by heaven, nor the earth, nor any other oath. Instead, let your yes, be yes, and the no, no, in order that you might not fall under judgment.

13 Is anyone among you suffering? Let him pray. Is anyone cheerful? Let him sing praises. 14 Is anyone among you ill? He should call the elders of the church, and they should pray over him, anointing him with oil in the name of the Lord. 15 And the prayer of faith will restore to health the one who is sick, and the Lord will raise him up; and if he has committed sins he will be forgiven.

16 Confess to one another the sins; and pray for one another that you might be healed. The earnest request of a righteous person is able to accomplish much.[o] 17 Elijah had the same kind of feelings and desires as us, and he prayed fervently that it not rain; and it did not rain upon the land three years and six months. 18 Then he prayed again, and the heaven gave rain,

and the land sprouted its fruit.

19 My brethren, if anyone among you wanders away from the truth, and anyone should restore him, 20 keep in mind that whoever restores a sinner from the error of his way will save a soul from death itself and cover a multitude of sins.

The Book of First Peter

The Book of First Peter was written ca. AD 62–64. Peter's first letter is a manifesto of what it means to be a Christian in an unchristian world: what to believe and how to act. Peter's doctrine is the same as Paul's doctrine, but expressed in simpler terms to an audience of believers not able to follow Paul's theological arguments.

FIRST PETER ONE

1 Peter, apostle of Jesus Christ, to elect[a1] expatriates[a2] of the diaspora, of Pontus, Galatia, Cappadocia, Asia, and Bithynia, 2 according to foreknowledge of God Father, in sanctification of spirit to obedience and sprinkling of blood of Jesus Christ: Grace to you and peace multiplied.

3 Blessed be the God and Father of our Lord Jesus Christ, who according to his great mercy regenerated[b] us to a living hope through resurrection of Jesus Christ out from the dead ones,[c] 4 to an inheritance not-corruptible and not-defiled and not-fading,[d] reserved in heaven for you, 5 the ones by the power of God being guarded through faith unto a salvation ready to be revealed in a last season.[e]

6 In which be now rejoicing, if need be for a little time at present you are made sorrowful in various trials 7 to the end that what is genuine in your faith—much more valued than gold that is perishing though tested by fire—is discovered for commendation and glory and honor by the revealing of Jesus Christ 8 (whom not having seen in person, you love; in respect to whom now not seeing but believing be rejoicing with joy inexpressible and glorious) 9 when you receive the completion of your faith, salvation of your souls.

10 Concerning which salvation prophets earnestly sought to understand and searched very diligently, who prophesied concerning the grace coming to you: 11 searching into what or what sort of season the Spirit of Christ in each was continually revealing,[f1] declaring beforehand the sufferings of Christ and the glory after these things.

12 To whom it was revealed that not to themselves, but to us they ministered these same things which have been declared unto you through the ones who preached the good news to you by the Holy Spirit sent out from heaven; toward which things messengers desire to look into more closely.

13 Therefore, having prepared your mind for work, being prudent, steadfastly hope upon the grace being brought to you in the revelation of Jesus Christ, 14 as obedient children not conforming to the former desires in your ignorance, 15 but according as the one who called you is holy, also yourselves become holy in all behavior. 16 For this reason it is written, "You be holy because I am

holy."

17 And if, as in fact you do, you call "Father" the *One* who without respect of persons judges according to each one's work, conduct yourselves in reverence and caution[f2] the time of your residence as expatriates,[f3] 18 knowing (as you do) that not by corruptible things—by silver or by gold—you were redeemed from your empty manner of life (traditions handed down from your fathers) 19 but with precious blood as of a lamb—Christ—without blemish and without spot.

20 Truly foreknown before the founding of the world, but made known during these last times for you, 21 who through him believe in God, the one having raised him out from *the* dead and having given him glory, so that your faith and hope are in God.

22 Your souls having purified by obedience to the truth through the Spirit to sincere brotherly love, you are to love one another earnestly out of a clean heart, 23 having been born-again not from corruptible seed but by the not-corruptible word of God which lives and abides forever, 24 because all flesh is as grass, and all its glory as the flower of grass. The grass withers and the flower falls off, 25 but the word of the Lord abides forever. And this is the word that was proclaimed good news to you.

FIRST PETER TWO

1 Therefore, having laid aside all malice, and all deceit, and hypocrisy, and envies, and all evil-speaking,[g] 2 as new-born infants you are to desire earnestly the reasonable sincere milk[h] that by it you may grow, 3 if, as is the fact, you have experienced that the Lord is good. 4 To whom coming, a living stone by men indeed rejected, but with God chosen and precious, 5 and yourselves as living stones being built a spiritual house, a holy priesthood, to offer spiritual sacrifices acceptable to God through Jesus Christ.

6 Therefore, also, it is contained in Scripture, "Behold! I lay in Zion a stone, a chosen cornerstone, precious; and the one that believes on him will never be put to shame." 7 Now, the honor is unto you who believe. But to those disbelieving the stone those building rejected, that one became for the head of the corner, 8 and a stone of stumbling, and a rock of ruin, which those who disbelieve the word fall against, to which also they were appointed. 9 But you are a chosen people, a royal priesthood, a holy people, a people purchased,[i] so that you may declare abroad the perfections of the one having called you out of darkness into his wondrous light. 10 Who at one time were not a people but now are God's people; who had not received mercy but now have received mercy.

11 Beloved, I exhort you as foreigners and expatriates to refrain from carnal desires which war against the soul, 12 having your conduct good among the peoples,[j] so that when they speak

against you as doing evil, out of the good works they behold, they might glorify God in the day of visitation.

13 Be in submission, then, to every human creation on account of the Lord, whether to the king as superior in rank, 14 or governors as by him being sent to execute justice for evil-doers, but reward him that does well. 15 For so is the will of God: by doing good to others to continue to silence the ignorance of foolish men. 16 As free, and not as having the freedom as the pretext for wickedness, but as servants of God. 17 Show honor to all. Love the brotherhood. Reverence[k] God. Honor the king. 18 The domestics[l] be subject to your masters with all respect, not only to the good and lenient, but also to the unjust.

19 For this is acceptable, if because of conscience toward God one endures trouble, suffering unjustly. 20 For what kind of glory is it if you sin and endure being beaten? But if you do good and endure suffering, this is acceptable with God. 21 For to this you were called, because Christ also suffered—for you—leaving you an example, so that you should follow in his footsteps. 22 Who did not do sin; neither was deceit found in his mouth. 23 Who being reviled did not revile in return, suffering did not threaten, but committed to him who judges justly. 24 Who himself bore our sins in his body on the tree; so that having died to sins we continually live to righteousness, having been healed by his wounds.

25 For you were as wandering sheep, but have now turned toward the shepherd and overseer of your souls.

FIRST PETER THREE

1 In like manner you wives put yourselves in submission to your own husbands, that even if any disbelieve the Word, by the wives' conduct they may be won without a word, 2 having contemplated your reverent, blameless conduct.

3 Whose adornment let it not be the outward braiding of hair and wearing of gold accessories or wearing of garments; 4 but the hidden person of the heart, in the incorruptible quality of the gentle and tranquil spirit, which is very precious to God.

5 For in this manner in the past the holy women trusting on God also adorned themselves, being subject to their own husbands, 6 as Sarah obeyed Abraham, calling him "Sir," of whom you became daughters, to do good, and not fearing not one fear. 7 Husbands in the same manner dwelling with *their wives* according to knowledge as with a weaker feminine vessel, bestowing respect as also joint heirs of the grace of life, so as to not cut off your prayers.

8 But this, finally, be all of one mind: compassionate, loving as brethren, tender-hearted, courteous, 9 not returning evil for evil, or reproach for reproach; but on the contrary, blessing, knowing that to this you were called, that

you may inherit blessing.

10 For the one who wants to love life and to see good times, let him stop his tongue from evil, even his lips from speaking deceit; 11 let him turn away from evil and let him do good; let him seek peace and let him pursue it. 12 Because the Lord's eyes are on the righteous, and his ears toward their prayer; but the Lord's face is against any doing evil.

13 And who is the one that will harm you, if you should be followers of that which is good? 14 But if also you should suffer for righteousness, you are blessed.

But you should not become afraid of them, neither should you be troubled, 15 but sanctify the Lord God in your hearts. And at all times be prepared to present a verbal defense[m] to everyone asking you a reason concerning the hope in you, but with meekness and fear, 16 having a good conscience, that when they speak against you as evildoers, they who falsely accuse your good manner of life in Christ may be made ashamed.

17 For better to suffer doing good, if wills the will of God, than doing evil. 18 Because even Christ suffered once for sins—righteous for unrighteous—in order that he might bring us to God; having indeed been put to death in flesh,[n1] but having been made alive in spirit,[n2] 19 in which[o] he preached, also having gone to the spirits in prison, 20 once upon a time having disbelieved, when once the longsuffering of God waited in the times of Noah, an ark being prepared, in which few, that is, eight souls, were saved through water.

21 Which antitype, immersion, now saves us—not the putting off of filth of flesh, but the response of a good conscience toward God through the resurrection of Jesus Christ, 22 who is at the right hand of God, having gone into heaven, messengers and authorities and powers having been subjected to him.

FIRST PETER FOUR

1 Christ, then, having suffered for us in flesh, you also arm yourselves with the same purpose; because the one having suffered in flesh is done with sin 2 to live the remaining time in flesh no more in men's lusts but God's will. 3 For our past life was enough time to live like the worldling,[p] having lived without restraint in lusts, in insatiable desire for wine, in riotous feastings, in drinking matches, and in unlawful idolatry. 4 In this they think you strange—of you not running around with them to the same debauched excess—speaking evil of you; 5 who shall give an account to him who is ready to judge the living and the dead. 6 For to this the good news was proclaimed even to those now dead, that they may be judged, indeed, according to men in flesh, but they might live according to God in spirit.

7 Now the end of all things is at hand; therefore use sound

judgment, and be observant to prayers. 8 But before all other things having continual godly love among yourselves—because godly love will cover a great many sins— 9 hospitable to one another without complaining. 10 Each, according to the spiritual gift they received, are to serve others as good ministers of the varied grace of God. 11 If anyone speaks—as the oracles of God; if anyone ministers—as from the ability which God supplies; that in all things God may be glorified through Jesus Christ; to whom is the glory and the dominion forever and ever. Amen.

12 Beloved, do not be surprised at the fiery trial coming to you (which is happening to test you) as though something unheard of is happening to you, 13 but as you have participated in the sufferings of the Christ, be rejoicing in order that also when his glory is revealed you may rejoice exceedingly. 14 If you are belittled[q] in respect to the name of Christ, you are blessed because God's glory and Spirit rests upon you. Indeed on their part it is slander; but on your part it is glory.[r]

15 For let not any of you suffer as a murderer, or thief, or evildoer, or as a busybody; 16 but if as a Christian, let him not be ashamed, but let him glorify God in this name.[s] 17 For the season is come to begin the judgment starting from the house of God; but if first from us, what will be the outcome of those disbelieving the good news of God? 18 And if the righteous is scarcely saved—in what place will the ungodly and sinner appear? 19 And therefore those suffering according to the will of God let them commit their souls in well-doing as to a faithful Creator.

FIRST PETER FIVE

1 I exhort the elders among you, I who am a fellow elder and witness of Christ's sufferings, who also am a partaker of the glory about to be revealed. 2 Shepherd the flock of God among you, overseeing not by constraint but voluntarily, by no means for dishonorable gain but willingly, 3 not as ruling those in your congregation,[t] but being to the flock an example to be imitated. 4 And the chief shepherd appearing, you will receive the crown of glory made of unfading amaranths.[u]

5 Likewise you younger submit to elders—but all submit to one another, putting on humility, because God opposes the proud but gives grace to the humble.

6 Therefore be humbled under the mighty hand of God, that he might exalt you in proper season, 7 having cast all your anxiety upon him, because he concerns himself in your behalf.

8 Be sober-minded, be mindful of threatening dangers: your enemy the devil walks here and there as a roaring lion, seeking someone he may swallow,[v] 9 whom resist immovable by faith, knowing the same sufferings are being experienced by your

brothers and sisters throughout the world.

10 Now the God of all grace, who called you to his eternal glory in Christ Jesus, after you have suffered a brief time, himself prepare, make steadfast, strengthen, and confirm you; 11 to him be the glory and the dominion to eternity, truly.

12 Through Silas,ʷ to you the faithful brother, as I reckon, through whom I wrote a little, exhorting and testifying this to be the true grace of God in which you stand. 13 The fellow elect in Babylon and Mark my son greet you. 14 Greet one another with a kiss of love. Peace to you: all those in Christ Jesus. Amen.

The Book of Second Peter

The Book of Second Peter was written ca. 64–67. Some notice stylistic differences and less cultured Greek in 2 Peter from 1 Peter, leading some to deny Peter as author of one or the other book (or both books). The differences are accounted for by 1 Peter 5:12. Silas (Silvanus) was the scribe for 1 Peter, writing what Peter dictated using better Greek than Peter spoke—the Holy Spirit inspiring each man to express the truth in suitable words. The Book of 2 Peter came direct from Peter's hand, no scribe. In 2 Peter the apostle addresses conflict and danger within the local church from false teachers.

SECOND PETER ONE

1 Simon Peter, a servant and apostle of Jesus Christ, to those having obtained equally precious faith with us in the righteousness of our God and our Savior Jesus Christ: 2 Grace to you and peace abound to you by the knowledge of God and of Jesus our Lord.

3 As his divine power has given to us all things needed for life and godliness, through the knowledge of him who called us by his own glory and moral excellence, 4 through which have been freely given to us great and precious promises, so that through these things you may become partakers of the divine nature, having escaped the corruption in the world by lust.

5 And this same also—bringing forth all diligence—add[a] with your faith, moral excellence; and with moral excellence, knowledge; 6 and with knowledge, self-control; and with self-control, perseverance; and with perseverance, godliness; 7 and with godliness, brotherly love; and with brotherly love, godly love. 8 For if these things exist in you and are abounding, they make you neither inactive nor unfruitful as to the knowledge of our Lord Jesus Christ.

9 For in whom these things are not present, he is slow to understand spiritual things, nearsighted, having taken forgetfulness of the purification of his former sins. 10 Wherefore, rather, brethren, be diligent to make certain your call and election, for in doing these things never no never should you fail at any time. 11 For in this manner will be abundantly supplied to you the way into the eternal kingdom of our Lord and Savior Jesus Christ.

12 Therefore I will not neglect[b] to always put you in remembrance of these things; although you know and have been made steadfast in the present truth. 13 But I regard as right (as long as I am in this tent) to wake you up with a reminder, 14 knowing that putting off my tent is near, even as our Lord Jesus Christ revealed to me. 15 And also I will always do my best to provide for you after my departure,[c] to cause a remembrance of these things.

16 For, not having copied[d] skillfully devised fables made to

deceive, we made known to you the power and presence of our Lord Jesus Christ; but indeed we were eyewitnesses of his majesty.

17 For, having received from God the Father honor and glory, so great a voice having come to him through the glorious glory, "This is my beloved Son in whom I am well pleased." 18 And this voice we heard coming from heaven, being with him in the holy mountain.

19 And we have more certain the prophetic word to which you do well to pay attention, as to a lamp giving light in a dark place, until the day dawns and the morning star springs up in your hearts. 20 This first knowing, that every prophecy of Scripture does not come from one's own[e1] interpretation,[e2] 21 for not at any time did prophecy come by the will of man, but men of God spoke being born along by the Holy Spirit.

SECOND PETER TWO

1 And also false prophets came among the people, as also false teachers shall be among you, who will smuggle[f] in destructive heresies, and denying the master who bought them will bring upon themselves impending destruction. 2 And many will conform to their destructive ways, through whom the way of the truth will be slandered. 3 And by their desire to have more, with deceitful words they will exploit you.

For whom the judgment of old does not rest, and their destruction does not sleep. 4 For God did not spare the messengers who sinned, but cast them to Tartarus[g] in chains of darkness, delivered and kept for judgment. 5 And did not spare the old world (but preserved Noah—one of eight—a preacher of righteousness) having brought a flood on an ungodly world. 6 And the cities of Sodom and Gomorrah, having reduced them to ashes, condemned them to destruction, having set them as an example to those who would thereafter live ungodly. 7 And rescued righteous Lot oppressed by the extremely wicked behavior of the immoral— 8 for seeing and hearing, that righteous man in dwelling among them from day to day, his righteous soul was tormented with their lawless works.

9 The Lord knows to deliver believers out of temptation; but to keep the unrighteous for a day of judgment to be punished, 10 but especially those who live after the flesh with lust of that which defiles, and who despise authority.

These are presumptuous, arrogant, unafraid to speak evil of authorities; 11 whereas God's messengers, being of greater strength and ability, do not bring a reviling judgment against them before the Lord. 12 But these, like unreasoning natural animals born for capture and destruction, speak evil of what they do not know; in their corruption they will utterly perish.

13 These take to themselves wages for unrighteousness as

those who esteem self-indulgence a daily pleasure. They are stains and blemishes, reveling in their deceits, feasting together with you, 14 having eyes full of adultery, unable to cease from sin, enticing unstable souls, having a heart exercised in the desire for more, accursed children, 15 having abandoned the right way, they go astray to follow the way of Balaam, the son of Beor, who loved the wages of unrighteousness. 16 But he had reproof of his transgression, a mute beast of burden having spoken with a man's voice restrained the prophet's folly.

17 These are wells without water, small clouds being driven by tempest, for whom the darkness of the spiritual darkness[h] is forever reserved. 18 For speaking vain boastings they entice by fleshly desires and wantonness those truly escaped from those who live in error, 19 promising freedom to them, themselves being slaves of corruption; for by what someone has been overcome he is also made a slave.

20 For if, having escaped the world's defilements by an experiential knowledge of our Lord and Savior Jesus Christ, and in these having again become entangled and overcome, their last state has become worse than the first. 21 For was better for them not to have known the way of righteousness than having known to turn from the holy commandment delivered to them. 22 But has happened to them the true proverb: a dog having returned to its own vomit, and a sow having washed to wallowing in mire.

SECOND PETER THREE

1 This, now, beloved, a second letter I write to you, in which I stir up your discerning mind by reminder, 2 to be mindful of the words spoken before by the holy prophets, and of the command by us the apostles of the Lord and Savior, 3 knowing this first of all: that will come during last of the days[i] scoffers living according to their own desires, 4 and saying, "Where is the promise of his coming? Because from when the fathers fell asleep all things thus remain the same as from the beginning of the creation."

5 For they are willingly ignorant of this, that of old were heaven and earth brought into existence out of water and through water by the word of God, 6 through which the then world having been flooded with water perished. 7 But now the heavens and earth[j] by the same word are reserved for fire, being kept to a day of judgment and the destruction of ungodly men.

8 But this thing, let it not be unknown to you beloved: that one day with the Lord is as a thousand years and a thousand years is as one day. 9 The Lord of the promise is not slow, as some reckon slowness, but is longsuffering to us, not wanting some[k] to perish but all to come to repentance. 10 But the day of the Lord will come

as a thief in the night in which the heavens will pass away with a rushing noise, and elements will be unbound with burning fire, and earth and the works in it will be burned up.

11 All these, then, being unbound, what manner is necessary for you to live in holy conduct and godliness, 12 expecting and waiting with eager desire the coming of the day of God, in which heavens being on fire will be unbound and elements burning will be unbound?

13 Now we expect a new heavens and a new earth according to his promise, in which righteousness resides. 14 Therefore, beloved, expecting these things, be diligent to be found with reference to him spotless and blameless, in peace.

15 And the long-suffering of our Lord esteem as salvation, even as also our beloved brother Paul, according to the wisdom given him, did write to you, 16 as also in all the epistles, speaking in them about these things, in which are some things hard to be understood, which the unlearned and unstable twist, as also the other Scriptures, to their own destruction.

17 You, then, beloved, knowing before, keep watch, so that you are not seduced by the error of the wicked to be led astray to fall from your own steadfastness. 18 But grow in grace and knowledge of our Lord and Savior Jesus Christ. To him be the glory both now and to the day of eternity. Amen.

The Book of First John

The Book of First John was written ca. AD 95. The early church testified of the apostle John as author and Ephesus as place of writing. Various reasons have been assigned as the occasion for the letter, e.g., a polemic against Gnosticism or secessionists. The letter is not a polemic but instructional. I agree with A. W. Pink [*Exposition*], "the object of his epistle is to delineate the character and distinguishing marks of God's regenerate sons." Throughout his letter John states many ways by which to affirm and diligently practice one's faith.

FIRST JOHN ONE

1 What was from the beginning, which we heard, which we perceived with our eyes, which we contemplated, and our hands touched, concerning the word of life—2 and the life was revealed, and we have looked intently,[a] and are testifying and declaring to you the eternal life that was with the Father, and revealed to us—3 what we perceived and heard we declare also to you, so that you also might have fellowship with us; and also our fellowship is with the Father and with his Son, Jesus Christ. 4 And these things we write, in order that our joy might be made full.

5 Now this is the message that we heard from him and make known to you: that God is light and darkness is not in him, none at all. 6 If we should say that we have fellowship with him, and habitually[b] live out our life in the darkness, we are lying and not doing the truth. 7 But if we habitually order our behavior in the light, as he is in the light, we have fellowship with one another, and the blood of Jesus Christ his Son is continually cleansing us from every sin.

8 If we should say that we have no sin,[c] we deceive ourselves and the truth is not in us. 9 If we continue to confess our sins, he is faithful and righteous to forgive us the sins, and to cleanse us from every unrighteousness. 10 If we should say that we have not sinned, and as a result are not now sinning, we make him a liar, and his word is not in us.

FIRST JOHN TWO

1 My little children, I am writing these things to you that you may not commit acts of sinning. Now if anyone should commit an act of sinning, we have one who represents us with the Father, Jesus Christ the righteous. 2 Now he is propitiation for our sins—but not for ours only but also for all the world.

3 Now in this we know that we have come to know him: if his commandments we are continually keeping. 4 The person saying, "I have known him," and his commandments he is not keeping, he is a liar, and the truth is not in him. 5 But whoever habitually keeps his word, truly in him the love of God has been brought to completion. In this we know that

we are in him: 6 the person claiming to abide in him is obligated, even as he lived his life, also himself to behave in the same manner.

7 Beloved ones, I am not writing a new commandment to you, but an old commandment, which you have had constantly[d] from the beginning. The old commandment is the word that you heard. 8 Again, a new commandment I am writing to you, which is true in him and in you, because the darkness is passing away, and the true light is already shining.

9 The person saying he is in the light but is habitually hating his brother, he is in the darkness up to this moment. 10 The person habitually loving his brother abides in the light, and there is no cause for stumbling in him. 11 But the person who as a habit of life is hating his brother is in the darkness, and in the darkness is habitually ordering his behavior, and does not know where he is going, because the darkness has blinded his eyes.

12 I am writing to you little children, because your sins have been permanently forgiven[e] because of his name. 13 I am writing to you fathers, because you have known and continue to know him who is from the beginning. I am writing to you young men, because you have overcome and continue to overcome the evildoer.[f]

I have written to you children, because you have known and continue to know the Father. 14 I have written to you, Fathers, because you have known and continue to know him who is from the beginning. I have written to you young men, because you are strong, and the word of God abides in you, and you have overcome the evildoer.

15 Love not the world, nor the things in the world. If anyone habitually loves the world the Father's love is not in him. 16 Because all that is in the world—the strong desire of the flesh, and the strong desire of the eyes, and the ostentatious pride of worldly life—is not from the Father but is from the world. 17 And the world is being caused to pass away,[g] and its strong desire. But the person habitually doing God's will abides for the age.

18 Little children, it is a last hour, and as you have heard that antichrist is coming, even now many antichrists have arisen, whereby we know that it is a last hour. 19 From among us they went out, but they were not of us—for if they had been of us they would have remained with us—but that it might be apparent that all are not of us.

20 And you have anointing from the holy One, and you know all things. 21 I have not written to you because you do not know the truth, but that you know it, and that no lie has its source in the truth. 22 Who is the liar if not the person denying that Jesus is the Christ? This is the antichrist: the

person who is denying the Father and the Son. 23 Every person who is denying the Son, neither has he the Father. The person who is confessing the Son has the Father also.

24 That which each one of you[h] have heard from the beginning, let it constantly abide in you. If that which you have heard from the beginning should abide in you, you will also abide in the Son and in the Father. 25 Now this is the promise that he promised us: the eternal life. 26 These things I have written to you concerning those leading you astray. 27 And you, the anointing that you received from him abides in you, and you have no constant need that anyone should continuously teach you, but as the same anointing teaches you about all things, and is true and is not a lie, and just as it has taught you, you will be constantly abiding in him.

28 And now, little children, abide in him, that when he appears we may have confidence, and not be put to shame before him at his coming. 29 If you understand that he is righteous, you also know that every person habitually practicing righteousness is born from[i] him.

FIRST JOHN THREE

1 Look at what manner of love the Father bestowed upon us, that we should be named children of God. And we are.[j] On account of this the world knows us not, because it knew him not. 2 Beloved ones, we now are God's children, and what we will be has not yet been revealed. We certainly know that when he is made visible we will be like him, because we will see him just as he is. 3 Now every person having this hope continually in him is constantly purifying himself, just as he is pure.

4 Every person habitually practicing sin also habitually practices lawlessness; and sin is lawlessness. 5 And you know that he was revealed in order that he might take away sins; and in him sin does not exist. 6 Every person habitually abiding in him is not habitually sinning. Every person habitually sinning has not discerned him, nor does he know him.

7 Little children, let no one mislead you. The person habitually practicing righteousness is righteous, just as he is righteous. 8 The person habitually practicing sin is from the devil, because from the beginning the devil has been sinning. For this purpose the Son of God was revealed: that he might destroy the works of the devil.

9 Every person who has been born from God does not habitually practice sin, because his seed abides in him, and he is not able to habitually sin, because from God he is born. 10 Through this the children of God are revealed and the children of the devil: any person not habitually practicing righteousness is not of God; also the person not habitually loving his brother.

11 Because this is the

message that you have heard from the beginning: that we should habitually love one another. 12 Not as Cain, who was out of the evildoer, and murdered his brother. And why did he murder him? Because his works were evil, those of his brother righteous.

13 Be not surprised, brethren, if, as is the case, the world hates you. 14 We know with certainty we have permanently passed[k] out of death to life, because we are habitually loving the brethren. The person not habitually loving is abiding in death. 15 Every person habitually hating his brother is a murderer; and you know that every murderer does not have eternal life abiding in him.

16 In this we have come to know love: because he for us laid down his life. And we are obligated to lay down our lives for our brethren. 17 Now whoever, perhaps, may have as a constant possession[l] the means of life in the world, and keeps on contemplating his brother having constant need, and may not have compassion for him, how does God's love abide in him?

18 Little children we should not love in word or in speech, but in action and truth. 19 In this we will know that we are of the truth, and will quiet[m] our heart in his presence, 20 because if our heart should condemn us, that God is greater than our heart, and he knows all things. 21 Beloved ones, if our heart is not condemning us, we have confidence toward God, 22 and whatever we keep on asking we keep on receiving from him, because his commandments we are habitually keeping, and the things pleasing before him we are habitually doing.

23 Now this is his commandment: that we should believe in the name of his Son, Jesus Christ, and we should be habitually loving one another, even as he gave a commandment to us. 24 Now the person habitually keeping his commandments, abides in him, and he in him; and by this we know that he abides in us, from the Spirit whom he gave to us.

FIRST JOHN FOUR

1 Beloved ones, stop believing every spirit, but examine the spirits, whether they are from God, because many false prophets have gone out into the world. 2 In this you know the Spirit of God: every spirit who agrees that Jesus Christ is come in the flesh is from God, 3 and every spirit who does not confess Jesus Christ is come in the flesh is not from God. Now this is that *spirit* of the antichrist, which you have heard that *spirit* is coming,[n] and now is already in the world.

4 You are of God, little children, and have conquered them, because greater is he who is in you than he who is in the world. 5 They are from the world. On account of this, from the world they speak, and the world listens to them. 6 We are from God. The person knowing God listens to us.

The person who is not of God does not listen to us. From this we know the Spirit of truth and the spirit of error.

7 Beloved ones, let us be habitually loving one another, because love is from God; and every person who is habitually loving has been born from God and knows God. 8 The person not habitually loving has not known God, because God is love. 9 In this God's love has been revealed in us: that God sent his Son, the only begotten, into the world, in order that we may live through him. 10 In this is the love: not that we have loved God, but that he loved us, and sent his Son, a propitiation concerning our sins.

11 Beloved ones, if God so loved us, we also are obligated to love one another. 12 No person has seen God at any time. If we habitually love one another, God abides in us and God's love has been brought to its fulness in us.

13 In this we know that in him we are abiding, and he in us, because of his Spirit he has permanently given to us. 14 And we have deliberately considered and we are testifying that the Father has sent the Son as Savior of the world. 15 Whoever confesses that Jesus Christ is the Son of God, God in him abides, and he in God. 16 Now we have known and do know, and we have believed and do believe, the love which God has for us. God is love, and the person abiding in love abides in God, and God abides in him.

17 In this, love has been brought to completion with us: that we might have confidence in the day of judgment; because even as he is, we also are in this world. 18 There is no terror in love. On the contrary, love completed casts out terror. Because the one with terror has torment,° the person who has terror does not have completed love.

19 We love because he first loved us. 20 If any person should say, "I am loving God," and is hating his brother, he is a liar. For the person not loving his brother, whom he has seen, is not able to be loving God, whom he has not seen. 21 Now this commandment we have from him: that the person loving God should also be loving his brother.

FIRST JOHN FIVE

1 Every person believing that Jesus is the Christ has been born from God; and every person loving the One who fathered, loves the One who has been begottenᵖ from him. 2 In this we know that we are habitually loving the children of God: when we habitually love God, and his commandments we are habitually doing.

3 For this is the love for God, that his commandments we are habitually obeying; and his commandments are not heavy burdens. 4 Because every person born from God constantly overcomes the world; and this is the victory that is constantly overcoming the world: our faith. 5 Who is the person overcoming the

world, if not the person believing that Jesus is the Son of God?

6 This is the One who came through water and blood, Jesus Christ; not by water only, but by the water and the blood. Now the Spirit is the One constantly testifying, because the Spirit is the truth. 7 Because there are three constantly bearing testimony: 8 the Spirit and the water and the blood. And these three are in the one [q].

9 If we habitually receive the testimony of men, the testimony of God is greater, because this is the testimony of God: that he has testified and is testifying concerning his Son. 10 The person believing on the Son of God has the testimony in himself; the person not believing God has made him a liar and presently considers him a liar, because he has not believed in the testimony that God has testified concerning his Son. 11 Now this is the testimony: that God gave us eternal life, and this life is in his Son. 12 The person who has the Son has life. The person not having the Son of God does not have life.

13 These things I have written to you, in order for you to have assurance that you do possess eternal life, to you who believe on the name of the Son of God [r]. 14 And this is the assurance that we are having before him, that whatever we keep on asking according to his will, he hears us. 15 Now if we are knowing that he hears us, whatever we are asking, we are knowing that we have the things which we have asked from him.

16 If anyone should see his brother sinning a sin not tending toward death, he should ask, and he will give him life—those not sinning toward death. There is a sin tending toward death; concerning that I do not say that he should ask. 17 All unrighteousness is sin; and there is a sin not tending toward death.

18 We know that everyone having been born from God does not keep on habitually sinning. But rather, the One having been born from God guards him,[s] and the evildoer does not influence him.

19 We know that we are from God, and the whole world is in the power of the evildoer. 20 And we know that the Son of God has come and is here, and has given us an understanding, in order that we may know him who is true. Now we are in him who is true, in his son, Jesus Christ. He is the genuine God and eternal life. 21 Little children, guard yourselves from idols.

The Book of Second John

The Book of Second John was written ca. AD 95, presumably in Ephesus. The book is a personal letter to Christians in a church other than Ephesus.

1 The Elder to an Elect Lady and her children, whom I love in truth, and not only I, but also all those knowing the truth, 2 according to the truth constantly abiding in us, and will be with us to the age. 3 Grace, mercy, peace will be with us from God who is Father[a] and from Lord Jesus Christ the Son of the Father, in truth and love.

4 I greatly rejoiced that I have found some of your children living their life in truth, even as we received commandment from the Father. 5 And now I am asking you, Lady, not as if I am writing a new commandment to you, but that which we have had from the beginning: that we should habitually love one another. 6 Now this is love: that we should habitually order our behavior according to his commandments. This is the commandment just as you have heard from the beginning: that we should order our behavior in love.

7 For many deceivers have gone out into the world—those not confessing Jesus Christ coming in flesh. Such a person is the deceiver and the antichrist. 8 Take heed to yourselves in order that you should not lose the things we accomplished, but that you may receive a full reward.

9 Any person who goes beyond and does not abide in the teaching of Christ does not have God. The person abiding in the teaching, that person has both the Father and the Son. 10 If any person comes to you, and does not bring this teaching, do not receive him into your house, and do not give him greeting. 11 For the person greeting him is partaking in his evil works.

12 Having many things to write to you, I was not inclined with paper and ink, but hope to come to you and speak face to face, in order that our joy might be complete. 13 The children of your elect sister greet you.

The Book of Third John

The Book of Third John was written ca. AD 95, presumably in Ephesus. The book is a personal letter to Christians in a church other than Ephesus.

1 The Elder, to Gaius the beloved, whom I love in truth. 2 Beloved, concerning all things I am praying that you prosper and be in good health, just as your soul prospers. 3 For I greatly rejoiced when brethren were constantly coming and constantly bearing witness of the truth in you, even as you are living your life in truth. 4 I have no greater joy than this, that I should hear my children are habitually ordering their behavior in the truth.

5 Beloved, you are doing faithfully whatever you may be doing for the brethren, and they strangers, 6 who testified of your love before a church; whom you will do good, having sent them forward in a manner worthy of God; 7 because for the sake of the Name they went forth, accepting nothing from the unsaved. 8 Therefore we are obligated to receive such, in order that we might be fellow workers in the truth.

9 I wrote something to the church, but that person loving to be first among them, Diotrephes, does not accept us. 10 On account of this, when I should come, I will bring to remembrance his works which he is doing, babbling against us with evil words; and not being satisfied with these, neither does he himself receive the brethren, and those so inclined he forbids and he casts them out from the church.

11 Beloved, do not follow after what is evil, but what is good. The person habitually doing good is from God; the person habitually doing evil has not seen God. 12 To Demetrius repeated testimony has been borne by all, and by the truth itself. And we, moreover, bear testimony, and you know that our testimony is true.

13 I had many things to write to you, but I am unwilling with ink and pen to continue writing to you.[a] 14 Now I am hoping to see you shortly, and we will speak face to face. Peace to you. The friends send greetings to you. Be greeting the friends by name

The Book of Jude

The Book of Jude was written ca. AD 67–70. The book was written to an unknown community of believers to oppose apostate Christianity in Jude's own times, using historical examples, current descriptions, and encouraging prophesy, ending with an exhortation to evangelize, and a doxology.

1 Jude, servant of Jesus Christ, also brother of Jacob. To those in God Father, sanctified, in Jesus Christ kept, called. 2 Mercy to you, and peace and love be multiplied.

3 Beloved ones, as I was making all diligence to write to you about the salvation we have in common, I felt compelled to write to you exhorting you to contend earnestly for the faith which was delivered once for all to the saints. 4 For certain persons came in deceitfully, those having been previously written long ago to this judgment: the godless perverting[a] the grace of our God into license, and denying the only master and Lord of us, Jesus Christ.

5 But I intend to remind you—at one time you knew this—that the Lord having saved a people out of the land of Egypt, the second time destroyed those not believing; 6 and messengers—those not having kept their original state but deserted their own dwelling—have been kept in eternal bonds under darkness unto judgment of a great day; 7 as Sodom and Gomorrah, and the cities around them in the same manner with them, having practiced fornication and having followed after strange flesh, are set forth as an example to suffer the penalty of eternal fire.[b]

8 Yet in like manner also these deceivers[c] indeed defile the flesh, and deny authority, and also speak abusively of those in authority. 9 However Michael the archangel, when contending with the devil in a dispute about Moses' body, did not presume to bring against him a judgment of slander, but rather said, "The Lord censure you."

10 But these! Indeed what they do not understand they speak evil of; but what naturally by instinct, as the irrational animals, they understand, in these they corrupt themselves. 11 Woe to them! Because in the way of Cain they lived, and to the wickedness of Balaam for hire they hurried, and in the rebellion of Korah they destroyed themselves.

12 These are hidden rocks in your love feasts, feasting together with you, providing for themselves[d] without fear, small clouds without water driven about by winds, autumn trees without fruit, utterly dead, uprooted; 13 turbulent waves of the sea foaming out their shameful conduct; wandering stars for whom the darkness of spiritual darkness[e] to eternity has been reserved.

14 Now Enoch, the seventh from Adam, also prophesied of these saying, "Behold! The Lord

came^f in the midst of his holy ten thousands 15 to do judgment against all, and to punish all the godless concerning all their ungodly works they did impiously, and concerning all the offensive words which godless sinners have spoken against him. 16 These are grumblers, fault-finders. They are living according to their own desires, and their mouth speaks flattery, admiring persons for the sake of advantage.

17 But you, beloved, remember the words, the forewarning, received from the apostles of our Lord Jesus Christ, 18 that said to you, that in the last time there shall be false prophets,^9 according to their own desires living a life of ungodliness. 19 These are those causing divisions; natural souls not having the Spirit.

20 But you, beloved, building up yourselves on your most holy faith, praying in the Holy Spirit, 21 you keep yourselves in the love of God, expecting the mercy of our Lord Jesus Christ to eternal life. 22 And truly have mercy on those who are doubting; 23 now others save snatching out of the fire; now to others show mercy with fear, hating even the clothing stained by the flesh.

24 Now *to* the one able to keep you free from stumbling and cause you to stand in the very presence of his glory, without blemish, in exuberant joy, 25 God only wise, our Savior, *be* glory, majesty, dominion, and authority, now and to all the ages. Amen.

The Book of Revelation

The Book of Revelation was written ca. 95–96 AD. John was not the author of the book of Revelation. Jesus Christ was the author, 1:1; 22:20. The apostle John was the scribe and publisher of the book. The contents follow the three point outline in 1:19. The first point, "the things you have seen," is an introduction to the Revelation. The second point, "the things that are" is commendation and judgment of spiritual conditions in the local churches during the entire New Testament church age. The third point, the "things about to be after these," may be subdivided into three sections: 4:1–20:6, the outworking of the Old Testament Day of the Lord to its consummation in the Davidic-Messianic Kingdom; 20:7–20:15, the end of this present creation and final judgment of the unsaved out of all the ages; 21–22, a new heaven and new earth for the saved out of all the ages.

REVELATION ONE

1 The revelation of Jesus Christ, which God gave him, to show to his servants what things must suddenly begin to be. And he made it known, having sent through his messenger to his servant, John, 2 who has testified to the word of God and to the testimony of Jesus Christ, all that he saw. 3 Blessed the one reading and those hearing the words of the prophecy, and attentive to the things having been written in it. For the appointed time is near.

4 John to the seven churches in Asia. Grace to you and peace from him who is and who was and who is coming, and from the seven spirits before his throne, 5 and from Jesus Christ, the faithful witness, the firstborn of the dead and the ruler of kings of the earth. To the one loving us and releasing[a] us from our sins by his blood. 6 And he has made us kings and priests to his God and Father. To him the glory and the dominion to the ages of the ages. Amen.

7 Lo and behold! He is coming with the clouds, and every eye will see him, and those who pierced him, and because of him all will lament, all the tribes of the earth, yes, truly.

8 "I, I am the alpha and omega," says the Lord God, "the one who is, and the one who had been, and the one who is coming, the ruler over all."

9 I John, your brother and sharing in the tribulation and kingdom and endurance of circumstances,[b] in Jesus, was on the island called "Patmos," on account of the word of God and the witness of Jesus.

10 I was in spirit on that day belonging to the Lord, and I heard behind me a loud voice, like that of a trumpet, 11 saying, "I, I am the alpha and omega, the first and the last"; and "What you see, write in a book, and send to the seven churches: to Ephesus, and to Smyrna, and to Pergamum, and to Thyatira, and to Sardis, and to Philadelphia, and to Laodicea."

12 And I turned to see the voice that was speaking with me. And having turned, I saw seven golden lampstands, 13 and amidst the lampstands—like Son of Man, being clothed to the feet, and wrapped around at the breasts with a golden belt. 14 And the head and the hairs white, as if wool, white as snow, and his eyes like a flame of fire. 15 And his feet like fine bronze, as by a furnace having been purified. 16 And his voice like a voice of many waters. 16 And he is holding in his right hand seven stars. And out of his mouth a two-edged sword proceeds. And his face like the sun shining in its full strength.

17 And when I saw him I fell at his feet as dead. And he put his right hand on me, saying, "Fear not. I am the first and the last 18 and the living one. And I was dead, and see, I am living to the ages of the ages. And I have the keys of death and of hades.[c] 19 Therefore, write the things you have seen, and the things that are, and the things about to be after these.

20 The secret[d] of the seven stars, which you saw on my right hand, and the seven golden lampstands. The seven stars are messengers of the seven churches, and the seven lampstands are seven churches."

REVELATION TWO

1 To the messenger of the church in Ephesus write. These things says the one holding the seven stars in his right hand, walking in the midst of the seven golden lampstands. 2 I know your works, and your toil, and endurance as to circumstances, and that you are not able to endure evil persons. And putting to the test those saying themselves apostles and are not, and you discover them false. 3 And you have perseverance as to circumstances, and have endured with patience on account of my name and not become wearied.

4 But I have against you that your first love you have forsaken. 5 Call to mind, therefore, from what place you have fallen, and repent, and do the first works. But if not, I am coming to you, and will remove your lampstand out of its place, if you may not repent. 6 But this you have, that you hate the works of the Nicolaitans, which I also hate.

7 The one having an ear, let him hear what the Spirit says to the churches. To the one who is prevailing I will give him to eat out of the tree of life, which is in the paradise of God.

8 And to the messenger of the church in Smyrna write. These things says the first and the last, who became dead and came to life. 9 I know your[e] tribulation and helpless poverty[f]—but you are rich—and the slander of those claiming themselves to be Jews and are not, but a synagogue of Satan.

10 Do not fear what you are about to suffer. Look, the devil is about to cast some of you into prison, so that you may be tempted. And you will have

affliction ten days. You be faithful unto death, and I will give to you the crown, the one of life. 11 The one having an ear, let him hear what the Spirit says to the churches. The one who is prevailing never no never may be injured by the second death.

12 And to the messenger of the church in Pergamum write. These things says the one having the sharp two-edged sword. 13 I know⁹ where you dwell: the place of Satan's throne. And you hold fast to my name, and you have not denied my faith, even in the days of Antipas, my witness, my faithful one, who was murdered among you, where Satan dwells.

14 But I have a few things against you, because you have *those* there holding the teaching of Balaam, who did teach Balak to throw a snare in front of the sons of Israel: to eat whatever is sacrificed to idols, and to commit sexual immorality. 15 So also you have in like manner *those* holding the teaching of the Nicolaitans. 16 Therefore repent. But if not, I am coming to you quickly. And I will make war against them with the sword of my mouth.

17 The one having an ear, let him hear what the Spirit says to the churches. The one who is prevailing, I will give to him the manna, the one hidden. And I will give to him a white stone, and on the stone a new name has been written, which no one knows except the one receiving.

18 And to the messenger of the church in Thyatira write. These things says the Son of God, the one having his eyes like a flame of fire, and his feet like fine bronze. 19 I know your works, and love, and faith, and service, and your perseverance, and your last works greater than the first.

20 But I have against you that you permit the woman Jezebel, the one saying herself a prophet, and teaching and deceiving my servants to commit sexual immorality, and to eat whatever is sacrificed to idols. 21 And I have given her time in order that she may repent, and she does not desire to repent of her sexual immorality. 22 Look, I will cast her into a bed, and those committing adultery with her into great affliction, except they may repent of her works. 23 And her children I will kill with death, and all the churches will know that I am the one searching minds and hearts. And I will give to each of you according to your works.

24 But to you I say, to the remaining ones of those in Thyatira, as many as have not this teaching, who have not known the depths of Satan, as they say, I will not cast upon you any other burden. 25 But to what you have, hold fast until when I may come.

26 And the one who is prevailing and keeping my works until the end, I will give to him authority over the nations. 27 And he will shepherd them with a rod of iron, as the vessels of the potter are broken in pieces, even as I also

have received from my Father. 28 And I will give to him the morning star. 29 The one having an ear, let him hear what the Spirit says to the churches.

REVELATION THREE

1 And to the messenger of the church in Sardis write. These things says the one having the seven spirits of God, and the seven stars. I know your works, that reputation you have that you are alive; and yet you are dead. 2 Be mindful and strengthen the things that remain, that are about to die. For I have not found your works complete in the sight of my God. 3 Remember therefore what you have received and heard; and keep and repent. Therefore, if not, though you may watch,[h] I will come, like a thief, and never no never shall you know at what hour I will come upon you.

4 But you have a few persons in Sardis who have not defiled their clothing, and they will live with me in white, because they are worthy. 5 The one who is prevailing, in this manner will be clothed in white garments. And never no never will I blot his name out of the book of life. And I will confess his name in front of my Father, and in front of his messengers. 6 The one having an ear, let him hear what the Spirit says to the churches.

7 And to the messenger of the church in Philadelphia write. These things says the holy, the true, the one having the key of David, the one opening and no one will shut, and shutting and no one opens. 8 I know your works. Look, I put in front of you an open door (which none is able to shut it) because you have little power, and have kept my word, and have not denied my name. 9 Look, I cause from the synagogue of Satan those declaring themselves to be Jews—and are not but they lie—look, I will make them that they will come and will fall prostrate in front of your feet, and they may know that I have loved you.

10 Because you have kept the word of my endurance as to circumstances, I also will keep you out of the hour of the trial that is about to come upon the whole inhabited earth, to test the earth dwellers.[i1] 11 I am coming with haste. Hold fast to what you have, in order no one may take your crown.

12 The one who is prevailing, I will make him a pillar in the temple of my God. And never no never might he go out anymore. And I will write upon him the name of my God, and the name of the city of my God, the New Jerusalem coming out of heaven from my God, and my new name. 13 The one having an ear, let him hear what the Spirit says to the churches.

14 And to the messenger of the church in Laodicea write. These things says the Truth,[i2] the witness faithful and true, the beginning of the creation of God. 15 I know your works, that you are not cold nor hot. Oh that you would be cold or hot! 16 So because

you are lukewarm, and you are neither hot nor cold, I am about to spit you out of my mouth.

17 Because you say, "I am rich, and I have grown rich, and I have need of nothing." And you do not know that you are miserable, and pitiable, and helplessly poor, and blind, and naked. 18 I counsel you to buy from me gold refined by fire so that you may be rich. And white clothing so that you might be clothed and may not make apparent the shame of your nakedness. And eye-salve to anoint your eyes, so that you might see.

19 As many as if I may love, I rebuke and discipline. Therefore be zealous and repent. 20 Look, I stand before the door and knock. If any should hear my voice and open the door, then I will come to him, and will eat with him and he with me. 21 The one who is prevailing, I will give to him to sit with me on my throne, as I also overcame and sat down with my Father on his throne. 22 The one having an ear, let him hear what the Spirit says to the churches.

REVELATION FOUR

1 After these things, I took heed, and look, a door opening and open in heaven. And the first voice that I heard, like a trumpet, was speaking with me saying, "Come up here and I will show you what is inevitable to happen after these things."

2 Immediately I was in spirit, and look, a throne was set in heaven, and upon the throne one sitting. 3 And the one sitting in appearance as stone, crystalline and blood-red.[j] And a rainbow encircling the throne, as in appearance many colors. 4 And encircling the throne, twenty-four thrones. And on the thrones twenty-four elders are sitting, being dressed in white clothing. And on their heads golden crowns.

5 And out of the throne came lightning flashes, and voices, and thunders. And seven lamps of fire are burning before the throne, which are the seven spirits of God. 6 And before the throne like a sea of glass, like crystal. And in the midst of the throne and encircling the throne four living creatures, full of eyes front and back. 7 And the first living creature like a lion, and the second living creature like a calf, and the third living creature having the face as of a human being, and the fourth living creature as an eagle flying.

8 And the four living creatures, they one for one each had six wings encircling and within full of eyes. And they do not have rest day and night, saying, "Holy, holy, holy the Lord God Almighty, the one having been, and the one being, and the one coming."

9 And when the living creatures will give glory and honor and thanksgiving to the one sitting upon the throne, the one living to the ages of the ages, 10 the twenty-four elders will fall before the one sitting upon the throne, and they will worship the one living to the

ages of the ages, and they will throw their crowns before the throne, saying, 11 "Worthy are you, our Lord and God, to receive glory and honor and power. Because you created all, and because of your will they have existed and were created."

REVELATION FIVE

1 And I saw on the right hand of the one sitting on the throne a little scroll, with writing inside and back side, being sealed with seven seals. 2 And I saw a strong messenger proclaiming in a loud voice, "Who is worthy to open the little scroll and loose its seals?" 3 And no one in heaven was able—nor on the earth, nor under the earth—to open the little scroll, nor to see it. 4 And I was weeping much, because no one was found worthy to open the little scroll, nor to see it.

5 And one of the elders is saying to me, "Do not weep. Look, the Lion of the tribe of Judah, the offspring of David, has prevailed to open the little scroll and its seven seals." 6 And I saw in the midst of the throne and of the four living creatures and in the midst of the elders, a lamb standing as though having been slain, having seven horns, and seven eyes which are the seven spirits of God being sent out into all the earth.

7 And he came and took out of the right hand of the one sitting on the throne. 8 And after taking the scroll, the four living creatures, and the twenty-four elders, fell down before the Lamb, each having a lyre, and gold basins full of incenses, which are the prayers of the saints. 9 And they are singing a new song, saying, "Worthy are you to take the little scroll, and to open its seals, because you were slain, and you did pay the price to God by your blood, out of every tribe, and tongue, and people, and nation. 10 And to our God you have made them kings and priests. And they will reign on the earth."

11 And I saw, and I heard voices of many messengers encircling the throne, and of the living creatures, and of the elders. And their number was ten thousands of ten thousands and thousands of thousands, 12 saying in a loud voice, "Worthy is the Lamb having been slain to receive the power, and riches, and wisdom, and strength, and honor, and glory, and blessing." 13 And every creature which is in heaven, and on the earth, and under the earth, and on the sea—and everything in them—I heard saying to the one sitting on the throne and to the Lamb, "The blessing, and the honor, and the glory, and the power to the ages of the ages." 14 And the four living creatures were continually saying, "Truly!" And the elders fell down and worshiped.k

REVELATION SIX

1 And I saw when the Lamb opened one of the seven seals. And I heard from one of the four living creatures, saying, as if a voice of thunder, "Go!"(l) 2 And I saw, and look, a white horse and

the one sitting on it having a bow. And to him a crown was given. And he went out prevailing and that he should have victory.

3 And when he opened the second seal, I heard the second living creature saying, "Go!" 4 And another horse went out, bright red. And to the one sitting on it was given to him to take the peace from the earth, and that one another they will kill. And to him was given a great sword.

5 And when he opened the third seal, I heard the third living creature saying, "Go!" And I saw, and look, a black horse, and the one sitting on it having a weighing balance in his hand. 6 And I heard as a voice in the midst of the four living creatures, saying, "A measure^m of wheat for a denarius, and three measures of barley for a denarius; and the oil and the wine you may not injure."

7 And when he opened the fourth seal, I heard the voice of the fourth living creature saying, "Go!" 8 And I saw, and look, a pale horse, and the one sitting on it. His name was Death. And hades was going with him. And to them was given authority over the fourth of the earth, to kill with sword, and with famine, and with plague, and by the beasts of the earth.

9 And when he opened the fifth seal, I saw under the altar the souls of those who had been killed because of the word of God, and because of the testimony which they had held fast. 10 And they were exclaiming in a loud voice, saying, "Until when, O Lord, holy and true, do you not judge and avenge our blood from those dwelling upon the earth?" 11 And to each were given white robes. And was said to them that they should rest yet a little time, until also might be completed their fellow servants and their brethren: those about to be killed even as them.

12 And I saw when he opened the sixth seal. And there was a great earthquake. And the sun was black as sackcloth of hair. And the whole moon was as blood. 13 Also the stars of heaven fell to the earth, as a fig tree scatters its unripe figs being shaken by a great wind. 14 And heaven was torn apart and the parts were^n as a scroll being rolled up. And every mountain and island were moved out of their places.

15 And the kings of the earth, and those of the highest rank, and the military commanders, and the rich, and the powerful, and every slave and free hid themselves in the caves, and in the rocks of the mountains. 16 And they say to the mountains and to the rocks, "Fall on us and hide us from the face of the one sitting on the throne, and from the wrath of the Lamb, 17 because the great day of their wrath has come, and who is able to stand?"

REVELATION SEVEN

1 After these things, I saw four messengers standing on the four corners of the earth, holding fast the four winds of the earth, so that no wind would blow on the

earth, nor on the sea, nor on any tree.

2 And I saw another messenger, ascending from the dawning° of the sun, having the living God's seal. And he called in a loud voice to the four messengers, to whom it had been given to them to damage the earth and the sea, 3 saying, "You may not damage the earth, nor the sea, nor the trees until we may have sealed the servants of our God on their foreheads." 4 And I heard the number of them being sealed: one hundred forty four thousand, having been sealed out of every tribe of the sons of Israel.

5 Out of the tribe of Judah twelve thousand having been sealed. Out of the tribe of Reuben twelve thousand. Out of the tribe of Gad twelve thousand. 6 Out of the tribe of Asher twelve thousand. Out of the tribe of Naphtali twelve thousand. Out of the tribe of Manasseh twelve thousand. 7 Out of the tribe of Simeon twelve thousand. Out of the tribe of Levi twelve thousand. Out of the tribe of Issachar twelve thousand. 8 Out of the tribe of Zebulon twelve thousand. Out of the tribe of Joseph twelve thousand. Out of the tribe of Benjamin twelve thousand.

9 After these things I saw, and look, a great multitude, which no one was able to number it, out of every nation, and tribes, and peoples, and languages standing before the throne and before the Lamb, clothed with white robes, and in their hands palm branches. 10 And they were exclaiming in a loud voice, saying, "Salvation to our God, the one sitting on the throne, and to the Lamb!"

11 And all the messengers stood encircling the throne, and the elders, and the four living creatures. And they prostrated themselves on their faces before the throne, and worshiped God, 12 saying, "Truly blessing, and glory, and wisdom, and thanksgiving, and honor, and power, and strength to our God to the ages of the ages. So be it!"

13 And one of the elders responded, saying to me, "These who were clothed in white robes, who are they, and from what place have they come?" 14 And I said to him, "My lord, you know." And he said to me, "These are the ones coming out of the great Tribulation. And they have washed their robes and made them white in the blood of the Lamb. 15 For this reason they are before the throne of God and serve him day and night in his temple. And the one sitting on the throne will spread his tent over them.

16 "They will not hunger anymore, nor will they thirst anymore, no neither shall the sun fall upon them nor any scorching heat. 17 Because the Lamb in the midst of the throne will shepherd them, and God will wipe off every tear from their eyes."

REVELATION EIGHT

1 And when he opened the

seventh seal, there was silence in the heaven about a half hour. 2 And I saw the seven messengers who stand before God. And there were given to them seven trumpets.

3 And another messenger came, and he stood at the altar holding a golden censer. And to him was given much incense that he will offer with the prayers of all the saints upon the golden altar before the throne. 4 And the smoke of the incense went up with the prayers of the saints out of the hand of the messenger in God's presence. 5 And the messenger took the censer and filled it out of the fire of the altar. And he threw it to the earth. And came thunders and rumblings and flashes of lightning and an earthquake.

6 And the seven messengers having the seven trumpets prepared themselves so that they might sound the trumpets. 7 And the first sounded his trumpet and there was hail and fire, mixed with blood, and it was thrown upon the earth. And a third of the earth was burned, and a third of the trees were burned, and all the green grass was burned.

8 And the second messenger sounded his trumpet, and *something* like a great mountain, burning with fire, was thrown into the sea. And a third of the sea became blood, 9 and a third of the living creatures in the sea died, and a third of the ships were destroyed.

10 And the third messenger sounded his trumpet. And out of the heaven fell a great star burning as a torch. And it fell upon a third of the rivers, and upon the springs of waters. 11 And the name of the star is spoken "Wormwood." And a third of the waters became as wormwood. And many of the people died from the waters, because they were made poison.

12 And the fourth messenger sounded his trumpet. And a third of the sun was afflicted, and a third of the moon, and a third of the stars, so that a third of them may be darkened, and a third of the day may not have light and the night the same. 13 And I looked and I heard one eagle[p] flying in mid-heaven, saying in a loud voice, "Woe, woe, woe, to the earth dwellers, from the remaining voices of the trumpet of the three messengers now about to sound their trumpets."

REVELATION NINE

1 And the fifth messenger sounded his trumpet. And I saw a star falling out of heaven to the earth. And given to it the key of the pit of the abyss. 2 And he opened the pit of the abyss. And smoke came out of the pit, as smoke of a great furnace. And the sun and the air were darkened by the smoke of the pit.

3 And out of the smoke came forth locusts to the earth. And to them was given as the scorpions of the earth have power. 4 And was said to them that they will not hurt the grass of the earth, nor any green thing, nor any tree, except

the people not having the seal of God on the foreheads. 5 And it was given to them so that they would not kill them, but that they will afflict them five months. And their affliction *was something* like the affliction of a scorpion when it might sting a person. 6 And in those times, people will seek death and never no never will find it. And they will desire to die and death will flee from them.

7 And the resemblance of the locusts *was* just like horses made ready for battle. And upon their heads as crowns, like gold. And their faces as the faces of humankind. 8 And they had hair like the hair of women, and their teeth were as of lions. 9 And they had breastplates as breastplates of iron. And the sound of their wings as the sound of many horse chariots running into battle. 10 And they have tails like scorpions and stingers. And in their tails their power to harm people for five months. 11 They have over them a king, the messenger of the Abyss. His name in Hebrew "Abaddon," and in the Greek he has the name "Apollyon."

12 The first woe has passed. Look, still two woes are coming after these things.

13 And the sixth messenger sounded his trumpet. And I heard one voice from the four horns of the golden altar in God's presence, 14 saying to the sixth messenger, the one having the trumpet, "Release the four messengers, those in bonds at the great river Euphrates." 15 And the four messengers were released, the ones made ready for the hour and day and month and year, in order that they might kill a third of humankind.

16 And the number of the armies of the calvary twice ten thousand ten thousands. I heard their number. 17 And in this manner I saw the horses in the vision, and those sitting on them, having fiery breastplates, and deep blue, and made of sulfur. And the horses' heads as heads of lions, and out of their mouths go out fire and smoke and sulfur. 18 By these three plagues was killed a third of humankind: by the fire, and by the smoke, and by the sulfur going out of their mouths. 19 For the power of the horses are in their mouths, and in their tails. For their tails are like serpents, having heads, and with them they harm.

20 And the rest of the people who were not killed by these plagues repented not of the works of their hands, so that they will not worship the demons, and the idols golden and silver and bronze and stone and wooden, which neither are able to see nor to hear nor to walk. 21 And they repented not of their murders, nor of their sorceries, nor of their sexual immorality, nor of their thefts.

REVELATION TEN

1 And I saw another mighty messenger coming out of heaven, clothed with a cloud, and a rainbow on his head. And his face was as the sun, and his feet as

pillars of fire. 2 And he had in his hand a little scroll that was open. And he placed his right foot upon the sea, and the left upon the earth. 3 And he exclaimed in a loud voice as a lion roars. And when he exclaimed, the seven thunders spoke their voices.

4 And when the seven thunders had spoken I was about to write. But I heard a voice out of heaven, saying, "Seal what the seven thunders have spoken, and do not write them." 5 And the messenger I saw standing on the sea and on the earth lifted his right hand to heaven. 6 And he made an oath by the one living to the ages of the ages, who created heaven and the things in it, and the earth and the things in it, and the sea and the things in it. "No longer will there be time. 7 But in the times of the voice of the seventh messenger, when he is about to sound a trumpet, then the hidden of God has been completed, as his servants the prophets have proclaimed."

8 And the voice that I heard out of heaven again was speaking with me, and saying, "Go, take the little scroll, that is open in the hand of the messenger standing upon the sea and upon the land." 9 And he says to me, "Take and eat it. And it will be bitter to your stomach, but in your mouth will be sweet as honey."

10 And I took the little scroll out of the hand of the messenger; and I ate it. And it was in my mouth sweet as honey. And after I had eaten it my stomach was made bitter. 11 And they say to me, "You must prophecy again about peoples, and nations, and languages, and many kings."

REVELATION ELEVEN

1 And a measuring stick, like a staff, was given to me, saying, "Get up and measure the entire temple of God, and the altar of sacrifice, and those worshiping in it. 2 And the courtyard outside the entire temple leave out and not measure it, because it is given to the nations. And the holy city they will trample upon forty-two months. 3 And I will give to my two witnesses, and they will prophecy a thousand two hundred sixty days clothed in sackcloth."

4 These are the two olive trees and the two lampstands who are standing before the Lord of the earth. 5 And if any should desire to harm them, fire goes out of their mouth and consumes their enemies. And if any may desire to harm them he must be killed in this manner.

6 These have the authority to shut the sky, so that no rain may fall in the times of their prophecy. And they have authority over the waters to turn them into blood, and to inflict the earth with every plague, as often as if they may desire.

7 And when they may have completed their testimony, the beast, the one arising out of the abyss, will make war with them, and will prevail over them, and will

kill them, 8 and *leave* their bodies upon the street of the great city, which is spiritually called Sodom and Egypt, where also their Lord was crucified. 9 And the peoples and tribes and languages and nations look upon their bodies three and a half days. And they will not let go their bodies to be put into a tomb. 10 And the earth dwellers are glad over them and rejoice, and will send gifts to one another, because these two prophets did afflict the earth dwellers.

11 And after the three and a half days, a spirit of life from God entered in them, and they stood upon their feet. And great fear fell upon those seeing them. 12 And they heard a great voice out of heaven, saying to them, "Come up here." And they went up to heaven in the cloud. And their enemies saw them. 13 And in that hour there was a great earthquake. And a tenth of the city fell. And seven thousand names of persons were killed in the earthquake. And the rest became terrified and gave glory to the God of heaven.

14 The second woe has passed. Look, the third woe is coming quickly. 15 And the seventh messenger sounded his trumpet. And there were great voices in heaven, saying, "The kingdom of the world has become our Lord's and his Christ, and he will reign to the ages of the ages." 16 And the twenty-four elders sitting before God on their thrones fell upon their faces and worshiped God,

17 saying, "We give thanks to you, Lord, the one being God Almighty, and who was, that you have taken your great power and have begun to reign. 18 And the nations were angered. And your wrath came, and the season for the dead to be judged, and to give your servants, the prophets, the reward, and to the saints, and to those fearing your name, the small and the great, and to destroy those who are destroying the earth."

19 And the temple of God in heaven was opened. And the ark of his covenant was seen in his temple. And there were lightnings, and voices, and thunders, and an earthquake, and great hail.

REVELATION TWELVE

1 And a great sign was seen in heaven. A woman clothed with the sun, and the moon under her feet, and on her head a crown of twelve stars, 2 and pregnant. And she cries out in laborious effort and pain to give birth.

3 And another sign was seen in heaven. And look, a great fiery red dragon, with seven heads and ten horns. And upon his heads seven diadems. 4 And his tail draws a third of the stars of heaven; and he threw them to the earth. And the dragon is standing before the woman who is about to give birth, so that when she gives birth he might eat her child.

5 And she birthed a male son who is about to rule all the nations by a rod of iron; and her child was caught up to God and his throne. 6

And the woman escaped into the wilderness, where she has a place prepared by God, so that they should nurture her there one thousand two hundred sixty days.

7 And war happened in heaven. Michael and his messengers made war against the dragon, and the dragon and his messengers made war; 8 and he had not strength. A place was not found for them anymore in heaven. 9 And the great dragon was thrown out, the serpent of the beginning, who is called "Devil," and "Satan," deceiving the whole inhabited earth. He was thrown down to the earth; and his messengers were thrown down with him.

10 And I heard a great voice in heaven, saying, "Now has come the deliverance, and the power, and the kingdom of our God, and the authority of his Christ, because the accuser of our brethren has been thrown down, the one accusing them before our God day and night. 11 And they did overcome him by means of the blood of the Lamb, and by means of the word of their testimony; they did not love their life even until death. 12 Through this, rejoice O heavens and those dwelling in them. Woe to the earth and the sea, because the Devil has come down to you, possessing great wrath, because knowing he has a brief time.

13 And when the dragon saw that he had been thrown down to the earth, he persecuted the woman who had birthed the male. 14 And to the woman were given the two wings of the great eagle, so that she may fly into the wilderness, unto her place, where she is nurtured there a time, and times, and half a time from the presence of the serpent.

15 And the serpent threw water out of his mouth behind the woman, as a river, so that he might make her to be carried away by a flood. 16 And the earth helped the woman, and the earth opened its mouth and swallowed the river, which the dragon had thrown out of his mouth. 17 And the dragon was angry with the woman, and went to make war with the others of her offspring, the ones keeping the commandments of God and holding to the testimony of Jesus.[q]

REVELATION THIRTEEN

1 And he stood upon the sand of the sea.[r1] And I saw a beast rising out of the sea, having ten horns, and seven heads, and on its horns ten diadems, and upon its heads names of slander against God. 2 And the beast I saw was as a leopard, and its feet as a bear's, and its mouth as the mouth of a lion. And the dragon gave to it his power, and his throne, and great authority. 3 And one of its heads as having been killed to death. And the wound of its death was healed. And the whole earth marveled after the beast.

4 And they worshiped the dragon who had given authority to the beast. And they worshiped the beast, saying, "Who is like the

beast, and who is able to make war against it?" 5 And was given to it¹² a mouth speaking great things and slandering. And was given to it authority to act forty-two months. 6 And it opened its mouth for slander against God, to slander his name and his tabernacle, those living in the heaven.

7 And was given to it to make war against the saints, and to prevail over them. And was given to it authority over every tribe, and people, and language, and nation. 8 And all earth dwellers will worship it, of whom their names have not been written in the book of life of the Lamb, the one that was slain from the founding of the world.

9 If anyone has an ear, let him hear. 10 If anyone into captivity, into captivity he goes. If anyone is to be killed by sword, by sword he must be killed. Here is the endurance and the faith of the saints.

11 And I saw another beast ascending out of the earth, and it had two horns like a lamb, and it was speaking as a dragon. 12 And it does all the authority of the first beast in its presence, and causes the earth dwellers that they will worship the first beast, of whom its death wound had been healed. 13 And it works great signs, so that it should cause even fire to come out of heaven to the earth in the presence of the people.

14 And it deceives the earth dwellers by means of the signs that were given to it to do in the presence of the beast, telling those earth dwellers to make an image to the beast that has the sword wound and has lived. 15 And it was given to it to give breath to the image of the beast, so that also the image of the beast might speak, and should cause as many as may not worship the image of the beast may be killed.

16 And it makes all the small and the great, and the rich and the helpless poor, and the free and the slaves, that it should give them a mark on their right hand or on their forehead, 17 in order that no one may be able to buy or to sell, except the one having the mark— the name of the beast or the number of his name. 18 Here is wisdom. The one having understanding, reckon the number of the beast. For it is a man's number, and the number of it is six hundred sixty six.

REVELATION FOURTEEN

1 And I saw, and look, the Lamb was standing upon Mount Zion, and with him one hundred forty four thousand, who had his name and the name of his Father, that had been written on their foreheads. 2 And I heard a voice out of heaven, as a sound of many waters, and as a sound of loud thunder. And the voice that I heard as of lyrists playing with their lyres. 3 And they are singing a new song before the throne, and before the four living creatures, and the elders. And no one was able to learn the song except the one hundred forty four thousand who had been redeemed from the

earth.

4 These are the ones not having been defiled with women, for they are pure, these the ones following the Lamb wherever he may go. These have been redeemed from humankind as firstfruits to God and to the Lamb. 5 And in their mouth was not found a lie; they are blameless.

6 And I saw another messenger, flying in mid-heaven, having the everlasting good news to proclaim to the earth dwellers, and to every nation, and tribe, and language, and people. 7 He was saying in a loud voice, "Fear God, and give him glory, because the hour of his judgment has come, and worship the one having made heaven, and the earth, and sea, and springs of waters."

8 And another messenger, a second, followed saying, "Fallen, fallen Babylon the great, who has given all the nations to drink out of the wine of the wrath of her immorality."

9 And another messenger, a third, followed them, saying in a loud voice, "If anyone worships the beast and its image, and receives a mark on his forehead or upon his hand, 10 he also will drink of the wine of God's anger, that has been mixed undiluted in the cup of his wrath; and he will be afflicted in fire and sulfur in the presence of the holy messengers, and in the presence of the Lamb. 11 And the smoke of their affliction goes up to the ages of the ages. And there is no rest day and night for those worshiping the beast, and its image, and if anyone receives the mark of its name. 12 Here is the endurance of the saints: those keeping the commandments of God, and the faith of Jesus."

13 And I heard a voice out of heaven saying, "Write, 'Blessed are the dead in the Lord dying from now on.'" "Yes," says the Spirit, "so that they will rest from their labors. For their works follow with them."

14 And I saw, and look, a white cloud. And upon the cloud one sitting like the Son of Man, having on his head a golden crown, and in his hand a sharp reaping hook. 15 And another messenger came out of the temple, proclaiming in a loud voice to the one sitting on the cloud, "Thrust out your reaping hook and reap, because the hour has come to reap, because the harvest of the earth has ripened." 16 And the one sitting on the cloud thrust his reaping hook upon the earth, and the earth was reaped.

17 And another messenger came out of the temple in heaven, he also having a sharp reaping hook. 18 And another messenger came out of the altar, having authority over the fire, and he called in a loud voice to the one having the sharp reaping hook, saying, "Thrust out your sharp reaping hook and gather the clusters from the vine of the earth, because its grapes have fully ripened."

19 And the messenger thrust his reaping hook into the earth,

and gathered the vine of the earth, and threw them into the winepress of God's great wrath. 20 And the winepress was tread outside the city, and blood flowed out of the winepress as high as the bridles of the horses, to a distance of one hundred eighty four miles.⁵

REVELATION FIFTEEN

1 And I saw another sign in heaven, great and wonderful, seven messengers having seven plagues, the last, because in them the wrath of God was completed. 2 And I saw as a sea of glass mixed with fire, and those prevailing over the beast, and its image, and the number of its name, standing upon the sea of the glass, having lyres of God.

3 And they are singing the song of Moses, the servant of God, and the song of the Lamb, saying, "Great and wonderful your works, Lord, God the Almighty. Righteous and true your works, O King of the nations. 4 Who might not fear, O Lord, and will glorify your name, that alone *is* holy? Because all the nations will come and will worship in your presence, because your righteous acts were made known."

5 And after these things I saw, and the temple of the tabernacle of the testimony was opened in heaven. 6 And the seven messengers having the seven plagues came out of the temple, being clothed in pure, bright linen, and wrapped around the chest with golden belts.

7 And one of the four living creatures gave to the seven messengers seven golden basins full of the wrath of God, the one living to the ages of the ages. 8 And the temple was filled with smoke from the glory of God and from his power. And none were able to enter into the temple until the seven plagues of the seven messengers were completed.

REVELATION SIXTEEN

1 And I heard a loud voice from within the temple saying to the seven messengers, "Go, and pour out the seven basins of God's wrath against the earth." 2 And the first went and poured out his basin against the earth, and it became an ulcer, hurtful and evil, upon persons having the mark of the beast, and those worshiping its image.

3 And the second poured out his basin into the sea, and it became blood, as of a corpse. And every living soul that was in the sea died.

4 And the third poured out his basin into the rivers and the springs of the waters, and they became blood. 5 And I heard the messenger of the waters saying, "You are just, the one who is and was, the holy, because you did judge these things, 6 because they poured out the blood of saints and prophets, and you are giving them blood to drink; they are deserving." 7 And I heard the altar saying, "Yes, Lord God Almighty, true and righteous your judgments."

8 And the fourth poured out his basin upon the sun. And there was given to it to burn people with fire. 9 And the people were burnt with great burning. And they slandered the name of God, the one having authority over these plagues, and they did not repent to give him glory.

10 And the fifth poured out his basin upon the throne of the beast, and its kingdom became darkened, and they chewed their tongues from the mental anguish, 11 and they slandered the God of heaven from their anguish, and from their ulcers. And they did not repent of their works.

12 And the sixth poured out his basin upon the great river Euphrates. And its water was dried, so that the way of the kings of the rising of the sun may be prepared.

13 And I saw out of the mouth of the dragon, and out of the mouth of the beast, and out of the mouth of the false prophet, three unclean spirits as frogs. 14 For they are spirits of demons doing signs, who go out to the kings of the whole inhabited earth, to gather them unto the battle of the great day of God the Almighty.

15 "Look, I come as a thief. Blessed the one mindful and guarding his clothing, so that he should not walk naked and they might see his shame." 16 And he assembled them unto the place called in Hebrew, "Harmagedon."(t)

17 And the seventh poured out his basin upon the air. And a loud voice came out of the temple from the throne, saying, "It is done." 18 And there were lightings, and voices, and thunders. And there was a great earthquake, such as there had not been since people began to be upon the earth, so mighty an earthquake, so great. 19 And the great city became into three parts. And the cities of the nations fell. And Babylon the great was remembered in God's presence, to give her the cup of the wine of the anger of his wrath.

20 And every island fled, and mountains were not found. 21 And a great hail, about eighty-five pounds,u came down out of heaven on the people. And the people reviled God because of the plague of the hail, for the plague of it is exceedingly great.

REVELATION SEVENTEEN

1 And came one of the seven messengers having the seven basins, and spoke with me, saying, "Come. I will show you the judgment of the great whore,v the one sitting upon many waters, 2 with whom the kings of the earth did commit fornication, and the earth dwellers have been made drunk with the wine of her fornication."

3 And he carried me away in spirit into a wilderness. And I saw a woman sitting upon a scarlet-colored beast, slanderous names filling it, having seven heads and ten horns. 4 And the woman was clothed in purple and scarlet, and adorned with gold and costly stone and pearls, having a golden cup in

her hand, abominations filing it. 5 And upon her forehead a name was written, "Hidden: Babylon the great, the mother of the whores and of the abominations of the earth." 6 And I saw the woman being drunk with the blood of the saints, and the blood of the witnesses of Jesus. And I marveled, seeing her with great wonder.

7 And the messenger said to me, "For what reason did you marvel? I will tell you the secret of the woman, and of the beast carrying her, the one having the seven heads and the ten horns. 8 The beast, the one you saw, was, and is not, and is about to ascend out of the abyss and go into damnation. And the earth dwellers will wonder, those whose names are not written in the book of life from the foundation of the world, seeing the beast that was, and is not, and yet will be.

9 "Here is the mind having wisdom. The seven heads are seven mountains on which the woman is sitting. 10 And there are seven kings: the five are fallen, the one is, the other has not yet come, and when he may have come he must remain a little while. 11 And the beast which was, and is not, is also himself an eighth, and is of the seven, and goes into damnation.

12 "And the ten horns you saw are ten kings, who have not yet received a kingdom, but one hour receive authority as kings, along with the beast. 13 These have one mind, and their power and authority they are giving to the beast. 14 These will make war with the Lamb. And the Lamb will prevail over them, because he is Lord of lords, and King of kings. And those with him are called and chosen and faithful."

15 And he says to me, "The waters that you saw, where the whore sits, are peoples, and multitudes, and nations, and languages. 16 And the ten horns that you saw, and the beast, these will hate the whore, and will make her desolate, and naked, and her flesh they will eat, and they will burn her with fire. 17 For God did put into their hearts to do his will, and to do one desire, and to give their kingdom to the beast, until God's words will be fulfilled. 18 And the woman whom you saw is the great city possessing dominion over the kings of the earth."

REVELATION EIGHTEEN

1 After these things, I saw another messenger descending out of heaven. He had great authority, and the earth was illuminated from his glory. 2 And he proclaimed in a mighty voice, saying, "Fallen, fallen is Babylon the great. And she has become a habitation of demons, and a gathering place of every unclean spirit, and a habitat of every unclean bird, and a lair of every unclean beast. 3 Because all the nations have drunk of the wine of the wrath of her immorality. And the kings of the earth have committed immorality with her. And the merchants of the earth

have become rich through the power of her luxury."

4 And I heard another voice from heaven, saying, "Come my people, out of her, so that you may not participate in her sins, so that you may not receive of her plagues. 5 For her sins they have joined together as high as heaven, and God has remembered her iniquities. 6 Give to her as also she has given, and give back two-fold according to her works. In the cup which she has mixed, you mix to her double. 7 As much as she has glorified herself and lived in luxury, so much give to her affliction and sadness, because in her heart she says, 'I sit a queen and am never a widow; and sorrow I shall never no never see.' 8 For this reason in one day her plagues will come: death and sorrow and famine. And by fire she will be consumed, because mighty is the Lord God judging her.

9 "And the kings of the earth will lament and will wail for her, the ones who committed immorality with her, and lived in luxury, when they see the smoke of her burning, 10 standing from afar, by reason of the fear of her affliction, saying 'Woe, woe, woe the great city Babylon, the strong city. Because in one hour has come your judgment.'

11 "And the merchants of the earth will lament and mourn for her, because no one buys their merchandise no more, 12 merchandise of gold and of silver, and of precious stone, and of pearls, and of fine linen, and of purple, and of silk, and of scarlet, and all evergreen wood, and every implement of ivory, and implements of most precious wood, and of bronze, and of iron, and of marble, 13 and cinnamon, and spice, and incense, and myrrh, and frankincense, and wine, and oil, and finest flour, and wheat, and cattle, and sheep, and of horses, and of chariots, and of slaves, and souls of men. 14 And the ripe fruit, the desire of your soul, has went away from you, and all the sumptuous things and splendid things have went away from you, and no more, never no never, will you find them.

15 "The merchants of these things, having been made rich from her, will stand from afar, by reason of the fear of her affliction, lamenting and mourning, 16 saying, 'Woe, woe, woe the great city, once clothed with fine linen and purple and scarlet, and adorned with gold and precious stone and pearl.' 17 For in one hour such great wealth has been laid waste."

And every captain, and all those sailing to a place, and sailors, and as many as trade by the sea, stood at a distance, 18 and seeing the smoke of her burning were crying out, saying, "What is like the great city?" 19 And they cast dust upon their heads, and were crying out, lamenting and mourning, saying, "Woe, woe the great city, in which all those having ships in the sea were enriched through her wealth. For in one hour she has been laid waste."

20 "Heaven rejoice over her, and saints, and apostles, and prophets because God did judge your judgment against her."

21 And one messenger took up a mighty stone, as a great millstone, and threw it into the sea, saying, "In this manner the great city Babylon will be thrown down with violence, and never no never may be found anymore. 22 And the sound of lyrists and musicians, and flute players and trumpeters, never no never might be heard in you anymore. And any craftsmen of any craft shall never no never be found in you anymore. And the sound of a millstone shall never no never be heard in you anymore. 23 And the light of a lamp shall never no never shine in you anymore. And the voice of a bridegroom and a bride, never no never might be heard in you anymore.

"For your merchants were the great ones of the earth, because by your sorcery all the nations were deceived." 24 And in her was found the blood of prophets and of saints, and of all those killed on the earth.

REVELATION NINETEEN

1 After these things I heard as a loud voice of a great multitude in heaven, crying out, "Praise to Yah!ʷ The deliverance and the glory and the power to our God. 2 Because true and righteous his judgments, because he has judged the great whore who had corrupted the earth with her immorality. And he has avenged the blood of his servants out of her hand."

3 And a second time they said, "Praise to Yah! And her smoke ascends to the ages of the ages." 4 And the twenty-four elders fell down and the four living creatures; and they worshiped God, the one sitting on the throne, saying, "Amen. Praise to Yah!" 5 And a voice came out of the throne, saying, "Praise our God, all his servants, and those fearing him, the small and the great."

6 And I heard as the voice of a great multitude, and as the sound of many waters, and as the sound of mighty thunders, saying, "Praise to Yah! Because our Lord God Almighty has reigned. 7 We should rejoice and should leap for joy, and will give the glory to him, because the wedding supper of the Lamb has come, and his bride has made herself ready. 8 And to her was given that she should be clothed in fine linen, bright, pure. For fine linen is the righteousness of the saints." 9 And he says to me, "Write: 'Blessed are those having been invited to the wedding supper of the Lamb.'"

And he says to me, "These are true words of God." 10 And I fell before his feet to worship him. And he says to me, "See you do not. I am a fellow servant with you, and of your brethren holding fast the testimony of Jesus. Worship God. For the testimony of Jesus is the spirit of prophecy."

11 And I saw that heaven was opened. And look, a white horse, and the one sitting upon it called

faithful and true. And in righteousness he judges and makes war. 12 And his eyes as a flame of fire, and upon his head many diadems, with a name having been written, which no one knows except himself. 13 And clothed in clothing that had been dipped in blood. And his name is called, "The Word of God."

14 And the armies who were in heaven were following him upon white horses, being clothed in fine linen, white, pure. 15 And out of his mouth went out a sharp sword, so that by it he might smite the nations. And he will shepherd them with a rod of iron. And he treads the wine press of the anger of the wrath of God the Almighty. 16 And he has upon his robe and upon his thigh a name that was written, "King of kings and Lord of lords."

17 And I saw one messenger standing in the sun. And he proclaimed in a loud voice, saying to all the birds flying in mid-heaven, "Come. Gather yourselves unto the great supper of God, 18 so you might eat flesh of kings, and flesh of commanders, and flesh of mighty, and flesh of horses and of those sitting on them, and flesh of all, both free and slaves, and small and great."

19 And I saw the beast, and the kings of the earth, and their armies, assembled to make war against the one sitting on the horse and with his army. 20 And the beast was captured, and with him the false prophet, the one who did signs in his presence, by which he deceived those who had received the mark of the beast and those worshiping its image. These two were thrown living into the lake of fire burning with sulfur. 21 And the rest were killed with the sword of the one sitting on the horse, going out of his mouth. And all of the birds were filled with their flesh.

REVELATION TWENTY

1 And I saw a messenger descending out of heaven, holding the key of the abyss, and a great chain in his hand. 2 And he took hold of the dragon, the serpent of the beginning, who is the Devil and Satan, and bound him for a thousand years. 3 And he threw him into the abyss, and shut and sealed it over him, so that he should not deceive the nations anymore, until the thousand years were completed. After these things he must be released for a little time.

4 And I saw thrones, and they sat upon them. And judgment was given to them. And the souls of those who had been beheaded by reason of the testimony of Jesus, and by reason of the Word of God, and those not worshiping the beast, nor his image, and did not accept the mark upon the forehead, and upon their hand. And they lived and ruled with Christ a thousand years. 5 The rest of the dead lived not again until the thousand years should be completed.

This is the first resurrection. 6 Blessed and holy the one having part in the first resurrection. Over these the second death has no power, but they will be priests of God and of Christ, and will rule with him a thousand years.

7 And when the thousand years should be completed, Satan will be set free out of his prison, 8 and will go out to deceive the nations in the four corners of the earth, the Gog and Magog, to gather them to make war, of whom the number of them *is* as the sand of the sea.

9 And they came up over the great expanses of the earth and encircled the camp of the saints and the beloved city. But fire came out of heaven and consumed them. 10 And the Devil, the one deceiving them, was thrown into the lake of fire and sulfur, where also is the beast and false prophet. And they will be afflicted day and night to the ages of the ages.

11 And I saw a great white throne, and the one sitting on it, from whose face the earth and heaven fled, and no place was found for them.

12 And I saw the dead, great and small, standing before the throne; and books were opened. And another book was opened, which is the one of life. And the dead were judged out of the things which had been written in the books, according to their works.

13 And the sea gave the dead the ones in it. And Death and hades gave the dead, the ones in them. And they each were judged according to their works. 14 And Death and hades were thrown into the lake of fire. This the second death is the lake of fire. 15 And if anyone was not found having been written in the book of life, he was thrown into the lake of fire.

REVELATION TWENTY-ONE

1 And I saw a new heaven and a new earth, for the first heaven and the first earth they had gone away; and there is no more sea.

2 And the holy city, New Jerusalem, I saw coming out of heaven from God, prepared as a bride adorned for her husband.

3 And I heard a great voice from the throne, saying, "Look, the tabernacle of God amid humankind. And he will dwell with them, and they will be his peoples, and God himself[x] will be with them. 4 And he will wipe off every tear from their eyes. And death will not be anymore, nor sorrow, nor wailing, nor pain. They will not be anymore because the first things have gone away."

5 And the one sitting on the throne said, "Look, I make all things new." And he says, "Write, because these words are faithful and true." 6 And he said to me, "It is done. I, I am the alpha and the omega, the beginning and the end. To the one thirsting I will give out of the spring of the water of life freely. 7 The one prevailing will inherit all things, and I will be his God, and he will be my son. 8 But to fearful,[y] and to unbelieving, and to having become abhorrent, and to murderers, and to sexually immoral, and to sorcerers, and to

idolators, and to all liars, their portion is in the lake burning with fire and sulfur, which is the second death."

9 And one of the seven messengers, one having the seven basins full of the last seven plagues, came and spoke with me, saying, "Come. I will show you the bride, the wife of the Lamb."

10 And he carried me away in spirit to a mountain great and high, and he showed me the holy city Jerusalem, descending out of heaven from God, 11 holding the glory of God, its luminance like a precious stone, like a crystalline stone, being clear as crystal. 12 Having a great and high wall, having twelve gates, and at the gates twelve messengers, and names inscribed which are of the twelve tribes of the sons of Israel. 13 From east three gates, and from north three gates, and from south three gates, and from west three gates. 14 And the city wall had twelve foundations, and on them twelve names of the twelve apostles of the Lamb.

15 And the one speaking with me had a golden measuring stick, so that he might measure the city, and its gates, and its wall. 16 And the city sits four-cornered, and its length the same as the width. And he measured the city with the stick at one thousand three hundred seventy-nine miles.[z] The length and the width and the height of it are alike. 17 And he measured its wall, two hundred forty-six feet,[aa] the measure of a man, that is, the messenger.

18 And the structure of its wall crystalline, and the city pure gold, like clear glass.[bb] 19 The foundations of the city wall adorned with every precious stone, first crystalline, the second blue, the third red, the fourth green, 20 the fifth milky-white with red stripes, the sixth blood-red, the seventh golden, the eighth sea-green, the ninth a transparent green with yellowish tinge, the tenth grass green, the eleventh deep purple, the twelfth violet. 21 And the twelve gates were twelve pearls, each one of the gates was of one pearl. And the city street pure gold transparent as glass.

22 And I did not see a temple in it, for the Lord God Almighty is its temple, and the Lamb. 23 And the city has no need of the sun nor of the moon, so that they should give light in it. For the glory of God gives it light, and its lamp is the Lamb. 24 And the nations will walk by its light, and the kings of the earth bring their glory into it. 25 And its gates may never no never be closed by day, for there will not be night. 26 And they will bring the glory and the honor of the nations into it. 27 And never no never may enter into it anything defiling, and those practicing anything detestable to God,[cc] and a lie; only those being written in the book of life of the Lamb.

REVELATION TWENTY-TWO

1 And he showed me a river of water of life radiant as crystal, going out of the throne of God and

of the Lamb. 2 The river was in the middle of the broad street. On this side and on that side a tree of life producing twelve fruits according to month, each giving its fruit. And the leaves of the tree for healing the nations.

3 And there will not be any curse anymore. And the throne of God and of the Lamb will be in it, and his servants will serve him. 4 And they will see his face, and his name is on their foreheads. 5 And there will not be night there, and they do not have need of a lamp, and of light of the sun, because the Lord God will shine upon them; and they will rule to the ages of the ages.

6 And he said to me, "These words are faithful and true: and the Lord, the God of the spirits of the prophets, sent his messenger to show his servants the things that must suddenly begin to be; 7 and 'Look, I come suddenly. Blessed the one heeding the words of the prophecy of this book.'"

8 And I, John, I am the one hearing and seeing these things. And when I heard and saw, I fell down to worship before the feet of the messenger showing me these things. 9 And he says to me, "See you do not. I am your fellow servant, and of your brethren the prophets, and those heeding the words of this book. Worship God."

10 And he says to me, "Do not seal the words of the prophecy of this book, for the time is near. 11 The one unrighteous, be yet unrighteous; and the one morally filthy, be yet morally filthy; and the one righteous, be yet practicing righteousness; and the one holy, be yet holy."

12 "Look, I am coming suddenly, and my reward is with me, to give to each as is his work. 13 I, I am the alpha and the omega, the first and the last, the beginning and the end. 14 Blessed those washing their robes, in order that their right will be to the tree of life, and by the gates they may enter into the city. 15 Without are the dogs and the sorcerers and the sexually immoral and the murders and the idolators, and everyone loving and practicing falsehood.

16 "I, Jesus, have sent my messenger to testify these things to you in the churches. I, I am the root and the offspring of David, the bright morning star. 17 And the Spirit and the bride say, 'Come.' And the one hearing let him say 'Come.' And the one thirsting—the one desiring—let him come, let him take freely the water of life.

18 "I testify to all hearing the words of the prophecy of this book: if any person might add to these things, God will add unto him the plagues that have been written in this book. 19 And if any person might take away from the words of the book of this prophecy, God will take away his part from the tree of life, and out of the holy city, of those that have been written in this the book.

20 "The one testifying these things says, 'Yes, I come suddenly.'" So be it, come Lord

Jesus! 21 The grace of the Lord Jesus Christ with all.

Matthew Translation Notes

a In 1:18, I have "genealogy," based on the Western manuscripts which have *génesis*, "origin" [Zodhiates, s. v. 1078]. The Byzantine manuscripts have *génnēsis*, "birth" [Zodhiates, s. v. 1083]. The word *génnēsis* has to do with birth, whereas *génesis* has to do with genealogy. Because Matthew is explaining the genealogy of Jesus, *génesis* seems the better choice, and it is the word used at Matthew 1:1 in both Byzantine and Western manuscripts, "Book of the genealogy of" etc. The word *génnēsis*, birth, came to be used in early Christian literature to describe the nativity of Christ. The similarity of the words in sound and letters led to the one being substituted for the other in 1:18 by the scribes copying Matthew's Gospel [Metzger, *Textual*, 7].

b In 1:20, the phrase, "having thought (his spirit was agitated)" is the translation of *enthuméomai* [Zodhiates, s. v. 1760]. This word means "the mind, thought, but also anger, wrath, indignation, a spirit that is aroused." Joseph was not necessarily agitated in a negative sense, but I think Joseph was, to use a common phrase, full of conflicting emotions.

c In 1:20, I have translated the Greek *ággelos*, "messenger," rather than transliterate it, "angel." (And so throughout the New Testament. See Preface.)

d In 2:2, The word translated "to do homage to" in vv. 2, 8, is *proskunéō*, "to worship, do obeisance, show respect, fall or prostrate before . . . literally to throw a kiss in token of respect or homage" [Zodhiates, s. v. 4352]. Literally the wise men (*mágos*) said "we have come to bow to him," but culturally they had come to recognize him as a king. They had not come to worship in the sense Christians think of worship toward Jesus Christ. *Proskunéō* is used several times in Matthew and I will translate the word "knelt before" or something similar, unless the context requires an act of worship.

e In 2:8, I have translated *paidíon* as "child." the KJV, NKJV, ASV, and BBE translate *paidíon* as "young child." When used literally *paidíon* means "a child recently born, a baby, infant . . . also those more advanced in age" [Zodhiates, s. v. 3813]. But Jesus is in a house, perhaps as old as seven months, having been born September, 5 BC, and Herod dying April, 6 BC [see Quiggle, *God Became Incarnate*]. I agree with other versions that translate *paidíon* without the adjective.

f In 3:6, and in other verses, I have translated the word *baptízō* as immerse or immersed, not transliterated it as "baptize." The word means "to immerse, to submerge for a religious purpose, to overwhelm, to saturate" [Zodhiates, s. v. 907]. (And so throughout the New Testament, for example, John the Immerser.)

g In 3:11, I have translated, "in the Holy Spirit." Other versions say, "with the Holy Spirit." The word I have translated "in" is the Greek *én*, a preposition meaning "in, with, by," and other uses. Here the use is either sphere of activity, requiring "in," or instrumental, requiring "with." The Holy Spirit is the person doing the immersion, he is not a thing as the instrument of immersion. He immerses the person into a living relationship with Christ, by his operation on and in the believer, thereby joining the believer to Christ.

h In 4:24, the words "being inhabited by demons" translate *daimonízomai*, "to be in the power of a demon" [Zodhiates, s. v. 1139]. Most name this "demon possession," but spirit beings can merely inhabit a soul, they cannot own it; every human soul belongs to God the Creator. (And so throughout the New Testament.)

i In 4:24, the word I used, "epileptic," is definitely anachronistic, but the alternative is "moonstruck" or "lunatic" (luna-tic), the proper translation of *seléniázomai* [Zodhiates, s. v. 4583]. The words "moonstruck" or "lunatic" do not communicate to the modern reader the kind of disease the boy was suffering. The word *seléniázomai* was used by the ancient peoples for certain observed disorders, because the ancient peoples thought the disease more pronounced during certain lunar phases. Epilepsy was first proposed as an organic disease in 1873, and studies from 1859–1906 defined it as a neurological disorder. "Epileptic" also occurs in 17:14 as the translation of *seléniázomai*, but there the problem is demonic habitation producing a condition that looked similar, but was not an organic disease.

j At 5:22 I have transliterated the Greek *rhaká* [Zodhiates, s. v. 4469] as "Raca." The full meaning of *rhaká* cannot be communicated in one word. It is "a word of contempt meaning empty, worthless, foolish." Jesus says that when you judge a person as worthless, you are saying that person is not fit to live.

k At 5:22, I have transliterated the word *mórós* [Zodhiates, s. v. 3474] as "Moros." The English word "moron" is derived from *mórós*. It is a more serious reproach than *rhaká*, which scorns a man by calling him stupid, whereas *mórós* scorns him concerning his heart and character." Jesus calls the attitude expressed by this word, murder.

l In 5:22 the word "Gehenna" is the transliteration of the Greek *géenna* [Zodhiates, s. v. 1067]. Gehenna is a place of "unquenchable fire," Mark 9:43, aka the "lake of fire," Revelation 20:14.

m In 5:48, the word *teleíōs* [Zodhiates, s. v. 5046], "complete, full grown,' is used two times of two persons with two distinct meanings. The person who lives a righteous life, per Christ's teaching in 5:1–47, is able to be as *teleíōs*, spiritually "mature," as his heavenly Father is *teleíōs*, perfect. The two uses are comparative, not absolute.

n In 6:13, I have translated the familiar "lead us not into temptation," as "bring us not into a state of trial." That is the translation suggested by Zodhiates [s. v. 3986]. The difference here is between the word used in the text, *peirasmós*, "a difficulty brought about by the circumstances, or adversity, affliction, or sorrow from God for the purpose of proving faith" [Zodhiates s. v. 3986], versus *peirázō*, "a temptation in a malicious effort to destroy faith" [Zodhiates, s. v. 3985]. God *peirasmós*, Satan *peirázō*.

o In 6:24, I have translated *mamōnás* as "god of materialism." The word is "a comprehensive word for all kinds of possessions, earnings, and gains, a designation of material value, the god of materialism" [Zodhiates, s. v. 3126]. Because the contrast is between a personal God and *mamōnás*, it seems likely Jesus is personifying *mamōnás* as an idol opposing God. Therefore I have translated the word as "god of materialism," i.e., the false deity people create when covetousness becomes idolatry.

p In 6:27, "lifespan" is *hēlikía*. The word has two meanings: age in the sense of physical maturity or lifespan; physical size in the sense of height [Bromiley, *Encyclopedia*, 2:941–943]. In classical Greek and the Egyptian papyri it is overwhelmingly used in the sense of age [Moulton, s. v. 2244]. In Matthew 6:27, the context "life" in 6:25 favors a translation indicating age, i.e., "lifespan." The associated *pḗchus*, "cubit" must here mean a measure of time, not physical height. The cubit was a measure of eighteen inches, which puts Jesus in the awkward position of asking, "which of you can change his height from five foot six to seven feet?" The better translation of cubit in this context is an unspecified measure of time.

q In 7:6, I have translated *katapatéō*, "to trample upon," in a figurative sense, "treat them with contempt." The word has the figurative meaning, "to treat with the utmost contempt and indignity" [Zodhiates, s. v. 2662].

r At 8:1, "knelt before" translates *proskunéō* [Zodhiates, s. v. 4352]. This word can mean to show respect to a person or it can mean to worship deity. It is highly unlikely a Jew would worship another human being, for Jesus of Nazareth was considered a prophet, or possibly the messiah, who according to 2 Samuel 7:13, 16; Psalm 2 was a descendant of David whom God would anoint to be king of Israel. The reader must view these Old Testament scriptures and the gospel account the same way the healed leper would have known them, in the complete absence of the New Testament revelation. His exemplar would have been the prophet Elisha healing the Syrian leader Naaman, 2 Kings 5.

s In 8:1, the word translated "sir" is *kúrios*. The healed leper was not a disciple, nor was he a servant, nor would he recognize God incarnate in a human being (at the time a pagan idea). "Sir" is the appropriate word in his mouth.

t In 8:6, the centurion uses the word *paralutikós*, "paralyzed, palsied ... loss of motor power in a muscle or set of muscles" [Zodhiates, s. v. 3885]. It is doubtful palsy is intended, as palsy affects the face. The centurion used *paralutikós* to describe the observed phenomena, not the medical condition. Paralyzed persons can experience "terrible pain." The "terrible pain" may indicate severe disc herniation, in which any movement causes terrible pain, resulting in the person lying down and making every effort not to move, effectively "paralyzing" the person.

u In 8:11, I have translated *anaklínō* [Zodhiates, s. v. 347] as "recline at the table." In Jesus' time *anaklínō* was used of reclining in order to eat. Instead of chairs, the ancients used a low couch set perpendicular to a low table. They leaned on their left elbow and took food from the dishes with their right hand.

v In 8:26 I have translated the word *epitimáō*, "to punish, rebuke, charge" as "restrained." Other versions translate "rebuke." Zodhiates [s. v. 2008], says, "followed by the dative of thing ["winds," noun dative masculine plural] and implying a desire to restrain, e.g., spoken of winds and waves (Matthew 8:26)."

w In 9:3, the word I have translated "slanders God" is *blasphēméō* [Zodhiates, s. v. 987], to speak evil of, to slander, usually transliterated "blasphemy." Note also that contrary to some versions I did not capitalize "man." The capitalization of "man" in some versions is completely inappropriate in the mouth and thoughts of Jesus' enemies. An historical-grammatical interpretation of the four gospels requires translators and interpreters to understand how Jesus' friends and enemies thought of Jesus, which was not in the capital letters of deity.

x At 9:13 the Byzantine text (KJV/NKJV) ends v. 13 with the words "to repentance." The words do not appear in any other textual family.

y At 9:15, "sons of the bride-chamber" is the literal translation of *huiós numphṓn*. In the Scripture "sons of," unless used of physical birth, is a gender-neutral term. These persons are in modern terms bridesmaids and groomsmen. They are not wedding guests (HCSB, ESV, NLT) or guests of the bridegroom (NIV). They are friends of the bridegroom (NKJV), but I chose the more literal translation.

z At 9:20, for "the fringe of his garment" see Numbers 15:38–39. Harris [*TWOT*, s. v. 103a], states, "It is debated whether [the Hebrew word] *sîsît* indicates the fringe around the edges of a garment or a tassel at each corner."

aa In 10:29, the "brass coin" is the Greek word *assárion*, a brass coin equal to the tenth part of a drachma. A Roman *denarius* was worth sixteen *as* (*assárion*). One bread, which was enough for one person, cost one *assárion* (bread in Jesus' time was about the size of pita bread). A day's wage for a common laborer was normally 10–12 *assárion*.

bb In 11:17, "beat your breast" is *kóptō* [Zodhiates, s. v. 2875]. When used in the middle voice, as it is here, it indicates the physical actions that accompany mourning or lamenting: "to strike or beat one's body, particularly the breast, with the hands in lamentation."

cc In 12:43, I have translated *ánudros tópos*, as "barren places." The word *ánudros* means a place that is without water, dry, barren, desert. Zodhiates states, "The Jews supposed that the abode of evil spirits was in deserts" [Zodhiates, s. v. 504]. But the point is not lack of water (dry, NKJV; waterless, HCSB; arid, NIV; desert, NLT). The natural abode for a fallen spirit being is in the spirit domain second heaven. Some fallen spirit beings desire to inhabit human souls. Such was the case here. The barren places were the spirit domain which human beings do not inhabit.

dd In 13:26 Jesus uses the word *chórtos*, "the grass or herbage of the field" [Zodhiates, s. v. 5528]. Both wheat and darnel are classified among the grasses.

ee In 13:55, the word I have translated "builder," is *téktōn* [Zodhiates, s. v. 5045]. Older language studies concluded this word meant "an artificer, a craftsman, especially a worker in wood." More recent studies have indicated this word described a builder, probably working in stone.

ff In 14:24, one set of manuscripts have, "and the boat was now amidst the sea." Other manuscripts have, "and the boat was many *stádion* from the land." In the John 6:19 parallel passage, the disciples had rowed about "twenty-five or thirty *stádion*." The Mark 6:47 parallel passage reads, "the boat was in the midst of the sea." I decided to combine the two Matthew texts and use the information in John to tell how far the men had rowed, "about three miles from land," as an indication of the strength of the contrary winds.

The word *stádion* indicates a measure of distance equal to about 606 English feet. John 6:19 says they were twenty-five or thirty *stádion* from the shore, which is about three English miles, or about halfway between Bethsaida-Julius, close to where they began, and Bethsaida-Galilee, about where they landed.

gg In 14:28 "master" is *kúrios*. Peter might have been saying "sir, master, or lord." I put "master" as the word a disciple would use toward the one of whom he was a disciple.

hh In 16:22, I have translated *kúrios* as "master." Peter did not think of Jesus as Lord in the sense of deity—he would not have rebuked God. Peter is speaking as a disciple to his master.

ii In 17:2 I have translated the word *metamorphóō* [Zodhiates, s. v. 3339] as "his form was changed." The word is a compound of *metá*, change of place or condition, and *morphóō*, to form. Most versions translate "transfigure." The HCSB and NLT translate "transform." Transform and transfigure are synonyms that mean "to change in outward form or appearance." I choose to give the direct translation of *metamorphóō*.

jj For "epileptic" in 17:15, see note "i" for a discussion. (The problem in 17:14 is not an organic disease but demonic activity imitating a neurological disorder.)

kk 17:21, is not included because evidence indicates it is a textual variant. As Metzger says [35], if the verse was originally in Matthew, there does not seem to be a valid reason to have omitted it "in a wide variety of manuscripts." The verse was probably inserted from Mark 9:29 by a copyist trying to make the accounts read the same. The sentence reads, "But this kind does not go out except but by prayer and fasting."

ll At 18:2, the "it" referring to the earlier mentioned "child" reflects the grammar of the pronoun in the Greek text, third person neuter singular. In inspiring the Scripture, the Holy Spirit always let the biblical writers express themselves within their own vocabulary and culture. Other translations change the grammar to the third person masculine "him." I chose to leave the grammar as it was written, in order to reflect the culture of the times and the style of the human author, just as the original readers would have seen the sentence.

The culture of the times evaluated every person, including children, in terms of their benefit to the family. Because small children could not contribute, they were not valued. Also, mortality before 5 years of age was a reality, so much so, many children in the Greco-Roman culture of the times were not given permanent names until their fifth birthday.

mm 18:11 is not included because assumed to be a textual variant. The verse reads, "For the Son of Man has come to save that which has been lost." Metzger says [*Textual*, 36], "There can be little doubt that the words are spurious here, being absent from the earliest witnesses representing several textual types (Alexandrian, Egyptian, Antiochian), and manifestly borrowed by copyists from Luke 19:10."

nn At 18:19 the word I have translated "truly" is *amḗn* [Zodhiates, s. v. 281], which Greek word is a transliteration of the Hebrew and `*āmēn*. In both Hebrew and Greek the word means "truth" or "truly."

oo At 19:16, I have followed texts that do not have the adjective "good" modifying the noun "teacher." The Byzantine texts have the word "good" as an adjective modifying "teacher." Most Alexandrian and Western texts do not [Metzger, *Textual*, 39]. The word was probably imported from the parallel accounts of Mark 10:17 and Luke 18:18. The scribe importing "good teacher" into Matthew from Mark and Luke must also change Matthew 19:17. The Matthew text is understandable without importing "good" to modify "teacher."

pp In 20:16, some manuscripts end the verse with, "for many are called, but few chosen." This was most likely imported by a scribe from 22:14, so as to summarize this parable.

nn In 20:22, 23, the phrase "be baptized with the baptism that I am baptized with" is "absent from early and good witnesses [manuscripts] representing several types of text [i.e., from several different sources] [Metzger, *Textual*, 42]. In the Byzantine texts (used by the KJV/NKJV) the phrase appears to have been imported into Matthew from the parallel account in Mark 10:38, 39.

oo At 21:3, what is the best translation of *kúrios*, "sir, master, lord," in the mouth of Jesus? He knew who he was, so "Lord" seems appropriate. Four reasons argue for "Lord." One, the word *kúrios* when spoken by Jesus most often refers to YHWH, in which case the proper translation would be "Lord."

Two, it is plausible the person receiving this message could interpret *kúrios* as referring to YHWH: "you will say, 'The Lord [i.e., YHWH] has need of them.'" Three, the owner could have understood "Lord" as a reference to the messiah, who was a king, so "Lord" is appropriate. Four, because Jesus is entering Jerusalem as the Davidic King and YHWH's Messiah, Zechariah 9:9, quoted in 21:5, then Jesus using *kúrios* in the sense of "Lord" to refer to himself is plausible.

qq In 21:30, in the Greek text, the second son says, "I sir." The Greek language often left out what was implied. Here it is implied the second son said, "I go, sir." Because "go" is implied but not in the text, I have put "*go*" in italic font. Every version supplies something explanatory between "I" and "sir."

rr At 23:4, some texts have "they bind heavy burdens and hard to bear." The preponderance of textual evidence is the words "hard to bear" were imported from Luke 11:46 [Metzger, *Textual*, 49].

ss The sentence 23:14 is not included because assumed to be a textual variant. The sentence is not in the Alexandrian and Western texts of Matthew's Gospel. In the Textus Receptus (KJV/NKJV) it is after v. 13. In other manuscripts it is before v. 13. The verse is considered to have been imported from Mark 12:40 or Luke 20:47 [Metzger, *Textual*, 50]. The sentence reads, "Woe to you, scribes and Pharisees, hypocrites! Because you devour widows' houses, and as a pretense are praying long prayers. On account of this you will receive greater condemnation."

tt In 24:29, the word I have translated "during" is *meta*, which is translated "after" by other versions. The word means "mid, amid, in the midst, with, among, implying accompaniment" [Zodhiates, s. v. 3326]. When used with the accusative case ("tribulation" is in the accusative case) it "strictly implies motion toward the middle or into the midst of something." The idea is one thing accompanies another thing, thus, the things happening to the sun, moon, etc., accompany—are part of—the Tribulation. Other translations view *meta* as indicating succession in time (thus, "after") because of the preceding "immediately."

uu In 25:13, the longer ending ("in which the Son of Man comes") is supported by some manuscripts, not supported by many more. The clause may have been added from 24:44 to provide a similar ending to a story with the same exhortation. The presence or absence of the clause does not materially affect the meaning. The shorter ending does require the reader to reflect on previous warnings.

vv At 27:2, the word I have translated "procurator" and which all other versions translate "governor" is *hēgemṓn*, "leader, chief, head" [Zodhiates, s. v. 2232]. Judea was part of the Syrian province, which had a governor. Therefore Pilate could not be a governor. In AD 33 Syria was an Imperial province governed by the Imperial Legate Flaccus. The lesser official who administrated the Judean region of the Syrian province was the procurator

Pontius Pilate.

ww At 28:19, the careful reader will note the translation does not say "make disciples," but "disciple all the peoples." That is because the Greek text is not *poiēma mathētés*, "make disciples," but is *mathētés*, "to disciple." The word *mathētés* is in the aorist tense: teach a person to follow. In this context *mathētés* means, "teach a person to follow Christ's commandments." By implication the commandments incorporate Christ's doctrine. The New Testament church is not to make disciples, but to disciple all those whom Jesus makes a disciple by salvation. Every saved person is a disciple of Jesus needing discipling.

xx The Byzantine texts end 28:20 with the word "amen." The older Western texts do not. If the word was originally present, there is no reason for eliminating it. The word *amén* is transliterated from Hebrew and Greek as "amen." The Hebrew word means "truly." Jesus often used *amén* at the beginning of a sentence, in the sense of "truly." Jesus never used *amén* at the end of a sentence.

Mark Translation Notes

a This translation note deliberately left blank.

b At 1:2, the Western and Alexandrian manuscripts read, "As written in Isaiah the prophet." The Byzantine manuscripts read, "As written in the prophets." In both manuscript families, the text of 1:2–3 combines prophecies from Isaiah and Malachi. Lightfoot [*Commentary*, 2:394] says, "It was very customary among the Jews . . . to hear many testimonies cited out of many prophets under this form of speech, *as it is written in the prophets*. If two or more [were cited] this was the most common manner of citing them, *as it is written in the prophets*. It is without all example [in the writings of the Jews], when two testimonies are taken out of two prophets, to name only the last." I believe it more likely the phrase "as it is written in the prophets" was the autograph. This is the phrase Peter would have heard growing up in the synagogues and would have used as an apostle as he lectured to his Roman audience.

c In 1:8, I have translated "in water" and "in the Holy Spirit" (cf. the ASV). The preposition is the Greek *én*. When used with the Dative case, as it is here, *én* may be instrumental, "with," or locative, "in." The water is both the means and the sphere in which water baptism was accomplished. The Spirit is both the means and the sphere in which spiritual baptism is accomplished. Compare Romans 8:9, "But you are not in flesh but in spirit" (and so all other translations except the NIV, NLT) where "flesh" and 'Spirit" are dative.

d In 1:12, I have translated *ekbállō*, "to cast, throw out, drive" [Zodhiates, s. v. 1544] as "urged." I believe the theological context of Scripture's testimony concerning the deity of the God-man and the nature of the Trinity must be considered, because the Trinity, being of one essence, operates together. The sense of *ekbállō* in this place is urge, send, led, but not "to force."

e In 1:19, the translation "those" is *autós*, usually translated "they" to indicate Jacob and John in the boat. But 1:20 indicates employees were also in the boat. The employees are part of the context, so I have translated *autós* as "those."

f In 1:20, I have used the modern word "employees," to translate *misthōtós*, "hired one" [Zodhiates, s. v. 3411]. Some versions translate *misthōtós* as "hired servants," others as "hired men." A person who has been hired is an employee.

g At 1:30, the verb form, "fevering" is unfamiliar to the reader because all other versions translate the verb in the text as a noun. The word *puréssō* [Zodhiates, s. v. 4445] is in the text a verb in the grammatical form present particle active.

h In 1:32, the word translated "demonized" is the Greek *daimonízomai*, "to be in the power of a demon" [Zodhiates, s. v. 1139]. There is no such thing as demon possession. A fallen messenger—a demon—cannot possess a person. All persons belong to God. A fallen messenger in a human soul is like a squatter inhabiting a house owned by another. A fallen messenger may oppress a person, but by *daimonízomai*, the gospel writers mean the fallen messenger is inhabiting the person's soul. The person who has been *daimonízomai* is more than oppressed, he/she is dominated by the demon's power. No saved person may be *daimonízomai*.

i In 1:34, a very few manuscripts add to the end of the verse the words from Luke 4:41, "to be Christ." If the words had been in the autograph of Mark's gospel, there would be no reason for a copyist to have deleted them.

j In 2:15, "reclining" is *katákeimai*, "to lie down" [Zodhiates, s. v. 3621]. Men, according to the customs of the times, lay on a bed or couch that was placed perpendicular to the table, propping themselves up on their left elbow, thereby eating with their right hand. I added "*to eat*" to clarify the meaning of "reclining."

k In 2:16 the KJV and NKJV have "the scribes and pharisees," but the text indicates Mark is speaking of scribes who were Pharisees. "Scribe" was an occupation, Pharisee (and Sadducee) was a religious denomination.

l At 2:19, the "groom's companions" translates *huiós* [sons] *numphṓn* [bridal chamber], literally, "sons of the bridechamber." In the Scripture "sons of," unless used of physical birth, is a gender-neutral term. These are in modern terms bridesmaids and groomsmen.

m In 2:27 the translation "humankind" is from *ánthrōpos*, a generic term used to identify a male human individual or humankind as a group of individuals, without regard to gender [Zodhiates, s. v. 444]. Context determines which is in view.

n In 2:28, the phrase "Son of Man" always emphasizes Jesus' connection to humanity. Only Jesus uses this term, always in reference to himself, so the term is capitalized, because Jesus knew who he was.

o In 3:28, 29, I have translated the word *blasphēméō* [Zodhiates, s. v. 987], defined as "to hurt the reputation with reports or words, speak evil of, slander," as "slanders" versus the transliteration "blasphemy" in other versions.

p In 4:26, 28 the kind of seed is not specified. I have used wheat as Christ's example in 4:28, "a stalk, then a head, then abundant grain in the head" versus the example of corn followed by most versions, "the blade, then the ear, after that the full corn in the ear." Corn, or more properly "maize," was first domesticated in what is now Mexico about 8,700 years ago. What we think of as corn was not known in the biblical world in Jesus' times.

q In 5:6, the fallen spirit being (demon) did not worship Jesus, he knelt before Jesus. The demon did not know Jesus the Christ was deity incarnate. See comments in the Preface. I discuss this thoroughly in my commentary on Mark's gospel. Briefly, 1) everything any demon said about Jesus is repeated from what they heard Gabriel tell Mariam, Luke 1:32–33; 2) would Satan have asked Jesus to give him worship if he had known Jesus was God the Son incarnate? see Matthew 4:9; 3) would the demon have asked Jesus to, "swear by God," 5:7, if he believed Jesus was God? The demon knelt as a position of submission. After the incident at Mark 1:23–26, the first encounter between Jesus and a demon, the demons knew God had given Jesus authority to cast them out.

r In Mark 5:27, the woman touches Jesus' *himátion*, his outer clothing. Matthew is more specific, she touched his *sísît* [Harris, *TWOT*, s. v. 103a], the fringe around the edges of his clothing or a tassel at each corner. The word *himátion* might also mean "a large piece of woolen cloth nearly square, which was wrapped around the body or fastened about the shoulders" [Zodhiates, s. v. 2440].

s In 6:3, the word I have translated "builder," is *téktōn* [Zodhiates, s. v. 5045]. Older language studies concluded this word meant "an artificer, a craftsman, especially a worker in wood." More recent studies have indicated this word described a builder, probably working in stone.

t Mark 6:11 the last sentence is not included because assumed a textual variant. It is not found in early manuscripts of Mark's Gospel. It appears only in the KJV/NKJV. Textual critics consider the sentence to be in Mark by scribal addition from Matthew 10:15. The sentence reads, "Amen, Amen I say to you, it will be more tolerable for Sodom or Gomorrah in a day of judgment than for that town."

u In 6:45, I have added the word "Galilee" to the text: Bethsaida-Galilee. There were two villages named "Bethsaida," one on the northeast side of the lake, one on the west side. The one on the west side was Bethsaida-Galilee, see John 12:21. The one on the northeast side was Bethsaida-Julius in Gaulanitis. The local village had been developed by Philip the Tetrarch into the city of Julius, named in honor of Caesar Augustus's daughter, Julia [Bromiley, *Encyclopedia*, s. v. "Bethsaida]. The gospel writers continued to call it Bethsaida.

v In 7:8, the last part of the sentence is not included because assumed a textual variant. These words are not found in the oldest manuscripts. Some consider it a scribal addition repeating 7:4. In some manuscripts it is at the beginning of 7:8 and in others it is at the end of 7:8. It seems unlikely to me that Peter would again list what was listed in 7:4. The KJV and NKJV end the sentence with "washing pots and cups—and many other similar things you do."

w In 7:24, some manuscripts do not have "and Sidon." "Sidon" was probably brought up from 7:31, or perhaps incorporated from Matthew 15:21. In 7:31, most texts, including the oldest, have "Tyre and Sidon," giving an indication of the way Jesus returned from that region.

x In 9:18, I have translated *xērós*, "dry" [Zodhiates, s. v. 3584], as "withering away," whereas modern versions translate "rigid." The word *xērós* is used seven times in the New Testament to describe a plant drying out, dry land as opposed to the sea, a hand that has been made unusable by a disease or injury, or persons with an injury or disease that has left them partly immobile. The translation "rigid," by some is an interpretation, based on the assumption the boy's problem was epilepsy, not demonic habitation.

y In 9:29, some manuscripts add at the end, "and fasting." The words may have been imported from the parallel passage in Matthew 17:21, to make the accounts harmonize. The words are missing from important manuscripts in the Alexandrian and Western texts [Metzger, 85]. For these reasons it seems unlikely the words "and fasting" were part of the autograph of Mark's gospel. Except for Matthew 17:21, fasting is never mentioned as part of casting out evil spirits. Fasting was seldom mentioned by Jesus, and usually in a negative sense, Matthew 6:16, 48; Mark

2:18. Fasting was a practice of Judaism, a religion of traditions.

z In 10:21, the Textus Receptus and many minuscules have "take up the cross" between the words "heaven" and "follow" [Metzger, *Textual*, 89]. The phrase here in 10:21 seems out of place to me and does not fit the context. The cross has been mentioned prior to this point only at 8:24, where Jesus is speaking of discipleship to the large group of people who had been following him, expecting some messianic manifestation. The rich man was not a follower and thought of Jesus as a teacher, not the messiah.

aa 11:26 is not included because assumed to be a textual variant. This verse is "missing from early witnesses that represent all text types" [Metzger, *Textual*, 93]. The verse appears to have been inserted by a copyist from Matthew 6:15. The verse reads, "But if you do not forgive, neither will your Father who is in heaven forgive your wrongdoing."

bb In 12:42, the widow put into the public treasury two *leptons*, which were the smallest Jewish coins, physically and in value, and made of copper. Two *leptons* were equal in value to one *quadrans*, the smallest Roman coin, also made of copper. The Roman *assárion*, the next Roman coin in value, was also made of copper. The Roman *denarius* was made of silver. The Jewish *lepton* was 1/128 of a *denarius*; the *quadrans* was 1/64 of a *denarius*; an *assárion* was 1/16 of a *denarius* [Schmidt, 28]. So, sixteen *assárion* made a *denarius*; sixty-four *quadrans* made a *denarius*; one hundred twenty-eight *leptons* made a *denarius*. In modern terms, think of the *quadrans* as a penny. A day's wage was 40–45 pennies. The widow put in one penny, "all her livelihood."

cc In Mark 13:13, I have translated *sózó* [Zodhiates, s. v. 4982], "to save, deliver, make whole, preserve safe from danger, loss, destruction," as "delivered," not "saved" as in other versions. The persons Jesus is speaking of are already saved from the penalty of their sins, else the Holy Spirit would not provide them the words to speak.

dd In 13:24, I have translated *metá* as "with." The word *metá* is a preposition meaning "mid, in the midst, with, among" [Zodhiates, s. v. 3326]. When *metá* is associated with the accusative case, as it is in Mark 13:24 ("tribulation" is accusative), then *metá* is normally translated "after," which accounts for other versions of Mark 13:24. However, Jesus is still speaking of the Tribulation period. The events given in 13:24–25 are during the tribulation period, not after, see Revelation 8:12, compare 6:12–13. Therefore, to translate *metá* as "after" the tribulation, in Mark 13:24, clearly presents a contradiction with later Scripture. The translation of *metá* in Mark 13:24 should agree with Revelation 8:12ff, and therefore I have use the primary meaning of *metá*, "with that Tribulation."

ee In 14:54, I have translated *hupērétēs* as "temple police." The word means "a servant, attendant, subordinate official" [Zodhiates, s. v. 5227]. The apostle John uses this word in his gospel at 18:3 to describe the men sent to arrest Jesus. These were officers of the temple who carried out the orders of the chief priests. In addition to its use in the arrest of Jesus, 18:3, 12, it is used at John 7:32, 45, 46; 18:22; 19:6 of officers of the temple. The *hupērétēs* were the company and officers sent to capture Jesus, wholly composed of Levites working in the temple (see my commentary on John's gospel, vol. 2). Thus, temple police.

ff In 14:70, the ending, "your speech is alike," is not present in the majority of manuscripts, only in the manuscripts used by the KJV/NKJV. This fact argues the words are not in the autograph but added by a scribe to give a reason as to how those standing by knew Peter was a Galilean. Its absence from other manuscripts fits with Peter's brevity, for he seldom gives explanatory asides.

gg In 15:25, the translation, "about midmorning," is Peter's "third hour." Literally, the third hour is about 9:00 a.m. Peter isn't saying the crucifixion occurred at 9:00 a.m., but that Jesus was condemned to be crucified at about 9 a.m., which agrees with the other gospels. Mark reports Peter's eyewitness testimony, given at Rome about twenty-five years after the crucifixion. So Peter's third hour, assuming he was one of those standing at a distance from the cross (Luke 23:49) is an extrapolation (a guess) derived from the time when he saw Jesus on the cross with darkness covering the land. If, as was the case, Jesus went to Pilate early in the morning—Peter does not appear to have followed John to the Praetorium—and now Peter sees Jesus on the cross about the sixth hour. i.e., about noon, he must have assumed Jesus had been condemned to crucifixion about mid-morning.

A "guesstimate" of the time by Peter does not conflict with the doctrine of scripture inerrancy. The Holy Spirit accurately reported, through Mark, what Peter believed to have been the time when Jesus was condemned, beaten, scourged, and then led out to be crucified. What Peter believed was historically accurate: Jesus was led out to be crucified sometime between the third hour (Mark) and the sixth hour (John), i.e., about midway between 9:00 a.m. and noon, and then there was darkness beginning about noon, Mark 15:33.

hh Mark 15:28 is not included because assumed to be a textual variant. The verse is not in the "earliest and best witnesses of the Alexandrian and the Western types of text" [Metzger, *Textual*, 99]. The verse is in several Byzantine texts (used by the KJV/NKJV). If the verse was part of the original text of Mark, there is no good reason it would be deleted from the earliest Alexandrian and the Western manuscripts. If the verse was added by later scribes it was borrowed from Luke 22:37. The scripture referred to is Isaiah 53:12. Peter does not usually point out the fulfillment of Scripture. The verse reads, "And the Scripture was fulfilled that says, and with the lawless he was numbered."

ii Mark 16:9–20. Based on an argument by David Alan Black, in the book, *Perspectives on the Ending of Mark*, and other arguments in Black's book, *Why Four Gospels*, I believe Mark 16:9–20 are part of the autograph. In essence, Black proposes when Peter gave his lectures on Jesus in Rome, he did not lecture on the resurrection, because he knew Matthew and Luke had covered that material. So, when first published, in Rome, Mark's Gospel ended where Peter's lectures had ended. Later, after Peter had died, Mark issued a second edition, from Alexandria, with the material found in Mark 16:9–20, to "round off" the final discourse. "These verses form a summary catalogue of references to the resurrection stories of Matthew and Luke" [Black, *Perspectives*, 29 (essay by Daniel B. Wallace).] See the referenced works, and the Introduction in my work. *A Private Commentary on the Bible: Mark's Gospel*.

jj In 16:18, the words "and with their hands" are present in some manuscripts, missing in others [Metzger, *Textual*, 107]. My decision was not to include the words, as there was no reason to delete them if they were original to the autograph.

Luke Translation Notes

a At Luke 1:3, it is possible "Theophilus," a compound word formed from *theós*, God, and *phílos*, loving, is not a proper name but literally means "lover of God." The sentence would then read, "... to write an orderly account to you, most noble lover of God," as addressed to believers in general. So also at Acts 1:1.

b At 1:19, the pronoun is plural, "these," not the singular "this" of several versions. The plural "these" refers to the prophecy of John's birth and the instructions following the prophecy. The "good news" is *euaggelízō* [Zodhiates, s. v. 2097], "proclaim the good news." *Euaggelízō* is in the grammatical form aorist infinitive middle voice, giving the sense "to announce or publish something as good news." The word "tidings" (KJV, ASV, NKJV), which means "news, information" is too archaic for modern readers.

c In Luke 1:28, the words "blessed are you among women," are present in a number of related manuscripts, but missing in a diverse group of manuscripts. The words were probably imported from 1:42, where their presence is undisputed. If they were original to 1:28 there is no reason they would have been omitted from such a wide diversity of manuscripts [Metzger, *Textual*, 108]. For that reason I have omitted the words from 1:28.

d At 2:2, I have translated *hēgemoneúō* as "procurator." A procurator was not a governor. In the times of which Luke writes, the *hēgemoneúō* Quirinius was ranked under the Syrian province governor Varus (7–4 BC). Quirinius' position was Legate of Augustus managing the military forces in the Syrian province. [See William Ramsay, *Was Christ Born in Bethlehem*, and *The New Schaff-Herzog Encyclopedia of Religious Knowledge*, s. v. Quirinius.]

e In 2:7, the word I have translated, "barn" is *phátnē* [Zodhiates, s. v. 5336]. The traditional translation "manger" gives the false impression the baby was laid in a feeding trough. The *phátnē* in which Mariam gave birth to Jesus was inside the cave under the tower of the flock, just as Micah 4:8 had prophesied.

Also in 2:7, I have translated *katáluma* [Zodhiates, s. v. "2646"] as "lodging." A *katáluma* could be a guest room in a house, or an open area surrounded by a wall with niches in the wall for people and animals, or a large open area where many people camped out in the open for the night. Considering many people had come to Bethlehem for the registration, the lack of room in any kind of *katáluma* was understandable, and providential. Jesus was born in the barn, Micah 4:8, where sacrificial lambs were birthed.

f At 2:11 I have given the translation "For has been born to you today a savior who is Christ Lord" in the order in which the words occur in the Greek text. The emphasis is the birth of a savior who is the Christ of Psalm 2:2, 7; Daniel 9:26, thus defining the kind of savior he will be, both king (Psalm 2) and redeemer (Daniel 9:26). The nouns "Christ" and "Lord" are of equal grammatical value (both nominative masculine singular), both equally the object of the pronoun ("who") and the verb ("is"), so there is no grammatical reason to reverse the order in which they appear in the text, "Christ Lord." Nor is there a grammatical reason to add to the text the definite pronoun "the" before "Lord."

g At Luke 2:52 the choices are "Jesus progressed in wisdom and maturity" or "Jesus progressed in wisdom and grew taller." Luke's meaning is not physical height but the maturity that comes with age.

h At 3:23–24, the consensus of opinion from ancient times is that Luke gives Jesus' physical descent through Mariam (Matthat—Heli—Mariam) and Matthew gives Jesus' royal heritage though Joseph (Matthan—Jacob—Joseph).

i In 6:1, the clause, "the second after the first," is the translation of *deuteróprōtos*, "second-first," coming after the word *sábbaton* (sabbath). Most Language Authorities delete *deuteróprōtos* as a "transcriptional blunder" [Metzger, *Textual*, 116]. However, *deuteróprōtos* makes sense within the biblical context. The reference is to Leviticus 23:15 (ESV), "You shall count seven full weeks from the day after the Sabbath, from the day that you brought the sheaf of the wave offering." The Holy Spirit through Luke used *deuteróprōtos* as a chronological marker in Luke's gospel to tell the reader of the AD 31 Passover not mentioned by the other gospels (although this incident is mentioned, Matthew 12:1; Mark 2:23). See my commentary on Luke's gospel, vol. 1.

j At 7:30 I have translated *nomikós* [Zodhiates, s. v. 6544] as "experts in the law," where other versions translate "lawyers." The HCSB and NIV are exceptions. The grammatical value of *nomikós* in 7:30 is an adjective, which is why I have translated the *kai* [Zodhiates, s. v. 2532] as explicative, "namely." As an adjective *nomikós* modifies the noun "Pharisees." The sentence is "but the Pharisees, namely the experts in the law," etc.

k In 8:44, Luke says she touched the *kráspedon*, the "fringe" of his clothing. This is the border of the clothing, corresponding to the Hebrew *kānāp*, "border or corner" [Zodhiates, s. v. 2440]. The Hebrews were to attach a *sîsît* on the *kānāp* of their clothing. The word *sîsît* means either a tassel or a fringe. Harris [*TWOT*, s. v. 103a] states, "It is debated whether *sîsît* indicates the fringe around the edges of a clothing or a tassel at each corner.

l In 8:45 some versions add the words, "and you say, 'Who has touched me?'" The form of the sentence varies in so many manuscripts it was likely imported from Mark 5:31 by a scribe trying to make the Mark and Luke accounts similar [Metzger, *Textual*, 122].

m At 9:10, I have added "Julius" to "Bethsaida" to give "Bethsaida-Julius." There were two villages named "Bethsaida," one on the northeast side of the lake, one on the west side. The one on the west side was Bethsaida-Galilee, see John 12:21. The one on the northeast side was Bethsaida-Julius in Gaulanitis. The local village had been developed by Philip the Tetrarch into the city of Julius, named in honor of Caesar Augustus's daughter, Julia [Bromiley, *Encyclopedia*, s. v. "Bethsaida"]. The gospel writers continued to call it Bethsaida.

n In 9:23–25 I have translated the third person singular pronouns as plurals: "them, they, themselves, their." Modern use has agreed "they, them, and their" may be used to reflect the singular or the plural. Jesus undoubtedly meant persons: male or female.

o In 9:54, some manuscripts add at the end, "as also Elijah did." The absence in early texts suggests this was a later scribal addition as an explanation to clarify for Gentile readers. On the other hand, for those to whom Luke was writing—an unsaved Gentile audience hearing about Jesus through Luke's gospel as an evangelistic document in the early church—such a reference would be unhelpful. The comment, if genuine, is in the mouth of Jacob and John to Jesus. One doubts either Jacob, John, or Jesus needed the reminder about Elijah. For those reasons I considered the words a scribal addition, not part of the autograph.

p In 9:55 and 9:56, two additions are not well attested in the ancient manuscripts, and for that reason I have not included them in the translation. The YLT examples these scribal additions: "55 and said, 'Ye have not known of what spirit ye are; 56 for the Son of

Man did not come to destroy men's lives, but to save.'"

q In 10:1 the evidence for "seventy" and "seventy-two" have equal representation in the ancient manuscript families. Which reading is the autograph does not affect any interpretation or doctrine. A reading must be chosen. I chose seventy-two.

r In 10:25, the text says *nomikós* [Zodhiates, s. v. 3544], "lawyer." I have put "skilled in the Mosaic Law" in place of the single word English translation, to bring out the fullest meaning of *nomikós* within the historical-cultural context.

s In 10:34, the word translated "khan" (inn, in most versions) is *pandocheíon* [Zodhiates, s. v. "3829"], which is not the same word as at Luke 2:7, which is *katáluma*, an open courtyard or a guest room in a house. The word *pandocheíon* means a structure specifically designed for receiving travelers, a "khan." A khan was a trading center and hostel in a city, with a square courtyard surrounded by rows of connected lodging rooms, usually on two levels. The "host" (the "innkeeper") is *pandocheús*. The khan was undoubtedly located in Jericho.

t At 10:38, some texts add "into her house," as explanatory of "Martha received him." If the phrase were in the autograph, there is no reason it should have been deleted [Metzger, *Textual*, 129].

u In 11:1–4, the differences between Luke's version and Matthew's version indicate this prayer in Luke was given at a different time and place than the similar prayer in Matthew's Gospel. The failure of various copyists to understand that the prayer in Luke was given at a different time and place than that in Matthew's Gospel has led to copyist additions to Luke's report. I have not included any of those additions. The Holy Spirit wanted us to have both Luke's and Matthew's versions of the prayer. Looking at how people have ritualized this prayer into various liturgies (versus using it to actually pray to the Father), or have used it as some kind of incantation, I believe the Spirit wanted readers to understand prayer does not require a certain set of words to be effective prayer. See my commentary on Luke's gospel, vol. 1 for the various scribal additions.

v In 11:24, "arid places," ties into the Jewish belief the abode of evil spirits was in deserts [Zodhiates, s. v. 504]. That belief was wrong (fallen angels live in the spirit domain second heaven), but Jesus often accommodated his lessons to certain current cultural beliefs. He wasn't giving a lesson on the living accommodations of fallen messengers.

w In 11:28 I have translated the word *menoúnge* [Zodhiates, s. v. 3304] "Yes, truly." Others translate with some form of "Yes, rather." This word is "a particle of affirmation . . . yes indeed."

x In 11:37, the word I have translated "eat lunch," is *aristáō* [Zodhiates, s. v. 709], "to breakfast but also to dine . . . any meal before the principle one." Looking at the context, I decided the Pharisee was asking Jesus to lunch, not breakfast.

y At 11:41, my translation reads, "But of the things within *your heart*, give compassionately, and see, all things are clean to you." Other translations speak of giving alms or charity or gifts. The word in question is *eleēmosúnē* [Zodhiates, s. v. 1654], "mercifulness, compassion." By a figure of speech, known as a metonymy (a substitution), *eleēmosúnē* is translated giving alms or giving to the poor, because such giving is being merciful or giving out of compassion. Because mercy and compassion are of the heart, giving is from the heart. The contrast in the passage is between inside and outside, a clean cup versus a clean heart.

z At 12:5, "two *assárion*." There were sixteen *assárion* in a *denari*. A day's wage for a common laborer was ten to twelve *assárion*.

aa In 12:25, the text literally reads (in the word order of the text) "which now of you being anxious is able to the *hēlikía* of him to add *pēchus*. The word *hēlikía* [Zodhiates, s. v. 2244] means "age, full-age, vigor, stature, size." The word *pēchus* [Zodhiates, s. v. 4083] means "a cubit, equal to the length of a man's arm from the elbow to the end of his middle finger, i.e., about twenty-one inches." In the literal sense of the words, Jesus asks, who by worry can add size to his height? In a metaphorical sense, *pēchus* might be used to indicate time. The metaphorical meaning might be, who by worry is able to add time to their age (lifespan)? There is no compelling cultural or textual evidence to value one option (height or age) above the other.

bb In 12:35, the phrase, "Let your clothes be pulled up and knotted," translates *perizōnnumi*, "to gird or wrap around" [Zodhiates. s. v. 4024]. The person would bend over, grab the lower edge of his garment (a dress-like robe) from the back, and pull it forward through the legs (thereby also gathering the front of the garment), pull the gathered garment up to the waist to free the lower legs, and then knot, or tie (using the sash/belt), the gathered garment in place at the waist. The mental image in the illustration is a servant prepared for work.

cc In 16:13, the word "material possessions" translates *mamōnás* [Zodhiates, s. v. 3126], by some transliterated "mammon," and by others translated "money." *Mamōnás* is "the comprehensive word for all kinds of possessions, earnings, and gains, a designation of material value, the god of materialism." In Luke 6:13, the point is not serving money, but serving all kinds of material possessions.

dd In 17:24 the text literally reads, "As for the lightening flashing, from the of the sky to the of the sky shines." Every Bible translation must add an explanatory word to "of the sky" to make the passage sensible for the non-Greek reader. I have followed the form suggested by the ASV and YLT.

ee At 17:36. The majority of texts are missing 17:36, and it is likely it was imported from Matthew 24:40 [Metzger, *Textual*, 142–143]. However, there is a possibility it was accidentally omitted because the repetition of the same words at the end of 17:34, 35, make it easy to omit the third repetition at 17:36. Manuscripts were copied without spaces between words, so it was easy for the eye to slip over a verse so similar to others as the scriptures were copied. For that reason I decided to retain the verse.

ff In 18:22, the word I have translated "helpless beggars" is the Greek *ptōchós* [Zodhiates, s. v. "4434"]. The Greeks had two words to describe the poor. One word was *pénēs* [Zodhiates, s. v. "3993"]. That word described the person who earned just enough to meet his or her daily needs for food and shelter. In modern terms, they were the "living paycheck-to-paycheck" poor. The word *ptōchós* referred to those who must beg to earn their daily needs for food and shelter. If they did not receive sufficient money by begging, they went without one or more or all of those daily needs. The *ptōchós* poor were in abject poverty, utter helplessness, complete destitution, and therefore a helpless beggar. In modern terms, it is those homeless who are completely dependent on the kindness of strangers for their survival.

gg In 20:30, the Textus Receptus, after the word "second," has the phrase, "as the wife and he died childless." The phrase appears to have been imported from Mark 12:21. Matthew also lacks the phrase. For those reasons I have not included the phrase in the translation.

hh In 21:2, the widow put into the public treasury two *leptons*, which were the smallest Jewish coins, physically and in value, and made of copper. Two *leptons* were equal in value to one *quadrans*, the smallest Roman coin, also made of copper. The Roman *assárion*, the next Roman coin in value, was also made of copper. The Roman *denarius* was made of silver. The Jewish *lepton* was 1/128 of a *denarius*; the *quadrans* was 1/64 of a *denarius*; an *assárion* was 1/16 of a *denarius*. So, sixteen *assárion* made a *denarius*; sixty-four *quadrans* made a *denarius*; one hundred twenty-eight *leptons* made a *denarius*. [Schmidt, *Biblical Measures*, 28.]

ii 23:17 is not included because assumed to be a textual variant. The verse is missing from a large number of early manuscripts; in those manuscripts where it does appear (manuscripts unrelated to one another), it appears in different places, in different forms, after 23:17 or after 23:19. The manuscript evidence indicates it was created by paraphrasing Matthew 27:15; Mark 15:6. [Metzger, *Textual*, 153]. The verse reads, "Now of necessity he had to release to them at least one."

jj At 23:23, the ending phrase, "and of the chief priests" appears in some manuscripts, where it seems an explanatory addition to the verse added by well-meaning scribes [Metzger, *Textual*, 153]. For that reason I have not included the phrase in the translation. The "they" at the beginning of 23:23 means all present, the multitudes and the priests.

kk At 23:43, the word I have translated "truly" is the Greek *amḗn* [Zodhiates, s. v. 281], transliterated from the Hebrew into Greek, and usually transliterated from the Greek into the English "amen." The Hebrew word means "truly," and is transliterated into Greek and English with the same meaning.

John Translation Notes

a1 At 1:14, the word I have translated "embodied" is *sárx* [Zodhiates, s. v. 4561], living flesh (versus a corpse) or body. The resurgence of the doctrine of physicalism led to me to make that translation. Physicalism says the deity person God the Son in his incarnation literally stopped being deity and became a human being, though retaining some abilities of deity. Other versions translate "made flesh" (KJV); "became flesh" (YLT, ASV, NKJV, ESV, HCSB, NIV); "became human" (NLT, a translation too much like Physicalism).

God the Son became embodied in the defined sense of the union of deity with a rational human soul and human body. Deity and human are integral parts of the one person formed by the union. The biblical doctrine is God the Son in his union (the incarnation) with Jesus of Nazareth became one person with one personality, that of God the Son, with two distinct natures, deity and human, both natures informing the personality, and by that incarnation became the God-man, Jesus the Christ. The Chalcedonian Creed continues to be the orthodox doctrine of the New Testament church. See the Chalcedonian Creed, AD 451, here: [https://www.theopedia.com/chalcedonian-creed].

a2 At 1:16, the many translations, such as "grace for grace" (KJV, ASV, NKJV); "grace upon grace" (ESV); "grace after grace" (HCSB); and the atrocious NIV, "one blessing after another," do not reflect the Greek text, *chárin antí cháritos*. The word *antí* [Zodhiates, s. v. 473], means "over against, in the presence of, in lieu of." John 1:17 indicates the comparison is between the grace that came through the Law given through Moses and the grace that came through Jesus Christ.

Chárin antí cháritos means that the *grace* in the Law given through Moses is being compared to the *grace* that came through Jesus Christ. What, then, is the comparison between grace in the Law and grace through Christ? In the Law the animal sacrifices atoned for sins and were a type of the spiritual truth of salvation through a substitutionary atonement. However, the fact that the sacrifices had to continue revealed they were not perfect, and therefore could not make the offeror perfect. The Law anticipated the need for a perfect sacrifice, and illustrated the form that perfect sacrifice would take: a substitutionary sacrifice with a perfect value to remit the penalty of all sin past, present, and future.

The animal sacrifices were acceptable when offered by faith in God's testimony that required those sacrifices. The believer's faith in God and God's testimony was made acceptable by God's grace to the forgiveness of sins, which is the salvation principle in Ephesians 2:8, through the merit of Christ's propitiation of God for sin, which God decreed in eternity past was the only merit for the forgiveness of sin. See my commentary on John's gospel vol. 1, for an extended discussion.

a3 At 1:34, the reader will have seen I did not capitalize "son" in John's mouth. Nor did I capitalize "lamb" at 1:29, 36. The reason is as I explained in the Preface, no one during the Christ's earthly ministry understood Jesus was God the Son incarnate. John seems to understand, but when we see read John's question at Matthew 11:3 (Luke 7:19), we see John has doubts if Jesus is the Christ. If John knew his relative Jesus was God incarnate, then he would not have had doubts. John knew Jesus was a righteous man, Matthew 3:14, but he did not know Jesus was the messiah until he had baptized Jesus, John 1:33, and he did not know Jesus was God incarnate.

a4 The translation "I tell you the truth," at 1:51 and multiple places throughout John's good news, is literally, "Amen amen, I say to you." The word *amḗn* [Zodhiates, s. v. 281] is the transliteration of the Hebrew `*āmēn*, as transliterated into Greek. In both Hebrew and Greek the word means "truth" or "truly."

a5 In 4:10, the translation "had known" (versus "knew" in most translations) is the pluperfect tense of the verb *eídō*, to see or to perceive. The pluperfect tense "is used to describe an action that was completed and whose effects are felt at a time after the completion but before the time of the speaker" [Mounce, *Basics*, 234]. Jesus is saying the woman did not know the gift of God prior to his speaking to her.

b In 4:20, I have replaced the plural pronoun *humeís*, "you" with the noun the pronoun represents, "Jews."

c In 4:22, I have replaced the plural pronoun *humeís*, "you" with the noun the pronoun represents, "Samaritans." The word "Jews" is inserted into text because implied by the context.

d In 4:36, The word translated "reward" is *misthós*, wages, hire, reward. The reaping is spiritual, therefore the *misthós* is spiritual.

e In 5:2, the word translated "sheep" is *probatikós*, meaning "pertaining to sheep." The reference could be to the Sheep Gate, but it could also mean the sheep "market" (KJV) near the temple. Most translators prefer "gate" in deference to Nehemiah 3:1, 32; 12:39.

f In 5:22, the translation turns on the words *oudé*, "not even" and *oudeís*, "not one." The idea of *oudé* is continuative: "and not, also not, and hence, neither, not even." I have given an expanded meaning of *oudé:* "from this time." The word *oudeís* is a compound of *ou* and *heís* literally meaning "not one." The basic idea is "no one," or "not even one." Putting the Greek grammar into English grammatical order translates as "For the Father from this time judges not even one."

g In 5:29, the translation turns on the synonyms *poiéō* [Zodhiates, s. v. 4160], and *prássō* [Zodhiates, s. v. 4238]. The word *poiéō* means "to make, cause, practice good." The word *prássō* means "to continually, habitually do evil." The difference between practice good and habitually do evil is the difference between saved and unsaved, respectively.

h In 5:39, 40 the "you" is in the plural form in the Greek text, which I have shown by translating "you all."

j In 6:10, the word translated "recline" is *anapíptō*, "to lie down in order to eat" [Zodhiates, s. v. 377]. In Jesus' first century culture people lay on a couch propped up on one elbow in order to eat.

k In 6:19, the "about three miles" translates "twenty-five or thirty *stádion"* in the text. The Roman *stádion* is equal to 606.9 feet. The distance rowed was between 2.87 miles and 3.44 miles.

l In 6:34, the translation "this the bread" reflects the definite article in the text. They were not asking for just any bread, but that particular bread coming out of heaven, 6:33.

m At 6:35 (also John 6:48, 51; 8:12; 10:7, 11; 14:6; 15:1; Revelation 1:8, 11; 22:16), the text for "I am" is "*egó* (I) *eimí* (I am)." The same translation, "I am," could have been achieved by *eimí* alone. The English translation and punctuation should emphasize *egó*, e.g., "I, I am the light of the world."

n In 6:69, the manuscripts diverge. The Western texts are as I have given in the translation, reading "that you are the holy one of God." The Byzantine texts read "that you are the Christ, the Son of the living God." The manuscripts that Metzger [*Textual*, 184] lists in support of the shorter reading include several second century manuscripts of John's Gospel. What seems to have happened in the Byzantine texts is a copyist changed the text to agree with Peter's much later confession at Matthew 16:16.

o In 7:22, most versions do not translate the *diá toúto*, "because of this."

p In 7:32, the word translated "temple police" is *hupērétēs*, a subordinate official [Zodhiates, s. v. 5257]. In Jewish contexts the word can mean the synagogue assistant who handed the scroll of Scripture to the reader, or an attendant of the Sanhedrin, or other kinds of subordinate officials. In terms of temple personnel, in this particular context, it means a constable or officer who executes the decree of a public official.

q In 7:38, the translation "heart," is from the Greek *koilía*, the belly of man. Metaphorically *koilía* means the inner person. In English the same metaphorical use is indicated by "heart." In Scripture when "heart" is used metaphorically the term refers to the personality: the seat of moral reflection, choice of the will, and pattern of behavior. The term includes all the mental processes, feelings, affections, and emotions, along with the internal motivations, leading to one's decisions and responses to life situations. That is the meaning in 7:38.

r1 At 8:3, most biblical scholars believe this story (the *pericope de adulterae*, or PA) is a genuine story about Jesus. Opinions divide as to whether the PA was written by John or someone else. For a discussion of the textual issues and reasons for believing the PA is authentically part of the autograph of John's good news, see my book, *A Private Commentary on the Bible: John 1–12*.

r2 In 8:6, the text reads in part, "that they might have to accuse him." It seemed appropriate to complete the sense by adding "some excuse." Other versions use "a basis" (NIV), "evidence" (HCSB), "something" (NKJV)..

s In 8:7, The adjective "first" seems better applied to the noun "stone." Most versions apply the adjective "first" to the pronoun "among you." The Greek text reads, "the *one* sinless among you first the stone at her let him throw."

t At 8:9–11, the translation is made difficult by possible scribal additions to the autograph, accumulating over time as explanatory glosses. Here is the verse with those additions in brackets. 9 Now those having heard [and by their conscience being convicted] they went out one by one, having begun from the eldest [until to the last]; and he [Jesus] was left alone, and the woman being in the midst. 10 Now Jesus having raised up [and saw no one but the woman] said to her, "Woman, where are [they who accuse you]? Has no one condemned you?" 11 Then she said, "No one, Sir." Then Jesus said [to her], "Neither do I condemn you; go and [from now] sin no more."

u At 8:11, the word *kúrios* in her reply is best translated "sir" as there is no estimate of her faith.

v1 In 9:35, the Byzantine manuscripts read, "Do you believe on the Son of God?" The Alexandrian manuscripts read, "Do you believe on the Son of Man?" I believe doctrine must decide this issue. In response to Jesus' question at 6:35, the man asked, 6:36, "Who is he, sir, that I might believe on him?" When Jesus, 6:37, identified himself as the person described in 6:35, the healed man believed and worshiped, 6:38. Son of God is more natural to belief and worship than Son of man.

v2 In 11:44, "sweat cloth," is a *soudárium* [Zodhiates, s. v. 4676], similar in size to a napkin or handkerchief, used for wiping perspiration, often worn around the neck in life, and used to cover the face in death. See Luke 19:20; John 20:7; Acts 19:12.

w In 12:4, the Byzantine texts read "Judas of Simon Iscariot." The Western texts read "Judas Iscariot." Earlier in John 6:7 we were told Judas Iscariot was the Son of Simon. At Matthew 26:6 and Mark 14:3 we are told this supper took place at the house of Simon the leper. The coincidence of the supper at the house of Simon the leper and Judas of Simon Iscariot at the same supper implies Simon the leper was the father of Judas. Based on those scriptures it seemed best to follow the Byzantine texts.

x In 12:7, most versions read, "burial" versus "embalming." The Greek word is *entaphiasmós* [Zodhiates, s. v. 1780], "to prepare a corpse for burial and to bury; the process of preparing a corpse for burial, a laying out, embalming."

y In 12:17, the English translation is awkward, but reflects the emphasis of the Greek language, which would put the most important words first in the text. "Bore witness" are the first words in the text. Other versions place those words at the end of the text.

z At 12:32, I have translated *eán* [Zodhiates, s. v. 1347] as "when," versus "if" in other versions. The word *eán* "implies a condition which experience must determine, an objective possibility, and thus always refers to something future." The word "all" in "will draw all persons" is in the grammatical form masculine plural, leading to the translation, "all persons."

aa In 13:24, the translation "if he will say" reflects the seldom used optative mood of Greek grammar. The optative mood is used when a speaker wants to portray an action as possible [Wallace, 480]. In this verse the optative implies the condition, "does Jesus wish to explain his comment?"

bb In 13:38, the translation "not at all" is the result of *ou mḗ*, the Greek double negative, strengthening the denial. My usual translation of *ou mḗ* is "never no never," but "not at all" seemed better in this place.

cc In 14:1, "keep on" reflects the continuous aspect of the Greek present tense. "You believe now, keep on believing."

dd In 14:7, there are two Greek words translated "perceived." The first is *eídō* [Zodhiates, s. v. 1492], "to perceive," which I have translated "perceived" in accordance with the grammar, which is the pluperfect tense. The second is *horáō* [Zodhiates, s. v. 3708] in the present indicative tense, to perceive with the eyes, implying not the mere act of seeing but the actual perception of the thing seen. Because they had seen Jesus, they had both seen and perceived the Father. Thomas (and the others) had already heard and seen everything they needed to understand Jesus and perceive the Father in Jesus.

ee In 4:16, the words I have translated "a Helper equal to me" is *állos parákletos*. The word *állos* means "another of the same kind, of equal quality." The Helper is deity, because Jesus the Christ is deity incarnate, and the Helper is another of the same kind as Jesus. (The Holy Spirit's indwelling the believer is not an incarnation).

The word *parákletos* [Zodhiates, s. v. 3875] "is properly a verbal adjective referring to an aid of any kind." The word *parákletos* does not mean "comforter," a different Greek word that does not appear in John's good news. Nor does "advocate" fit here, as it does at 1 John 2:1, because that is Jesus' role as propitiator of God and high priest of his people. The designation "helper" [Kittel, 5:804] does fit in John 14:16, and should not be avoided just because it was used in the Mandean Writings (Mandean Gnosis) of the third century AD as "helpers sent from heaven to souls on earth" [Kittel, 5:807].

ff In 14:18, I have translated *orphanós* [Zodhiates, s. v. 3737] as "disciples." The modern "orphans" of other translations, while literally correct, fails to capture Jesus' meaning. The figurative sense is 'abandoned.' [Kittel, 5:488]. The Greek philosopher Epictetus, AD 50–130 (thus a contemporary of John and near contemporary of Jesus), used *orphanós* of pupils who felt abandoned or bereaved when left by their teacher. Because Jesus *is not* representing himself as a father and his disciples as children who will be orphaned when he leaves them, it seemed the better choice to translate this use of *orphanós* in the sense of disciples abandoned by their master.

gg In 15:12, in "as I loved you," the word "loved" is a verb in the grammatical form aorist indicative. The aorist says the action happened, usually but not necessarily in the past. Christ is not saying his love has an end, but that his continuing love is the basis for, and example of, the kind of love the disciples are to have for one another.

hh In 18:1, "winter-flowing stream" is *cheímarros* [Zodhiates, s. v. 5493], a stream that flows only in the winter (the rainy season in Israel) because swollen with rains.

ii In 18:29, notice they "led Jesus from Caiaphas into the Praetorium," i.e., to Pilate, but in 18:13 they first took Jesus to Annas. John's Gospel tells us about the trial before Annas, where Peter denied Jesus three times, 18:15–18, 25–27. The Synoptic gospels tell us about the trial before Caiaphas, where Peter denied Jesus three more times, and also tell us about the trial before the Sanhedrin.

jj In 18:28, my translation, "keep the festival," is literally, "eat the Passover." I have made that translation because most believers do not know the New Testament gospel writers combined the Passover and the Feast of Unleavened Bread into one feast, called either "Passover" or "Unleavened." For example, Mark 14:12, "On the first day of the feast of Unleavened Bread when they sacrificed the Passover." But the Passover lamb was sacrificed the day before Unleavened began. The Passover was Nisan 14, the first day of Unleavened Bread began Nisan 15. The priests are saying they must remain undefiled in order to eat of the sacrifices made during the Feast of Unleavened Bread (Nisan 15–21), which were known as *chagigah*. Others commentators who agree with this explanation are Zodhiates, Edersheim, Geldenhuys, Lightfoot, and Carson, for which see their respective commentaries.

For example, Geldenhuys [*Luke*, 663], "The usage of the

expression 'to eat the Passover' loosely and popularly [refers to] the entire seven days . . . beginning with the slaughter of the Passover lamb . . . John in 18:28 means the celebration of the seven days feast which included the eating of the sacrificial meals during the whole seven days feast, and . . . in particular to the eating of the *chagigah* ('Festival-offering') which had to be eaten [by the priests] during the forenoon after the first Passover day."

Compare Deuteronomy 16:2, "You will sacrifice the Passover . . . from the flock and the herd." The sacrifice on Passover day was a lamb from the flock. The reference to the herd in the Deuteronomy passage can only mean cattle and oxen sacrificed daily during Unleavened Bread, Nisan 15–21.

Lightfoot [*Commentary*, 3:421], quotes several ancient Rabbis, "R. Solomon [says], 'The flocks are meant of the lambs and the kids; the herd of the *chagigah*' . . . R. Bechai, The flocks are for the due of the Passover; the herd for the sacrifices of the *chagigah*' . . . R. Nachmanid, 'The herd for the celebration of the *chagigah*, the flock for the Passover, the oxen for the *chagigah*.' . . . They ate, and drank, and rejoiced, and were bound to bring their sacrifice of *chagigah* on the fifteenth day [Nisan 15]."

The daily *chagigah* for the seven days of the Feast of Unleavened Bread were known as Passover offerings long before gospel times. John's words conform to the common expression of the times. See my commentary on John's Gospel, vol. 2.

kk In 19:1, John uses the word *mastigóō* [Zodhiates, s. v. 3146], to whip or scourge, for this first flogging, described by the Latin word *fustigatio*. This was a less severe beating meted out for relatively light offences. Pilate had Jesus given the *fustigatio* in an effort to appease the Jews and release Jesus. John and Luke (Luke uses *paideúō*, to instruct by chastisement [Zodhiates, s. v. 3811]) to tell us about the *fustigatio*. The second flogging, the *verberatio*, took place between John 19:16a–16b. The *verberatio* was used as capital punishment for people sentenced to death by flogging, or as preparation for crucifixion. Matthew and Mark tell us about the *verberatio* flogging, both using the word *phragellóō* [Zodhiates, s. v. 5417], to scourge with a whip. Jesus was two times scourged with the whip, first receiving the *fustigatio*, then after Pilate condemned him to crucifixion he received the *verberatio*.

ll At 19:31, the word "particular" translates the definite article before "Sabbath." The Jews identified Sabbaths occurring during a feast as a "high day." There was no scriptural reason for doing this. John uses the terminology in use by the Jews at the time of the crucifixion.

mm At 19:39, "seventy-five pounds" is in the Greek text "one hundred *litras.*" The *lítra* was a Roman measurement of weight equal to about twelve ounces [Zodhiates, s. v. 3046], thus, 100 *litras* X 12 ounces = 1200 ounces / 16 ounces = 75 pounds. Naturally Nicodemus did not carry this burden himself, but his household servants (or his pupils/disciples?) helped him.

nn In 19:40, "linen cloths" is *othónion* [Zodhiates, s. v. 3608], strips of linen cloth. Jesus was wrapped in strips of linen cloth "as is customary among the Jews, to prepare for burial."

oo In 20:7, "sweat cloth," is a *soudárium* [Zodhiates, s. v. 4676], similar in size to a napkin or handkerchief, used for wiping perspiration, often worn around the neck in life, and used to cover the face in death. See Luke 19:20; John 11:44; Acts 19:12.

pp In 20:19, the Greek text is "the first of the Sabbaths," not the "first of the week" as in other translations. It was "evening the same day," i.e., the same day as the resurrection, being close to or just after sunset. By "the first of the Sabbaths," John means one of two things, possibly both. John may be counting the first of the seven Sabbaths from Unleavened Bread to Pentecost, Leviticus 23:15–16. The sheaf of the firstfruits was waved that very day Jesus resurrected. John may also mean sunset had occurred (the evening before Mary and others came to the empty tomb) and the day had become day 1, the first day of the week. These two views are not mutually exclusive. I chose to give the text as it exists, not an interpretation. In either view, the day was Day 1, the modern Sunday, the first day of the week after the Sabbath day that ended the previous week.

qq At 21:25, the "Amen" in the Textus Receptus after the end of the sentence was added to later manuscripts through liturgical use, and from there into the Textus Receptus. If the word was part of the autograph there is no sensible reason it would have been deleted in earlier manuscripts.

Acts Translation Notes

a1 At Acts 1:1, it is possible "Theophilus" a compound word formed from *theós*, God, and *phílos*, loving, is not a proper name but literally means "lover of God." The sentence would then read, "The first discourse indeed I produced concerning all things, O lover of God," as addressed to believers in general. So also at Luke 1:3.

a2 At 1:6, the word "then" translates the two conjunctions, *mén oún*, literally "indeed therefore," which are translated "so when" or "when" by other versions. Zodhiates, s. v. 3303, suggests "then."

a3 At 2:4, I have translated *glóssa* [Zodhiates, s. v. 1100] as "language," and so also at every occurrence of *glóssa* in the Book of Acts. The word literally means "tongue" as an organ of the body. Because speech is formed by the tongue, the word was also used as a metaphor for a spoken language. In Acts *glóssa* means the metaphorical use. In Acts 2 the context indicates known languages and dialects, 2:6–11.

b At 2:38 I have translated *metanoéō* [Zodhiates, s. v. 3340] as "convert," versus "repent" in other versions. Peter is calling for repentance to a purpose: to believe and be saved, Acts 2:21, 40, cf. 2:38, "for the forgiveness of your sins." So also at 3:19.

c1 At 9:5, there are two translation issues to be discussed. The first is the change from the traditional "Who are you, Lord?" to the more accurate, "Who are you, Sir?" If Saul knew it was YHWH or Jesus, he would not have asked. The Greek word used, *kúrios* [Zodhiates, s. v. 2962] may mean master, sir, lord, depending on context. Saul probably knew deity was speaking to him, but did not believe he was persecuting YHWH, and he did not believe in Jesus as Messiah, Savior, or deity, so not understanding who was speaking, he said *kúrios*, which I have translated as "Sir" to indicate his confusion.

The second translation issue is the best manuscripts end with "Jesus, whom you are persecuting." The following is sometimes attached to the end of 9:5 or the beginning of 9:6 [Metzger, *Textual*, 317–318]. "Hard it is for you to kick against the goads." He, both trembling and astonished, said, "Lord, what do you want me to do?" The fact the sentences appear in different locations in different manuscripts is itself suspicious. The fact that the sentence parallels 26:14–15 decides the issue. A scribe assimilated the 26:14–15 passage to 9:5 or 9:6, and other scribes repeated the error. The sentence came into the Textus Receptus through the Latin Vulgate used by Erasmus.

c2 At 10:25, I have translated *proskunéō* [Zodhiates, s. v. 4352] as "publicly showing him respect. The word *proskunéō* may mean to prostrate oneself, to publicly show respect, or to worship. The issue is difficult to decide. Peter's response, "I myself am also a man" will support both the worship point of view and the great respect point of view. My decision was Cornelius fell down in front of Peter, either on his knees or prostrated, to publicly show Peter great respect. I made that decision because Cornelius was a God-fearer, a worshiper of YHWH, having received some instruction in the Mosaic Law and traditions of Judaism, and would not knowingly would worship a human being. Notice Cornelius did not *proskunéō* toward the "holy messenger," who was delivering a word from God. There was nothing about Peter to suggest he was a manifestation of deity requiring worship. When Peter said he was also a man, he meant a man like you, Cornelius, not requiring such a show of respect.

d At 12:15, the end of the sentence reads, in the word order of the Greek text, "the *ággelos* it is of him." As I have done elsewhere throughout the New Testament, I have translated *ággelos* as "messenger."

e1 At 13:43, the word I have translated "gentile converts" is *prosélutos* [Zodhiates, s. v. 4339], a convert from paganism to Judaism. Other versions transliterate *prosélutos* as proselytes.

e2 In Acts 15:16–17, Jacob is quoting Amos 9:11–12, which ends with the words "doing these things." The words in 15:18, "known from eternity," are Jacob's comment on the prophecy. The addition to 15:18 in the KJV-NKJV, "known unto God are all his works from the beginning of the world" are by later scribes attempting to explain what they thought an incomplete sentence. [See Metzger, *Textual*, 379.]

f Acts 15:34 is not in the translation because it is almost certainly a scribal addition to explain 15:40. The sentence reads, "But it seemed good to Silas to remain there."

g 24:6b–8a is not in the translation because assumed to be a textual variant. The passage is found only in the Western family of manuscripts, and from there into the Textus Receptus [Metzger, *Textual*, 434]. Of the modern versions only the HCSB includes it, but in brackets. The passage makes sense with or without the part in brackets. The passage is, "6b and according to our Law wished to judge. 7 But Lysias the commander coming up with great violence took him away out of our hands, 8a commanding his accusers to come to you."

What seems likely is some scribe thought some background information was needed for the reader. However, one doubts Tertullus would have accused a soldier under Felix of interfering with a lawful assembly. Bringing it up was a distraction from the focus of their case against Paul. Tertullus would have assumed the Roman commander had written a letter to Felix presenting the event differently than what is in 24:6b–8a. Considering all these things, I chose not to include the passage in the translation.

h At 28:16, certain words are not in the translation because assumed to be a textual variant. The words appear late in the Western family of manuscripts, and from there into Byzantine texts and the Textus Receptus [Metzger, *Textual*, 443]. The words are "the centurion delivered the prisoners to the captain of the guard; but."

i Acts 28:29, is not in the translation because assumed to be a textual variant. The sentence appears only in certain manuscripts of the Western family, and from there into the Byzantine texts [Metzger, *Textual*, 444]. The lack of clear textual support indicates it is probably a scribal addition to make a transition from 28:28 to 28:30. The sentence is, "And when he had said these words, the Jews left, and had much reasoning among themselves."

Romans Translation Notes

a1 At 1:4, where I have translated "*his* spirit," others translate "Spirit," indicating the Holy Spirit. The definite article ("the") is not present in the text, and I have followed the general rule that when the writers meant the Holy Spirit they put a definite article before "spirit," or preceded "spirit" with "holy" (which is not the case in Romans 1:4). Certainly that was Paul's standard practice. Additionally, in 1:3, 4 Paul gives notice of Jesus Christ's human nature and his deity nature: the Son of God born of the offspring of David. This is the same kind of statement Peter makes, 1 Peter 3:18, "having indeed been put to death in flesh, but having been made alive in spirit." Jesus Christ participated in his own resurrection, John 10:17; Romans 1:4, with the Father, Romans 6:4, and the Holy Spirit, Romans 8:11.

a2 In 1:29, the Textus Receptus inserts "fornication" (*porneía*, Zodhiates, s. v. 4202) before "malevolence" (*ponēría*, Zodhiates, s. v. 4189), following those manuscripts where *porneía* appears. Textual evidence does not support the addition.

b In 2:16, some manuscripts have "Jesus Christ" and others have "Christ Jesus." The reading "Christ Jesus" is the older reading [Metzger, *Textual*, 448].

c In 2:17, the Textus Receptus reads *íde* (lo, behold), whereas the older Alexandrian and Western texts read *ei dé*, (but if). The diphthong *ei* and the character *i* are pronounced the same, giving rise to *íde* in later texts.

d In 3:22, the Textus Receptus combines two diverse readings in different texts to give "unto all and upon all." The reading "toward all" is sufficiently clear.

e In 3:28, there is textual evidence the sentence begins with "therefore" and there is textual evidence the sentence begins with "for." The interpretive difference is "therefore" makes 3:28 a conclusion of 3:27, and "for" makes 3:28 a reason for 3:27. The word "for" seems more reasonable to the argument.

f In 4:1 the Greek text is (word order), "What then shall we say to have found Abraham the father of us according to flesh?" Put into an English syntax, "What then shall we say Abraham our father according to flesh to have found?" Within the context, Abraham is the physical father of the Hebrew ethnicity, all Hebrews being descended from Abraham through Isaac. The ASV and NKJV so arrange the text that the thing Abraham found was according to flesh. The NIV deletes the word "flesh," as does the NLT.

g In 4:19, most versions translate the perfect passive participle of *nekróō* [Zodhiates, s. v. 3499] as "already dead" (NKJV, HCSB), or "as good as dead" (ESV, NIV). Zodhiates says the word in the perfect passive participle can mean "impotent" (referencing this verse and Hebrews 11:12) and given the context I agreed. The word translated "already" in some texts seems a scribal addition to emphasize Abraham's faith was not weak.

h In 5:2, the manuscript evidence for the words, "by the faith" after "access" is balanced for and against their presence in the autograph [Metzger, *Textual*, 452]. The sense of the passage is not changed by the presence or absence of the words. Because Paul has already stated in 5:1 the believer's faith in Jesus Christ, the words seemed redundant to me. "By faith," 5:1, "we have peace," 5:1, and "have access into this grace in which we stand," 5:2.

i In 6:11, at the end of the verse, the Textus Receptus adds the words "our Lord." There is no valid reason for the words to have been omitted in other manuscript families if they were in the autograph. Their addition fits into later liturgical practices. For those reasons I have not included the words in the translation.

j In 7:18, some manuscripts and most translations add explanatory words after "not." The sentence is understandable as I have translated the text. Compare the ASV, "but to do that which is good (is) not."

k In 8:1, after "Christ Jesus," later manuscripts add, "whose manner of life is not according to flesh" and other manuscripts add to that, "but according to spirit." The shorter text, as I have given it in the translation, is supported by the earlier texts [Metzger, *Textual*, 456] without the two additions. For those reasons I have not included the words in the translation. In my opinion, the additions are scribal attempts to define what it means to be in Christ Jesus or not in Christ Jesus.

l1 At 9:12, the translation, "The older will serve the younger," is an interpretation of the Greek text, "the greater will serve the lesser." All versions make this interpretation.

l2 At 9:28, the translation turns on two words, "For the word he *synteleō* and *syntémnō* the Lord will do on the earth." The word *synteleō* [Zodhiates, s. v. 4931] means to finish entirely, so may also be translated accomplish or perform. The word *syntémnō* [Zodhiates, s. v. 4932] means cut short, make concise, but may also be translated to determine, to decree. In this verse Paul is drawing from the LXX, combining parts of Isaiah 10:23; 28:22.

> Isaiah 10:23 (LXX), He will finish the work, and cut it short in righteousness: because the Lord will make a short work in all the world.
>
> Isaiah 28:22 (LXX), Therefore do not ye rejoice, neither let your bands be made strong; for I have heard of works finished and cut short by the Lord of hosts, which he will execute upon all the earth.

Other versions either reproduce the LXX or paraphrase the LXX. However, Paul seldom directly quotes the LXX, but usually only applies it to his argument. Zodhiates suggests "performs" and "decrees" are valid translations in Romans 8:28. Therefore I have translated Romans 9:28 in a way that seems sensible to the context and argument. Romans 9:28, "For the word he performs and decrees the Lord will do on the earth."

m In 10:9, after "confess" some manuscripts add the phrase, "the word."

Because Paul has twice used the phrase, "the word," in the sentence, the addition seems a scribal clarification, and therefore I have not included the phrase in the translation.

n At 11:6, I have not included what others think to be the ending sentence because assumed to be a textual variant. The sentence exists in several variations in some manuscripts. As Metzger says [*Textual*, 464], if the sentence was in the autograph, there seems to be no reason it should have been deleted from the majority. The sentence reads, "But if out of works, no more is it grace. For otherwise the work is no more work." The sentence is a scribal addition that restates what Paul has previously stated.

o In 11:21, after "neither you," some texts add *mḗ pṓs*, "not at all," giving the reading, "not at all neither you." The words "not at all" seem redundant, but the expression *mḗ pṓs* is "a typically Pauline expression" [Metzger, *Textual*, 465]. I decided to retain "not at all," but in brackets.

p In 14:6 I have not included what others think to be the ending sentence because assumed to be a textual variant. The Textus Receptus and later manuscripts [Metzger, *Textual*, 468] add the sentence, "And the one not keeping the day, to the Lord does not keep." This is a typical, but unnecessary, scribal addition to balance the statement in imitation of the next part of the sentence.

q In 14:10, the best manuscripts and early church fathers (Marcion, Polycarp, Tertullian, and Origen) give the reading "God" at the end of the sentence. The reading "Christ" at the ends of the sentence is in later manuscripts, probably an assimilation from 2 Corinthians 5:10.

r In 14:15, the word I have rendered "ruin" is *apóllumi* [Zodhiates. s. v. 622]. This word means to destroy, to cause to perish. Yet, in both secular and biblical literature, it never means annihilation, but ruin or loss. The most commonly used sense is "ruin," e.g., Matthew 9:17. Various lexicons (Moulton, *Vocabulary*; Kittle, *TDNT*; Silva, *NIDNTTE*) give secular examples: the loss of money, the loss of clothing, the loss of life, loss of two pigs, to kill in battle, to suffer loss of money, to trifle away one's life.

The word *apóllumi* derives from *ólethros* [Zodhiates, s. v. 3639], ruin, destruction. The prefix *apó* intensifies the meaning. This word, *apóllumi* is seldom used with the saved person. When it is, as it is here, we must ask what is it that is ruined? Not salvation, but some other spiritual loss. Although almost all other translations use "destroy," I choose "ruin" to express the spiritual damage done to faith and fellowship in the sinning believer. Certainly 14:23 is applicable here, "now all that is not of faith is sin."

s In 14:21, the Textus Receptus adds "or is led into sin or is made weak." The clause has various forms in various manuscripts [Metzger, *Textual*, 468–469], suggesting it was added as an explanation, or perhaps as an expansion of 1 Corinthians 8:11–13.

Romans Translation Notes

t At 16:24, Metzger says the earliest and best witnesses omit 16:24. I chose to retain the verse.

u 16:27 has many different endings in diverse manuscripts. I chose to omit "of the ages" after "glory to the ages."

First Corinthians Translation Notes

a In 2:1, the ancient manuscripts are divided between "testimony" and "mystery" [Metzger, *Textual*, 480]. Of the sixteen versions I consulted, only two (NLT, BBE) preferred "mystery."

b In 2:7, "God's hidden wisdom" is my translation of the literal text, "of God wisdom in a *mustérion*." The word *mustérion* [Zodhiates, s. v. 3466] means hidden or secret, but is often transliterated "mystery." A *mustérion* is something God has not yet revealed, which cannot be discovered by searching the Scriptures, but when mentioned in the New Testament is now being revealed.

c In 2:13, The majority of Greek manuscripts texts have "spirit." When the Holy Spirit is in view Paul prefaces the word "spirit" with the definite article ("the") or the word "holy." (Unless, as at 2:10, the second use of "spirit," the context explicitly requires otherwise.) Only the Textus Receptus has "holy" before the word "spirit" in 2:13. Other translations insert a definite article into the text before "spirit." But in 2:13 the human spirit is in view. The point of 2:13 is the spiritual man is taught internally, in his spirit, versus being taught externally by man's words. Taught in spirit requires the spiritual perception given by the Holy Spirit to the saved, regenerated human nature; thus the difference between a natural person (see note "d") and a spiritual person.

d In 2:14, all the translations read "the natural man." However, the Greek text does not have the definite article, so an indefinite article is more appropriate, "a natural man." Paul is not speaking of any particular unsaved person, but is speaking of the unsaved as a group lacking spiritual perception, because none in that group are regenerated and none in that group are taught by the Holy Spirit, 2:13. The best translation is "a natural person," incorporating all the members of the group.

e In 3:2, I have "food for chewing," the translation of *brōma* [Zodhiates, s. v. 1033] whereas other translations have "solid food." This word *brōma* means meat and vegetables, food that must be chewed, as opposed to milk, which is drunk.

f In 3:5, the Textus Receptus has "who" versus "what" in both instances. As Metzger [*Textual*, 483] states, "since the answer [to Paul's questions] is 'nothing' the question can scarcely have been 'who?'"

g1 In 4:1 the word I have translated "previously hidden things" is again *mustérion*, see note b. The apostles were revealing things previously hidden in the counsels of God, but were now to be revealed to the New Testament church.

g2 At 4:5, the word is not *mustérion* but is *kruptós* [Zodhiates, s. v. 2927], "hidden, concealed, secret." The "*kruptós* of darkness" are not the *mustérion* of God but things men hide in their hearts.

g3 In 4:10, the Greek text has no verbs, which must be supplied by the reader or translator.

h In 6:9, the word translated "nor effeminate with other males" is *malakós* [Zodhiates, s. v. 3120], literally "soft," figuratively "effeminate," indicating a sexually penetrated male. In Roman culture it was expected men of higher social status would sexually penetrate men and boys of lower social status, whether born free, freedmen (a freed slave), or slave. The word was sometimes used of males who were prostitutes for other males. See Translation Notes Resources for commentaries on 1 Corinthians.

i At 6:18, the words, "committing unlawful sexual intercourse," translate *porneúō* [Zodhiates, s. v. 4203], to commit fornication.

j At 6:20, I have not included the words in the Textus Receptus that follow after "in your body." Those Textus Receptus words are "and in your spirit which are God's." The words are missing from the earliest and best manuscripts, and from church fathers such as Irenaeus. Tertullian, Origen, and Cyprian [Metzger, *Textual*, 488]. The words are unnecessary to Paul's argument, which concerns the body, not the soul.

k1 At 7:6, the word I have translated "counsel" is *suggnómē* [Zodhiates, s. v. 4774], "to think alike, agree with," translated "concession, permission, leave" in other versions. The point of Paul's argument is 7:1–2, and his remark at 7:7 relates to marriage. Paul is saying, "being unmarried is better considering the times, but I am not commanding any one to be single. I am giving you wise counsel on marriage to fit the times."

k2 At 7:12, Paul is not saying his words are not inspired counsel from God, but that he is giving instructions on marriage to fit the circumstances of the New Testament church, where in a marriage two unbelievers might become one believer and one unbeliever, a circumstance Jesus did not address. Should the believer leave the unbeliever, so he or she might not be unequally yoked? In the gentile world that would be an acceptable outcome. But not in Christianity.

Notice Paul repeats in 7:10 Jesus' instructions concerning divorce. Nothing Paul says in 7:11–16 contradicts what Jesus' said about marriage and divorce. The party who had unwillingly suffered the violence of divorce, was always free to remarry; hence in Israel the certificate of divorce Moses required to prove a woman was not married, thus free to remarry. Read Jesus at Mark 10:11–12.

Paul by the inspiration of the Holy Spirit applies what Jesus said, giving us new revelation, one of the duties of an apostle.

l In 7:23, the phrase "do not let" translates the Greek word *mḗ* [Zodhiates, s. v. 3361]. The Greek language had two words for the negative. One was *ou* [Zodhiates, s. v. 3756], which is the absolute negative: never, not possible. This one, *mḗ* is the conditional or subjective negative: it may not happen; may it not happen. Though both words are usually translated "no" or "not," I wanted to communicate the subjective possibility that exists in *mḗ*. Because the verb, "become" is in the imperative mood, I have translated, "do not let [*mḗ*] yourselves."

m At 7:25, the words "virgin women of marriageable age," translate *tón parthénos*, literally, "the virgins" (*parthénos* is plural). Paul's readers would have understood *parthénos* [Zodhiates, s. v. 3933] as a female who is unmarried but of marriageable age. What, culturally, constituted a marriageable age for women? In Paul's Jewish culture, a female could be betrothed one day after her twelfth birthday, but not married until after the onset of puberty (menstruation). Gentiles had similar customs. The translation reflects the historical-cultural setting.

n At 7:29, I have translated *sustéllō* [Zodhiates, s. v. 4958], "full of distress," as suggested by Zodhiates. The word *sustéllō* means "to repress, withdraw oneself, contract, shrink, to wrap up." Metaphorically *sustéllō* means "distressed, anxious." The word in this text is a verb in the passive voice, meaning the action of *sustéllō* has come upon them. Most translate *sustéllō* as "the time is short," which is an eschatological interpretation. The passage is speaking of "the necessity at hand," 7:26, not some yet-future necessity.

o At 7:31 Paul describes the world as *schḗma* [Zodhiates, s. v. 4976], which I have translated "external form." Kittel [7:954] says the Greeks used this word to mean "the outward form or structure perceptible to the senses," and he defines the word in this verse as "distinctive manifestation (or form)" [7:956]. Other translations give "fashion; present form; current form." The physical world is not currently perishing, only what human beings have made of this world is currently perishing.

p In 7:37, other translations make the verse about the woman. But the text is "*heautoú parthénos.*" The word *heautoú* [Zodhiates, s. v. 1438] is a reflexive pronoun meaning "himself, herself, itself." In note "m" I discussed *parthénos*, which normally means "a female who is unmarried but of marriageable age." But here the context is whether or not to marry, so *parthénos* has the sense of "unmarried." The subject of 7:37 is the male; every other pronoun in the verse is the male gender. Therefore the proper translation is "himself unmarried." Let us remember that in these ancient cultures, the male decided to marry, the female was given in marriage.

q In 9:4 the unfamiliar translation, "is it possible we have no," in this verse and in 9:5, is the result of the double negative, *mḗ ouk*, used in a question. The word *mḗ* [Zodhiates, s. v. 3361], is the subjective conditional negative: something may or may not exist. The word *ouk* [Zodhiates, s. v. 3756] is the objective absolute negative: something definitely does not exist.

r In 9:6, as in 9:4, 5, there is an interplay between the objective negative *ouk* and the subjective negative *mḗ:* "have no [*ouk*] authority to work or not [*mḗ*]?"

s1 For the ending of 10:28 the Textus Receptus repeats 10:26. The absence of the repetition in the majority of older manuscripts argues the repetition was not in the autograph [Metzger, *Textual*, 495].

s2 I have placed the first sentence of 11:1 at the end of chapter 10, where it rationally belongs. Chapters and verses are not inspired. The current chapter-verse divisions were created by the French printer known as Robert Estienne, aka Robert Stephanus, 1503–1559, for the Geneva Bible, and subsequently used in later Bible translations up to the present day.

t At 11:6, the choices for *aischrós* [Zodhiates. s. v. 150] are "indecent, indecorous, dishonorable." I chose "indecent" because Paul seems to be referring to one of three different cultural customs, perhaps all three. One, the custom of prostitutes to cut their hair short so as to be readily identified by potential customers. Or two, short hair on a woman was considered humiliating. Or three, in some cults (despised by even pagans) women wore their hair short. See Translation Notes Resources for commentaries on 1

Corinthians.

u At 11:24, the Textus Receptus begins the sentence, "This is my body," with "take, eat." These words are not in most manuscripts [Metzger, *Textual*, 496], and were added to conform to Matthew 26:26.

v I have placed the first sentence of 14:1 at the end of chapter 13, where it rationally belongs. Chapters and verses are not inspired. The current chapter-verse divisions were created by the French printer known as Robert Estienne, aka Robert Stephanus, 1503–1559, for the Geneva Bible, and subsequently used in later Bible translations up to the present day.

w In 14:2, I have given the in-context sense of *akoúō* [Zodhiates, s. v. 191], "to hear," as "understands." The sense of the passage is that the language being spoken, although a known language in the world, is not a language known by those hearing, so they lack understanding of what is being said.

x In 14:2, the word "hidden" translates *mustérion* [Zodhiates, s. v. 3466], hidden, secret, not fully made known. The word *mustérion* is usually used in Scripture to indicate "something which man is capable of knowing, but only when it has been revealed to him by God, and not through any searching of his own" [Trench, *Commentary*, 55]. In this passage Paul uses *mustérion* in a less technical sense as something hidden because not being communicated in a language those hearing understand.

y At 15:5, most versions have "appeared" where I have "was seen." The verb in question, *horáō* [Zodhiates, s. v. 3708] "to see" is in the aorist tense, indicative mood, passive voice. In the passive voice the subject receives the action of the verb. Christ did not "appear," which would be the active voice, he "was seen," the passive voice. So also at 15:6, 7. The issue here is not doctrine but grammar: Christ was seen because he chose to appear.

z At 15:9, where others translate "called" I have translated "named.' The word is *kaléō* [Zodhiates, s. v. 2564], "called, named." This word is used in three main senses. One, to call someone to come; two, to appoint to a position; three, to give a name. Paul cannot be saying he is not fit to be appointed (called) to the office of apostle, because obviously Jesus thought otherwise, and to say he was not fit to be an apostle would contradict the choice Jesus made. Paul says because he was such an ardent persecutor of the church he is not fit to be named among the apostles.

aa At 16:2, the words "you may be successful" translate *euodóō* [Zodhiates. s. v. 2137]. Literally this word means "good journey," or "prosperous." The meaning in context is not "yield or profit from gainful activities," which the English "prosper" implies. The meaning is success in gathering the gift, "gathering all that he can . . . The idea of success is linked with the result of gathering or saving" [Kittel, *Dictionary*, 5:113–114]. The instruction is not "give as you have financially benefitted" but "be successful in gathering all you can for the gift." Each is to set something aside, week by week, accumulating it as he may be successful in saving it.

Second Corinthians Translation Notes

a At 1:3 and following verses, the word I have translated "encourage" is *paráklēsis* [Zodhiates, s. v. 3874], an exhortation, admonition, or encouragement. Other versions translate "comfort." I chose to translate the word in a positive, active sense: encourage, encouragement, encouraged, encouraging.

b At 1:13, the word I have translated "aware" is *anaginōskō* [Zodhiates, s. v. 314], to perceive accurately, to recognize. Other versions translate "acknowledge" or "understand."

c At 1:17 the word "shallow-minded" is *elaphría* [Zodhiates. s. v. 1644], literally lightness with regard to weight, metaphorically shallow-minded, inconstant. The word is only used here. Every version struggles with this word: lightly (NKJV), lightness (KJV, NIV), fickleness (ASV) vacillating (ESV), irresponsible (HCSB), carelessly (NLT). I chose to use the word's meaning.

d At 1:22 the word translated "guarantor" is *arrabōn* [Zodhiates, s. v. 728]. The meaning of *arrabōn* is "earnest money, a pledge, something which stands for part of the price and paid beforehand to confirm the transaction." We must be careful here, as we are speaking of God the Holy Spirit. He is a person, not a thing, and therefore is neither "earnest money, pledge, or part of the price." Other versions make the Holy Spirit to be the *arrabōn*. Just as the sealing is not the Sprit himself, but the work of the Spirit, even so the *arrabōn* is not the Spirit himself, but the work of the Spirit.

If the Holy Spirit is a guarantee (NKJV, ESV), down payment (HCSB), earnest (KJV, YLT, ASV), deposit (NIV), or first installment (NLT) then we have not only made him a thing but divided him into parts distributed to each believer, so each can receive their personal deposit or down payment guaranteeing their inheritance. God the Holy Spirit is not divided among believers but always present in whole in every believer.

The *arrabōn* is not a pledge, because a pledge is returned when the full payment is made. The *arrabōn* is not a deposit, because a deposit can be returned if the transaction is cancelled. The *arrabōn* is not a down payment, because a first down payment implies additional payments until the sum of the payments equals the whole amount.

The Spirit himself is none of these, he is the guarantor of the whole that has been given each believer as his or her inheritance in Christ. The Holy Spirit is himself the guarantor that we will receive the full inheritance. Sealing by the Holy Spirit is the assurance that salvation is eternal, and therefore the inheritance is reserved in heaven for each believer.

e At 2:9 the word "character" is *dokimḗ* [Zodhiates, s. v. 1392], proof of genuineness, trustworthiness. The verb, "I might know," is in the aorist subjunctive so the meaning is "prove yourselves true," or "prove yourselves genuine."

f At 2:11, the word I have translated "ways" is *nóēma* [Zodhiates, s. v. 3540]. The basic meaning of this word is "to perceive, to observe." Depending on context it might be translated thought, concept, device, contrivance, understanding. Other translations have "devices" (KJV, NKJV, YLT, ASV), "designs" (ESV), "intentions" (HCSB), "schemes" (NIV, NLT).

g At 2:15; 4:3, the word I have translated "not saved," is *apóllumi* [Zodhiates, s. v. 622]. At Matthew 15:24 the word means unsaved. In 2:15; 4:3 Paul is making a contrast to "saved" so "not saved" seemed the better translation.

Others translate this word "perishing." Literally this word means to destroy, but it is never used in the sense of annihilation in either biblical or secular Greek. The most commonly used sense is "ruin," e.g., Matthew 9:17. Various lexicons (Moulton, *Vocabulary*; Kittle, *TDNT*; Silva, *NIDNTTE*) give secular examples: the loss of money, the loss of clothing, the loss of life, loss of two pigs, to kill in battle, to suffer loss of money, to trifle away one's life.

h At 2:17, the phrase "professing ... for personal gain" translates *kapeleúō* [Zodhiates, s. v. 2585], to treat as if for personal profit. The KJV and ASV translated "corrupting." The NKJV, ESV, NIV use peddling, peddlers, peddle. The NLT says "hucksters." In modern times these persons are the ones selling the Prosperity Gospel.

i At 3:6 is one of those places where the definite article is not used with "spirit" but most translations add a definite article and capitalize "spirit" to interpret the passage as the Holy Spirit. But Paul, following his usual style, means the human spirit, not the Holy Spirit. The contrast is the letter of the New covenant does not give life, but the spirit of the New covenant gives life. The spirit of the New covenant is spiritual and eternal life in Christ. Then in 3:7–9

Paul explains this spirit of life comes out of the ministry of the Holy Spirit.

j At 3:17, there is no verb in the Greek text in the second sentence. Other translations insert two verbs in the second sentence.

k At 4:4, the word I have translated "clearly appear" is *apaúgasma* [Zodhiates, s. v. 826], to shine. Other versions translate "shine" or "shine forth," or "seeing the light" (ESV), "see the light."

l At 5:1, the word I have translated "perpetual" is *aiōnios* [Zodhiates, s. v. 166], eternal, endless, perpetual. This word is translated "eternal" by others. The meaning of *aiōnios* depends on context. Of God *aiōnios* means without beginning or ending. When speaking of the eternal life of the saved *aiōnios* means both quality of life and duration of life, and therefore is more properly that endless life God gives the believer which regenerates his or her human nature in this mortal life and transforms his or her human nature to be sinless in the endless life to come. In 2 Corinthians 4:18 the context is spiritual realities, which are endless. In 2 Corinthians 5:1, the context is the mortal body versus the immortal body. The resurrected body is incorruptible, therefore immortal (deathless), and the appropriate translation at 2 Corinthians 5:1 is "endless" or "perpetual." In Scripture, something is perpetual until the conditions affecting that "something" change. Because the resurrected body will be incorruptible, the condition never changes, therefore the "house not made with hands" is perpetually deathless, which is to say the life of the resurrected body is endless.

m At 5:19, where most versions translate the preposition *én* as "in," I have translated "by" [Wallace, *Greek Grammar*, 372]. The reason is doctrinal. God was not in the Christ, God the Son is the Christ. The "messiah" or "christ" is an office of the incarnate God the Son, Psalm 2:2, 7. Therefore the instrumental means whereby God effected the reconciliation was the Christ, the God-man, propitiating God for human sin.

n At 5:20, the word I have translated "exhorting" is *parakaléō* [Zodhiates, s. v. 3870], which others translate "beseech, pleading, appeal, appealing." The word means "to aid, comfort, encourage." Various translations throughout the New Testament are "comfort, exhort, desire, call for, beseech." At 5:20, the subject is salvation. God does not beseech or plead, he commands all to believe and be saved. "Exhorting" is the appropriate translation.

o At 5:21, every version enlarges on the text of this verse in translation to effectively communicate the meaning. The Greek text is "the not having known sin for us made sin so that we might become righteousness of God in him."

p At 6:13, I have translated the word *antimisthía* [Zodhiates, s. v. 489], to recompense, as "in return." The word is formed from *anti* [Zodhiates, s. v. 473], used here in the metaphorical sense of an equivalent exchange, and *misthós* [Zodhiates, s. v. 3408], a reward. The translation turns on the meaning of 6:11–12. Paul says, 6:11, our heart is enlarged, meaning we (Paul and his companions in ministry) have great affection for you Corinthians. But 6:12, you Corinthians seem restrained in your affections toward us. The word *antimisthía* is being used as an idiom to say the Corinthians owe Paul the same affection as he has for them.

q At 6:17, the word "gather" translates *eisdéchomai* [Zodhiates, s. v. 1523], to receive in favor or communion. The word is used only here. Paul seems to be quoting from Jeremiah 32:37–38, where the corresponding word is *qābas* [Harris, *TWOT*, s. v. 1983] gather, assemble.

r At 7:1, the translation "may we" reflects the subjunctive mood of the verb. The subjunctive is the mood of possibility or probability, which is why I translated "may we." Most versions translate the subjunctive here as "let us."

s At 8:2, the word I have translated "helpless poverty" is *ptōchós* [Zodhiates, s. v. 4432], poor and helpless. The word *pénēs* [Zodhiates, s. v. 3993] identified those poor who had daily work to supply daily needs. The word *ptōchós* identified those poor dependent on begging as the only means for survival.

t At 8:2, the word I have translated "faithful benevolence" is *haplótēs* [Zodhiates, s. v. 572], simplicity, sincerity, faithfulness, plenitude. Paul's point is not liberality or generosity, (some versions) but faithful benevolence out of proper motivation. The contrast is their affliction and poverty motivated them to be faithful in helping others.

u At 8:4, the careful student of the Word will have noticed I translated the verse much differently than some versions. That is because some versions have interpreted the verse for the reader. Contrary to the KJV/NKJV, the words "receive the gift" are not in the Greek text. Contrary to the ESV, the word "relief" is not in the text, and the ESV has translated "grace" as "favor." The HCSB and

NIV have translated "grace" as "privilege." The NLT "gift for the believers" is not in the text. Paul's focus is not the act of giving, but the motivation in giving, which was to participate in the grace and fellowship of the ministry they were doing toward fellow saints in need.

v1 At 9:5, literally, "and not as covetousness."

v2 At 9:7, a "glad giver" not a "cheerful giver." A glad giver gives without regret or unwillingness, thus it is pleasing to him to give.

v3 At 9:10, the word I have translated "rewards" is *génnēma* [Zodhiates, s. v. 1081] that which is born or produced. Strong's and other translations do not distinguish *génnēma* from *génēma*, fruit. The use of *génnēma* in 9:10 is metaphorical of the virtue of willingly blessing others through giving, thus there is a reward for the righteousness that gives bountifully.

w at 9:15, the word "ineffable" means "too great or extreme to be expressed or described in words."

x In 10:1, the word I have translated "gentle strength" is *praútēs* [Zodhiates, s. v. 4240]. This word indicates that middle ground between anger and apathy. It is that balance in one's character that does what is right, in the right measure, for the right reason. The translation "gentle strength" is meant to indicate that balance.

y At 10:1, the word I have translated "virtue" is *epieíkeia* [Zodhiates, s. v. 1932], the virtue that sets things right.

z At 11:2, the word I have translated "marry" is *harmózō* [Zodhiates, s. v. 718], occurring only here in the New Testament. In secular Greek the word meant to adjust, to fitly join. In 11:2 the words "husband" and "virgin" indicate the joining in view is marriage.

Most translations use some variation of betrothed, conforming to the theory put forward by Reformed theology that the New Testament church is the bride of Christ.

The New Testament writers never name the New Testament church as Christ's bride. Expositors making the New Testament church Christ's bride make an unjustified inference from the Bible's figurative use of marriage to indicate the spiritual fidelity required between the believer and Christ. I invite the reader to do what I have done, examine every use of the word "bride" in the New

Testament. In no use is the New Testament church associated with the word "bride," unless the expositor inserts the New Testament church into the passage.

Because this issue is so controversial, an extended comment is warranted. Let's examine the concepts and then the context of 2 Corinthians 11:2. First, "virgin" is being used in a spiritual sense. No sinner is a virgin in a spiritual sense, having "fornicated" with the world. Salvation and regeneration cleanse the sinner from the defilement of sin, making that sinner a spiritual virgin.

In context, Paul is speaking of the kind of life the spiritual virgin, the believer, is to live in Christ: not succumbing to temptation, or false doctrine, or a false gospel. In preaching the gospel by which Christ saved these people, Paul gave them the promise of a pure relationship with Christ which they were to maintain—not maintain their salvation, but by their behavior maintain that spiritual purity they received when saved. See how he contrasts virgin with vv. 3, 4, Satan's deceptions, corruption, a false gospel, false teachers.

So Paul's point is not betrothal or marriage, but spiritual fidelity toward Christ, using *harmózō* as a figure of speech, to adjust one's behavior so as to fitly join Christ.

This passage fits into the main theme of the letter. Paul, not others, is the one who brought the good news to the Corinthians. Their salvation was proof of that ministry. So why are they paying attention to others contrary to that good news? They are to maintain their spiritual purity.

aa At 11:4, the exclamation "—you have endured it very well!" The Greek manuscripts do not have punctuation (exception: the interrogative is indicated by the grammar), so punctuation is part of translation. Other translations also treat this phrase as sarcastic or ironic.

bb At 11:5, the word I have translated "messengers" is *apóstolos* [Zodhiates, s. v. 652], "one sent, ambassador, messenger." This word is usually transliterated "apostle." I have done the same at 11:13, "false messengers." The reason is Paul was the only apostle to have come to Corinth. (In 11:14 the word messenger is *ággelos* usually transliterated "angel.")

cc At 11:13, the word I have translated "changing their outward form" (so also vv. 14, 15) is *metaschēmatízō* [Zodhiates, s. v. 3345]. This word may be translated "transform" but the transformation is outward only, only in appearance. To effectively communicate that change in outward appearance only I translated "changing their outward form" and added "to seem."

dd In 12:11, as at 11:5, 13 (see note bb) I have translated *apóstolos* [Zodhiates, s. v. 652] as messengers, because Paul was the only apostle to have come to Corinth. He is not comparing himself to the Twelve, but to those falsely naming themselves as *apóstolos*, as messengers sent by God. The adjective "worthy" is sarcastic.

ee At 12:12 the phrase "one sent by God" is again *apóstolos* [Zodhiates, s. v. 652], translated more literally, because Paul is saying "I was sent by God [*apóstolos*] but those others you have received (11:4) were not sent by God.

ff At 13:9, the word I have translated "complete readiness" is *katártisis* [Zodhiates, s. v. 2676]. This word means "to make fully ready, put in order, the act of completing, perfecting." The text reads (word order) "We are praying the of you *katártisis*." Other versions have "be made complete (NKJV), restoration (ESV), maturity (HCSB)." I chose to translate "complete readiness" to reflect Paul's repeated warnings they should be spiritually ready for his coming.

gg At 13:14, the Textus Receptus ends with "Amen." The better attested manuscripts do not.

Galatians Translation Notes

a1 At 1:5, "truly" translates *amḗn* [Zodhiates, s. v. 281]. The Greek *amḗn* is a transliteration of the Hebrew '*āmēn*, which is transliterated into English as "amen." In both Hebrew and Greek the word means "truth" or "truly."

a2 In 1:6, 8, 9 there is an interplay of two words. The translation "good news" in 1:6 is the Greek word *euaggélion* [Zodhiates, s. v. 2098], which is the good news itself. The words "proclaim" and "proclaiming" in 1:8, 9 are *euaggelízō* [Zodhiates, s. v. "2097"], "to proclaim, to preach." What does not agree with the *euaggélion* (good news) is a false *euaggelízō* (proclamation). Other versions translate *euaggelízō* as "preach a gospel," which is an interpretation, not a translation.

b In 1:15, there is a textual variation. Some texts have, "But when it pleased *ho theós* (the God)," and other texts have "But when it pleased *ho* (the one.)" Manuscripts considered the most reliable have only the definite article *ho* in the masculine singular, thus, "the one." The translator must ask, why would *ho theós* be replaced by *ho* if *ho theós* was the original reading? Nor is it likely *theós* was accidentally deleted, considering *ho* is supported by many reliable manuscripts [Metzger, *Textual*, 521–522]. Most Bible versions have followed the reading *ho theós*, but the reading *ho* seems more likely to be the autograph.

c In 2:11, I added the words "of Syria" for clarification. There were seventeen cities named "Antioch" in the ancient world. The two mentioned in the Scripture are Antioch of Syria, e.g., Acts 11:26, and Antioch of Pisidia, Acts 13:14.

d In 3:1, it seems likely the phrase added after "crucified" in the Textus Receptus, "that you should not obey the truth" (KJV, YLT, NKJV), is imported from 5:7, "Who hindered you, not to obey the truth?" [Metzger, *Textual*, 524.]

e In 3:8, the translation issue is word order and punctuation. Most translations say it is the Scripture that foresees, on the theory Paul is figuratively personifying "scripture." The Greek text reads (the Greek texts were copied without punctuation),

> Having foreseen then the Scripture that by faith justifies the gentiles God foretold the gospel to Abraham will be blessed in you all the nations.

Although the majority opinion is the Scripture is personified, I have given what I believe is the more natural translation, indicating God foresees. "Having foreseen, then, the Scripture that justifies the gentiles by faith, God foretold the good news to Abraham: 'In you all the peoples will be blessed.'"

Also in 3:8, I have translated *éthnos* [Zodhiates, s. v. 1484] as "peoples," not "nations." The word means "a multitude, people, race, belonging and living together."

f1 At 3:24, the word translated "guardian" is *paidagōgós* [Zodhiates, s. v. 3807]. The original meaning of this word was a slave who guarded the heir when a minor from moral and physical danger. Therefore, the slave accompanied the child everywhere, including taking the child to and from school. In later Greek the destination, to the educator, became the meaning of the word. The KJV "schoolmaster," and the ASV, NKJV "tutor," were not the meaning in Paul's times. The NIV "put in charge to lead us to Christ" gives the Law an evangelistic purpose it did not have. The NLT "kept in protective custody" carries the idea of guardian too far. The Law was to be the guardian of morality for those of faith, reminding them of God's moral values, and requiring them to live out those values, a function now served by the born-again nature of the believer, and the indwelling Holy Spirit, through the law of Christ.

f2 In 4:7, the multiple variations across eight diverse manuscripts [Metzger, *Textual*, 527] indicates the simpler manuscript version, "an heir through God," is most likely the autograph.

g In 4:15, the first sentence of the Greek text reads, "Where, then, your blessedness?" Paul's question was, what has become of your blessedness (or joy, happiness) toward me? I have tried to communicate the intent of the question with a paraphrase, "What has become of your blessedness?" Other translations do much the same.

h In 5:12, the word I have translated "would separate themselves from you" is *apokóptō* [Zodhiates, s. v. "609"] in the future tense. The word *apokóptō* means "to cut off, amputate." Paul is making a macabre play on words with circumcision. The use of *apokóptō* is figurative. A spirit of malice or vengeance is not agreeable with the values of Christianity. Hence translations such as "emasculate" (ESV, NIV), or "castrated" (HCSB), or "mutilate themselves" (NLT), miss the point. I cannot think of any occasion in Acts or his other letters where Paul had desired physical harm to any person.

i In 5:23, the word I have translated "gentleness in strength" is *praútēs* [Zodhiates, s. v. 4240]. This word indicates that middle ground between anger and apathy. It is that balance in one's character that does what is right, in the right measure, for the right reason. The translation "gentleness with strength" is meant to indicate that balance.

j In 6:1, the word I have translated "detected" is *prolambánō* [Zodhiates, s. v. "4301], literally "to overtake." Some believe the word should be translated in 6:1 as "surprised in," or "surprised by." However, an act of sinning by a believer is a choice, not a surprise, even if the act is the result of a pre-salvation habit. I have translated "detected" versus "surprised" for clarity [see Lightfoot, *Galatians*, 215]. The thought is not habitual sinning (the condition of the unsaved), but occasional acts of sinning, a condition that affects all Christians.

k At 6:8, Paul writes "sowing to the *pneúma*," and "from the *pneúma*." My usual translation practice is to capitalize *pneúma* when preceded by the definite article. In this verse, I believe the first *pneúma* is in contrast to "flesh" and therefore the first *pneúma* is the human spirit, meaning sowing spiritual things out of the spiritual born-again human nature. When a saved person sows spiritual things, then he or she reaps spiritual things from the Holy Spirit.

Ephesians Translation Notes

    a In 1:4, I have translated *kósmos*, an ordered arrangement, usually translated "world," as "before the beginning of the universe," i.e., before the universe was created. The change from "world" (all other versions) to "universe" fits the modern and biblical conception of the creation as more than this physical earth. Genesis 1:1 informs us God created the heavens (note the plural) and the earth. By this phrase is intended both the material domain and spirit domain. The heavens consist of the atmospheric sky, the starry sky (outer space), and the immaterial heavens (the spirit domain) where the holy and fallen angels dwell.

    b In 1:4, the translation "without blemish," is the from Greek *ámōmos*, "spotless, without blemish" [Zodhiates, s. v. 299]. This word is usually translated "without blame" or "blameless," which is an interpretation, not a translation.

    c In 1:5, the word most versions translate adoption or adopted is *huiothesía*. This word does not appear in secular Greek and is used in the New Testament only in Paul's writings. In secular Greek, *thetós huiós*, "to place as a son," is used to identify an adopted son. Paul, in combining *thetós* and *huiós* to create the compound word *huiothesía*, undoubtedly intends to indicate the same action by God toward a believer: adoption as an adult son or daughter. I have chosen to translate the word as "sonship," because every believer is adopted by God as an adult son or daughter to become both an heir of God and God's legacy out of this present universe. "Sonship" is not a gender-specific word, but indicates the status of every believer before God.

    d In 1:9, the word I have translated "hidden *things*" is *mustérion* [Zodhiates, s. v. 3466], hidden, secret, not fully made known. The word *mustérion* is usually used in Scripture to indicate "something which man is capable of knowing, but only when it has been revealed to him by God, and not through any searching of his own" [Trench, *Commentary*, 55].

    e At 1:11, the word I have translated "made his heirs and his inheritance" is *ekleróthemen* [Zodhiates, s. v. 2820]. The word may be translated as "obtained an inheritance" (NKJV, ESV) or "made his inheritance" (ASV, HCSB). I chose to incorporate both ideas, because both are true.

    f In 1:13, The preposition *én* which other versions translate "with" should be translated "by" [Wallace, *Grammar*, 372] The seal is not the Holy Spirit himself, but sealing is a work of the Holy Spirit as God's witness that the believer is genuinely and eternally saved. The sealing by the Spirit keeps the believer secure in his or her salvation, for no one can break God's seal. The seal is impressed with God's mark—the image of Christ the Savior—indicating the believer is God's property.

g In 1:14, I have translated *arrabṓn* as "guarantor" versus the "guarantee" used by other versions. Just as sealing is a work "by" the Holy Spirit, he himself is not the guarantee but the guarantor. If the Holy Spirit is a thing, then he can be a seal and guarantor. But the Holy Spirit is a person. His works are to seal the believer and be the guarantor of the believer's inheritance. See the extended discussion at Translation Notes on 2 Corinthians, note "d" for 1:22. See also discussion in my commentary on Ephesians.

h In 2:2, the phrase, "the lower spirit world," is my translation of the Greek *aḗr* [Zodhiates, s. v. 109]. The New Testament usually identifies *aḗr* with the atmosphere, perhaps extending into the airless space immediately above the earth. In Ephesians 2:2, the "ruling ruler" (*árchōn*) is a spirit being, Satan, ruling the lower spirits, i.e., the other fallen angels. The word *aḗr* must certainly refer to a place in the spirit domain in which he exercises authority.

Satan does not live in the physical atmosphere/outer space, nor does he live in/on the physical earth. These are all material realms, and Satan is a spirit-being suited for life in the spirit domain. He is a ruler in it, because the region of his dominance is part of it.

Paul used a familiar word and concept to teach the power of Satan. The teaching method is known as "apperception," using the known to teach the unknown. See discussion in my commentary on Ephesians.

i In 2:5, 8, the phrase "by grace you are having been saved" is clumsy English but required by the grammar. The word *esté*, "you are," is in the present tense indicative mood, which in Greek speaks of contemporaneous action. The word "saved," *sōzō*, is a participle in the perfect tense, which speaks of a past completed action with continuing results in the present time. The combination of present and perfect tenses is difficult to express in English. The combination indicates the present continuing result of a past completed action. God saved the believer by his grace in the past, and by his grace God maintains the believer's salvation in the present. Therefore, "by grace you are having been saved," indicates the present continuing result of the past completed action "saved."

(A less grammatically accurate translation is "by grace you are saved." but that translation requires the reader to understand "are" as a present state of being, and the verb "saved" as indicating a past completed action with continuing present results. The debate over the eternal security of salvation shows some readers do not understand.)

j In 2:22, "in the Spirit," is God indwelling his saved people. The translation "by the Spirit" (ESV, NIV) makes the Holy Spirit the means or instrument of God's indwelling. Because the Holy Spirit is a person, not an instrument, the proper translation is "in the Spirit" whether speaking of each believer's human spirit, or of the Holy Spirit himself.

k In 4:17, where I have translated "You are no longer to conduct your manner of life" *peripatéō* [Zodhiates, s. v. 4043], the Textus Receptus reads, "no longer walk as the rest [*loipós*, Zodhiates, s. v. 3062] of the Gentiles." The majority of texts do not have *loipós* but *peripatéō*, literally to walk, as a metaphor behavior or the manner of life. Most versions translate *peripatéō* as "walk," I have given a translated that reflects the obvious figurative sense of the passage, "your manner of life."

l In 4:26, two kinds of anger are mentioned. The word "angry" translates *orgízō* [Zodhiates, s. v. 3710], anger as a state of mind. The translation "violent, seething, exasperated anger" is *parorgismós* [Zodhiates, s. v. 3950], the "irritation, exasperation, or anger to which one is provoked."

m In 5:3, "greediness" is *pleonexía* [Zodhiates, s. v. 4124], the desire to have more. The word is usually translated "covetousness."

n In 5:5, the translation "prostitute themselves sexually" is from *pórnos* [Zodhiates, s. v. 4205], to sell sex. Selling sex is not necessarily for money, but may also be for immaterial gain.

o In 5:30, the part in brackets, "out of his flesh and out of his bones." has good external evidence to be in the autograph, but there are good reasons to suspect it is a scribal edition to smoothly transition to the Genesis 2:24 quote in 5:31. As Hoehner says, it "is accepted with great hesitation." Because the text is disputed I have enclosed it in brackets. See Metzger, *Textual*, 541. Hoehner, *Ephesians*, 769ff., including footnote 3.

Philippians Translation Notes

a In 1:1, "overseers" translates *epískopos* [Zodhiates, s. v. 1985]. In Greek culture, an *epískopos* was a magistrate sent to outlying cities to organize and govern them. In the Septuagint *epískopos* described those overseeing public works (2 Chronicles 34:12, 17) or cities (Isaiah 60:17, a prefect, aka: magistrate). In the New Testament *epískopos* describes those persons designated to manage a local church body. The KJV, ASV, NKJV "bishops" is an anachronism of later ecclesiastical hierarchy. The NLT "elders" is a different Greek word not in the text.

b In 1:19, Paul is speaking to saved persons about himself, a saved person. Therefore, contrary to the YLT, KJV, ASV, I have translated *sōtēría* [Zodhiates, s. v. 4991], ("safety, deliverance, preservation from danger or destruction") as "deliverance," in the sense of acquitted of the legal charges brought against Paul by the Jews.

c In 1:28, I have translated *ptúrō* [Zodhiates, s. v. 4426], "to frighten," as "intimidated." In Paul's context "intimidated" seemed a better translation than "frightened" (most translations).

d In 3:2, the word I have translated "discern" is *blépō* [Zodhiates, s. v. 991], "to see," here used in the sense of mental perception, to be aware, to observe. The exhortation is a warning to perceive the false doctrine. The "look out, watch out, beware" of other versions fails to communicate Paul's intent.

e In 3:3, I have translated *latreúō* [Zodhiates, s. v. 3000], as "serving." The word means "to serve, in the sense of serving God" (all occurrences: Romans 1:9, 25; Philippians 3:3; 2 Timothy 1:3). The KJV, ASV, ESV, NIV, NLT translate *latreúō* as "worship."

f In 3:7, 8, the words "having no value," are *zēmía* [Zodhiates, s. v. 2209], "damage, loss, detriment", or "disadvantage" [Kittel, 2:888]. The word "lost" in 3:8 is also *zēmía*, but in the aorist indicative passive

Zēmía "is not the objective loss of the thing itself. It is the subjective loss of its value. These verses mean everything that was once valuable to Paul have now in Paul's estimation lost its value for him. Paul now regards it all as definitively deprived of value in virtue of the superiority of the knowledge of Jesus Christ for the sake of which he has experienced this comprehensive devaluation" [Kittel, 2:890].

g In 3:8, the word other versions translate as "rubbish, dung, refuse, filth, garbage" is *skúbalon* [Zodhiates, s. v. 4657]. Literally this word means "excrement." I have translated this word "worthless." Paul's use here corresponds with *zēmía* on 3:7, 8, see note "f." In "general the word carries with it the thought of what is worthless and useless, also abhorrent and unclean" [Kittel, 7:446]. Although the word "dung" may be used in a metaphorical sense ("this is crap"), I have chosen to translate *skúbalon* as "worthless" to fit with *zēmía*, "loss of value."

h In 4:6, the words "not even one thing or person," are my interpretative translation of *mēdeis* [Zodhiates, s. v. 3367] "not even one," to correspond to *en pás*, "in everything."

i I have translated 4:13 much different than other versions, except the YLT. The Greek text simply does not say, "I can do all things." The text states (Greek word order), "all things I have strength in the one strengthening me."

(A small number of later Greek texts have *christós* [Metzger, 550], which is why it is found in Erasmus' Greek text [the so-called Textus Receptus, named that by Erasmus' Dutch publishers]. If *christós* had been in the autograph, there is no rational reason it would have been omitted in earlier texts.)

The verse opens with the adjective "all things," and requires a preposition, "for" or "in," to make a complete sentence in English. "*In* all things I have strength in the One strengthening me."

The verse has nothing to do with what you want to do. The all things you can do are all those things God requires of you through the One, Christ, strengthening you, in order that you will be able to do all those things God requires of you. Within the context, the "all things" Paul refers to are those things he has previously mentioned in 4:11–12.

Colossians Translation Notes

a1 In 1:2, the Greek text is "to the saints in Colossae and faithful brothers in Christ." The word "saints" is a noun, which indicates the word "and" is probably epexegetical. I have indicated this by making "faithful brothers and sisters in Christ" descriptive of "saints."

a2 In 1:2, I have translated *adelphós*, "brothers," as "brothers and sisters." *Adelphós* is being used in the sense of "brethren" to refer to all the saints—those who are saved—at Colossae. Women are members of the same church family as the men, which is to say that all were brethren of the church of Christ in Colossae. Therefore I have given what I believe was the intended meaning, "brothers and sisters."

b In 1:3, some texts read "We always give thanks to God and the Father," some texts read "We always give thanks to the God and Father," and some texts read "We always thank God, the Father" [Metzger, *Textual*, 552]. I have used the shorter reading.

c In 1:10, the translation, "to behave," is from the Greek word *peripatéō* [Zodhiates, s. v. 4043], literally "to walk," figuratively, the manner in which one lives out his/her life.

d In 1:14, the phrase "through his blood," occurring in the KJV/NKJV after "redemption" and before "the forgiveness," is an interpolation from Ephesians 1:7 and without support in the many Alexandrian, Western, and Byzantine manuscripts [Metzger, *Textual*, 554].

e In 1:16, the words "stand created" indicate the grammatical form perfect indicative passive of the verb *ktízō* [Zodhiates, s. v. 2936], "to create." The perfect tense emphasizes the continuing state of "having been created" as a result of the past event of creation. All things have been brought into existence by creation and remain in their created state of existence.

f1 At 1:27, and other verses in Colossians, the word I have translated "hidden *things*" is *mustérion* [Zodhiates, s. v. 3466], hidden, secret, not fully made known. The word *mustérion* is usually used in Scripture to indicate "something which man is capable of knowing, but only when it has been revealed to him by God, and not through any searching of his own" [Trench, *Commentary*, 55].

f2 At 2:2. There are fifteen different endings for 2:2 in about thirty-five manuscripts, plus minuscules. I have chosen the "of God—of Christ—" reading, which cannot be derived from any of the others, a fact which argues it is the original. The reading of the KJV has the greater number of manuscript witnesses, but analysis indicates it conflates two other readings [Metzger, *Text of the New Testament*, 236–238].

g In 2:8, where other versions translate *sulagōgéō* [Zodhiates, s. v. 4812] as "cheat" (NKJV) or "captive" (NIV, HCSB), I have translated "rob you of the riches of Christ," based on Zodhiates' definition, "to lead off as prey, carry off as booty, rob, or kidnap, figuratively of false teachers who rob believers of the complete riches available in Christ and revealed in the gospel." The NIV, HCSB translation "captive" implies the Colossians themselves are being carried off, versus their spiritual treasures [see Moulton, *Vocabulary*, s. v. 4812]. The translation "rob" has the advantage of conforming to the two words that form *sulagōgéō: súlon*, "a prey" (from *suláō*, "to strip, rob") and *ágō*, "to carry away." Thus to carry away riches, i.e., to rob.

h In 2:12, the translation, "through your faith in the effective power exercised by God," was suggested by Harris [*Colossians*, 94], who understands the genitives "faith" and "working" as subjective and objective, respectively.

i In 2:14, I have translated the text as, "He cancelled the bond that testified against us." The word beginning the phrase is *exaleíphō* [Zodhiates, s. v. 1813], "to blot out, to expunge, wipe off." However, as Robertson says [4:494], the meaning is "cancelled." That is because the object receiving the action of *exaleíphō* is *cheirógraphon* [Zodhiates, s. v. 1813], "a record of debt." The *cheirógraphon* was a certificate of indebtedness, or more simply, an IOU. Harris [*Colossians*, 96] states *to cheirógraphon* may be translated "the bond that stood against us," or "the bond that testified against us." Because the thing that either "stood against us" or "testified against us" is the *dógma* [Zodhiates, s. v. 1378], "the law," the translation "testified against us" seemed the better choice.

j1 In 2:18, as explained in the Preface, I have translated the word *ággelos* as "messenger." I added the adjective "celestial" to make clear these messengers were spirit beings. "Celestial messengers," is a context-driven translation, an interpretation based on what I and others believe to be the meaning of the passage.

j2 In 2:18, the question mark (prying into?) is meant to indicate the arrogance or impertinence implied by *embateúō* [Zodhiates, s. v. 1687], of pretending to know what one cannot know.

k In 3:2, I have translated *phronéō* [Zodhiates, s. v. 5426], "to think, have a mindset," a verb in the present imperative active voice, as "constantly fix your thoughts on." The subject of the verb is implied: "you, Christian reader, constantly fix your thoughts" etc. The idea is, "to give your mind to, to set your mind on something." The translation was suggested by Harris [*Colossians*, 120].

l In 3:6, the ending phrase, "on the sons of disobedience," may be a scribal addition copied from Ephesians 5:6, or may be original to the text. The words are absent from some manuscripts and works of the early church Fathers, and present in other manuscripts and early church Fathers. Colossians and Ephesians were written about the same time, and I know by personal experience an author does not hesitate to repeat in one place something he wrote in another place, if applicable to the immediate context.

m In 3:15, some manuscripts have "the peace of God" and others have "the peace of Christ." Deciding which was the autograph and which the scribal emendation was difficult. Both God and Christ give peace, Romans 1:7; 1 Corinthians 1:3; 2 Corinthians 1:2; Galatians 1:3; Ephesians 1:2; 6:23; Col 1:2; 1 Thessalonians 1:1; 2 Thessalonians 1:2; 1 Timothy 1:2; 2 Timothy 1:2; Titus 1:4; Philemon 3; 2 Peter 1:2; 2 John 3; Revelation 1:4, 5. What seemed most likely the autograph is, "the peace of God." This seems even more likely when we look at 3:16, where the expression is "the word of Christ," thus, the peace of God through the message of Christ.

n The translation of 3:16 is debated among commentators. See my commentary on Colossians for examples. I made my decision based on the following: though songs and hymns may teach through lyrics, teaching is more than singing songs. Paul didn't teach through singing, but preaching and writing. Therefore, he means use songs as a way to express thankfulness, which is part of worship and praise. Others agree with my translation, e.g., the HCSB, John Eadie, James D. G. Dunn (see my commentary on Colossians in the Sources section).

o In 3:20, where the Greek text has "for this is" I have "for such behavior is," etc. I have exchanged the pronoun "this" for its referent: the Christian child's obligation to obey his/her parents.

In 3:20 I have translated *euárestos* [Zodhiates, s. v. 2101], "well-pleasing, acceptable," according to the sense of the exhortation: a child's obedience to his/her parent is proper behavior for those who are in Christ Jesus.

p In 3:21, I translated as "antagonize" the Greek word *erethízō* [Zodhiates, s. v. 2042], "arouse, excite; provoke, irritate, exasperate" (or in a positive sense, stimulate) [see also Harris, *Colossians*, 156]. Looking to the context, the words "exasperate" (HCSB) or "vex" (YLT) seemed appropriate, but did not quite capture what I believed the apostle was trying to communicate. (The NIV "embitter" is a different Greek word not in this text.) The KJV/NKJV and ASV use "provoke." Looking to my own responses as a child and later actions as a father, I felt "antagonize" better communicated the sense of irritation or resentment or anger that fathers sometimes provoke in their children, when the father's parental authority conflicts with the child's growing need for independence.

q In 3:22, "earthly masters" translates "the according to flesh masters." The word translated "reverence" is *phobéō* [Zodhiates, s. v. 5399], "to become fearful, afraid, terrified." In regard to the Lord it indicates reverence; what the Old Testament named the "fear of the Lord." The grammatical form here is a verb, present participle. "The participle ... is probably causal [versus circumstantial]: "because of your reverence for the Lord" [Harris, *Colossians*, 158].

r In 3:23, the phrase "work at it with enthusiasm" is an interpretive translation of *psuchḗ ergázomai* [Zodhiates, s. v. 5590, 2038], literally "from your soul work."

s In 4:1, the translation of the first part follows O'Brien [see his commentary on Colossians, 214]. The Greek text reads "masters that which is *díkaios* (righteous, just [Zodhiates, s. v. 1342]) and that which is *isótēs* (what is equitable [Zodhiates, s. v. 2471]) to your slaves *paréchō* (to present, offer, bestow [Zodhiates, s. v. 3930])." The grammatically neuter *díkaios* indicates a Christian master's treatment of his slaves is to be "what is just [or] what is right" [Harris, *Colossians*, 162; Robertson, 4:509]. The grammatically neuter *isótēs* indicates fairness of treatment [Harris, *Colossians*, 162]. The neuter gender treats *díkaios* and *isótēs* as abstract principles guiding behavior, rather than concrete instances of right and fair. "Paul is not enjoining social equality through the emancipation of slaves but rather even-handedness of treatment" [Harris, *Colossians*, 162]. Thus, "justly" and "fairly" are accurate translations of Paul's thought.

The more difficult word is the imperative *paréchō* in the middle voice. The modern translations follow the view that "the middle stresses the required involvement and initiative of the masters: they were to act voluntarily, from their own resources" [Harris, *Colossians*, 162]. I am following Lightfoot's view [*Colossians*, 230] that the middle voice points to the slave-owners' reciprocal obligation: "exhibit on your part." I agree with O'Brien that "treat" is the better translation of *paréchō* in context.

† In 4:5, the words translated "making the most of every opportunity" are *kairós exagorázō*, to buy or redeem time [Zodhiates, s. v. 2540, 1805]. The word *kairós* is not time in the chronological sense, but time in the sense of "season, a period of opportunity." The word *exagorázō* means "to buy out of, redeem." Used together the idea is to gain opportunity.

First Thessalonians Translation Notes

a1 In 1:1, the text reads the name *Silouanós*, which transliterated is "Silvanus" [Zodhiates, s. v. 4610]. The name *Silouanós* is the same person as *Sílas* [Zodhiates, s. v. 4609], appearing at Acts 15:22, 27, 32, 34, 40; 16:19, 25, 29; 17:4, 10, 14, 15; 18:5. Luke calls him Silas but Paul always refers to him as Silvanus. I have substituted *Sílas* for *Silouanós* to maintain the relationship with the many verses where the person Silvanus is identified as Silas.

a2 In 1:1, after the words "Grace to you and peace," some manuscripts have variations of, "from God our Father and Lord Jesus Christ." If any of those variations had been in the autograph there is no reason why it would have been deleted from the majority of manuscripts [Metzger, *Textual*, 561]. For that reason I have used the shorter text.

b1 In 1:3, I have translated the word *adialeíptōs* [Zodhiates, s. v. 89] as "at every opportunity." The word means "without ceasing, continually, without intermission." To translate the word literally would exclude all other activities. "An old papyrus letter, lately discovered in Egypt but written as far back as the apostles' days, speaks of an 'incessant cough,' thus not continuous but continually recurring. Thus, not uninterrupted prayer, but continually recurring prayer is the thought here" [See Vine & Hogg commentary on Thessalonians, 27]. I have translated the intended and rational sense of the word.

b2 In 1:3, in the Greek text the nouns faith, labor, and hope are in the Genitive case, indicating the intimate relationship between work and faith, labor and love, perseverance and the hope given to us by Jesus Christ. My translation was influenced by George Milligan [commentary on Thessalonians]: "your faith works, and your love toils, and your hope endures," and William Tyndale [AD 1549 Matthew Bible], "your work in the faith and labor in love and the perseverance in the hope."

c In 2:11–12, the Greek text places "encouraging you and comforting and solemnly charging you," after Paul's "father" metaphor. Chrysostom (d. AD 407), Archbishop of Constantinople, places "encouraging you" etc., after the "father" metaphor, showing the antiquity of the reading. The KJV-NKJV and ASV arrange the text differently.

d In 3:1, I have translated the word *stégō* [Zodhiates, s. v.

4722], "forbear, endure," as "restraining the impulse." The text is literally "therefore no longer forbearing/enduring." The sense is Paul could no longer endure not knowing the circumstances of his friends in Thessalonica. See 2:17, he was "exceedingly eager, with great desire, to see your face." He had "restrained the impulse," the meaning of "forbear," to leave Athens and go to Thessalonica.

e In 3:2, the word translated "fellow worker" is *sunergós* [Zodhiates, s. v. 4904], "fellow laborer or worker, helper." Other manuscripts have *diákonos* [Zodhiates, s. v. 1249], "minister, servant, deacon." See Metzger, *Textual*, 563.

f In 4:1, the words some translate "finally" are *loipón oún*. The word *oún* is a conjunction, here indicating a connection between what has gone before with what is about to come [Zodhiates, s. v. 3767]. The word *loipón* [Zodhiates, s. v. 3063] is the neuter singular of *loipós*, "remaining" [Zodhiates, s. v. 3062]. Together the words mark a transition to a different subject. Paul has more to say, thus, "As to the rest."

g In 4:4, I have translated the word *skeúos*, "vessel" [Zodhiates, s. v. 4632] as "his or her sexuality," to fit the subject, which is *porneía*, 4:3, sexual immorality. In the context of, "abstain from sexual immorality," Paul obviously meant *skeúos* to refer not merely to the body, but to the way the body may be used sexually.

h In 4:5 the word I have translated "peoples" is *éthnos* [Zodhiates, s. v. 1484], "people, race," in the plural form. The KJV, NKJV, HCSB, ASV, ESV translate "gentiles," the NIV, "heathen," the YLT, "nations," and the NLT, "pagans." To the Jew the word *éthnos* meant every non-Jew. But Paul's Thessalonica readers were mostly gentile. To his mostly gentile readers *éthnos* described people in general. But Paul is not making Hebrew persons an exception by using *éthnos*. Even the Hebrews, especially those living in gentile countries, were not immune to the temptations of the passions of sexual lust. The Hebrew believers in the Thessalonian congregation would have known that. What Paul does mean is the division between Christian and non-Christian, between saved and unsaved. The phrase, "the *éthnos* not knowing God," are those persons who are unsaved. Christians are not to act like the unsaved peoples.

i In 5:9, the word I have translated "deliverance" is *sōtēría* [Zodhiates, s. v. 4991], safety, deliverance, preservation from danger or destruction. This word is most often translated "salvation" and so here also by most other translations. But Paul is speaking of a day of God's wrath to people who are already saved. Therefore *sōtēría* in this place means "deliverance" from that day of God's wrath.

j In 5:19, the word usually translated "quench," *sbénnumi* [Zodhiates, s. v. 4570] I have translated "hinder." This word literally means quench when used of a literal fire or a literal light (such as from a lamp). But the use here is figurative. In this context of submission to God's will (do good, rejoice, pray, give thanks), to hinder the Holy Spirit is to refuse to submit to God's will. When God's will is resisted, the Holy Spirit's work of teaching, guidance, and blessing turns to conviction of sin in order to prompt repentance. In context, God's will is resisted when the believer fails to pursue the good, fails to find contentment in God's will, fails to give thanks in everything, or fails to pray at every opportunity.

Second Thessalonians Translation Notes

a In 1:1, the text reads the name *Silouanós*, which transliterated is "Silvanus" [Zodhiates, s. v. 4610]. The name *Silouanós* is the same person as *Sílas* [Zodhiates, s. v. 4609], appearing at Acts 15:22, 27, 32, 34, 40; 16:19, 25, 29; 17:4, 10, 14, 15; 18:5. Luke calls him Silas but Paul always refers to him as Silvanus. I have substituted *Sílas* for *Silouanós* to maintain the relationship with the many verses where the person Silvanus is identified as Silas.

b At 1:9, the word I have rendered "ruin" is *apóllumi* [Zodhiates. s. v. 622]. This word means to destroy, to cause to perish. Yet, in both secular and biblical literature, it never means annihilation, but ruin or loss. The most commonly used sense is "ruin," e.g., Matthew 9:17. Various lexicons (Moulton, *Vocabulary*; Kittle, *TDNT*; Silva, *NIDNTTE*) give secular examples: the loss of money, the loss of clothing, the loss of life, loss of two pigs, to kill in battle, to suffer loss of money, to trifle away one's life.

c At 2:2, some texts read "the day of Christ," versus the majority that read "the day of the Lord. The substitution of *christós* (christ) for *kúrios* (lord), is due to failure to consider how Paul used "day of the Lord, and a misunderstanding of the grammatical interaction between the words *enístēmi* [Zodhiates. s. v. 1764] "present" in 2:2 and *proton* [Zodhiates, s. v. 4412], "first" in 2:3.

The usage argument. A review of Paul's use of "day of the Lord," indicates he always distinguishes between the Old Testament "Day of the Lord," 1 Thessalonians 5:2; 2 Thessalonians 2:2, and the second advent, the "day of the Lord Jesus," 1 Corinthians 5:5; 2 Corinthians 1:14. The texts with "day of the Lord" are the correct texts of 2:2, based on Paul's use of the term.

The grammatical argument. The Thessalonians had been told by someone, 2:2, their persecutions meant the Day of the Lord was "present," *enístēmi*. The word *proton* in 2:3 relates to the condition in 2:2, when is the Day of the Lord present? That day is not present unless two things come first, the *apostasía* and the man of lawlessness. The sense is the occurrence of those two events reveal the Day of the Lord is present. Grammatically, those two events do not come and then comes the Day of the Lord, but those two events are sequenced events occurring within the Day of the Lord, whereby one knows the eschatological time is the Day of the Lord. Paul gives the sequence of events as the *apostasía* ("departure," aka rapture) and the man of lawlessness declaring himself to be God. By those two events, in that order, one may know the time of the Old Testament Day of the Lord has arrived.

By Paul's usage and his grammar indicate the correct text is "day of the Lord," not "day of Christ."

Virtually all commentators translate "day of the Lord" but base their comments on the belief Paul meant the second advent. Their view is a falling away of the NT church (see note "d" below), the man of lawlessness, then the second advent. The reason is their eschatology (Amillennialism or Postmillennialism) does not allow for a literal Old Testament Day of the Lord. When one's eschatology (premillennialism) does incorporate a literal Old Testament Day of the Lord, then it is plain from the events of the Revelation the *apostasía* and man of sin are sequenced events indicating when the Old Testament Day of the Lord has arrived. Thus there is also a prophetic argument: the "lion of the Tribe of Judah, the offspring of David," Revelation 5:5 are specific Old Testament symbols for Messiah the King of Israel. The events of Revelation 6–19 are the Old Testament Day of the Lord. (See my commentary on the Revelation.) The correct texts for 2 Thessalonians 2:2 are the ones reading the "day of the Lord."

d In 2:3, the word I have translated, "departure," is *apostasía* [Zodhiates, s. v. 646]. The word *apostasía* means "departure." The word has been transliterated as "apostasy," and translated as "falling away, revolt, rebellion, turning away from God, definite rejection of God," in seventeen versions from AD 1532 to the present times, a trend begun with Justin Martyr (AD 100–165), in *Dialogue with Trypho*, chapter 110, who wrote, "He [Jesus Christ], shall come from heaven to glory, when the man of *apostasía* ... shall venture to do unlawful deeds." Since that time those translating Justin's works have transliterated *apostasía* into "apostasy," or translated *apostasía* as does the LXX to mean religious rebellion. But *apostasía* means "departure," and I have translated it according to its meaning. For a thorough discussion of *apostasía* in 2:3 see my book, *A Private Commentary on the Bible: Thessalonians*, 207–217.

d In 2:13, where I and most translations have "from the beginning," the ESV has "as the firstfruits." The reading "from the beginning has strong support" in many manuscripts [Metzger, *Textual*, 568]. Many today prefer the reading "as the firstfruits" because the Greek text *apó arché*, "occurs nowhere else in the Pauline corpus" [same reference]. To deny a strongly supported reading because of the way the author chose to express himself in one of thirteen letters seems unrealistic.

The issue is not doctrinal. The firstfruits are indicative of the greater harvest, for example, 1 Corinthians 15:23. But for Paul to say God chose the Thessalonians "as the firstfruits" seems unlikely, because they were neither the first gentiles saved, nor the first saved in Macedonia or Achaia.

First Timothy Translation Notes

    a In 1:3, the several Bible versions are divided between placing "I going to Macedonia" at the beginning or the middle. The word order of the text is, "Just as I urged you to remain in Ephesus—I going to Macedonia" etc. I chose to follow the word order.

    b In 1:3, the word I translated "teach different" is *heterodidaskaléō* [Zodhiates, s. v. 2085], a compound word (possibly created by Paul) formed from *didáskalos*, "teacher" and *hèteros*, "other but different." The meaning is another teacher who does not teach the same as Paul but teaches that which is different. I did not supply the word "doctrine" as do other translations, preferring to let the context supply the meaning.

    c At 1:4, the word translated "administration ... purpose" is *oikonomía* [Zodhiates, s. v. 3622], "to administer, to manage." An administrator-manager conducts himself in order to accomplish a purpose. Literally the text reads, "administration of God." Because Timothy's actions, not those of God, are the subject, I have translated, "administration of God's purpose," to make plain Paul has charged Timothy to be the manager of God's purposes in the Ephesian church.

    d At 1:9, The two words I have translated "the ones abusing fathers and mothers" are nouns joined together by the conjunction "and." The coordinating conjunction makes the two nouns equal elements. These are compound words formed by a noun+verb. The words are *patralóas*, "father+smite/beat," and *metralóas*, "mother+smite/beat." [Respectively, Zodhiates, s. v. 3964, 3389.] Although the word "smite" might be extended in meaning to "murder," the idea of murder is captured by the next word, *androphónos* [Zodhiates, s. v. 409], "manslayer, murderer." The better choice is "abusing," which fits Paul's culture and every culture from then to now.

    e At 1:17 I have translated "incorruptible" versus "immortal" in other versions. The word here is *áphthartos* [Zodhiates, s. v. 862], "not corruptible." The word for immortal is *athanasía* [Zodhiates, s. v. 110], "without death." The word *áphthartos*, means "not subject to death or decay," thus better translated "incorruptible," versus "immortal." God is not immortal, which requires a beginning, God is eternal, without beginning or end, he is the, "not subject to death or decay," God.

    f At 2:9, "fashionable hairstyles" is literally "braided hair," which was the high fashion among the women of the day, usually decorated with jewelry.

g At 2:15, "childbearing" means more than the physical act of conceiving and birthing a child. Childbearing also looks to parental love and care, which is to say, the act and process of raising a child to maturity.

h At 3:2, "one-wife kind of husband" See translation note "j."

i In 3:8 the first clause literally reads, "in the same manner deacons respectable," etc. All versions add some kind of verb for the reader.

j At 5:9, a "one-husband kind of wife" is the same idiomatic expression as at 3:2, a "one-wife kind of husband." The expression does not mean only one spouse in a lifetime, but means married until the marital relationship ends naturally in the death of one of the spouses, with remarriage assumed and allowed. In Paul's times, the death of a spouse was the common end of many marriages, through childbirth, disease, sepsis, war, and other causes. And so marriage after the death of a spouse was common. If the idiom meant only one spouse in a lifetime, then Paul's instruction for younger widows, 5:14, to remarry, would contradict his instruction at 5:9, and contradict the Old Testament moral value to care for the widow.

k In 6:5, the sentence "Withdraw from such" has support from some of the church fathers, but is missing from the Alexandrian and Western group of manuscripts [Metzger, 575]. The instruction "withdraw from such," does not quite fit into the tenor of the letter, and therefore I have accepted the judgment of the textual critics that "withdraw from such" is not in the autograph. If the text had been "rebuke such" it would be more agreeable as a genuine instruction from Paul.

l In 6:11, the word I have translated "patience with things and circumstances" is *hupomonē* [Zodhiates. s. v. 5281], usually translated "endurance" or "patience." There is a different Greek word for patience with people, which is *makrothumía* [Zodhiates, s. v. 3115], and often translated "longsuffering."

m At 6:11 "gentleness in strength" is *praütēs* [Zodhiates, s. v. 4240]. This word indicates that middle ground between anger and apathy. It is that balance in one's character that does what is right, in the right measure, for the right reason. The translation "gentleness with strength" is meant to indicate that balance.

Second Timothy Translation Notes

a At 1:10, the word I have translated "incorruptibility" is *aphtharsía* [Zodhiates, s. v. 861]. This is the word other versions have wrongly translated "immortality." The word *aphtharsía* means "incorruption, incorruptibility, incapacity for corruption." A much different word, *athanasía* [Zodhiates, s. v. 110], "the absence of death," means immortality, 1 Corinthians 15:53, 54; 1 Timothy 6:16.

b At 2:15, the KJV-NKJV translation "rightly dividing" is not supported by the context. The word in question is *orthotoméō* [Zodhiates, s. v. 3718]. This is a compound word formed from *orthós*, "right," and *témnō*, "to cut or divide." But the meaning and use of a compound word is not formed by adding together the meaning of the parts, but by cultural use and context

In secular use, *orthotoméō* meant to cut straight, and was used in contexts such as building a straight road.

In 2 Timothy 2:15, the context is properly handling the Word of God. The contextual meaning of *orthotoméō* is: to handle correctly, skillfully (Zodhiates s. v. 3718); set forth truthfully (Mounce, *Dictionary*, p. 1226, s. v. 3982); correctness, rightly explaining (Silva, s. v. 3981). Therefore, I have translated, "skillfully teaching the word of truth."

Titus Translation Notes

a In 1:1, I have translated both occurrences of the Greek preposition *katá* [Zodhiates, s. v. 2596], as "according to." Modern versions, such as ESV, HCSB, NIV, translate the first *katá* in this verse as "for" and ignore the second *katá*. The difference is my translation states Paul is an apostle according to the faith, whereas other translations state Paul is an apostle for the purpose of the faith. As Paul himself teaches, the origin and source of faith is God. e.g., Ephesians 2:8. Paul was called and appointed to testify about the faith and according to the faith, Acts 9:15. The proper translation of *katá* in Titus 1:1, both occurrences, is "according to."

b At 1:6, a "one-wife kind of husband" is the same idiomatic expression as at 1 Timothy 3:2, and the same as at 1 Timothy 5:9, a "one-husband kind of wife." The key to understanding this expression is the culture of Paul's times and his instructions to Timothy concerning widows. In Paul's times, the death of a spouse was the common end of many marriages, through childbirth, disease, sepsis, war, and other causes. And so marriage after the death of a spouse was common. If the idiom meant only one spouse in a lifetime, then Paul's instruction for younger widows, 5:14, to remarry, would contradict his instruction at 5:9, and contradict the Old Testament moral value to care for the widow. The expression at Titus 1:6, a "one-wife kind of husband," does not mean only one spouse in a lifetime, but means married until the marital relationship ends naturally in the death of one of the spouses, with remarriage assumed and allowed.

c In 2:9, I have translated *doúlos* [Zodhiates, s. v. 1401] as "servants" not "slaves" because the believer reading this translation (and my commentary on the Pastoral Letters) will almost certainly not own slaves. Slavery is ongoing in the modern world, but in these modern times it is illegal in the world. Nevertheless, Paul is referring to those believers who were slaves in the Roman Empire and in Christian homes within the Roman Empire. The application is this: whether one is a slave, servant, or employee in the world, the moral values, principles, and applicable precepts of Christianity apply at all times.

Philemon Translation Notes

a In Philemon 2, I have translated "our sister." Some manuscripts have "the beloved." This was most likely a scribal emendation to conform to "Philemon the beloved."

b In Philemon 12, I have not included the words "you therefore receive him" after "even him" (KJV-NKJV), which words are one of several scribal additions to the text.

c In Philemon 25, most versions have "grace ... be with your spirit." The Greek text has the preposition *metá*, "with," but not the verb. The question is, if a verb is added to the preposition, should it be the verb "be" or the verb "is?" Now we are into interpretation. If we translate "grace ... be with your spirit," we have interpreted the sentence as a prayer or a benediction. If we translate "grace ... is with your spirit," we have interpreted the sentence as a declaration. My choice is to translate, not interpret, so I have not added a verb. "The grace of the Lord Jesus Christ with your spirit."

d In Philemon 25, some manuscripts append "amen." If present in the autograph, there is no rational reason for it to have been deleted in any manuscript.

Hebrews Translation Notes

☦ My translation is affected by my belief the Hebrews Writer was a companion of the apostle Paul. I believe the Writer traveled with Paul on one or more of Paul's missionary journeys, and thus heard many of Paul's synagogue addresses. I believe the Writer used Paul's synagogue addresses as the doctrinal sections of the letter, on which he built his exhortations to his readers. Therefore, Paul's doctrine as expressed in his letters supports the translation of some words and phrases.

a1 In 1:1 God has spoken *én tois prophétais* "by the prophets," not the NIV, NLT "through," which is never a proper translation of the preposition *én* [see Wallace, 372]. The translation "by" indicates instrumentality. The prophets were the instrument by which God spoke to others. This translation becomes important when we consider 1:2, *én huiós*, see note a2.

a2 The Greek text in 1:2, *én huiós*, is a preposition and a noun, translated in this context as "in Son." The noun is in the Dative case, so the preposition *én* might be translated as "in" or "by." The difference is "in" indicates the sphere of activity, whereas "by" indicates instrumentality. The Writer's point is God is speaking in person in the God-man. The God-man is not God's instrument, as were the prophets, but God incarnate. Therefore *én huiós* is the sphere in which God himself spoke versus the instruments (the prophets) by which God previously spoke. When Jesus the Christ spoke, God himself was speaking directly, not speaking through others as had been the case before the incarnation.

b1 In 1:3, the translation "exact" is from the Greek word *charaktér* [Zodhiates, s. v. 5481]. The word occurs only here in the New Testament. The original meaning of this word described an engraving tool. Then, as metal coins came into use, it indicated a die used in minting coins to impress an image onto the coin. From that use *charaktér* came to denote the impress or image made on the metal, which is why the ESV translates "exact imprint." The idea of moral character follows from the original meaning. The Writer, by combining *charaktér* with *hupóstasis* (see note b2) communicates that the incarnate Son is the exact same essence as the Father. Jesus exactly represents the Person God: "he who has seen me has seen the Father," John 14:9, cf. Colossians 2:9.

b2 In 1:3, the word translated "essence" is the Greek word *hupóstasis* [Zodhiates, s. v. 5287]. The base meaning of *hupóstasis* is "to stand under," or "support." However, its scientific use was predominant in Greek as a special term for "everything that settles, hence the philosophical 'existence,' 'reality'" [Kittle, 7:572]. The word *hupóstasis* is used three times in Hebrews (1:3; 3:14; 11:1). In 1:3 the meaning is best represented by the English "essence." Jesus is the *apaúgasma*, shining, of God's *dóxa*, glory, and is the *charaktér*, the exact image, of God's *hupóstasis*, essence. Jesus Christ is visibly the character or express image of God manifest in the flesh. Christ is the whole divine essence, and all the divine properties are possessed by and communicated to him.

c Hebrews 1:6. How one understands the first few words will determine the interpretation of the verse. The first words of the verse are "*hótan dé pálin eiságō*." Literally, "When but again he brings." The question is whether *pálin* (again) should be connected to *hótan* (when) or to *eiságō* (he brings). The choice of translation affects one's view concerning the timing of the angelic worship, "Let all God's messengers worship him." If one translates the text as, "when he again brings," that translation leads the interpreter to the conclusion that the verse is referring to an appearance of Christ subsequent to his incarnation.

This is a place where doctrine impacts translation. The Christ is an office of the incarnate God the Son; he is Jesus the Christ. The office of "Christ" is announced at Psalm 2:2, the Hebrew *māshîah*, "anointed." The office was fulfilled in the incarnation of God the Son, Psalm 2:7; God the Son became the Christ when he incarnated. Therefore, the Christ cannot have appeared prior to the incarnation. What some call appearances of the "pre-incarnate Christ," are in reality appearances of the pre-incarnate God the Son appearing as the Messenger of YHWH.

The word *pálin* (again) may also mean "furthermore" or "on the other hand." If one translates *pálin* according to these meanings, the translation would read, "And furthermore, when he brings the firstborn into the world, he says," etc. The meaning of "furthermore" connects the quote in 1:6 with the quoted verses in 1:5.

"It seems preferable, therefore, to construe *pálin* as a connective, following the interpretative tradition of the Old Latin, and the Syriac versions. Its force is continuative ('and again he says') or mildly adversative ('but he says')" [see Lane, *Hebrews 1–8*, p. 26]. *Pálin* occurs ten times in Hebrews. Only in 5:12; 6:1, 6 is it used in the sense of repetition. The use of *pálin* as a continuative is the Writer's habit, seven out of ten occurrences, e.g., 1:5, 6; 2:13 (x2); 4:5, 7; and 10:30.

I have chosen to translate as the continuative, "Then again," as introducing item three in the list of things (1:5–6) the Father said about the incarnation of the Son.

d In 1:8, the translation "to the age of the age" is *eis ton aiōna tou ainōs*. The Greek word *aiōn* [Zodhiates, s. v. 165], "age," means a period of time. The duration is determined by context. Most versions translate as "forever and ever," but here the phrase means from eternity to eternity. The difference is "forever" has a beginning from which the duration "forever" is counted, but "eternity" does not have a beginning. The Greek phrase *eis ton aiōna tou ainōs* looks to the past, present, and future: eternity to eternity. The God-man, being deity incarnate, is ruler from eternity.

e In 1:9, "exuberant joy" translates *agallíasis* [Zodhiates, s. v. 20], "exultation, exuberant joy." Other versions repeat Psalm 45:7 instead of translating the text.

f1 In 2:1, where I have translated "transgress," others have translated "drift away." The word is *pararréō* [Zodhiates, s. v. 3901]. This word occurs only here in Scripture. The word is a compound formed from two words meaning "beyond" and "to flow." The meaning of a compound word is not determined by setting the definition of each part side by side, but by the use of the word. Because this word is used only one time, one cannot compare multiple uses in scripture to develop meaning. Biblical doctrine must be considered to determine the meaning. A person does not "drift away" from truth, because an act of sinning is always a choice. One should not translate in such a way that the translation contradicts another part of Scripture. If one ignores the truth, he has not drifted away but has transgressed.

f2 In 2:7, I have not shown the Hebrews Writer as quoting from the Old Testament. He is definitely quoting at Hebrews 2:6, because he uses a variation of the "it is written" formula, "someone somewhere has testified," to show he is quoting Psalm 8:4. But in Hebrews 2:7 he changes Psalm 8:5 with the addition of the neuter pronoun *tis* (who?, which?, or what?) to narrow "what is man," Psalm 8:4, to one man, Jesus the Christ. Other versions, in their eagerness to identify an Old Testament quote, ignore the neuter pronoun *tis*, which I translated "a certain one." The Hebrews 2:7

text literally reads "you made lower him a little who than angels ...."

g In 2:10, the Greek word translated "originator and leader" is *archēgós* [Zodhiates, s. v. 747]. The word is formed from two words meaning "beginning" and "to lead." Single word translations such as "source, captain, pioneer, leader" fail to capture both concepts of beginning and leadership. Through Jesus, the originator and leader of salvation, God brings many sons to glory and honor. In the New Testament *archēgós* refers to Jesus only, Acts 3:15; 5:31; Hebrews 2:10; 12:2.

h In 2:10, the translation "fully qualified" is from *teleióō* [Zodhiates, s. v. 5048]. The basic thought of *teleióō* is whole, complete (not "perfect" as in other translations). It means that nothing has been left out. Often in Scripture it bears the meaning of "mature." In 2:10, the Writer uses *teleióō* in the sense of "fully qualified." In the present context, "God has fully qualified Jesus the Son to come before him in priestly action. He has done so by the suffering (2:10) in which Jesus confirmed his obedience, 5:8ff." [Kittle, 1:487–488].

i In 2:14, "render ineffective" translates *katargéō* [Zodhiates, s. v. 2673], "to render inactive, or ineffective." Other versions translate "destroy." Death was not destroyed, which would contradict 9:27. Through his work on the cross Jesus Christ rendered ineffective the power of both spiritual and physical death for those whom he has saved. The power of spiritual death is separation from God's effective presence. The power of physical death is to confirm the unsaved in their state of spiritual death. By salvation both physical and spiritual death are rendered ineffective to harm the believer.

j In 3:6, I have note included the clause, "firm to the end." after "hold fast." This scribal addition is in the Textus Receptus and several other manuscripts [Metzger, *Textual*, 595]. Comparison with many manuscripts indicates the clause was added to 3:6 from 3:14 by an ancient scribe in an attempt to make the two verses agree.

k In 4:9, "sabbath-keeping" translates *sabbatismós*, "a keeping of the sabbath, a rest as upon the sabbath" [Zodhiates,. s. v. 4520]. The sabbath was not a day of worship (every day was a day of worship) it was a day in which no work (employment of man, woman, or beast) was to be done. (See my book, *The Old Ten in the New Covenant.*)

l In 5:8, the Greek text is (word order), "though being a son he learned from the things he suffered the obedience." Obedience was what Christ learned through his suffering. Obedience was natural to his sinless human nature. But the Hebrews Writer never forgets Christ was man as well as God. The God-man learned obedience through the experience of choosing to deny the temptation to disobey, the very temptation Adam chose to commit.

m For 5:9, "fully qualified," see translation note h.

n In 6:2, I have translated *baptismós* [Zodhiates, s. v. 909] as "immersions." Others have translated as "washings" or transliterated as "baptisms."

o In 6:20, the three words interpreted as "forever" by other versions and by me as "to the age," are *eis tón aiṓn*. The Greek word *aiṓn* [Zodhiates, s. v. 165], "age," means a period of time. The duration of *aiṓn* is always an interpretation from context.

p In 7:11 I have translated *teleiōsis* [Zodhiates, s. v. 5050] (from *teleióō*, s. v. 5048), as "perfection" versus its primary meaning of "complete." The reason is in 7:19 the law is said to have made nothing *teleióō*, "complete, perfect." If we translate *teleiōsis* and *teleióō* as complete, then we are in the position of saying Christ came to complete the Mosaic Law. He did not. He fulfilled the Mosaic covenant and replaced it with a New covenant, Hebrews 8:6–13; 10:16–17. Therefore we must give *teleiōsis* and *teleióō* a translation that fits the context and the doctrine. "Truly then, if the Levitical priesthood (was so complete as to be) perfection" etc.

q In 7:16, the word translated, "indissoluble," is *akatálutos* [Zodhiates, s. v. 179], literally, "without dissolve." The idea is not so much the eternality of that life, but the character of that life, as "a life that was not acquired and that cannot be done away with." The eternal life that animates Jesus Christ is an increate life, therefore an unending life.

r1 In 7:28, the **perfect participle of** *teleioo* is difficult to translate into English. The Greek perfect tense indicates an action completed in the past whose effects are felt in the present. There is no English equivalent, and the tense is properly translated "having been." The word *teleioo* means to make perfect by reaching the intended goal. The **perfect participle of** *teleioo* is properly translated "having been perfected." But the intended goal of *teleióō* in 7:28 is not well-expressed by "perfected." In 7:28 the Writer summarizes the entire argument of chapter 7, Jesus is fully qualified in every way to forever be the high priest of those whom he has saved. I chose to give the sense of the **perfect participle of** *teleioō* in the context of chapter 7, "always fully qualified."

r2 In 8:2, the word translated "pitched" is *pḗgnumi*, "to fix, fasten, make fast and firm, fasten together, construct, build" [Zodhiates, s. v. 4078]. Here the meaning is to erect or set up a tent. The word "pitch" is an older word for setting up a tent: to pitch a tent.

s In 8:5, the tabernacle Moses built in the wilderness was not a "copy" (most versions), nor a "shadow" or "example" (some versions). The tabernacle was a "representation" [Zodhiates, s. v. 5262] of heavenly realities. Nor was it a "shadow" (most versions), but a *skiá* [Zodhiates, s. v. 5639], not a literal shadow but figuratively a foreshadowing of heavenly realities.

t In 9:7, the word "errors" translates *agnóēma* [Zodhiates, s. v. 51], "error." Other versions give an interpretive translation: NKJV, sins in ignorance; ESV, unintentional sins; HCSB, NIV, sins ... committed in ignorance. The interpretive translation assumes an atonement for only unintentional sins on the Day of Atonement, because there was no sacrifice specified for presumptuous sins. However, the Writer may have stated "errors of the people," rather than "sins of ignorance" because presumptuous sins may have received atonement on the Day of Atonement. Five times the instructions for the Day of Atonement say the sacrifice for the people is: "because of their transgressions"; "for all their sins"; "for all their iniquities." Leviticus 16:16, 21, 22, 30, 34. In this instance, translators should translate, expositors should interpret.

u For 9:23, "representations," see translation note s.

v For 10:1, "representation," see translation note s.

w For 10:1, "complete" see translation note h.

x In 10:14, "completed continually" is the translation of *teleioō* [Zodhiates, s. v. 5048], in the present tense. The Greek present tense indicates the action is in progress or ongoing. In this context the action, sanctification, was accomplished in the past and is ongoing into the future.

y In 11:1, the translation "title deed" reflects *hupóstasis* [Zodhiates, s. v. 5287], the real presence. The word *hupóstasis* was used in the sense of ownership of property in ancient Egyptian documents [Moulton, 659–660]. A title deed describes real property, such as land, a home, or a car. When one legitimately possesses the title deed, then he holds physical proof of possession of the property, whether or not it is in his immediate presence. Therefore, in 11:1 *hupóstasis* refers to that certain reality in which one's faith is resting. In a figure, faith is a title deed to that reality we possess in Christ.

z In 11:1, "objective evidence" is *élegchos* [Zodhiates, s. v. 1650], which may mean subjective or objective evidence. Because it is in parallel with *hupóstasis*, then *élegchos* must mean objective evidence.

aa At 11:5, the word "translated" is *metatíthēmi* [Zodhiates, s. v. 3346]. The word means "to transpose, put in another place, hence to transport, transfer, translate." Modern versions avoid the lesser known definition of the English "translate," which is "to move from one place or condition to another" and use the ambiguous taken away, taken up, or taken from.

bb In 11:13, "expatriates" is from *parepídēmos* [Zodhiates, s. v. 3927], a foreigner who has settled down among native people. With the word *patrís* [Zodhiates, s. v. 3968], "homeland," which I have translated "native country" in 11:14, the sense is the earth is not the believer's native country, the believer is an expatriate from heaven, living temporarily on the earth, waiting to return. He/she writes home (prayer), and receives care packages from home (grace, blessings, mercy).

cc In 12:14 the word I have translated "perceive" is *horáō* [Zodhiates, s. v. 3708], "to see ... implying not the mere act of seeing, but also the actual perception of some object, thus differing from *blépō*, to see." Here the sense is not literal but figurative, to perceive with the mind or sense. If pursuing peace was all we needed to physically see the Lord, why salvation from sin's penalty? Other Bible versions do the believer a great disservice by translating "see."

dd At 12:17 the word "place" is *tópos* [Zodhiates, s. v. 5117], "place." A figurative sense of this word is "opportunity" or "occasion." Esau had both opportunity and occasion, but not place, because the blessing once given could not be withdrawn or changed. The opportunity had been lost, a harsh reality, but nevertheless a reality for the sinner who rejects salvation until his place—his life—is lost, and then there is no place for repentance. If someone should we despise the blessings of the Lord as Esau did, what has happened cannot be changed, and even the believer must live with the consequences of his sin. Some decisions to commit sin take the believer down a path he should never have taken, deliver him to a place he should never have come to, prevent him from returning to his starting point to begin anew, requiring him to live with the consequences of his sin.

James Translation Notes

‡ Chapter introduction, and 1:1. The first word in the Greek text is the name *Iakōbos* [Zodhiates, s. v. 2384]. The epistle was written by someone named *Iakōbos*, which translated is "Jacob." The name "James" is from "the Old French 'Gemmes,' a variation of the later Latin 'Jacomus,' itself a variation of the early Latin 'Jacobus'" [Vlachos, *James*, 9]. The Jacob of the gospels (Jacob son of Zebedee) and Acts 12:17; 15:13; Galatians 1:19; 2:9 is the most likely author of the letter.

a At 1:17, I have translated *pás dósis agathós* as "every good giving." The key word *dósis* [Zodhiates, *WSDNT*, s. v. "1394"], can mean a gift, but when considered with the many other Greek words meaning "gift," *dósis* stresses the act of giving and looks to the intent in giving. When *dósis agathós*, beneficial giving, becomes *pan dōrēma téleios*, every perfect gift, it has reached its goal.

b At 2:1, I chose to reorder the text so as to have a positive command, versus the negative in other translations.

c At 2:2, the word translated "congregation" is *sunagōgḗ* [Zodhiates, s. v. 4864], assembly. Here the word is without the definite article, which suggests Jacob is speaking "of the people assembled, not the building itself" [Vlachos, *James*, 69]. Hence the translation "congregation."

d At 2:5, several versions add in the verb "to be" before the words "rich in faith." The verb is not in any text, and to insert it is contrary to the contrast Jacob is making. The saved person who is poor according to the world's values is rich in faith and heir to greater riches in the coming kingdom.

e At 2:7, the phrase I have translated "the one having been called upon you," is a literal, word order translation of the text. Jacob used this same phrase a few years later at Acts 15:17, quoting from Amos 9:12, "upon whom my name has been called in them." The idea is that the rich slander the good name by which the believer is called, i.e., the good name is Christ.

f At 2:11, the subjunctive mood ("may") of the verbs for adultery and murder acknowledges the possibility of these sins, but does not give permission for committing these sins.

g1 At 2:14, the text has the definite article, "the faith." The use of the definite article points to a specific kind of faith, the kind that does not have works.

g2 At 2:17, the text has the definite article "the faith," which refers to "that kind of faith" in 2:14. The Greek text at 2:17 reads, "so also the faith if not it may have works dead is by itself." In an English syntax, "so also the faith, except it may have works, by itself is dead."

h At 2:26, "the faith," refers back to 2:14, the kind of faith that does not have works.

i At 3:2, The word translated "control" occurs here and at 1:26. Many versions translate this word "bridle" (the bit in a horse's mouth). It is a compound word [Zodhiates, *WSDNT*, s. v. "5468"] formed from the words for "bridle" and "to lead, govern." The meaning of a compound word is not the meaning of the parts, but how the word is used in the culture. A "dandelion" is a compound word formed from parts meaning "teeth" and "lion" but there is neither a lion nor lion's teeth in my yard. Figuratively the meaning in 2:14 is to restrain, govern, or control.

j At 3:6, the reading "appoints itself" is a translation of *kathístemi* [Zodhiates, *WSDNT*, s. v. "2525"], in the grammatical form present indicative middle. In the middle voice the subject performs the action on him or herself. The idea is not of the literal tongue but figurative of the activity of one's sin acting through one's speech.

k At 3:16, there are no verbs in the Greek text, "For where envy and self-interest, there confusion and every evil practice." The verbs are supplied by the reader, or translator.

l At 4:5, Jacob means the saved human spirit, not the Holy Spirit, which is why God gives greater grace, that the saved human spirit may be focused on the things of God. (In Paul's letters, the presence of the definite article would indicate the Holy Spirit. Jacob is not Paul, and writes with a different style than Paul.)

m At 4:7, the verse opens with *oún*, "therefore, then." The verb is "to be subject," i.e., to be under God's authority, and may be understood in three senses. If the verb is a true passive, then the sense is "therefore, allow yourselves to be subjected"; if the verb has a middle sense, then the reading is "therefore, subject yourselves"; if the verb is an ingressive aorist, then it means "therefore, become subject to God" [Vlachos, *James*, 142]. I have chosen to interpret the grammar as an ingressive aorist and use Young's Literal Translation: "be subject, then, to God."

n At 5:1, Robertson [6:57] identifies the grammatical form of "weep" as the ingressive aorist and translates "burst into weeping." Vlachos agrees [*James*, 158], citing Robertson. The grammatical form ingressive aorist emphasizes the beginning of an action, denoting entrance into a state or condition.

o At 5:16b, the Greek text is "much able petition of a righteous accomplishes," *polús ischúō déēsis díkaios energéō*." I have translated "The earnest request of a righteous person is able to accomplish much."

First Peter Translation Notes

a1 At 1:1, I have translated "elect expatriates." There has been an on-going discussion among commentators throughout the centuries as to whether *eklektós* should be joined with *parepídēmos*, expatriates, or with *prógnōsis*, "foreknowledge." I believe *eklektós* should be understood as an adjective modifying *parepídēmos:* "elect expatriates." Peter is not discussing how people get saved, but what happens after salvation. The election of the expatriates has to do with their security in a foreign land—the world of sinners. God has known them from eternity-past, keeps them secure in their historic-present, and will bring them home into eternity-future.

a2 At 1:1, the word I have translated "expatriates" is *parepídēmos* [Zodhiates, s. v. 3927]. This word means "a foreigner who has settled down, however briefly, next to or among the native people." Other versions translate pilgrims (NKJV), strangers (KJV), strangers in the world (NIV), sojourner (YLT, ASV), elect exiles (ESV), temporary residents (HCSB).

I have translated it "expatriates" because that word exactly communicates the position of God's people in the world. The Writer of Hebrews said the Old Testament believers dwelt in a foreign country and looked for a homeland and a city prepared for them, Hebrews 11:9–10, 13–16. So too, New Testament believers look for Christ to return and take them home to heaven.

Believers, whatever their natural origin may be, are citizens of a heavenly country and city, and therefore while in this world are expatriates of heaven, waiting to go to their homeland. While we wait, we receive "care packages" from home: things such as answered prayer, spiritual blessings, and letters from our heavenly Father, Jesus, and the Holy Spirit. First Peter is one such letter from home.

b At 1:3, the word I have translated "regenerated" is *anagennáō* [Zodhiates, s. v. 313]. *Anagennáō* is a compound word formed from *aná*, "again" (equal to the English "re-" implying repetition), and *gennáō*, to be born; thus *aná-gennáō*, to be born-again, to be regenerated. It is used only here and at 1:23. Other versions translate begotten (KJV, NKJV), begat (ASV), beget (YLT), caused us to be born again (ESV), new birth (HCSB, NIV).

c At 1:3, the phrase, "out from the dead ones," translates *ek nekrós*. This phrase is often translated "from the dead." The word *ek* [Zodhiates, a. v. 1537] is a preposition meaning out of, from. The word *nekrós* [Zodhiates, s. v. 3498] means dead. My translation is intended to emphasize Jesus was truly physically dead and was truly raised out from that state of physical death.

d At 1:4, the unfamiliar "not" translates the Greek character α, alpha, which when preceding a word (known as the alpha privative) negates the meaning. For example, *áphthartos*, is the alpha privative "not" and *phthartós*, corruptible. So *áphthartos* means not-corruptible.

e At 1:5 the word translated "season," is *kairós* [Zodhiates s. v. 2540]. The Greeks had two words for time, One was *chronós* [Zodhiates, s. v. 5550], time measured by the succession moments, such as by a clock. The *chronós* as I write this is 8:53 a.m. The word *kairós* refers to some quality or characteristic of a moment or period of time. As I write this the *kairós* is during the morning, and the season (*kairós*) is autumn. At 1 Peter 1:5 "a salvation ready to be revealed in last season" means a fit or opportune time when the foreordained event will take place. The salvation of the believer will be revealed at the last [*éschatos*, Zodhiates, s. v. 2078], most extreme opportune time. In context Peter refers to full receipt of the promised inheritance.

f1 At 1:11, the words "continually revealing" translate the imperfect tense of *dēlóō* [Zodhiates. s. v. 1213], which means to make manifest, known. The imperfect tense indicates continuous or linear action in past time. I have chosen to understand the word from the prophets' point of view, thus translating it "continually." Although the Spirit worked without cessation (continuously), the prophets received the prophetic word at intervals (continually), just as the Writer of Hebrews said, "in many parts and in many ways," 1:1.

f2 At 1:17, the word I have translated "reverence and caution" is *phóbos* [Zodhiates, s. v. 5401]. This word means "fear," but when used in relation to God means a "deep and reverential sense of accountability toward God." I incorporated the ideas of reverence and accountability in the translation.

f3 At 1:17, "residence as expatriates" is *paroikía* [Zodhiates, s. v. 3940], "residence in a foreign land without the right of citizenship." At 1:1, Peter used *parepídēmos* [Zodhiates, s. v. 3927], "a foreigner who has settled down, however, briefly, next to or among the native people." The concepts are similar, and I translated using the same word, expatriates.

g At 2:1, other translations (the KJV is the exception) obscure Peter's use of an important figure of speech: the polysyndeton, or many-ands. When several words are connected by "and, there is never any climax at the end . . . we are asked to stop at each point, to weigh each matter that is presented to us, and to consider each particular that is thus added and emphasized [Bullinger, *Figures of Speech*, 208].

h At 2:2, "reasonable sincere milk" is the literal translation of *logikós ádolos gála* [Zodhiates, s. v. 3050, 97, 1051]. The key word is *logikós*, pertaining to reason and therefore reasonable. The word *ádolos* is *dólos*, (2:1) deceit, guile, with the alpha privative negating the meaning, so *ádolos* means without deceit or guile, thus sincere. Some translations use "pure"; others "unadulterated."

i At 2:9, "a people purchased" is *peripoíesis* [Zodhiates, s. v. 4047], a word which means "a people acquired or purchased to Himself in a peculiar or unique manner."

j At 2:12, the word translated "peoples" is *éthnos* [Zodhiates, s. v. 1484]. The word means "a multitude, people, race, nation" The Jews used *éthnos* to mean all who were not Jews, i.e., they were gentiles. Most versions translate "gentiles," but that assumes at 1:1, "elect expatriates of the dispersion" Peter is writing only to saved Hebrews, which he is not, as 1:2 and the entire letter indicates. At 2:9, *éthnos* describes Christians, a "holy *éthnos*," that is, a "holy people."

k At 2:17 I have translated *phóbos* [Zodhiates, s. v. 5399] as "reverence." The Old Testament phrase was "fear of YHWH." I used "reverence" to indicate a desire springing up in every believer to manifest God's glory, to bring him honor, to proclaim his goodness and love, and to be known as his child.

l At 2:18, the word "domestics" is *oikétēs* [Zodhiates, s. v. 3610]. The word identified a domestic servant, one of the household, belonging to the family, but not necessarily born in the house. In common terms the *oikétēs* was a slave. There were also slaves who worked in the fields or in the mines. Peter meant any believer who was a member of a household as a slave, regardless of where he worked.

m At 3:15, the word translated "verbal defense" is *apología* [Zodhiates, s. v. 627], to give an answer or speech in defense of oneself.

n1 At 3:18, the words "in flesh" accurately reflect the Greek text, which does not have the definite article. See translation note n2.

n2 At 3:18, the word *pneúma*, "spirit," is not capitalized as in some other versions. Peter is making a comparison between "in flesh" and "in spirit." Jesus died in the sphere of activity of flesh and was made alive in sphere of activity of spirit. He was dead in the material domain but alive in the spirit domain.

o At 3:19, I have translated *én ho* as "in which." The preposition *én* can mean "by" as in instrumentality, but 3:18 has established "in spirit" means the sphere of activity is the spirit domain, and so *én* in 3:19 must be translated "in" [Wallace, *Greek Grammar*, 372]. The point of Peter's words is "in which" sphere of spiritual activity, 3:18, "also having gone to the spirits in prison, he preached." The identity of those human spirits in the spirit domain, is in 3:20.

p At 4:3, the word "worldling" translates *éthnos*. Peter is speaking of the unsaved, who are devoted to the interests and pleasures of this present world. "Worldling" is a word I and others use to describe all persons who are not devoted to the interests and glory of God.

q At 4:14, the word I have translated "belittled" is *oneidizō* Zodhiates, s. v. 3679], to defame, reproach, or disparage with abusive words. I chose "belittled" as a suitable synonym for "reproach" because it communicates the verbally abusive aspect of *oneidizō*.

r At 4:14, the sentence "Indeed on their part it is slander; but on your part it is glory" is thought by many to be an explanatory scribal addition. I chose to include the sentence. Ancient evidence for the sentence includes Cyprian, (A.D. 200–258) in Epistle LV, *To the People of Thibaris, Exhorting to Martyrdom*, paragraph 2, and his treatise *On the Exhortation to Martyrdom*, paragraph 9 [Roberts and Donaldson, *Ante-Nicene Fathers*, 5:348, 501]. The textual evidence is divided. See discussion in my commentary on 1 Peter.

s At 4:16, where I have "in this name" [*ónoma*, Zodhiates s. v. 3686]," the Textus Receptus has "in this matter" [*méros*, Zodhiates, s. v. 3313]. The sentence is about suffering "as a Christian" therefore "glorify God in this name" Christian, through your suffering.

t At 5:3, the word I have translated "congregation" is *klḗros*

[Zodhiates, s. v. 2819], a lot, in the sense of a portion, allotment, part, share, or inheritance. The NKJV, NIV, HCSB translate "those entrusted to you," whereas the KJV used "God's heritage." Because Peter is speaking of pastoral oversight of "the flock," *poímnion* [Zodhiates, s. v. 4169], it seemed best to view *kléros* as in parallel with *poímnion*, and translate it "congregation."

u At 5:4, "unfading amaranths" is *amárantinos* [Zodhiates, s. v. 262], made of amaranths. Amaranth is a plant used as a food source for its grain and leaves. The flower of the plant is long-lasting, giving rise to its use in ancient times as a symbol of immortality. The sentence is not, as in other translations, receive the unfading crown of glory, but receive the crown of glory made of unfading *amárantinos*, which symbolize the glory received is endless.

v At 5:8, the word I have translated "swallow" is *katapínō* [Zodhiates, s. v. 2666], literally to swallow as in drinking, whether in a natural or figurative sense. This fits with the lion imagery, as lions do not chew their food but tear off and swallow chunks of flesh. The same term is used in the LXX concerning the great fish which was "to *swallow up* Jonas" [Brenton, 1075].

w At 5:12, the text reads the name *Silouanós*, which transliterated is "Silvanus" [Zodhiates, s. v. 4610]. The name *Silouanós* is the same person as *Sílas* [Zodhiates, s. v. 4609], appearing at Acts 15:22, 27, 32, 34, 40; 16:19, 25, 29; 17:4, 10, 14, 15; 18:5. Luke calls him Silas but Paul and Peter always refer to him as Silvanus. I have substituted *Sílas* for *Silouanós* to maintain the relationship with the many verses where the person Silvanus is identified as Silas.

Second Peter Translation Notes

a At 1:5, the word translated "add" is *epichorēgéō* [Zodhiates, s. v. 2023], to add more unto. To develop one virtue in the exercise of another. "In your faith supply virtue, and in your virtue knowledge,' etc." [Vincent, 1:679].

b At 1:12, some manuscripts have *ameléō* [Zodhiates, s. v. 272], to neglect. Other manuscripts have *méllō* [Zodhiates, s. v. 3195], to intend. The difference is not in meaning but in expression: *ameléō*, "I will not neglect"; *méllō*, "I will always."

c At 1:15 Peter doesn't use the specific Greek word for death, *thanátos*, but wrote *éxodos*, a departure [Zodhiates, s. v. 1841]. Death, the believer's *éxodos* from the world, is the beginning of eternal life.

d At 1:16, the word I have translated "copied" is *exakoulouthéō* [Zodhiates, s. v. 1811], literally to follow, but metaphorically, as it is used here, to copy after, to conform to.

e1 At 1:20, the word I have translated "one's own" is *ídios* [Zodhiates, s. v. 2398], "one's own, private, particular, individual."

e2 At 1:20, the word "interpretation" is the Greek word *epílusis* [Zodhiates, s. v. 1955], meaning exposition, interpretation. Peter means the writers of Scripture did not interpret the word God gave them, but wrote what God gave them. One could more expansively translate, "no prophecy . . . is the prophet's own interpretation."

f At 2:1, the word translated "smuggle in" is *pareiságō* [Zodhiates, s. v. 3919], to bring in by the side of, to introduce along with others.

g At 2:4, the word other versions translate "hell" is *tártaróō* [Zodhiates, s. v. 5020], "Tartarus," which is not the same as hades or hell. Hades is the location of unsaved human beings between physical death and final judgment, Luke 16:23. Hell is the location of unsaved human beings in the lake of fire after final judgment (known as *géenna*, aka Gehenna, in the gospels). *Tártaróō* is the location in the spirit domain for certain fallen angels, known otherwise as the abyss, Luke 8:31; Revelation 9:1; 20:1, who demonized (inhabited, indwelt) human beings, or committed other, unknown, crimes requiring immediate imprisonment. See my commentary on 2 Peter for a discussion of *tártaróō*.

h At 2:17, the phrase "the darkness of the spiritual darkness" are the words *zóphos* [Zodhiates, s. v. 2217], "darkness" and *skótos*

[Zodhiates, s. v. 4655], "spiritual darkness." The word *skótos* is literally physical darkness, figuratively spiritual darkness, cf. Matthew 8:12; John 3:19; Romans 2:19; Jude 1:13. The word *zóphos*, is not literal darkness, because that would contradict a lake of fire, but the darkness of those who are spiritually dark, the unsaved spiritually dead.

i At 3:3 what others translate as "the last days" is properly "last of the days." The word "last," and the definite article, and the word "days" are plurals in the Genitive case. See 1 Peter 1:5; 1 John 2:18; Jude 18. What was a "last hour/last time/last of the days" to Peter, John, and Jude was before the Day of the Lord, 2 Peter 3:10, and the coming Antichrist, 1 John 2:18. Those three persons, Peter, John, and Jude, said the first century times in which they were living were the "last hour/last time/last of the days." Thus the "last hour/last time/last of the days" is the entire NT church age ending at the rapture.

j At 3:7 the word "earth" is *gê* [Zodhiates. s. v. 1093], the physical earth, versus in 3:6 the word "world" is *kósmos* [Zodhiates, s. v. 2889], an ordered system. The world human beings had made in Noah's time, a *kósmos*, perished in the flood, but the earth, *gê*, remains reserved for judgment by fire.

k At 3:9, where other versions have "not willing any should perish, the Greek text does not have a word corresponding to "any." The text is this, "not willing *tís* to perish." The word *tís* [Zodhiates, s. v. 5100] means "one, someone, a certain one." God is not wanting some to perish, indicating his action to save certain ones (*tís*). But at the same time God is also willing all [*pás*, Zodhiates, s. v. 3956] come to repentance, indicating God does not prevent any from coming and believing. Looked at doctrinally, election guarantees the salvation of those whom God has chosen, but says nothing pro or con about those whom God has not chosen. Election speaks of the elect, no one else.

First John Translation Notes

a. At 1:2, the Greek word I have translated "intently" is *horáō*, to see with perception. The same word was used at 1:1 and there I translated it "perceived." I chose to translate this occurrence as "intently" to convey the sense of evaluation leading to understanding, which in turn led to eyewitness testimony, resulting in proclamation of the Word who is the Life.

b At 1:6 is the first use of the word "habitually, which I use throughout 1 John. I also use "continually" or a similar word. These words reflect the present tense of the verb. In the present tense the action is viewed as in progress, e.g., "I am reading." Using a word to indicate the present tense in 1 John is controversial. For a discussion of the issues see my book, *A Private Commentary on the Bible: John's Epistles*, Appendix One: Translating the Present tense in 1 John.

c At 1:8–10, two words are used for sin. In 1:8 the word is *hamartía*, [Zodhiates, s. v. 266], the sin attribute resident in human nature. In 1:9, 10, the word is *hamartánō* [Zodhiates, s. v. 264], acts of sinning.

d At 2:7, the translation "you have had constantly" reflects the imperfect tense of the verb *échō*, to have [Zodhiates, s. v. 2192]. The imperfect indicates past action that is in progress or ongoing.

e At 2:12, the translation "permanently forgiven" from *aphiēmi* [Zodhiates, s. v. 863] to forgive. The word is in the grammatical form perfect indicative passive. The perfect tense indicates a completed action or condition having continuing results. The condition "forgiven" having taken place, it continues into the future: permanently forgiven.

f At 2:13, the translation "evildoer" is *ponērós* [Zodhiates, s. v. 4190], evil in a moral or spiritual sense. Things are not evil, people are evil. Adjectives modify nouns, but no noun is present for the adjective *ponērós*. Because people, not things, are evil, we could supply a noun: "the evil person." Most versions supply a noun: KJV, NKJV: wicked one; ASV, HCSB, NIV, ESV: evil one.

g At 2:17, the translation "being caused to pass away" may not seem right to some. The verb "passing" is in the passive voice. The reason it does not seem right is readers are used to every other translation, which change the passive voice to the active voice. In the active voice the world is doing the action, causing itself to pass away. In the passive voice John uses, the action is being done to the world, it is being caused to pass away.

In John's letter, the "world" is what sinner's create. The "cause and effect" relationship between God's laws and the world naturally results in the impermanence of all sinners have created. The inflexible nature of God's laws causes the world to be passing away. But "the person habitually doing God's will abides for the age." Why? Same reason, God's laws. The person "habitually doing God's will" is the saved, born-again believer in Christ as Savior. God's works are naturally permanent, because they don't to violate God's laws. So also the believer and his or her works done within God's will.

h At 2:24 the translation "each one of you" reflects the plural number of *humeís* [Zodhiates, s. v. 4771] meaning John is writing to each reader, and so throughout this paragraph.

i At 2:29, where I have translated "born from him," most versions translate "born of him." The proposition is *ek* [Zodhiates, s. v. 1537], which may be translated "out of, from, because of, by" in respect to source, cause, or means. Here *ek* indicates source.

j At 3:1, the words "and we are," *kai esmén*, are not in the Textus Receptus used by the KJV and NKJV, but are in many of the Alexandrian and Western manuscripts [Metzger, *Textual*, 642] used by the ESV, HCSB, NIV. I have chosen to include the words. The question implied by the aorist subjunctive of *kaléō*, "should be named," seems to require a response: "and we are." The subjunctive is the mood of possibility or probability ["the verbal action (or state] as uncertain but probable," Wallace, 461]. Because of the love the Father has given to believers, believers should be and are named children of God.

k At 3:14, "we have permanently passed" is from the verb *metabaínō* [Zodhiates, s. v. 3327] in the perfect tense. The meaning of *metabaínō* is "to pass or go from one place or state to another." The perfect tense indicates an action completed in the past but having continuing results; a continuing state of affairs or condition. The state or condition John describes is the transition from spiritual death to eternal life experienced through salvation. The perfect tense indicates the new state of eternal life is permanent.

l At 3:17, the translation, "may have as a constant possession" reflects the present subjunctive form of the verb *échō*, "to have."

The use of the subjunctive in this context expresses probability: "may have." The present tense indicates continuous action: "constant possession."

m At 3:19, the translation "quiet" reflects the meaning of *peíthō*, to persuade [Zodhiates, s. v. 3892]. When our conduct is according to God's laws, our conscience persuades us all is well. I have substituted the result, a quiet conscience, for the cause, to persuade. The KJV, NKJV, ASV, YLT, and ESV translate *peíthō* with "assure," but this is certainly not correct, because that is not what the word means. Nor does it mean "rest" (NIV), nor "convince" (HCSB, NET). The Tyndale (AD 1526) and Geneva (AD 1560) translations used "quiet."

n At 4:3b, the Greek text literally reads, "now this is that of the antichrist which you have heard that is coming." I have inserted the word "spirit" (although "disposition" is another good word choice) because the subject is "every spirit (*pneúma*) who does not confess Jesus Christ is come in the flesh."

o At 4:18, the word I have translated "torment" is translated by others as "punishment." This word is *kólasis* [Zodhiates, s. v. 2851]. The word does have the idea of punishment for correction. The correct translation is a matter of the relationship between a sinning believer and God. God acts toward sin in one of three ways: Retribution, in judicial vengeance for the crime, with no view toward redemption or restoration. Redemptive, to save the sinner from his sin. Remedial, to discipline and correct his saved children in order to restore them to righteousness and fellowship. What is in view in 4:18 is God's remedial action toward his saved people, which is why I have translated *kólasis* as "torment." Translating *kólasis* as "punishment" may be misunderstood as retribution, an action God never takes toward his saved people, cf. Romans 8:1. The believer who is not abiding (thus love is not completed) will experience fear (*phóbos*) and torment (*kólasis*), but the believer who is abiding does not have torment (*kólasis*) because he does not have fear (*phóbos*).

p At 5:1, the three uses of *gennáō* [Zodhiates, s. v. 1080], "to be begotten or be born," pose a translation problem for the newer versions. The NIV, HCSB, ESV, and NLT want to avoid using the older words "begot" and "begotten." In so doing they interpret, rather than translate, *gennáō*.

q In 5:7, 8, the Textus Receptus adds "in heaven: the Father, the Word, and the Holy Spirit—and these three are one." These words are only in later editions of Erasmus' Greek text (christened "Textus Receptus" by its Dutch publisher). In his first edition (1515) Erasmus did not include the words. When challenged, he replied he would add them if they could be found in any Greek text. A manuscript (now known as manuscript 61) was produced and Erasmus added the words into the third, 1522 edition.

The passage is present in only eight Greek manuscripts from the 10th, 14th, 16th, and 18th centuries, and in four of those it is not biblical text but has been added as a marginal note. The passage is not in any of the ancient versions: Syriac, Coptic, Armenian, Ethiopian, Arabic, Slavonic. It is not found in the Old Latin of Tertullian (AD 155–240), Cyprian (AD 200–258), or Augustine (AD 354–430), nor in Jerome's Vulgate (copy of AD 541–546), nor the codex Amiatinus (copied before AD 716) [Metzger, *Textual*, 648]. The passage does not appear in the Latin Vulgate before AD 800 [Metzger, *Text*, 102]. It is not quoted by any of the Greek Fathers. The weight of manuscript evidence and church history is against the text being genuine.

r In 5:13, In did not include the words "and that you may continue to believe on the name of the Son of God," These words, are found in three Greek manuscripts (K L P) and most Greek minuscule manuscripts (minuscule: written in all lower case letters). Through these manuscripts the words found their way into the Textus Receptus. The reading without those words is found in Alexandrian manuscripts B and ℵ, and Syriac manuscripts. It is possible the shorter reading came into being to remove an original reading that was perceived to be a redundancy created by copyists in earlier manuscripts; or some copyists might have believed the longer reading was an assimilation of John 20:31 [Metzger, *Textual*, 649]. The interpretation is not affected by the words. The shorter reading seemed most likely the autograph.

s At 5:18, the translation issue is the identity of the "one" having been born from God. In some manuscripts the "him" in the phrase "guards him" is the pronoun *autón*. In other manuscripts the pronoun is *èautón*, "himself." I have used those manuscripts with the pronoun *autón*. The translation is, "The One [the God-man] having been born from God guards him [*autón*, the believer]." I believe it is more consistent with the Scripture that Christ keeps the believer.

Second John Translation Notes

a At 1:3, the translation "God who is Father" reflects the grammar in which both God and Father are nouns in the genitive case, a genitive of apposition. The nouns "God" and "Father" are equal terms describing the same Person, but the second genitive (Father) is part of the larger category of the first genitive (God) [Wallace, *Grammar*, 95–96]. God is Father, but not only Father.

Third John Translation Notes

a At 1:13, the translation is based partly on Robertson's [6:266] understanding of the Greek text.

Jude Translation Notes

a At 1:4, the word translated "perverting" is *metatíthēmi* [Zodhiates, s. v. 3346], to transpose, transfer, translate. The idea in Jude is to transfer to another use or purpose, in other words, to pervert the proper use or purpose, hence the translation "perverting."

b I have structured 1:7 to capture the grammatical relationship between the verbs and the nouns. The nouns "Gomorrah" and "cities" are feminine gender in the nominative case. The noun "Sodom" is neuter gender in the nominative case. The verbs "having practiced fornication" and "having followed after strange flesh" modify the nominative feminine and neuter nouns. I have also tried to capture the syntax revealed in the text word order: "as Sodom and Gomorrah and the around them cities the same with them manner having practiced fornication and having followed after strange flesh" etc. The meaning is the cities practiced fornication and went after strange flesh, just like Sodom and Gomorrah practiced fornication and went after strange flesh. The example the cities provide for Jude's exhortation is eternal punishment for one of the characteristics of apostasy: defilement.

c At 1:8, I have translated *enupniázō* [Zodhiates, s. v. 1797], as deceivers instead of the usual translation "dreamers." The point is not that they are dreaming, but that their philosophies and actions are as empty and vain as dreams.

d At 1:12, the words "providing for themselves" translate *poimaínō* [Zodhiates, s. v. 4165]. This word means "to feed and tend a flock of sheep." Figuratively it means to care for and provide for others. Apostates shepherd only themselves; they provide for themselves only.

e At 1:13, the phrase "the darkness of the spiritual darkness" are the words *zóphos* [Zodhiates, s. v. 2217], "darkness" and *skótos* [Zodhiates, s. v. 4655], "spiritual darkness." The word *skótos* is literally physical darkness, figuratively spiritual darkness, cf. Matthew 8:12; John 3:19; Romans 2:19; Jude 1:13. The word *zóphos*, is not literal darkness, because that would contradict a lake of fire, but the darkness of those who are spiritually dark, the unsaved spiritually dead.

f At 1:14, "the Lord came" correctly translates the third person singular in the aorist tense indicative mood, active voice. The aorist indicative expresses a single act without a specific reference to the time of the act: the act happened. The third person singular of "I come" is "he came." The result is the past expression of a future event, "the Lord came." God coming to punish the ungodly was a future event to Enoch—the Noahic Flood. Enoch spoke as though the action had happened in order to indicate the certainty of the event. Jude uses this prophecy to speak of Christ's yet-future coming to punish the ungodly is just as certain to happen.

g At 1:18, the word I have translated "false prophets" is translated "scoffers" by others. The word is *empaíktēs* [Zodhiates, s. v. 1703], which means "a mocker, scoffer, spoken of imposters, false prophets." Considering Jude's theme of apostates in the church teaching false doctrines, "false prophets" is the correct translation.

Revelation Translation Notes

a At 1:5 older translations say "washed" where I translate "releasing." The difference is in the texts. The Byzantine texts have *luou*, washed, the Alexandrian texts read *luo*, loosed. As you can see the difference is one letter. Scribes may have added a letter, or deleted a letter, at some point as the autograph, or copies of the autograph, were being copied. Either word clearly indicates the teaching of Scripture, that Jesus redeemed believers from the penalty, power, and pleasure of sin, and will shortly deliver the believer from the very presence of sin.

A choice had to be made. On the one hand, there is the figure of "washing of water with the Word," Ephesians 5:26, and "washing of regeneration and renewing of the Holy Spirit," Titus 3:5. In Revelation 7:14, "they have washed their robes and made them white in the blood of the lamb." On the other hand, *luo*, loosed is in the older manuscripts. Sinners loosed or released from sins by Christ's death (his blood) is directly related to forgiveness, Romans 3:25; 5:9. A choice had to be made. I chose to use *luo*, loosed, as more consistent with redemption "from our sins."

b At 1:9, I have translated *hupomonē* [Zodhiates, s. v. 5281], usually translated "endurance, patience", as "endurance of circumstances." The reason is another Greek word, *makrothumía* [Zodhiates, s. v. 3115], also means endurance or patience. But whereas *makrothumía* means endurance or patience with people, *hupomonē* means endurance or patience with things or circumstances.

c At 1:18 and throughout the translation, I have not capitalized the word "hades." "Hades" is capitalized when referring to a location, e.g., the Greek mythological "Hades" or the Greek god "Hades." I have made a choice not to capitalize hades or hell to avoid any confusion with Greek mythology. The Scripture hades is a location in the spirit domain where the souls of unsaved human beings go after physical death to await resurrection and final judgment, Luke 16:23. The Scripture hell is the lake of fire, the place of endless conscious torment for unsaved human beings and fallen angels. Revelation 20:4–6, 10–15.

d At 1:20 I have translated *mustérion* [Zodhiates, s. v. 3466] as "secret," versus other versions that transliterate the word as "mystery." In Scripture, a *mustérion* is secret or hidden knowledge that is about to be revealed.

e At 2:9, some manuscripts in the Byzantine group, on which the Textus Receptus is based, have the words "works and" between "I know your" and "tribulation." The words are not present in older manuscripts. If the words were present in the autograph, there is no rational reason to have removed them. Some long-ago scribe added "works" to make all the letters begin the same.

f At 2:9 the word I have translated "helpless poverty" is *ptōchós* [Zodhiates, s. v. 4432]. The Greeks had two words for poor/poverty. The *pénēs* [Zodhiates, s. v. 3993] poor was the person working daily to provide for himself. The *ptōchós* poor was completely helpless and must beg daily to provide for himself. Christians are often *ptōchós*, not because of disability, but hindered by persecution from employment.

g At 2:13, Some Byzantine text types (from which the Textus Receptus was derived) have the words "your works" between "I know" and "where you dwell." These words are missing in all older manuscripts, and are likely the result of some long-ago scribe trying to make all the letters begin the same. If they were present in the autograph there is no rational reason to have removed the words.

h At 3:3, I have translated *grēgoreúō* [Zodhiates., s. v. 1127], as "though you may watch." The Greek grammar is the subjunctive mood, indicating possibility. Literally the verse reads, "if therefore not you may watch." I translated, "Therefore, if not, though you may watch" etc. Other versions translate as though Christ's coming is dependent upon their not watching, "If you will not watch I will come like a thief." He is coming whether one watches, or not. Many watch but fail to do what Christ requires. That is the point.

i1 At 3:10 a phrase occurs that is used repeatedly in Revelation to identify the unsaved. The phrase is literally, "those dwelling upon the earth." I have consistently given this phrase as "earth dwellers" wherever it occurs in the text of the Revelation.

i2 At 3:14, the word I have translated "Truth" is *amḗn* [Zodhiates, s. v. 281]. The Greek *amḗn* is the transliteration of the Hebrew ʾ*āmēn*, and is usually transliterated into the English "amen." I chose to give a translation versus a transliteration. The word means truth, truly, trustworthy, firm, steady, and at the end of a prayer can mean "so be it," as an expression of desire. When the original readers read "these things says the *amḗn*," they understood Jesus to be saying, "These things says the Truth," for they knew Jesus had said in another place, "I, I am the way, and the truth, and the life," John 14:6.

j At 4:3, I have translated *líthos íaspis kai sárdios* (vocabulary forms) as "stone, crystalline and blood-red." The word *íaspis* [Zodhiates, s. v. 2393] is usually translated "jasper." The word *sárdios* [Zodhiates, s. v. 4556] is usually translated "sardius." These are modern names derived by transliterating the ancient words.

Modern sciences of chemistry and crystallography classify stones according to mineral composition and structure. The ancients essentially classified stones according to color, shape, and use, so modern names do not correspond. I have made a choice not to use the modern names for the stones, but to use the colors. In the Scripture and in John's historical-cultural context, colors had meaning.

See *A Private Commentary on the Bible: Revelation 1–7*, for a lengthy discussion.

Revelation Translations Notes

k At the end of 5:14, I have not included the words, "Him who lives for the ages of the ages." These words appear in the AD 1516–1633 editions of Erasmus' Greek text (the "Textus Receptus," so named by the Dutch publisher of the 1633 edition), and translations using Erasmus' Greek text.

l At the end of 6:1, most versions translate *érchomai* [Zodhiates, s. v. 2064] as "come" which led certain scribes to add the words "and see," as though the word *érchomai* was addressed to John [Metzger, *Textual*, 667]. The word *érchomai* means "to come, to go, to move along." Because John saw something "went out" when the seal was broken, it seems *érchomai* is directed toward the mounted horseman telling him to "Go!" This is confirmed when we see *érchomai* is not said when the fifth and sixth seals are broken. If the living creatures were saying "Come" to John when a seal is broken, there is no rational reason "Come" is not said to John when the fifth and sixth seals are broken.

m At 6:6 the word "measure" is *choinix* [Zodhiates, s. v. 5518] a word indicating a certain Greek measure for dry things. The English equivalent is thought to be a pint, but is in reality unknown. Some translations say "measure," and others "quart." For all we know a *choinix* was equivalent to the smallest Roman dry measure of .28 pints.

n At 6:14 I have translated *apochōrízō* [Zodhiates, s. v. 673] as "torn apart and the parts were." This word means to separate, to disjoin. To disjoin is to take apart, to separate the pieces.

o At 7:2, some versions say, "ascending from the east," KJV, NIV, NKJV, NLT. The word these versions are translating "east" is *anatolé* [Zodhiates, s. v. 395], "the dawn." The word is used ten times in the New Testament. This word may be translated as the geographic direction east or as the dawning of the sun. In one scripture, Luke 1:78, the word has a metaphorical sense. For Revelation 7:2 I chose the literal "dawning," indicating direction and possibly the time of day.

p At 8:13 where I have written "eagle," from *aetós* in the Alexandrian manuscripts, the Byzantine manuscripts have *ággelos* (messenger; angel). The weight of textual evidence at 8:13 supports *aetós*, eagle. The use of "one" (in both manuscript types) rather than "another" is against the word being *ággelos*. The scriptural support for *ággelos* in 8:13 versus *aetós* raises the question why any scribe would substitute *aetós* for *ággelos* if *ággelos* was the autograph. For these reasons I have retained the reading *aetós*. There are also scriptural reasons for *aetós*, see *A Private Commentary on the Bible: Revelation 8–16*.

q The last sentence of 12:17, "And he stood upon the sand of the sea," or as some number it 12:18, is properly the first sentence of 13:1. I remind the reader the division of the Bible into chapters and verses was made by the French printer Robert Estienne (1503–1559, aka Robert Stephanus) for the Geneva Bible, and was after adopted by all versions.

r1 At 13:1, in some manuscripts the sentence reads, "And he stood upon the sand of the sea," referring to the dragon. In other manuscripts the sentence reads, "And I stood upon the sand of the sea," referring to John. Contextually, the dragon is the proper subject of the sentence, which is why in some manuscripts the sentence is attached to 12:17, or numbered as 12:18.

r2 At 13:5, some versions have "he." The Greek text has the neuter pronoun "it." Throughout the passage the text has the neuter "it" for the beast and false prophet.

s At 14:20, the measurement "184 miles" is in the text "one thousand six hundred stadia." One Roman stadia was 606.9 feet. The math (606.9' X 1600 stadia)/5,280' = 183.9 miles. I rounded up.

t At 16:16, the word "Harmagedon" transliterates the Greek word *àrmagedṓn* [Zodhiates s. v. 717]. In Greek the rough breathing accent over the initial *à* is transliterated "*ha*." I have transliterated *àrmagedṓn* to Harmagedon for the same reason I transliterate *Iēsoús* to "Jesus" and *Iàkōbos* to Jacob (versus the substitution "James"). Those words are names, and in most translations names are transliterated.

u At 16:21, the words "about eighty-five pounds" translate the Greek word for "talent," a unit of weight. The weight of one talent varies with the source consulted. I used 39 kg/85.98 lbs. as about midway way in the estimates. [Schimdt, *Biblical Measures and their Translation*.]

v At 17:1 the word translated "whore" is *pórnē* [Zodhiates, s. v. 4204]. This word means to sell sex, thus prostitution. This word is translated harlot, whore, prostitute in the various translations. I did not use the word "prostitute" like many modern versions, because the woman does not sell sex, but represents false religion. A whore is sexually promiscuous, but does not necessarily sell sex.

w At 19:1, 3, 4, 6 the word I have translated "Praise to Yah" is *allēlouía* [Zodhiates, s. v. 239], more commonly transliterated "alleluia" or "hallelujah." The word "Yah" is a shortened form of God's name in the Old Testament, YHWH, occurring twenty-four times in the Psalms. The word *allēlouía* occurs only in Revelation 19.

x At 21:3, some texts have after "God himself" the words "their God."

y At 21:8, the word I have translated "fearful" is *deilós* [Zodhiates, s. v. 1169], "timid, fearful." Modern versions translate this word "cowardly" or "cowards." Although cowards or the cowardly may be timid or fearful, the translation "cowards" or "the cowardly" is not a translation but an interpretation. The word is used three times in the New Testament. Matthew 8:26; Mark 4:40; Revelation 21:8. In no use does it mean cowards or the cowardly.

z At 21:16, twelve thousand stadia = 1,379.3 miles. I rounded down.

aa At 21:17, one hundred forty four cubits = 246 feet.

bb For 21:18–21, the stones, see translation note j.

cc At 21:27, the words I have translated "anything detestable to God" are literally "make abomination." An abomination, *bdélugma* [Zodhiates, s. v. 946] may be defined in this context as, "generally that which is detestable to God."

Primary Translation Resources

The ASV, ESV, HCSB, KJV, NIV, NKJV, NLT, YLT, sourced from PC Study Bible®, version 5, release 5.2. Copyright © 1988–2008, by BibleSoft, Inc.

The AD 1535 New Testament translation by William Tyndale, sourced from the New Matthew Bible (NMB), copyright 2016 by Ruth Magnusson (Davis).

The New Testament text at www.biblehub.com was used as the primary text and for grammatical and lexical information.

The Greek New Testament, Kurt Aland, ed. 3rd ed. 1975.

Brenton, Sir Lancelot, C. L. *The Septuagint with Apocrypha: English*. London: Samuel Bagster & Sons, 1851. Reprinted http://ecmarsh.com, 2010.

Green, Jay P. Sr. *The Interlinear Bible, Hebrew-Greek-English*. Peabody, MA: Hendrickson Publishers, 1986.

Kittel, Gerhard, and Gerhard Friedrich. *Theological Dictionary of the New Testament*. 10 vols. Translated by Geoffrey W. Bromiley. Grand Rapids, MI: Eerdmans Publishing, 1967.

Metzger, Bruce M. *A Textual Commentary on the Greek New Testament*. 2nd ed. USA: United Bible Societies, 1994.

_____. *The Text of the New Testament, Its Transmission, Corruption, and Restoration*. London: Oxford University Press, 1964.

Moulton, J. H., and G. Milligan. *Vocabulary of the Greek Testament*. 1930. Reprinted, Peabody, MA: Hendrickson Publishers, 1997.

Schmidt Peter. *Biblical Measures and their Translation*. SIL Electronic Working Papers 2014-003, February 2014, © 2014 Peter Schmidt and SIL International®. All rights reserved.

Wallace, Daniel B. *Greek Grammar Beyond the Basics*. Grand Rapids, MI: Zondervan, 1996.

Zodhiates, Spiros. *The Complete Word Study Dictionary New Testament*. Revised. Chattanooga, TN: AMG Publishers, 1993.

Translation Notes Resources

In addition to the primary translation resources, the following were consulted for translations of specific scriptures, or mentioned as a resource for additional information.

Black, David Alan. *Why Four Gospels.* 2nd ed. Gonzalez, FL: 2010.

Black, David Alan. Ed. *Perspectives on the Ending of Mark.* Nashville, TN: Broadman and Holman, 2008.

Bock, Darrell L. and Gregory J. Herrick. *Jesus in Context.* Grand Rapids, MI: Baker Academic, 2005.

Brenton, Sir Lancelot, C. L. *The Septuagint with Apocrypha: English.* London: Samuel Bagster & Sons, 1851. Reprinted http://ecmarsh.com, 2010.

Bromiley, Geoffrey W. Gen. Ed. *The International Standard Bible Encyclopedia.* Revised 1982. Reprinted, Grand Rapids, MI: William B. Eerdmans Publishing Company, 1992.

Bullinger, E. W. *Figures of Speech Used in the Bible.* 1898. Reprinted, Grand Rapids, MI: Baker Book House, 1968.

Carson, D. A. *The Gospel According to John.* Pillar New Testament Commentary. Grand Rapids, MI: William B Eerdmans Publishing, 1991.

Ciampa, Roy E. *The First Letter to the Corinthians.* PNTC. Grand Rapids, MI: Eerdmans Publishing, 2010.

Edersheim, Alfred. *The Life and Times of Jesus the Messiah.* 1883. Reprinted, Grand Rapids, MI: Eerdmans Publishing, 1971.

Fee, Gordon D. *The First Epistle to the Corinthians.* NICNT. Grand Rapids, MI: Eerdmans Publishing, 2014.

Garland, David E. *1 Corinthians*, ECNT. Grand Rapids, MI: Baker Academic, 2003.

Geldenhuys, Norval. *Commentary on the Gospel of Luke.* NICNT. Grand Rapids, MI: Eerdmans Publishing, 1951.

Harris, Murray J. *Exegetical Guide to the Greek New Testament: Colossians and Philemon.* Nashville, TN: Broadman and Holman, 2013.

Harris, R. Laird; Gleason L. Archer, Jr.; and Bruce K. Waltke. *Theological Wordbook of the Old Testament.* 2 vols. Chicago, IL: Moody Press, 1980.

Hoehner, Harold W. *Ephesians, An Exegetical Commentary.* Grand Rapids, MI: Baker Academic, 2002.

Hogg, C. F. and W. E. Vine. *The Epistle to the Galatians.* 1921. Reprinted, London: 1959.

Hollingsworth, David R. and James D. Quiggle. *New Testament Chronology.* Amazon/KDP, 2014.

Lane, William. *Hebrews 1–8.* Word Biblical Commentary. Waco, TX: Word Inc. 1991.

Lightfoot, John B. *Commentary on the Epistles of St. Paul: Colossians and Philemon.* 1875. Reprinted. Peabody, MA: Hendrickson Publishers, 1995.

_____. *Commentary on the Epistles of St. Paul: Galatians.* 1865. Reprinted. Peabody, MA: Hendrickson Publishers, 1995.

_____. *Commentary on the New Testament from the Talmud and Hebraica.* 1859. Reprinted. Peabody, MA: Hendrickson Publishers, 1995.

Milligan, George. *St. Paul's Epistles to the Thessalonians.* 1908. Reprinted. Minneapolis, MN: Klock & Klock Publishers, 1980.

Mounce, William D. *Basics of Biblical Greek Grammar.* Grand Rapids, MI: Zondervan, 2009.

_____. *Complete Expository Dictionary of Old and New Testament Words.* Grand Rapids, MI: Zondervan, 2006.

O'Brien, Peter T. *Colossians, Philemon.* WBC, vol. 44. Waco, TX: Word Books, 1982.

Perkins, Larry J. *The Pastoral Letters, A Handbook on the Greek Text.* Waco, TX: Baylor University Press, 2017.

Pink, A. W. *Exposition of First John 1 & 2.* 1950–1953. Reprinted, Lafayette, IN: Sovereign Grace Publishers, 2001.

Quiggle, James D. *A Private Commentary on the Bible: 1 Peter.* Amazon/KDP, 2012.

_____. *A Private Commentary on the Bible: 2 Peter.* Amazon/KDP, 2012.

_____. *A Private Commentary on the Bible: Ephesians.* Amazon/KDP, 2012, 2020.

_____. *A Private Commentary on the Bible: John 1–12.* Amazon/KDP, 2014.

_____. *A Private Commentary on the Bible: John's Epistles.* Amazon/KDP, 2016.

_____. *A Private Commentary on the Bible: Luke's Gospel 1:1–12:59.* Amazon/KDP, 2021.

_____. *A Private Commentary on the Bible: Mark's Gospel.* Amazon/KDP, 2016.

_____. *A Private Commentary on the Bible: Matthew's Gospel.* Amazon/KDP, 2016.

_____. *A Private Commentary on the Bible: Revelation 1–7.* Amazon/KDP, 2022.

_____. *A Private Commentary on the Bible: Revelation 8–16*. Amazon/KDP, 2022.

_____. *A Private Commentary on the Bible: Thessalonians*. Amazon/KDP, 2021.

_____. *The Old Ten In the New Covenant*. Amazon/KDP, 2022.

Roberts, Alexander, and James Donaldson. *Ante-Nicene Fathers*. Vol. 5. *Hippolytus, Cyprian, Caius, Novation, Appendix*. 1886. Reprinted, Peabody, MA: Hendrickson, 1995.

Robertson, A. T. *Word Pictures in the New Testament*. Vol. 6. Nashville, TN: Broadman Press, 1932.

Silva, Moisés. Revision Editor. *New International Dictionary of New Testament Theology and Exegesis*. Grand Rapids, MI: Zondervan, 2014.

Trench, Richard C. *Commentary on the Epistles to the Seven Churches in Asia*. London, 1897.

Ramsay William M., Sir. *Was Christ Born at Bethlehem?* 1898. Reprinted. Minneapolis, MN: James Family Publishers, 1978.

Vincent, Marvin R. *Word Studies in the New Testament*, 1887. Reprinted. Grand Rapids: MI: Eerdmans, 1977.

Vlachos, Chris A. *Exegetical Guide to the Greek New Testament: James*. Nashville, TN: Broadman and Holman, 2013.

Internet

The New Schaff-Herzog Encyclopedia of Religious Knowledge.

BOOKS BY JAMES D. QUIGGLE

DOCTRINAL SERIES

Biblical History
Adam and Eve, a Biography and Theology
Angelology, a True History of Angels

Essays
Biblical Essays
Biblical Essays II
Biblical Essays III
Biblical Essays IV

Marriage and Family
Marriage and Family: A Biblical Perspective
Biblical Homosexuality
A Biblical Response to Same-gender Marriage

Doctrinal and Practical Christianity
First Steps, Becoming a Follower of Jesus Christ
A Christian Catechism (with Christopher McCuin)
Why and How to do Bible Study
Thirty-Six Essentials of the Christian Faith
The Literal Hermeneutic, Explained and Illustrated
The Old Ten In the New Covenant
Christian Living and Doctrine
Spiritual Gifts
Why Christians Should Not Tithe

Dispensational Theology
A Primer On Dispensationalism
Understanding Dispensational Theology
Covenants and Dispensations in the Scripture
Dispensational Soteriology
Dispensational Eschatology, An Explanation and Defense of the Doctrine
Rapture: A Bible Study on the Rapture of the New Testament Church
Antichrist, His Genealogy, Kingdom, and Religion

God and Man
God's Choices, Doctrines of Foreordination, Election, Predestination

Books By James D. Quiggle

God Became Incarnate
Life, Death, Eternity
Did Jesus Go To Hell?

Small Group Bible Studies

Elementary Bible Principles (with Linda M. Quiggle)
Counted Worthy (with Linda M. Quiggle)

COMMENTARY SERIES

The Old Testament

A Private Commentary on the Bible: Judges
A Private Commentary on the Book of Ruth
A Private Commentary on the Bible: Esther
A Private Commentary on the Bible: Song of Solomon
A Private Commentary on the Bible: Daniel
A Private Commentary on the Bible: Jonah
A Private Commentary on the Bible: Habakkuk
A Private Commentary on the Bible: Haggai

The New Testament

James Quiggle Translation New Testament

The Gospels

A Private Commentary on the Bible: Matthew's Gospel
A Private Commentary on the Bible: Mark's Gospel
A Private Commentary on the Bible: Luke 1–12
A Private Commentary on the Bible: Luke 13–24
A Private Commentary on the Bible: John 1–12
A Private Commentary on the Bible: John 13–21
A Private Commentary on the Bible: Acts 1–14
A Private Commentary on the Bible: Acts 15–28
Four Voices, One Testimony (a Gospel harmony)
Jesus Said "I Am"
The Parables and Miracles of Jesus Christ
The Passion and Resurrection of Jesus the Christ
The Christmas Story, As Told By God

Pauline Letters

A Private Commentary on the Bible: Galatians

A Private Commentary on the Bible: Ephesians
A Private Commentary on the Bible: Philippians
A Private Commentary on the Bible: Colossians
A Private Commentary on the Bible: Thessalonians
A Private Commentary on the Bible: Pastoral Letters
A Private Commentary on the Bible: Philemon

General Letters

A Private Commentary on the Book of Hebrews
A Private Commentary on the Bible: James
A Private Commentary on the Bible: 1 Peter
A Private Commentary on the Bible: 2 Peter
A Private Commentary on the Bible: John's Epistles
A Private Commentary on the Bible: Jude

Revelation

A Private Commentary on the Bible: Revelation 1–7
A Private Commentary on the Bible: Revelation 8–16
A Private Commentary on the Bible: Revelation 17–22

REFERENCE SERIES

Dictionary of Doctrinal Words

Translation of Select Bible Books

Old and New Testament Chronology (With David Hollingsworth)

(Also in individual volumes: Old Testament Chronology; New Testament Chronology)

TRACTS

A Human Person: Is the Unborn Life a Person?

Biblical Marriage

How Can I Know I am A Christian?

Now That I am A Christian

Thirty-Six Essentials of the Christian Faith

What is a Pastor? / Why is My Pastor Eating the Sheep?

Principles and Precepts of the Literal Hermeneutic

(All tracts are in digital format and cost $0.99)

Formats

Print, Digital, Epub, PDF. Search "James D. Quiggle" or book title.